Studies in the Eighteenth Century

Studies in the Eighteenth Century

II

*Papers presented at the Second
David Nichol Smith Memorial Seminar
Canberra 1970*

Edited by
R. F. Brissenden

1973
Australian National University Press
Canberra

First published 1973

Printed in Australia at The Griffin Press, Adelaide, for Australian National University Press, Canberra, A.C.T. 2600

United Kingdom, Europe, Middle East, Africa, and Caribbean.

Angus & Robertson (U.K.) Ltd, London

Registered in Australia for transmission by post as a book

National Library of Australia Card no. and ISBN 0 7081 0092 9
Library of Congress Catalog Card no. 68-18428

Contents

Illustrations

Preface

THE PAPERS BROUGHT together in this volume have been selected from those delivered at the Second David Nichol Smith Memorial Seminar in Eighteenth Century Studies. The Seminar, under the sponsorship of the National Library of Australia, the Australian National University, and the Australian Academy of the Humanities, was held in Canberra during the week 23-29 August 1970. Like the first Seminar, which took place in 1966, it was designed to honour the memory of David Nichol Smith, whose books constitute a large and important part of the National Library's Rare Book collection, and to stimulate the further growth in Australia of scholarly activity in the field of eighteenth-century studies. That the Seminars have in fact had this effect is indicated by the recent formation of the Australasian and Pacific Society for Eighteenth Century Studies and by the decision to hold a third Seminar in 1973.

The Second Seminar was officially opened by his Excellency the Governor General, the Right Honourable Sir Paul Hasluck. We greatly appreciated his interest and his consenting to honour the occasion in this way.

During the course of the Seminar an exhibition of paintings, prints, documents, and books, titled *The Eighteenth Century*, was staged at the National Library, where the Seminar was held. The exhibition was designed by Mr Arthur Robinson, and it included not only material drawn from the Library's own collections but also eight oil paintings by Joseph Highmore and forty-five mezzotints which were very kindly lent for the occasion by the Trustees of the National Gallery of Victoria. This material was selected by Dr Ursula Hoff, Assistant Director of the Gallery.

As a contribution to the Seminar the National Library published a *Supplement* to the Cameron and Carrol *Short Title Catalogue* of eighteenth-century imprints held in the libraries of the A.C.T. This catalogue, which was prepared to mark the first David Nichol Smith Memorial Seminar in 1966, is the largest list so far published devoted exclusively to eighteenth-century British books. The *Supplement* was edited by Mr Ivan Page, the Keeper of Rare Books.

In addition Mr J. C. Eade, a research scholar in the Department of English at the Australian National University, prepared a *Bibliographical Essay on Studies in Eighteenth-Century European Culture in Australia since 1958*. The publication of the *Essay* was sponsored by the Australian Academy of the Humanities.

The organisation of the Seminar could not have been undertaken without generous assistance from a number of institutions. It is a pleasure to express our gratitude in particular to the Australian-American Educational Foundation, the British Council, the Government of the Federal Republic of Germany, the Australian Department of Foreign Affairs and the American Council of Learned Societies. With their aid, and the assistance of a number of universities throughout the world, we were able to bring together in Canberra for the Seminar scholars from Asia, Europe, North America, and New Zealand. The publication of this volume has been made possible by grants from the James N. Kirby Foundation and the Ian Potter Foundation. To them also we extend our thanks.

As editor of these papers I owe a particular debt of gratitude to Ian Donaldson, John Hardy, Ann Duffy and J. C. Eade: their help at various stages in the editing has been invaluable.

R.F.B.

Australian National University,
Canberra, 1972

Notes on Contributors

ALLENTUCK, Marcia, B.A., PH.D., Associate Professor of English and Art History at the City College of the City University of New York and Senior Research Fellow, Dumbarton Oaks, Harvard University. Professor Allentuck's main area of interest is the relationship between literature and the fine arts. Her publications include *The Works of Henry Needler, Henry Fuseli: the Artist as Critic and Man of Letters, The Achievement of Isaac Bashevis Singer* and *John Graham's System and Dialectics of Art*.

BELL, A. S., M.A., Assistant Keeper of Manuscripts, National Library of Scotland. A graduate of Cambridge, Mr Bell is interested in literary correspondence of the eighteenth and nineteenth centuries, and is at present revising the Clarendon Press edition of *The Letters of Sydney Smith*.

CARROLL, John, M.A., PH.D., Professor of English and Chairman of the Department, University College, Toronto University. Professor Carroll is a graduate of the universities of Illinois, Oxford, and Harvard. He has edited *Selected Letters of Samuel Richardson, Samuel Richardson: a Collection of Critical Essays* and *Clarissa* in the Oxford English Novels series. His main scholarly interests lie in the field of eighteenth- and twentieth-century fiction.

CASHMERE, J. J., B.A., DIP.ED., M.A. Mr Cashmere is a graduate of the universities of Sydney and Tasmania. He is a lecturer in the Department of History at La Trobe University. At present he is working on a study of the Toleration controversy in France and Holland, 1670-1715.

DONALDSON, Ian, B.A. (Melbourne), M.A. (Oxon.), Professor of English at the Australian National University, Canberra. From 1962 to 1969 he was a Fellow of Wadham College, Oxford, and from 1965 to 1969 co-edited *Essays in Criticism*. His publications include *The World Upside-Down: Comedy from Jonson to Fielding*.

ELKNER, Brian, M.A., D.U., Lecturer in French, University of Melbourne. Dr Elkner was educated at the universities of Melbourne and Lyons. He has published *French Aesthetic Thought in the XVIIIth Century*, an annotated catalogue of works available in reprint, and is at present working on an edition of the principal aesthetic texts in the *Encyclopédie*.

FABIAN, Bernhard, DR.PHIL., Professor of English, Westf. Wilhelms-Universität, Münster. Professor Fabian is the author of numerous articles on eighteenth-century literature; and is one of the four editors of the facsimile reprint series, *Anglistica & Americana*. At present he is working on a book on the bibliography of English Literature.

GREENE, Donald, B.A., M.A., PH.D., Leo S. Bing Professor of English, University of Southern California. Professor Greene has degrees from the Universities of Saskatchewan and London and Columbia University. He is the author of *The Politics of Samuel Johnson, The Age of Exuberance,* and *Samuel Johnson* (Twayne's English Authors). He has edited a collection of critical essays on Johnson (Twentieth Century Views), a bibliography of Johnsonian studies (with James L. Clifford), and a volume of Johnson's political writings in the Yale Edition of Johnson's works. He is secretary of the American Society for Eighteenth-Century Studies and co-editor of the journal *Eighteenth-Century Studies.*

HAINSWORTH, J. D., M.A., Professor of English, University of New England. Professor Hainsworth's special interests are in drama and in contemporary literature, and the articles he has published are mainly in these fields. He is at present working on a study of the eighteenth-century London theatre and editing a selection of verse by David Garrick.

HAY, John A., M.A., M.A.C.E., Lecturer in English, University of Western Australia. Mr Hay read English at Cambridge, and his publications include articles on various eighteenth-century topics. He is at present editing the poetry of Edward Young.

KORSHIN, Paul J., PH.D., Associate Professor of English, University of Pennsylvania. Professor Korshin received his graduate training at Harvard University. He has published numerous articles on poetics, bibliography, and on Swift and Johnson. He recently completed a study of the development of poetic theory in the later seventeenth century and is now writing a book on typology.

LANDA, Louis A., A.B., M.A., PH.D., Professor of English Emeritus, Princeton University. In numerous articles and books Professor Landa has made a most distinguished contribution to the study of eighteenth-century English literature. His major publications include *Swift and the Church of Ireland* and editions of *Gulliver's Travels* and Defoe's *Journal of the Plague Year.*

LEITH, James A., M.A., PH.D., Professor of History and Chairman of the Department, Queen's University. Professor Leith is a graduate of the University of Toronto and Duke University. His publications include *The Idea of Art as Propaganda in France 1750-1799: A Study in the History of Ideas,* and *Media and Revolution: Moulding a new Citizenry in France during the Terror.*

PEARSON, W. H., M.A., PH.D., Associate Professor of English at the University of Auckland. Professor Pearson is a graduate of the Universities of New Zealand and London. His doctoral research was on the nineteenth-century poets Patmore, Hopkins, and Thompson. His publications include a novel, *Coal Flat,* several essays on New Zealand life and literature, an edition of Frank Sargeson's *Collected Stories,* and a part-biographical, part-critical work, *Henry Lawson among Maoris.* He was a Senior Research Fellow in Pacific History at the Australian National University from 1967 to 1969, working on a long-term study of imaginative writing in English set in the Pacific islands.

RAE, Thomas I., M.A., PH.D., Assistant Keeper of Manuscripts, National Library of Scotland. Dr Rae is a graduate of St Andrews University and is Secretary of the Scottish Historical Society. He is the author of *The Administration of the Scottish Frontier, 1513-1603*; and is at present interested in Scottish historical thought from the late sixteenth to the early eighteenth centuries.

RAWSON, C. J., M.A., B.LITT., Professor of English, University of Warwick. Professor Rawson has published *Henry Fielding* in the Profiles in Literature series, and has edited a collection of critical articles, *Focus Swift*. His book, *Henry Fielding and the Augustan Ideal under Stress,* has recently appeared.

ROBINSON, Roger D., M.A., PH.D., Lecturer in English, University of Canterbury, New Zealand. Dr Robinson was educated at Queens' College, Cambridge, and taught at the University of Leeds before moving to New Zealand. He is working on a book on Fielding and on some nineteenth-century novelists, especially Dickens and Butler.

SHACKLETON, Robert, M.A., D.LITT. (Oxon.), HON.LITT.D. (Dublin), DOCTOR H.C. (Bordeaux), F.B.A., F.S.A., F.R.S.L., Bodley's Librarian, Oxford. Dr Shackleton is a Fellow of Brasenose College and a Vice-President of the International Society for Eighteenth-Century Studies. He has published a critical edition of Fontenelle's *Entretiens sur la pluralité des mondes* and *Montesquieu, a critical biography.* He is interested in French eighteenth-century literature, especially in Montesquieu, and the *Encyclopédie,* and in Anglo-French and Franco-Italian literary relations.

STOUT, Gardner D., Jr, PH.D., Associate Professor of English, University of California, Berkeley. Professor Stout has published the standard critical edition of Laurence Sterne's *Sentimental Journey*; at present, he is writing a book on Swift's *Tale of a Tub* and working on a study of Augustan satire.

WILDING, Michael, M.A., Senior Lecturer in English, University of Sydney. Mr Wilding was educated at Lincoln College, Oxford. He is the author of *Milton's Paradise Lost* and co-author of *Cultural Policy in Great Britain.* He edited *Marvell* in the Modern Judgments series, and co-edited *Australians Abroad*. At present he is working on a study of the political novel.

Studies in the Eighteenth Century

Pope's Essay on Man *and the French Enlightenment*

Robert Shackleton

May I begin this essay with a personal reminiscence? In the summer term of 1939 I was approaching the end of my second year as an undergraduate at Oriel, reading French. I was proposing to offer as a special subject 'the influence of England on French literature in the second half of the eighteenth century'. In the Oxford Modern Languages School special subjects were not then usually taught. One was left to one's own devices: a healthy training. My tutor, A. D. Crow, suggested that I might usefully, nevertheless, seek general advice on what to read from the Merton Professor. I went accordingly to 20 Merton Street and made the acquaintance of Nichol Smith. The hour and a half which I spent in his study I remember vividly and regard as having had a decisive influence in my career. I can see him now taking book after book from his shelves to show me, calf-bound eighteenth-century volumes, for the most part French translations of English works: *Joseph Andrews*, the *Night Thoughts*, Ossian, and as like as not the *Essay on Man*. I was not, before this, without an interest in books and I had started a modest collection. But I had never seen so many together in a private house. It was then that I saw, in my undergraduate way, that the physical objects we call books are the bone structure of literature and began to understand that bibliography and literary history are inseparable disciplines. Now, thirty years later, as a librarian responsible for one of the world's greatest libraries, I look back to this first encounter with Nichol Smith and see it as a great moment in my life.

In the cosmopolitan age which the eighteenth century was, few if any writers enjoyed greater international renown than Pope: a renown which received its final expression in 1801 in a magnificent polyglot edition of the *Essay on Man* from the presses of Bodoni at Parma. The history of this vogue has not been written. Emile Audra, who was well qualified by knowledge and experience to write it, was working in the last years of his life on the influence of Pope in France, but his work never saw the light of day. Of all Pope's works the most famous in France and (after *Eloisa to Abelard*) the most frequently translated and most frequently reprinted was the *Essay on Man*. Voltaire was to call it 'the most beautiful, the most useful, and the most sublime didactic poem ever written in any language'.

Although when the *Essay on Man* appeared the alignment of the rival forces whose struggles are characteristic of the Enlightenment had not been effected, most of the salient doctrines of the *philosophes* had received expression in France, and many of them were of English inspiration. The rationalist attack on authority and prejudice which the Cartesian method had encouraged culminated in the deist movement in late seventeenth-century England. Side by side with this, and to some extent within it, existed elements of materialism, likewise attributable in part to the influence, albeit in distorted form, of Cartesianism; for it was inevitable, as Douglas Bush has said, 'that the materialistic cat should swallow the spiritual canary'. In opposition to Descartes and inspired largely by Locke, though affiliated to a much more ancient tradition, is found the sensationalist doctrine that all ideas come from the senses: the real litmus test of a *philosophe*. Accompanying these doctrines are an intense interest in psychology and human motivation, and a real preoccupation with the problems of teleology: a preoccupation more important in itself than for specific answers to the problems. The exemplifiers of these various positions are Shaftesbury and, by way of counterpoise, Mandeville in England in the quarter century preceding the *Essay on Man*, and in France, more remotely but still vivid in the public's mind, still read and still reprinted, Fontenelle and Bayle, and closer in time and great in significance, the *Lettres persanes* of Montesquieu. To these early Enlightenment views in philosophy and religion should be added new ideas in politics: criticism of authority, the belief in toleration, the acceptance of natural law.

Pope, in spite of occasional disclaimers and his deathbed repentance, falls into the pattern of the early Enlightenment. The clear cult of the deist inspires the *Universal Prayer*:

> Father of All! in every age,
>   In every clime adored,
> By saint, by savage, and by sage,
>   Jehovah, Jove, or Lord!

The pre-eminence given by the deist to morality over faith (succinctly defined by Addison in the 459th *Spectator*) is stressed in the *Essay on Man*:

> For modes of faith, let graceless zealots fight;
> His can't be wrong whose life is in the right.
>
> (III, 305-6)

The method of argument outlined in the first book of the *Essay on Man* is again that of natural religion. Little is left to revelation by the man who asks the rhetorical question:

> Say first, of God above or man below,
> What can we reason, but from what we know? (I, 17-18)

In 1742, in book IV of the *Dunciad*, he commits himself to sensationalism in deriding and dissociating himself from the gloomy clerk who declaims:

> Let others creep by timid steps, and slow,
> On plain experience lay foundations low,
> By common sense to common knowledge bred,
> And last, to Nature's cause through Nature led.
> All-seeing in thy mists, we want no guide,
> Mother of arrogance, and source of pride!
> We nobly take the high priori road,
> And reason downwards, till we doubt of God. (465-72)

Many of the *philosophes* confined themselves to problems of moral philosophy, and left political thought alone. Pope, on the contrary, in the third book of the *Essay on Man* discusses the rise of social organisations. Society, he says, is natural, as the animals show us:

> Great nature spoke; observant man obeyed;
> Cities were built, societies were made. (III, 199-200)

Kings were then appointed by general agreement: the origin of monarchy. Then monarchy declined, through the corrupt and unnatural influence of individuals, into tyranny. Pope shows himself here a modest follower of Locke and a modest precursor of Rousseau.

There may indeed be ambivalence and contradiction in Pope's attitudes. In the *Essay on Man* he may, in Maynard Mack's words, 'have wished to have it both ways' and appear an advocate of the new ideas without abandoning the old.[1] But there is no doubt that his ideas made him appear a friend and ally to at least the more moderate among the French *philosophes*, and it is in that role that he is cast when the *Essay on Man* first became known in France.

The first French writer to take cognisance of the *Essay on Man* was Voltaire. The two poets were already acquainted. Pope had formed a judgment on Voltaire before meeting him which their encounters were not to ratify:

---

[1] *An Essay on Man*, M. Mack (ed.), The Twickenham Edition of the Poems of Alexander Pope, London, Vol. III, i, 1950, p. xxv.

> I esteem him for that honest, principled spirit of true religion
> which shines through the whole [of *La Ligue*] and from whence
> . . . I conclude him at once a freethinker and a lover of quiet;
> no bigot, but yet no heretic.[2]

Two years later Voltaire, writing to Thieriot, describes Pope as 'the
best poet of England, and at present, of all the world'.[3] Praise is
renewed in the twenty-second letter of the *Lettres philosophiques*,
entitled *Sur M. Pope et quelques autres poètes fameux*, where reference is made to the *Rape of the Lock* and the *Essay on Criticism*.
It is only in a variant dating from 1756 that the *Lettres philosophiques* mention the *Essay on Man*; and though the poem has
affinities with the twenty-fifth letter, *Sur les Pensées de M. Pascal*,
these have been thought fortuitous.[4] It is worth while, however, to
look at them in the light of accurately established texts.

The *Lettres philosophiques* had a curious if well-known bibliographical history. The first text to appear was an English translation
published at London in 1733. This was followed in the next year
by two editions in French, each with a false imprint. The first said
'Bâle' but appeared at London, the second, with the imprint
'Amsterdam', was published at Rouen, the printer being Jore and
Voltaire's friend Cideville seeing the edition through the press. The
second of these editions contains an important section lacking in
the first: the twenty-fifth letter on Pascal. On or shortly before
1 July 1733 Voltaire sent the manuscript of this twenty-fifth letter
to his Rouen printer.[5]

The four epistles which make up the *Essay on Man* were first
published separately, on 20 February, 29 March, and 8 May 1733,
and 24 January 1734.[6] In a letter to the Abbé Du Resnel, editorially
dated between 6 and 15 May 1733, Voltaire announces 'J'ai reçu
les essais de Pope sur l'homme' which must refer to the first two
epistles, and on 14 July he asks Thieriot, surprisingly, if the *Essay
on Man* is by Wollaston or Pope.[7] Thus epistles I and II were in
his hands for seven weeks before he despatched the commentary on
Pascal to his printer at Rouen. During this time he was presumably
completing its preparation for the press.

2 *The Correspondence of Alexander Pope*, G. Sherburn (ed.), Oxford, 1956,
Vol. II, p. 229 (Pope to Bolingbroke, 9 April 1724).
    3 Best.D303 (references to Voltaire's correspondence, when in this form, are to
the definitive edition in *The Complete Works of Voltaire*, Th. Besterman (ed.),
Geneva, 1968-; when in the form Best.5939, are to *Voltaire's Correspondence*,
Th. Besterman (ed.), Geneva, 1953-65).
    4 R. Pomeau, *La Religion de Voltaire*, Paris, 1956, p. 129.
    5 Best.D626.
    6 R. H. Griffith, *Alexander Pope, a Bibliography*, London, 1968, Vol 1, pp. 223,
236-7, 242, 255-6.
    7 Best.D609, D 631.

I do not propose now to make a systematic examination of the relationship between the *Essay on Man* and the commentary on Pascal, but will point out some resemblances.[8]

One concerns a famous passage:

> Hope humbly then; with trembling pinions soar;
> Wait the great teacher death, and God adore!
> What future bliss he gives not thee to know,
> But gives that hope to be thy blessing now.
> Hope springs eternal in the human breast:
> Man never is, but always to be blessed:
> The soul, uneasy and confined from home,
> Rests and expatiates in a life to come. (I, 91-8)

Compare this with paragraph XXII of the commentary on Pascal:

> Il faut, bien loin de se plaindre, remercier l'auteur de la nature de ce qu'il nous donne cet instinct qui nous emporte sans cesse vers l'avenir. Le trésor le plus précieux de l'homme est cette *espérance* qui nous adoucit nos chagrins, et qui nous peint des plaisirs futurs dans la possession des plaisirs présents.

Two other passages from the first epistle find their echo in paragraph XXVIII. Here Voltaire insists that rational reflection shows that man's imperfections are not to be lamented, that man is the most perfect and the happiest of all creatures, and that only through pride and temerity can we claim that we ought to be other and better than we are. The ideas are commonplaces of the 'cosmic toryism' of the age, but the words are close to Pope's:

> Then say not man's imperfect, heaven in fault;
> Say rather, man's as perfect as he ought. (I, 69-70)

and

> In pride, in reasoning pride, our error lies;
> All quit their sphere and rush into the skies. (I, 123-4)

Voltaire's third paragraph begins with a quotation from Pascal: without the mystery of original sin, man is wholly incomprehensible. How, Voltaire asks, would Pascal reply to one who could explain man in wholly rational terms, including the mixture of good and evil in his nature? Such an interlocutor would argue:

> Ceux qui sont le mieux organisés sont ceux qui
> ont les passions les plus vives.

Likewise Pope:

> Hence different passions more or less inflame,
> As strong or weak, the organs of the frame. (II, 129-30)

[8] References to the commentary on Pascal are to paragraph numbers in *Lettres philosophiques*, G. Lanson and A.-M. Rousseau (eds.), Paris, 1964.

The interlocutor says that self-love is equal in all men and is as necessary to them as the five senses. Pope had declared:

> Self-love, the spring of motion acts the soul. (II, 59)

Voltaire's spokesman says that man has his rightful place in nature, above the animals and below other beings, Pope evokes the

> Vast chain of being, which from God began,
> Natures ethereal, human, angel, man,
> Beast, bird, fish, insect. (I, 237-9)

The Frenchman insists that man is a mixture of good and evil, endowed with passions to act, and reason to control his passions. Likewise Pope:

> Virtuous and vicious every man must be,
> Few in the extreme, but all in the degree. (II, 231-2)

A recurrent theme for Pope is the balancing in man of self-love or the passions (which he equates: 'Modes of self-love the passions we may call') and reason:

> Two principles in human nature reign;
> Self-love to urge and reason to restrain. (II, 53-4)

If man were perfect, Voltaire's spokesman concludes, he would be God. The apparent contradictions in man are part of his nature. Man is what he ought to be, 'ce qu'il doit être'. To this one can quote Pope again:

> Then say not man's imperfect, heaven in fault;
> Say rather, man's as perfect as he ought. (I, 69-70)

The resemblances between Voltaire and Pope are striking. Voltaire later was to praise the *Essay on Man* and to quote from it. Is it not reasonable to believe, in the light of these textual affinities, that he was borrowing from it also in 1733, at a time at which we know the first two epistles were on his desk?

I have laboured this demonstration, partly because Voltaire's indebtedness has been denied, but more because it shows an extraordinarily rapid penetration of Pope's poem on the Continent within a few weeks of its publication. But there is more. The *Lettres philosophiques* were, upon their publication, condemned by the Parlement of Paris and burnt by the public hangman, and Voltaire had to take refuge away from Paris to avoid arrest. More than any other part of the work, it was the commentary on Pascal which was objected to, and which Voltaire was therefore most anxious to disavow—though perfectly willing, incompatibly with this disavowal, to use in an attempt, vain in its outcome, to ingratiate himself with the government as an anti-Jansenist, Pascal being the idol of the Jansenist party. The *Lettres philosophiques* were the first book of popular philosophical appeal to be condemned by the civil power during the reign of Louis XV. The persecution of the controversial works of the Enlightenment started with the *Lettres philosophiques* and with that persecution, as a corollary, come the first signs that the *philosophes* were consolidating themselves into a party. It is at this point that the influence of the *Essay on Man* becomes articulate.

The direct blast against the *Essay on Man* was not to come, however, until the work had been translated into French.

Two translations were quick to appear. The first was the prose translation of Etienne de Silhouette. One of the more interesting minor figures in French intellectual life of the century, and once, briefly, a major figure in public life since he held the office of *contrôleur-général*, Silhouette had published a book on China before he came of age. After travelling in Italy, where he met Montesquieu, likewise travelling, he crossed to England and while there wrote and published a prose version of the *Essay on Man*. His translation, which was praised by Pope as giving the sense very well,[9] appeared in 1736. The Abbé du Resnel produced a verse translation. He had already translated the *Essay on Criticism* and in his capacity as royal censor signed the approbation for Silhouette's translation of that work. He was a friend of Voltaire, who encouraged his enterprise and may well have lent him the English text. Described by Voltaire as a man who could think, feel, and write, and even addressed by him as 'mon cher Pope',[10] the Abbé's version first appeared in 1737. Madame du Châtelet, when he presented a copy to her, said that Voltaire would read the work with great pleasure, and that the Abbé had demonstrated to her that metaphysical ideas could be well expressed in French poetry.[11] His rendering, which appeared with the title *Principes de la morale*, enjoyed an unusually great success throughout the century.

The Jesuit *Journal de Trévoux* published a eulogistic review of Silhouette's translation upon its appearance, and the Jesuit Tournemine wrote to Silhouette that Pope was 'un philosophe profond et un poète vraiment sublime', whose work would be harmful only to those corrupt minds which turn everything to poison. The following year, however, the *Journal de Trévoux* retraced its steps and denounced the *Essay on Man* as an impious work teaching deism and fatalism. In October 1737 the *Journal des Savants* published a

[9] Joseph Spence, *Observations, Anecdotes, and Characters of Books and Men*, J. M. Osborn (ed.), Oxford, 1966, §308.
[10] Best.D715, D 2726.
[11] *Lettres de la marquise du Châtelet*, Th. Besterman (ed.), Geneva, 1958, Vol. I, pp. 189-90.

long article on du Resnel's translation. The author of the article, who was the Abbé Trublet,[12] gave an analysis of the poem with lengthy quotations but included little personal comment except on the principles of translation. One passage of philosophical purport, however, he quotes, comparing the versions of du Resnel and Silhouette. It is the naturalist passage in the second epistle which includes the line 'Teach us to mourn our nature, not to mend' and sitting characteristically on the fence Trublet exclaims:

> Voilà de ces pensées, vraies et salutaires dans la bouche du chrétien, mais fausses et dangereuses dans celle du libertin.

The story of the attacks on the *Essay on Man* by Jean-Pierre de Crousaz, and of the subsequent polemical pieces in the quarrel, has been elucidated by Emile Audra, L. F. Powell, Maynard Mack, Jacqueline de La Harpe, and George Sherburn, and is not to be repeated here. Crousaz was not a man of mean intellect, as is sufficiently attested by his aesthetic writings, though he is best known in England from the *Dunciad*'s sneer at 'German Crousaz' and from Gibbon's scorn:

> Mr de Crousaz the adversary of Bayle and Pope is not distinguished by lively fancy or profound reflexion, and even in his own country at the end of a few years, his name and writings are almost obliterated.[13]

His two criticisms of the *Essay on Man*, the *Examen* and the *Commentaire*, were published respectively in 1737 and 1738. Both were based not on the English text but on translations, the first following Silhouette, the second du Resnel. They advanced the uneasily compatible accusations that Pope was a disciple of Leibniz and a disciple of Spinoza, and in this way placed him at the forefront of European controversy: fatalism, materialism, deism, optimism, were all discerned in his lines. Pope, *nolens volens*, became now the spokesman of a school, a protagonist of the Enlightenment; nor, in Continental opinion, did the fact that the eminent ecclesiastic and future bishop Warburton came to his defence rescue him for orthodoxy. Rather did it procure for Warburton the reputation of a liberal divine sympathetic to the philosophical movement, a reputation clearly evidenced by the surviving letter which Montesquieu wrote to him.[14]

Warburton's *Vindication of Mr. Pope's Essay on Man* was published in 1740. A year earlier the *Commentaire* of Crousaz had been

---

12 C.-P. Goujet, *Bibliothèque francaise*, Vol. VIII, 1744, p. 246.
13 E. Gibbon, *Memoirs of my Life*, G. A. Bonnard (ed.), London, 1966, p. 73.
14 See R. Shackleton, 'Montesquieu's Correspondence: additions and corrections', *French Studies*, Vol. 12, 1958, pp. 341-2.

translated into English by no less a person than Samuel Johnson. In 1742 were published Silhouette's *Lettres philosophiques et morales*, a defence of the *Essay on Man* which Pope himself had revised before it appeared. The controversy had grown and new fuel was provided by Pope's publication of the *Universal Prayer* in 1738.

In 1742 Louis Racine, son of the tragic poet, published his poem *La Religion*, which attempts a rational justification of revealed religion. In the second canto he criticises optimism, saying that on the banks of the Thames,

> Quelque abstrait raisonneur, qui ne se plaint de rien,
> Dans son flegme anglican, répondra, *Tout est bien*.

Pope is named in the author's own footnote. A few weeks at most after the publication of *La Religion* Pope's friend the Catholic, Jacobite, and freemason Andrew Michael Ramsay wrote to Louis Racine in protest against false interpretations of Pope, asserting the poet's orthodox catholicism and denying charges of fatalism and Spinozism. When Racine learned that Pope was a Catholic, not an Anglican, says the rarely facetious author of the historical volume of the *Encyclopédie méthodique*, he dared no longer think him irreligious.[15] Racine expressed gratification to Ramsay, and asked leave to publish his letter. Ramsay did better than grant the leave requested: he sent Racine a letter from Pope himself, dated 1 September, destined for publication, in which the poet asserted his religious orthodoxy. The letter is famous. Though often published it has been thought spurious. But Audra discovered the manuscript, which is in Pope's hand, and its authenticity cannot be denied. It ends:

> I have the pleasure to answer you in the manner you most desire, a sincere avowal that my opinions are entirely different from those of Spinoza, or even of Leibniz; but on the contrary conformable to those of Mons. Pascal and Mons. Fénelon, the latter of whom I would most readily imitate, in submitting all my opinions to the decision of the Church.[16]

Does this mean that the sentiments of the *Essay on Man* were sincerely unsaid? A possible answer is a statement made by Joseph Spence on the authority of Pope, unpublished until Dr James Osborn's recent edition: 'Mr. Pope's letter to Racine [is] a scarce concealed satire'.[17]

15 G.-H. Gaillard, *Encyclopédie méthodique, Histoire*, Paris, 1790, Vol. IV, pp. 362-3.
16 L. Racine, *La Religion, poème*, Paris, 1742, p. 32; Paris, 9e édition, 1775, pp. 249-63; E. Audra, *L'Influence française dans l'œuvre de Pope*, Paris, 1931, frontispiece.
17 Spence, *Observations*, §307.

Louis Racine's personal religion was Jansenist in inspiration. Jansenist likewise was the outlook of Jean-Baptiste Gaultier, a theologian much given to denunciations of the works of the *philosophes*. He was later to write attacks on Voltaire's *La voix du sage et du peuple* and on Montesquieu's *Lettres persanes*. In 1746 he published *Le Poème de Pope intitulé Essai sur l'homme convaincu d'impiété*. The first of the three letters into which this work is divided is a catechism taken from the *Essay on Man*, in the verse translation of Du Resnel. It is a painstaking demonstration of the impiety of Pope: fatalism, natural morality, uncertainty of immortality, similarity of men and animals. The second letter compares the *Essay on Man* with two other works, the *Lettres philosophiques* (notably the twenty-fifth letter on Pascal) and an anonymous work which Gaultier has before his eyes in manuscript: *Examen sur la religion en général*. This is one of those clandestine manuscripts described by Ira Wade in 1938, which placed in circulation the daring thought of the early Enlightenment. Wade listed twenty-seven copies of this particular work, which came into print in 1745 under the title *Examen de la religion dont on cherche l'éclaircissement de bonne foi; attribué à Mr de Saint-Evremond*. The imprint, following the usage of the day, was Trévoux, *aux dépens des Pères de la Société de Jésus.* The authorship has been attributed to many writers, including, remarkable to relate, Gilbert Burnet, but opinion now accepts an army officer called La Serre who was hanged as a spy at Maestricht in 1748.

Gaultier quotes Pope's insistence that man is as perfect as he ought to be. He likens it to Voltaire's similar claim in the commentary on Pascal. He finds that the *Anonyme*, as he calls the author of the impious manuscript, declares that man is what his nature requires him to be. 'Vous voyez', he goes on, 'que Pope, Voltaire, et mon Anonyme s'accordent parfaitement'. They are three voices in unison, whose inspiration is Spinoza, and he quotes from the *Tractatus Theologico-Politicus* that it would be inappropriate for human nature to have more perfection than it now has, and than God has given it as a consequence of the immutable laws of nature.

Gaultier says that Pope sees self-love as the eternal bond of society, and that Voltaire expresses the same view in the *Lettres philosophiques*, while the *Anonyme* goes further and asserts that Christianity is harmful to society. Gaultier again proclaims Spinoza as the common source, and quotes his famous assertion that it is by natural law that fish enjoy water, and by natural law that the big fish eat the small.

Angrily the critic goes on to advert to such passages as the famous
'For modes of faith let graceless zealots fight', to the praise given to
the good man:

> Slave to no sect, who takes no private road,
> But looks through nature up to nature's God. (IV, 331-2)

In his concluding letter he deplores the general advance of free
thought. In England, France, Holland, Germany, and all the North,
irreligion is striding forward. It is assisted particularly by freemasonry, since the *Framassons*, as he quaintly calls them, seek in
spite of their profession of faith to spread deism throughout society.
He sees a general conspiracy against religion, 'une conspiration
générale contre la religion'. Bayle, Pope, Voltaire, and their peers
are advancing false doctrines; they are abandoning the source of
light for thick darkness, illuminated at best by the faint glimmer-
ings of human reason; they are following the lead of Spinoza. Their
ideas he pronounces dangerous in their practical consequences: their
notion of self-love inspired the War of the Austrian Succession, and
Pascal is quoted as saying that self-love is the cause of war.[18] Jansenist that he is, Gaultier, after mentioning Pascal, proceeds to cite
Saint Augustine on the co-existence of the earthly city and the
heavenly city, of Babylon and Jerusalem. If men are to aspire to the
city of God they must resist the evil ideas now in circulation. The
Lettres philosophiques were burnt by the hangman, but Pope's
Essay has escaped all pursuit—an immunity which cries for rectifica-
tion.

I have lingered over the work of Gaultier, first because it has
received scant attention from scholars, secondly because of its
unusual clarity in establishing the Spinozism of the *Essay on Man*,
and finally because it is the first sustained exposition of the conspiracy interpretation of the Enlightenment. What at the end of
the century the *émigré* Abbé Barruel and the Scot John Robison
were to say of the *philosophes*, that they were conspirators seeking
to subvert society and religion, using freemasonry as an instrument
and a disguise, Gaultier is saying now in 1746. The sage of Twickenham is the arch-conspirator.

The reputation, like a Nessus shirt, began to stick, and Pope,
having died in 1744, could not even try to take it off. There was no
one to protest when in 1748 La Mettrie, in the dedication to
L'Homme machine, the most extreme work any of the *philosophes*
had yet produced, spoke in eulogistic terms of the *Essay on Man*. In

---

18 'La pente vers soi est le commencement de tout désordre en guerre, en police,
en économie' (Pascal, *Pensées*, éd. de Port-Royal, ch. IX, §5; éd. Lafuma
(Delmas), 2e éd., no. 313).

1749 the *Nouvelles ecclésiastiques,* a journal which gave a black account week by week of the progress of the new ideas, and was the mouthpiece of the hidebound sector of the Jansenist party, contained an article which was to be much discussed. This was a review by the Abbé de La Roche of *L'Esprit des lois* which Montesquieu had published the previous year. It was violently hostile. How much wiser, says the Abbé, was the young Montesquieu when he consigned his first productions to the flames. *L'Esprit des lois* is based on the system of natural religion, which is the same as the system of Spinoza, which is the same as the system of Pope: equations proved, he contends, in Gaultier's attack on Pope. Does not Montesquieu's definition of laws as 'rapports nécessaires' reaffirm Pope's 'Whatever is, is right'?

This article evoked two replies in the following year. One was Montesquieu's own *Défense de l'Esprit des lois,* where to the accusation that he has followed the system of Pope he replies with chaste elegance:

Dans tout l'ouvrage, il n'y a pas un mot du système de Pope.

The second reply came from Voltaire, not specially a friend of Montesquieu but a friend to anyone he thought a victim of injustice. His ironical *Remerciement sincère à un homme charitable* is addressed to the Abbé de La Roche. You have done well, he writes, to attack dangerous works. You have preserved the world from the poison contained in the *Essay on Man,* a work which I unceasingly reread in order to convince myself more and more of the strength of your reasons and the importance of your services.

Gaultier had deplored the impunity of the *Essay on Man.* An attempt was made to end it. On 1 August 1750 the Sorbonne began to act against dangerous books, appointing a committee of twelve deputies for initial investigation. Their first act was to acquire a set of the *Nouvelles ecclésiastiques.* So aided, they drew up a list of suspect books. These included *L'Esprit des lois,* the *Histoire naturelle* of Buffon, and the two translations of the *Essay on Man.* Condemnation by the Sorbonne could lead to prohibition by the civil power or by the Holy See. Du Resnel and Silhouette panicked. They retracted their errors and the storm was averted.[19] But the juxtaposition of the *Essay on Man* with the masterpieces of Montesquieu and Buffon shows how far in French opinion the work of Pope was held characteristic of the new and heterodox ideas.

In the winter of 1741-2 a friend of Rousseau, Conzié, Comte de Charmettes, had lent him a third and new translation of the *Essay on Man,* by Seré de Rieux, along with a commentary which has not been identified. Rousseau wrote a letter of thanks on 17 January

[19] *Nouvelles ecclésiastiques,* 23 janvier 1752 (p. 13).

1742.[20] This letter, unpublished until 1962, is a long one, and closely discusses Pope's ideas, notably the concept of the great chain of being. One line preoccupies him:

> Tout est lié. Qui sait où la chaîne se perd?

The original of this rendering by Seré is:

> The chain holds on, and where it ends, unknown. (III, 6)

Does the great chain of being, embracing all elements in the creation, ascend to God himself? Can there be a relationship between God who is infinite and the creatures who are finite? Pope insists that such a relationship exists:

> Vast chain of being, which from God began,
> Natures ethereal, human, angel, man,
> Beast, bird, fish, insect. (I, 237-9)

But can the finite and the infinite be matched? Rousseau asserts that Pope is raising a question which man is incompetent to answer. In the chain of being we are acquainted only with those links which are closest to ourselves, and are invincibly ignorant about the extremities. If the intervals between the links are equal (an assertion made more explicitly by Du Resnel than by Pope), then the distance from God to a creature is equal to the distance between two creatures. Rousseau will not have this: the opinion is offensive both to religion and to reason. For the rest, however, Rousseau rejects the accusations of irreligion raised against Pope. He declares that Pope's critics have not understood him, and turns against them an anecdote from the seventeenth century. The Cardinal de Retz asked Ménage to teach him an understanding of poetry. That would take too long, said Ménage. When people show you poetry, say simply that it is no good ('Cela ne vaut rien'); you will almost always be right. So the critics of Pope, says Rousseau, whenever they read a passage they do not understand, cry 'impiety!'

Rousseau was then not yet thirty. He was to return to the theme in the famous open letter to Voltaire of August 1756, meticulously edited by R. A. Leigh.[21] I have so far considered Voltaire's attitude to Pope only as shown in the *Lettres philosophiques*. Pope's influence is shown later in the *Discours en vers sur l'homme*, the sixth and seventh of which, published in 1737, deal with the nature of man and of true virtue. Ten years later *Zadig*, under its original title of *Memnon*, shows the marked imprint of the *Essay on Man*, above all in the eighteenth chapter where the angel Jesrad, in

---

[20] *Correspondance complète de Jean Jacques Rousseau*, R. A. Leigh (ed.), Geneva, 1965-, No. 43 (= Leigh 43).

[21] Ibid., No. 424.

dialogue with Zadig, holds forth on the problem of evil in the world. Here his ideas could well be summed up as 'All partial evil, universal good'. The chain of being, the variety of the creation, and the all-pervasive influence of providence, find expression in Jesrad's words. The influence of Pope on Voltaire, linked with that of Leibniz, here reaches its apogee.

On 1 November 1755 came the Lisbon earthquake. Voltaire's optimism was rudely shaken. He found the disaster a practical refutation of Pope's 'Whatever is, is right'. On 28 November he asks his friend Elie Bertrand whether Pope, if he had been at Lisbon, would have dared to say 'Tout est bien'.[22] In the next year he published his *Poème sur le désastre de Lisbonne* with its fierce critique of those misled philosophers who cry 'Tout est bien' and with its preface in which a distinction is drawn between Pope, whom he still reveres, and the disciples who exaggerate and distort his thought. Voltaire expresses doubts about the great chain of being; denies the equality of the intervals in the chain; rejects fatalism; insists that evil exists on the earth. He looks forward, however, to a brighter future and proclaims, in words that might still have been Pope's, that God's greatest gift to mankind is hope.[23]

It was in reply to the *Poème sur le désastre de Lisbonne* that Rousseau wrote his long letter to Voltaire. With remarkable consistency over fourteen years, he praised the older man's criticism of Pope's chain of being. With less consistency, he denied ever having read Crousaz, whom he had cited in 1742. With respect but with skill he took issue with Voltaire on the problem of evil. Particular evil and general evil are not the same. Particular evil certainly exists, but general evil would be incompatible with the existence of God. We should not say, 'tout est bien' but 'le tout est bien', not 'all is well' but 'the whole is well'. Pope's system does not prove the existence of God; it is the existence of God that proves Pope's system.

These are wise words which Rousseau is speaking, wiser than those of most of his contemporaries when they discuss Pope. It is a wisdom based on similarity of outlook, for Rousseau's position is one of substantial sympathy with the *Essay on Man*. Voltaire's attitude has changed. In the *Lettres philosophiques* he had used Pope, without acknowledgment. Just as the enthusiasms he showed in that work for Shakespeare and for Locke were attenuated in his later years, so, though he still respects the name of Pope, he has retreated from discipleship.

Pope's disciples, indeed, were diverse since his influence was many-

22 Best. 5939.
23 Voltaire, *Oeuvres*, L. Moland (ed.), Paris, 1877-85, Vol. IX, p. 471.

sided. The constructive deism of the *Essay on Man* and the *Universal Prayer* could not fail to appeal to the author of the *Vicaire savoyard* and to the French deists of the first half of the century. The optimism and corrected teleology discussed at the time of the Lisbon earthquake were popular when Leibniz was popular and came into their own again towards the end of the century when, under the influence of Bernardin de Saint-Pierre, men began to look again for a divine purpose and intended harmonies in the creation; and new translations of the *Essay on Man* were published by Fontanes and Delille.

Finally there was Spinozism. The early accusations were given a firmer base by Gaultier's critique and, though Pope had probably never looked at the *Tractatus Theologico-Politicus*, the similarities were not few and were striking. They served to give Pope a place in the vanguard of the French philosophical movement. This is his greatest importance on the continent: a role which was outside his intention, but which might well not wholly have surprised the man who wrote:

> What's Fame? a fancied life in others' breath,
> A thing beyond us, ev'n before our death. (IV, 237-8)

The Hero as Clown: Jonathan Wild, Felix Krull and Others[1]

C. J. Rawson

Two related assumptions about *Jonathan Wild* have seldom been questioned: that the tone of the novel is 'acrid, incisive, mordant, implacably severe'[2], and that its 'hero' is a figure of unrelieved and unsoftened villainy. These assumptions are shared by Coleridge and by Scott, who differ substantially from one another in their valuation of the work.[3] They have held firm among all the other interpretative reappraisals and disagreements of more recent critics. Even when the conventional view of the novel's moral formula, as a simple opposition of 'good' and 'great', has been challenged as incomplete, it is Heartfree and not Wild who has been felt to need reinterpretation.[4] This is understandable because the figure of Heartfree lacks vitality, and because the Preface to the *Miscellanies* offers a third category, 'the great and good', by which we may measure the insufficiencies of mere 'goodness'. Conversely, there seems to be no external invitation to revise the official notion of Wild as a diabolically sinister villain, and Fielding's formulaic harping, within the novel, on Wild's wicked 'greatness' is very insistent. These indications seem conclusive, but they point in fact to a central uncertainty of the novel.

For it is partly because of Fielding's failure to embody his mock-heroic in a live, coherent and self-sustaining fable (like, say, the *Dunciad*'s) that the ostensible schematic certainties hold sway. The

1 A fuller version of this, with more elaborate documentation, will appear as Chapter IV of my book, *Henry Fielding and the Augustan Ideal under Stress*, London and Boston, 1972.

2 F. Homes Dudden, *Henry Fielding, His Life, Works, and Times*, Oxford, 1952, Vol. I, p. 485.

3 S. T. Coleridge, *Literary Remains*, London, 1836-9, Vol. II, pp. 376-7; Walter Scott, 'Henry Fielding', *Lives of Eminent Novelists and Dramatists*, London, n.d., p. 428, and also 'Tobias Smollett', p. 465.

4 Allan Wendt, 'The Moral Allegory of *Jonathan Wild*', *E.L.H.: A Journal of English Literary History*, Vol. XXIV, 1957, pp. 306-20.

mock-heroic has to be activated largely by verbal insistence, so that its moral implications are continually being abstracted into formulaic ironies of linguistic usage, and a tendency to the simplifications of 'moral allegory' inevitably results. Because the formulaic ironies about 'greatness' are pressed with almost obsessional emphasis and consistency, it is easy for the reader to become mesmerised by this dimension of the work, and to attend more to the ironic commentary on Wild than to what the action reveals about him. There are, however, two sides to this verbal abstraction of the mock-heroic element. If the verbal mock-heroics are unsustained (or very imperfectly sustained) by a live core of mock-heroic fiction, they do on the other hand co-exist, as it were in parallel, with another fiction which *is* live, but whose main energies are outside the domain of heroic pretensions. This fiction might be called comic in something like the sense intended by Fielding in the Preface to *Joseph Andrews*, when he distinguished 'comic epic' from mock-heroic: as embodying a humbler and more 'realistic' conception of the 'ludicrous', to which the mock-heroic adds marginal, not radical, ingredients of stylised fun. The comparison requires caution, for the overt conception of Wild obviously resembles that burlesque of 'sentiments and characters' (rather than of mere 'diction'), that 'exhibition of what is monstrous and unnatural', which Fielding describes as the antithesis of anything we shall find in *Joseph Andrews*; and it is even possible that Fielding had *Jonathan Wild* partly in mind when he made the distinction.[5] There is, however, a paradoxical sense in which mock-heroic is more integral in *Joseph Andrews* or *Tom Jones* than in *Jonathan Wild*, because, being less indiscriminately pervasive, it more easily finds its proper place, blending naturally and expressively into Fielding's *own* ironic manner, rather than sustaining an inflexibly schematic pseudo-speaker: to this extent *Jonathan Wild* appropriates the Preface to *Joseph Andrews* to itself, standing it on its head.

Nor, in speaking of the unofficial 'comic' fiction in *Jonathan Wild*, would it be right to insist unduly on the 'realistic' overtones of the term 'comic', and I shall be drawing attention to stylisations which systematically modify any tendency to naked factuality, notably the stylisations of drollic farce. But such stylisations are also, after all, prominent in *Joseph Andrews* and *Tom Jones*, and are a crucial if sometimes unacknowledged part of Fielding's novelistic manner. In some ways, the vitality of Wild as a fictional creation proceeds almost more actively from the budding comic

---

[5] This would presuppose that *Jonathan Wild* was sufficiently advanced in composition when the Preface to *Joseph Andrews* was written. I believe Dudden, *Henry Fielding*, Vol. I, pp. 482-3, to be right in his view that the main, mock-heroic or 'great man' section, was drafted about 1740.

novelist in Fielding than from the experienced practitioner of mock-heroic. It was Fielding's undoubted purpose to transform burlesque into serious moral satire, in the approved manner. Pope turned his dunces into a menace of epic gravity, and Fielding tried to do as much for Wild. One of the unexpected charms of the novel is that he failed to take the villain as seriously as the mock-heroic commentary purports, and that Wild comes alive less as a diabolical Machiavel than as a not unengaging comic figure, drawn on a smaller and more human scale.

In the Preface to the *Miscellanies*, Fielding draws attention to the unsuccess of Wild's villainy. He tells us in general of the 'bitter anxiety' which attends 'the purchases of guilt', and that villains seldom prosper:

> And though perhaps it sometimes happens, contrary to the instances I have given, that the villain succeeds in his pursuit, and acquires some transitory imperfect honour or pleasure to himself for his iniquity; yet I believe he oftener shares the fate of my hero, and suffers the punishment, without obtaining the reward.[6]

The passage is often overlooked by critics, because their emphasis tends to be on Wild's energy and cunning, not on his failure. One might argue that the passage's main points seem too obvious to need special mention. The moral that crime does not pay is covered by the poetic justice of Wild's execution, and we should anyway expect Fielding to draw prefatory attention to 'the doctrine which I have endeavoured to inculcate in this history', even if the didactic statement turns out to be somewhat reductive. If the novel's ironic scheme ensures a more frequent and declaratory emphasis on the exploits of 'greatness' than seems compatible with an unproblematic prefatory insistence on the victory of good over evil, the fact can be put down to the formal exigencies of the ironic scheme. On the other hand, the confidence expressed in the Preface might not seem altogether appropriate to the presumed earnestness of the novel's political satire. The fact that Walpole had fallen by the time the novel was published, and that Fielding may have gone through a pro-Walpole phase after he had drafted the anti-Walpole part of the novel but before he prepared the whole novel for publication,[7] does not resolve the inconsistency (although it might help to prepare

---

6 *The Complete Works of Henry Fielding*, W. E. Henley (ed.), London, 1903, Vol. XII, p. 244. Hereafter cited as *Works*.
7 See Martin C. Battestin, 'Fielding's Changing Politics and *Joseph Andrews*', *Philological Quarterly*, Vol. XXXIX, 1960, pp. 39-55. A different view is expressed by W. B. Coley, 'Henry Fielding and the Two Walpoles', *Philological Quarterly*, Vol. XLV, 1966, pp. 157-78. See also Hugh Amory, 'Henry Fielding's *Epistles to Walpole*: A Reexamination', *Philological Quarterly*, Vol. XLVI, 1967, pp. 236-47.

us for certain ambiguities of feeling): the more generalised attack on abuses in high places, and on the corrupting 'doublethink' of social attitudes and political language,[8] must be presumed to remain firm and urgent, and is so taken by the critics. Nor does Fielding's tentativeness in asserting that the wicked sometimes flourish in real life ('though perhaps it sometimes happens') ring true to our notion of his real thinking, or conform with the bitter severity which Fielding seems to have intended for the novel, and which the critics conventionally assume. We may feel surprised at the Preface's implication that Wild, unlike other villains 'perhaps', never 'succeeds in his pursuit' or gains any 'transitory or imperfect honour or pleasure to himself for his iniquity'. Are we to take 'transitory' in a large sense, to mean 'of this life' rather than eternity, the other villains being punished only after death, whereas Wild comes to a bad end in his own lifetime? Partly, no doubt: but Fielding also insists on the temporal miseries of wicked 'greatness', the 'difficulty and danger, and real infamy', the 'bitter anxiety'. If the Preface is ambiguous, so is its relation to the novel. It is true that Wild suffers the insecurity and restlessness which proverbially afflict the 'great', but does he not gain considerable 'transitory imperfect honour or pleasure', leadership (while it lasts) of his gang, the satisfaction of getting his own way in this or that piece of trickery or bullying?

The orthodox answer would be yes, in spite of the Preface. But the fact is that in the novel Wild continually displays a comic self-imprisonment, and almost invariable failure in crime and in love. He is repeatedly outwitted by his partners and accomplices, and robbed, betrayed, or cuckolded by his women.[9] On this point, the Preface spoke more truly, perhaps, than Fielding meant. If the Preface seems out of phase, it is not in noting Wild's unsuccess, but in solemnifying the moral lesson. The 'bitter anxiety' and insecurity attributed by the Preface to the 'great' is readily transformed into a genial comedy of self-entrapment, as when Wild (tricked by La Ruse, robbed by Molly, and variously humiliated by Laetitia) complains, in his soliloquy on the vanity of human greatness:

> In this a *prig* is more unhappy than any other: a cautious man may, in a crowd, preserve his own pockets by keeping his hands in them; but while the *prig* employs his hands in another's pocket, how shall he be able to defend his own?
>
> (II. iv)

[8] See Glenn W. Hatfield, *Henry Fielding and the Language of Irony*, Chicago and London, 1968, esp. pp. 89-108, 157-8.

[9] The real-life Wild of historical accounts had, by contrast, great 'personal magnetism', was held in awe by fellow criminals, and was very successful with women. See Gerald Howson, *Thief-Taker General. The Rise and Fall of Jonathan Wild*, London, 1970, p. 245.

This compulsiveness has its bearings on Fielding's official themes, notably his analysis of Hobbesian insatiability and restlessness.[10] But if the compulsiveness is partly Hobbesian, it is also partly Bergsonian. It belongs to an undercurrent of almost affectionate comicality which flows right through the work, culminating in the final glimpse of Wild, on the gallows, stealing the parson's 'bottle-screw, which he carried out of the world in his hand' (IV. xiv). The examples reveal an exquisite effrontery of self-realisation. They also show Wild made absurdly defenceless by his compulsion to pick pockets.

Self-entrapment is not necessarily endearing, and the great conqueror's 'abject slave[ry] to his own greatness' leads the narrator to reflect on the bitter unreason, the cruel gaping folly, of 'great' doings:

> when I behold one great man starving with hunger and freezing with cold, in the midst of fifty thousand who are suffering the same evils for his diversion; when I see another, whose own mind is a more abject slave to his own greatness, and is more tortured and racked by it than those of all his vassals; lastly, when I consider whole nations rooted out only to bring tears into the eyes of a great man, not, indeed, because he hath extirpated so many, but because he had no more nations to extirpate, then truly I am almost inclined to wish that nature had spared us this her MASTERPIECE, and that no GREAT MAN had ever been born into the world. (I. xiv)

This passage only emphasises how far Wild, as an imaginative creation, is removed from the 'heroic' analogies of the abstract 'moral allegory'. Self-imprisonment in motiveless vice in his case also readily turns to a vacuous automatism, but one which Fielding fantasticates into a charming comic routine:

> the two friends [Wild and La Ruse] sat down to cards, a circumstance which I should not have mentioned but for the sake of observing the prodigious force of habit; for though the count knew if he won ever so much of Mr. Wild he should not receive a shilling, yet could he not refrain from packing the cards; nor could Wild keep his hands out of his friend's pockets, though he knew there was nothing in them. (I. vi)

The disparity is not merely between Wild and those 'great men' in higher places to whom the ironic formula compares him, and whose mischief is on an international rather than a merely private scale. If that were the only disparity, one might see it as a simple mock-heroic diminution of Wild, even though, given an intention to make Wild seem very sinister, such a diminution might feel

[10] See W. R. Irwin, *The Making of Jonathan Wild*, New York, 1941, pp. 59-60.

oddly counterproductive. But the disparity (between grim satiric exposure, and a more genial comedy) also exists within the presentation of Wild himself, and creates some revealing uncertainties, as well as unexpected enrichments.

The end of II. v, for example, is bitter. Thomas Fierce has been sentenced to death for a crime he did not commit, as a result of machinations by Wild, who outwardly befriended him:

> His only hopes were now in the assistances which our hero had promised him. These unhappily failed him: so that, the evidence being plain against him, and he making no defense, the jury convicted him, the court condemned him, and Mr. Ketch executed him.

This summarising brevity is very shocking, especially at the end of a chapter in which the narrative has been conducted with a certain particularising amplitude. Fielding's narrator rounds things off by saying that the event shows Wild to have been 'the most eminent master' of 'policy, or politicks, or rather pollitricks'.

But running against this official view of Wild is the long build-up of this and immediately preceding chapters, where the 'eminent master' is outwitted at every turn with mechanical inevitability and a comic frenzy of plot and counterplot. Wild had set out, in II. ii, 'to impose on Heartfree by means of the count, and then to cheat the count of the booty'. In II. iii, he takes from the count (by arrangement) a casket of jewelry bought on credit from Heartfree, and then arranges for Heartfree to be robbed of money paid by the count (as part of the plot) in down payment. Wild then meets Molly Straddle, who robs him of this money in the course of 'amorous caresses'. He then goes on to his true love, Letty Snap, who is busy playing him false with a preferred lover, Bagshot. She condescends to see him when she is told by her sister that Wild has some jewels for her, and hides her lover. Meanwhile, Wild discovers the theft of the money, and when Laetitia appears, it turns out that the jewels had been extracted by the count and replaced with counterfeits. Laetitia, who knows a real jewel from a false, vociferously taunts and berates Wild. He leaves in rage and multiple humiliation, while she returns to her lover. Wild rushes to the count's house:

> Not the highest-fed footman of the highest-bred woman of quality knocks with more impetuosity than Wild did at the count's door, which was immediately opened by a well-dressed liveryman, who answered that his master was not at home.

This mock-heroic simile opens II. iv. It gives a deflating glimpse of Wild, as though in the role of a footman, and then has him *actually* rebuffed by a *real* footman. The latter's 'polite' formality makes

Wild's oafish fury look even sillier, and comically compounds his humiliation. Wild nevertheless bursts into the house, but fails to find the count or the jewels. After a fruitless pursuit of the count, he retires to a night-cellar, takes 'a sneaker of punch', and delivers his soliloquy on the vanity of human greatness, including the passage about the defencelessness of pickpockets, whose hands are, occupationally, prevented from guarding their own pockets. He endures one or two further subsidiary frustrations, and, 'cocking his hat fiercely', struts out.

The next chapter, II. v, which is to end with Wild's grim plot against Fierce, begins with Laetitia eagerly returning to Bagshot (who has, however, absconded!). It then returns to Wild, who has spent the night in 'successless search for Miss Straddle' and the money, and who now, 'with wonderful greatness of mind and steadiness of countenance went early in the morning to visit his friend Heartfree'.

The 'steady countenance' is continually emphasised (see I. xiv, II. ii, II. iii, a further example in II. v, and III. xi). It supposedly denotes an undeviating brazenness in villainy, and a highly efficient subordination of feelings to expediency. But by this time, the comic diminutions of Wild (his bustling oafishness, the preposterous dandy-ferocity of his cocked hat, the almost charming and definitely subheroic detail of the 'sneaker of punch') incline us to think not so much of a Machiavellian self-command, as of the deadpan expression of a stage comic. A stage-comparison had already been made explicitly in II. iii, when Wild discovers in Laetitia's house that his money had been stolen by Molly: 'as he had that perfect mastery of his temper, or rather of his muscles, which is as necessary to the forming a great character as to the personating it on the stage, he soon conveyed a smile into his countenance . . .'. Several other comparisons draw our attention to the world of the farce and the puppet-show (II. iii, III. xi). And the relentless sequence of snubs and defeats, after which Wild so quickly and automatically presses on undeterred, suggest not mainly a 'heroic' singleness of purpose, but the stylised resilience of a clown, who rises instantly to his feet each time he has been knocked down.

These overtones of stylised farce are essential to the novel, and are often drawn attention to overtly. In II. v, their presence is powerful but not entirely overt, and their relationship to the very harsh passage about Fierce's death is possibly awkward and problematical. But their existence is inescapable. The somewhat frenetic ups and downs of Wild's fortunes and doings in the preceding chapters, for example, lend to the plot itself an air of somewhat extravagant automatism. This is continued and elaborated in II. v. The framing of Fierce, planned in Heartfree's house by Wild and Molly Straddle, for what was actually Molly's theft from Wild of money which Wild had stolen from Heartfree, has, as sheer narrative arrangement, a zaniness which fantasticates the cruelty of the deed itself out of some of its horror.

This zaniness of plot combines with a certain comic speeding-up of narrative tempo, and a slightly routinised presentation of Wild's motions. And such narrative stylisation is inseparable from the 'character' of the hero, whose touch of absurd compulsiveness nourishes and gives point to the narrator's manner, as well as feeding upon it. Consider the operations of the 'wonderful . . . steadiness of countenance' as Wild goes to Heartfree's house, knowing Heartfree to have been robbed and wounded by Wild's men. Wild enters 'with a cheerful air', which he immediately 'changed into surprise' on seeing Heartfree's wounded state. As he listens to Heartfree's account of the robbery, he evinces 'great sorrow', and 'violent agonies of rage' against the thieves. This results in a preposterous reversal, in which Heartfree is grieved by Wild's sorrow and tries to cheer him up. He does so partly by assuring Wild that he managed to save La Ruse's (fraudulent!) note from the robbery (by Wild!), upon which Wild 'felicitated' him, and also 'inveigh[ed] against the barbarity of people of fashion' who failed to pay their debts to the poor tradesman. All the while, he is also 'meditating within himself whether he should borrow or steal from his friend, or indeed whether he could not effect both': at such a moment he seems nothing so much as a kind of twin-engined mechanism, outwardly producing all the appropriate words and appearances, inwardly ticking away at possible further schemes, both equally compulsively.

At this point, Heartfree's apprentice comes in from the shop with 'a banknote of 500*l.*' which a lady 'who had been looking at some jewels, desired him to exchange'. Heartfree recognises the note as 'one of those he had been robbed of', which makes it clear to Wild (and to the reader) that the lady must be Molly Straddle, who had stolen the money from Wild, and for whom Wild had been searching everywhere. Wild ought by rights to be astonished, delighted, and also confused, for Molly's appearance at Heartfree's house could create obvious embarrassments and difficulties. Instead of any hint of these warring feelings, let alone any such blowsy elaboration of the presumed perplexity as Fielding sometimes provides in other contexts (an example might be Lady Booby's 'opposite passions distracting and tearing her mind different ways' in *Joseph Andrews*, I. ix), there is a flat resolution of the whole crisis in, once again, Wild's absolute control of his facial muscles: Wild instantly, 'with the notable presence of mind and unchanged complexion so essential to a great character, advised [Heartfree] to proceed cautiously . . .'. Wild offers to see the lady privately, puts on a 'great ferocity in his looks' and addresses an indignant, threatening, and moralising speech to her, which Fielding, however, 'omits', coming quickly to Wild's proposal to Molly that they should frame poor Fierce (this, Wild makes plain, is her only way of escaping conviction herself). The novel's first edition flattens her reaction to a pure and laconic automatism: 'The lady readily consented; and Mr. Wild and she embraced and kissed each other in a very tender and passionate manner'. The revised version of 1754 expands the passage, cutting out the passionate embrace and adding a conversation in which Wild asks Molly for the rest of the stolen money, and she confesses that she gave half of it to 'Jack Swagger, a great favorite of the ladies', and spent the rest on 'brocaded silks and Flanders lace'. If the terse automatism of the first edition is abandoned at this point, the revised version shows us Wild even more thoroughly deceived by one of his women. He takes this without fuss, and the machinations against Fierce take their course. The outcome is, as we have seen, very sinister, but it is not easy to be sure whether the grimness is altogether successfully given intensity and point by the contrast with what goes before, or whether the earlier overtones of comedy or farce have softened the whole chapter pervasively. Nor are we certain at all times of the extent to which these overtones are themselves fully under Fielding's control: to what extent, for example, they purposefully modify the bleakness, preserving urbanity, proportion, and a sense of authorial control, and to what extent they are subversive of the serious intentions.

In *Joseph Andrews* and *Tom Jones*, Fielding found a tone capable of holding moral urgency and comic modifiers in a coexistence enriching to both and subversive of neither. What prevents this in *Jonathan Wild* is the stridency of the ironic framework. The stiff acerbities of the commentary on 'greatness' exist in a schematic separation from the action, and sometimes fail to blend with it. The action, on its own, tends against odds towards the more integrated amplitude of Fielding's novelistic manner, with fitful success. At times, the collision is untidy, fragmenting. The gap between what is said about Wild and what we see in the action is too great. At others, the wholeness and vitality of a scene or episode are strong enough for the action to assert its independent force, and even to bend the commentary to itself, as though the comic novelist had for the time found his true voice within an alien genre of prose satire and a foreign idiom of 'Swiftian' ironic negation.

One area of genuine uncertainty is that of the scale or magnitude of Wild's operations. In the affair of Heartfree's jewels, despite the undercurrent of comic deflation, the scale is undoubtedly large. Thomas Fierce loses his life, Heartfree is temporarily ruined, and eventually the liberty and indeed survival of Heartfree and his family come to be in grave jeopardy, as a more or less immediate consequence of the affair. The sums of money involved in the initial series of frauds and thefts are, as it happens, relatively large (by the standards of the novel), running into many hundreds of pounds. Against this runs a certain unreality. Since Fierce never appears in the novel, except to be briefly disposed of off-stage in II. v, his fate has a somewhat disembodied air: his oddly chosen name adds to this, since no ferocity ever emanates from him and since the only impression he is allowed to make on us is that of a somewhat distant pathos. The Heartfrees are much more central, and their distresses are undoubtedly particularised, but their schematic role is to be suffering victims whose troubles will be resolved by a happy ending once the 'moral allegory' has had its say.

As to the more technical question of sums of money, it should be said that while the sums involved on this occasion are large enough to ruin a defenceless tradesman like Heartfree (and need, for reasons of plot, to do this), many of the other incidents in the novel involve sums which are pointedly, and sometimes ludicrously, small. The settlements for the marriage between Wild and Laetitia Snap involve fussy parental machinations over 'a pint silver caudle-cup' and conclude thus:

> At length, everything being agreed between the parents, settle-ments made, and the lady's fortune (to wit, seventeen pounds and nine shillings in money and goods) paid down, the day for their nuptials was fixed, and they were celebrated accordingly.
> (III. vii)

The parenthesis, as so often in Fielding, is the most pointed part of the sentence, masquerading as an afterthought only for added emphasis, and its whole implication is of the small-scale shabbiness of the business.

On an earlier occasion, Wild loses money at play, takes on a henchman to rob the most prosperous-looking gamester, and finds that the total takings amount to two shillings. Fielding highlights this episode strongly. He not only (in a manner which was to become characteristic of his novelistic style) closes a Book on it:

> This was so cruel a disappointment to Wild, and so sensibly affects us, as no doubt it will the reader, that, as it must dis-qualify us both from proceeding any farther at present, we will now take a little breath, and therefore we shall here close this book. (I. xiv)

but returns to it, with a pointed elaboration, at the start of the new
Book. Despite the smallness of the sum, Wild has troubled to bully
his accomplice out of the larger share, and the second paragraph
of II. i opens thus:

> But to proceed with our history: Wild, having shared the booty
> in much the same manner as before, *i.e.,* taken three-fourths of
> it, amounting to eighteen-pence, was now retiring to rest, in no
> very happy mood, when by accident he met with a young
> fellow. . . .

Again, the deflating details of the petty cash appear in a syntactic-
ally subordinate place, and again we may feel that the offhand
manner of the disclosure is deceptive, a function of the pointedness
itself. But if the detail kindles the subordinate clause with its spark
of comic significance, the main clause in this case also commands
weighty attention. For the 'young fellow' whom Wild met is, of
course, Heartfree, and the meeting initiates the most crucial part
of the entire action. It is, moreover, made clear beforehand that the
newly introduced character (and his wife) will have a momentous
role. The *first* paragraph of II. i, which immediately precedes the
passage about the 'eighteen-pence', gives us Fielding's other and
perhaps more sober reason for starting a new Book just here:

> One reason why we chose to end our first book, as we did, with
> the last chapter, was, that we are now obliged to produce two
> characters of a stamp entirely different from what we have
> hitherto dealt in. These persons are of that pitiful order of
> mortals who are in contempt called good-natured; being indeed
> sent into the world by nature with the same design with which
> men put little fish into a pike-pond in order to be devoured
> by that voracious water-hero.

The two tendencies of the very self-conscious transition from Book I
to Book II (the comic reduction of Wild's operations, and the sign-
posting of major and sinister new developments) are aspects of an
ambiguity which seems, at this moment, not fully in Fielding's
control.

Some degree of assimilation of Wild's villainy to the domain of
clowning and farce is, of course, not only intentional but explicit.
Whether it is always meant to disarm the harsher ironies is more
uncertain. An extended and elaborate series of theatrical and
literary analogies in III. xi compares Wild to a puppet-master, who
makes his puppets do his bidding whilst himself remaining unseen.
It goes on to take up the now familiar image of the actor's 'solemnity of countenance' in order to compare the doings of the great
world with those of village farces:

> It would be to suppose thee, gentle reader, one of very little
> knowledge in this world, to imagine thou hast never seen some
> of these puppet-shows which are so frequently acted on the
> great stage; but though thou shouldst have resided all thy days
> in those remote parts of this island which great men seldom
> visit, yet if thou hast any penetration, thou must have had some
> occasions to admire both the solemnity of countenance in the
> actor and the gravity in the spectator, while some of those farces
> are carried on which are acted almost daily in every village in
> the kingdom.

Arguably, the allusion to farce does not attenuate the acerbity here.
The comparison of the world, and of government, to a farce is only
a familiar kind of cynical commonplace, not a humorous stylisation.
The address to the reader has a tart and somewhat nagging quality,
and the passage goes on to make a wry reflection on mankind's
positive willingness to be deceived, like 'the readers of romances'
(the passage, like other reminders of farce, belongs with a larger
network of analogies, in this novel, between life and art—serious
plays, farces, puppet-shows, romances—to which I shall return).

    If there is little geniality, and little affectionate diminution of the
'hero' in this instance, what are we to make of the information in
I. iii that Wild, as a schoolboy, not only admired some disreputable
exploits of epic heroes, but that 'the Spanish Rogue was his favorite
book, and the Cheats of Scapin his favorite play'? Or of the sustained drollic allusion when, in II. iii, Wild opens the casket of
jewels for Laetitia, and finds that counterfeits have replaced the
real thing:

> He then offered her the casket, but she gently rejected it; and
> on a second offer, with a modest countenance and voice, desired
> to know what it contained. Wild opened it, and took forth
> (with sorrow I write it, and with sorrow will it be read) one of
> those beautiful necklaces with which, at the fair of Bartholo-
> mew, they deck the well-bewhitened neck of Thalestris, queen
> of Amazons, Anna Bullen, Queen Elizabeth, or some other high
> princess in Drollic story?

Besides being in themselves disarmingly funny, these two instances
explicitly link Wild with a not unamiable tradition of clowning
roguery, in fiction and on the stage. The substitution of counterfeit
jewels, or of mere stones, for the genuine contents of a casket or
other container, is a stock situation in the 'literature of roguery',
occurring, notably, in Alemán's *Guzmán de Alfarache*[11] *(The*

---

[11] I have used throughout the translation by James Mabbe, *The Rogue* (1622),
London and New York, 1924, 4 vols. This is described by Alexander A. Parker,
Literature and the Delinquent, Edinburgh, 1967, p. 100, as 'despite certain free-
doms, fundamentally faithful to the tone and to the plot of the original'. Field-

Spanish Rogue: Part II, Book II, ch. ix),[12] and recurring in Smollett's *Ferdinand Count Fathom* (1753, ch. XX), the novel which Scott, in a well-known passage, preferred to *Jonathan Wild*.[13] The Spanish rogue Guzmán is also, like Wild, robbed by a woman during amorous caresses (II. III. i),[14] and in general Wild's career in the novel has many resemblances to that of the picaresque hero of his 'favourite book' (cuckoldry, spells in prison, a proneness to comic discomfitures, etc.). Moreover, the picaresque hero, from Guzmán to Thomas Mann's Felix Krull, has had a close traditional relation to the stage comic or clown. Guzmán and other characters in Alemán's long work are repeatedly involved in a variety of clownish pranks and in some scenes of scatological slapstick of a sort which one might associate with 'the fair of Bartholomew' and Guzmán serves for a time as a professional fool or jester (II. I.iff.).[15] The connection between rogue and clown, in the specific case of Fielding's novel as well as in the picaresque tradition at large, is reinforced by such a figure as Scapin, hero of Wild's 'favourite play' (Otway's adaptation of Molière).[16] The more recent type of picaro, in fiction or farce, was usually not a detestable villain, but a combination of

---

ing's title, 'The Spanish Rogue', suggests, however, that he was probably referring to *The Life of Guzman d'Alfarache, or The Spanish Rogue* (1707), translated from Sébastien Brémond's French translation of 1695. This, and Lesage's very free translation (1732), both play down the serious moral and theological elements of the Spanish original, and Brémond expands the comic elements (Parker, pp. 115ff.). Parker argues that the more genial novel of roguery, the more good-humoured conception of the picaresque, which we associate with Lesage's *Gil Blas* (1715-35), is really a phenomenon of the eighteenth century (Parker, pp. 120ff., 136-7). These facts are of crucial relevance to our understanding of the picaresque overtones of *Jonathan Wild*. Parker's important book seems nevertheless to exaggerate the lack of comedy or lightheartedness in the earlier, Spanish forms of picaresque, of which *Guzmán* is a prototype (see the review of Parker by C. A. Jones, *Modern Language Review*, Vol. LXIII, 1968, p. 726, and Vivienne Mylne's view that 'the comparison of the *pícaro* with the delinquent occasionally seems rather forced', *French Studies*, Vol. XXII, 1968, p. 246). The English term 'rogue' could of course carry both more and less severe senses.
  The relationship of *Guzmán* to *Jonathan Wild* is touched on by A. Digeon, *The Novels of Fielding*, London, 1925, pp. 99, 108n.2, who cites Lesage's version; and Irwin, *The Making of Jonathan Wild*, pp. 94 and 131nn.45-7. Irwin plays down the picaresque element against Digeon. F. W. Chandler, *The Literature of Roguery*, London, and Boston, and New York, 1907, Vol. II, pp. 302-7, devotes several pages to *Jonathan Wild* but notes that it is in some ways outside the Spanish picaresque tradition (II.306).
  12 Mabbe, *The Rogue*, Vol. IV, pp. 19ff.
  13 Scott, 'Tobias Smollett', *Lives of Eminent Novelists*, p. 465.
  14 Mabbe, *The Rogue*, Vol. IV, pp. 93-4.
  15 Ibid., Vol. III, pp. 41ff.
  16 A ballad-opera based on this play, *A Cure for Covetousness or the Cheats of Scapin*, and other versions or adaptations of the play were performed in Bartholomew Fair and Southwark Fair in the 1730s and early 1740s (Sybil Rosenfeld, *The Theatre of the London Fairs in the 18th Century*, Cambridge, 1960, pp. 38-9, 42, 47, 50, 94, 148). Otway's play was frequently performed on the more orthodox stage throughout the first half of the eighteenth century.

mischief-maker and social outcast who arouses admiration, or at least a degree of affectionate tolerance and complicity, in the reader. Scapin in particular is a prankster whose mischief is beneficently devoted to the service of the young lovers in the play. To the extent that Wild, unlike Guzmán or Scapin, *is* a detestable villain, he has to be thought of as outside the more amiable forms of the picaresque tradition. But it is specifically to Guzmán and to Scapin that Fielding alludes, and the allusion actively defies the novel's official insistence on Wild's villainy. Fielding seems to admit this when he says that these particular literary tastes, unlike Wild's predilection for heroic writings, were a 'blemish' to his 'true greatness' (I. iii). The force, and the functions, of this defiance will need further definition, but some of its limits should be stated at once. The official insistence against which it tends is by no means totally overcome, and this is natural and right: all Fielding's purposes would be deeply violated if it were otherwise. In particular, the analogy between rogue and clown stops well short of any transfiguration of the hero into an exalted symbolic role, of wise fool, or existentialist outsider, or (as in the case of Mann's Felix Krull, who offers himself for instructive comparisons) of the artist as immoralist, above the crowd and its common rules. Such transfigurations would be unlikely not only in a profoundly conformist author like Fielding, but also at a stage in the cultural history of Europe when a basic consensus of moral values was, or could be felt to be, solid and secure enough at least to discourage radical reversals of this kind. Various adumbrations of reversal were, of course, already well-established in several literary conventions: not only in the figure of the amiable picaresque outcast, but in wise fools and 'praises of folly', and in the ancient poetic persona of the proud, defiantly lonely satirist. But these reversals seldom became radical. 'Praises of folly' came nearest to doing so, but their insistence on a wisdom opposed to the worldly remains deeply rooted in traditional Christian and humanist values: where they seem more fundamentally subversive than this, as in Swift's *Tale of a Tub*, the effect is not only largely unintended, but also exceptionally 'modern'. The rogue outcast, when he is a sympathetic rather than a mainly reprehensible figure, is normally a wily and more or less charming scamp, set in a stylised world (inverted Arcadia, or 'Newgate pastoral'),[17] in which his exploits score against the pompous and the wicked of the social establishment: a sanctioned challenge to existing society

---

[17] Swift to Pope, 30 August 1716, suggested that Gay might write 'a Newgate pastoral, among the whores and thieves there', a suggestion which later bore fruit as the *Beggar's Opera* (Swift, *Correspondence*, Harold Williams (ed.), Oxford, 1963-5, Vol. II, p. 215).

(part disaffection and part holiday), but from within and, basically, in the name of traditional moral values.

As to the outsider as artist, and especially as satirist, he is an outsider precisely because he upholds traditional values, not because he defies them. This artist, moreover, is almost invariably a poet, not an actor (whose status would be much lower), and least of all a clown. Swift wrote to Pope on 20 April 1731 that 'The common saying of life being a Farce is true in every sense but the most important one, for it is a ridiculous tragedy, which is the worst kind of composition'.[18] The constatation about life is bitterly felt, but the rule of theatrical decorum against which life offends remains, for Swift, firm and unbending. The order of art must be preserved, in the teeth of life's unruliness (a notion relevant, as we shall see, to Fielding's interest in the analogy of theatre and life in *Jonathan Wild*), and 'ridiculous tragedies', mixtures of the tragic and comic modes, are for Swift impermissible. Those of Swift's contemporaries and those later eighteenth-century authors who theorised in favour of, or actually attempted, the celebrated mixture of genres, did so at a level, precisely, of *mixture* rather than fusion, and sentiment- ality was the normal result. In later writers, like Mann or, say, Ionesco with his 'tragic farces', the fact that life is a 'ridiculous tragedy' entails a radical intermerging of comic and tragic, not (as for Swift) a defiant categorisation, and this intermerging is often achieved at the highest imaginative pressure. The kind of serious- ness (not sublimity, for that belongs to another, though related, mode, of Shakespearian fools and Dostoievskian saints)[19] with which the clownesque protagonists are treated in Beckett's *Waiting for Godot*, even as we laugh at zany dialogue and music-hall routine, would seem unthinkable to Swift or Fielding. They would react to the clown on a single level, as mainly or 'merely' funny, and the clown would seem to them an 'outsider' only in the sense that he was entirely beneath notice except as someone to be amused by for a few pence[20] (Fielding was, however, interested in 'low' farce, and

18 Swift, *Correspondence*, Vol. III, p. 456.
19 This complex question is discussed more fully in *Henry Fielding and the Augustan Ideal under Stress*, pp. 140-2. Lear's Fool was in any case impossible on the eighteenth-century stage. He was omitted in Tate's version (1681) and was not restored until 1838 (D. Nichol Smith, *Shakespeare in the Eighteenth Century*, Oxford, 1928, pp. 20-5).
20 See some contemptuous remarks in Swift's 'Hints towards an Essay on Con- versation' *The Prose Works of Jonathan Swift*, Herbert Davis (ed.), Oxford, 1939-68, Vol. IV, p. 91; hereafter 'Swift, *Prose Works*'. Cf. Nichol Smith's comment on Tate's omission of the Fool in *Lear*: 'Tate appears to have regarded the Fool as a senseless jester whose only function was to amuse the theatre-goers of an unrefined age' (*Shakespeare in the Eighteenth Century*, p. 21; see also Garrick's attitude, cited p. 22).

was for a time involved in puppet-theatre).[21] Thus, when Wild is
equated with the clown we seem simply invited, for the moment, to
laugh, more or less genially, *at* him and from above. In the case of
Felix Krull, we laugh *with*, not *at*, and his splendid arrogance and
ease makes us feel inferior rather than superior.

If it is easy for Fielding and his contemporaries to equate the rogue
with the clown, it is not easy for them to equate either with the
artist in any serious sense, as does Mann, inheriting Nietzsche's view
of the artist as joker, illusionist, swindler.[22] Robert Alter remarks
that this equation, in the positive or mainly non-pejorative form in
which it is found, notably, in *Felix Krull*, is 'distinctively modern',
resting on 'the tension between the artist and society' characteristic
of our own time. Alter also notes suggestively that there is an old
form of this equation which works in the reverse direction: 'at least
as far back as Boccaccio's Bruno and Buffalmacco, writers on occasion have chosen to present the artist as a rogue or trickster'. But
even the positive equation can be found, in an unformed or potential state, early in the picaresque tradition. Unlike the 'ordinary
man', to whom 'things happen', the picaro, 'in his aspect of master-
of-his-fate, actually handles experience much the way an artist
handles the materials of his art', and, as Alter further notes,

21 Martin C. Battestin, 'Fielding and "Master Punch" in Panton Street', *Philological Quarterly*, Vol. XLV, 1966, pp. 191-208.
22 If Swift identifies any artist with the mountebanks of the stage itinerant, it
is only the Grubstreet authors of such works as '*Six-peny-worth of Wit*, Westminster *Drolleries, Delightful Tales, Compleat Jesters*, and the like' (*Tale of a
Tub*, §I in Swift, *Prose Works*, Vol. I, p. 38). Contrast Mann's celebration of 'the
primitive origin of all art, the inclination to ape, the jester's desire and talent to
entertain' in his essay on 'Chekhov', *Last Essays*, trans. R. and C. Winston and
T. and J. Stern, London, 1959, p. 182. For the view of the artist as clown, joker,
illusionist, swindler etc., and its Nietzschean elements, see R. Hinton Thomas,
Thomas Mann: The Meditation of Art, Oxford, 1963, pp. 9, 60-1, 121, 124, 151,
172, 176; H. P. Pütz, *Kunst und Künstlerexistenz bei Nietzsche und Thomas
Mann*, Bonn, 1963, esp. pp. 39-40. A certain ambiguity enters into Mann's
feelings over this, and its corresponding tendency to assert the artist's immoralism; and indeed into Mann's whole attitude to Nietzsche, which finally became
fraught with deep misgivings (*Thomas Mann: The Mediation of Art*, pp. 138ff.;
Last Essays, pp. 141ff.).
Sterne is perhaps a transitional figure here, as in so many ways. His jester-like
posturings are an important exploration of the connections between artist and
clown, and look forward to more modern treatments. But his coyness and self-
undercutting contain a shrinking from the full implications of the connection,
a kind of refusal to take the clowning, and his claims for it, as boldly and with
such serious gaiety in paradox as does Mann in his *Felix Krull* mood. But there
is an affinity between the two, and Mann praised Sterne (Herman Meyer, *The
Poetics of Quotation in the European Novel*, trans. Theodore and Yetta Ziol-
kowski, Princeton, 1968, pp. 233-4, a context in which Fielding is also mentioned;
see also Oskar Seidlin, 'Laurence Sterne's *Tristram Shandy* and Thomas Mann's
Joseph the Provider', *Modern Language Quarterly*, Vol. VIII, 1947, pp. 101-18).

he has from the start been a master of illusionism and disguise.[23] It is the extension of the disguise analogy, beyond the clown or the mountebank, and even beyond the actor, to the figure of the creative artist, and the high valuation placed on the artist as 'illusionist' and impersonator, which we cannot, I think, expect to find in Fielding. Conceptions of the artist as merging his personality in his creations, so that the two are not simply separable, have an old ancestry; but they probably do not reach their greatest maturity and completeness, or achieve their highest importance and estimation, until Romantic and post-Romantic times, in Keats's account of the 'camelion Poet' (letter to Woodhouse, 27 October 1818) and its many contemporary and future analogues.[24] Ben Jonson, in verses 'On the Author, Worke, and Translator' prefixed to Mabbe's translation of *Guzmán*, speaks warmly of 'this Spanish Proteus'.[25] But the description, though applied to Guzmán, is not primarily a celebration of his Protean talents (and still less of his 'immoralism'), but a compliment to the literary work of which he is the hero, and which captures his vices so truthfully. Contrast Hazlitt's praise of Shakespeare as 'the Proteus of human intellect' or Thomas Mann's exploration of the positive connection between genius and a Protean immoralism, in *Lotte in Weimar* and elsewhere.[26]

This account should prepare us to expect certain precise distinctions between Mann's confidence man and Fielding's. But some analogies, which make the juxtaposition instructive, may be noted first. Like Wild, Krull is repeatedly spoken of as an exceptional or pre-eminent figure, above common mortals, and reserved or 'born' for a special fate (for Wild this means hanging, for Krull a high success in his progress through the world, a difference obvious and piquant, but which, I shall argue, is in some ways much less than it seems). Krull used to play, as a boy, at being emperor and hero,[27] and Wild, in his schooldays (and after) 'was a passionate admirer of heroes, particularly of Alexander the Great' (I. iii): a further amus-

[23] Robert Alter, *Rogue's Progress: Studies in the Picaresque Novel*, Cambridge, Mass., 1964, pp. 128-9.
[24] For some romantic examples, see M. H. Abrams, *The Mirror and the Lamp: Romantic Theory and the Critical Tradition*, London, 1960, pp. 245ff. and notes on pp. 375ff.
[25] Mabbe, *The Rogue*, Vol. I, p. 31.
[26] Hazlitt, *Complete Works*, P. P. Howe (ed.), London and Toronto, 1930-4, Vol. VIII, p. 42, cited Abrams, p. 245; Andrew White, *Thomas Mann*, Edinburgh and London, 1965, p. 51; Thomas Mann, *Lotte in Weimar*, Ch. III, trans. H. T. Lowe-Porter, Harmondsworth, 1968, pp. 73-4.
[27] *Confessions of Felix Krull, Confidence Man*, I.ii; trans. Denver Lindley, Harmondsworth, 1958, pp. 10-11. A parallel exploration of the relation of artist and prince occurs in Mann's early novel, *Royal Highness* (1909), finished just before Mann started *Felix Krull* (see Ignace Feuerlicht, *Thomas Mann*, New York, 1968, pp. 22ff., 92). Mann never finished *Felix Krull*. Part of the work was published in 1937, and the novel as we have it now in 1954.

ing coincidence is that Krull's sister, Olympia, bears the name of Alexander's notorious mother! In the important episode of Krull's visit to the circus the confidence man's relation to clowns and other circus artists is explored, more concentratedly than in *Jonathan Wild*, but clearly within the same time-honoured tradition.[28] It is at this point, where analogy and difference are elaborately intertwined, that the most meaningful distinctions (from our present point of view) may be felt to crystallise.

Krull, 'with a thoughtful fellow-feeling', thinks of the circus artists, 'these ageless, half-grown sons of absurdity', painted and masked and grotesque, as outside the 'human' world of 'every-day daily life'. He does not, of course, think of himself literally as a circus performer, but he embraces his shared identity with them 'as a member of a more general profession, as an entertainer and illusionist'. The acrobats and others also evoke notions of the deep impersonality of art, and its separateness from and superiority to the 'unheroic, gaping crowd', which, as in Jonathan Wild's final 'apotheosis' (IV. xiv), wildly applauds. Amusingly, many of them have names of mock-epic or mock-imperial resonance: 'the star of the circus' is a trapeze artist called Andromache, and the lion-tamer Mustafa rules over lions with names like Achille and Nero, a touch of slipshod grandeur not unlike that evoked by Fielding when he lists the 'high princess[es] in Drollic story', who are enacted in Bartholomew Fair farces (II. iii), or when he otherwise links the heroic with low farce.

These relations between confidence trickster and circus artist are, in Mann's novel, self-consciously explored by the confidence trickster himself. Or rather, there is a fluid interplay between the relations which occur in the consciousness of Krull, and those which are authorially given. For example, the mock-heroic names of the performers are not presumed to have been invented by Krull, but they convey the ironic poignancy, the sense of shabby splendour, of Mann's identification not only of roguery with art, but of both with such gaudy tinsel. It is not only because Krull is his own first-person narrator that his activities and reflections seem much more internalised than those of Wild. Mann's own self-involvement with Krull, which has led one critic to describe the novel as 'A Portrait of the Artist as a Young Swindler', is felt vividly and at a high creative pressure.[29] Krull's disguises, like Wild's poker-faced decep-

28 Mann, *Felix Krull*, III.i, pp. 166ff.
29 Feuerlicht, *Thomas Mann*, p. 92 (title of Ch. VIII). On Mann's feeling that *Felix Krull*, with its 'new twist [partly inspired by the memoirs of the Rumanian swindler Manolescu] to the theme of art-and-the-artist, to the psychology of the unreal, the illusionary form of existence', was perhaps his 'most personal' work, see *A Sketch of My Life*, trans. H. T. Lowe-Porter, London, 1961, pp. 41-2.

tions, are usually in pursuit of some technically criminal end: how-ever, not only does Krull enjoy them *per se*, as artistic achievement and as ever-renewable modes of self-realisation, but Mann himself (as the novel's tone unmistakably reminds us throughout) casts a festive and triumphant verve over, and into, all Krull's operations. Where the multiplicity of Krull's deceptions and disguises is a pro-clamation of plasticity, of the fluidity of boundaries, of the inappro-priateness to a fully human life of simplified or static postures, Wild's deceptions are frozen into a sharply defined criminal-cum-comic role. Of course, the underlying comedy of Wild (like much of Fielding's comedy elsewhere) rests also on an ideal of spontaneous and vital plasticity, and on a corresponding proto-Bergsonian view of the rigid and the mechanically self-entrapped. But for Fielding, the ideal of vital plasticity is different from that celebrated in Mann's novel, partly because for Fielding plasticity meant carrying one's full humanity within one's appointed social role, whereas for Mann plasticity is a transcendence or even a denial of any given role. Moreover, Fielding's notion of an ideal plasticity was at the same time contained within a securely held and strongly manifested moral outlook. It is always clear that Wild is doing wrong, but never conceded that Krull is, a distinction not unconnected with the fact that, by roughly similar misdemeanours, Wild reduces life into routine (thus losing his plasticity), while Krull frees himself from the routines of common life.

Fielding's well-known externality, here as elsewhere, is an aloof-ness which not only asserts the author's moral and social superiority, but suggests the poise of one who is sufficiently sure of his standards not to need to involve himself in the unduly intimate scrutiny of a nasty situation. Or, for that matter, of any other situation: if character is determined by its relation to a moral code, it will seem correspondingly natural to feel that a personality can be con-fidently defined. Where Krull is endlessly various and elusive (truly Protean beyond the reach of Guzmán's or any other mere picaro's skills), Wild shows to the end a notable 'conservation of character' (IV. xiv). Fielding's uses of this and related phrases suggest that the notions of 'self-consistency' and of the referrability of character to a fixed moral standard are interwoven in his mind with a profound intimacy. The topic exercises his irony throughout *Jonathan Wild*, and makes its first appearance in I. i, when Fielding sarcastically rebukes the historians who 'destroy the great perfection called uniformity of character' by attributing to 'great' personages like Alexander and Caesar certain alien touches of 'goodness'. This ironically overstated postulate of an unmixed purity of good or evil should not, in itself, be exaggerated. It has a fictive or rhetorical pole that belongs naturally among the work's formulaic contrasts of 'greatness' and 'goodness', and it is moreover undercut in the same chapter and elsewhere by reminders that no man is perfect and that even a 'great' man like Wild has a few 'weaknesses' (I. i; IV. iv; IV. xv). Furthermore, in the Preface to the *Miscellanies* Fielding tried to rectify what in sober truth, as opposed to the novel's ironic extravagance, would seem an over-simple division, by adding a third category of the 'great and good'.[30] On the other hand, the concessions in the novel over Wild's 'weaknesses' are themselves mainly rhetorical (they are, in the words of the closing paragraph of I. i, 'only enough to make him partaker of the imperfection of humanity, instead of the perfection of diabolism'), and the mixed category of the 'great and good' in the Preface seems to extend only to a very few rare persons. In any event, even this mixed category hardly weakens the connection between the notion of character as a fixed and coherent thing, and the very straightforward moral norms against which it is tested.

But a more interesting convergence between a categorisable self-consistency of character, and the domain of stable and predictable moral judgments (notably the domain of the merited rewards and punishments which constitute 'poetic justice'), occurs in the two closing chapters. First, in the important and memorably comic paragraph in IV. xiv in which Wild swings 'out of the world' with the ordinary's bottle-screw in his hand, we read of the 'admirable conservation of character in our hero' which makes him maintain his pickpocketing habits 'to the last moment'. It is not clear, and does not need to be clear, whether it is Wild who is 'admirable' for having retained his selfhood unflinchingly, or whether 'nature' is to be congratulated for creating such a consummately self-consistent personality, or whether the author of the novel has achieved a triumph of artistic coherence. The three notions closely intersect, without blurring each other's sharp and witty clarity (just as the genial humour of Wild's mortal exit does not blur the firmness with which it is brought home to us that Wild deserved his fate). The parallels and reciprocities between 'art' and 'nature' exercised Fielding as much and as buoyantly as they did Mann, differently though the two novelists interpret them. In IV. xv Fielding returns, in a slightly modified form, to the point first raised in I. i, that Wild's 'greatness' was unflawed by those uncharacteristic ingredients of 'goodness' which 'weak writers' have commended in Alexander and Caesar, and 'which nature had so grossly erred in giving them, as a painter would who should dress a peasant in the robes of state, or give the nose or any other feature of a Venus to a satyr'. A few lines later, as part of the 'finishing' (a pun) of Wild's 'character', we are reminded of 'the conformity above mentioned of his death to his life'. This 'conformity' is a reference to the moral logic of events: he was hanged, as any 'hero' should be, hanging being not only the end for which he was born, but also the properest end for 'great' men, though 'so few GREAT men can accomplish' it.

The ideal congruence between Wild's moral character and the judgment of fate upon him, which makes hanging a 'finishing' of 'character', establishes itself as very close to 'conservation of character' in the other senses. An elaborate assimilation occurs at the beginning of IV. xiv, the hanging chapter, where the operations of life are, with grandiloquent fuss, judged by standards derived from stage drama:

> The day now drew nigh when our great man was to exemplify the last and noblest act of greatness by which any hero can signalize himself. This was the day of execution, or consummation, or apotheosis (for it is called by different names), which was to give our hero an opportunity of facing death and damnation, without any fear in his heart, or, at least, without betraying any symptoms of it in his countenance. A completion of greatness which is heartily to be wished to every great man; nothing being more worthy of lamentation than when Fortune, like a lazy poet, winds up her catastrophe awkwardly, and bestowing too little care on her fifth act, dismisses the hero with a sneaking and private exit, who had in the former part of the drama performed such notable exploits as must promise to every good judge among the spectators a noble, public, and exalted end.
>
> But she was resolved to commit no such error in this instance. Our hero was too much and too deservedly her favourite to be neglected by her in his last moments; accordingly all efforts for a reprieve were vain, and the name of Wild stood at the head of those who were ordered for execution.

The reference to a hoped-for reprieve may, as we shall see, be a playful glance at the *Beggar's Opera*, where Macheath is saved at the last minute because 'an opera must end happily'.[31] It is as though, in the opera, the rules of art have exerted their domination upon the action in a way that prevents, instead of furthering, the 'completion of greatness' in a fit catastrophe. This 'completion', like the next chapter's 'finishing of . . . character', means simultaneously due punishment, a satisfying end, and a self-fulfilment for the hero. For this intermerging of moral propriety (or poetic justice) and true coherence of character in some kind of *actual* sense, Fielding at

---

[31] John Gay, *Beggar's Opera*, III.xvi.

least once attempted an explanation in terms of psychological truth
or 'probability'. The passage, from *Tom Jones*, VIII. i, is particularly relevant here, because it explicitly links 'conservation of
character' (which requires of authors 'a very extraordinary degree
of judgment, and a most exact knowledge of human nature') with
the kind of poetic justice that sends or ought to send villains of
plays to the gallows. After noting a type of unnatural characterisation ('Should the best parts of the story of M. Antoninus be ascribed
to Nero, or should the worst incidents of Nero's life be imputed to
Antoninus, what would be more shocking to belief . . .'), Fielding
goes on to say:

> Our modern authors of comedy have fallen almost universally
> into the error here hinted at: their heroes generally are
> notorious rogues, and their heroines abandoned jades, during
> the first four acts; but in the fifth, the former become very
> worthy gentlemen, and the latter, women of virtue and dis-
> cretion: nor is the writer often so kind as to give himself the
> least trouble, to reconcile or account for this monstrous change
> and incongruity. There is, indeed, no other reason to be
> assigned for it, than because the play is drawing to a conclu-
> sion; as if it was no less natural in a rogue to repent in the last
> act of a play, than in the last of his life; which we perceive to
> be generally the case at Tyburn, a place which might, indeed,
> close the scene of some comedies with much propriety, as the
> heroes in these are most commonly eminent for those very
> talents which not only bring men to the gallows, but enable
> them to make an heroic figure when they are there.

This assertion of a link between propriety and probability is not,
of course, to be taken as a bald and literal truth. Here, as in
Jonathan Wild, Fielding is exploring ironic connections, imaginative meeting-points, with a cautious indirection which guards him
against imputations of undue facility, and in a context which
guarantees that he is fully aware of the actual turpitudes and disorders of real life. But he is also assuming, in this passage as in the
overall shape of *Tom Jones*, a greater notional congruence between
the patterned ideal and the actual shape of things than we find in,
say, Swift, when in the *Project for the Advancement of Religion*,
Swift similarly complains of the perverse kinds of 'distributive
Justice' in modern playwrights.[32] Probability, realism and the rest,

32 *Project for the Advancement of Religion* (1709), Swift, *Prose Works*, Vol. II,
pp. 55-6. It is true that many years later, in praising the *Beggar's Opera*
in *Intelligencer*, No. III (1728), Swift did not complain of the opera's happy
ending. But he describes the work in a way which implies that it nevertheless
has all the poetic justice that the strictest morality requires: 'It shews the miserable Lives and the constant Fate of those abandoned Wretches: For how little
they sell their Lives and Souls; betrayed by their *Whores*, their *Comrades*, and

do not enter, and their absence is attributable almost as much to Swift's temperamental resistance to any feeling that actuality can in itself be orderly, as to the overriding didactic preoccupation of his *Project*. The order of art is conceived by Swift as *holding down* the subversive unruliness of the actual, not as shaping that unruliness into its potential coherence, nor as exploring any live and meaningful mutualities or adaptabilities between energy and rule. Appropriately, the *Project*'s solutions are external and reductive: for example, let a censor be appointed 'to strike out every offensive, or unbecoming Passage from Plays already written, as well as those that may be offered to the Stage for the future'.[33]

For Swift, a fifth-act reprieve is simply an offence against moral order, an official sanctioning by art of the all too evidently existing gap, in life, between what is and what ought to be. Fielding is by contrast hanging on to the notion that the actual is not wholly disconnected from the ideal. Last minute reprieves, and other artificially imposed happy endings, are objected to not merely because they violate an absolute standard of moral decorum, but because they are an extension of untrue notions of character: it is no more 'natural in a rogue to repent in the last act of a play, than in the last of his life'. Nature is seen as at least *sometimes* behaving in such a way that the actual, the 'characteristic' and the morally appropriate coincide. Hence a feeling (playfully elaborated throughout *Jonathan Wild*) that nature and art are engaged, no doubt imperfectly, in a parallel *and* collaborative enterprise. This means partly the familiar notion that art must correct nature where the latter is deficient, even doing (Fielding says at the end of IV. xiv) 'a violence to truth' in cases where the factual arrangements of fortune are imperfectly shaped. Thus, in the novel, not only Wild but 'all the other persons mentioned in this history in the light of greatness' suffer 'the fate adapted to it' (i.e. hanging), except two: Theodosia Snap, for whom Fielding had a soft spot because her main lapse was sexual and because she was reviled by the canting Laetitia for giving birth to a bastard (III. xiii; at the end of the novel, Theodosia 'was transported to America, where she was pretty well married, reformed, and made a good wife'), and Count La Ruse, who was 'broke on the wheel' (an elegant variation, morally equivalent to hanging) (IV. xv, *ad fin.*).

But if Fortune sometimes behaves like a lazy poet, and needs real poets to put her right, she committed 'no such error' in the case of Wild, whose real-life end happened (happily!) to be morally

---

the *Receivers* and *Purchasers* of those Thefts and Robberies' (Swift, *Works*, Vol. XII, p. 36).
[33] Swift, *Prose Works*, Vol. II, p. 56.

deserved, and appropriately grand. Fielding almost festively celebrates this convergence of the real with the due order of things.
Wild's failure to get a reprieve is a triumphant instance of life
imitating art, a point which emerges all the more sharply if a tacit
contrast with Macheath's reprieve is intended. The pattern had
already appeared in reverse in IV. vi, when Heartfree's reprieve,
which *does* come (unlike Wild's) but which is also and this time
explicitly contrasted with Macheath's, is cheekily presented as an
example of art imitating life:

> lest our reprieve should seem to resemble that in the Beggar's
> Opera, I shall endeavor to show [the reader] that this incident,
> which is undoubtedly true, is at least as natural as delightful;
> for we assure him we would rather have suffered half mankind
> to be hanged than have saved one contrary to the strictest rules
> of writing and probability.

This sense of the reciprocity of life and art is very buoyant in
Jonathan Wild. That it is at the same time playful need not be
laboured. But the playfulness and the sense of reciprocity differ
greatly from Gay's (Fielding admired Gay, of course, and imitated
him in his plays). Gay's playfulness, though it has a very sharp tang,
expresses itself with a lightly carried panache, while Fielding's in
this novel is a heavier exfoliation of oafish grotesquerie. Gay's preoccupation with 'strict poetical justice' in the matter of Macheath's
hanging is aired by the Beggar, before the Player overrides it with
his reference to the operatic proprieties, which demand a reprieve
(*Beggar's Opera*, III. xvi). But in the 'Introduction' to *Polly*, he
makes the Poet, who now replaces the Beggar, say that he had been
'unjustly accused of having given up my moral for a joke, like a
fine gentleman in conversation', but that this time he 'will not so
much as seem to give up my moral'. Macheath is accordingly hanged
in this sequel, the last Air proclaiming that 'Justice long forbearing
. . . Hunts the villain's pace'.

In *Polly*, Macheath is less charming than in the *Beggar's Opera*,
shadier, more ponderous, somewhat trapped in his own sexuality,
rather than a gay easygoing and successful rogue. His character in
these respects is (like his ending) closer to that of Wild, and closer
also to that of his own Brechtian reincarnations, in the *Threepenny
Opera* and also the *Threepenny Novel*. Brecht's *Opera*, however,
like the *Beggar's Opera* and unlike *Polly*, ends with a reprieve, but
a grotesque reprieve to which are added (while Macheath is standing at the gallows) elevation to the peerage, a castle, and 'a pension
of ten thousand pounds a year', all by order of the Queen.[34] Brecht

---

34 *Threepenny Opera*, trans. Desmond I. Vesey and Eric Bentley, in *Three
German Plays*, Martin Esslin (ed.), Harmondsworth, 1963, p. 225.

not only does not provide the kind of 'poetical justice' with which
Polly had closed, but also converts the reprieve in Gay's earlier
opera from merry inconsequence to an absurdly apt and pregnant
social criticism in its own right. In one sense, its heaving grotesquerie may be felt to resemble the hanging chapter of *Jonathan
Wild*, despite its contrary outcome, because both share an element
of deliberately ponderous fantastication, in service of a similar satiric
irony. In such a style, Gay is not at home. An approximation to the
later Macheath may be sensed in *Polly*, but *Polly* is an unsuccessful
work. In the less alien idiom of the *Beggar's Opera*, the hero is an
attractive and charming rogue for whom a bad end might seem out
of place. When he is saved by the rules of opera, we know that some
mockery of operas is taking place, but Macheath's attractiveness
throughout the work has been such that the ending has a primary
and not mainly a parodic aptness.

This is not to say that the *Beggar's Opera* ends by giving up its
'moral for a joke'. After the Beggar and the Player have agreed on
the reprieve 'to comply with the taste of the town', the Beggar gets
his moral in. He says that 'through the whole piece' the 'similitude
of manners in high and low life' is such that 'it is difficult to determine whether . . . the fine gentlemen imitate the gentlemen of the
road, or the gentlemen of the road the fine gentlemen'. More important, he adds to these often-quoted words a further biting irony:

> Had the play remain'd, as I at first intended, it would have
> carried a most excellent moral. 'Twould have shown that the
> lower sort of people have their vices in a degree as well as the
> rich: And that they are punish'd for them.

This closes the dialogue, and the scene in which it occurs (III. xvi).
The Beggar is not only allowed the last word, but uses it to give a
bitter final countertwist to his moral. It might be felt that Gay is
thus enabled to get all the moral effect of that stricter 'poetical
justice' which the Beggar 'at first intended', merely by stating the
intention; and that he does so with even greater point for this
sharp rhetorical underplaying. After all, *Polly*, where Macheath is
finally executed, ends unmemorably, with deadening commonplaces
about how truth and justice must always prevail.

The ending of the *Beggar's Opera* differs chiefly from that of
Jonathan Wild, however, because it lacks that sense of the reciprocity of art and life which is characteristic of Fielding's work.
Gay's ending, like Fielding's, is festive as well as bitter, but the two
notes are kept separate and not, as in Fielding, in a grotesque
unison. 'Art' is given its head, and a sharp moral follows, separately.
Nor is it a simple case of bad art being mocked in Macheath's
reprieve. Such mockery exists also in Fielding's contrary ending, and

Gay's joke at the expense of operas, as I suggested, also gives primary satisfaction, because Macheath is so likable. This effect is so far from being cancelled by the Beggar's closing words, that it is reaffirmed in a further scene and a final song. For the Beggar's last words occur in the penultimate, not the last, scene. In the last, Macheath celebrates the reprieve by starting a dance of the assembled company, pairing off all present and himself taking Polly 'for life'. The final Air is on the theme that 'The wretch of to-day, may be happy to-morrow'. It is this separation of the realm of aesthetic order and aesthetic satisfaction from both actuality and the relevant moral comments made within the work that we do not find in Fielding. It is not that Fielding insists that his work exactly reproduces what actually happened (he specifically denies this in the Preface, asserting his more 'general' satiric concerns and refusing to compete with 'authentic' biographical accounts of Wild),[35] although Wild did, of course, actually die on the gallows in real life. Still less does Fielding say that life always fulfils those universal or ideal patterns of moral coherence for which art properly speaks. Wild differs from his own historical original in not offering a final gesture of repentance, in the style of those real-life criminals mentioned in *Tom Jones*, VIII. i, who complete their lives like a bad play. Fielding's insistence that 'poetical justice' and 'conservation of character' have been not only scrupulously observed but shown to be interrelated, in the construction of his book as in the career of his fictionalised hero, asserts a reciprocal interplay rather than any identity between art and life. Fielding's joke that his book is well constructed, and ends as such books should, means also that the course of events described there (unlike the facts on which the story is based) has the superior truth of art. Gay's joke about opera endings, on the other hand, insists only on the greater fun of art, and stays distinct from the graver and harsher truths which his opera also proclaims.

The fitness of Wild's finishing, and the care bestowed by Fortune on the 'fifth act' of his drama, are no merely local or isolated quips. They are prepared for throughout the novel by a whole series of allusions to the fact that Wild was born to be hanged, and that Fortune and Nature (though not always to be relied on to govern the lives of men with a proper consistency) jealously reserved Wild for this due end. In II. xii, Wild is alone at sea and in mortal danger, but he is saved from drowning in fulfilment of the proverb that he who was born to be hanged shall never be drowned. The point is elaborated in a facetious and wordy application of Horace's *Nec deus intersit*: Wild's astonishing survival was due not to 'super-

35 Fielding, *Works*, Vol. XII, p. 242.

natural' but to 'natural' causes, because it was Nature's intention to hang him! When Wild is stabbed by Blueskin in IV. i, Fortune, like an Iliadic goddess, 'carefully placed his guts out of the way' of the knife, so that the wound is not mortal and Fortune's 'purpose' to hang Wild is safeguarded. In IV. xii, when Wild is sentenced, the familiar sarcastic comparison is made between this 'proper end' and Fortune's remissness in not finishing off some other great men in the same way. And in IV. xiv, some paragraphs after the elaborate stage metaphor about the fit 'fifth act', Wild's eleventh-hour attempt to kill himself with laudanum to avoid hanging is again foiled by Fortune.

In all these passages, the play of literary (and especially theatrical) allusion is very pointed. It is part of a larger network, which includes not only the references to clowns and Bartholomew Fair farces, but also a host of other references to the 'stage of life' (I. iii; II. xii), to Nature as a 'dramatic poet' (I. iii), to epic and historiographic parallels ' passim. The cumulative effect of these is to reinforce the playful sense of cosmic tidy-mindedness which comes, notably, from the fulfilment of Nature's and Fortune's purposes in the matter of Wild's hanging. A certain sense of life as a well-made play survives, even when the analogies are negative (when certain kinds of art are seen to falsify actuality or to violate moral standards, or when real life is said to be less orderly than art). This is even true when 'the stage of the world differs from that in Drury Lane' in a way that is unflattering to both:

> the stage of the world differs from that in Drury-Lane principally in this—that whereas, on the latter, the hero or chief figure is almost continually before your eyes, whilst the under-actors are not seen above once in an evening; now, on the former, the hero or great man is always behind the curtain, and seldom or never appears or doth anything in his own person. He doth indeed, in this grand drama, rather perform the part of the prompter, and doth instruct the well-dressed figures, who are strutting in public on the stage, what to say and do. To say the truth, a puppet-show will illustrate our meaning better, where it is the master of the show (the great man) who dances and moves everything, whether it be the king of Muscovy or whatever other potentate *alias* puppet which we behold on the stage; but he himself keeps wisely out of sight, for, should he once appear, the whole motion would be at an end. Not that anyone is ignorant of his being there, or supposes that the puppets are not mere sticks of wood, and he himself the sole mover; but as this (though every one knows it) doth not appear visibly, *i.e.* to their eyes, no one is ashamed of consenting to be imposed upon. . . . (III. xi)

This is one of the more acrid of the novel's theatrical comparisons, and hardly implies sympathy for Wild's behind-the-scenes manipulation of his accomplices, or for the willingness of mankind to be taken in by such perfunctory concealments.[36] The image, of course, points particularly to Walpole who was commonly presented by satirists as a theatrical manager or an actor, and specifically as a Colley Cibber, patentee of Drury Lane.[37] The anti-Walpole, anti-Cibber allusion, with its attendant implication that Walpole's government is a farce, links the passage with several of Fielding's plays, as well as with the *Dunciad*. It also provides a specific satiric charge within the more general and continuous theatrical metaphor in the novel as a whole. Such specific implications, against Walpole and Cibber, might not seem calculated to soften the passage very much. On the other hand, the characteristic glint of uppish humour at Cibber's expense, and the patronising chatter about puppet-shows, do introduce a note of comicality sufficient to suggest that the viciousness of Wild and Walpole stops short of destroying the narrator's emotional poise. The puppet 'king of Muscovy', like the roll-call of 'high princess[es] in Drollic story' in II. iii, and the circus figures with the heroic or imperial nicknames in *Felix Krull*, is lit by the inherent fun which belongs to such hobbling stylisations in the lower theatrical arts, and by the added fun of stylised allusion to these stylisations in a sophisticated and highly articulate ironic fiction. References to the order of art, the setting up of stylised frames to surround the action or the moral commentary, are, with Fielding, in themselves signs that the author is in control. The naked rawness of circumstance and any undue immediacy of authorial feeling are distanced into a world where artifice and moral irony combine to reassure us of certain essential stabilities. The fact that differences between art and life are noted as often as analogies is less significant than the fact that relations as such, whether positive or negative, are insistently explored. It is the meaningful existence of relations, and the positive turn which is almost always

[36] This may be seen as a specifically political form of that '*Possession of being well deceived*; The Serene Peaceful State of being a Fool among Knaves' which Swift exposed in the 'Digression Concerning Madness' (Swift, *Prose Works*, Vol. I, p. 110), and which it is Felix Krull's life work buoyantly to exploit.
[37] See John Loftis, *The Politics of Drama in Augustan England*, Oxford, 1963, pp. 134-5; Maynard Mack, *The Garden and the City. Retirement and Politics in the Later Poetry of Pope, 1731-1743*, Toronto, 1969, pp. 158ff.; Malcolm G. Largmann, 'Stage References as Satiric Weapon: Sir Robert Walpole as Victim', *Restoration and 18th Century Theatre Research*, Vol. IX, 1970, pp. 35-43, where Walpole appears as rogue, clown, strolling player, as well as puppet master. Largmann gives several Fielding references. See further *Champion*, 22 April 1740 (*Works*, Vol. XV, p. 289), and *Tom Jones*, VII.i, which also contains one of Fielding's larger discussions of the traditional analogy of world and stage.

sensed as a potential in Fielding's irony (but seldom in Swift's), which matter.

Behind these relations lies the notion, tentative and exploratory but also (for Fielding) vitally active, of life imitating art. The agent of this process is often called Nature, that ordering principle which was for Fielding and others part metaphor of an ideal, part object of aspiration, seldom totally an actuality but always a potential to which actuality tends or against which it can be measured. When life imitates art, Fielding is always (except in his last works) able to seem buoyantly in control, partly because this imitation makes life seem amenable to that wisdom of the artist-gentleman-moralist which he likes to project as his own. This is true even when the imitation is incomplete, for a degree of comparability is pre-supposed, and there is also a sense (again absent in Swift) that a vital interaction between the two domains is at every moment possible. Hence the positive quality in Fielding's ironic negations, even in the formulaically negative *Jonathan Wild*, and especially in a context of continuous parody, that is of continuous awareness of the domain of art as a measure (this effect of the systematic parody in *Jonathan Wild* may be contrasted with the much more radically destructive quality of the parody in Swift's *Tale of a Tub*). When 'greatness' is played off against heroic ideals of which it is part imitation and part travesty, when these ideals as celebrated by epic poets and imperial biographers are played off against a humbler 'goodness', when the events of the story are discussed in terms of what does or does not happen on the stage or in novels, or when these events are asserted to be unlike everyday life but better, or unlike fiction but truer, the result is a cumulative proclamation of the living relevance of the confrontation between life and art.

In III. vii, after the marriage of Wild and Laetitia, Fielding says that, unlike 'most private histories [novels], as well as comedies', his story does not end with the wedding of the principals and its happy-ever-after implications. Apart from the obvious fact that there is more of the story to come, the marriage was not happy:

> Now there was all the probability imaginable that this contract would have proved of such happy note, both from the great accomplishments of the young lady, who was thought to be possessed of every qualification necessary to make the marriage state happy, and from the truly ardent passion of Mr. Wild; but, whether it was that nature and fortune had great designs for him to execute, and would not suffer his vast abilities to be lost and sunk in the arms of a wife, or whether neither nature nor fortune had any hand in the matter, is a point I will not determine.

The uncertainty whether Nature and Fortune had 'great designs' or no 'hand in the matter' is playful, and can afford to be. There are no real or pressing doubts, no ambiguous valuations. We know what the 'great designs' are, and how Wild is destined to end anyway. 'I will not determine' really means 'I (and you, reader) know very well': the marriage will not be happy because Laetitia is a mercenary wanton, and Wild an oafish, unattractive, dupable and foultempered lecher. Moreover, Fortune, truer than any novel or play, but in this novel also morally truer than in everyday life (yet also literally true to the career of the historical Wild), is reserving Wild for hanging. When Fortune is noted elsewhere (e.g. in IV. xii) as failing to reward other great men with a similar fate, the fact appears as a lapse in the cosmic plan, deplorable indeed but also incapable of seriously undermining one's faith in the ideals which the plan embodies: contrast the very cruel sense of the violation of Nature's laws in a late work like *Amelia*. In the present passage, the irony is so confidently in control of itself as to be self-enjoying, without smugness, *containing* rather than denying an evil whose foetid energies are made very clear. The two personified terms, 'nature' and 'fortune', are so lightly carried as to be little more than idiomatic usages. Any additional resonance which they have is derived from the fact that they occur a good deal in the novel as a whole, in mutually echoing contexts, and that they are at all times, as here, brought into relation with great and disorderly forces of character and circumstance. When Fielding shows us life imitating art in a work of art imitating life, he makes us feel (not least because the imitations, in both directions, are incomplete) that the process, though not flawlessly circular, is vitally and genuinely reciprocal, loose ends and all.

These reciprocities are, paradoxically, most vividly felt when Fielding can be playfully ironic about them, as normally happens in his fiction before *Amelia*. It is a measure of the 'positive' quality of his irony that this should be so. In *Amelia*, where a note of bald literalness governs some of the main assertions of the art-life relationship, the matter is rigidified to something more like mere analogy than live interplay:

> Life may as properly be called an art as any other; and the great incidents in it are no more to be considered as mere accidents than the several members of a fine statue or a noble poem. The critics in all these are not content with seeing anything to be great without knowing why and how it came to be so. By examining carefully the several gradations which conduce to bring every model to perfection, we learn truly to know that science in which the model is formed: as histories of this kind,

therefore, may properly be called models of HUMAN LIFE, so, by observing minutely the several incidents which tend to the catastrophe or completion of the whole, and the minute causes whence those incidents are produced, we shall best be instructed in this most useful of all arts, which I call the ART of LIFE.

(I. i)

In *Amelia*, the 'art of life' is assumed to be practised by the characters, whereas in *Jonathan Wild* (and the other novels) it is visibly shaped and dominated by the author. For the characters in *Amelia* this is hard, uphill work, often unsupported by displays of authorial confidence. The author is now a subdued presence, making a few passionate bids (out of eloquent but also harsh survivals of his earlier style) to create order out of the chaos of cruel circumstance, but often lapsing into cantankerous sentimentality. In *Jonathan Wild*, the author is master of circumstance, like Felix Krull but *unlike* Wild. Fielding's distinct separation from his character means first that in his novel the figure of the artist is exclusively authorial, and secondly, since Wild is sometimes seen in the role of a clown, that the artist and the clown are very distinct beings. In Mann, there is instead a deep interpenetration: Mann himself, Krull the confidence man, and the circus artists, are not simply identical, but their interinvolvement is close and the boundaries between them fluid.

The fact that Krull has no 'single identity to preserve'[38] is itself his triumph as an artist. It is a kind of 'triumph' which Swift foresaw long ago as 'modern', and mockingly pre-enacted in the *Tale of a Tub*. The *Tale*'s 'author' (not without his own associations with, among others, the mountebank of the *Stage-Itinerant*), represents, however, a *deplorable* fluidity, the engulfing vitality of moral and intellectual chaos. In some ways, Swift's 'author', in his characterless and subterranean energy, even more resembles (or is a negative version of) that 'undifferentiated man' whom Lawrence was to describe as buried beneath all our civic roles, alive in the 'fecund darkness' of our primal being.[39] The closeness (in which mutually opposing valuations are sometimes hard to disentangle from elements of essential agreement) of Swift to his satirised 'author' and of both to Lawrence becomes vivid if we set the *Tale*'s Clothes' Philosophy beside, say, Ursula's cherished conception of the inner man of every civic puppet as 'a piece of darkness made visible only by his clothes', and her contempt for their daylight

---

38 Susan Meikle, *Clownesque Elements in Works of Four Modern German Writers*, Unpublished M.A. Dissertation, University of Birmingham, 1969, p. 186. On Krull's non-identity, see also White, *Thomas Mann*, p. 56.
39 D. H. Lawrence, *The Rainbow*, Harmondsworth, 1950, ch. XV, pp. 453-7.

manner of assuming 'selves as they assume suits of clothing'.[40] Fielding never gets entangled in his own satirised opposites as Swift does.
Where Swift and Lawrence see the retreat from roles as a descent
into an undifferentiating inner darkness (whether nasty or vitally
creative), Fielding and Mann think in terms of a multiplication or
variegation of being: criminal hypocrisies, mendacities of clownish
facial expression in Wild, gay adoption of disguises and 'double'
identities by Krull. But there is an overriding difference, which is
cultural, between the eighteenth-century authors on the one hand,
and the twentieth-century ones on the other. For both Swift and
Fielding, our civic roles, our appointed functions in society, though
subject to uppish ridicule for their tendency to self-entrapment or
professional rigidity, are nevertheless essential to the order on which
society rests. For Lawrence and Mann, that order is so far from
being sacrosanct, and its categorisations so untrue or irrelevant,
that they need to be destroyed or at least transcended, in an overriding plasticity of being, and a correspondingly fluid system of
values. 'Conservation of character' and 'poetical justice' not only
cease to have the importance which they had for Fielding, but also
lose their reciprocal tendency to merge the concepts of character
consistency and moral propriety, in their more simply definable
forms at least, into one another. It is by emphasising this convergence in the 'finishing' of Wild that Fielding makes the artist
(i.e. himself) triumph over life, whereas Krull triumphs over life by
remaining unpunished, and striding from success to success.[41] It is
as right for the earlier confidence man to be hanged, as for the
later one to flourish. Both are victories for the artist, and proud
consummations for the confidence man, but in Fielding the two are
different persons, the artist having kept Nature in order (or corrected her unruly tendency to the fortuitous) by ensuring that the
confidence man is eliminated. If both authors say that life is a
confidence game, Fielding wants the artist to expose the confidence
game by appeal to a truer morality, while Mann wants him to play
the system by being the supremest confidence trickster of all. Mann
belongs to a century which can think, scientifically and without
necessary attribution of blame, of human behaviour as an interplay

40 Ibid., p. 453. For Lawrence's puppet imagery, see p. 454.
41 Krull's story is unfinished, though in its existing form ends on a triumphant
climax. In the novel's opening paragraph, moreover, we see Krull sitting down
to write his memoirs 'at leisure and in complete retirement—furthermore, in
good health, though tired', a beginning which seems to show us Krull in a happy
prosperous retirement after a successful career (see Feuerlicht, *Thomas Mann*, p.
93). R. B. Heilman says, however, that 'The story was to end conventionally:
the picaresque hero exposed and jailed' ('Variations on Picaresque *(Felix Krull)*',
Sewanee Review, Vol. LXVI, 1958, p. 573). I have not been able to find the
evidence for this.

of fictive roles, a puppet-show or a circus act, and which can likewise present the analogy between society and a confidence game as a sober sociological fact rather than as a moral scandal.[42] The sociologist might, for example, note the 'sincerity' of Nazi murderers who subsequently describe themselves as having been merely 'bureaucrats faced with certain unpleasant exigencies':

> Their human remorse is probably just as sincere as their erst-while cruelty. As the Austrian novelist Robert Musil has put it, in every murderer's heart there is a spot in which he is eter-nally innocent. The seasons of life follow one another, and one must change one's face as one changes one's clothes. At the moment we are not concerned with the psychological difficulties or the ethical import of such 'lack of character'. We only want to stress that it is the customary procedure.[43]

Mann's thinking on such questions has not the scientific objectivity of the sociologist, nor is it necessarily true that his thinking was shaped by developments in scientific psychology and sociology. Like Yeats and some other twentieth-century authors who have been pre-occupied with the problems of role and mask, Mann is not con-cerned merely with the sociological fact of role-playing, nor even with the practical exploitation of the sociologist's understanding of human trickery, but with the artist's high and special function in relation to these. In a world of relative deceptions and delusive appearances, the *radical* trickery of art becomes the only reality or truest fiction, the most authentic assertion of selfhood.[44]

It is not a simple question of immoralism. The sociologist I have quoted certainly does not condone Nazis (neither, to put it mildly, did Mann). But Swift and Fielding would not have been able thus to separate 'ethical import' from mere psychological fact. For them, 'changes of clothes' in this sense are overridingly culpable, and not only when the gravest moral or political issues (such as tyranny or mass murder) are involved. The traditional image of hollowness and unreality which occurs in satirical Clothes' Philosophies ('Is not Religion a *Cloak* . . .'),[45] and in their most reductive exemplar, the Beau (as when in *Jonathan Wild*, I. x, Fielding says of Tom Smirk that 'As we take dress to be the characteristic or efficient quality of a beau, we shall . . . content ourselves with describing his

---

42 See, for example, Peter Berger's excellent discussion, *Invitation to Sociology: A Humanistic Perspective*, Harmondsworth, 1967, pp. 159-160, 187 *et passim*.
43 Ibid., pp. 127-8.
44 I speak here of Mann's more buoyant, art-asserting mood, which seems to me dominant in *Felix Krull*. That there are ambiguities in his view of the artist as swindler, and moral reservations about the value of art, is an important part of Mann's outlook. See above, n. 22, and Hinton Thomas, *Thomas Mann, passim*.
45 Swift, *Prose Works*, Vol. I, p. 47.

dress only . . . '), makes a simple moral judgment about hypocrisy, or a culpable triviality. When Lawrence talks of the hollowness of the 'dressed-up creatures', it is more in terms of an inauthenticity in respect of their most vital selves, than in respect of any simply definable moral code.[46] The insufficiency of the handsome and elegant Skrebensky (very deeply and sympathetically explored in a manner unthinkable not only in Swift or Fielding, but perhaps even in the Richardson of *Clarissa*) is in particular seen as a matter of 'unreality' rather than 'immorality', although some critics would feel that such redefinitions have, in Lawrence, a rewritten Puritanism, a new morality as binding as the old.

What Lawrence's 'puritanism' could not be expected to emphasise is that element of deception in serious art which Mann constantly asserted. A festively conceived exhibition of the artist as swindler was outside the range of his sympathies, as it would (for other but not unrelated reasons) be outside the range of Swift's or Richardson's, but perhaps not Fielding's. The figure of the author in *Jonathan Wild* gets away with a great deal of sleight-of-hand when talking about the relation of his art to truth, and about the identity of real-life truths themselves. This sleight-of-hand, moreover, is at times cheekily transparent, and the cheek is not entirely unlike Krull's. Something of Krull's 'life's task of making the world respond gladly to the reality his own imaginative powers can create'[47] is sensed in Fielding's signposted projection of events through the ordering and distorting rearrangements of art. But Fielding holds back from any full commitment to the artist as swindler. The parts of Fielding which resemble Krull are different from the parts of Wild which resemble Krull, even when Wild is seen, in his small way, as himself an artist (i.e. a clown). Where Krull the artist appro-

---

[46] Lawrence, *The Rainbow*, p. 453. In 'Art and Morality', Lawrence rejected 'the common claptrap that "art is immoral"', and said that art 'substitutes a finer morality for a grosser'. He elaborates on this in 'Morality and the Novel', saying that 'morality is that delicate, for ever trembling and changing *balance* between me and my circumambient universe'. It is not a 'stable equilibrium'. 'Everything is true in its own time, place, circumstance, and untrue outside of its own place, time, circumstance.' A crude moralising in art is as immoral as licentious freedom. In the closing paragraph of 'Why the Novel Matters' occurs the clearest statement of the opposition between a deadeningly fixed morality, and the 'finer morality' which the novel can most fully express, by giving '*all* things . . . full play', realising their true vitality. 'In life, there is right and wrong, good and bad, all the time. But what is right in one case is wrong in another . . . And only in the novel are *all* things given full play, or at least they may be given full play, when we realize that life itself, and not inert safety, is the reason for living. For out of the full play of all things emerges the only living that is anything, the wholeness of a man, the wholeness of a woman, man alive, and live woman' (*Phoenix. The Posthumous Papers of D. H. Lawrence*, London, 1936, pp. 521, 525, 528-9, 538).

[47] Meikle, *Clownesque Elements*, p. 32.

priates to himself the picaro's mastery over his own fate, Fielding claims mastery only over his characters' fate, and Wild ends up with no mastery at all. Wild's hanging and Krull's successful survival are both triumphs of art over the apparent disorders of life, but the triumph in Fielding is not only a victory and not a defeat for traditional moral values, but is also the triumph of Fielding alone. If Wild also triumphs in a sense, in that he proudly maintains his oafish selfhood to the end, the triumph is of a different nature from that of his author, although it is part of the author's triumph to have brought about that of the character. In the case of Krull's continuing brilliant success, Mann the artist is inextricably interwoven with Krull the artist. Mann confers some of his own authorial superiority on Krull, Fielding keeps his authorial superiority to himself. Krull as clown differs from Wild as clown. Krull has the clown's freedom from the conventional restrictions of common life, Wild the clown's entrapment in stock situations and the clown's mechanical limitation of response. This means that Fielding can patronise him and that, where Krull's arrogance charms and slightly awes the reader, Wild's arrogance has an oafish helplessness of which we can take a genial view.

This happens in spite of Wild's moral disrepute, and in spite also of the fact that for Fielding the 'art of life' is a moral more than an aesthetic matter. A reason for this may be that, as in *Joseph Andrews* and *Tom Jones*, he is able to establish himself visibly as master of the unruly turpitudes which he describes, to project that feeling, so familiar to readers of both these novels, of a sense of order, a power of containment and of wise definition, strong enough to outclass *without denying* the energies of evil. The stylisations of art were for Fielding live symbols of this order, except in the very last works. Even there, in *Amelia* and the *Voyage to Lisbon*, they figure prominently, as the pointedly and painfully visible shell of an ideal which has been shattered by cruel fact. They retain, in the much earlier *Jonathan Wild*, all their force, and make this work, despite the asperity of the ironic formula, very different from the bitter writings of the last years. The formulaic schematism has often disguised this, by competing, in its often wooden insistence, with the real fictional life, and by directing the attention of critics to more prominent but more inessential things: the pseudo-Swiftian irony, the 'moral allegory'. In terms of these, Wild is bound to seem what Robert Alter, and so many before and after him, have called 'an absolutely unmitigated scoundrel'.[48] Critics, and among them some of the best, also remind us that *Jonathan Wild* is in some

48 Alter, *Rogue's Progress*, p. 26.

sense not a novel, but 'prose satire', 'formal satire', or the like.[49] This is true in a strictly formal sense, and it is in some contexts important to say so. But there is another sense in which *Jonathan Wild* comes nearer to Fielding's novelistic manner than is often acknowledged. In the Preface to *Joseph Andrews*, Fielding dismissed 'blackest villainies' from the realm of the 'ridiculous', and this and other remarks in the Preface may seem partly intended to distinguish in his own mind between the mock-heroic *Jonathan Wild* (unpublished but probably substantially completed when the Preface to *Joseph Andrews* was written) and the 'comic epic' *Joseph Andrews*. But it is precisely the containment of Wild by the comic spirit that takes some of the sting out of his viciousness. If this containment is sometimes unintended, and too intermittent to ensure a total artistic success, it is strong enough to release that blend of moral confidence and rich ironic understanding in which Fielding found his truest voice as a writer. The energies of the author of *Joseph Andrews* and *Tom Jones* are continually encroaching on the 'formal satirist', and it is this, more than the strenuous schematics, that it seems proper to take note of now.

---

[49] Robert H. Hopkins, 'Language and Comic Play in Fielding's *Jonathan Wild*', *Criticism*, Vol. VIII, 1966, pp. 214-15; Robert Alter, *Fielding and the Nature of the Novel*, Cambridge, Mass., 1968, p. 149.

Richardson at Work: Revisions, Allusions, and Quotations in Clarissa

John Carroll

I

After the death of Clarissa, John Belford remarks, in one of those many outbursts of praise wrung from her grieving friends, 'There never was a lady so young, who wrote so much and with such celerity. Her thoughts keeping pace . . . with her pen, she hardly ever stopp'd or hesitated; and very seldom blotted out, or altered.'[1] Samuel Richardson was as ready with his pen as Clarissa with hers; seldom has there been a novelist who wrote 'so much and with such celerity'. In a span of fourteen years, he not only ran a busy, highly successful printing house but wrote three of the longest novels in English and rejoiced in a voluminous correspondence with his friends. Richardson was unlike Clarissa, however, in that he 'blotted out' and 'altered' extensively.

Unfortunately, the manuscript of *Clarissa* does not survive. Nor does his correspondence tell us precisely how and when he conceived of the novel and began to write it. However, from a series of letters beginning in 1744, we can see that the novel went through many alterations before its serial publication in 1747-8. The precise nature of these changes cannot always be determined, though the general tendency is clear from his correspondence. The second and third editions of the novel put us on solid ground in discussing Richardson's revisions.[2] After collating the first, second, and third editions, I am very impressed—indeed at times overwhelmed—with

1 Samuel Richardson, *Clarissa*, London, 1747-8, VII, p. 228.
2 Throughout this essay the phrase 'third edition' refers to the duodecimo edition published in 1751. An octavo edition was printed simultaneously. I have not as yet had the opportunity to examine the 'fourth edition' of 1759. However, W. M. Sale points out that this edition reprinted the third edition page for page. It therefore seems unlikely that there are major alterations in this edition. See Sale, *Samuel Richardson: A Bibliographical Record*, New Haven, 1936, p. 57.

Richardson's meticulous care in revising his work. Nothing was too minute to escape his attention—not even the typography. As the printer of his own works, Richardson was unique in his ability not only to get what he wanted on the page but also to determine how it looked. This is a subject to which I shall return, but I think it noteworthy—to provide one example at this point—that his care may have extended even to the printing ornaments. Certainly it is appropriate that the ornament at the conclusion of the last volume of the third edition portrays the rape of Europa, an ornament also used in this edition at the end of volume five, in which the rape actually occurs.

In discussing his revisions, I shall turn first to the information we have from the years before publication.[3] He had many problems, but two difficulties seemed to have been paramount. These were the length of the novel and the characterisation of Lovelace. In the first surviving letter from Richardson which mentions *Clarissa*, written to Edward Young in December 1744, he laments, 'I have run into such a length!—And am such a sorry pruner, though greatly luxuriant, that I am apt to add three pages for one I take away!' And he also confesses, 'The unexpected success that attended the other thing [*Pamela*], instead of encouraging me, has made me so diffident!'[4] Richardson obviously felt that he now had a reputation to be treated with care.

By 20 January 1746, a little over one year later, Richardson writes to Aaron Hill, 'I send you the First Part of the Piece I am upon; mostly new, or alter'd much from what you saw it before. I wish you may be able to read it, because of the Interlineations, &c. But yet the succeeding Parts I doubt are worse than this'. Richardson was apparently worrying every line. And then, immediately, the continuing problem of length is mentioned: 'Length is my principal Disgust, at present. Yet I have shorten'd much more than I have lengthen'd . . . The fixing of Dates has been a Task to me. I am afraid I make the Writers do too much in the Time'.[5] He not only feared that a long novel would daunt potential readers but he was also concerned about the credulity of those who would venture into its depths: how could Clarissa write so much in so little time? No lady would believe it, Richardson sighed, who was not an early riser herself.

[3] For a more detailed account of the writing of the novel than space permits here, see T. C. D. Eaves and Ben Kimpel, 'The Composition of *Clarissa* and its Revisions before Publication', *Publications of the Modern Language Association*, Vol. LIII, 1968, pp. 416-28.

[4] *Selected Letters of Samuel Richardson*, John Carroll (ed.), Oxford, 1964, p. 61. Hereafter this work will be referred to as *Selected Letters*.

[5] Ibid., p. 63. Here, as in other passages from the *Selected Letters*, I have omitted marks indicating deletions and alterations.

He enlisted Hill's help in abridging, but Richardson's heart was not really in the task. He professed paralysis in the face of conflicting advice. Colley Cibber was 'for taking away whole Branches', but 'these very Branches Dr. Young would not have parted with'.[6] The manuscript (or perhaps manuscripts) seem to have been in constant circulation. Richardson was in a perpetual, and apparently pleasant, dither about the opinions of his friends. When Hill finally took action and produced a sample abridgment which reduced thirty-seven of Richardson's close 'sides' to fifteen, Richardson was mightily distressed: 'All that I design'd by it, I doubt cannot be answer'd in so short a Compass without taking from it those simple, tho' diffuse Parts, which some like, and have (however unduly) complimented me upon, as making a new Species of Writing'.[7] Hill's lack of delicacy, by the way, permits him to put the exclamation 'By Heaven' in the mouth of Arabella. At this point, Richardson added a footnote to Hill's manuscript: 'To what Regiment of Guards could this Lady belong?'[8] Hill retreated from the whole business in confusion. Cuts were made, but still the first edition comprised seven volumes. In fact, Richardson cheated a bit in order to make the novel appear shorter than it actually was. In the first edition, most of the sixth volume and all of the seventh are printed in smaller type than he used in the preceding volumes.

The second problem—that of Lovelace's characterisation—arose in large part because Richardson the novelist was sometimes at odds with Richardson the moralist. The novelist made Lovelace too attractive. In 1746, he remarked,

> Lovelace's Character I *intend* to be unamiable, as I hinted: I once read to a young Lady Part of his Character and then his End; and upon her pitying him, and wishing he had been rather made a Penitent than to be killed, I made him still more and more odious, by his heighten'd Arrogance and Triumph, as well as by vile Actions, leaving only some Qualities in him, laudable enough to justify her first Liking.[9]

The last phrase comes close to the centre of his problem. Lovelace must be a 'match' for Richardson's Clarissa as a writer and as a combatant in the battle of the sexes. And just as important, he must be winning enough to convince us that Clarissa could fall in love with him. He must also have a mental and spiritual depth that will make his tragedy as moving as that of Clarissa.

Hill argued while the work was still in manuscript that Richard-

6 Ibid., p. 71.
7 Ibid., pp. 75-6.
8 Ibid., p. 76.
9 Ibid., pp. 73-4.

son had made Lovelace too odious: no woman would think *her* lover could possibly be as bad as the hero, and thus the power of the example would be lost. But Hill was a poor judge. After the opening of the novel had been published, Richardson lamented, 'It has been matter of Surprize to me, and indeed, of some Concern, that this Character has met with so much Favour from the good and the virtuous, even as it stands from his two or three first Letters'.[10] On the other hand, when it was suggested by one reader that Lovelace *was* completely evil, Richardson turned around and asked,

> Is he not generous! Is he not, with Respect to *Meum* and *Tuum* Matters, just? Is he not ingenuous? Does he not on all Occasions exalt the Lady at his own Expence? Has he not therefore many Sparks of Goodness in his Heart; tho', with regard to the Sex and to carry a favourable Point against them he sticks at nothing?[11]

In the long run, the novelist did win out over the moralist. Lovelace, like Clarissa, is created *con brio, con amore*. The didactic writer, say what he might in footnotes, could not turn the hero into a mere exemplum of evil.

I have not mentioned one other problem Richardson had during the composition and, indeed, during the piecemeal publication of the novel. I have not mentioned it because the problem really lay with his audience rather than with the manuscript. As we know, reader after reader pleaded with him to save Clarissa. When the novel was still in manuscript, Laetitia Pilkington came upon Cibber while he was reading it. She proceeded to inform him that Lovelace eventually rapes Clarissa. Down went the manuscript. Tears stood in Cibber's eyes: 'What! (said he) shall I, who have loved and revered the virtuous, the beautiful Clarissa, from the same motives I loved Mr. Richardson bear to stand a patient spectator of her ruin, her final destruction . . . I cannot bear it!' Mrs Pilkington continued, 'When I told him she must die, he said, "G-d d-n him, if she should; and that he should no longer believe Providence, or eternal Wisdom or Goodness governed the world, if merit, innocence, and beauty were to be so destroyed".'[12] Not everyone was so passionate about the matter, but a great many readers, including Henry Fielding, who had laughed so wickedly at Virtue Rewarded, preferred a happy ending.

The method of publication may have been used to arouse suspense. Volume two, published with volume one in November 1747,

---

[10] Ibid., p. 92.
[11] Ibid., p. 89.
[12] *Correspondence of Samuel Richardson*, A. L. Barbauld (ed.), London, 1804, Vol. II, pp. 128-9.

ends with the sudden news of Clarissa's being tricked away. Volume four, published with volume three in April 1748, ends with Lovelace announcing Clarissa's recapture in Hampstead. The final words are: 'And now, dressed like a bridegroom, my heart elated beyond that of the most desiring one . . . I am already at Hampstead'.[13] Readers had to wait till November for the next instalment. Although the method of publication would have allowed time for him to provide a different ending, Richardson never wavered from his belief that the book must end tragically. Undoubtedly, however, he was immensely pleased by his ability to stir up so many alarums and excursions among the admirers of Clarissa and Lovelace.

I should like to turn now to the alterations made in the novel after its debut. Richardson anticipated the demand for a second edition by printing enough copies of volumes five through seven to provide a complete set of both editions. Volumes one through four were, however, reset for the second edition that appeared in 1749. One of the more interesting points about the second edition is the inclusion of a table of contents, which summarises the letters volume by volume. This table of contents, Richardson writes, 'will not only point out the principal Facts, and shew the Connexion of the Whole; but will enable the *youthful Readers* of both Sexes to form a judgment as well of the *blameable* as of the *laudable* Conduct of the principal persons'.[14] In the table, Richardson summarises every letter and, by italic type, draws our attention both to important facts and to how those facts should be interpreted. The second edition contains, in the first four volumes, hundreds of alterations; many of these are small but others are of significance. The third edition (1751) continues alterations in style, and, according to the title-page, 'Many Passages and some Letters are restored from the Original Manuscript'. For the benefit of readers who had purchased the first or second edition, he printed an octavo volume of some 300 pages containing these 'restored' passages. It was the act of an honest—and shrewd—tradesman.

In discussing the revisions, I should like to examine first of all those changes which are of a less immediately obvious character than those of the so-called restorations. To begin with, the pages of the second and third editions have a somewhat different dress typographically from those of the first. In the first edition, for the most part, only proper nouns are capitalised. In the second and third editions there is a marked increase in the use of capital letters for other nouns. Spelling changes, so that, for example, *inquire* becomes *enquire* in the third edition but not the second. Long

---

13 *Clarissa*, 1747-8, IV, p. 362.
14 *Clarissa*, 1749, I, pp. iii-iv.

paragraphs in the first edition are broken into smaller units, a device which gives more urgency and point to passages of narrative. In the first edition, a syllable is italicised in a word to give the exact emphasis of the speaker; in the later editions, the whole word is italicised.

Now most of these changes are relatively unimportant. But one change after the first edition is highly significant. This is the greatly increased use of italics, not to give the rhythm of the speaker's voice, but to draw the attention of the reader to an important statement. I suppose that, like most readers, my inner reading voice simply becomes more emphatic when I run across these italics, which are especially prevalent in the letters of Lovelace as the time of the rape approaches. Before long, the reader feels that he is being cudgelled into observing important matters that he can see perfectly well for himself. Still another typographical device calls attention to itself in the third edition; for the benefit of his readers, Richardson placed turned full points (or periods) in the margin to indicate 'restored' passages. Again the rhythm of the reader is broken: What do we have here? What new revelation has come to us from Mr Richardson's manuscript?

Of the thousands of changes made in the second and third editions, a great many are alterations in syntax and grammar. The general trend of these changes, begun in the second and continued in the third, is toward 'correctness'. For example, somebody had apparently told Richardson that a preposition is a poor word to end a sentence with. Consequently, he went through the novel tucking prepositions back inside the sentences. Other changes are clearly meant to improve the rhythm of a sentence. One seemingly minor but perhaps significant change is the consistent alteration of the words 'mamma' and 'papa' in the first edition to 'mother' and 'father' in the second and third. Engaged in the wearisome task of collating, the editor tends to put such an alteration under the microscope, especially when he has noted it for the fiftieth time in volume one. There is, I think, one marked result of this change. The use of 'mother' and 'father' slightly lessens the air of common, domestic, kitchen wrangling that threatens to dominate the first two volumes. One advantage of this alteration is that when Clarissa does use 'mamma' and 'papa' in the later editions, the words indicate her tenderness of feeling for them, an effort to go back to a time when she was their favourite child. The slightly increased formality here is, however, on the whole, symptomatic of that trend toward 'elevation' which we find in the corrections of syntax and grammar. Indeed, there is a tendency in both the second and third editions to starch the ruffles more heavily.

On the other hand, one characteristic of the style, of Lovelace's in particular, does not change. And that is the use of rare, obsolete, colloquial, or newly coined words. It is Clarissa who asks, 'What are *words*, but the *body* and *dress* of thought? And is not the mind indicated strongly by its outward dress?'[15] Lovelace's dress, in his letters, is always consciously that of a man free of intellectual restraints. He says to Belford, 'I love to plague thee, who art a pretender to accuracy, and a *surface-skimmer* in learning, with out of the way words and phrases'.[16] Fortunately, Richardson's concern about correctness did not lead him to geld Lovelace's style. I might add that it is very interesting indeed to see how many words in the *Oxford English Dictionary* were first—and sometimes last—used by Richardson.

Lovelace's pyrotechnic style would be too dazzling if his were the only voice in the novel, but in truth that prose is often a relief from the style of reason and sensibility espoused by Clarissa. Both write to the moment; both embody their impulses in their letters; but Clarissa's impulse is usually curbed by deliberation. To be fair to Clarissa, she is just as adept as Lovelace at recreating lively dialogue and recording seemingly trivial stage business that has subtle and far-extending significance. Indeed, in retracing his steps, Richardson saw the value of presenting as many encounters as possible in direct dramatic form. Several episodes in the first edition, presented as indirect narrative, become direct 'scenes' in the second and third editions.

Some of the smaller changes were undoubtedly the result of Richardson's well-known concern with delicacy. For example, in the first edition, there is a passage in which Lovelace day-dreams of Clarissa nursing twin boys he has fathered on her: 'I now me-thinks behold this most charming of women in this sweet office, pressing with her fine fingers the generous flood into the purple mouths of each eager hunter by turns'.[17] In the second edition, the sentence stops at the word 'office'. She no longer presses her nipples to provide milk for the boys. And that fine baroque emblem is lost.

Many of these changes must have been the result of afterthoughts by Richardson himself. But there is no doubt that the reactions of his audience to the first and second editions affected his handling of material. Richardson by no means pandered to their taste; on the contrary, his inclination was to drive home his point of view more firmly when he was criticised or questioned. In his advertise-ment to the second edition, Richardson commented that no 'material

15 *Clarissa*, 1747-8, III, p. 322.
16 Ibid., III, p. 145.
17 Ibid., IV, p. 260.

objection' had come to his knowledge but 'what has either arisen from want of attention (occasioned perhaps by its being at first published at distant periods of time) or been obviated in the POST-SCRIPT'. Undoubtedly, Richardson had a point about the difficulties created for readers of the first edition by its serial publication. Keeping the threads of this intricate story together, especially when crucial action turns on fine points of psychology, is not easy at the best of times. But there were also those, in Richardson's opinion, whose attention simply strayed.

One matter plaguing Richardson from the beginning was that too many readers came away from the novel thinking Clarissa had voluntarily eloped with Lovelace. In 1747, Aaron Hill, who certainly should have known better after reading the manuscript so many times, dropped a remark about Clarissa's running away from her father's house with a worse man than Solmes and that of her own choosing. Richardson was close to anguish:

> I am very unfortunate, good Sir, let me say, To have *given*
> *Reason* to be so little understood: And how can I but doubt
> my own Conduct in this Story, when, if I did not, I must ques-
> tion your Attention to it, in the most material Point of all,
> respecting my Heroine's Character, and, as I may say, one of
> the principal Morals that I proposed to be drawn from my
> Story.[18]

One can understand the feeling of hopelessness. After expending all those pages showing how Lovelace tricked her into his carriage, one of Richardson's most devoted readers missed the whole point. In Richardson's eyes, the story would have had a different turn entirely if Clarissa had been guilty of so grievous a fault as eloping.

One method by which Richardson hoped to prod readers into attentiveness was by means of footnotes. In the second edition, he remarks in one of these notes that several readers

> have attributed to Mr. Lovelace, on his behavior to his Rose-
> bud, a greater merit than was due to him; and moreover
> imagined that it was improbable that a man who was capable
> of acting so generously . . . in *this* instance should be guilty of
> any *atrocious* vileness. Not considering that Love, Pride, and
> Revenge, as he owns in Vol. I Letter xxxi, were ingredients of
> equal force in his composition; and that Resistance was a
> *stimulus* to him.[19]

This is one of many instances when the editor signals his readers to a halt and proceeds to discourse on the correct interpretation of

18 *Selected Letters*, p. 82.
19 *Clarissa*, 1749, II, p. 146.

what the characters are doing and saying. Even in the first edition, he busied himself giving cross-references between letters, thus reminding us of the whole context in which a given passage must be considered.

At this point, I think we must raise the question of the nature and value of the major additions and restorations in the second and third editions. In 1959, M. Kinkead-Weekes broached the problem of whether those passages marked in the third edition were really resurrected from the manuscript or were passages that Richardson wrote to answer objections that had arisen during and after the publication of the first edition.[20] There is no question that some material marked with the turned full points is intended as a counterblast to critics or a corrective to misreadings. In volume three, for example, he adds a footnote in both the second and third editions scolding those female readers who accused Clarissa of being over-nice, too punctilious in her interviews with Lovelace before the rape. They thought her super-delicacy prevented him from making a successful plea for marriage. 'Surely', Richardson says, 'those who have thought her to blame on this account, have not paid a due attention to the story'. He goes on to point out how artfully Lovelace reminds Clarissa again and again that she has placed conditions on his behaviour which now she 'would gladly have dispensed with'.[21]

After putting in the footnote, Richardson goes on to insert in the third edition (but not in the second) a lengthy scene which dramatises the cat-and-mouse game Lovelace plays with her. The scene vivifies the way in which he offers marriage so that Clarissa cannot accept his proposal. Now there is no question that the footnote is an addition rather than a restoration, but the lengthy scene cannot easily be classified. It may have been added to show erring readers how difficult it was for Clarissa to accept the proposal without humiliating herself; on the other hand, the scene is not a flat, prosy, didactic elaboration of the point made in the footnote. The scene is lively, direct, animated; it might well be a passage restored from the manuscript.

Because of the criticism of Clarissa's punctilio, some clauses and sentences were omitted from the later editions. In the first edition, Lovelace on one occasion seemingly urges Clarissa to marry him as soon as possible. Clarissa then writes to Anna, 'But what could I say? I wanted somebody to speak for me. I could not, all at once, act as if I thought that *all punctilio was at an end*. I was unwilling

20 M. Kinkead-Weekes, '*Clarissa* Restored?', *Review of English Studies*, N.S., Vol. X, 1959, pp. 156-71.
21 *Clarissa*, 1751, III, p. 14.

to suppose it *was* so soon'.[22] In the third edition (though not in the second) the last two sentences are omitted. Clarissa was indeed sounding too punctilious here, especially in the light of the criticisms levelled at her.

Another long addition in volume three, a letter from Joseph Leman to Lovelace, can easily be seen as part of Richardson's effort to blacken the hero's character. This letter brings up a previous episode in Lovelace's life in which he seduced a Miss Betterton, who later died in childbirth. Richardson is engaging in a tactical manoeuvre here; Lovelace's treatment of Miss Betterton is so mean that the reader is further discouraged from wanting Clarissa to accept him. A passage added in volume four shows Lovelace daydreaming about his imagined triumph over Clarissa; in these pages she is all humility while he crows in triumph. Anyone who admires Clarissa for her integrity (and 'anyone' presumably includes all readers of the novel) must be repelled by this passage. And, to give one further example of this blackening, Richardson inserted in the third edition a letter by Lovelace in which he talks at great length about a plan to kidnap and ravish Anna Howe, her mother, and her maid. It ends with his imagining the scene in the courtroom:

> Every eye dwells upon Miss!—See, see, the handsome gentleman bows to her!
> To the very ground to be sure, I shall bow; and kiss my hand.
> See her confusion! See! She turns from him—Ay! that's because it is in open court, cries an arch one!—While others admire her—Ay! that's a girl worth venturing one's neck for!
> Then we shall be praised—Even the Judges and the whole crowded Bench will acquit us in their hearts; and every single man wish he had been me!—The women all the time, disclaiming prosecution, were the case to be their own. To be sure, Belford, the sufferers cannot put half so good a face on the matter as we.[23]

So it goes throughout the scene, with Lovelace preening himself as a Macheath. There is little question that this episode was at one time in the manuscript since Richardson's young friend Sophia Westcomb objected to it before the publication. If Richardson wanted to darken Lovelace's character by this episode, he certainly succeeds in that purpose. On the other hand, the restoration is not merely a gratuitous introduction of another example of Lovelace's malignity. There is a vicious humour in the letter quite characteristic of him; in short, this restored letter is not merely a way of distancing us from Lovelace. There is a kind of outlaw

---

[22] *Clarissa*, 1747-8, III, p. 96.
[23] *Clarissa*, 1751, IV, p. 258.

vigour here that, in terms of Richardson the novelist rather than Richardson the moralist, elicits an amused and interested response. The most important counterbalance to Lovelace in the novel is Belford. This dedicated rake, this ally of Lovelace who reforms under the influence of Clarissa, is the centre of all intelligence in the novel. He is the one who knows Lovelace's plans and who also knows Clarissa's true worth; it is appropriate that he eventually becomes the keeper of the correspondence, the supposed editor of the novel, since he bridges the worlds of the hero and heroine. Richardson's friend Johannes Stinstra thought that Belford was probably modelled on the author himself. Richardson immediately denied it, of course, but Stinstra's remark has a kind of truth in it. Like Richardson, Belford can live in the worlds of both Lovelace and of Clarissa, understanding each of them.

Mr Hickman, the suitor of Anna Howe, is also a foil for Lovelace. In this novel about unique, or at the very least unusual people, Hickman is a rarity—a Christian gentleman in the mould of Steele's Christian hero. Richardson wants us to admire him for his gentleness, good manners, and good sense. But even Lady Bradshaigh, one of Richardson's most devoted admirers, thought Hickman ridiculous in his inability to handle Miss Howe. A passage added in the third edition is, I think, calculated to show him in a more amiable and honourable light and to reduce criticism of him for being such a fool as to pursue Anna when she treats him so badly. This passage occurs in volume two. Here he writes a letter to Miss Howe's mother withdrawing from his courtship, but Mrs Howe reassures him that Anna will capitulate and make him a good wife. Unfortunately, even these letters cannot alter the feeling of many readers that Hickman is not only weak and meek but simply foolish.

The critical question arising for the editor of *Clarissa* is, in the last analysis, which edition is the best novel? Kinkead-Weekes concluded that the third edition is cruder than the first because of Richardson's reaction to the criticisms and misinterpretations of his audience. But it is not at all easy to choose between the first and third editions. Some of the so-called restorations are lively, illuminating, and dramatically effective. Unquestionably, however, the heavy use of italic type to emphasise significance or meaning rather than the rhythm of the voice becomes tiresome and distracting. Most of the footnotes and some of the new passages in the third edition have a slightly shrill, nagging tone.

Despite the alterations from indirect to direct narrative, the first edition is closer to the tradition of the 'dramatic' novel, the novel that has come to have the sanction of James, Ford, and Joyce. In the first edition, the author is more content than in the third to remain in the wings. In the third edition, and to a certain extent in the second, Richardson too often comes down into the audience, grabs it collectively by the lapels and discourses on what we ought to think of a particular passage. There is also a freshness, a directness in the first edition that has been somewhat blighted by the third. 'Correctness' in grammar and syntax is all very well, but it sometimes appears less appropriate in letters written to the moment than does the freedom taken with rules which Richardson allowed his characters in the first edition. Further, the second and third editions were warped in certain ways by failures among his readers; the first edition, then, it might be argued, is the true novel, the second and third editions are heavy with encrustations, some valuable, others not, which tell us as much about the audience as about Richardson. In any event, I have concluded that the first edition should be reprinted with textual notes including all of the restorations and any other alterations that have critical significance. By this means, the reader is allowed to exercise his own judgment on the importance—and value—of these changes.

II

If the revisions in the first three editions tell us a good deal about Richardson's narrative and didactic problems and how he attempted to solve them, the allusions and quotations tell us something—but not everything—about his own reading and knowledge. To a certain extent, the allusions are also a gauge of what Richardson expected from his audience. He remarked to Aaron Hill that *Clarissa* was written for males under twenty and females under thirty. But he was not addressing himself solely to the young, the ignorant, and the idle. The diffidence that he confessed when writing *Clarissa* resulted from his knowledge that the novel would come under the scrutiny and judgment not only of flighty ingenues and silly young men but of the leading authors of the day. It might be added here that Richardson's awareness of an audience varying enormously in worldly experience and literary knowledge suggests an area of study that has been too little regarded in eighteenth-century fiction: it is clear that such writers as Richardson, Fielding, and Sterne knew very well that they were exploring a new genre, one that was 'popular', but they were as aware as, let us say, Dryden or Pope of the value gained by a reference or an allusion intelligible only to the most sophisticated readers. I am not suggesting that one could write on Richardson and the novel as Reuben Brower wrote on the poetry of allusion in Pope. Nonetheless, Richardson, like Fielding and Sterne, often sets up interesting reverberations by a casual allusion or quotation.

In both his letters and his novels, Richardson clearly stood on the side of the moderns in the battle of the books. The moderns, above all, had the advantage of being Christian. He wrote to Lady Bradshaigh in 1749 of the *Iliad*,

> Scholars, judicious scholars, dared they to speak out, against a prejudice of thousands of years in its favour, I am persuaded would find it possible for Homer to nod, at least. I am afraid this poem, noble as it truly is, has done infinite mischief for a series of ages; since to it, and its copy the Eneid is owing, in a great measure, the savage spirit that has actuated, from the earliest ages to this time, the fighting fellows, that, worse than lions or tigers, have ravaged the earth, and made it a field of blood.[24]

Richardson also ridicules scholars such as Parson Brand who are ignorant of experience and learned only in languages.

Although Richardson was critical of those who worshipped the ancients, he nonetheless made frequent use of classical literature, history, and mythology. For the most part, anyone who was moderately well read could spot the significance of these immediately. Many of these classical allusions draw our attention to an important and familiar theme in the eighteenth century—that of the 'great man'. The peculiar interest of the theme in this novel lies in the way Lovelace compares himself with the great conquerors of the past. These comparisons begin when Anna Howe quotes Lovelace's remark that he is like Julius Caesar, who 'perform'd great actions by day, and wrote them down at night: And valued himself, that he only wanted Caesar's outsetting, to make a figure among his contemporaries'.[25]

Before the rape, Lovelace constantly compares himself to 'great men' of antiquity because in so doing he makes his campaign against Clarissa rank in stature with those of the great conquerors. Indeed, he says, on one occasion, that subduing the heroine would be a rape worthy of Jupiter; should he succeed he may be titled the 'greatest conqueror in the world'. In the imagination of Lovelace, the man who has three imperial passions—'Love, Revenge . . . [and] a desire of conquest'[26]—his triumph over her would be the supreme triumph in the war of the sexes. After the hero's pyrrhic victory, Belford attempts to arouse the conscience of Lovelace by recalling those 'imperial' aspirations. 'Hadst thou been a king, and done

24 *Selected Letters*, p. 134.
25 *Clarissa*, 1747-8, I, p. 68.
26 Ibid., IV, p. 283.

as thou *hast* done by such a meritorious innocent, I believe in my heart, it would have been adjudged to be a national sin, and the sword, pestilence, or famine, must have atoned for it!'[27]

Lovelace, on the other hand, uses these previous comparisons to soothe his conscience. If he is ready to magnify his exploits before the rape by these parallels—always aware, of course, of the irony of comparing his exploits with women to those of the 'great'—he is now, after the rape, prepared to reverse the telescope, to minimise his actions in comparison with those of the scourges of humanity. How trivial, he asserts, his crimes are compared to those of Caesar and Alexander. If Hannibal had been a private man and plotted against women and if Lovelace had been a general, 'Hannibal would have done less mischief;—Lovelace more.—That would have been the difference'.[28] On another occasion he says that Christian princes 'every day are guilty of ten times worse breaches of faith, and . . . commit devastation upon devastation; and destroy for their *glory*! . . . And are dubb'd *Le Grand*; praised, and even deified, by orators and poets for their butcheries and depredations'.[29] The reader of *Jonathan Wild* would have little difficulty in seeing the total implications of these remarks since, in both works, goodness is true greatness.

Another set of references ties Lovelace, through quotation and allusion, to Milton's Satan. Indeed, there are constant references to Lovelace's diabolism both by Clarissa and Anna. Even Lovelace is willing to make such comparisons, and one in particular is, I think, quite important. In a letter to Belford before the rape, justifying the trials of Clarissa, Lovelace writes,

> Satan, whom thou mayest, if thou wilt, in this case, call my instigator, put the good man of old upon the severest trials.—To his behaviour under these trials, that good man owed his honour and his future rewards. An innocent person, if doubted, must wish to be brought to a fair and candid trial.[30]

The allusion to Job is especially significant because, as her death approaches, Clarissa's Bible is opened again and again to the Book of Job and many of her 'meditations' are based on passages from it. For Richardson, indeed, Clarissa was a contemporary Job. How *could* one account for the disasters visited on this pious human being?

There are also allusions linking the novel with the story of Faust. After the rape, Clarissa writes:

27 Ibid., VI, pp. 170-1.
28 Ibid., IV, p. 283.
29 Ibid., VII, p. 336.
30 Ibid., III, p. 109.

O Lovelace, you are Satan himself; or he helps you out in every thing; and that's as bad!

But have you really and truly sold yourself to him? And for how long? What duration is your reign to have?

Poor man! The contract *will* be out; and then what will be your fate.[31]

Richardson's attentive reader will recall this, and similar passages, when Lovelace says near the conclusion, 'Living or dying, she is mine—and only mine. Have I not earned her dearly?—Is not Damnation likely to be the purchase to me, tho' a happy Eternity will be hers?'[32] These references constantly remind us that the engagement of Clarissa and Lovelace is fought against the background of all eternity. The issue is salvation versus damnation. And thus the tragedy is two-fold: Clarissa's loss to the world, which issues, to be sure, in sainthood, and the destruction of the energy, brilliance, and wit of Lovelace, as well as of his soul.

There are also many allusions which place the action in the context of English and Continental history. The greater part of these are made by Lovelace, who uses them, as he used the classical references, to justify his ways to Clarissa: He writes to Belford,

Have I used Miss Harlowe, as our famous Maiden-Queen, as she was called, used one of her own blood, a Sister-Queen; who threw herself into her protection from her rebel-subjects; and whom she detained prisoner eighteen years, and at last cut off her head? Yet (credited by worse and weaker reigns, a succession four deep) do not honest Protestants pronounce *her* pious too?—And call her particularly *their* Queen.[33]

On another occasion, Lovelace remarks that he does not one half the mischief already in his head. 'And even *good folks*, as I have heard, love to have the *power* of doing mischief, whether they make *use of it*, or *not*. The late Queen Anne, who was a very good woman, was always fond of *prerogative*. And her ministers, in her name, in more instances than one, made a *ministerial* use of this her foible'.[34]

These references to modern history, like those to classical literature, have a curious two-fold effect. On the one hand, they reduce kings and queens to the level of the familiar and domestic. This is a trick of satire familiar to Swift, Pope, and Fielding: the actions of the great are demeaned by reminding us that the same motivations operate at the imperial as well as the domestic level. On the

31 Ibid., V, p. 241.
32 Ibid., VII, p. 212.
33 Ibid., VI, p. 280.
34 Ibid., V, p. 265.

other hand, as with the classical references, Lovelace also magnifies himself—and Clarissa—by these allusions. They are, in his eyes, worthy to be compared with the rulers of empires. In general, Lovelace's historical references also show, characteristically, a lack of reverence for anyone who is esteemed by tradition.

It is, of course, a telling stroke of characterisation that Lovelace knows far more of literature and history than he does of the Bible. Even Josephus is more readily available to him than Scripture. Thus, for example, when writing to Belford about his dying uncle, Lovelace suggests that wealthy old men who keep their heirs from wealth should be quickly dispatched:

> Let me see, if I mistake not, it is in the Bible, or some other good book: Can it be in Herodotus?—O I believe it is in Josephus; A half-sacred and half-profane author. He tells us of a king of Syria, put out of his pain by his prime minister, or one who deserved to be so for his contrivance. The story says, if I am right, that he spread a wet cloth over his face, which killing him, he reigned in his place. A notable fellow! Perhaps this wet cloth, in the original, is what we now call *laudanum*; a potion that overspreads the faculties, as the wet cloth did the face of the royal patient.[35]

This is a reference to the passage in Josephus, as translated by L'Estrange, where Hazael 'strangled' Adad 'with a wet Cloth, and took Possession of his Palace and Government'.[36]

Now it is of some interest that Richardson knew Josephus, but it is more interesting that Richardson uses the passage to darken Lovelace's character. A section added shortly after this in the third edition even more directly urges Belford to kill his uncle; to be sure the whole business is one of Lovelace's *jeux d'esprit*—he wants to shock Belford—but his malign gaiety is a result of that hard-heartedness so alien to Clarissa's world. Secondly, and even more important, the motif of drugging is introduced shortly before the rape. Drugs are a way of getting one's will; in retrospect, this passage seems a foreshadowing of the drugging of Clarissa; he already has that possibility in mind.

In still another reference to Josephus, which comes after the rape, Anna remarks that though the 'horrid wretch' loves Clarissa it is 'with *such* a love as Herod loved his Mariamne'.[37] The allusion again suggests striking parallels with the situation of Lovelace and Clarissa. Like Clarissa, Mariamne had all the charm of beauty, wit,

35 Ibid., IV, p. 84.
36 *The Works of Flavius Josephus*, trans. Roger L'Estrange, Edinburgh, 1751, Vol. I, p. 579.
37 *Clarissa*, 1747-8, IV, p. 340.

and youth. To assure possession of her, Herod killed her brother and her father. Ultimately, Herod suspected that she plotted to poison him and had her killed. But after her death, 'he used to rave for his Mariamne, and to call upon her in his distracted Fits'.[38] The pre-eminence of Mariamne among women, Herod's violence against her family, and his raving after he had caused her death provide notable parallels to the lives of Lovelace and Clarissa.

It is passages such as these I have just mentioned that raise questions about what Richardson expected from his audience. The story of Herod and Mariamne was not all that removed; it would have been familiar to readers of the *Spectator* and to those who went to the contemporary theatre. But the references in themselves suggest that Richardson hoped for a quick-wittedness from his audience that Pope or Swift or Fielding expected from theirs.

On another occasion, Lovelace boasts that he is of Montaigne's taste, who 'thought it a glory to subdue a girl of family.—More truly delightful to me the seduction-progress than the crowning act: —For that's a vapour, a bubble!'[39] This is, I think a reference to the essay translated by Florio under the title 'Of Three Commerces or Societies'. Florio's translation of the relevant passage reads:

> I have coveted to set an edge on that sensuall pleasure by difficultie, by desire, and for some glory. And liked *Tiberius* his fashions, who in his amours was swaied as much by modesty and nobelenesse as by any other quality . . . Surely glittering pearles and silken cloathes adde some-thing unto it, and so doe titles, nobilities, and a worthie traine. Besides which, I made high esteeme of the minde, yet so as the body might not justly be found fault withall.

It is indeed a fine summary of Lovelace's view of women, and still another passage, in the same essay, is also in the Lovelace vein: 'It is a being, but not a life, to bee tied and bound by necessity to one onley course. The goodliest mindes are those that have most variety and pliablenesse in them'.[40]

Lovelace's casual allusion undoubtedly flew past the ears of the young, the ignorant, and the idle like an arrow in the night. But for those to whom the allusion struck home, this would be a reminder that Lovelace had predecessors in life as well as in literature. The last passage I quoted from Montaigne on his hatred of being 'tied and bound by necessity to one onley course' is especially telling when applied to Lovelace's whole mentality. He is called, in

---

[38] See Josephus, *Antiquities of the Jews*, Book XV, chapters iv and x.
[39] *Clarissa*, 1747-8, IV, p. 94.
[40] *The Essays of Montaigne*, translated by John Florio, New York, 1933, pp. 744. 737.

one of the most illuminating references to classical mythology, a Proteus. His career as a Don Juan has been so successful because he can assume a variety of roles, as he does with Clarissa—roles ranging from the adoring lover to the tyrant. And we also find during the course of the novel that he is compared to Tiresias. Lovelace 'has a good deal of the soul of a woman and so, like Tiresias, can tell what they think, and what they drive at, as well as themselves'.[41] Lovelace identifies his own love of power with his feminine aspect: 'I . . . as to my will, and impatience, and so forth, am of the true *lady make!* and can as little bear control and disappointment as the best of them!'[42] The identifications of Lovelace with Proteus and with Tiresias are, then, highly useful ways of suggesting his essential nature.

Richardson's use of direct quotations, on the other hand, is not always functional. He seemed to regard his quotations from poets and playwrights, generally speaking, as embellishments. Thus, unfortunately, one cannot always take a quotation from a poem or a play as evidence that Richardson knew the work. As A. D. McKillop and A. Dwight Culler have indicated, a great many of these quotations may have come from Bysshe's *Art of English Poetry*. When Richardson needed a 'beauty' from the English poets on death or madness or on nearly any other topic, he knew where to find it.[43] There are, however, occasions when Richardson discusses the context of a quotation, and of course this is solid proof that he was familiar with the source.

The really telling use of drama and poetry comes not through direct quotation but through dramatic devices of the kind Richardson used when Lovelace takes Clarissa to see *Venice Preserved*. The story of Belvidera, who married in opposition to her father's wishes, would, Lovelace thought, soften Clarissa's emotions by making her identify herself with the heroine.

Aside from those allusions and references meant to increase the significance of an episode, there are also those that give indications of certain critical views held by Richardson. Clearly, for example, he was no admirer of Swift. In a letter to Lady Bradshaigh, Richardson said of him, 'Swift, your Ladyship will easily see by his writings, had bitterness, satire, moroseness that must make him insufferable both to equals and inferiors, and unsafe for his superiors to countenance'.[44] In *Clarissa*, Lovelace's frequent allusions to Swift are

---

41 *Clarissa*, 1747-8, III, p. 131.
42 Ibid., IV, p. 153.
43 See A. D. McKillop, *Samuel Richardson, Printer and Novelist*, Chapel Hill, 1936, p. 141, and A. D. Culler, 'Edward Bysshe and the Poet's Handbook', *Publications of the Modern Language Association*, Vol. LXIII, 1948, p. 871.
44 *Selected Letters*, p. 214.

undoubtedly intended by Richardson as strokes of characterisation. Lovelace has the type of mind which readily absorbs the outpourings of a depraved imagination; therefore, in Richardson's view, the hero is susceptible to the wit of Swift. Significantly, a phrase from *A Tale of a Tub* becomes the hero's justification for deceiving Clarissa: 'Are we not told, that in being *well* deceived consists the whole of human happiness?'[45]

More direct criticism of Swift is also included. When Belford describes the rooms of Mrs Sinclair and her prostitutes, Richardson introduces a footnote contrasting the passage with Swift's 'Lady's Dressing Room' and suggests that Belford's description is 'not only more natural but more decent painting as well as better justified by the design, and by the use that may be made of it'.[46] His summary comment on Swift occurs in the last volume when Anna recalls Clarissa's indictment of him: 'She often pitied the celebrated Dr. Swift for so employing his admirable pen, that a pure eye was afraid of looking into his works, and a pure ear of hearing anything quoted from them'.[47] She also held it as an aggravation of the crime of writers such as Swift 'that they who were so capable of *mending the heart*, should in any places show a *corrupt one* in themselves'. For Richardson, Swift was not only a man of corrupt heart, but, like Lovelace, one in whom intellect and wit ran wild.

Like so many eighteenth-century writers, Richardson provided in his work the standards of criticism by which he thought it should be judged. These standards may be present in the form of miniature essays, as when Clarissa writes to Anna on the subject of wit, or they may appear in the form of a short, casual comment by one of the characters, or in a short essay by the editor in a footnote.

The harmless drudgery of editing *Clarissa* has proved to me that Richardson was not being merely vain or captious when he demanded from his readers the utmost attention to his work. Mrs Barbauld was right in comparing him to the great Dutch painters; Richardson, at least in *Clarissa*, was a master of detail and design. He almost fulfils the claim he once made in a set of notes from a preface to the novel: 'Judges will see, that long as the Work is, there is not one Digression, not one Episode, not one Reflection, but what arises naturally from the Subject, and makes for it, and to carry it on'.[48] It might be added that even the final ornament of Europa and the bull 'carries on the subject' after the last word has been read.

[45] *Clarissa*, 1747-8, IV, p. 249.
[46] Ibid., VII, p. 258.
[47] *Clarissa*, 1751, VIII, p. 214.
[48] *Clarissa: Prefaces, Hints of Prefaces, and Postscript*, edited with an introduction by R. F. Brissenden, Los Angeles, 1964, p. 4.

Rhetoric and Historiography: Tristram Shandy's First Nine Kalendar Months

John A. Hay

In the course of his discussion of the Dido-Aeneas anachronism in Virgil's *Aeneid*, Dryden describes Virgil as 'the Apollo who has [a] dispensing power. His great judgement made the laws of poetry; but he never made himself a slave to them; chronology, at best, is but a cobweb-law, and he broke through it with his weight'.[1] In *Tristram Shandy*, Sterne creates a world of people enmeshed in a variety of cobweb-laws, and none of these people seems to have Virgil's 'dispensing power'.

To Toby Shandy 'cobweb-laws' would appeal as a singularly appropriate description of the obfuscating rhetoric which enslaves his brother. Walter Shandy, who 'was born an orator', is at once fascinated and dominated by the niceties of, for example, *apostrophe, ploche, anaphora, enthymeme, synathroesmus, paramologia,* and *argumentum ad hominem* or *ad rem*.[2] Although versed in the mechanics of minute analysis, he is not their master. Not only does he fail to distinguish *argumentum ad hominem* from *argumentum ad ignorantium*, he seems forever unable to dispose reality within a rational, let alone an orderly, perspective. His role of orator enables him to cope with the news of Bobby's death, and it affords him occasional, exquisite escapes from rage, as in his confrontation of Obadiah after nothing better than a mule had resulted from the favourite mare and the Arabian stallion:

[1] John Dryden, 'Dedication' of *Aeneid* in *Essays of John Dryden*, W. P. Ker (ed.), 2 vols., Oxford, 1900, Vol. II, p. 193.
[2] For a discussion of Sterne's use of the devices of classical rhetoric, see G. Petrie, 'Rhetoric as Fictional Technique in *Tristram Shandy*', in *Philological Quarterly*, Vol. XLVIII, October 1969, pp. 479-94.

> —See here! you rascal, cried my father, pointing to the mule,
> what you have done!—It was not me, said *Obadiah*.—How do
> I know that? replied my father.[3]

Occasionally, as with Yorick's reaction to the preliminary remarks
upon auxiliary verbs, it excites curiosity. But, generally, the
response is Toby's: 'You puzzle me to death'. Walter's inability
to communicate through his beloved rhetoric exemplifies, like
Locke's substrational hypothesis of substance,[4] the inaccessibility
to one man of another man's visions or concerns. Ironically, however, whereas Walter's rococo flights of rhetoric fail to communicate his ideas, falling, like Swift's 'dead bird of Paradise, to the
ground', his accidental gestures or inflections, such as his prostra-
tion upon his bed, achieve a direct and compelling eloquence. On
the very page preceding the demonstration that he cannot distinguish *ad hominem* from *ad ignorantium*, he effectively defends his
theory of names 'in that soft and irresistible *piano* of voice, which
the nature of the *argumentum ad hominem* absolutely requires'.[5]
In the defeat of Walter's rhetorical strategies can be seen a paradigm for Sterne's comic treatment of the frustrating clash of
expectation and achievement. One of the instances for which
Walter's frustration serves as a paradigm is Tristram's attempt to
organise an account of his own history, and an analysis of this
instance provides a further example of Sterne's 'curious feeling for
order'[6] which expresses itself in the ostensible disorder typical of
the Scriblerian tradition which includes *A Tale of A Tub*, the
Memoirs of Martinus Scriblerus, as well as *Tristram Shandy*.

In pleading with the reader to forbear with Walter Shandy,
Tristram ignores the possibility that, equally with his father's
oratory, his historical narrative will require the reader's forbear-
ance:

> —Will not the gentle reader pity my father from his soul?—
> to see an orderly and well-disposed gentleman, who tho'
> singular,—yet inoffensive in his notions,—so played upon in
> them by cross purposes;—to look down upon the stage, and
> see him baffled and overthrown in all his little systems and
> wishes; to behold a train of events perpetually falling out

[3] *Tristram Shandy*, Vol. V, Ch. iii, p. 27 (all quotations are taken from the set
in the Nichol Smith Collection which is made up as follows: Vols. I and II
(1760) and V (1767) are of the second edition; Vols. III and IV (1761), VI (1762),
VII and VIII (1765) and IX (1767) are all first editions).

[4] John Locke, *An Essay concerning Human Understanding*, A. C. Fraser (ed.),
Oxford, 1894, II, xxiii, paras. 1-37.

[5] I, xix, 117.

[6] The phrase is D. W. Jefferson's, and occurs in his important article '*Tristram
Shandy* and the Tradition of Learned Wit', in *Essays in Criticism*, Vol. I, 1951,
pp. 225-48.

against him, and in so critical and cruel a way, as if they had purposedly been plann'd and pointed against him, merely to insult his speculations.[7]

Tristram, with characteristic self-consciousness, assumes a distinction to exist between his way, and that of his father:

> —My way is ever to point out to the curious, different tracts of investigation, to come at the first springs of the events I tell;—not with a pedantic *Fescue*,—or in the decisive Manner of *Tacitus*, who outwits himself and his reader;—but with the officious humility of a heart devoted to the assistance merely of the inquisitive;—to them I write,—and by them I shall be read,—if any such reading as this could be supposed to hold out so long, to the very end of the world.[8]

It is, of course, one of the principal ironies of the book that, long before the completion of the ninth volume, it is clear that Tristram's instrument is, often, the Fescue, and his manner that of Tacitus. Narrator and reader are both outwitted.

Tristram's self-appointed task is akin to historiography and, like Walter Shandy, he has a complex notion of his task, and of an appropriate methodology. Although he directs his energies towards a full account of his life and opinions, his notion of this task, and the methodology he chooses, conspire to frustrate him. What is accomplished is a 'rhapsodical work', suspended between two anecdotes of a sexual nature, and organised within a chronological framework which at first glance is of minus five years, but upon closer inspection deepens to minus seventy years.[9] Nor is the chronological framework a simply stable one. As A. A. Mendilow shows,[10] it is varied by relocations of viewpoint from, for example, what he calls 'writer's present' to 'reader's present', or from 'fictional time' to 'actual time'. It is scarcely surprising, then, that there were among Sterne's contemporaries a sufficient number to attend several performances, in 1783 and 1784, of Leonard MacNally's *Tristram Shandy, a Sentimental, Shandean Bagatelle, in Two Acts*,[11] and buy two editions of this work. MacNally's adaptation of Sterne's novel is interesting for its chronological re-arrangements. In order to allow the successive presentation of the main 'scenes' of the novel, MacNally made chronologically simultaneous the death of Le Fever, the birth of Tristram and Uncle Toby's courting of the Widow

---

[7] I, xix, 127-8.
[8] I, xxi, 148.
[9] From 1689 to 1759.
[10] A. A. Mendilow, *Time and the Novel*, London, 1952, pp. 158-99.
[11] The reaction to this work of some eighteenth-century critics is mentioned by A. B. Howes in *Yorick and the Critics: Sterne's Reputation in England, 1760-1868*, New Haven, 1958, p. 64.

Wadman. There is, of course, no artistic justification for MacNally's tamperings: even if one reads no further than the motto from Epictetus, included on the title page of the second edition, they are shown to be specious. But he does illustrate the real problems of chronology which confront the reader of Tristram's curious narrative.

In 1936, in an important, if not exhaustive article,[12] Theodore Baird identified both the carefully planned framework of calendar time within the novel, and a particular source for the dates used. In his demonstration that, at least in matters of chronology, Sterne did not simply 'begin with writing the first sentence—and trusting to Almighty God for the second',[13] Baird facilitated later studies of the structural coherence of the novel. Of such studies, which reject the tradition that Sterne's novel was 'a salmagundi of odds and ends recklessly compounded',[14] the one most pertinent to the present concern is Wayne Booth's demonstration that Sterne did not stop his book because he had grown tired of it, but because the ninth volume 'represented the completion of a plan, however rough, which was present in his mind from the beginning'.[15] One consequence of the comprehensiveness of Baird's work, however, has been the direction of critical attention away from further consideration of the *minutiae* of the framework of calendar time and towards qualitative analyses of Sterne's uses of the subtle and often complex implications of John Locke's concept of duration.[16] In view of the quality of much of this criticism, it might appear odd to regret this trend. But the chronologies presented in *Tristram Shandy* reveal at least one more interesting facet of the work, and it is my intention, in this paper, to examine this.

The labyrinthine structure Tristram makes of his history does not proceed from the accidental abortion of a carefully conceived

12 T. Baird, 'The Time Scheme in *Tristram Shandy* and a Source', in *Publications of the Modern Language Association of America*, Vol. LI, 1936, pp. 803-20.
13 VIII, ii, 5.
14 E. A. Baker, *The History of the English Novel*, London, 1930, Vol. IV, p. 244.
15 W. C. Booth, 'Did Sterne Complete *Tristram Shandy*?', *Modern Philology*, Vol. XLVIII, 1951, pp. 172-83.
16 Locke, *An Essay*, especially II, xiv and II, xv. Of the many studies of Locke's influence upon Sterne, the best is undoubtedly J. L. Traugott's *Tristram Shandy's World: Sterne's Philosophical Rhetoric*, Berkeley and Los Angeles, 1954. (See especially Ch. 2.) K. MacLean's *John Locke and English Literature of the Eighteenth Century*, New Haven, 1936, makes some curious conclusions concerning Sterne's understanding of the Lockean concept of duration. Other interesting studies are those of Mendilow, *Time and the Novel*; C. Parish, 'The Nature of Mr. Tristram Shandy, Author', in *Boston University Studies in English*, Vol. V, 2, 1961, pp. 74-90; A. H. Cash, 'The Lockean Psychology of *Tristram Shandy*', *ELH: A Journal of English Literary History*, Vol. XXII, 1955, pp. 125-35; and B. H. Lehman, 'Of Time, Personality, and the Author', in *Studies in the Comic*, University of California Publications in English, Vol. VIII, 2, 1941, pp. 235-50.

plan but, rather, represents the inevitable result of his working definition of historiography:

> Could a historiographer drive on his history, as a muleteer drives on his mule,—straight forward;—for instance, from *Rome* all the way to *Loretto*, without ever once turning his head aside either to the right hand or to the left,—he might venture to foretell you to an hour when he should get to his journey's end;—but the thing is, morally speaking, impossible: For, if he is a man of the least spirit, he will have fifty deviations from a straight line to make with this or that party as he goes along, which he can no ways avoid. He will have views and prospects to himself perpetually solliciting his eye, which he can no more help standing still to look at than he can fly; he will moreover have various
>
> > Accounts to reconcile:
> > Anecdotes to pick up:
> > Inscriptions to make out:
> > Stories to weave in:
> > Traditions to sift:
> > Personages to call upon:
> > Panegyricks to paste up at this door:
>
> Pasquinades at that:—All which both the man and his mule are quite exempt from. To sum up all; there are archives at every stage to be look'd into, and rolls, records, documents, *and endless genealogies, which justice ever and anon calls him back to stay the reading of* [my italics]:—In short, there is no end of it;—for my own part, I declare I have been at it these six weeks, making all the speed I possibly could,—and am not yet born:—I have just been able, and that's all, to tell you *when* it happen'd, but not *how*;—so that you see the thing is yet far from being accomplished.[17]

The exigencies of his task determine even his diet. In Volume VI he notes: 'By the help of a vegitable diet, with a few of the cold seeds, I make no doubt but I shall be able to go on with my Uncle *Toby*'s story, and my own, in a tolerable straight line'.[18] The ideal of the straight line proves chimerical. However much it might recommend itself as 'the path-way for Christians to walk in', or 'the [Ciceronian] emblem of moral rectitude', or 'the *best line* [for] cabbage-planters', its place is abrogated by those famous emblems,[19] drawn long before Dorothy Van Ghent[20] visualised as curious lozenges the plot lines in *Pride and Prejudice*:

[17] I, xiv, 79-81.
[18] VI, xl, 152.
[19] VI, xl, 152-3.
[20] D. Van Ghent, *The English Novel, Form and Function*, New York, 1953, p. 105.

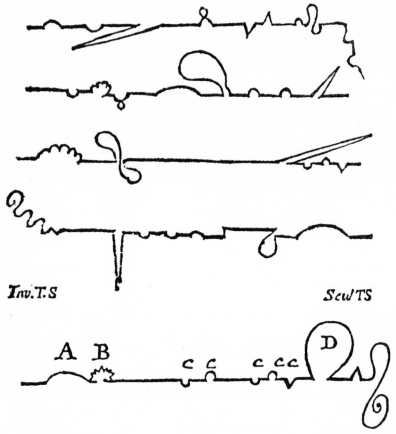

As stones get in the way of Berkleian toes, and stray facts impede Walter's rhetorical flights, so Tristram's Lockean notions make impossible any simply chronological exposition. It is no casual observation of his that Locke's *Essay upon* [sic] *the Human Understanding* may be described as 'a history-book'. In proportion as he is able to describe the *Essay* as history, so is it appropriate to characterise Tristram's history by Locke's definition of wit:

> For wit lying most in the assemblage of ideas, and putting those together with quickness and variety, wherein can be found any resemblance or congruity, thereby to make up pleasant pictures and agreeable visions in the fancy.[21]

21 Locke, *An Essay*, II, xi, 2. In 'The Author's PREFACE', *Tristram Shandy*, III, ii, Sterne rejects Locke's 'wit-judgement' distinction, and refers to 'wit' in a way reminiscent of Pope's use of the notion of 'true wit' in *An Essay on Criticism*.

It is not that Tristram, in writing his history, lapses into digression, rather that he seeks it. As Coleridge suggested, 'the digressive spirit [is] not wantonness, but the *very form* of his genius'.[22]

Tristram, as narrator, reveals a hyperdeveloped awareness of his audience. He continually demands of the reader prodigious caution, and a liveliness to the subtlest innuendo. The result is a tyranny. Addressed variously as 'the Christian reader', 'my Lord', 'Madam', 'Sir', 'you' or 'your worship', the reader is warned of the many 'nice and ticklish discussions' in the book;[23] addressed to the question: '*Whether my father should have taken off his wig with his right hand or with his left*';[24] sent back to re-read the chapter in which Mrs Shandy is shown to be no Papist; allowed half a day to guess at certain procedural grounds;[25] admonished, in order to determine 'who was *Tickletoby*'s mare?' to 'read, read, read, my unlearned reader! read';[26] warned that 'we live amongst riddles and mysteries';[27] and advised, in the course of a comparison of trespasses against truth and beauty, of the need to understand certain things '*cum grano salis*'.[28] Yet if he is not to misunderstand the book, the reader must submit to a tyranny which extends even to black pages, blank pages, marbled endpapers and delayed chapters. And in submitting, he is oddly rewarded. He may perceive, like Baird, the finely wrought pattern of calendar time within the novel, or notice Tristram's failure to fulfil promises to provide 'a map, now in the hands of the engraver, which . . . will be added to the end of the twentieth volume',[29] and to give 'a most delectable narrative' of his 'travels through *Denmark* with Mr. *Noddy*'s eldest son'.[30]

He may also notice some teasing discrepancies in the chronologies presented, the most interesting of which was first noticed in *Notes and Queries*, in 1895, by a correspondent signing himself HRPC, Southsea:

> In *Tristram Shandy* by Sterne there is a curious mistake, which was brought to my notice some years ago by a more observant man than myself. In vol. i. chap. iv., Tristram says, 'I was begot in the night between the first Sunday and the first Monday in the month of March, one thousand seven hundred and eight-

[22] This quotation is a reconstruction by Hartley N. Coleridge of MS. notes by S. T. Coleridge, and is to be found in T. M. Raysor's edition of *Coleridge's Miscellaneous Criticism*, Cambridge, Mass., 1936, p. 411.
[23] VI, xvii, 69.
[24] III, ii, 9.
[25] I, x, 34.
[26] III, xxxvi, 167-8.
[27] IV, xvii, 123.
[28] II, iv, 24.
[29] I, xiii, 77.
[30] I, xi, 52-3.

een'. In chap. v. he says, 'on the fifth day of November, 1718, which to the era fixed on was as near nine calendar months as any husband could in reason have expected, was I, Tristram Shandy, gentleman, brought forth into this sorry and disastrous world of ours'. Now, instead of this being nine, it is only eight months; and it is, in the first place, remarkable how such a mistake occurred, and, further, how it escaped the critics. I wonder has the editor of the new edition of Sterne's 'Works' noticed it.[31]

The editor did not, and critics seem to have offered no explanations before 1961 when, in a footnote to his important article, Charles Parish observed: 'There seems to be, however, only eight months in this proposed pregnancy. Are Tristram's figures wrong? On the other hand, he does say that many things went awry at his begetting'.[32] Parish might well be right to suggest that, if blame is to be assigned, then Tristram rather than Sterne may be the relevant narrator. But it is merely tantalising to suggest that 'many things went awry at his begetting'. In the body of his article, Parish claims that the chronological discrepancy demonstrates the hollowness of Tristram's formal statement of his time of begetting. This, I feel, is plausible, and consistent with much else in the book. But the case is more complex than either he, or HRPC allows, and susceptible of a different explanation. Simply to assume that the discrepancy is an error is to risk earning the rebuke Tristram gives to the reader who fails to see that Mrs Shandy is not a Papist:

> —'Tis to rebuke a vicious taste which has crept into thousands besides herself,—of reading straight forwards, more in quest of the adventures, than of the deep erudition and knowledge which a book of this cast, if read over as it should be, would infallibly impart with them.—The mind should be accustomed to make wise reflections, and draw curious conclusions as it goes along; . . . so wholly intent are we upon satisfying the impatience of our concupiscence that way;—that nothing but the gross and more carnal parts of a composition will go down: —The subtle hints and sly communications of science fly off, like spirits, upwards;—the heavy moral escapes downwards; and both the one and the other are as much lost to the world, as if they were still left in the bottom of the ink-horn.[33]

The dates identified by Baird as the co-ordinates of the framework of calendar time in *Tristram Shandy* are, often, less accessible and less extensively corroborated than those which show a discrepancy between the putative and actual length of Tristram's time spent

---

31 *Notes and Queries*, Eighth Series, Vol. V, 12 January 1895.
32 Parish, 'The Nature of Mr. Tristram Shandy', p. 81.
33 I, xx, 130-3.

in utero. It is Tristram's first task as narrator to locate precisely in terms of calendar time the unhappily interrupted events with which the novel begins. Addressing himself, characteristically, to the 'curious and inquisitive', and, literally, closing the door to all matters not directly related to his immediate historiographical task, Tristram outlines a sequence of interrelated evidences which locate his exact time of conception, and which justify his emphatic exclamation concerning this: 'I am positive I was'. The 'extreme exactness' to which Walter Shandy 'was in truth a slave' gave to his conjugal activities an exceptional orderliness in so far as calendar time is concerned. That it was his rule, 'on the first *Sunday night* of every month throughout the whole year . . . to wind up a large house-clock which we had standing upon the back-stairs head, with his own hands', as well as bringing into the same period 'some other little family concernments . . . in order . . . to get them all out of the way at one time, and be no more plagued and pester'd with them the rest of the month'[34] is ratified not only by Toby's testimony, since Walter had often spoken to him of the matter, but also by the hilarious association of ideas suffered by Mrs Shandy who 'could never hear the said clock wound up,—but the thoughts of some other things unavoidably popp'd into her head,—& *vice versâ*:—'.[35] To this is added the unimpeachable evidence in Walter's pocket book:

> That on *Lady-Day*, which was on the 25th of the same month in which I date my geniture,—my father set out upon his journey to *London* with my eldest brother *Bobby*, to fix him at *Westminster* school' [and, as it appears from the same authority], 'That he did not get down to his wife and family till the *second week* in *May* following'.[36]

The *sermocinatio* figure[37] is then introduced by Tristram to answer the question posed by the feigned interrogator. Thus Tristram's disjunctive syllogism is capped by the evidence that a sciatica disabled Walter all December, January, and February. It is sciatica, of course, that gives the Widow Wadman cause to complain of her first husband. And, it is whimsically revealed in Volume IV, Walter's particular sciatica was contracted from the damp lining of the coach bearing on its door the *bend sinister* of illegitimacy, across the field of the Shandy coat of arms.

Imprecise documentation of the events of *the* Sunday night would

34 I, iv, 12-13.
35 I, iv, 13.
36 I, iv, 14.
37 Identification of Sterne's use of this figure was first made by Traugott, *Tristram Shandy's World*, p. 137.

have been impossible for any chronicler of the Shandys, let alone Tristram. Not only did Walter Shandy 'oft, and heavily, complain' of the events of that night, but their very recollection elicits from him a tear, uncharacteristic of a man accustomed to managing his afflictions otherwise.

Not surprisingly, the chapter containing the formal statement of the time of Tristram's conception is succeeded by a chapter which begins with an ostensibly formal statement of his time of birth. This, in turn, is partially substantiated by reference to a calendar of astrological time: 'I wish I had been born in the Moon . . .'.[38] However, in the most famous of all the examples of the digressive artistry of this novel, a description of Tristram's birth is delayed for two further volumes, and, even then, is given indirectly by a reference which is elucidated in the following chapter, when 'bridge' is seen to refer to Tristram's unhappy nose. Chronologically simple exposition is thus interrupted by the only homunculean narrative in English literature.

If for the fifty-six years old Walter Shandy the act of propagation had 'not a jot' to do with pleasurable sensuality, it nonetheless seemed to him to require, like the niceties of rhetoric, not only 'due care', but 'all the thought in the world'.[39] To a man sophisticated in obstetrical and gynaecological controversies, and familiar with such works as Licetus's *De Ortu Animae Humanae*, the time spent *in utero,* especially by a little man cruelly unescorted by animal spirits, would scarcely seem an inconsiderable issue. Indeed, Walter showed his concern with the calendar arithmetic of pregnancy in Elizabeth Mollineux's 'marriage settlement'.[40] Judicious conclusions are based on a woman's 'full reckoning, or time of supposed and computed delivery'. In Volume I, Chapter iii, Walter observes '*My Tristram's misfortunes began nine months before ever he came into the world*' and, again, in My FATHER'S LAMENTATION, reference is made to 'a course of nine months gestation'.[41] Tristram, too, refers to the melancholy dreams perturbing the 'little gentleman . . . for nine long, long months',[42] as well as referring to the same figure in the sentence announcing his date of birth. Yet conception on the first Sunday night in March (2 March), and birth on 5 November 1718, allows a gestation of two hundred and forty-eight days: eight months on the narrator's calendar.

In the unlikely event that such meticulous care over two points of calendar time should result in an error, it is instructive to compare

[38] I, v, 15.
[39] II, xix, 171.
[40] I, xv, *passim.*
[41] IV, xix, 133.
[42] I, ii, 6.

the 'nine months' problem with an undoubted arithmetical error in Volume I.[43] Towards the latter end of September 1717, Walter was 'whistled up to *London,* upon a *Tom Fool's* errand'. The consequence of this was Mrs Shandy's forfeit of a right to a London confinement, thereby dooming Tristram to birth in the country. The forfeiture clause in Mrs Shandy's 'marriage settlement', inserted by Walter upon uncharacteristically worldly advice from Toby, concerning the deceptions of women, is shown to have been in Walter's mind from the moment that Mrs Shandy's case was proven to be 'wind or water,—or a compound of both,—or neither', to the time of their grave conversation in bed after the conclusion of some small family matter on *the* Sunday night: 'nor was it till the very night in which I was begot, *which was thirteen months after* [my italics], that she had the least intimation of his design'. This, of course, is five, not thirteen months.

On the other hand, if the relevant date had been that of Tristram's birth, and not of his conception, then the arithmetic would be accurate. No subsequent historiographical evidence is introduced to suggest that the figure of thirteen months is other than an arithmetical error, proceeding, in all probability, from the accidental interchange in the narrator's mind of the respective dates of Tristram's conception and birth. The 'nine months' problem, however, is less simply explicable.

In a novel in which the reader is warned: '—never O! never let it be forgotten upon what small particles your eloquence and your fame depend',[44] it is interesting that the first ambivalent implication of the chronological discrepancies concerning the nine months should be reflected in the very syntax with which Tristram's date of birth is announced. The cautious reader, like the 'admirable grammarian', will notice that the formal statement: 'On the fifth day of *November,* 1718 . . . was I *Tristram Shandy*, Gentleman, brought forth'[45] is interrupted with the words: 'which to the æra fixed on, was as near nine kalendar months as any husband could in reason have expected'. This curious qualifier of the formal statement seems to make equivocal the precise nature of a husband's reasonable expectations, and, in so doing, suggests that just how near to 'nine kalendar months' Tristram's period *in utero* was could be of importance to Walter Shandy, as well as to Tristram. With this in mind, it is tantalising to read, in a rather miscellaneous, and occasionally contradictory entry under the heading DELIVERY in *Chambers Cyclopaedia: or an Universal Dictionary of Arts and*

43 I, xv-xviii, 91-8.
44 II, vi, 48-9.
45 I, v, 15.

Sciences, that 'A *legitimate delivery* is that which happens at the just term . . . and an *illegitimate,* that which comes . . . sooner . . . as in the eighth . . . Hoffman says that the usual time of gestation is nine solar months'.[46] Sterne may have owned a copy of the 1738 edition of *Chambers Cyclopaedia,* and he certainly had access to the 1734 edition kept at York Minster. In either case, the work is a known source of many arcane facts in *Tristram Shandy,* and such an entry cannot have escaped the attention of an author who made such parodic capital out of Dr Slop. Juxtaposing the *Chambers Cyclopaedia* entry with the evidence which Tristram painstakingly documents seems to strengthen the latent suggestion that Walter is not Tristram's father. It would seem that a witty proof of Walter's dictum: 'Every thing in the world . . . is big with jest', is being offered to the reader through a proof that Tristram ought not refer to Walter Shandy as 'my father'.

Tristram's illegitimacy seems to be substantiated by a complex set of allusions to illegitimacy, cuckoldom, and impotence which pervade the novel. Perhaps the wittiest of these is Yorick's observation that no one has erased the *bend sinister* of illegitimacy which was accidentally painted across the field of the Shandy coat of arms when Walter married Elizabeth Mollineux. It is curious, too, that Walter's hierarchy of the ways in which a father gains right and jurisdiction over his child gives legitimation a higher place than procreation.[47]

In adopting the self-deprecating role akin to that described as the *eiron* in Northrop Frye's *Anatomy of Criticism,* Tristram so details instances of what Walter Shandy describes as Tristram's 'unaccountable obliquity' as to imply that illegitimacy might account for them. And in choosing, for pecuniary reasons, to publish Yorick's sermon, Tristram unwittingly provides a text to head this catalogue of evidence of 'obliquity':

> The surest way to try the merit of any disputed notion is, to trace down the consequences such a notion has produced, and compare them with the spirit of Christianity;—'tis the short and decisive rule which our Saviour hath left us, for these and such-like cases, and it is worth a thousand arguments,—*By their fruits ye shall know them.*[48]

---

[46] I quote from the 1752 edition. Sterne seems to have owned a copy of the 1738 edition: see *A Facsimile Reproduction of a Unique Catalogue of Laurence Sterne's Library,* London, 1930, p. 10, No. 236. See also B. L. Greenberg, 'Sterne and Chambers Encyclopaedia', *Modern Language Notes,* Vol. LXIX, 1954, pp. 560-2.

[47] V, xxxi, 111.

[48] II, xvii, 147.

The text from Matthew VII, 20 seems, too, to lie beneath the amusing inference in Walter's remarks concerning the cruelty which was Commodus's particular obliquity:

> —I know very well, continued my father, that *Commodus*'s mother was in love with a gladiator at the time of her conception, which accounts for a great many of *Commodus*'s cruelties when he became emperor.[49]

Nowhere, however, is the effect upon Walter of Tristram's obvious 'obliquity' better exemplified than in Volume VI, Chapter xviii, in the 'bed of justice' scene, which takes place, appropriately, on one of *the* Sunday nights. Not only is Walter frustrated in his attempts to converse with his wife, he becomes the victim of those bawdy innuendoes which seem to reverberate after his slightest remark. Like the short-nosed Shandy men before him, Walter is the object of constant, derisive insinuations of sexual inadequacy. In seeming to show himself to be illegitimate, Tristram points to an off-stage cuckolding as the culmination of Walter's misfortunes. Volume VIII begins, as the 'curious and inquisitive' will recall, with a surprising claim: 'It is with LOVE as with CUCKOLDOM—'.

In an interesting study, W. B. Piper describes the rich fabric of allusion, at once comic and tragic, to the themes of impotence and frustration in *Tristram Shandy*.[50] These, clearly, can reinforce the case for Tristram's illegitimacy, and add an absurd quality to his role as 'the tragi-comical memorialist' of the Shandys: like Ossian, or Melville's Ishmael, he is the last survivor of a sorrowful story. Bobby died young, and Toby celibate. Tristram approaches death both impotent and consumptive and, as memorialist, seems to show that the legitimate Shandy line ended with the lapsing of Walter's progenitive achievements some time before 1718, at which time he was fifty-six years old.

The most exquisite irony to emerge from Tristram's curious proof concerns Kysarcius's conclusion that the mother is not of kin to her child. Walter Shandy finds Kysarcius's claim both seductive and compelling. As Louis Landa's fascinating study shows, Walter, like Boswell, is in the van of the animalculists who, against the ovo-ists, support the concept of male primacy in generation, holding 'the female [to be] no more than a nidus, or nurse, as Mother

---

49 VI, v, 12.
50 W. B. Piper, *Laurence Sterne*, New York, 1965; see especially, chaps. 4 and 5. See also the article by the same author, 'Tristram Shandy's Tragi-comical Testimony', *Essays in Criticism*, Vol. III, 1961, pp. 171-85.

Sterne's use of bawdy innuendoes is examined in A. R. Towers's article, 'Sterne's Cock and Bull Story', *ELH: A Journal of English Literary History*, Vol. XXIV, 1957, pp. 12-29.

Earth is to plants of every sort'.[51] Not only does Tristram accidentally disprove Kysarcius and Walter, he seems to show Walter to have
been no agent at all. The consequence is to suggest that Yorick's
observation might well be accurate:

> —and as the mother's is the surest side—Mr. *Shandy*, in course,
> is still less than nothing—In short, he is not as much akin to
> him, Sir, as I am—
> —That may well be, said my father, shaking his head.[52]

In his ostensible, if unconscious demonstration of his own illegitimacy, Tristram inadvertently locates his narrative within a
numerous eighteenth-century tradition of books entitled *The Life
and Adventures* . . . (or some of the many variant forms of such a
title), in which the nominal hero is illegitimate. This indigenous
tradition[53] comprises not only such factual, or quasi-factual criminal
biographies as the two volume *History of the Lives and Robberies
of the Most Noted Highway-Men, Foot-Pads, House-Breakers, Shop-
Lifts and Cheats of both Sexes in and about London and Westminster* (1713), but also such purely imaginary works as *The Scotch
Rogue* (1706), or *Tom Merryman* (1725). *Moll Flanders* (1722) and
Tom Jones (1749)—in very different ways—part of this tradition.
A measure of the strength of the tradition can be seen in the popularity of novels which parody it, such as Francis Coventry's *The
History of Pompey the Little: or The Life and Adventures of a
Lap Dog* (1751-2). In *Tom Jones*, too, is foreshadowed the teasing
device of delaying until the end of the novel clear proof of the
hero's genealogy. Fielding manipulates the movements of Mr Dowling so that the contents of the explanatory letter he carries are not
prematurely revealed.

An interesting device employed in such novels of this tradition
as Defoe's *Life and Adventures of Duncan Campbell* (1720), is to
include very early in the narrative an encapsulated history of the
life of the hero's father. Thus the life of Duncan's father, Archibald
Campbell, is begun in Chapter I, on the same page as Duncan's date
of birth is announced. Yorick, who bears a closer physical resemblance to Tristram than does the short Walter Shandy, is introduced
soon after the first references to Tristram's conception and birth
are announced, and the encapsulated history of Yorick occupies a
significantly large proportion of Volume I. Mr Geoffrey Day, of

51 L. A. Landa, 'The Shandean Homunculus: The Background of Sterne's
"Little Gentleman"', in *Restoration and Eighteenth Century Literature: Essays
in Honour of Alan Dugal McKillop*, C. Camden (ed.), Chicago, 1963, p. 57.
52 IV, xxx, 201.
53 This is discussed in J. J. Richetti's book, *Popular Fiction Before Richardson,
Narrative Patterns, 1700-1739*, Oxford, 1969, pp. 23-59.

the University of Sydney, has suggested to me that, rather than merely teasing the reader with the possibility that Yorick is Tristram's father, Sterne makes out a subtle proof that he *is* Tristram's father. I find it difficult to imagine Yorick with Mrs Shandy, and prefer to take the suggestion as another of the strands in a curious, cobweb structure in which both Tristram and his reader are enmeshed. Nonetheless, an ambivalence is contained within the parenthetical comment which Tristram includes among his observations concerning Yorick:

> —but it was his misfortune all his life long to bear the imputation of saying and doing a thousand things of which (unless my esteem blinds me) his nature was incapable. All I blame him for—or rather, all I blame and alternately like him for, was that singularity of his temper, which would never suffer him to take pains to set a story right with the world, however in his power.[54]

What emerges as the essential feature of Tristram's demonstration of his ostensible illegitimacy is that he did not set out to show any such thing. In attempting to reconcile with his own heteroclite notion of writing history the demands of those 'who find themselves ill at ease unless they are let into the whole secret from first to last, of everything which concerns them', he makes possible what he could only describe as an unimaginable interpretation of the facts of his history. His self-conscious methodology makes nothing simple or lucid. Rather, it ties a knot in his history which begins to resemble the 'good, honest, devilish tight, hard' one[55] which Obadiah makes in that memorable chapter where Dr Slop cuts his thumb.

Like Walter Shandy, and Kysarcius, Tristram becomes a victim of his own methodology, a rider of his own hobby horse. And, being unaware of the dilemma he has occasioned, he cannot consciously resolve it. If there is to be a resolution, it must be imposed either unconsciously, or *ab extra*, just as Toby Shandy both confounds and refutes Kysarcius with his objective, straightforward and commonsense question (of which Yorick so readily approves): 'And what said the Duchess of *Suffolk* to it?'[56] In failing to include in his history what Mrs Shandy could have said upon the matter, Tristram reflects Walter's indifferent attitude to her opinions. In relation to the one historiographical knot which she could easily cut, Mrs Shandy is left on the staircase throughout the novel. By omitting such a testimony, Tristram unwittingly adopts in his way of writing

54 IV, xxvii, 183-4.
55 III, x, 30.
56 IV, xxix, 197.

history a favourite rhetorical device of Walter Shandy, that of *epitropis,* which Puttenham describes as:

> When we will not seeme, either for manner sake or to avoid tediousness, to trouble the judge or hearer with all that we could say, but having said enough already, we referre the rest to their consideration.[57]

As Graham Petrie indicates, it is through Tristram's varied use of this device, as well as of the device of *paradeigma,* that, as narrator, he builds up a close and intimate relationship with the reader.[58] In this instance, however, enough has *not* been said, and the curious and inquisitive reader is lured into, perhaps, the most bizarre of the saurian jokes of the novel. The trap is made fast by Tristram's unconscious use of *synathroesmus,* that 'multiplication or heaping togeather of manye wordes, sygnifyinge dyuers thinges of like nature'.[59]

The manner in which the knot is cut is foreshadowed in Volume II, in the episode in which the speculations of the hypercritic are overthrown by the device of *paramologia,* or *joint concession,* 'when we graunt many things to our aduersaryes, and at the last bringe in the one thinge that overthroweth all that were graunted before'.[60]

> If my hypercritic is intractable,—alledging, that two minutes and thirteen seconds are no more than two minutes and thirteen seconds,—when I have said all I can about them;—and that this plea, tho' it might save me dramatically, will damn me biographically, rendering my book, from this very moment, a profess'd ROMANCE, which, before, was a book apocryphal:—If I am thus pressed.—I then put an end to the whole objection and controversy about it all at once,—by acquainting him, that *Obadiah* had not got above threescore yards from the stable-yard before he met with Dr. *Slop.*[61]

The error of the hypercritic is not that he insists that calendar time may be a measurable and reliable criterion, but that he insists that the evidence available to him is sufficient to build an incontrovertible case. If the hypercritic is put down by Tristram's conscious use of the *paramologia* device, the 'nine months' problem is resolved by his accidental, unconscious use of the same device.

There would seem to be more than accidental parallelism in-

[57] George Puttenham, *The Arte of English Poesie,* London, 1589, p. 189.
[58] Petrie, 'Rhetoric as Fictional Technique', p. 493.
[59] John Holmes, *The Art of Rhetoric Made Easy,* 1739, p. 56, quoted in Petrie, 'Rhetoric as Fictional Technique', p. 483.
[60] Holmes, *The Art of Rhetoric,* p. 50.
[61] II, viii, 57-8.

volved in a novel which concludes as it began, with an anecdote about a Shandean progenitive scheme. And in view of all that is set out in the nine volumes, it seems inevitable that, six weeks after Obadiah's cow had been led on her '*pop-visit*' to Walter's bull, one day or other the preceding summer, she should not calve. 'Obadiah's suspicions (like a good man's) fell upon the Bull'. In peremptorily dismissing Walter's characteristic question, Dr Slop raises an issue crucial to the speculations concerning Tristram's supposed illegitimacy:

> —But may not a cow be barren? replied my father, turning to Doctor Slop.
> It never happens: said Dr. Slop, *but the man's wife may have come before her time naturally enough* [my italics]—Prithee has the child hair upon his head?—added Dr. Slop—[62]

This conversation, however, took place some five years before Tristram was born. That Walter should subsequently take the matter of prematurity for granted seems a reasonable consequence of the adamant and silencing finality of Dr Slop's pronouncement. The one fact unaccounted for in the case for Tristram's illegitimacy is, of course, the possibility that he was premature. Indeed, the use of the term illegitimacy in *Chambers Cyclopaedia* is mainly to describe births which occur before or after a gestation of nine solar months. Prematurity, then, can be seen as the first instance of Tristram's obliquity, thwarting as it does his father's arithmetical speculations.

Because of Tristram's way of writing his history, however, the reader must wait until the end of the ninth volume to see accidentally ratified, through a most haphazard use of *paramologia*, the right and common-sense solution to the 'nine months' dilemma. In summarily disentangling the intricate cobweb of evidence of Tristram's illegitimacy that his puppet-narrator weaves, Sterne not only insists upon the validity of the method by which Toby refutes Kysarcius, but gives another instance of his pervasive technique of wittily deflating learned ephemera by subjecting them to the hard objections of the common man:

> —Let the learned say what they will, there must certainly, quoth my uncle *Toby*, have been some sort of consanguinity betwixt the duchess of *Suffolk* and her son—
> The vulgar are of the same opinion, quoth *Yorick*, to this hour.[63]

In an interesting way, Sterne makes use of the device of *enthymeme* in presenting Tristram's history to the reader. The

62 IX, xxxiii, 144.
63 IV, xxx, 201.

suppressed premiss, that Tristram could have been premature, is
obscured by the fascinating suggestions of illegitimacy, so that when
it *is* revealed at the end of the work, the reader finds himself, again,
to have been the manipulated victim of a perverse puppet master.
The same puppet master may be seen at work in *A Sentimental
Journey*, inviting elaborate speculations as to just what did take
place on the bed between Yorick and the *fille de chambre*, in the
chapters entitled 'The Temptation. Paris' and 'The Conquest'.[64]

In delaying his resolution of the problem until the end of the
work, Sterne, like Swift in his parodic attacks in *A Tale of a Tub*
upon 'the Philosopher's Way in all Ages . . . of erecting certain
Edifices in the Air'[65] and upon such bookish distinctions as that
between *meum* and *tuum*, becomes part of the Baconian tradition
of ridiculing those who 'like Spiders spin out their own Webs'.[66]
It is, too, a subtle proof of Matthew VII. 20, that in writing his
own history Tristram constructs something as elaborately fantastic
as the structures Walter fashions with his own astonishing rhetoric.
The bewildered reader, confronted with all this, might be pitied
for becoming, like the hypercritic or the admirable grammarian,
the ironically observed manipulator of insufficient, and occasionally
inappropriate devices of measurement:

> —And how did *Garrick* speak the soliloquy last night?—Oh,
> against all rule, my Lord,—most ungrammatically! betwixt the
> substantive and the adjective, which should agree together in
> *number, case* and *gender*, he made a breach thus,—stopping,
> as if the point wanted settling;—and betwixt the nominative
> case, which your lordship knows should govern the verb, he
> suspended his voice in the epilogue a dozen times, three seconds
> and three fifths by a stop-watch, my Lord, each time.—Admir-
> able grammarian!—But in suspending his voice—was the sense
> suspended likewise? Did no expression of attitude or counten-
> ance fill up the chasm?—Was the eye silent? Did you narrowly
> look?—I look'd only at the stop-watch, my Lord.—Excellent
> observer!
> And what of this new book the whole world makes such a
> rout about?—Oh! 'tis out of all plumb, my Lord,—quite an
> irregular thing!—not one of the angles at the four corners was
> a right angle.—I had my rule and compasses, &c. my Lord, in
> my pocket.—Excellent critic![67]

[64] Laurence Sterne, *A Sentimental Journey through France and Italy by Mr.
Yorick*, G. D. Stout, Jr (ed.), Berkeley and Los Angeles, 1967, pp. 234-8.
[65] Jonathan Swift, *A Tale of a Tub*, A. C. Guthkelch and D. Nichol Smith
(eds.), 2nd ed., Oxford, 1958, p. 56.
[66] Francis Bacon, *Novum Organum*, I, xcv, J. Devey (ed.), London, 1911, p. 427.
[67] III, xii, 57-9.

In the curious intricacies of the 'nine month' problem in *Tristram Shandy* is illustrated a possible use of the fragment from Archilochus with which Isaiah Berlin begins his essay on Tolstoy's view of history: 'The fox knows many things, but the hedgehog knows one big thing'.[68] To understand Sterne's masterpiece is, in a real sense, to reconcile the hedgehog with the fox.

[68] Isaiah Berlin, *The Hedgehog and the Fox: An Essay on Tolstoy's View of History*, London, 1953, p. 1.

Henry Fielding and the English Rococo

Roger Robinson

> Mazes intricate,
> Eccentric, intervolv'd, yet regular
> Then most when most irregular they seem.
> *Paradise Lost*

I want to start, with what is only partly wantonness, at what might
be called the bottom left-hand corner of *Tom Jones.* The Man of
the Hill's long digressive narrative in Book VIII is interrupted by
Partridge, who insists on telling a longwinded ghost story. Before
he gets to the point, he rambles through a legal anecdote:

> Well, at last down came my Lord Justice Page to hold the
> assizes; and so the fellow was had up, and Frank was had up
> for a witness. To be sure, I shall never forget the face of the
> judge when he began to ask him what he had to say against
> the prisoner. He made poor Frank tremble and shake in his
> shoes. 'Well, you fellow,' says my lord, 'what have you to say?
> Don't stand humming and hawing, but speak out.' But, how-
> ever, he soon turned altogether as civil to Frank, and began to
> thunder at the fellow; and when he asked him if he had any
> thing to say for himself, the fellow said he had found the horse.
> 'Ay!' answered the judge, 'thou art a lucky fellow: I have
> travelled the circuit these forty years, and never found a horse
> in my life; but I'll tell thee what, friend, thou wast more lucky
> than thou didst know of; for thou didst not only find a horse,
> but a halter too, I promise thee.' To be sure, I shall never
> forget the word. Upon which everybody fell a laughing, as how
> could they help it? Nay, and twenty other jests he made, which
> I can't remember now. There was something about his skill in
> horseflesh which made all the folks laugh. To be certain, the
> judge must have been a very brave man, as well as a man of
> much learning. It is indeed charming sport to hear trials for life
> and death. One thing I own I thought a little hard, that the
> prisoner's counsel was not suffered to speak for him, though
> he desired only to be heard one very short word; but my lord
> would not hearken to him, though he suffered a counsellor to

talk against him for above half an hour. I thought it hard, I own, that there should be so many of them; my lord, and the court, and the jury, and the counsellors, and the witnesses, all upon one poor man, and he too in chains. Well, the fellow was hanged, as to be sure it could be no otherwise, and poor Frank could never be easy about it. (VIII, 11)

Another, even more remote, extract: Partridge, in his own life story, which is the last major digression of the novel, is complaining about the crooked practices of attorneys, and Fielding adds the following footnote:

This is a fact which I knew happen to a poor clergyman in Dorsetshire, by the villainy of an attorney, who, not contented with the exorbitant costs to which the poor man was put by a single action, brought afterwards another action on the judgment, as it was called. A method frequently used to oppress the poor, and bring money into the pockets of attorneys, to the great scandal of the law, of the nation, of Christianity, and even of human nature itself. (XVIII, 6)

The preamble to an interruption of a digression; and a footnote to an incidental detail from another digression: in each case we are apparently on the outer peripheries of the novel's structure, four removes from the main narrative and a very long way indeed from either the cause or the outcome of Tom Jones's own career in the novel.

Fielding's discursiveness has always been a major critical problem. Even the enthusiastic author of *An Essay on the New Species of Writing Founded by Mr Fielding* thought that 'the long unenliven'd story of *the Man of the Hill* . . . neither interests nor entertains the Reader, and is of no more Service than in filling up so many Pages';[1] and this irritation with the digressions remained the dominant attitude until after Cross, who said curtly, 'at best, episodes may be bad art'.[2]

Recent criticism has been more thoughtful. Since R. S. Crane defined the stories of the Man of the Hill and Mrs Fitzpatrick as 'negative analogies to the moral state of the listeners',[3] there has developed some fairly intense competition to perceive the relevance of other interpolated narratives, extending even to the confessedly irrelevant 'Story of the Unfortunate Jilt' and outwards from Fielding to credit even the unsuspecting Defoe with operating hidden systems of moral order.

[1] *Essay* (1752), A. D. McKillop (ed.), Los Angeles, 1962, p. 44.
[2] W. L. Cross, *The History of Henry Fielding*, New Haven, 1918, Vol. II, p. 188.
[3] R. S. Crane, 'The Concept of Plot and the Plot of *Tom Jones*', in *Critics and Criticism Ancient and Modern*, R. S. Crane (ed.), Chicago, 1952, p. 643.

Perhaps the main failing of this surely important critical revalua-
tion has been that its anxiety to admire order and unity has
prevented it from enjoying discursiveness and variety. Fielding was
a habitually discursive writer, as was shown before he took to the
novel by the 'incongruous episodes'[4] of his farces and the widely
ranging subject matter and reference of his periodical essays. *Joseph
Andrews* is to a considerable extent a variety show, while *Tom Jones*
is positively a virtuoso performance, with the introductory chapters
contributing to the variety of expertise displayed and also explicitly
drawing attention to it, making us aware of the actual processes of
literary creation and replacing the pretence of authenticity of Defoe
and Richardson with an open invitation to enjoy the artifice.
The exuberant variety of manner within *Tom Jones*—picaresque
adventure, military romance, social satire, comedy of manners, bed-
room farce, mock-heroic, formal sermon, rhetorical dialectic, etc.—
is matched by the copiousness and miscellaneity of matter. It is an
illuminating experiment to compile an index to a randomly selected
chapter. For instance, Tom goes into the bushes with Molly Seagrim
—not the most likely opportunity for Senior Common Room intellectual fireworks—and within two pages Fielding has quoted from
Aristotle (twice), Virgil (twice, once with Dryden's translation
appended), Cleostratus, Pittacus, and Pope, and has indulged in
detailed accounts of the life cycle of the fallow deer, the ecology
of Hampshire, and the art of boxing rendered through the terminology of music; there are passing references to the laws of
drunkenness and illegitimacy, the function of ornamental plumage
in animals, the relationship between pupil and master and the
acoustical properties of a full stomach: all this in an episode by no
means outstanding for extensiveness of reference and containing the
pronouncement that 'I shall keep my learning to myself, and return
to my history' (V, 11).

With the major interpolations now generally regarded as contributing to Fielding's central moral and artistic purposes, what is
perhaps most needed is a critical view which can reconcile his
habitual diversity and virtuosity with the long-established claim of
his mastery of composition; a view which will account for the lavish
texture of exuberant digressiveness through which the whole narrative is presented, even crucial episodes of the main story like the
coitus interruptus with Molly; and which will attempt to explain
why Fielding should seemingly have been attracted to the novel
for the freedom offered by a new and infinitely flexible form and
then have immediately claimed for it, in the Preface to *Joseph*

---

[4] See George Sherburn, '*The Dunciad*, Book IV', *Texas Studies in English*,
Vol. XXIV, 1944, pp. 174-90.

Andrews, the highest possible artistic integrity, status, and ancestry.

Hoping to resolve this paradox of diversity and unity, I began as far out as possible on the novel's diverse and extensive structure. Partridge's sub-sub-digression about Sir Francis Page has an obvious immediate impact—Page, 'the hanging judge' of his age, was, Johnson tells us, notorious for 'insolence and severity', had been satirised by Pope, and was still powerful when *Tom Jones* was published.[5] The story was a true one, the trial having taken place at Salisbury assizes in 1739, and would obviously have been current during Fielding's time on the Western Circuit. The bite of topicality is further sharpened by the fully engaged earnestness of Fielding's concern, and the searingly ironic tone which asserts itself through the inanity of Partridge's voice—'It is indeed charming sport to hear trials for life and death'.

But the real power of the anecdote comes from the strength of its connection to a whole texture of recurrent reference to the issue of judicial conduct and the problematic relation between punishment and compassion in true justice. The novel is packed with myriad demonstrations of acts of judgment and punishment, amounting by sheer amplitude of material to a considerable disquisition on the subject, and exploring through the whole range of formal resources available to the novel as Fielding conceived it what the modern reader would surely call a 'theme'.

Mr Allworthy, of course, is throughout a model. Fielding reserves Allworthy's most crucial pronouncement on the subject until the end, for a purpose which I hope to show; but his treatment of Jenny Jones and Partridge in the opening chapters illustrates the discrimination inherent in his administration of justice. The sentencing of Partridge is followed by an explicit statement of this attitude, which, although without the formal rhetoric of his sermons on sexual conduct and marriage, stands like them as a memorable initial statement on what is to be a major moral theme:

> These solicitations [on Partridge's behalf] were nevertheless unsuccessful: for though Mr Allworthy did not think, with some later writers, that mercy consists only in punishing offenders; yet he was as far from thinking that it is proper to this excellent quality to pardon criminals wantonly, without any reason whatever. (II, 6)

Authorial comment makes sure that the value of Allworthy's example is not lost, particularly where the story necessitates his making a mistake. In the middle of his examination of Partridge,

<hr/>

[5] Samuel Johnson, 'Life of Savage', in *Lives of the English Poets*, G. B. Hill (ed.), Oxford, 1905, Vol. II, pp. 348-9; Pope, *Imitations of Horace*, Satire II, i, 82 and *The Dunciad*, IV, 30.

for instance, the narrator praises his 'natural love of justice, joined to his coolness of temper'; and the quibble over his committal of Molly without 'regular information' serves only to stress that 'his intention was truly upright' and to sharpen the contrast between his practice and the 'many arbitrary acts daily committed by magistrates who have not this excuse to plead for themselves' (IV, 11).

Squire Western, of course, gives fictional shape to this hint of a general abuse, in the half-serious accounts of his administration of the poaching and swearing laws, and the more direct censure that he was 'charmed with the power of punishing' (III, 10). Later, his angry and ignorant attempt to commit Mrs Honour provides another opportunity for Fielding to extend the relevance of the implied criticism outwards, by Miss Western's account of the syco- phantic London justice 'who would commit a servant to Bridewell at any time when a master or mistress desired it' (VII, 9).

Then, at Upton, Fielding presents a mock trial which is almost as broad a burlesque of justice as those in *Joseph Andrews* (X, 7). The scene is the kitchen of an inn, at 'scarcely daylight'; the charge is fatuously trivial—the 'theft' of Sophia's muff—and the magistrate is weakminded, ignorant, sleepy, and reluctant to act at all; the motives of the main witnesses on either side are blatantly prejudiced, Western's by desire for revenge and the chambermaid's by desire for Tom, and the senior legal authority referred to, of all people, is Fitzpatrick. Yet this farce is played out seriously in the formal terminology of the courts—Fitzpatrick, 'so learned a coadjutor', speaks of 'felony' and 'evidence of the fact', Susan 'deposed', the magistrate 'declared', and the incident is concluded on a tone of high-court gravity: 'The justice then arose, acquitted the prisoner, and broke up the court.' It all makes a fine piece of 'solemn mockery', that favourite eighteenth-century technique, exploiting the ironic incongruity of style and subject. There is at the same time a deeper irony in the contrast between the ludicrous proceedings and the serious consequences of criminal committal for Tom which they so nearly produce. The most important irony works outwards from the incident itself—in the sharp contrast with Allworthy's less for- mal but much more just proceedings.

Fielding's intention to sustain this pattern of contrast to All- worthy's conduct as magistrate is apparent earlier in the Upton scenes, when immediately after the brawl he reveals that the land- lord whose boorish insults provoked it is, in fact, 'the principal magistrate of the town' (IX, 3-4). Pressure of narrative prevents any extension of this piece of incongruity, and Fielding appears to have forgotten it when he introduces the magistrate for the muff case from among the guests.

Western, Miss Western's London magistrate, Sir Francis Page, the Upton landlord and the sleepy justice make an oddly mixed list, ranging from one of the major characters of the novel to the briefest passing reference: cumulatively they cast a shadow of judicial incompetence and malice which persists until the final chapters and darkens the dangerous situation of Tom under arrest, trapped by Dowling's manipulation of a law under which, we now amply know, he will most probably be deprived of a proper defence and a fair judgment.

In the meantime, in the long section between Malvern and Upton and the later situation of Tom's arrest, various formal devices keep the issue alive and ensure the interaction of the two groups of episodes. Fielding's similes are, I think, more constructively used in this respect than has been recognised.

He employs them to reiterate aspects of themes such as this at periods when the main action provides no opportunity. Thus Sophia's fear of her father's pursuit is compared to 'the common fault of a justice of peace, . . . apt to conclude hastily from every slight circumstance, without examining the evidence on both sides' (XI, 8). Reflections on the force of repetition in argument lead to a jibe against empty repetitiveness at the bar (XII, 9); Lady Bellaston leading astray Lord Fellamar is compared to a 'Newgate solicitor' corrupting a young witness (XV, 4); and shady court techniques are again exposed in the comments on the effects of surprise on the dishonest (XVIII, 5). There is a more precise literary purpose behind such figurative diversions than is immediately apparent in their incidental conversational tone—they form a vital link, in fact, in the pattern of reference which connects Page's sarcasm and Fitzpatrick's officiousness with the situation of the hero at the crisis of his career.

Another important recurrence of this issue of magisterial authority, again on the peripheries of the action, is the interlude of Tom's encounter with the gipsies (XII, 12). This provides the opportunity for the portrayal of a microcosmic society governed by 'one great magistrate', in whom Fielding presents an ideal judge and embodies his conception of the responsibilities of judicial power. The Gipsy chief, like the king-to-be in *A Journey from this World to the Next* (ch. 5), and the magistrate of the wild country where Mrs Heartfree is shipwrecked in *Jonathan Wild* (IV, 11), is conscious of the burdens rather than the glories of authority:

> me assure you it be ver troublesome ting to be a king, and always to do justice.

This discourse, and the incident of Partridge's misbehaviour which makes possible the king's demonstration of ideal judicial fairness, lead to a digression in the author's own voice on the significance of the episode. The formal arrangement and style of this passage (which is too long to quote) indicate its importance; the fact that it is introduced as a sub-digression to a digression, as I hope is becoming apparent in my argument, does not detract from its centrality to the novel's meaning. It contains Fielding's most fundamental reflections on the issue of authority and society, considering the merits and faults of absolute monarchy, and ultimately arguing the superiority of the rule of law, despite individual 'inconveniences', over any system of absolute power. This conclusion, in a passage obviously demanding serious attention, gives a philosophical totality to the particular and practical aspects of the theme demonstrated throughout the novel.

And so on. The consequences of undeserved or harsh punishment are similarly demonstrated at every level of relevance to the main action—by the later career of the hero himself, by Partridge's sad digressive tale of prison and poverty, by Mrs Miller's account of the Anderson family's sufferings, by a series of incidental similes referring to the debt laws, and even, as with the threat of Bridewell for Jenny and Molly, by the indication of what *could* have happened. It is another form of Fielding's extensiveness that he likes to suggest possible outcomes for his characters, often tragic, alternative to those dictated by the comic direction of his plot.[6]

And the solution of the problem of justice and mercy is finally and significantly integrated with the resolution of the central plot. It centres on Black George. From the beginning he has posed a particularly knotty judicial problem, and the hare-stealing incident in fact brings Jones and Blifil into direct contrast for the first time precisely in these terms. Our attention to the contrast is ensured by the chapter heading, 'In which Master Blifil and Jones appear in different lights' (III, 10), and the opening sentence sets out the crucial problem in categorically simple terms:

> Master Blifil fell very short of his companion in the amiable quality of mercy; but he as greatly exceeded him in one of a much higher kind, namely, in justice.

Square and Thwackum open the debate, both, despite lip-service, rejecting mercy absolutely in favour of the more severe virtue:

6 Sheldon B. Sacks, in *Fiction and the Shape of Belief*, Berkeley, 1965, has convincingly argued that the major digressions, the Man of the Hill, Mrs Fitzpatrick and Mrs Bennet in *Amelia*, contain this kind of 'threat' to the main characters as well as the comic reassurance described by Crane 'that nothing that may happen to them will be, in comparison, very bad'. (Crane, *Critics and Criticism*, p. 643, cited Sacks, p. 250.)

Square held it to be inconsistent with the rule of right; and
Thwackum was for doing justice, and leaving mercy to heaven.

The debate is continued when Jones and Partridge argue about
the highwayman near Barnet (XII, 14). At the time Fielding is
deliberately equivocal about Tom's forgiveness of the man. Certainly, in the context of all Tom's other acts of benevolence, we are
intended to approve his 'extraordinary humanity'; but the arguments on the other side, advanced both in the authorial voice and
by Partridge, insisting on the rights of the innocent and the general
benefit of dispassionate justice, are made wholly plausible and are
subjected to no ironic undermining. The crux is the unloaded pistol.
Tom 'began to believe all the man had told him' only after he had
examined it, and his argument defending his compassion makes
this moderation of the offence a vital condition:

> I mean only those whose highest guilt extends no farther than
> to robbery, and who are never guilty of cruelty nor insult to
> any person.

The vindication of his mercy in this particular instance comes
a few chapters later when the highwayman is revealed as the deserving Anderson, whose innocence and extremity of distress exonerate
the illegality of his final resort (XIII, 10). Vindication of Tom's
general principle comes only at the end of the novel, when Allworthy's final resolution of the problem takes as its basis exactly
the distinction between degrees of culpability which Tom argued
in the dispute with Partridge, and which was the deciding factor
in prompting his mercy towards Anderson.

Tom's soft-hearted pleas for Black George are the occasion of
this, the last of Allworthy's sermons (XVIII, 11).[7] It is short but
succinct. The convention of the sermon form, established in the
first word, 'Child', ensures that it is read with attention and
approval, and Fielding emphasises its forcefulness by the extremely
authoritative tone of the opening—' "Child," cries Allworthy, "you
carry this forgiving temper too far" '—and the concluding comment that 'This was spoken with so stern a voice, that Jones did
not think proper to make any reply'. The reader, clearly, is meant
to find it equally unanswerable.

Allworthy's first point is to make the familiar juxtaposition of
mercy and justice, not, this time, in the crude antithesis which
Thwackum set up, but reconciling the two as facets of the same
quality:

2 See H. K. Miller, *Es ays on Fielding's* 'Miscellanies': *Commentary on Vol. 1*,
Princeton, 1961, for a general discussion and justification of the term 'sermon'
for passages such as this (esp. pp. 149-50).

Such mistaken mercy is not only weakness, but borders on injustice, and is very pernicious to society, as it encourages vice.

Allworthy goes on to expound the merciful concessions which may justly be made: temptation may be suffered 'to atone for dishonesty', and a highwayman driven by distress deserves the plea for mercy which Allworthy has 'more than once' made. He places the crucial distinction, however, precisely where Tom previously put it in exonerating Anderson: between excusable 'dishonesty' and any 'blacker crime'. The Anderson decision depended simply on the pistol, and hence the clear line between robbery and murder; but Black George's guilt hangs on the less palpable offence of ingratitude. No single incident could demonstrate this crux, and Fielding, in any case, has deliberately sustained an equivocal view of George's character, and presented the theft of the banknote as a highly complex moral issue. Allworthy's pronouncement settles all doubt. The relationship between Tom and George previous to the theft is now, for the first time, shown to be decisive, and ingratitude is classed without equivocation alongside murder and cruelty. The standard Allworthy here lays down justifies in retrospect Tom's compassion towards Anderson, who intended no violence; but sets George's ingratitude outside the scope of rightful mercy.

Under the circumstances of such 'blacker crime', Allworthy goes on, 'compassion and forgiveness become faults'. This assertion, in a book which has done so much to recommend compassion and forgiveness, must constitute a vital link in the novel's ultimate meaning. In effect, it is the culmination of another central theme: the lesson taught here is the final piece of 'prudence' which Tom has to acquire in order to take his place in society. Having eliminated his faults, he now has to learn how prudently to moderate his instinctive virtues, to add the 'distinguishing faculty' to what would otherwise, as Fielding said in the *Enquiry into the Late Increase of Robbers* (sec. viii), be 'the benevolence of a child or a fool'.

Allworthy's sermon, conclusive as it is, is not quite the final appearance of the theme of punishment and compassion. Two pages later, Tom himself faces the most important moment of judgment in the whole novel—his final interview with Sophia (XVIII, 12). Their conversation has often been recounted and analysed, but never, I believe, with any reference to the crucial pronouncement made in the sermon which immediately precedes it. Yet the two are integrally related, and Fielding's juxtaposition of them in the action has certainly more purpose in it than convenience. Until Allworthy's sermon, the novel has propounded no firm standard for assessing the conflicting demands of mercy and punishment. The dismissal of Tom, the forgiveness of Anderson, are complex decisions equivocally presented, proved right or wrong to the reader only by insight into personal circumstances which would not be available outside fiction, nor even there, except in retrospect. Black George, too, provides a tangle of moral ambiguities—until Allworthy's short sermon settles the problem. His solution is entirely in accord with the most authoritative Christian social thought of the time. Bishop Butler's sermon, 'Upon Resentment', for instance, anticipates Fielding so closely in the crimes which are to be excluded from compassion—'injury, injustice and cruelty'—that a direct influence seems probable.[8]

Having set this standard, Fielding then demonstrates its relevance to the main plot. The values established by Allworthy's sermon enable Sophia, in the next chapter, to forgive Tom. The decision she must make is set out at the beginning of the interview in terms which instantly relate it to the theme which has just been resolved. Tom pleads: ' "It is mercy, and not justice, which I implore at your hands." ' Justice, he admits, must 'condemn' him—but we have just read Allworthy's exposition of the conditions under which justice may rightly give way to mercy—when true justice, indeed, consists of mercy. In this light, Tom's explanation of his letter to Lady Bellaston must be allowed in his defence, since it frees him from the accompanying disqualification. A real intention to make a profitable marriage to Lady Bellaston was the only 'blacker crime' of which he could have been guilty. His innocence of any such intention makes the worst of his offence merely mistaken gallantry. Thus, when he goes on to plead his 'situation', his 'despair' and the apparent hopelessness of his love, he is appealing, in Allworthy's terms, for Sophia's consideration of the 'mitigating circumstances' which entitle him to mercy. At this point, indeed, Sophia's forgiveness is obtained, precisely in accordance with the guiding principles which Allworthy laid down. The comic prolongation of the interview concerns only Tom's proof of his repentance; the application for merciful justice has been granted.

The values of a legal and social theme are thus integrated with the resolution of the main personal narrative. Perception of this interaction will, I believe, remove the difficulties which some critics have found in the final scenes. William Empson, for instance, is troubled by an 'unanswered ambiguity' in Allworthy's severity against George;[9] yet if Allworthy's strict edict really did fall short of Tom's 'perfect Gospel Christianity', as Empson claims, the final

[8] Joseph Butler *Works*, W. E. Gladstone (ed.), Oxford, 18961, Vol. II, p. 147. See also 'Upon Forgiveness of Injuries', Miller, *Essays on Fielding's* 'Miscellanies', pp. 150-67.
[9] William Empson, '*Tom Jones*', The Kenyon Review, Vol. XX, 1958, pp. 233-5.

resolution of the book's central narrative could not have been achieved so precisely within the terms his sermon lays down. Fielding enables Sophia to forgive Tom without becoming a fraction less credible, less sensible, or less deserving of Allworthy's fullest approval.

The circle, then, is complete. The theme of merciful judgment, begun as an offshoot of the main personal narrative, and diffused through the complex of the novel's formal techniques, is brought to its culmination in the conventional device of the sermon; this resolution in turn refers the values which have been formulated from this extensive and flexible demonstration back again to the main narrative, which is duly resolved in accordance with them. In this way all the apparently subordinate formal devices—the sub-sub-digression of the horse-thief's trial, the authorial digression from the gipsy interlude, the farce of the muff trial, the simile which compared Western's remorselessness with that of the Newgate turn-key, the chapter heading contrasting Jones and Blifil—all these help to make possible Sophia's forgiveness of Tom. The theme is diffusely and diversely rendered: but it is also made integral to the very centre of the novel.

The second of my opening quotations can be much more briefly dealt with. I chose it, rather than any other major theme such as sexual conduct or honour, to show how the broad scope and miscellaneity of Fielding's form allows him to achieve a remarkable cumulative impact even with minor issues—in this case, the hardships suffered by poor clergymen. No fewer than eight cases are mentioned: Mrs Seagrim's father, Mrs Honour's father, Mrs Miller's husband, Uncle Nightingale's father-in-law and son-in-law, this Dorsetshire victim of attorneys' swindles, Tom's grandfather, and Parson Adams. Such persistence is not accidental. Fielding indicates very clearly the kind of connection he means us to draw between these references when he reminds us in a footnote of the similarity between the social declines suffered by Mrs Honour and Mrs Seagrim:

> This is the second person of low condition whom we have recorded in this history to have sprung from the clergy. It is to be hoped such instances will, in future ages, when some provision is made for the families of the inferior clergy, appear stranger than they can be thought at present. (IV, 14)

Clearly we are being invited to make the same connection, and apply the same constructive social comment, to all the subsequent instances of the same situation.

Each of these references must be called marginal to the main action, especially the attorney's victim. He is nevertheless categorised as a 'poor clergyman' and so plays his part (almost subliminal) in Fielding's process of propaganda by repetition.

Not that he allows even this issue to remain entirely extraneous to the narrative. At the end, it is revealed that this deficiency in society's treatment of some of its most deserving members has, in fact, had an effect of some importance on the main action itself. Since Tom's father, 'the son of a clergyman of great learning and virtue', had to be 'bred up' and 'maintained' by Allworthy, it may fairly be said, without being over-ingenious, that Tom's illegitimacy is a consequence of his grandfather's poverty (XVIII, 7). There need have been no subterfuge if the Summer family had possessed an income in keeping with the parson's abilities and the value of his social function. This revelation is, of course, passed over quickly in the hurry of the dénouement, but it does reflect a heightened significance on the situations of Mrs Honour and Nancy Miller and Uncle Nightingale's daughter. The various transgressions of these characters are seen as at least partly due to society's neglect of its responsibilities towards the clergy.

I said at the beginning that my wantonly obscure quotations seemed a long way from the cause or outcome of Tom Jones's career in the novel. I have been trying to show that Fielding's extraordinary cohesive control over the diverse abundance of his material makes even such peripheral embellishments neither wanton nor obscure; and that, by a sustained patterning of accumulated detail, they do contribute relevantly to the reader's understanding of, in the one case, the outcome and in the other, one cause of that career. My argument is that Fielding pursued the dual objectives of diversity of form and unity of theme, and that a footnote to a digression, just as much as a long interpolated narrative, may be fully relevant or even pivotal to a central theme of the novel. He warned us to be alert for this method of procedure, after all:

> First, then, we warn thee not too hastily to condemn any of the incidents in this our history as impertinent and foreign to our main design, because thou dost not immediately conceive in what manner such incident may conduce to that design. This work may, indeed, be considered as a great creation of our own; and for a little reptile of a critic to presume to find fault with any of its parts, without knowing the manner in which the whole is connected, and before he comes to the final catastrophe, is a most presumptuous absurdity. (X, 1)[10]

[10] This concept of the artist as creator, and particularly as one who reveals invisible order, will be seen to underlie the whole attitude to form which I am describing, as I hint in the quotation which ends this paper. See also Ian Watt, in *The Rise of the Novel*, London, 1957, on the plot of *Tom Jones*: 'the supreme task of the writer was to make visible in the human scene the operations of universal order' (p. 271).

Much of the book's unique character, I believe, comes from this remarkable combination of inventive miscellaneity and serious compositional unity.

Fielding's attitudes to the magistracy and the clergy may also have seemed wantonly remote from my professed subject; but being far more certain than Fielding could be that my audience consists entirely of the very uppermost graduates in criticism, I have trusted that my use of terms like 'wanton', 'maze', 'lavish', 'copious', 'miscellaneous', and 'embellish' will have sufficiently indicated the direction of my confessedly serpentine route. In support of my view of the form of *Tom Jones* I may, I think, cite Henry Knight Miller and William Hogarth—strange bedfellows, perhaps; and when I add Sir Thomas Browne, Pope and Handel, Mario Praz, Joseph Burke, and R. F. Brissenden, I may seem to have not so much a bedful as a baroque bacchanal.

However, it was reassuring, after formulating with some trepidation the main argument of my reading, to find H. K. Miller, in his article on 'Some Functions of Rhetoric in *Tom Jones*'[11] reaching a very similar conclusion about what I have called Fielding's dual objectives from a learned analysis of Fielding's rhetoric and style. Great comedy, Miller argues, requires a mixture of the incompatible worlds of ordered light and illogical confusion, distilled by an alembic which 'can ultimately be identified as style'. He goes on,

> Fielding found, I think, the perfect style to answer these demands: an easy and elegant dignity, a formal syntax, an assured control, that all reflect the certainties of an Ideal order; and at the same time, a joyful sense of the ambivalences in language itself, an inbred habit of ironic qualification, a narrative exuberance, that mirror in all its frightening, hilarious complexity the world of the Contingent.[12]

The same combination, I have been arguing, directs what Miller here calls 'narrative exuberance'; the narrative material is indeed exuberant in its copiousness and unpredictability. But at the same time it is ordered with the same 'assured control' as Fielding's style, into patterns creating 'the certainties of an Ideal order'.

We need not be embarrassed at this apparent co-existence of Rococo and Augustan. George Sherburn was saying nearly thirty years ago, in an essay relating *The Dunciad* to Fielding's plays, that Pope 'seeks diversity of episode fully as much as he does structural unity of the whole. The tendency, in spite of all the learned have said, is quite typical of English neo-classicism, and in this as in most of Pope's poems episodes follow loosely in diverse and con-

11 *Philological Quarterly*, Vol. XLV, 1966, pp. 209-35.
12 Ibid., p. 228.

trasting moods, just as in a suite by Purcell or Handel an allegro is followed by an andante, or a courante by a rigadoon'.[13]

An even more illuminating comparison is with Hogarth, if only because, as Mario Praz has recently said, the coupling of his name with Fielding's 'is almost a commonplace'[14]—and yet the commonplace preoccupation with caricature, gin laws, and Bridget Allworthy has failed to lead to an appreciation of the profound similarity in their art. Sir Nikolaus Pevsner has described Hogarth's storytelling with the same word used by Miller about Fielding's—exuberant.[15] Like *Joseph Andrews* and *Tom Jones*, Hogarth's pictures create an initially confused impression of sheer amplitude of content, especially those in his later 'epic' style, as Joseph Burke has pointed out, with their enlarged scope and variety deliberately designed to fulfil the definition of epic in the Preface to *Joseph Andrews*.[16] Perhaps, as Burke suggests, this was a matter of 'collaboration' rather than 'influence', since even the earlier 'dramatic cycles', painted before 1742, display the same dual objectives on which I have been arguing Fielding based his version of epic form. They are crowded with apparently digressive material, yet any descriptive attention soon reveals the relevance of the profuse individual details to the picture's main purpose, its moral preoccupation. One particularly close parallel to Fielding's digressions is the use of pictures on the wall to extend or comment on the main situation portrayed. Thus in the first scene of *The Rake's Progress* the Rake's miserly father is shown in a wall portrait gloating over stacks of coin, and the room is littered with other evidence of avarice (Plate I), so that the story is extended backwards in time to include the accumulation of the fortune which the Rake is already beginning to dissipate, and to imply, of course, an ironic comment through what may fairly be called the 'negative analogy' between the two kinds of folly. Elsewhere, Hogarth uses the background pictures, again as Fielding does his digressions or heroic similes, to bring out implications in the main situation which cannot be stated directly at that stage, or to emphasise the implied moral comment on the action. In the Levée scene (Plate II), for instance, the fourth of the *Marriage à la Mode* series, the affable conversation between the Viscountess and Counsellor Silvertongue is seen to take place beneath Correggio's openly sensual *Jupiter embracing Io*, a juxtaposition which places

13 Sherburn, *Texas Studies*, Vol. XXIV, p. 184.
14 Mario Praz, *Mnemosyne. The Parallel between Literature and the Visual Arts*, Princeton, 1970, pp. 148-9.
15 Nikolaus Pevsner, *The Englishness of English Art*, London, 1956, p. 23.
16 Joseph Burke and Colin Caldwell, *Hogarth. The Complete Engravings*, London, 1968, p. 21. My long-standing debt to Professor Burke's work on Hogarth was increased by the advice and encouragement he offered me during the seminar at which this paper was delivered.

their relaxed sociability and meaningful glances at their true carnal level as decisively as Fielding does by using the simile of rutting animals about Tom and Molly—or, on another topic, by inserting the Sir Francis Page story to give a more grave perspective to the hero's later legal plight. The other paintings round the room— Lot being intoxicated and seduced by his daughters, Correggio's *Rape of Ganymede* (placed ironically above the castrato singer)—emphasise the Viscountess's sensual tastes and the unnaturalness of the relationship presented, while a more precise comment is of course made by the black servant-boy pointing mischievously to the horns on the head of the statuette of Actaeon.

One could multiply examples. The two pictures of Cupid with his toy rocket in the *Before and After* pair are just like one of Fielding's facetious heroic parodies. Mock-heroic on a much grander scale is incorporated in the comically parodic references in both the general structure and incidental details of the *Election* series (Plate III). *The Distressed Poet* includes a topical reference—another habit of Fielding's, of course—to the reputation of Pope, who appears as 'Pope Alexander' in a print on the garret wall (in the painted version, he is shown giving the notorious thrashing to Curll). Pevsner refers to the technique as 'the baroque trick of a picture within a picture'.[17] Fielding's equally purposeful technique of putting a story within a story is, I would suggest, a very close literary equivalent to this Baroque device in painting.

The same technique also operates in less obvious ways in both artists. Hogarth, like Fielding in the Man of the Hill's story or the strong hint of the likelihood of Tom's execution, likes to imply possible alternative directions which his main narrative could take. The scene of the Harlot's arrival in London as an innocent country girl, for instance (Plate IV), contains indications of two possible outcomes other than the encounter with Mother Needham which is actually portrayed. One is an alternative road to ruin—the notorious seducer and rapist Colonel Francis Charteris is seen lurking with his pimp in a doorway casting a connoisseur's eye over the incoming girls[18]—while happier courses which the Harlot's career could have followed are indicated by the preoccupied clergyman, the homeliness of her goose and the address of the relative for whom it was intended, and the simple, honest labours of the serving-girl or housewife on the balcony in the background.

The main action is also extended through its incidental contact with other characters. The various background characters who are

---

17 Pevsner, *English Art*, p. 51.
18 See Ronald Paulson's superlative commentaries in *Hogarth's Graphic Works, First Complete Edition*, Yale, 1965, Vol. II, p. 144.

in the same predicament as the Rake in Bedlam or the Harlot in Bridewell deepen both the human and the social significance of the scenes presented in the same way as Fielding does in the Newgate section of *Amelia*, or, over a longer period, the series of other sufferers from poverty and social injustice whom Tom encounters on his travels. Hogarth is even capable of introducing moral equivocation, as Fielding deliberately does in Partridge's case against mercy to highwaymen. Sir John Gonson[19] is admirable when arresting the Harlot in Scene III, but when we see him crudely caricatured on the shutter in Bridewell in Scene IV, it arouses, if not a shift in our sympathies, at least a reflection on human complexity very like that aroused by Fielding's handling of legal issues. Similarly the Idle Apprentice's ride to Tyburn (Plate V) is both well-deserved retribution and a sordid ritual which instructs the small boys in the foreground not in morality but in pickpocketing dexterity.

There are other similarities. Both artists are as lavish in style as in narrative material and ironic reference. The rich verbal surface of Fielding's prose, with his constant pleonasms and extensions, ambiguities and afterthoughts, similes and parentheses, has an immediate similarity with the lavish and open brushwork of Hogarth's technique—what Pevsner has called his 'rich, fluid, Baroque paint'.[20]

The same exuberant copiousness is evident in Fielding's narrative and descriptive techniques. Andrew Wright, analysing the 'static' quality of Fielding's stage-like scenes, describes how these 'tableaux' are set within a 'rococo framework'. He refers to the Hogarthian exuberance of the 'almost labyrinthine construction' of authorial intrusion, mock-pompous generalisation, classical allusion, etc., through which Fielding tortuously conducts his reader to the 'scantily reported scene that follows'.[21]

One crucial factor in giving what Hogarth calls 'fit proportion' to the elaborations of his and Fielding's compositions is the realism of the component details themselves. Fielding's digressive excursions are not the remote fantasies which are interspersed into *Don Quixote* and the French romances, but are fully as realistic and topical as the main narrative itself. (This is even true in some respects of the story of Leonora.) The Man of the Hill's story is fixed as firmly to Monmouth's rebellion as Tom's is to Bonnie Prince Charlie's. And the copious topical references—to Pope, Cibber, Dr Misaubin, Rock, Peter Walter, Jack Broughton, George Whitefield, Rich's pantomime, and many others—all help to con-

19 Paulson, *Hogarth's Graphic Works*, Vol. I, p. 146.
20 Pevsner, *English Art*, p. 122.
21 Andrew Wright, *Henry Fielding: Mask and Feast*, London, 1955, p. 24.

vince the reader of the contemporary relevance of what is depicted and asserted. The names in this list have been deliberately selected, since every one of them appears in the same way—giving incidental topicality—in the works of Hogarth. Similarly, both place their actions in recognisable real life settings—Rich's Masquerade in *Tom Jones*, Vauxhall Gardens in *Amelia*, Horace Walpole's drawing-room in *Marriage à la Mode* II, Misaubin's 'Museum' in *Marriage à la Mode* III, and so on.

Paradoxically, such precise realism was a principal characteristic of the English rococo. In architecture and interior decoration, the French style of lavish ornamentation was adapted to an equally ornate, but representational mode of decoration. Isaac Ware's *Complete Body of Architecture* (1756) recommends 'variety and elegance' in the 'French' manner, but suggests that the decorations should be confined within a classical frame, and that realistic forms such as flowers and musical instruments be substituted for 'unmeaning' ornament. The French fashion of decoration, in fact, became fused with the English passion for 'things of a natural kind', expressed most influentially for this period by Shaftesbury. This is the fusion which Christopher Hussey has described as the 'naturalisation of the English rococo',[22] and which was in part responsible for the *jardin anglais* and Gothic architecture, as well as the 'regular intricacy' of Hogarth. There was also an enormous vogue for this sort of representational realism of ornament in the applied arts, its more vulgar excesses being ridiculed by Hogarth himself, of course, in the mantelpiece ornaments of *Marriage à la Mode* II, especially the clock with its fish swimming among dense foliage surmounted by a hideously smirking cat.

Reynolds was to express neo-classicism's interest in the sublimation of low material (in his Sixth Discourse). Hogarth's realism is rather the demonstration of his belief that his perfect line of grace, intricate, varied and serpentine, is to be universally observed in nature, which is why, in *The Analysis of Beauty*, he illustrates beauty with cacti, candlesticks, and corsets. The same may be said of the adaptation made by Fielding of the French romances and the classical epic, retaining their rich diversity of character, scene and incident, but 'naturalising' it.

This peculiarity of the English rococo was left out of account by Herbert Dieckmann in his recent warning against the use of rococo as a period concept.[23] Yet it is closely related to what was perhaps the main bond uniting a distinctive group of artists—their humanitarian interests. Fielding, Hogarth, Handel, Roubiliac, and

[22] Christopher Hussey, *Early Georgian Country Houses*, London, 1955, p. 24.
[23] In *The Disciplines of Criticism*, Peter Demetz, Thomas Greene and Lowry Nelson Jr (eds.), New Haven and London, 1968, pp. 419-37.

Garrick were among the leaders of the 'Slaughter's' coffee-house set. They united in what Trevelyan called a 'joint-stock' manner in philanthropic ventures like Captain Coram's Foundlings' Hospital, and their humanitarian inclinations may have been as important in forming their taste for the representational rococo (or, in more conventional literary terms, for diverse realism) as the English love of naturalism. (The 'puff' which Fielding inserted in *Amelia* for Vauxhall Gardens, incidentally, was for the benefit of the many rococo designers and craftsmen among his 'Slaughter's' friends who found employment there.) Thus to equate Hogarth and Fielding in terms of rococo composition is not incompatible with equating them in terms of propaganda against gin or public hangings.[24]

Even apart from realism and social purpose, in terms of compositional principles alone, the equation seems to me remarkable. Antal has described the development of Hogarth's composition as a move from 'anticipated rococo' in the *Progresses* to 'full rococo' in *Marriage à la Mode*.[25] *The Analysis of Beauty* advocates 'composed intricacy of form'. And when Hogarth defines this 'intricacy' as 'that peculiarity in the lines, which compose it, that *leads the eye a wanton kind of chace*', by adding the epithet 'wanton', as Joseph Burke comments in his Introduction to the *Analysis*, 'he has transformed the principle from a baroque to a rococo one'.[26]

The relevance of this formula to literature has been perceived in an essay on 'Sterne and Painting' by R. F. Brissenden, who applies it to the 'intricacy and variety', the 'wanton and delightful "chace"', of *Tristram Shandy*.[27] 'It is tempting to describe Sterne's work as rococo', Brissenden says. Mario Praz is another who has more recently succumbed to the temptation, speaking in *Mnemosyne* of Sterne as 'supreme master of the arabesque in the rococo manner'.[28] What makes Hogarth's principles of beauty of form even more relevant to Fielding is that he speaks not just of 'intricacy' but of 'composed intricacy'. The combination of the visual with the literary in this concept is shown in the quotation from Milton with which Hogarth illustrates it:

> Mystical dance! . . . Mazes intricate,
> Eccentric, intervolv'd yet regular
> Then most, when most irregular they seem.

---

[24] I am indebted at several points in this paragraph to Mark Girouard's articles, 'English Art and the Rococo', *Country Life*, 13, 27 Jan., 3 Feb. 1966.

[25] F. Antal, *Hogarth, and His Place in European Art*, London, 1962, pp. 106-7.

[26] William Hogarth, *The Analysis of Beauty*, ed. with intro. by Joseph Burke, Oxford, 1955, pp. 45, 42, 1 i.

[27] In *Of Books and Humankind*, John Butt (ed.), London, 1964, pp. 106-7.

[28] *Mnemosyne*, p. 148.

The rococo 'wantonness', in fact, is the surface elaboration of a highly wrought structure, a composition which is 'regular' in its ultimate conception, for all its eccentric intricacy of execution.

Such a formula—this 'composed intricacy of form'—is remarkably apt to describe *Tom Jones*.[29] The reader, and indeed the hero himself, are led an apparently 'wanton kind of chace' through a complex plot complicated further by chance encounters, irrelevant incident, and seemingly arbitrary and miscellaneous intruded comment. Yet for all this copious rococo informality at the surface of the action, the baroque principle of unity which Hogarth elicited from the Milton quotation applies equally here: when the maze seems most irregular, then it is likely to fit most cogently into the true 'composition' of the whole, which is to be found not in the external connections of the narrative, but in the controlling regularity at the level of meaning.

Thus Allworthy's performances as magistrate, Black George's treachery, the Man of the Hill's offences and sufferings, the Gipsy King's judgment, the two meetings with Anderson, and much else, however arbitrary, discontinuous, and 'contrasting' as units of a narrative sequence, all contribute positively and coherently to the presentation of the theme of right judgment, and, by a masterstroke of intricate composition, illuminate and justify the ultimate resolution of the central action.

Having opened with Milton, I may perhaps be permitted to end with Sir Thomas Browne:

> This is the ordinary and open way of His Providence, which Art and Industry have in a good part discovered; whose effects we may foretel without an Oracle: to foreshew these, is not Prophesie, but Prognostication. There is another way, full of Meanders and Labyrinths, whereof the Devil and Spirits have no exact Ephemerides; and that is a more particular and obscure method of His Providence, directing the operations of individuals and single Essences: this we call Fortune, that serpentine and crooked line, whereby He draws those actions His Wisdom intends, in a more unknown and secret way.[30]

I hope it will seem appropriate to my subject to end with a quotation which both closes my argument, and simultaneously extends it infinitely outwards.

---

[29] *Joseph Andrews* is formed on the same principles, I believe, though without the same copiousness or consistency of composition. *Amelia* retains some of the techniques of 'intricacy'—digression, allusion, simile, etc.—but 'composition' has become dominant and variety is no longer an end in itself.

[30] *Religio Medici*, Part I, section 17.

An Early Theory of Genius: Alexander Gerard's Unpublished Aberdeen Lectures

Bernhard Fabian

I

The history of the concept of genius is still incomplete. Some later phases, especially in France and in Germany, have been studied in detail.[1] Attempts have also been made to trace the antecedents of the concept back to the Renaissance and even to classical antiquity.[2] Surprisingly little, however, is known of the crucial period in England about the middle of the eighteenth century when the concept of original genius made its historically significant appearance and *the* genius came to be recognised as a distinct human

[1] See, for instance, Herbert Dieckmann, 'Diderot's Conception of Genius', *Journal of the History of Ideas*, Vol. II, 1941, pp. 151-82; Hubert Sommer, 'A propos du mot "génie"', *Zeitschrift für Romanische Philologie*, Vol. LXVI, 1950, pp. 170-201; Hermann Wolf, *Versuch einer Geschichte des Geniebegriffs in der deutschen Ästhetik des 18. Jahrhunderts: I. Band: Von Gottsched bis auf Lessing*, Beiträge zur Philosophie, 9, Heidelberg, 1923; Kurt Bauerhorst, *Der Geniebegriff: Seine Entwicklung und seine Formen unter besonderer Berücksichtigung des Goetheschen Standpunktes*, Dissertation, Breslau, 1930; Hans Hecht, *T. Percy, R. Wood und J. D. Michaelis: Ein Beitrag zur Literaturgeschichte der Genieperiode*, Göttinger Forschungen, Heft 3, Stuttgart, 1933; B. Rosenthal, *Der Geniebegriff des Aufklärungszeitalters (Lessing und die Popularphilosophen)*, Germanische Studien, Heft 138, Berlin, 1933; Hellmuth Sudheimer, *Der Geniebegriff des jungen Goethe*, Germanische Studien, Heft 167, Berlin, 1935; Pierre Grappin, *La théorie due génie dans le préclassicisme allemand*, Paris, 1952; Giorgio Tonelli, 'Kant's Early Theory of Genius (1770-1779)', *Journal of the History of Philosophy*, Vol. IV, 1966, pp. 109-31, 209-24.

[2] Edgar Zilsel, *Die Entstehung des Geniebegriffs: Ein Beitrag zur Ideengeschichte der Antike und des Frühkapitalismus*, Tübingen, 1926.

This paper is part of a project financially assisted by the Deutsche Forschungsgemeinschaft. I should like to thank the University Libraries of Aberdeen and Edinburgh for permission to quote from their manuscripts.

type.[3] Addison's essay in the *Spectator* and Pope's praise of Homer are the *loci classici* in the early part of the century,[4] Young's *Conjectures* is the familiar document of the latter part. But what, precisely, were the important contributions towards the formation of the concept after Pope and before Young?

My answer to this question is intended to draw attention to the Aberdeen professor Alexander Gerard as one of the pioneer thinkers in the field of *Genielehre*. Gerard, as is well known, published *An Essay on Genius* in 1774. Occasional critical attacks notwithstanding, this book has, from his day to the present, been credited with providing the most incisive and systematic account of genius in the eighteenth century.[5] However, due to the late publication date, the *Essay* is frequently regarded as a summary of established views and accepted ideas rather than as an original contribution to the study of genius. In the efflorescence of works on genius during the 1750s and 1760s Gerard is felt to have been a comparative latecomer writing at a moment when the historically important statements had already been made.

In reality, Gerard was one of the early theoreticians of genius. He did most of his work in the 1750s. He preceded Young, his fellow-countryman William Duff, and other writers who are usually given priority over him. He was among the first, perhaps the very first, to attempt a comprehensive theory of genius designed to explain the nature of the creative endowment and the quality of the creative achievement.

II

In Gerard's early work, with which I am here concerned, three stages must be distinguished. The first is represented by his *Essay on Taste*, written in 1756, though not published until 1759.[6] This does not yet contain the complete theory. Because of the nature of the subject Gerard confined himself to what he termed the 'connexions'

3 See Paul Kaufmann, 'Heralds of Original Genius', in *Essays in Memory of Barrett Wendell*, Cambridge, Mass., 1926, pp. 191-217, supplemented by R. S. Crane's remarks in *Philological Quarterly*, Vol. VI, 1927, pp. 168-9; Hans Thüme, *Beiträge zur Geschichte des Geniebegriffs in England*, Studien zur englischen Philologie, LXXI, Halle, 1927; Logan Pearsall Smith, 'Four Romantic Words', in *Words and Idioms: Studies in the English Language*, London, 1957, pp. 95-114; Margaret Lee Wiley, 'Genius: A Problem in Definition', *Texas Studies in English*, Vol. XVI, 1936, 77-83; the most recent inclusive study is Ralph F. B. King, *An Analytical History of the Conception of Genius in English Literature and Thought from 1700 to 1775*, unpublished dissertation, Toronto, 1960.
4 *Spectator*, No. 160; Preface to the translation of the *Iliad* (1715).
5 See, for instance, Immanuel Kant's *Menschenkunde oder philosophische Anthropologie: Nach handschriftlichen Vorlesungen herausgegeben von Fr.Chr. Starke*, Leipzig, 1831, p. 233; King, *Analytical History*, p. 172.
6 See *An Essay on Taste*, Walter J. Hipple Jr (ed.), Gainesville, Fa, 1964.

of taste with genius. But from here he proceeded to a thorough analysis. As he informed the reader of his *Essay on Genius,*

> the attention which he bestowed on this latter faculty [of genius], in that one point of view, convinced him, that its Nature and its Principles admitted and required a fuller investigation than had ever been attempted, and determined him to enter on that investigation immediately after finishing his former work.[7]

The final results of this 'fuller investigation' were, prior to their publication in the *Essay on Genius,* presented as lectures to the Aberdeen Philosophical Society, a club formed in 1758 at the suggestion of Thomas Reid. Gerard was among the first elected members of this small and reticent group, from which the Scottish philosophy of Common Sense originated. Its history remains to be written, but its importance can perhaps be indicated by the fact that, besides the *Essay on Genius,* Reid's *Inquiry into the Human Mind,* Beattie's *Essays,* Campbell's *Philosophy of Rhetoric,* and other works were at least in part communicated to it as discourses.

The sequence of lectures delivered by Gerard extended from December 1758 at least to November 1772. In his 'Advertisement' to the *Essay* Gerard obviously refers to these lectures (without mentioning the Aberdeen Society) when he says that 'his plan was formed, the first part composed, and some progress made in the second part, so long ago as 1758' (p. iii). The progress of his work can be followed in the unpublished 'Minutes of the Aberdeen Philosophical Society', even if some phases must be reconstructed conjecturally.[8] The discourses themselves, which in accordance with the rules of the club were entered into a 'Book for inserting Discourses', do not seem to be extant. At any rate, they are not preserved in the parts of the book which I have recently rediscovered.[9]

It should be mentioned that, independently of Gerard's *Essay,* genius was a subject proposed to the Aberdeen philosophers for discussion. As entered in the 'Book for Questions', the question suggested by John Farquhar, a minister from a neighbouring village, reads: 'In the Perfection of what Faculty does Genius consist? Or if in a Combination of Faculties, what are they?'[10] When it was due for debate in December 1758, it was marked 'superceded because the subject of Mr Gerards Discourses'. Nevertheless, Farquhar's

7 *Essay on Genius,* London, 1774, p. iii.
8 See *An Essay on Genius,* Bernhard Fabian (ed.), Theorie und Geschichte der Literatur der Schönen Künste, 3, München, 1966, pp. XII-XVII.
9 'David Skene and the Aberdeen Philosophical Society', *The Bibliotheck,* Vol. V, 1968, pp. 81-99.
10 'Original Minutes of the Aberdeen Philosophical Society', Aberdeen University Library (AUL) MS. 539, Question 18.

question may serve as signpost to the historian of the concept. It indicates that as late as 1758 there was apparently no standard explanation for the phenomenon of genius and, moreover, that a psychological answer such as Gerard's in his *Essay* was expected.

When Gerard joined the Aberdeen Philosophical Society he had already outlined a theory of genius which, chronologically, holds an intermediate position between the *Essay on Taste* and the lost discourses. It is to be found in the 'Lectures on Moral Philosophy' which he delivered in the Marischal College of the University of Aberdeen until 1760, when he was succeeded by James Beattie. These lectures are preserved in two sets of student notes taken during the academic years of 1757/58 and 1758/59 by one George Forbes and one Robert Morgan. The first manuscript is now in Aberdeen, the second in Edinburgh.[11]

The interest of these lectures is threefold. First, they contain *in nuce* leading ideas of the *Essay on Genius* and thus verify Gerard's statement about the early origin of his book. Second, the theory here outlined is broader in scope than the theory which Gerard published. Whole areas of inquiry not touched upon in the *Essay* are at least roughly mapped out and correlated with other fields. Third, and most important, the theory is here placed within a larger frame of reference. While in the *Essay* the phenomenon of genius is singled out for isolated analysis, it is here embedded in a system of school philosophy.

Before presenting this theory in detail I should like to make two more points about Gerard's lectures. To begin with, they should be seen in a larger context. They are one of the various systems devised in eighteenth-century Scotland for the instruction of the university student. As such they should be placed side by side with Francis Hutcheson's *System of Moral Philosophy* (1755), James Beattie's *Elements of Moral Science* (1790-3), Adam Ferguson's *Principles of Moral and Political Science, Being Chiefly a Retrospect of Lectures Delivered in the College of Edinburgh* (1792), and a host of others published and unpublished, some of which may hold surprises similar to Adam Smith's recently unearthed *Lectures on Rhetoric and Belles Lettres*.[12] With few exceptions, these systems have hitherto

11 AUL MS.M. 205.2. Not yet listed under Gerard's name, Forbes belonged to the class of 1754-8: see P. J. Anderson, *Fasti Academiae Mariscallanae Aberdonensis*, Aberdeen, 1898, Vol. II, p. 325. At the end of the final chapter on 'Metaphysics' there is the following entry: 'Geo. Forbes Aberdeen, April 8th 1758'. Edinburgh University Library (EUL) MS.Dc.5. 61-2 (the order of the volumes must be reversed). Reference: Edinburgh University Library, *Index to Manuscripts*, Boston, 1964, Vol. I, pp. 4 and 592. Morgan belonged to the class of 1755-9: see Anderson, *Fasti Academiae*, Vol. II, p. 329. Morgan's name appears several times in the MS. The latest of several dates is 13 March 1759.

12 Adam Smith, *Lectures on Rhetoric and Belles Lettres*, John M. Lothian (ed.), London and Edinburgh, 1963.

received but scant attention. They remain to be evaluated for their intrinsic merits and for their educational significance.

Above all, the lectures given by Gerard and his colleagues have to be examined as the systematic background of a good number of the philosophic and aesthetic treatises then issuing from Scotland. Most of what the eighteenth-century Scottish professors wrote was, in one way or another, related to their systems. The lectures were the matrix of their thought, the point from which they proceeded and to which they often silently referred. In what they published they frequently gave, as Beattie did in his *Dissertations Moral and Critical* (1783), 'only a few detached passages', expecting the reader to accept them 'as separate and distinct Essays'.[13]

Secondly, it should be noted that Gerard's lectures were conceived as an advanced system. They were based on a program announced in 1755 as a *Plan of Education in the Marischal College and University of Aberdeen*. This document was drafted by Gerard for the faculty. It was translated into German and presented as a useful contribution to university reform in a country where comparable systems of instruction prevailed.[14] In deviating 'from the hitherto received method' Gerard's principal concern was to replace the traditional scholastic system of teaching philosophy by a system commensurate with what he called 'the reformed state of Philosophy'. As 'an image, not of human phantasies and conceits, but of the reality of nature, and truth of things', philosophy as taught in Aberdeen was to have as its basis 'an accurate and extensive history of nature, exhibiting an exact view of the various phenomena for which Philosophy is to account'. The various sciences were therefore made 'to follow one another, according to the natural connexion of their subjects' (pp. 3, 5, 6-7).

The most consequential innovation was a reconsideration of the place of logic. Logic was no longer to be taught, in the scholastic way, as an introduction to the study of the sciences but rather 'as a critical review of the sciences'. Its function was to 'explain the different methods of invention, at once suited to the constitution of the mind, and to the varieties of the objects it is conversant with'. As the last and crowning part of the program logic was to embrace 'the laws and rules of inventing, proving, retaining, and communicating knowledge' (pp. 20, 8-9, 33). From this derive some of the most interesting features of Gerard's theory of genius.

---

13 *Dissertations Moral and Critical*, London, 1783, p. ix.
14 The *Plan* was published in Aberdeen in 1755. For its background see P. J. Anderson, *Notes on the Evolution of the Arts Curriculum in the Universities of Aberdeen*, Aberdeen, 1908, pp. 7-9. The German translation, *Alexander Gerards Gedanken von der Ordnung der Philosophischen Wissenschaften*, appeared in Riga in 1770.

It will be noticed—and the Aberdeen professors did not fail to stress it—that this teaching program 'in the main agrees with the partitions of science laid down by LORD VERULAM, and perfectly suits the genius of his Philosophy' (p. 34). In particular, the concept of logic stems from *The Advancement of Learning*; it is modelled directly upon Bacon's four 'intellectual arts'.[15] Thus a Baconian background must be assumed for Gerard's theory of genius, and the *Essay on Genius* cannot but be regarded as a book in the Baconian tradition—a tradition, incidentally, that was hardly less pervasive in eighteenth-century Scotland than it was in seventeenth-century England.

III

'The constitution of man, and his several active powers', declares Gerard in the *Plan of Education*, 'must be explained, before his business, his duty, and his happiness can be discovered' (p. 23). Thus psychology as a subdivision of pneumatology, defined as 'the Natural Philosophy of Spirits' (p. 33), was taught by Gerard, as by some of his Scottish colleagues, as the first and fundamental discipline. As a 'faculty' of man, indeed the highest of his faculties, genius was consequently dealt with as a psychological phenomenon. The lectures on pneumatology constitute the first systematic context in which Gerard's theory of genius is encountered.

Psychology as viewed by Gerard consisted of four parts: '1.º Of yᵉ primary principles & fundamental operations of yᵉ human Mind. 2.º Of its Speculative operations & principles. 3.º Of its active operations & principles. 4.º Of yᵉ Nature & States of yᵉ Human Mind'.[16] Of these only the first two dealing with the cognitive aspects of the human mind are here of interest. Gerard subdivided the first part into a general and a special section. In the general section such constituent elements of his theory as the analysis of the imagination and of the association of ideas are included in the argument. The special section is almost exclusively devoted to external and internal sensation. In the second, more compact part, comprising those 'oyʳ powers of yᵉ mind peculiarly appropriated for Speculation', especially 'some Divisions of our perceptions qᶜ are chiefly subservient to Knowledge' (p. 160) are given attention. Simple modes, complex modes, distinct and confused perceptions, and innate ideas are some of the topics dealt with.

It is at the end of this second part that the chapter on genius is placed. In both the sets of notes, knowledge and judgment are

[15] *Works*, Spedding-Ellis-Heath (eds.), repr. Stuttgart, 1963, Vol. III, pp. 383 ff.
[16] EUL MS.Dc.5.62, p. 13.

discussed before, but the reflections on genius do not immediately arise from this discussion. In the earlier notes the chapter is followed, in the later it is preceded, by one on taste. This establishes a strong connection between the two concepts. Whether or not the *Essay on Taste* was preceded by a still earlier set of lecture notes (the Aberdeen program started in 1755 at the latest), the extant notes presuppose the approach of the *Essay on Taste.*

In the *Essay on Taste* Gerard determined for the first time what he called 'the nature and principles of genius'. At first sight this account bears a close resemblance to the theory in the *Essay on Genius.*[17] The basic ideas seem to be the same. From the beginning Gerard averred (quite conventionally when Pope's dictum is remembered)[18] that 'the first and leading quality of genius [was] *invention*' and that it 'consist[ed] in an extensive comprehensiveness of imagination'. Upon closer analysis, however, the account in the *Essay on Taste* is less a theory of genius than a description of the process of artistic production in the manner of traditional rhetoric. The three phases of the *tractatio materiae* can be clearly recognised. Invention as the 'first and leading quality' is followed by the 'qualities' or 'capacities' of disposition (synonymous, as frequently, with design), and execution or expression. Though the function of the imagination is explained in a rudimentary way, the process of invention is not really analysed. It is merely divided into three successive stages.

Before this account appeared in print Gerard dictated to the class of 1758 a 'brief consideration' of genius which represents the first stage of his 'fuller investigation'. It is based on the *Essay on Taste* and contains a précis of what Gerard intended to publish. Genius, he pointed out,

> includes two Parts.—1st Invention, or the Designing Power, it arises from an Extensive Comprehensiveness in[19] Imagination, or from a readiness of associating the remotest Ideas that seem to form Invention;—The uniting Principles must be so Vigorous & Quick, that whenever any Idea is present to the Mind, they bring into View at once all others that have any Connection with it.—
>
> Genius presents these wt so great propriety, that one would imagine almost that all possible Conceptions had been present to our View & in our Choice; it may first Collect these Materialls in[20] a Confused Heap, but when we view them, they [sic] same associating Power which formerly Made us sensible of their Connection, leads us to perceive the different Degrees of that

17 For the text see Appendix A.
18 'It is the Invention that in different degrees distinguishes all great Genius's' (Preface to *Iliad*).
19 Preceded by an illegible (deleted?) short word.
20 Written over '&'.

Connection, disposes them most strongly related into the same Member, & setts all the Members into that Position which it points out as the most naturall.—This is the Nature of Invention in Musick, Painting, Poetry, Rhetorick, Philosophy, & even Mathematicks.—The Variety which each of those kinds implys arises either from the Degree of Extent of Fancy, or from the Particular Prevalence of some one of the associating Qualitys, or from the Minds being more turned to one kind of Subject or other.—

The Second kind of Genius Consists in a Capacity to Express or Execute it's Designs, in[21] Materialls; without this Power it should never shew itself, & from the Varietys of this Capacity the Diversity of Genius's may be farther accounted for—

This Part of Genius is much more Capable of being improved by Culture than the other.—

We may farther Notice the [sic] Genius is alwise attended with some Exertion of the Understanding, which as it were reviews, examins, confirms & approves the Structure it has raised; this Exertion in the Sciences is Knowledge, Reason & Judgement, and in the Arts is Taste.[22]

Despite its dependence on the *Essay on Taste* this passage must be regarded as a theory in its own right. It differs from the earlier version in at least two respects. First, it is more extensive in scope. In the *Essay on Taste* Gerard was exclusively concerned with what he termed 'genius for the Arts'. Hence his attempt to approach the phenomenon from the rhetorical point of view. In the lecture notes he introduces for the first time the corresponding concept of scientific genius, which was to gain increasing importance. Though it makes only a tentative appearance at the end of the argument, it has a perceptible influence on the theory as a whole. Genius is now genius in general, and it is throughout assumed that the theory holds good for different kinds or varieties of genius. In addition, we shall see (when we turn to the chapter on logic) that owing to the inclusion of scientific genius the key term invention has assumed a wider, even a different meaning.

The other distinctive feature is the division of genius into two parts. It indicates that the rhetorical approach is basically retained, but significantly modified. The third phase of the rhetorical triad, the capacity for expression or execution, is carried over from the *Essay on Taste* without change, and reappears as part two. Gerard's insistence that this part was 'much more capable of being improved by culture than the other' solved a problem in the contemporary

---

21 Written over an illegible word.
22 AUL MS.M.205.2, fol. 464ᵛ—472ʳ.

discussion of genius. It made it possible for Gerard to allow for 'improvement' without implying that genius was a matter of acquired learning and knowledge, as William Sharpe had asserted shortly before in his *Dissertation of Genius*.[23]

The 'first part' was the result of a combination of the phases of invention and disposition. The new unit called 'invention, or the designing power' was obviously intended to remove one of the characteristic difficulties of the rhetorical theory: the virtual impossibility of experiencing invention and disposition as separate acts. In reviewing his initial scheme Gerard seems to have realised that the act of invention was too complex to be reduced to two simple stages of performance. In view of the further evolvement of Gerard's theory the two-part division may be regarded as a recognition of the fact that the study of genius required holistic concepts which could not be provided by traditional rhetoric.

What had Gerard accomplished so far? As early as 1757 he had devised—in admittedly embryonic form—a theory that was potentially capable of explaining artistic and scientific genius as parallel manifestations of the same creative endowment. He had arrived, at least negatively, by modifying the traditional rhetorical divisions, at a distinct notion of the complexity of the inventive process. He was about to disclose the psychological mechanism of the creative mind in terms of the then available concepts. By insisting that the imagination was 'alwise attended with some exertion of the understanding' (taste in the arts; knowledge, reason, and judgment in science) he developed a holistic view of the mental operations and thereby transcended the inherent limitations of the traditional faculty psychology.

In the following year (1758/59) Gerard dictated an entirely different text to his students. Not that he had changed his views. He had elaborated a number of points and arrived at formulations precise and definite enough to be incorporated, fifteen years later, into the *Essay on Genius*. The text as found in Morgan's notes is essentially an epitome of the first part of the book ('Of the Nature of Genius'). All of its five sections ('Of the Province and Criterion of Genius', 'To what Faculty of the Mind, Genius properly belongs', 'How Genius arises from the Imagination', 'Of the Influence of Judgment upon Genius', and 'Of the Dependence of Genius on other intellectual Powers') can be traced back to corresponding passages of the manuscript. Throughout, the text is so continuously

---

[23] *A Dissertation upon Genius: Or, an Attempt to show, That the Instances of Distinction, and Degrees of Superiority in the human Genius are not, fundamentally, the Result of Nature, but the Effect of Acquisition*, London, 1755.

readable as to suggest that Gerard's first lecture to the Aberdeen Society was based on it.[24]

I should like to select two significant aspects of the theory to illustrate its further evolution. First, the submersion of the rhetorical framework. In revising his theory Gerard seems to have increasingly felt the need for unifying concepts. While the earlier notes only implied a fusion of invention and disposition, the indivisibility of the two phases is now explicitly recognised. 'A certain Disposition of ye Materials', Gerard insisted, 'is necessarily implied in Invention'.[25] In the *Essay on Genius* this statement is even more emphatic: 'In every case, some degree of regular disposition is implied in the very notion of invention, and comes within the province of genius' (p. 60). The footnote reference which Gerard makes to Cicero's *Partitiones oratoriae* (I. 3) is a conspicuous, though hardly successful, attempt to place this position in the tradition of classical rhetoric.

The solution of Gerard's problem consisted in the replacement of rhetoric by a new conceptual framework. Unfortunately the lecture notes do not reveal the process of substitution. Only the result can be seen in the *Essay on Genius*:

> To collect the materials, and to order and apply them, are not to genius distinct and successive works. This faculty bears a greater resemblance to *nature* in its operations, than to the less perfect energies of *art*. When a vegetable draws in moisture from the earth, nature, by the same action by which it draws it in, and at the same time, converts it to the nourishment of the plant: it at once circulates through its vessels, and is assimilated to its several parts. In like manner, genius arranges its ideas by the same operation, and almost at the same time, that it collects them. (p. 63)

In other words: the vegetative analogy was the holistic concept which superseded the rhetorical partitions.

In view of the importance in the late eighteenth and early nineteenth centuries of the vegetative analogy as an archetypal model in aesthetics and psychology[26] one should try to fill the gap between the notes of 1758/59 and the *Essay* of 1774. In 1759, it will be recalled, Young's *Conjectures* appeared, a classic exposition of the vegetable concept of genius. Did Gerard assimilate Young's ideas? Their juxtaposition in the standard works on genius gives the impression that Gerard depended upon Young. Considering the consistency of Gerard's approach, one hesitates to accept this view.

24 See Appendix B.
25 EUL MS.Dc.5.62, p. 215.
26 See M. H. Abrams, 'Archetypal Analogies in the Language of Criticism', *University of Toronto Quarterly*, Vol. XVIII, 1948-9, pp. 313-27.

The rise of the vegetative analogy presupposes, about the middle of the century, a transition from physics to biology as the background discipline from which analogies and metaphors could be derived. In Scotland the key figure in this process is David Skene, an Aberdeen physician and founding member of the Philosophical Society.[27] In the words of his biographer, he 'pursued the study of nature to an extent and with an accuracy previously unknown in Scotland'.[28] From 1762 onwards, when Gerard was at work on the details of the psychological analysis of genius, Skene delivered to the Society a series of discourses on natural history. They were designed to draw the attention of his fellow members to natural history as 'the present most fashionable Study', to acquaint them with the work of Linnaeus (to whom 'the very being & spirit of Natural History is in a great measure owing'), and, finally, to advance a plan for the study of natural history based on Bacon but revised 'to include the History of the Human Mind'.[29] It is hardly possible to imagine a more favourable environment for the growth of botanical analogues. All I want to say is that Gerard listened to Skene's first discourse on 12 January 1762.[30]

The second aspect to be noted is Gerard's conception of the imagination as the inventive faculty. That genius, as the *Essay* has it, 'properly belongs' to the imagination was an axiom of the theory, though Gerard later presented it as the result of a process of reasoning (see I, ii). According to the early notes, genius 'arises from an Extensive Comprehensiveness in Imagination, or from a readiness in Associating the remotest Ideas'. The disjunction may be due to a mistake in note-taking, but the corresponding passage in the *Essay on Taste* (pp. 173-5) reveals that Gerard's notion of the structure and function of the imagination was far from distinct.

Gerard now added two more criteria: regularity, and activity and alertness of imagination.[31] The resulting triad not only refined the analysis: it also appeared sufficiently exhaustive to be retained in the *Essay on Genius* (I, iii). While the first criterion seems to have been suggested by the very notion of the inventive mind, the additional ones had different origins. The third is in all probability the conversion into a psychological category of the common thought, as Gerard called it, 'yᵗ a kind of Enthusiasm is inseparable from Genius. This can scarce be oyʳwise, as Enthusiasm consists in a live-

27 See n. 9.
28 Alexander Thomson, *Biographical Sketch of David Skene, M.D., of Aberdeen: With Extracts from Correspondence between Dr Skene and Linnaeus and John Ellis, about the Year 1765*, Edinburgh, 1859, p. 3.
29 Discourse I on Natural History, AUL MS.37, fol. 215r.
30 'Original Minutes . . .', AUL MS. 539, 12 January 1762.
31 EUL MS.Dc.5.62, pp. 214-15.

liness & Elevation of the Imagination'.[32] The second seems to have been derived from the chapter on the association of ideas. To association, Gerard noted, was 'owing in a great measure, Memory & Genius' (p. 29). Without the principle of association, 'as Imagination can separate & alter any Ideas, its exertion shou'd be perfectly irregular' (p. 28). Association, then, defined as 'a kind of mental Attraction analogous to ye Attraction of Bodies' (p. 29) gave rise to the concept of regularity, and the concept of regularity in turn suggested the introduction of the associative categories. The framework for the psychological analysis was complete.

Gerard's lectures on the imagination and the association of ideas were based exclusively on Hume's *Treatise of Human Nature*.[33] If from a 'Romantic' point of view they appear disappointingly conventional, it must be remembered that Gerard's system was a product of the 1750s. His psychology was mechanistic in origin, but the *Essay on Genius* shows that he transcended the inherent limitations both of mechanism and faculty psychology. When the book was translated into German, Immanuel Kant regarded Gerard as one of the exponents of the concept of 'productive Einbildungskraft'.[34]

IV

In addition to the psychology of genius Gerard's lectures contain a separate logic of genius. The justification for this treatment of the same subject in two different contexts is found in the chapter on knowledge. 'Lord Bacon', Gerard observes, 'makes a just distinction between ye explication of ye faculties of ye mind, & ye Explication of y^r Use; ye former belongs to Psychology, ye latter to Logic & Ethics; and y^{se} different views separately prosecuted, wou'd throw Light upon one anoy^r'.[35] In the *Essay on Genius* this distinction is wholly obliterated.

The Baconian logic which Gerard expounded to his students consisted, in accordance with the *Plan of Education*, of four parts. Defining logic as 'y^t Science q^e from the consideration of ye powers of human Understanding Compar'd w^t ye different Subjects about q^e 'tis employed, Directs it in ye investigation, ye Proof, ye Retention, & ye Communication of truth',[36] Gerard divided it into '1° Diacritics q^e direct ye mind in judging of Truth—2° Analytics or Eruditics

[32] Ibid., p. 216.

[33] I,i: 'Of the Ideas of the Memory and Imagination' and 'Of the Connection or Association of Ideas'.

[34] See *Menschenkunde*, pp. 107 ff.

[35] EUL MS.Dc.5.62, p. 200. There is no corresponding passage in the earlier notes. Gerard would seem to re er to 'Advancement of Learning', *Works*, Vol. III, p. 379.

[36] EUL MS,Dc.5.61, p. 505.

qᵉ directs yᵉ mind in the invention of Truth—3⁰ Mnemoneutics
assisting yᵉ mind in explaining of Truths—Lastly, Rhetoric, used in
a larger Sense than ordinary, qᶜ directs yᵉ mind in yᵉ communication
of Truth to others' (p. 507). One word is misheard. Instead of
'eruditics' Gerard dictated 'ereunitics', from Greek 'ερευνα', investigation.

It will be noted that this scheme is one of drastic rearrangement.
Under a unifying concept it draws together a number of disciplines
which traditionally existed apart from one another. Logic and
rhetoric, for instance, though also joined by other Scottish professors in compound courses,[37] are so correlated as to transform
rhetoric from an art of persuasion into a theory of communication.[38]
Diacritics and ereunitics, on the other hand, are meant to form a
general theory of knowledge. The function of ereunitics (which
Gerard regarded as the 'fundamental part of Logic . . . as Truth
must be invented before it can be judged of')[39] is clearly a double
one: to explain the nature of existing inventions and to provide
the basis for future inventions.

This approach resulted in a two-part division of ereunitics in
respect to genius as 'yᵉ leading faculty of yᵉ mind'. 'The Invention
of Arts & Sciences', Gerard proposed, 'may be considered either in
a Historical or in a Philosophical Light'.[40] Consequently the lectures present a history of invention and a philosophy of invention
as distinct, though complementary, fields of inquiry. In this they
differ most notably from the *Essay on Genius*. Whereas in the *Essay*
the psychology of genius and the philosophy of invention are
integrated, irrespective of their former place and function in the
system, the history of invention is excluded *in toto*. Though historical allusion is frequent in the *Essay*, history plays no part in
it. The lectures may thus be said to open up a much wider perspective of the phenomenon of genius.

What Gerard calls the history of invention consists of a series of
reflections which should be quoted in full since they have no
counterpart in the *Essay on Genius*:

> In yᵉ former view yˢᵉ Circumstances may be considered qᶜ
> operating as regular causes, have contributed to yᵉ Invention
> or Cultivation of Arts & Sciences or have prompted mankind to
> yᵉ Investigation of 'em. 'Tis indeed a matter of considerable

---

[37] See John M. Lothian's introduction to Adam Smith's *Lectures* (note 12),
pp. xxix-xxxi.
[38] See Bernhard Fabian, ' "The Fourth Part of Logic": Neue Quellen zur
schottischen Schulrhetorik des achtzehnten Jahrhunderts', in *Festschrift für
Edgar Mertner*, Bernhard Fabian und Ulrich Suerbaum (eds.), München, 1969,
pp. 231-71.
[39] EUL MS.Dc.5.61, p. 563.
[40] Ibid.

difficulty to determine how far ye Cultivation of Arts & Sciences in particular ages & places has been owing to Chances, & how far to discoverable Causes.—In general, y^{se} Events q^c depend on a few persons are ascribed to Chance, & y^{se} q^c depend on ye many to regular Causes. For if regular Causes take place, 'tis naturally to be expected y^t they will affect ye generality, tho' a few may escape y^r influence: & y^{se} Causes q^c operate on ye many, are generally of a grosser & more constant nature than y^{se} q^c affect only a few, & therefore may be more easily investigated. As therefore ye Improvement of Arts & Sciences depends chiefly on a few whom Nature has endowed w^t Genius, it must be acknowledged to be in a great measure accidental or to proceed from Causes beyond y^e reach of our Discovery, but still, as y^e Tincture of Knowledge in enlightened Ages is pretty general, tho' a few only excell, there is some room for ascribing Improvement of Knowledge to Discoverable Causes. And— $1.^o$ 'Tis evident y^t Arts & Sciences cannot be successfully invented or cultivated except in a State of Civil Society, for w^t out y^s State, every thing wou'd be too precarious, & too much Labour wou'd be requisite for supplying y^e necessities of Life to leave men leisure or Curiosity for Investigation.—Again, Arts & Sciences can scarcely take y^r Rise or be first invented except under a Government y^t is in some degree Moderate & free, for Despotic power makes every thing insecure, & engages ye Attention of mankind almost wholly to the avoiding of Inconveniences, & debases y^r minds in such a way as to make 'em little capable of making new Discoveries. A free & Moderate Government by introducing Law gives Security, y^s begets Curiosity, & Curiosity Knowledge.—Again, Nothing can be more favourable to ye Cultivation of Arts & Sciences than a number of neighbouring States separate from one anoy^r, & yet connected by y^r Language & Customs. This Situation produces Emulation among ye men of Genius belonging to different States, & at ye same Time it confines ye Authority of any one man of Genius w^{th}in Moderate Bounds, & prevents y^{se} who come after him from stopping y^r Enquiries of it, in Deference to him.[41]—Again, Arts & Sciences when they are once invented may be transplanted, & flourish for some time almost under any Government. & ye nearer y^t a Government approaches a Republican form, ye more favourable it will be to ye Sciences by allowing ye greatest Liberty of Enquiry: but Monarchy is on ye oy^r hand most favourable to ye fine Arts, as it gives ye greatest Encouragement to 'em, by means of ye inequalities of Rank & Fortune q^c are essential to y^s form of Government.— Again, 'tis observable y^t whenever ye Arts & Sciences have come to perfection in any Nation, they have immediately begun to

---

[41] 'Enquiries': 'ies' written over deleted part of the word; 'in Deference': 'in' written over 'of'.

decline again, & y^s is not only matter of fact but is also founded on reason, for when they are perfected, y^{se} who wou'd continue to pursue 'em, compare y^r own imperfect Essays w^t ye more finished works of y^r Predecessors, & by discovering y^r inferiority to y^{se}, are discouraged from prosecuting 'em. 'Tis further observeable y^t natural Causes as well as Moral have a great influence upon ye Cultivation of Arts & Sciences, by putting men in Circumstances q^c either give 'em peculiar opportunities for improving a particular Branch of knowledge, or render it necessary for them to apply to it. It seems also to appear from History, y^t natural Causes have in many oy^r ways, q^c we can't explain, an influence on ye Revolutions of Arts & Sciences.[42]

In calling these observations historical Gerard must be understood to have used the term history in a special sense. Strictly speaking, they are not historical statements. They do not refer to any specific event or situation. Some may have been derived from ancient history; others—like that concerning the 'Emulation among ye men of Genius belonging to different States'—would seem to stem from modern, if not contemporary experience; still others must be regarded as hypothetical constructs. Even if considerably added to, they would not form a continuous record of the outstanding inventions of the past. The question is if they were at all intended to constitute a conventional account of the 'rise and progress' of the inventive faculty.

It is possible to see in Gerard's observations a pre-historic kind of history such as Hume defined when he declared that history's chief use was 'only to discover the constant and universal principles of human nature'.[43] This would in part explain his attempt to establish generally applicable propositions like the confrontation of the uncivilised and civilised states of society and of the despotic and republican forms of government. But his intention went further. In pointing out 'y^{se} Circumstances . . . q^c operating as regular causes, have contributed to ye Invention or Cultivation of Arts & Sciences or have prompted mankind to ye Investigation of 'em', he obviously had in view a theory, based upon historical evidence, of the conditions under which invention was likely to occur in a given society. Had the name and the concept been available to him, he might have called it a sociology of genius. For this is essentially what he tried to produce.

From the beginning Gerard realised that the project was attended with considerable difficulties, and it must be said that the task ultimately proved beyond his reach. The history of invention is the

---

[42] EUL MS.Dc.5.61, pp. 563-7. The corresponding section in the first set of notes is AUL MS.M.205.2, fourth pagination, fol. 144r—152v.
[43] *An Enquiry concerning Human Understanding*, VIII, i.

only section of his theory which does not show any noteworthy improvement in the second set of notes. Still, it is to Gerard's credit that he asked a question that none of his contemporaries appears to have asked with the same precision,[44] and that he attempted to find the answers. Years later, Gerard took up the problem once more. On 12 December 1769, the Aberdeen Philosophical Society discussed the following question suggested by him: 'Whether any account can be given of the causes, why great Geniuses have arisen at the periods which have been most remarkable for them, and why they have frequently arisen in clusters?'[45] Nothing could better illustrate the turn of his thought. Unfortunately the abstract which Gerard was ordered to make does not survive.

V

Like the history of invention the philosophy of invention was a field which in Gerard's view had been 'Extremely little Cultivated'.[46] Again this meant that there was no coherent theory at once detailed and comprehensive enough to explain the basic aspects of invention in the arts and sciences. Assigning to the second branch of the logic of genius as its proper sphere 'y^{se} methods & Instruments q^c assist ye mind in ye discovery of Truth',[47] Gerard expected from a theory of invention that it remove the appearance of irregularity from 'the Phaenomena of our inventive Powers' by reducing them to 'Generall laws & Causes'.[48]

While the history of invention remained outside the sphere of the *Essay on Genius*, the philosophy of invention transcended it in scope and intention. The Baconian distinction between the explication of the faculties and the explication of their use resulted, for the purposes of the lectures, in the subordination of the concept of genius to that of invention. In the *Essay* invention is, so to speak, a constant (and therefore never defined) because Gerard intends to analyse genius; in the lectures genius (as previously examined in the pneumatology) remains the constant and Gerard proceeds to analyse invention. The lectures, then, contain that discussion of the concept of invention which more than one reader has found missing in the *Essay on Genius*.

In both sets of notes the argument can be divided into at least three parts. In the introductory part Gerard establishes the necessary

---

44 See, for instance, Young's *Conjectures*, London, 1759, pp. 46 ff.
45 See 'Original Minutes . . .', AUL MS.539, Question 104 and 12 December 1769.
46 AUL MS.M.205.2, fourth pagination, fol. 144r.
47 EUL MS.Dc.5.61, p. 567.
48 AUL MS.M.205.2, fourth pagination, fol. 154v.

connection between the former psychological and the new philosophical approach. The early version of this part can be disregarded.
In the later version the notes embody an important element of the
theory which Gerard transferred from the psychology of genius: the
notion, first expressed in the *Essay on Taste*, that the varieties of
genius 'will arise principally from ye different turn of Imagination,
or from ye different associating principles q^c chiefly prevail in a
particular person'.[49] Gerard did not elaborate the short remark
but from it was to grow Part II of the *Essay on Genius*, called 'Of
the general Sources of the Varieties of Genius'. From the 'Minutes'
of the Aberdeen Philosophical Society it can be gathered that in the
1760s Gerard delivered a number of lectures on the various aspects
of this topic.

In the context of the lectures the significance of this remark is not
immediately obvious but it can hardly be overrated. With a theory
of invention in view Gerard felt that 'in order to discover y^e
proper helps & Instruments for ye Invention of Truth, it wou'd be
extremely useful, y^t not only ye nature of Genius in general, but
also of all its different kinds & forms were accurately enquired
into'.[50] That is to say: Gerard hoped that the analysis of genius
would turn out to be a reversible process. As the concept of invention led to a knowledge of genius, so the knowledge of genius could
be used in devising the ways and means of invention.

Logically the next step in the argument was the differentiation
of the kinds of genius. Gerard began by distinguishing four: historical genius, poetical genius, mathematical genius, and inductive
or philosophical genius.[51] This consideration of genius 'with regard
to its Subjects' is to be found in the early notes in which, it will
be recalled, the concept of scientific genius makes its tentative
appearance. Gerard was then under the impression that each kind
of genius could be assigned a particular principle of association,
and that there were at least as many distinct kinds of genius as
there were principles. (Their number, incidentally, increased from
three in the lectures to five in the *Essay on Genius*.)[52] Historical
genius, he asserted, 'arises from a Disposition to associate chiefly
Ideas connected by Contiguity & particular Causes & Effects'.[53] In
the same way poetical genius was tied to the principle of resemblance. Whereas inductive or philosophical genius could be related
to the principle of causation and co-existence, the scheme did not

---

49 EUL MS.Dc.5.61, p. 567.
50 Ibid.
51 AUL MS.M.205.2, fourth pagination, fol. 153v—161r.
52 See EUL MS.Dc.5.61, p. 29, and *Essay on Genius*, II,i.
53 AUL MS.M.205.2, fourth pagination, fol. 153v.

work with mathematical genius—'which has less Dependence on the Imagination than any other kind, tho' still it has some & we fancy in this Subject Abstract Understanding is Combined'.[54] Additional explanations were required and Gerard suggested that the two last kinds of genius consisted principally of sagacity and illation.

Thus, far from being implied in Gerard's approach, the basic distinction of artistic and scientific genius in the later notes was the result of a process of revision. 'Genius', Gerard now proposed, 'may in general be reduced to two kinds'.[55] Artistic genius is further subdivided into several sorts, 'vizt. Genius in ye Mechanical Arts, in Musick, in Painting, in History, in Poetry, & Eloquence'. Of these, Gerard thought that 'a Genius for History is most a kin to y^t for the Sciences & perhaps borrows greatly from it' (p. 569). Scientific genius, in turn, consisted of only two sorts: 'Inductive genius or a Capacity of inferring Truth from Experiments & Observations' and mathematical genius. The latter, as now characterised, required 'a considerable Vigour of ye Imagination by q^c proper intermediate Ideas may be found out' (pp. 569, 570).

Since Gerard retained the distinction of the two kinds of genius and indeed expanded the contents of the notes into Part III of the *Essay on Genius*, this is the place to observe that, while the first part of the book consists of what originally was a psychology of genius, the remaining two-thirds derive from the logic of genius. The different origins are carefully concealed from the reader, but Gerard does not succeed in totally obliterating them. The announcement that in Part III 'a different method' (p. 317) must be pursued is an otherwise inexplicable admission that initially, as the lecture notes will reveal, Gerard had in mind a somewhat different and more ambitious project.

In connection with the distinction of the two kinds of genius Gerard's later definitions of genius make their first appearance. Artistic genius is said to be 'a Capacity for producing new Beauties', scientific genius that 'for inventing new truths'.[56] In 1774 the two halves were put together: 'The ends to which Genius may be adapted, are reducible to two; the discovery of *truth*, and the production of *beauty*. The former belongs to the *sciences*, the latter to the *arts*. Genius is, then, the power of invention, either in science or in the arts, either of truth or of beauty'.[57] There are two slight, though momentous changes: the word 'new' has disappeared, and discovery is substituted for invention as the criterion of scientific

54 Ibid., fol. 154r.
55 EUL MS.Dc.5.61, p. 567.
56 Ibid., pp. 567, 569.
57 *Essay on Genius*, p. 318.

genius. The definition in Part I of the *Essay on Genius* again differs from the composite one in Part III: 'Genius is properly the faculty of *invention*; by means of which a man is qualified for making new discoveries in science, or for producing original works of art'.[58] In other words: novelty is the distinctive mark of scientific genius, originality of artistic genius. And invention is clearly a primary notion under which, surprisingly enough, discovery and production are subsumed.

The re-phrasing of the definition was not a matter of style. It was, rather, an attempt to escape a serious dilemma which resulted from Gerard's analysis of the process of invention in the third section of the logic of genius. In both the sets of notes he follows Bacon in distinguishing two modes of invention. In the earlier version they are labelled, as in the *Advancement of Learning*, the invention of arguments and the invention of arts and sciences. Explaining the difference between them, Gerard paraphrases Bacon: 'The former is not properly an exercise of Invention, but is rather the Application of what we remember and know already to a particular Subject. It is only Using the knowledge which we have, and not making an Addition to it'.[59] In short, rhetorical invention, with the topics and commonplaces as its instruments, is disqualified as pseudo-invention.

Where was the place of literature and the fine arts in this scheme? Since they are not assigned to the first mode of invention it must be assumed that in speaking of 'the invention of arts and sciences' Gerard implies that they belong with the sciences and that, consequently, artistic and scientific invention are fundamentally the same process. This assumption is not borne out by the notes. The subsequent discussion is restricted to the 'useful' arts, all of which are found to be 'reduceable to 2 Classes—1.st Such as hold of Chymistry, & 2.ly Such as hold of Mechannics'.[60] Thus in Gerard's earliest theory of invention the fine arts are passed over in silence. Obviously the status of artistic invention was not easy to determine.

The solution of the problem is to be found in the later notes. Whether the reconsideration of the kinds of genius led to a determination of the status of artistic invention or whether the two-

[58] Ibid., p. 8. It has recently been suggested that Gerard took over his definition from David Hartley's *Observations on Man* (1749: I, 434). See Herbert Mainusch, *Romantische Ästhetik: Untersuchungen zur englischen Kunstlehre des späten 18. und frühen 19. Jahrhunderts*, Bad Homburg, 1969, p. 36. In view of the consistency of Gerard's approach the suggestion has little to commend it. Hartley is not mentioned in the lectures.
[59] AUL MS.M.205.2, fourth pagination, fol. 162r. 'Application' and 'already' written over other words. *Advancement of Learning*, *Works*, Vol. III, p. 384.
[60] AUL MS.205.2, fourth pagination, fol. 174v.

part division of invention suggested a corresponding two-part division of genius is difficult to ascertain. At any rate, artistic invention now comes under the head of rhetoric:

> Invention has been generally considered by Logicians as of two kinds, vizt: The Invention of Arguments and y^t of Sciences: ye former is not so properly Invention, as the recollecting what was formerly known, & so far as it implies Invention, it belongs most properly to that kind of Genius which regards the Arts. The method by which Logicians have ordinarily attempted to assist the mind in this, has been by their Topics, or certain general Heads which they considered as the Sources of Arguments in every Subject . . . But tho' Arguments may be reduced to certain common Heads, yet a knowledge of these common Heads will be of little use for suggesting Arguments . . . There are some Rules tho' usefull, yet are not sufficient to lead the Mind to new Discoveries.[61]

Though rhetorical invention was 'not so properly invention', Gerard had to admit that it implied at least a certain amount of inventiveness. Otherwise the criterion of genius would have been inapplicable to artistic genius and the system would have contradicted itself—especially in view of the fact that Gerard, in making his revision, had transferred the modified rhetorical interpretation of genius from the psychology of genius to that section of the logic which dealt with artistic genius.[62]

When read against the background of the theory of invention, Gerard's definition reveals an inescapable compromise. The repetition involved in the rhetorical process excluded artistic genius by definition from that realm of new discovery which he regarded as the province of genius. On the other hand, given the intellectual milieu of Gerard, he was hardly in a position to devise an alternative to the rhetorical conception of artistic genius. The way out of this difficulty was to subsume the manifestations of artistic genius under the term invention. In regard to artistic genius, invention meant no more than 'producing original works of art'. Contrary to the assumptions of many readers of the *Essay on Genius*, production is not opposed to imitation, and originality is used to denote an inferior species of invention. Gerard's formula, then, does not anticipate any of the Romantic ideas about art.

In contrast to artistic invention Gerard regards scientific invention as the only genuine kind of invention. He defined it, in the Baconian tradition, as the invention of 'New Truths'—a definition in which each of the two words carries a special emphasis. Scientific

[61] EUL MS.Dc.5.61, pp. 570-2.
[62] Ibid., pp. 567-70.

invention, Gerard asserted, was 'of yᵉ greatest importance'. Nevertheless, it had so far been 'very little considered in Logic',[63] so that a pioneer effort was to be made in producing at least a rudimentary equivalent to the well-established rhetorical theory of invention.

The superior ontological status assigned to scientific invention reveals the overruling importance which the concept of scientific genius had gained in Gerard's theory. In the *Essay on Taste* genius is exclusively artistic genius (to be analysed in rhetorical terms); in the *Essay on Genius* genius is, first and foremost, scientific genius. Though Gerard considered the two kinds of genius as parallel manifestations of the same creative endowment, the lecture notes show that the process of scientific invention had become the basic conceptual model which controlled his thought. While 'producing original works of art' was a slightly forced interpretation of invention, 'making new discoveries in science' was an almost natural synonym for it.

In defining scientific invention as the discovery of new truths Gerard gave the term a meaning which is now obsolete and which was perhaps even then less common than that of contrivance, construction, and creation. In fact, he was looking not ahead towards the later eighteenth century but back on the later seventeenth. His concept of scientific genius is closely related to that of the natural scientist which the spokesmen of the New Philosophy developed during the Restoration period. Whether one turns to Bishop Sprat, to Joseph Glanvill, or to Robert Hooke, the natural scientist is always regarded as an inventor or discoverer who finds out something 'new' for the benefit of mankind.[64] Under the spell of the emblem of Bacon's *Instauratio Magna* the early theorists of science considered the scientist a new Columbus who ventured to sail beyond the pillars of Hercules to arrive, in Joseph Glanvill's words, in 'an America of secrets' or in 'an unknown *Peru* of Nature'.[65] Under the same spell Gerard, and for that matter a number of eighteenth-century Scottish philosophers, conceived of invention as a continuous process of discovery, the final result of which was a complete exploration of nature.

Though by the middle of the eighteenth century the concept of invention had been divested of the fanciful seventeenth-century conceits, a naive philosophical realism remained at the core of it. Scientific invention still was a simple act of discovering existing

---

[63] Ibid., p. 573.

[64] See Bernhard Fabian, 'Der Naturwissenschaftler als Originalgenie' in *Europäische Aufklärung: Herbert Dieckmann zum 60. Geburtstag*, Hugo Friedrich und Fritz Schalk (eds.), München, 1967, pp. 47-68.

[65] *The Vanity of Dogmatizing* (1661), Bernhard Fabian (ed.), repre. Hildesheim, 1970, p. 178.

reality. In so far as genius was defined as the capacity of invention, this seventeenth-century and ultimately Baconian concept of scientific invention persisted. It forms the basis of Gerard's theory. It is also in the background of Young's *Conjectures* and William Duff's *Essay on Original Genius*. It appears to be one of the chief characteristics of what I should like to call the classical phase of English *Genielehre*, that is to say, the *Genielehre* which preceded Immanuel Kant's *Critique of Judgment*.[66]

Taken as a whole, Gerard's theory of scientific invention is an attempt to indicate the ways and means which lead to the discovery of nature. Its first section contains some 'general Rules qᶜ may prepare yᵉ Mind for Invention on any Subject'. These occur, as Gerard noted, 'in yᵉ most ordinary Systems'.[67] They give the impression of having been adapted from Gerard's colleague William Duncan. Duncan's *Elements of Logic* (originally published in Dodsley's *Preceptor*) is one of the few treatises on the subject which includes a non-rhetorical theory of invention.[68]

The remaining two sections are related to the two kinds of scientific genius. They deal at length with 'yᵉ instruments yᵗ are to be made use of first in Mathematical Subjects, or concerning yᵉ Relations of our general Ideas, & Secondly, Concerning Natural Subjects, or yᵉ Connections of real things'. 'Mathematical Discoveries', Gerard noted, 'are made Chiefly by means of Arithmetic, Algebra & Fluctions. In all yˢᵉ, yᵉ mind is chiefly employed in discovering unknown Quantities by means of yᵉ relations qᶜ they are known to bear to quantities yᵗ are known'.[69] Though Gerard does not refer to the pertinent sections in the chapter on psychology, it is obvious that this program of invention is determined at least as much by the doctrine of the association of ideas as by strictly mathematical considerations.

In the second section Gerard is predominantly concerned with natural philosophy. 'This Branch', he points out, 'is much more imperfect than yᵉ oyʳ, qᶜ seems to have been owing chiefly to men's imagining yᵗ it was to be improved in yᵉ same way wᵗ Mathematical knowledge, by Contemplation & yᵉ Comparison of our Ideas'. The remedy consisted in procuring 'a genuine & extensive History of Nature. This History must contain a quantity & variety of Observations qᶜ may serve as a foundation for Philosophical Conclusions'.[70] As might be expected, the program is that of Natural

66 See *Kritik der Urteilskraft*, §47, Karl Vorländer (ed.), Leipzig, 1924, pp. 161ff.
67 EUL MS.Dc.5.61, p. 573.
68 See the third edition, London, 1752, pp. 269ff.
69 EUL MS.Dc.5.61, pp. 574, 575.
70 Ibid., pp. 576, 577.

History as outlined in the *Advancement of Learning*.[71] Since the 'proper method' for invention in natural history was the experiment, Gerard added a long section concerning the making of experiments. It is the most detailed passage of the chapter on invention.[72]

Like the history of invention, Gerard's philosophy of invention is hardly more than an attempt to provide a theory, and it should be judged as such. If it is found deficient, it must be remembered not only that it forms part of a fairly elementary course of university instruction, but also that it was a pioneer attempt made about the middle of the eighteenth century. As a postscript it should be added that Gerard's grand scheme collapsed even before the *Essay on Genius* was published. His successor James Beattie dismissed the whole theory with a Scottish commonsense remark. 'Wherever there is Genius', a new generation of students jotted down, 'it will always find out a Method of Invention for itself, and where Genius is wanting, it is in vain to teach Invention by rule'.[73]

Appendix A

An Essay on Taste, London, 1759, pp. 173-5

The first and leading quality of genius is *invention*, which consists in an extensive comprehensiveness of imagination, in a readiness of associating the remotest ideas, that are any way related. In a man of genius the uniting principles are so vigorous and quick, that whenever any idea is present to the mind, they bring into view at once all others, that have the least connection with it. As the magnet selects from a quantity of matter the ferruginous particles, which happen to be scattered through it, without making an impression on other substances; so imagination, by a similar sympathy, equally inexplicable, draws out from the whole compass of nature such ideas as we have occasion for, without attending to any others; and yet presents them with as great propriety, as if all possible conceptions had been explicitly exposed to our view, and subjected to our choice.

At first these Materials may lie in a rude and indigested chaos: but when we attentively review them, the same associating power, which formerly made us sensible of their connection, leads us to perceive the different degrees of that connection; by it's magical

---

[71] Compare ibid., pp. 577ff. and *Advancement of Learning*, in *Works*, Vol. III, p. 330.

[72] See Appendix C.

[73] EUL MS.Dc.5.117, p. 288. For the ascription to Beattie see Fabian (note 38) and Vincent M. Bevilacqua, 'The Authorship of "Alexander Gerard's Lectures on Logic and Rhetoric": Edinburgh University Library, MS.DC.5, 117', *English Language Notes*, Vol. V, 1967, pp. 101-5.

force ranges them into different species, according to these degrees; disposes the most strongly related into the same member; and sets all the members in that position, which it points out as the most natural. Thus from a confused heap of materials, collected by fancy, genius, after repeated reviews and transpositions, designs a regular and well proportioned whole.

This brightness and force of imagination throws a lustre on its effects, which will for ever distinguish them from the lifeless and insipid productions of inanimated industry. Diligence and acquired abilities may assist or improve genius; but a fine imagination alone can produce it. Hence is derived its inventive power in all the subjects to which it can be applied. This is possessed in common by the musician, the painter, the poet, the orator, the philosopher, and even the mathematician. In each indeed, its form has something peculiar, arising either from the degree of extent and comprehension of fancy; or from the peculiar prevalence of some one of the associating qualities; or from the mind being, by original constitution, education, example, or study, more strongly turned to one kind than the others.

Appendix B

Edinburgh University Library, MS.Dc.5.62, pp. 213-18

[At the beginning of the section there is a gap in the text. According to the index at the end of the volume, pages 207-11 dealt with 'Taste, its nature, delicacy, refinement and correctness'. Page 212 contained the start of the section on Genius. Someone has altered the number of page 213 to 207 thinking that the numbering was at fault. The missing pages do not appear to have been bound in anywhere else in the volumes and it seems likely that the lacuna existed before they came to Edinburgh University Library. The section on genius now comprises pages 213 (changed to 207) to 218.]
. . . wanting, a man may have of Intellectual Powers in perfection, but has not Genius, but when a man shows Invention, he is acknowledged to have proportional Genius, whatever oy^r Intellectual Defects he lies under; on y^s account, ye first place is generally assigned to y^{se}, who have invented w^{t}out any Model, or hint from y^r Predecessors, & they who prosecute ye Hints, or improve ye Discovery of oy^{rs} are for ordinary only entitled to ye Second Rank. But whenever an Improvement or addition shows as great Invention as ye first Essay, 'tis looked upon, as Evidencing equal Genius; & if the first Trial be very imperfect, we will not allow so great Genius on account of it, as we allow to y^{se} who afterwards carry it to Perfection. Neither Truth nor Beauty can be invented oy^{r}wise

than by assembling Ideas in various positions y^t we may obtain new views of 'em; The only faculty of ye mind y^t fits us thus, for assembling Ideas is ye Imagination, from y^s faculty therefore, Genius immediately derives its Origin, tho' it may receive assistance from many oy^r faculties; & Genius consists in a particular structure of ye Imagination arising from ye Strength & Turn of ye Associating principles.—1.º Genius implies such extent of Imagination as enables a man to call in from all Quarters ye Ideas y^t are necessary for executing his Designs, & this arises from ye strength & vigour of ye Associating principles, enabling [p. 214] them to suggest Ideas from all Quarters of ye Universe, q^c are connected w^t ye Subject proposed, or ye Design y^t is formed. This Strength of ye Associating principles produces Fertility or Copiousness of Invention, w^{t}out q^c Genius cannot subsist—2.º Genius implies a certain regularity of Imagination, so y^t no unnecessary or foreign Ideas are introduced to perplex us at ye same time y^t all necessary Ideas are collected.— Irregularity of Fancy arises from a mans following any Association y^t occurs, w^{t}out Choice, or w^{t}out Reserve.—This Irregularity always diminishes Genius, even when it cannot entirely destroy it by producing disagreeable perplexity, excessive Splendour, or a disorderly Method. Sometimes indeed an Irregularity of fancy when not entirely ungoverned will lead to bold Inventions, by pursuing an uncommon Road, but still Regularity of Fancy is necessary to ye perfection of Genius, & y^s Regularity arises in a great measure from such a turn of Imagination as leads to a strong Association of ye Design of ye Whole w^t every particular Idea y^t is introduced, for in y^s case, any conception y^t is present, will most readily introduce y^{se} Ideas y^t are related to ye main Design as well as y^{se} related to itself, because y^{se} are associated by a double bond of Union, whereas oy^{rs} connected w^t itself, but foreign to ye Design, have but a Single Bond of Union, & if a foreign Idea shou'd [p. 215] break in, ye Idea of ye Design will immediately occur & lead us to repeat it.—'Tis necessary y^t y^{se} Qualities shoud be united in perfect Genius, by y^r Union they will be both improved & enable us to select Ideas w^t so great propriety y^t tho' only y^{se} q^c we make use of, have been actually present to our view, yet we shoud seem to have had all possible Ideas subjected to our Choice.—Again Genius implies an Activity & Allertnes of Imagination, by q^c it disposes ye Ideas, y^t are presented to us in a very different point of Light, w^t ye greatest Quickness. This proceeds from ye strength of ye Associating Principles constantly exerting 'emselves & not allowing ye mind to be unemployed for a moment, & tho' many Dispositions of ye Ideas y^t are started, shou'd fail of answering ye end proposed, an active Imagination will be indefatigable in trying oy^{rs} till at last it light upon one y^t is proper. Without y^s Activity, Invention shou'd be very slow & Laborious.—Again, A certain Disposition of ye Materials is necessarily implied in Invention, & y^s too is in a great measure accomplished by Fancy, by means of ye Associating principles; at first our Notion of ye order of ye parts may be but confused, afterwards various views of y^s Order occur to us & perplex our Choice; but in time ye same [p. 216] force of Association q^e makes us perceive ye Connection of all ye Ideas w^t ye Subject, will lead us also to perceive ye various Degrees of y^r Connection w^t one anoy^r. The most nearly connected will of course be united w^t Fancy in ye same member, & it will determine ye order of ye Members according to y^r Degree of Connection w^t ye End. It has been commonly thought y^t a kind of Enthusiasm is inseparable from Genius. This can scarce be oy^{r}wise, as Enthusiasm consists in a liveliness & Elevation of ye Imagination, & hence 'tis y^t a Genius in a particular way generally discovers itself even in ye most unfavourable circumstances, & is attented w^t a strong propensity to exert itself. But tho' Genius is properly a comprehensive, regular & active Imagination, it needs ye Assistance of Judgement for its perfection. The Vigour of Imagination produced Invention, but Judgement must regulate its Motions. We find in fact y^t ye greatest Genius's have always possessed Accurate Judgement. Judgement revises every Idea q^e fancy presents & either adopts or rejects it. It prevents fancy from presenting such as are Superflous & unnecessary, or such as are foreign or unsuitable. Regularity of Imagination can be formd only by Judgement exerting itself along w^t it & often correcting it, & after Regularity is acquired. Judgement must [p. 217] attend ye exertions of fancy to correct its wandering, to determine what Ideas are fittest for ye purpose, & what Light they may be placed in, so as effectually to produce it. The Activity of Imagination shoud be entirely useless, if ye various Arrangements q^e it forms were not subjected to ye Scrutiny of Judgement, y^t it may perceive q^e of 'em is right & q^e of 'em wrong.—Judgement too, not only assists in ye Disposition of a work, but also 'tis its Decision alone y^t can assure us y^t ye Disposition is right; & Judgement not only attends Genius thro' ye whole course of Invention, but also gives it farther Assistance by receiving ye Work when 'tis finished, & when on y^s account, it can see many things q^e regard it q^e it cou'd not when imperfect, & as fancy can introduce Ideas only by means of ye Connection w^t some present perception, ye Decisions of Judgement as being Perceptions present to ye mind, will lead fancy to discover Ideas proper for its purpose.—Genius also receives assistance both from Sense & Memory, 'tis from some perception of y^{se} powers y^t it must always at first set out in search of its Idea.

Besides yᵉ Ideas qᶜ Imagination introduces, tho' they be suggested by it, are really such perceptions as have been derived either entire or in yʳ parts from Sense & Memory.—Memory also often assists Imagination in yᵉ very act of [p. 218] introducing perceptions by means of yᵉ Connection qᶜ different Ideas have in yᵉ Memory itself.—

Appendix C

Edinburgh University Library, MS.Dc.5.61, pp. 577-84.

[The following passage illustrates Gerard's line of reasoning.]

As Experience is yᵉ Sole foundation of our knowledge of Real Existence, yᵉ fundamental Instrument for yᵉ Invention of Natural knowledge, must be such as tends to improve our experience & afford us a sufficient number of observations concerning yᵉ real Phenomena of things, yˢ can be affected only by a genuine & entensive History of Nature. This History must contain a quantity & variety of Observations qᶜ may serve as a foundation for Philosophical Conclusions, & it must consider generations or yᵉ Effects of Natures ordinary Course. Præter-generations or yᵉ extraordinary & uncommon productions of Nature, & Arts, or yᵉ changes yᵗ are made in yᵉ natural appearance of things by yᵉ intervention of human operations. It ought thus to be formed according to yᵉ extent or measure of yᵉ Universe [?]. A Natural History qᶜ is designed to serve as a foundation for Philosophy must be Conducted by [p. 578] very different Rules from one yᵗ is intended merely to gratify Curiosity by yᵉ knowledge of yᵉ facts themselves. 'Tis of great importance yᵗ yˢ end (yᵉ Subservience of it to Philosophy) be steadily kept in view in compiling a History of Nature, for it is yᵉ end yᵗ directs to the proper means; Every thing yᵗ is superfluous ought to be avoided & excluded from it: On yˢ account, all Antiquities, Quotations & Authorities, all trifling Controversies & all unnecessary Ornaments ought to be avoided, as what will no ways contribute to yᵉ Discovery of just Conclusions. Such a History shoud not run out into Descriptions of yᵉ curious Variety of Species qᶜ however entertaining contribute little to Philosophical Conclusions. All Superfluitous [?] Relations, unworthy of Credit, are to be entirely rejected, as what wou'd lead into Errour instead of discovering Truth. Of yᵉ three parts of Natural History, yᵗ of Arts is yᵉ most useful for yᵉ improvement of yᵉ Sciences, as it shows nature in Motion, & discovers its most hidden forms & operations. Tho' yᵉ Arts qᶜ as it were alter yᵉ materials of Natural Bodies are much more conducive to Philosophy than yˢᵉ qᶜ are only [p. 579] conversant about yᵉ larger portions of Nature, & qᶜ derive yʳ Merit merely from ye Address y^t is shown in ye practice of them. Not only y^{se} Experiments shoud be received into y^s History q^c tend to ye particular end of y^t art in q^c they occur, but also all such as accidentally cast up, for y^{se} may be very fit to lead to the Discovery of Truth, ye Commonest things ought to be received into an Inductive History of Nature, for till ye causes & Laws of obvious & familiar Phæno-mena be explained, uncommon & remarkable things cannot properly come under examination. . . . [p. 580]

In order to procure such a History as has been described, it is plain y^t it will be necessary to make many experiments of set purpose, & as one can scarcely expect to procure usefull experiments by making trial at random, it will be proper to take notice of ye different ways in q^c one Experiment may suggest & lead to anoy^r.— And 1.º We [p. 581] may proceed by Variation of ye Experiment, & y^t may be done in Three ways.—1.º By varying ye Materials, or making a Trial on oy^r Materials of what has been only attempted on one kind; This variation often tends directly to enlarge ye power of Man by enabling him to work equally w^t several kinds of Materials as they suit his Convenience; It also tends to discover ye Communities of things, & by y^s means to render our Conclusions general.—2.º The Experiments may be varied in respect of ye Efficient, when an attempt is made to produce an Effect already experienced by a different cause. And Lastly, The Experiment may be varied, by varying ye Quantity & making trial whither ye Effect will be encreased[1] in ye same proportion to y^t. This men are apt to take for granted, but nothing can be more fallacious, & therefore it ought not to be imagined, till it be confirmed by actual Trial.— Again, We may not only vary but also produce an Experiment, & y^t first, either by simply repeating it in order to find whither ye additional Effect produced by a Second application will be proportionable to what was produced at first.—2.º An Experiment may be produced by Extension, when 'tis brought to greater Subtility, & [p. 582] so contrived as to discover w^t greater exactness what was only observed in general before.—Again, Experiments may be transferred & y^t first from Nature or Accident into Art, for ye carefully observing ye several Phænomena & Processes of Nature will often suggest extremely useful experiments. 2.º—An Experiment may be transferred from one Art in q^c it has been already made to another Art.—Lastly, An experiment may be transferred from one part of an Art to anoy^r part of ye same. The Translation of ye experiment is in short nothing else but carefully catching at every thing y^t can give a hint at a new Discovery & diligently prosecuting it.—Again,

---

[1] 'encreas' written over 'produc'.

an experiment already tried may be inverted, or trial may be made of yᵉ contrary of what we have already found yᵉ Experiment to hold in.—Again, We may proceed by Compulsion of yᵉ Experiment, when 'tis urged & pushed as it were till yᵉ Virtue & Effect be annihilated & destroyed.—Again, An Experiment may be applied, or ingeniously traduced as it were to some other useful Experiment, qᶜ is a Consequence of it. Again, Experiments may be conjoined, when two methods of effecting yᵉ same thing are united together, to see whither [p. 583] they will produce yᵉ Effect by yʳ Union in a greater Degree than they did singly.—Lastly, tho' 'tis Irrational & foolish to make Experiments at Random, only because the like has never been tried before, yet such Chance Experiments may in some Cases be extremely usefull, when there is any particular Reason to expect great effects from yᵉ trial. In making Experiments one ought not to be disappointed, tho' they shou'd not answer his expectation, or tho' they shou'd not be immediately subservient to any usefull purpose, for they may notwithstanding be subservient to yᵉ Sciences.—By carefully making Experiments in such ways as have been mentioned, a Genuine natural History may be obtained, yᵉ want of it is yᵉ chief hindrance to yᵉ improvement of yᵉ Sciences.— On yˢ account when a Philosopher addressed himself to any particular Enquiry, instead of finding yᵉ Observations & Experiments conducive to it, already collected to his hand, he has been obliged to contrive & make them himself & thus to turn Historian & go & search Materials instead of being at Leisure to reason from them, & yˢ has cost greater Pains & longer Time than drawing Conclusions from 'em.—[p. 584] The Imperfection of Natural History has thus not only retarded but also corrupted Philosophy, by leading men to build Hypotheses upon few & insufficient observations, instead of drawing certain Conclusions from an extensive Experience. No Genius is sufficient for inventing genuine Science wᵗout a proper, Natural, & Experimental History, but if such was Collected, yᵉ perfecting of yᵉ Sciences woud be an easy & Compendious work, for the History woud supply & recommend to yʳ Attention, all yᵉ Facts qᶜ are either necessary to lead them into true Conclusions, or to prevent false ones qᶜ do not agree with the Phænomena of things.

Diderot and the Sublime: The Artist as Hero

Brian A. Elkner

One of the more popular of the after-dinner entertainments offered by d'Holbach to guests at his country estate seems to have been baiting Diderot about the sublime. On one occasion, after Diderot had defended at some length the essential goodness of man and his capacity to rise to the sublime, d'Holbach prevailed upon his friend to read from Voltaire's *Histoire universelle*. After twenty pages of crimes and atrocities, Diderot had to push the book aside and d'Holbach, seeing his obvious emotion, could not let the moment pass without remarking ironically: 'Voilà le sublime de la nature, le beau inné de l'espèce humaine'.[1] Diderot's well-known capacity to let his feelings get the better of him in an argument, together with his over-readiness to spring to the defence of mankind, made him an easy target for the rigorous and cynical mind of his fellow materialist. What seems to have upset Diderot most in these encounters, and there are several of them mentioned in the *Correspondance*,[2] was not the baron's mocking laughter so much as Diderot's own inability to refute the evidence against sublimity. There is no doubt, surely, that these constant assertions about the sublimity of nature and the innate goodness of the human species look somewhat out of place in the mouth of a materialist philosopher, whose own *Rêve de d'Alembert* will effectively discount the existence of anything of value in a universe where 'Tout change, tout passe, il n'y a que le tout qui reste',[3] and where man, as an individual component of universal flux, enjoys no privileges, is undistinguished from the constantly fermenting heap of matter. Individuals, sublime

[1] *Correspondance*, G. Roth (ed.), Paris, 1955–, Vol. III, p. 196.
[2] See, for example, a further letter written only two days later (ibid., pp. 203-4), telling of Diderot's reaction to the story of a Persian who decapitated his children: 'Et moi, je jette le livre . . . Et puis le baron se met à rire: Et le beau moral? et la dignité de la nature humaine?'
[3] *Oeuvres philosophiques*, P. Vernière (ed.), Paris, 1964, pp. 299-300.

or otherwise, simply do not exist,[4] and moral essences are totally inappropriate to a world in which 'whatever is, is right'.[5] Our ideas of the sublime correspond to no reality in a universe composed only of matter, even of sensitive matter: they are elaborate structures built on purely physical foundations. In a letter to Falconet in 1767, Diderot is obliged to admit that, despite his animosity to those philosophers who would put man on all fours and ascribe all his noble feelings to a few drops of fluid, voluptuously shed, there was, all the same, 'un peu de testicule au fond de nos sentiments les plus sublimes'.[6]

Diderot was not unaware, then, of the contradictions involved for a materialist who believes in sublimity, any more than he ignored the paradox involved in editing an encyclopædia aimed at bettering the condition of a creature who was, apparently, all that he should be.[7] No doubt there is a sense in which the sublime was Diderot's 'prop', something in which he had to believe in order to keep going on a project—the *Encyclopédie*—the disappointments of which constantly outweighed the rewards. But this equation of sublimity with virtue, with innate qualities, is only one aspect of Diderot's use of the word 'sublime'. In his aesthetic writings, the sublime appears less as a vague aspiration to set against the facts of bitter experience, and more as a concept the very definition of which depends on the tenets of empiricism, sensualism, and materialism. Even the sensitive clavichord can experience moments of delirium: it can imagine itself to be the only clavichord in the world, with the harmony of the entire universe passing through it.[8] The impression of sudden elevation above the ordinary, of transcendence of one's immediate situation, of having escaped for a moment from the laws of cause and effect, action and reaction, are experi-

[4] Ibid., p. 312: 'Et vous parlez d'individus, pauvres philosophes! laissez là vos individus; répondez-moi. Y a-t-il un atome en nature rigoureusement semblable à un autre atome? . . . Non . . . Ne convenez-vous pas que tout tient en nature et qu'il est impossible qu'il y ait un vide dans la chaîne? Que voulez-vous donc dire avec vos individus? Il n'y en a point, non, il n'y en a point . . . Il n'y a qu'un seul grand individu, c'est le tout.'

[5] Bordeu tells Mlle de l'Espinasse, in the final section of *Le Rêve* (p. 380), that 'Tout ce qui est ne peut être ni contre nature ni hors de nature', echoing the *Essay on Man* and going on to develop the moral implications of Pope's maxim.

[6] Quoted by Charly Guyot, *Diderot par lui-même*, Paris, 1953, p. 37.

[7] The correspondence with Falconet in particular has, as its main theme, the problem of reconciling the belief in determinism with the belief in progress. Diderot generally adopts the position that man is 'modifiable' within a determined framework. See the edition of the letters by Yves Benot, *Le Pour et le Contre*, Paris, 1958.

[8] *Le Rêve de d'Alembert*, p. 279: 'Il y a un moment de délire où le clavecin sensible a pensé qu'il était le seul clavecin qu'il y eût au monde, et que toute l'harmonie de l'univers se passait en lui'.

Published according to Act of Parliament . . . 10. 17. 1751

Proverbs CHAP. I. Vers: 27, 28.
When fear cometh as desolation, and their
destruction cometh as a Whirlwind; when
distress cometh upon them; then they shall
call upon God, but he will not answer.

Designed & Engraved by W.m Hogarth

ences that do not exist any the less for the materialist than for other men. And it is this feeling of going beyond our limitations that Diderot characterises as 'sublime', not in any systematic way (Diderot never wrote a *Traité du Sublime*), but in his constant use of the word in certain exclusive contexts, especially in the *Salons* and in the *Correspondance*. The sublime response to art goes beyond the limitations of art-as-a-language, the sublime artist goes beyond the limitations imposed by the flux of nature, and the sublime criminal goes beyond the mediocrity of a society founded on moderation and convention. I shall examine these three aspects of Diderot's thought in the following pages, in order to show that a belief in sublimity is not altogether incompatible with a material-ist philosophy, and to indicate at the same time the manner in which Diderot gives to the sublime artist, as to the sublime criminal, the status of hero.

Early in his philosophical career, Diderot was tempted by the idea of a sublimity contained in things, in the objects of the external world, in nature. His translation, in 1745, of Shaftesbury's *Inquiry concerning Virtue, or Merit* contains several illuminating footnotes in which Diderot comments or enlarges on the ideas of the English philosopher. One of these notes is particularly relevant to the sublime. Diderot adapts (one hesitates to say translates) the passage in which Shaftesbury maintains that it would be as much an affecta-tion to deny the existence of a special moral sense in man, as to disbelieve in the moral qualities inherent in things;[9] and the trans-lator adds:

> S'il n'y a ni beau, ni grand, ni sublime dans les choses, que deviennent l'amour, la gloire, l'ambition, la valeur? A quoi bon admirer un poéme ou un tableau, un palais ou un jardin . . .?[10]

Here, if you like, is the 'sublime de la nature' about which d'Holbach was later to tease his friend: sublimity, beauty, and virtue float upon the surface of things, exist as objective entities which man perceives by means of an inner moral sense peculiar to him. The experience of art, by elevating man towards the sublime, takes him beyond himself and provides him with a sudden and delicious apprehension of the ultimate harmony that exists between man and nature.

But Diderot's idea of the sublime was not long to remain under the influence of Shaftesbury's neo-Platonism; the belief in the essential sublimity of things can hardly be maintained by a disciple

---

9 *Characteristics*, I, ii, 3.
10 *Oeuvres complètes*, J. Assézat and M. Tourneux (eds.), Paris, Vol. I, p. 33.

Plate VI Servandoni, *Ruines d'un temple ionique*. Reproduced with the permis-sion of L'Ecole des Beaux-Arts, Paris.

of Locke, and Diderot's aesthetic thought evolves more and more towards the subject who experiences the emotion and away from the object which is the immediate cause of the emotion. In a letter to Sophie Volland, written in 1759, Diderot expresses most clearly his attitude towards things, towards natural phenomena:

> Les choses ne sont rien en elles-mêmes. Elles n'ont ni douceur ni amertume réelles. Ce qui les fait ce qu'elles sont, c'est notre âme . . .[11]

Things in themselves are nothing: neither sublime nor beautiful; nor, without someone to perceive them, would they even exist. What would happen to the sublime spectacle of nature, asks Diderot in the article *Encyclopédie* (published in 1765), if there was nobody there to see it? It would become an indescribable process, rather reminiscent of T. S. Eliot's changing scenery in *East Coker*, 'a movement of darkness on darkness': the whole universe would be reduced to a vast solitude in which unobserved phenomena, soundless and obscure, succeed each other in the cosmic silence.[12] Shaftesbury's idealism, like that of Berkeley, would have allowed beauty to exist in a flower growing in the silence of a deserted planet (for, after all, God would behold it); but for Diderot, especially after 1749, the first requirement is a human spectator. The sublime does not exist in nature, but is a value invested in objects by the human being who perceives them: the experience of sublimity, like all experience, is relevant only to the subject.

Moreover, the experience of art enjoys no special privileges. It does not depend on a mysterious sixth sense contained in man,[13] any more than it depends on a mysterious quality inherent in things. The idea put forward by Hutcheson, Smith and others, says Diderot in the *Salon* of 1767, of a special moral sense in man whose function it is to perceive beauty and goodness, is a vision which poetry might well accept, but which must be rejected by philosophy. 'Tout est expérimental en nous . . .': our habits are learned at such an early age that we call them natural, innate; but nothing

---

[11] *Correspondance*, Vol. II, p. 189.

[12] '. . . si l'on bannit l'homme ou l'être pensant et contemplateur de dessus la surface de la terre, ce spectacle pathétique et sublime de la nature n'est plus qu'une scène triste et muette; l'univers se taît, le silence et la nuit s'en emparent. Tout se change en une vaste solitude où les phénomènes inobservés se passent d'une manière obscure et sourde'. Quoted by Jean-Louis Leutrat, *Diderot*, Paris, 1967, p. 7.

[13] The idea is found in J.-B. Du Bos, *Réflexions critiques sur la poésie et la peinture* (1719), Geneva, 1967, p. 225: 'C'est ce sixiéme sens qui est en nous, sans que nous voyions ses organes. C'est la portion de nous-mémes qui juge sur l'impression qu'elle ressent, & qui, pour me servir des termes de Platon, prononce, sans consulter la règle et le compas'. But the idea was popularised throughout the eighteenth century by Francis Hutcheson's *Inquiry into the Original of our Ideas of Beauty and Virtue* (1725).

is natural, nothing innate, apart from nervous fibres more or less flexible, more or less stiff, more or less disposed to oscillate.[14] Like Condillac, Diderot is more interested in exploring the labyrinth of human experience than with hurrying to get outside into the problematical world beyond the cave,[15] especially if the clew that leads us towards 'reality' is an invisible one. Sublime feelings preoccupy the empirical philosopher much more than the definition of *the* sublime, that abstract entity towards which our feelings may or may not be directed. Accordingly, Diderot's evolving aesthetic presents us with a view of art which turns away from nature and becomes increasingly subjective in its concerns. Diderot's theory of the imagination liberates the image from reality, pointing towards a notion of the sublime in which nature can no longer be said to be 'at once the source, and end, and test of Art'.[16]

In a recent study of Diderot's aesthetic, David Funt stresses the point that, for Diderot, art is a language, a symbolic system distinguished from conventional language by its capacity to *illuminate* our experience. Where ordinary language seeks only to analyse, art seeks to synthesise.[17] But, if art *is* a language, what is its object, its *signifié*, as some structuralists would say? I think it is true to say that most of Diderot's commentators, apart from Funt, have seen the object of art as the representation of nature, of the external world of things and phenomena. The same commentators sometimes go on to accuse Diderot of being unfaithful, in his aesthetic, to the ideas put forward in his philosophy, and of having lacked sufficient courage to break with the conventional theory of the imita-

14 *Oeuvres complètes*, Vol. XI, p. 25: 'Croire avec Hutcheson, Smith et d'autres, que nous ayons un sens moral propre à discerner le bon et le beau, c'est une vision dont la poésie peut s'accommoder, mais que la philosophie rejette. Tout est expérimental en nous . . . Nos habitudes sont prises de si bonne heure, qu'on les appelle naturelles, innées; mais il n'y a rien de naturel, rien d'inné que des fibres plus flexibles, plus raides, plus ou moins mobiles, plus ou moins disposées à osciller'. R. F. Brissenden has kindly pointed out to me that, in fact, Adam Smith does not follow Hutcheson with regard to the moral sense innate in man. See Smith's *Theory of Moral Sentiments* (1759), Part VI, section 3, in which he argues for the existence of an internal monitor, formed as a result of our experience in the sight of others. In this respect, his position is not unlike that of Diderot.
15 E. B. de Condillac, *Tranté des systèmes* (1749), in *Oeuvres philosophiques*, G. Le Roy (ed.), Paris, 1947, Vol. I, p. 127: 'Nous naissons au milieu d'un labyrinthe, où mille détours ne sont tracés que pour nous conduire à l'erreur: s'il y a un chemin qui mène à la vérité, il ne se montre pas d'abord; souvent c'est celui qui paroît mériter le moins notre confiance. Nous ne saurions donc prendre trop de précaution. Avançons lentement, examinons soigneusement tous les lieux par où nous passons, et connoissons-les si bien, que nous soyons en état de revenir sur nos pas. Il est plus important de ne nous trouver qu'où nous étions d'abord, que de nous croire trop légèrement hors du labyrinthe'.
16 *Essay on Criticism*, I, 73.
17 'Diderot and the Esthetics of the Enlightenment', in *Diderot Studies XI*, O. Fellows and D. Guiragossian (eds.), Geneva, 1968, p. 54.

tion of *la belle nature*.[18] However, in the *Lettre sur les sourds et muets* (1751), which was until recently the most neglected of Diderot's aesthetic works, we find put forward a view which makes it abundantly clear that conventional language, by concerning itself only with the representation and analysis of phenomena, fails to apprehend the totality of the soul:

> Notre âme est un tableau mouvant, d'après lequel nous peignons sans cesse: nous employons bien du temps à le rendre avec fidélité: mais il existe en entier, et tout à la fois: l'esprit ne va pas à pas comptés comme l'expression: Le pinceau n'exécute qu'à la longue ce que l'œil du peintre embrasse tout d'un coup. La formation des langues exigeait la décomposition; mais *voir* un objet, le *juger* beau, *éprouver* une sensation agréable, *désirer* la possession, c'est l'état de l'âme dans un même instant . . . Ah, monsieur! combien notre entendement est modifié par les signes; et que la diction la plus vive est encore une froide copie de ce qui s'y passe![19]

The language of art tries to go beyond the level of the understanding (modified continually by the signs of ordinary language) in order to reach the inner world of chaotic sensations, impressions, associations. Conventional language is a de-composition of experience, but art sometimes manages to re-constitute, to put back what was lost in the process of reduction and analysis. Art does not try to represent the external world except as a means of provoking in the spectator a reaction which corresponds exactly to the *tableau mouvant* of his soul. Then, and then alone, does the aesthetic experience become sublime. Poetry is occasionally capable of creating this moment, theatre manages to succeed more often than poetry, and painting, the most sublime of the languages of art, gets closest to the instantaneity of our subjective experience.

Diderot demonstrates, in the *Lettre sur les sourds et muets*, the manner in which poetry transcends the limitations of ordinary language by re-juxtaposing words so as to rob them of their conventional meaning as signs, and to let them act on each other in new and exciting ways. The power of poetry is not in the *rapports*, in the cumulative associations that Du Bos had defined as sublime,[20] but in the capacity of the words to create 'emblems' which fit the images contained within the reader's soul. The presence of this

[18] The most systematic attempt at relating *la belle nature* to the aesthetic judgment was made by Batteux in *Les Beaux-arts réduits à un même principe* (1746), but the idea had been in vogue for more than half a century. See Jean Ehrard, *L'Idée de Nature en France dans la première moitié du XVIIIe siècle*, Chambéry, 1963, Vol. I, pp. 253-328, for a comprehensive account of the dialectic which develops between *la belle nature* and *la vraie nature*.

[19] *Oeuvres complètes*, Vol. I, p. 369.

[20] *Réflexions critiques*, p. 29.

power in poetry has the effect of reaching the *tableau mouvant* so that 'les choses sont dites et représentées tout à la fois'[21] (surely a tempting explanation for the sublime effect of *And there was light*, of which Longinus and Boileau make so much). Where Du Bos and other theorists of poetry had seen the sublimity of the medium in its cumulative effect, Diderot sees the poem as a total experience which no longer depends on the energetic arrangement of thoughts —the sublime *style* of the rhetoricians—but on the piling-up of what Diderot calls 'hieroglyphs' which make themselves immediately felt, instantly apprehended.[22] But even the most vivid poetry depends, in the end, on words; and words ask to be translated by the understanding, they speak to the memory as well as to the imagination, and they end up by limiting the possibilities for sublimity.[23] The *Lettre sur les sourds et muets* offers, as superior to poetry, a *sublime de situation* to be found in the 'language' of pantomime, where eloquent gestures replace the spoken word. The particular domain of this kind of sublimity is, of course, the theatre.

The old Le Sage had told Diderot that he never really began to enjoy the theatre until he went deaf,[24] and Diderot himself often went to plays, blocking his ears (as he put it) 'pour mieux entendre'.[25] The actor who goes beyond even the heightened language of poetry, who uses gesture and mime to express himself in silence, uses a symbolic language which the spectator finds hard to eradicate from his imagination. The most sublime thoughts are soon forgotten, but these images do not disappear.[26] The *sublime de situation* is directed towards imprinting in the beholder an ineffaceable image that has no need to be 'translated', that does not depend on the current 'value' of certain words. The theatre is not the domain of expression, says Diderot in the *Discours de la poésie dramatique* (1758), but of impression.[27] Gesture and mime oblige the spectator to supply his own 'meaning' to what he sees before him; his imagination is not limited by written signs that speak to his understanding as well. And, just as silence is more conducive to the sublime than is sound, so stillness creates a deeper

[21] *Oeuvres complètes*, Vol. I, p. 374.
[22] Ibid.: '. . . le discours n'est plus seulement un enchaînement de termes énergiques qui exposent la pensée avec force et noblesse, mais que c'est encore un tissu d'hiéroglyphes entassés les uns sur les autres qui la peignent. Je pourrais dire, en ce sens, que toute poésie est emblématique'.
[23] Ibid., p. 369: Diderot quotes some lines from Racine's *Phèdre* and comments: 'Voilà une des peintures les plus ressemblantes que nous ayons. Cependant, qu'elle est encore loin de ce que j'imagine!'
[24] Ibid., p. 360.
[25] Ibid., p. 359.
[26] Ibid., p. 355: 'On oublie la pensée la plus sublime; mais ces traits ne s'effacent point'.
[27] *Oeuvres esthétiques*, P. Vernière (ed.), Paris, 1965, p. 197.

impression in the spectator than movement. If poetry surpasses ordinary language by liberating the imagination, if gesture triumphs over poetry by going beyond mere words, the absence of gesture goes even further towards the sublime than the body language of the mime.[28] Diderot tried to introduce, on stage, not only an increased amount of pantomime, but also the occasional tableau, in which all movement was suspended. In a letter about the theatre to Madame Riccoboni in 1758, he shows his preference for the suggestive above the explicit in the use of the tableau:

> Savez-vous quels sont les tableaux qui m'appellent sans cesse?—
> Ceux qui m'offrent le spectacle d'un grand mouvement?—Point
> du tout; mais ceux où les figures tranquilles me semblent
> prêtes à se mouvoir.[29]

And yet, Diderot has to admit that even the dramatist cannot entirely do away with words, with some kind of exposition. A tragedy composed uniquely of silence and stillness, even if it *was* the ultimate work of Samuel Beckett, would not hold the audience's attention for very long.[30] The *sublime de situation* depends on the creation of a situation, on the careful development of themes, memories, associations, which the spectator must remember. Words are as indispensable in the theatre as they are in poetry. A third medium does, however, exist which offers more scope for the sublime, for the total liberation of the subjective imagination, than either theatre or poetry. The painting is silent *and* immobile, its figures suggest more than they supply and, most of all, the painting has an instantaneous effect. As Jonathan Richardson had put it in his *Essay on the theory of painting* (1715):

> Painting . . . pours ideas into the mind, words only drop them.
> The whole scene opens at one view, whereas the other way
> only lifts up the curtain little by little.[31]

Diderot's search for the sublime in art turns quite logically towards painting, towards the instantaneous representation of the *tableau mouvant* which poetry and theatre only partially succeeded in creating. But because painting is instantaneous in its effect, because it dispenses with the accumulation of linguistic pat-

---

28 *Oeuvres complètes*, Vol. I, p. 355: Diderot sees the absence of movement of the two princes in Act IV, Scene iv, of Corneille's *Héraclius* as more evocative than any speech or gesture.

29 *Correspondance*, Vol. II, p. 98.

30 It is interesting to note that Fénelon had already suggested a theatre without formal language in his *Lettre à l'Académie* of 1714 (section VI), in which cries and gestures would replace the discourse. Du Bos retorted that it would be rather difficult to write a tragedy composed uniquely of cries. See Wladyslaw Folkierski, *Entre le Classicisme et le Romantisme*, Paris, 1925, p. 175.

31 Quoted by Folkierski, p. 174.

terns—whether words, hieroglyphs, or gestures—it is the only medium where sublimity is an absolute obligation. The painter has no more than a moment in which to create his effect upon the spectator,[32] and he can descend from the sublime only to the dreadful: 'Point de milieu . . . le simple est sublime ou plat'.[33] There is no middle way for the painter or, for that matter, for the sculptor: Diderot tells Vassé, in the *Salon* of 1761, that it is no excuse to say the work is tolerable when the genre requires it to be sublime.[34] The plastic arts, and painting in particular, must bypass the memory and the understanding, communicating directly and immediately to the imagination, of which the work then forms an integral part:

> L'imagination me semble plus tenace que la mémoire. J'ai les tableaux de Raphaël plus présents que les vers de Corneille, que les beaux morceaux de Racine. Il y a des figures qui ne me quittent point.[35]

But, if painting gets closest to the subjective reality of the spectator because of its inherent freedom from language, it must be admitted nevertheless that the image on canvas can be as much a 'sign' as the spoken word or the gesture, and that painting is still therefore liable to the limitations of conventional meanings which inhibit the freedom of the beholder's response, precluding the possibility of a totally sublime experience. Painting which resembles the world of objects, for example, may evoke a purely mental response in which the beholder carefully compares the copy to the original he has in his memory, noting with cerebral satisfaction the points of comparison and those elements which the painter has changed in order to provide a unity lacking in the 'original'. The signs of painting, when they seek only to express *la belle nature*, can be as restrictive as the signs of the other media. This is surely why Diderot makes a distinction between the finished painting and the sketch. For sketches have a fire which finished paintings lack, he tells Grimm in the *Salon* of 1765: the vaguer the expression, the more the imagination is at ease; in the finished painting, Diderot sees a thing pro-nounced: but in the sketch, he finds a multitude of things which are hardly even an-nounced.[36]

> Pourquoi une belle esquisse nous plaît-elle plus qu'un beau tableau? c'est qu'il y a plus de vie et moins de formes. A mesure qu'on introduit les formes, la vie disparaît.[37]

---

[32] *Essais sur la peinture* (1765), in *Oeuvres esthétiques*, p. 721.
[33] *Salon de 1767*, in *Oeuvres complètes*, Vol. XI, p. 70.
[34] *Salon de 1761*, in *Oeuvres complètes*, Vol. X, p. 146.
[35] Ibid., p. 141.
[36] Ibid., pp. 351-2.
[37] *Salon de 1767*, p. 245.

The forms of painting, the visual 'language', interfere with the *life* of painting. Forms, like words, like gestures, call attention to themselves, evoke an experience only to contain it within a restricted framework. The absence of form, like the absence of words, leaves the spectator free to elaborate on the impression received, to give it his *own* meaning and, in so doing, to go beyond the language of art in order to reach the sublime.

Diderot's descriptions of paintings depicting ruins offer obvious analogies to his ideas on the sketch. Just as the sketch has more life than the finished canvas, so the ruin has more power to excite the imagination than has the complete building. Ruins themselves, as objects, are only the point of departure for the imagination of the subject; what gives them their peculiar power, what makes them sublime, is the flood of accessory ideas which they provoke and which are not contained or restricted. In the *Salon* of 1765, Diderot talks less about the ruins themselves in a painting by Servandoni (see Plate VI), than about the associations which they evoke in him:

> Ici, il se joint encore aux objets un cortège d'idées accessoires et morales de l'énergie de la nature humaine, de la puissance des peuples . . . Où régnait la foule, et le bruit, il n'y a plus que le silence et la solitude.[38]

It is not the concrete, representational, aspects of the work which determine the response of the spectator, but the accessory ideas which the spectator himself supplies; and it is precisely these accessories that make all the difference between the sublime and the merely agreeable. Carle Van Loo's *Madeleine dans le désert* is no more than a 'tableau très agréable', but the painter could have made it sublime had he imbued his painting with the solitude, the silence, and the horror of the desert.[39] Deserts, like ruins, offer incomplete prospects in which absent objects are more important than present ones, in which the image on canvas makes the spectator think about the littleness of man, the vastness of time and space, and so on. But these accessory ideas are not the product of considered judgment and careful reflection: they occur in a flood of lived experience which takes the spectator beyond himself and places him on the threshold of eternity.[40] In this sublime experience of ruins, a

---

[38] *Oeuvres complètes,* Vol. X, p. 308.

[39] *Salon de 1761,* p. 110: 'Combien la sainte n'en serait-elle pas plus intéressante et plus pathétique, si la solitude, le silence et l'horreur du désert étaient dans le local?'

[40] *Salon de 1767,* p. 229: 'Les idées que les ruines réveillent en moi sont grandes. Tout s'anéantit, tout périt, tout passe. Il n'y a que le monde qui reste. Il n'y a que le temps qui dure. Qu'il est vieux ce monde! Je marche entre deux éternités.' Cf. d'Alembert's vision of the universe in *Le Rêve* (note 3 above).

pre-eminently subjective experience, the accessories are, for once, more important than the vehicle.

The parallels between Diderot's implicit theory of the sublime and Edmund Burke's explicit one should be obvious. Burke, like Diderot, turns to his own subjective experience in order to discover the nature of the sublime; Burke, like Diderot, sees the ideas of silence, solitude, terror, obscurity, as the most productive of sublime feelings. 'A clear idea', Burke tells us, 'is . . . another name for a little idea',[41] and the tangle of impressions and associations is a far more powerful mainspring for the aesthetic emotion than any logical functioning of the mental process. Madame Gita May has already shown us the many points of comparison between Burke's *Enquiry* and Diderot's *Salon* of 1767,[42] but I think that we need to add to this case for an 'aesthetic affinity' an important qualification. For Burke sees all art, including sublime art, as imitation, deriving its power from that of the original, whereas we have seen that Diderot bases his notion of the sublime on a kind of imaginative freedom which is at its best when the amount of imitation is at its least. Burke's ideas derive closely from those of Du Bos, and both writers draw heavily on Locke's sensationalism. Du Bos had seen the human organism as preoccupied with avoiding repose: it seeks above all to be diverted, to maintain itself in a state of movement. The most pleasurable forms of movement are those which have connotations of violence and danger, but these constitute drastic ways of escaping from boredom since they lead, ultimately, either to the destruction of the self or to the immolation of others. Civilised society, through its art, provides the possibility of enjoying violent sensation without occasioning actual bodily harm. Art is therefore at its most powerful when the spectator is utterly convinced of the reality of the spectacle. The empathy experienced in front of the work of art must not be destroyed by the awareness that it is, after all, only an imitation. Nevertheless, the emotion involved in this aesthetic experience will always be of an inferior and superficial kind since the work cannot help being an imitation, an inferior copy of the real thing.[43] Burke develops this imitative theory of Du Bos and applies it specifically to tragedy, which he has no qualms in relegating to the level of superficiality:

41 *A Philosophical Enquiry into the Origin of our Ideas of the Sublime and the Beautiful* (1757), J. T. Boulton (ed.), London, 1958, p. 63.
42 'Diderot and Burke: A Study in Aesthetic Affinity', in *Publications of the Modern Language Association of America*, Vol. LXXV, 1960, pp. 527-39.
43 *Réflexions critiques*, p. 14: ' . . . L'imitation la plus parfaite n'a qu'un être artificiel, elle n'a qu'une vie empruntée, au lieu que la force & l'activité de la nature se trouvent dans l'objet imité. C'est en vertu du pouvoir qu'il tient de la nature même que l'objet réel agit sur nous'.

The nearer it approaches the reality, and the further it removes us from all idea of fiction, the more perfect is its power. But be its power of what kind it will, it never approaches to what it represents. Chuse a day on which to represent the most sublime and affecting tragedy we have; appoint the most favourite actors; spare no cost upon the scenes and decorations; unite the greatest efforts of poetry, painting and music; and when you have collected your audience, just at the moment when their minds are erect with expectation, let it be reported that a state criminal of high rank is on the point of being executed in the adjoining square; in a moment the emptiness of the theatre would demonstrate the comparative weakness of the imitative arts, and proclaim the triumph of the real sympathy.[44]

Now, Diderot is never attracted by the idea, a common one in eighteenth-century aesthetics, that art is necessarily inferior to nature, and he quickly dismisses Burke's argument by saying, in the *Salon* of 1767, that the empty theatre is a result of curiosity and not of any inherent weakness in the art itself. The audience reaction is conditioned in this case by social habit, but decapitate a state criminal every day and the people will quickly go back to Cato.[45] Burke, like Du Bos—and, one might add, Rousseau[46]—failed to take into account the possibility that the distance between the imitation and the reality might well be at the source of our aesthetic pleasure. Obviously, if the strength of our response can only increase as art draws nearer to nature, then there is a 'ceiling' beyond which we cannot go: reality itself. No matter how sublime the art, nature is always more sublime, and the imitation can never be more than a *pis aller*, safer perhaps than the real thing, but decidedly inferior. Despite the predominant subjectivism of his aesthetic, Burke tends

---

[44] *A Philosophical Enquiry*, p. 47.
[45] *Salon de 1767*, p. 120: 'On prétend que la présence de la chose frappe plus que son imitation; cependant on quittera Caton expirant sur la scène, pour courir au supplice de Lally. Affaire de curiosité. Si Lally était décapité tous les jours, on resterait à Caton'.
[46] See, for example, the often neglected little essay, *De l'imitation théâtrale*, which Rousseau omitted from his famous *Lettre à D'Alembert* (1758).: '. . . si quelqu'un pouvait avoir à son choix le portrait de sa maîtresse ou l'original lequel penseriez-vous qu'il choisît?' *Oeuvres complètes*, Paris, 1828, Vol. I, p. 448. What was, for Du Bos and Burke, an argument for the relegation of art to the level of harmless stimulation is, for Rousseau, yet another reason for condemning the deceptions practised by society. In the case of Burke, distance is an essential ingredient of the sublime emotion—'When danger or pain press too nearly, they are incapable of giving any delight, and are simply terrible; but at certain distances, and with certain modifications, they may be, and they are delightful, as we may every day experience' (*A Philosophical Enquiry*, p. 40). But he nevertheless distinguishes between the distance which separates the spectator from reality, and that which separates him from a mere imitation. In the second case, the distance is too great to exercise as compulsive a grip on the imagination.

to fall back on a kind of sublimity contained in things, a force inherent in nature which art can only feebly transmit to us.[47] But for Diderot, not only is art generally seen as being superior to nature,[48] but sublime art is sublime, as we have seen, precisely because of its independence of natural objects, because of the imaginative freedom which it creates in the perceiving subject. The difference between the sublime and the beautiful, for Diderot, must be formulated in terms of the difference between an evocation and an imitation; the sublime emotion does not transport us towards an external reality which art has tried to represent: the sublime emotion breaks free from reality and leaves the spectator in a state of suspension and delight.

A painting the effect of which is purely imitative, representative, might well be considered beautiful, but Diderot saves the word sublime for something else. In the *Salon* of 1761, he describes a painting by Vien with all the relish and satisfaction of a man coming from a good dinner:

> Rien ne m'en paraît sublime; mais tout m'en paraît beau. Je n'y trouve rien qui me transporte, mais tout m'en plaît et m'arrête . . . Les natures ne sont ici ni poétiques ni grandes; c'est la chose même, sans presque aucune exagération.[49]

The painting is beautiful, completely satisfying, leaving nothing to be desired, because it is firmly attached to the reality it represents: 'c'est la chose même'. Beautiful things sometimes ask to be copied, so that the number of pleasant moments may be doubled, but there is nothing sublime in the experience, precisely because the painting contains all the meaning intended for it; there is no metaphysical flight, no procession of accessory ideas, no astonishing suspension of the imagination. But the painting is not any the less to be enjoyed as an imitation, as a limited exercise in symbolic language. And yet, this implicit distinction, in Diderot's aesthetic, between the (sublime) evocation and the (beautiful) imitation does not hold when we look at the passages in the *Salons* which describe the landscape paintings of Vernet and, especially, the still life paintings of Chardin. Diderot sees in the exact imitation of the works of these two painters, not something pleasant and diverting, but a

---

[47] This point has already been noted by Samuel Monk, *The Sublime*, Ann Arbor, 1960, p. 86.

[48] See, for example, the *Pensées sur l'interprétation de la nature* (1753): 'La nature est opiniâtre et lente dans ses opérations . . . L'art, au contraire, se hâte, se fatigue et se relâche', in *Oeuvres philosophiques*, p. 211; or again, the *Pensées détachées...*: 'Quelquefois la nature est sèche, et jamais l'art ne le doit être, in *Oeuvres esthétiques*, p. 771.

[49] *Oeuvres complètes*, Vol. X, p. 122.

sublime de technique[50] which can only leave him mute with admiration. What then is the difference between a beautiful imitation by Vien and a sublime imitation by Chardin?

Diderot dwells, in a letter to Sophie Volland, written in 1760, on the intricate fantasies of Chinese art, and on the aesthetic behind them. The Chinese, instead of taking nature as their model, try to get as far away from it as possible, reasoning that, however talented the painter may be, however much trouble he may take over his work, he can never get anywhere near the effect of nature itself. Imitative art does no more than excite pity and derision in the beholder, whereas the free-ranging forms of fantasy can hardly be accused of falling short of an ideal with which they are not concerned.[51] The theory has obvious attractions for Diderot, particularly in the light of his growing awareness of the practical impossibility of ever rendering a single human hair as it appears in nature.[52] And yet, Vernet and Chardin have produced canvases which seem to defy the laws of nature by capturing and freezing in paint, by containing within a two-dimensional framework, that which never stands still. Because nature is in constant flux, because our perceptions of nature are always relative to our sensations, the achievement, of Chardin especially, is all the more remarkable. If it is true, says Diderot, that there is nothing real apart from our sensations, that neither the emptiness of space nor the very solidity of things is, in itself, anything like our impression of it, then let these philosophers explain the difference, four feet from a Chardin canvas (see Plate VII), between the creator and the painter.[53] For God to create a universe is not all that remarkable: He is, after all, omnipotent. But for a man to repeat the performance in paint and, moreover, to give his work a stillness which God could not give to the universe, is a feat which can only be called 'sublime'. Chardin the painter, like Diderot's ideal actor in the *Paradoxe sur le comédien*, casts a 'cold eye on life, on death', looks without flinching at the constant permutations of the universe, and rises above his human limitations in order to capture reality. The coldness of Chardin, which Diderot contrasts more than once with the passion of Greuze,[54] takes him beyond the *sensibilité* of the artist who merely wants to imitate objects which, in themselves, give him

[50] *Salon de 1765*, in *Oeuvres complètes*, Vol. X, p. 295.
[51] *Correspondance*, Vol. III, p. 145.
[52] *Salon de 1767*, p. 9: 'Vous avez senti la différence de l'idée générale et de la chose individuelle jusque dans les moindres parties, puisque vous n'oseriez pas m'assurer, depuis le moment où vous prîtes le pinceau jusqu'à ce jour, de vous être assujetti à l'imitation rigoureuse d'un cheveu. Vous y avez ajouté vous en avez supprimé . . .'.
[53] *Salon de 1765*, p. 299.
[54] Ibid., p. 342.

pleasure and comfort: the sublime artist, when he imitates nature, does so in order to assert his own superiority, in order to rise above the very things he imitates:

> suspendus entre la nature et leur ébauche, ces génies portent alternativement un oeil attentif sur l'une et l'autre.[55]

The imitation can at times be sublime by its very existence in the face of nature's laws: if art has not yet become a protest against nature, as it will with Baudelaire,[56] it has at least broken with the belief in an ultimate harmony with nature. All art, even imitative art, is capable of being sublime when it proclaims the energy of the human spirit, when it asserts against nature the impulse to create.

It is often seen as a profound contradiction in Diderot's thought that he should embrace the cause of art for morality's sake, while advancing at the same time a philosophy according to which both art and morality are determined by factors beyond man's control. Diderot's admiration for Greuze and Chardin is often seen as a sentimental 'sell-out' of his deterministic materialism, which he never had the courage to apply fully to his aesthetic. But we need to be careful here in distinguishing Greuze from Chardin for, although both painters use techniques of exact imitation, Chardin is seen to be 'sublime' and Greuze, apart from a grudging exception or two, is never allowed to be more than beautiful. The distinction between the two is more than an accident of vocabulary. Greuze's *peinture morale*, Sedaine's *drame bourgeois*, and Richardson's *roman sentimental*, all attract Diderot's enthusiastic approval and reflect his commitment to art as a means of changing society, by touching the heart of the wicked, by awakening the sensibilities of the virtuous. But to see the *Salons* as no more than art criticism directed against the aristocracy by a champion of the Third Estate[57] is to miss Diderot's quite 'aristocratic' use of the word 'sublime', a term which he denies to Greuze, Sedaine, and Richardson, and which is applied only to a kind of art to which moral values and social commitment seem totally inappropriate. Chardin is sublime, not because he confronts society, but because he stands up against nature. The beauty of a Greuze canvas might speak to our emotions, it might present us with a situation in which we feel immediately

---

55 *Paradoxe sur le Comédien*, in *Oeuvres esthétiques*, p. 309.

56 See for example, the *Salon de 1846*, XII: 'Un éclectique ignore que la première affaire d'un artiste est de substituer l'homme à la nature et de protester contre elle. Cette protestation ne se fait pas de parti pris, froidement, comme un code ou une rhétorique; elle est emportée et naïve, comme le vice, comme la passion, comme l'appétit', in *Curiosités esthétiques*, H. Lemaître (ed.), Paris, 1962, p. 169.

57 I. K. Luppol, *Diderot*, Paris, 1936, p. 373.

involved: but the sublimity of a Chardin still life depends on our admiration of the artist as an individual, as a man endowed with exceptional talent. The sublime artist is no use to society; his coldness makes us suspect him, his inventiveness tends to rock the social order too much, and his keen observation earns him more enemies than friends. In fact, the sublimity of the great artist puts him in the company of another individual with whom society wants little to do: the great criminal.

Rameau's nephew has no illusions about the relative merits of good and evil as domains of the sublime:

> S'il importe d'être sublime en quelque genre, c'est surtout en mal. On crache sur un petit filou; mais on ne peut refuser une sorte de consideration a un grand criminel. Son courage vous etonne. Son atrocité vous fait frémir. On prise en tout l'unité de caractere.[58]

The renegade of Avignon, in befriending the Jew who is to be his victim, resists the temptation to reach for the pear before it is ripe; he prepares his part with consummate *sang-froid*, putting on a mask of friendship and compassion until it is time to act. But the sublimity of his wickedness is not in his treachery or his hypocrisy or even in the fact that he manages to steal all of the Jew's wealth. The renegade is sublime because he denounces the Jew to the Inquisition after the swindle has been successfully completed. A common thief would have been content with the money of the infidel, but the sublime criminal will have nothing less than the Jew's death, which he justifies quite cynically by alleging the motive of revenge on that tribe who persecuted Our Lord.[59] La Rochefoucauld's maxim, that there are heroes in evil as well as in good, is demonstrated admirably, not only in *Le Neveu de Rameau*, but also in the sub-plot of Madame de La Pommeraye's terrible revenge, related in *Jacques le Fataliste*.[60] This single-minded pursuit of a faithless lover, this coldness with which she is able to look upon the dreadful result of her scheme, distinguish her from the ordinary human being, whose pity and compassion make him a creature abandoned to the discretion of his diaphragm.[61]

---

[58] *Le Neveu de Rameau*, J. Fabre (ed.), Geneva, 1950, p. 72.

[59] Ibid., p. 75.

[60] *Oeuvres romanesques*, H. Bénac (ed.), Paris, 1962, p. 651: 'Vous entrez en fureur au nom de Mme de La Pommeraye, et vous vous écriez: "Ah! la femme horrible! ah! l'hypocrite! ah! la scélérate! . . ." Point d'exclamation, point de courroux, point de partialité: raisonnons. Il se fait tous les jours des actions plus noires, sans aucun génie. Vous pouvez haïr; vous pouvez redouter Mme de La Pommeraye: mais vous ne la mépriserez pas. Sa vengeance est atroce; mais elle n'est souillée d'aucun motif d'intérêt'.

[61] *Le Rêve de d'Alembert*, p. 356: 'Mais qu'est-ce qu'un être sensible? Un être abandonné à la discrétion du diaphragme'. The main argument of the *Paradoxe sur le Comédien* is, of course, based on this principle.

Diderot's *Correspondance* is full of accounts of sublime heroes in evil: he sees Lovelace as a 'sublime brigand',[62] and Damiens, the regicide, as an example of criminal sublimity unsurpassed by any of the archetypes of virtue.[63] The *Salons* themselves contain several interesting accounts of paintings which depict horrible actions in such a way as to make us suspend our moral judgments, forcing us to turn away, if we *do* turn away, in terror, not in disgust.[64] Rubens's *Judith* (Plate VIII) provides a perfect example of the sublime: she plunges the knife into Holophernes's neck with a *sang-froid* that makes us shudder.[65] On the other hand, Pierre's painting of the *Décollation de Saint-Jean* fails to reach the sublime precisely because the painter has Herodias betray an involuntary expression of horror as she looks on her bloody work; she should have been ferocious in her joy, able to gaze without flinching on her triumph, and instead she lowers herself to the level of the ordinary person, capable of no more than ordinary feelings.[66] The sublime—in crime as in art—depends essentially on self-control, on tranquillity and coldness in the face of death, on self-assertion in the face of hopeless odds.

But, although Diderot seems to think that the criminal is, on the whole, more likely to exhibit sublime qualities than is the virtuous man, it is important to stress that these qualities are sublime, not because they are evil, but because they embody a form of human energy. He tells Sophie Volland, for example, that strong passions are what he most admires in man; if they motivate the criminal to commit a horrible action, they also motivate the artist who paints the criminal in his true colours. The essential thing is to feel strongly, to do evil rather than to do nothing, since the mediocre man lives and dies like a brute.[67] In an aside to Grimm

---

[62] *Correspondance*, Vol. III, p. 311.

[63] Ibid., pp. 141-2.

[64] *Salon de 1761*, p. 115.

[65] Ibid., p. 116.

[66] Ibid., p. 115: 'Il faut d'abord qu'elle soit belle, mais de cette sorte de beauté qui s'allie avec la cruauté, avec la tranquillité et la joie féroce. Ne voyez-vous pas que ce mouvement d'horreur l'excuse, qu'il est faux, et qu'il rend votre composition froide et commune?'

[67] *Correspondance*, Vol. IV, p. 81: '. . . j'ai de tout tems été l'apologiste des passions fortes. Elles seules m'émeuvent. Qu'elles m'inspirent de l'admiration ou de l'effroi, je sens fortement. Les arts de génie naissent et s'éteignent avec elles. Ce sont elles qui font le scélérat et l'enthousiaste qui le peint de ses vraies couleurs. Si les actions atroces qui déshonorent notre nature sont commises par elles, c'est par elles aussi qu'on est porté aux tentatives merveilleuses qui la relèvent. L'homme médiocre vit et meurt comme la brute'. See also the opening lines of the *Pensées philosophiques* (1746): 'Cependant il n'y a que les passions, et les grandes passions, qui puissent élever l'âme aux grandes choses. Sans elles, plus de sublime, soit dans les moeurs, soit dans les ouvrages; les beaux-arts retournent en enfance, et la vertu devient minutieuse', in *Oeuvres philosophiques*, pp. 9-10.

in the *Salon* of 1765, Diderot again defends sublime evil because it constitutes a guarantee that human energy has not yet exhausted itself:

> Je ne hais pas les grands crimes: premièrement, parce qu'on en fait de beaux tableaux et de belles tragédies; et puis, c'est que les grandes et sublimes actions et les grands crimes portent le même caractère d'énergie. Si un homme n'était pas capable d'incendier une ville, un autre homme ne serait pas capable de se précipiter dans un gouffre pour la sauver. Si l'âme de César n'eût pas été possible, celle de Caton ne l'aurait pas été davantage. . . .[68]

Energy might not be 'Eternal delight' for Diderot, but it is at least a positive quality to point out to those cynics who see the man-machine totally dominated by the forces which produce him, and totally unable to rise above his situation. Perhaps we do not transcend our condition, but the undeniable existence of sublime energy does allow us to extend it. If society establishes a new 'level' above the amoral and determined world of nature, the sublime individual, artist or criminal, stands above both, affirming his value in the face of an indifferent nature, a mediocre society.[69]

I have been obliged, throughout this paper, to yoke together many ideas which occur quite independently of each other in Diderot's encyclopædic work; obviously, the word 'sublime' occurs in such a variety of contexts that to reduce it to a single meaning would be not only an impertinence, but a falsification of the wide range of implications which Diderot puts into a word best left undefined. I think, nevertheless, that we can offer a common attribute which manages to link most of the uses of the word. That attribute is the idea of suspension. In the sublime response to art, the imagination is carried beyond the normal operations of the understanding and the memory, which are suspended in favour of the freedom of the subjective reaction. The accessory ideas which flood into the mind as a result of this subjective freedom have the further effect of suspending the spectator in time and space, giving him a profound sense of his own littleness without exposing him to complete despair: 'L'univers me comprend et m'engloutit comme un point; par la pensée, je le comprends'.[70] Pascal's assertion about thought could equally be applied to Diderot's attitude to sublime art, and for Diderot, as for Pascal, there is something heroic in being able to look into the abyss without falling. The sublime artist

---

[68] *Salon de 1765*, p. 342.

[69] For an interesting account of the 'levels' of nature which it is possible to discern in Diderot's thought, see Robert Mauzi's *Idée du Bonheur*, Paris, 1967, p. 254.

[70] *Pensées*, L. Brunschvicg (ed.), Paris, 1950, p. 126.

is suspended between nature and his sketch, looking alternately on one and the other, able to contemplate both without succumbing to normal feelings, able to suspend the operations of the diaphragm in order to create great art. And the sublime criminal provokes in us an uncomfortable suspension of our moral values, obliging us to confess our admiration and to discover an energy which overflows the bounds put down by society. The sublime continually escapes the normal categories by which we comprehend our experience, and indeed there is no framework within which we are able to contain the experience of sublimity. Perhaps that is why Diderot never offered us a definition of the concept (it was the Chevalier de Jaucourt who wrote the very derivative and dull article *Sublime* in the *Encyclopédie*). Diderot does, however, give us a model which, for all its tongue-in-cheek jocularity, does stress this essential notion of suspension.

In a letter to Sophie Volland, we find Diderot examining the sublime more closely than he ever does in his formal works:

> Les grands effets naissent partout des idées voluptueuses entrelacées avec les idées terribles; par exemple de belles femmes à demi-nues qui nous présentent un breuvage délicieux dans les crânes sanglants de nos ennemis. Voilà le modèle de toutes les choses sublimes. C'est alors que l'âme s'ouvre au plaisir et frissonne d'horreur. Ces sensations mêlées la tiennent dans une situation tout à fait étrange; c'est le propre du sublime de nous pénétrer d'une manière tout à fait extraordinaire.[71]

One can imagine what some contemporary anthropologists might make of these half-naked women serving drinks in the bleeding skulls of their lovers' enemies: Diderot's model of the sublime would not look out of place among the sex-death archetypes that adorn Georges Bataille's *Erotisme*, and, after all, Diderot is a near contemporary of Sade.[72] Indeed, this model of sublimity does present precisely that kind of suspension between attraction and repulsion which Bataille defines, in the work of Sade and elsewhere, as the essence of the erotic. The women are beautiful, but cruel; the drink is delicious, but the container is rather nasty; the soul opens with pleasure, only to shiver with horror. But it must

[71] *Correspondance*, Vol. IV, p. 196.
[72] See, for example, the opening paragraphs of the *120 Journées de Sodome*: '. . . la nature . . . malgré son désordre est souvent bien sublime, même quand elle déprave le plus. Car, osons le dire en passant, si le crime n'a pas ce genre de délicatesse qu'on trouve dans la vertu, n'est-il pas toujours plus sublime, n'a-t-il pas sans cesse un caractère de sublimité qui l'emportera toujours sur les traits monotones et efféminés de la vertu?' in *Oeuvres complètes*, G. Lely (ed.), Paris, 1966, Vol. XIII, p. 7.

be pointed out that where Bataille and others would see the sublime experience, especially in the religious domain, as a model for the erotic, Diderot sees the erotic as merely another model for the sublime. The world of art and the aesthetic response, the world of men's deeds in good and evil, constitute other examples of sublimity, and although Diderot admits the existence of *un peu de testicule* at the basis of our sublime ideas, he nevertheless maintains that the sublime experience establishes something on behalf of humanity, the very humanity which Sade's sublime individual would prefer to reduce to the status of victim. Diderot's sublime artist, like his sublime criminal, acts alone, stands apart from convention, apart from mediocrity, but his act is seen to be relevant and exemplary by those who admire and who feel, at the same time, the littleness and greatness of man. Diderot's most original contribution to the history of the sublime was to proclaim the relative and terrestrial nature of sublimity, without abdicating his faith in human possibility, and without turning his back on the material universe in terms of which this possibility must be defined.

Fuseli's Translations of Winckelmann: A Phase in the Rise of British Hellenism with an aside on William Blake

Marcia Allentuck

In the private collection of Sir Geoffrey Keynes, there exists one of the few remaining volumes from William Blake's personal library, with his signature boldly inscribed. Blake acquired it while he was still apprenticed to James Basire, and thus it may be said to have communicated its messages to him while he was still a young man, open to new currents of ideas and insights. Despite the importance of this book in Blake's artistic and critical development, it has never been discussed in detail in this connection and, indeed, has on the whole been lamentably neglected by art critics and intellectual historians. It is not my purpose here, however, to do more than suggest its influence upon Blake. Rather, I wish to provide the backgrounds for the publication of the eighteenth-century volume, to demonstrate Fuseli's decisive roles in connection with it, and finally to adumbrate its effects upon both Fuseli and Blake as artists and critics. Exigencies of space and time permit me to do no more on this occasion.

The full title of the book is: *Reflections on the Painting and Sculpture of the Greeks: With Instructions for the Connoisseur, and An Essay on Grace in Works of Art. Translated from the German Original of the Abbe Winkelmann, Librarian of the Vatican, F.R.S. &c. &c. By Henry Fusseli, A.M.* The first edition, published in 1765 under the imprint of Andrew Millar, was the one which Blake owned. He obviously acquired it before he had actually met Henry Fuseli, with whom he was to form a mutually

---

I am now completing a book with the same title as this paper, in which this volume of Blake's figures largely.

enriching friendship, and who became for Blake 'the only Man that e'er I knew/Who did not make me almost spew'. This grotesquely affectionate epigram characterised the nature of the relationship between these two eccentric originals, and we may be certain that in their meetings and conversations Fuseli's early translation of one of the first books (if not *the* first) actually to find its way into Blake's library, was an important subject for subsequent analysis and, in their maturity, for partial repudiation. We must turn, then, to the beginnings of Fuseli's enterprise as translator and disseminator, and later repudiator of Winckelmann, and then trace some consequences of this involvement for both Fuseli and Blake.

I

We know of only two things that Henry Fuseli took with him when he departed from his birthplace, Zürich, in 1763, eventually to reach London in 1764: an engraving after a painting by Raphael, and a package containing all of the letters which Johann Joachim Winckelmann had written to Fuseli's father, Johann Caspar Füssli, himself an artist and an art-historian, from the inception of their correspondence in 1758 until the time of Fuseli's leave-taking. These letters Henry Fuseli treasured for several years, and he was distraught, as his letters showed, when, together with many of his drawings and manuscripts, they were destroyed in a spectacular fire in his London lodgings in 1770. Only a few of these letters had been copied in Zürich before Fuseli took them; hence, when Leonard Usteri published a collection of Winckelmann's letters to his Swiss friends in 1778, Johann Caspar felt it incumbent upon himself to publish another work, a small, now exceedingly rare pamphlet, to account for the gap in the published correspondence and to give some idea of what had been lost. Fuseli's father wrote of Winckelmann:

> Sein Herz giesst in seinen Briefen . . . seine Freuden, seine Wünsche, seine Empfindungen in den Busen seiner Trautesten aus, als sein blosser Verstand, seine Ideen, seine reiche Einbildungskraft, ihre Schäze—Nirgends aber verdunkelt weder sein Herz seinen Verstand, noch sein Verstand sein Herz.
> (In his letters he pours out his heart . . . his joys, his hopes, his emotions—to the responsive hearts of those he trusts most —he offers them his unadorned understanding, his ideas, his rich imagination as treasures—Nowhere, however, do his emotions obscure his understanding, nor his understanding his emotions.)[1]

[1] Usteri's edition of Winckelmann's letters to Swiss intellectuals, *Winckelmanns Briefe an seine Freunde in der Schweiz* (Zürich, 1778) was almost im-

And of the fate of the letters Johann Caspar spoke specifically:

> Die Briefe von Herrn Winckelmann vom Julius 1758, bis 1764, schwollen zu einem grossen Paquete zusammen.—Meistens war ihr Genenstand die Kunst und seine eigenen Werke.—Ich konnte meinem Sohn, bey seiner Abreise nach England, seine Bitte nicht versagen, diese Briefe, als sein schäzbarstes Reisegeräthe, mit sich zu nehmen.—Viele Dienste haben sie ihm bey Uebersetzung der Winckelmannischen Schriften geleistet.
> (The letters from Winckelmann, dating from July 1758, until [the beginning of] 1764, had swollen into a large bundle.—They dealt mostly with art theory and with his own work.—When my son left for England, I could not refuse him his request: to take these letters with him as his most treasured parting gift.—They were of inestimable value to him during his work upon the translations of Winckelmann's writings.)[2]

Fuseli, who was born in 1741, spent the most formative period of his adolescence, the years between seventeen and nineteen, under the spell of his father's frequent and stimulating correspondence with Winckelmann. Johann Caspar had been approached in 1758 on Winckelmann's behalf by the engraver Wille, then in Paris, to try to raise sufficient funds in Zürich to enable Winckelmann, who appeared to be in financial straits in Italy, to undertake an important journey to Naples. There he hoped to extend his studies of classical antiquity and to include the results of his work in his history of art among the ancients. Johann Caspar did not know Winckelmann, nor was he ever to meet him. But so impressed had he and other members of the Swiss intelligentsia been by Winckelmann's *Gedanken über die Nachahmung der griechischen werke in der Malerei und Bildhauerkunst* (1755) that, at considerable inconvenience to themselves, they managed to raise the required sum. Winckelmann meanwhile had already received the money from other sources; the Swiss collection reached him when he was already in Naples. But Winckelmann did not return the funds; he would not, as he told Wille, 'der Grossmuth Ihrer Seelen nicht zu nahe tretten' (impinge upon the magnanimity of your souls).[3] And while Winckelmann elevated sponging into what can only be called an art, he appeared sincere in this instance, for he had no notion of Johann Caspar's statement to Wille that he had put himself upon the rack to obtain the funds. To Johann Caspar, Winckelmann

---

mediately followed by Johann Caspar Füssli's work: *Geschichte von Winckelmanns Briefen an seine Freunde in der Schweiz* (Zürich, 1778). The quotation in the text occurred on p. 4.

[2] Füssli, *Geschichte*, p. 13.

[3] Winckelmann, *Briefe*, Berlin, 1952-7, I, 348. For the remainder of this essay this collection of letters from and to Winckelmann will be referred to as WB.

dispatched a glowing letter of gratitude, one which was to set the tone for their correspondence for the rest of Winckelmann's life. In it, Winckelmann called Johann Caspar 'Freund, mit einer grossen Tugendhaften Seele begabt' (Friend, endowed with a great and virtuous soul), and assured him that 'die Welt wird mir ein Paradies und das Laben eine Wollust durch Kenntniss von Menschen ersterer Grösse, wie mein Fuessli ist' (the world had become a paradise for me, and life a pleasure, since I have come to know men of the greatest worth, like my Füssli).[4]

The letters that survive from Winckelmann to Johann Caspar substantiate the claims about their contents which Fuseli's father made in 1778. Winckelmann told Johann Caspar something that the Swiss, out of modesty, did not reveal in the 1778 edition: the German avowed that he had taken special pains to be specific in all of his discussions of art and antiquities, because he recognised that Johann Caspar was both an artist and an estimable critic of the arts.[5] When Winckelmann's monumental history of ancient art began to appear in 1764, Johann Caspar, who had been thanked in its preface, had already received a presentation copy from Winckelmann, who insisted: 'Ich erwarte nunmehro Ihr Urtheil über meine Geschichte' (I am eagerly awaiting your evaluation of my history).[6] And Winckelmann informed his friends that he wished Johann Caspar to supervise the printing of the second edition of his work, a project which Winckelmann's pathetic death in 1768 cut off. Moreover, when Johann Caspar's nephew, Hans Heinrich Füssli, came to Rome in the early 1760s, Winckelmann was delighted to serve as his cicerone, in addition, it appeared, to being his erotic admirer as well.

While a few of Winckelmann's letters to Füssli were copied and survived, there are no records now of any communications from Johann Caspar to him. Nevertheless, we can assume that when young Fuseli got into difficulties in Zurich over his politically Rousseauistic leanings, Johann Caspar described the entire matter to Winckelmann. For in April of 1763, Winckelmann obviously responded to Johann Caspar's request that he intercede for his son who would soon be arriving in England. Johann Caspar had perhaps known of Winckelmann's somewhat sycophantic friendships with Englishmen on the Grand Tour, and with Lady Mary Wortley Montagu's son. Yet Winckelmann had to inform Füssli that he was not as well known in England as the Swiss believed:

4 Ibid., p. 349.
5 Ibid., pp. 398-400 *passim.*
6 Ibid., II, p. 343.

Sie versprechen sich zu viel, Mein Freund, von mir in Engeland, für Ihren Herrn Sohn: ich bin wenigen bekannt, und vermeide diese inhospitale Nation, wo ich kann. Ich werde aber allezeit ein grosses Vergnügen haben, wenn der Sohn meines würdigsten Freundes sich mit mir unterhalten will. Vielleicht findet er in Engeland einen Freund von uns beyden, welcher ihm statt aller seyn würde. Es ist sehr glaublich dass Herr Mengs nach Engeland gehen wird, wohin ihm vier von der reichsten Herren rufen.

(You anticipate too much, my friend, from my [influence] in England for the benefit of your son: actually, I am little known there, and I avoid that inhospitable nation as much as I can. However, it would always be a pleasure if the son of my worthiest friend would stay with me awhile. And perhaps in England he will find our mutual friend, who will help him along. For it is very probable that Mengs will go to England, where four of the richest men in the country have called him [to execute commissions].)[7]

Fuseli was to make Winckelmann known in England; he would reach Rome two years after Winckelmann's death; and the painter Anton Mengs went from Spain to Rome, not England. But Winckelmann's interest was unquestionably sincere, for in August of the same year, he complained: 'Von Ihren Herrn Sohne habe ich keine Nachricht. Ich wünschte dass er nach der weiten Reise das Glück habe, Rom zu sehen, und ich ihn, um ihm den Freund seines würdigen Vaters zu zeigen' (I have had no news of your son. I wish that during his far-flung travels he may have the good luck to see Rome, and that I may be fortunate enough to see him, and to greet him as the friend of his worthy father.)[8]

II

Fuseli was more than an interested spectator of his father's relationship with Winckelmann. The fact that he took the letters speaks for itself, but whether he meant then to use them as guides for the translation of Winckelmann's works, or merely as touchstones of what had been extremely moving and valuable to him as an adolescent cannot be determined. It is certain, however, that during his stay in Germany with the aesthetician Sulzer in 1763 the works of Winckelmann were discussed, not only for themselves, but for the aid they were giving Sulzer in his composition of the lexicon on the fine arts which was later to bring him enormous honours. And most interesting of all: Sulzer himself had translated

[7] Ibid., p. 309.
[8] Ibid., p. 332.

Winckelmann's *Gedanken* into French almost immediately after its appearance in 1755.

In Leipzig, before he joined Sulzer, Fuseli had met the painter Adam Oeser, who, in the early 1750s, had given Winckelmann every encouragement, even house space, while he was composing this work in Dresden. It may be assumed with a reasonable degree of certainty that Fuseli pumped Oeser about Winckelmann; Fuseli had just burst out of the cocoon of his father's house, and he wanted to know everything about everyone. In Leipzig, Fuseli had also met Nicolai, who, in his periodical *Bibliothek der schönen Wissenschaften*, had earlier published some of Winckelmann's shorter pieces on aesthetics which Fuseli would incorporate into his edition and translation of the *Gedanken*. He too may have been a willing feeder of Fuseli's boundless curiosity. Moreover, Winckelmann's great *Geschichte* was about to appear in print, and the German art historian had written detailed descriptions of his progress to most of the intellectual circles in the German-speaking states. What would be more natural, then, for Winckelmann's name to be on everyone's lips? Indeed, Fuseli's letters of this period and of the time of his London year of admirable adjustment (1764-5) revealed his vibrant interest in both the man and his work—for he ranked Winckelmann with Klopstock and Rousseau, his current divinities upon his arrival in London.

By 1765, then, when Fuseli's first translation from Winckelmann appeared, he had already been exposed to the influence of Winckelmann on the continent, and he had himself participated in an intense movement of adulation of him. It is more than likely that it was Fuseli, and not his publishers, who took the initiative in suggesting a series of translations from Winckelmann. It is quite likely too that Fuseli was seeing himself in the role for which his teacher, the Swiss aesthetician J. J. Bodmer, had prepared him: as a middle-man between cultures, importing and exporting the best ideas for the edification of all. But no matter how strong Fuseli's zeal was, the shrewd London publishers would not have encouraged him if they themselves were not convinced that Winckelmann's writings would appeal to the literate British public.

And they had every reason for such a conviction. By 1765, the so-called 'Grecian Gusto' was becoming the touchstone of taste, and the faint strains of romantic hellenism were beginning to be heard in the land. While Greek studies in the British universities were moribund during the first half of the eighteenth century, Greek antiquities were commanding the interest and the funds of the wealthy at an increasingly significant rate. The Arundel marbles, collected in the previous century, were again a focus of enthusiasm when the Earl of Pembroke bought many of them to form the nucleus of the Wilton collection, to which he added scores of antique sculptures which had originally belonged to Cardinal Mazarin. In 1734 the Society of Dilettanti consolidated its resources to become an arbiter of taste, supporting the surveying trip to Greece of two young artists, Stuart and Revett, whose imaginations had been fired by the new excavations at Herculaneum in 1738. The result of their expedition, the great first folio of *Antiquities of Athens* (1762), was garnished with a magnificent list of subscribers, among whom were Reynolds, Sterne, Walpole, and Garrick. Robert Wood's *Ruins of Palmyra* (1753) and *Ruins of Balbec* (1757) fed the flames of the connoisseurs' desires; Joseph Nollekens was in Rome working with the astute dealer Thomas Jenkins to restore antiques for the lucrative British market; and Robert Adam's brother James pulled a coup for George III when, in 1762, he acquired from Winckelmann's patron, Cardinal Albani, the superb collection of Dal Pozzo drawings of classical antiquities.[9] By 1752, thirteen years before the Winckelmann translations, some Englishmen had had enough of the collecting of the remains of classical art as a status symbol. In his play *Taste*, the dramatist Samuel Foote was determined to

> shew the absurdity of placing an inestimable value on . . . a parcel of maimed busts, erazed [sic] pictures, and inexplicable coins, only because they have the mere name and appearance of antiquity, while the more perfect and really valuable performances of the most capital artists of our own age and country . . . are totally despised and neglected, and the artists themselves suffered to pass through life unnoticed and discouraged. . . . I was determined to brand those Goths in Science, who had prostituted the useful Study of Antiquity to trifling superficial Purposes.[10]

But these protests, like those of Hogarth against the 'brown masters', had virtually no effect. The rise of neo-hellenism was part of the shift in sensibility that began increasingly to take hold after the first half of the century, and no single group of dissidents could block it. Byron's 'Greece, sad relic', was, however, for the connoisseurs of the eighteenth century, still non-existent; the Greece with which they were concerned was the source of newly acquired adornments of their estates and collections. The 'Ubi sunt' theme was yet to be heard.

[9] Cornelius C. Vermeule, III, 'The Dal Pozzo-Albani Drawings of Classical Antiquities in the British Museum', *Transactions of the American Philosophical Society*, Vol. L, May 1960, pp. 1-78. The drawings from the Dal Pozzo Collection that are not now in the British Museum (an important group is) are in the Royal Library at Windsor.
[10] Samuel Foote, *Taste*, in *Works*, London, 1809, I, 15.

III

Both Fuseli and his publishers, then, were actuated by substantial reasons for undertaking the Winckelmann translations. It is curious, however, that these translations, despite their considerable influence upon the development of British aesthetic theory, should thus far have commanded scant modern reference. Even the opportuneness of their appearance, let alone their contents, was not remarked in Stockley's ostensibly thorough discussion of translations from the German between 1750 and 1830; 'it is hoped that nothing of importance has been overlooked', stated Stockley, after having claimed that his was the 'complete survey'.[11] And on the rare occasions when Fuseli's work is referred to, it is confused with a pirated Glasgow edition of 1766, which was hardly based upon his renderings.[12] Actually, however, one could do worse than venture the conclusion that if Fuseli's literary career had been limited only to his Winckelmann translations, he would still merit study as a mediator of values, the major disseminator in Great Britain of the doctrines of Winckelmann.

But not the first. The news that Fuseli was working on some Winckelmann texts must have got round the small, cut-throat London publishing world, for he was 'scooped' by two weeks. In mid-December 1764, the *London Chronicle* ran a series of letters containing a very loose and often incorrect translation of Winckelmann's *Gedanken,* which ended in February 1765, one month after Fuseli's first translation from Winckelmann appeared in the *Universal Museum.* The *Chronicle* translation, still anonymous, with the same errors, was then reprinted by the *Scots Magazine,* and formed the basis for the 1766 Glasgow edition mentioned in the preceding paragraph, an edition which confined itself solely to the *Gedanken.* There is a strong possibility that the *Chronicle* series was based on Sulzer's free French translation, for I have found similar errors in both. Further, it is a revealing commentary upon the lack of the knowledge of German in the British Isles that the *Chronicle* series was not based upon the original texts by Winckelmann, as was Fuseli's work, but upon a French translation in which Sulzer did not shine. Readers in Scotland had been prepared by the 'analytical extracts' which they had found in the *Scots Magazine*[13] for the Glasgow edition.[14] The unnamed trans-

---

11 V. Stockley, *German Literature as Known in England, 1750-1830,* London, 1929, p. xii.

12 An instance of this confusion may be found in John Fleming's work, *Robert Adam and His Circle,* London, 1962, p. 355.

13 Vol. XXVII, 1765, especially pp. 505-10, 270-2, and 690-4.

14 *Reflections Concerning the Imitation of the Grecian Artists in Painting and Sculpture in a Series of Letters. By the Abbé Winkelman,* Glasgow, 1766.

lator claimed to have known Wincklemann in Rome, but his deplorable performance demonstrated him to be either of limited linguistic capacities, or non-existent, merely a figment to serve as the publishers' come-on. This translation vanished into oblivion after it was published; and future references in Fuseli's lifetime and afterwards to the specific works by Winckelmann which he translated were to his English versions of them.

IV

Fuseli's first translation from Winckelmann (and the first work in English to bear his name, although it was given as 'Henry Tussle') appeared in the first issue of the first volume of the *Universal Museum*, in January 1765. The periodical had just been started by Thomas Payne, a friend of Johnson's and one of the group which was encouraging Fuseli's literary ambitions after he arrived in London. Fuseli's contribution, 'A Description of a Marble Trunk of Hercules, commonly called the Torso of Belvedere. Translated from the German of John Winckelmann, Librarian of the Vatican', occupied only a small space (pp. 16-18) in the periodical, but it pregnantly prefigured most of Fuseli's later techniques of translation.

Space does not permit a systematic comparison of the original German texts and the English versions which Fuseli diffused[15] yet some broad aspects of his treatment must be at least adumbrated. Behind his handling of texts for translation there stood two convictions: that a translation could have creative validity in its own right; and that every original text is itself a translation of intuitions and concepts into palpable form. He would not have subscribed to the frequent and facile comparison of translations to women who, if they are beautiful are not faithful, or if faithful, not beautiful; this comparison would for him have diminished the complex function of the translator as mediator between the source and the receptor languages, between the texts' indicative and allusive values. Fuseli could not have escaped some formation of attitudes regarding the art of translation during his formative years as an undergraduate in Zürich, for both his professor J. J. Bodmer and J. J. Breitinger were actively engaged in translations which were calculated to enrich German literature. Fuseli's own youthful attempts to render *Macbeth* into German were pursued under their watchful eyes. Breitinger especially had made clear what was required of the translator:

15 In my book on Fuseli, Blake, and Winckelmann this aspect is treated in great detail.

Von einem Uebersetzer wird erfordert, dass er eben diesselben
Begriffe und Gedanken, die er in einem trefflichen Muster
vor sich findet in eben solche Ordnung, Verbindung, Zusam-
menhänge, und mit gleich so starken Nachdrucke . . . so dass
die Vorstellung der Gedancken unter beyderley Zeichen einen
gleichen Hindruck auf das Gemüte des Lesers, mache.
(It is required of a translator that he convey the same concepts
and thoughts that he finds so admirably presented with similar
order, relation, and integration, and with the same strength
and effect, so that the representation of thoughts in either
tongue can have a similar effect upon the responsiveness of
the reader.)[16]

Both Bodmer and Breitinger transferred to Fuseli not merely the
notion of fidelity to the original, but also that of the paradox of
the translator, who must be both subservient and original at the
same time—for 'starken Nachdrucke' could not be achieved without
originality. The disciplined sympathy they advocated, the balance
between the translator's own power and that of the text to which
he must remain, more or less, faithful, the awareness, at all times,
of the invisible audience that needed to be persuaded—all of these
considerations took root in Fuseli's evolving conceptions of the
role of the translator. And for the remainder of his life, Fuseli,
whether he knew it or not, abided by Sir Thomas Browne's idea
of deuteroscopy—the second intention of words. Any apparently
gratuitous additions which Fuseli made to his originals were intended to enhance the suggestiveness of the text: ultimately they
were not blatant distortions but purifying ministrations. In later
life Fuseli would always be critical of translations that lacked
clarity, force, effect, that did not make 'bolder use of the strong,
natural language of passion'[17] that refused to study 'well the
genius of both idioms, in order to transfer the true meaning of one
language into another . . . with justness, perspicuity and energy'.[18]
Fuseli's own method of translation turned out to be neither ser-
vilely metaphrastic, nor boldly imitative, but accommodatingly
paraphrastic—as John Dryden had defined it in the previous
century. It was 'translation with latitude, where the author is kept
in view . . . but his words are not so strictly followed as his sense;
and that too is admitted to be amplified, but not altered'.[19]
Fuseli's translations were neither pale copies of their originals
nor wild variations upon them, but inventive, yet faithful renderings of their substance. In the case of Winckelmann, he plasticised

---

16 J. J. Breitinger, *Critische Dichtkunst*, Zurich, 1770, Vol. II, pp. 18-19.
17 *Analytical Review*, Vol. XXI, March 1795, p. 288.
18 Ibid., Vol. III, March 1789, p. 286.
19 *Essays of John Dryden*, W. P. Ker (ed.), 2 vols., Oxford, 1900, Vol. I, p. 237.

the German's somewhat static, abstract style where it was especially
clogging, making it more *malerisch*, painterly. Yet he maintained
as many of Winckelmann's syntactical relationships as were consistent with the loose Senecan style of much of English prose in
the 1760s.

In the case of Fuseli's first translation from Winckelmann, the
rendering of the *Beschreibung des Torso im Belvedere zu Rom*,[20]
much of what he was striving for and brought off in the larger
series of Winckelmann translations done a few months later was
apparent. In this essay much of Winckelmann's style was
rhapsodic; Fuseli curbed it where he appeared to have felt that it
would distract the reader from the material described, and he enhanced it when he felt that the reader needed an extra prod to
perceive the merits of the torso. The piece by Fuseli, which was
quite popular, for it was immediately reprinted, with only minor
changes, by the receptive *Annual Register* a few months later,[21]
merits brief examination.

The English style had overtones of Milton; where Winckelmann
wrote: 'Wie prächtig ist die anhebende Rundung ihres Gewölbes',
Fuseli translated: 'How magnificent is its vaulted orb.' And where
Winckelmann was excessively adjectival—'Die Wirkung und Gegen-
wirkung ihrer Muskeln ist mit einem weislichen Maasse von abwech-
selnder Regung und schneller Kraft wunderwürdig abgewogen'—
Fuseli was lucid and precise: 'The elasticity of the muscles is admirably balanced between rest and motion.' Finally, even when Fuseli
was as literal as he could be in English, he still telescoped and
sharpened Winckelmann's meanings; Winckelmann's injunction,
embodied in the sentence: 'Scheint es unbegreiflich, ausser dem
Haupt in einem andern Theile des Körpers eine denkende Kraft
zu zeigen, so lernt hier, wie die Hand eines schöpferischen
Meisters die Materie geistig zu machen vermögend ist', was conveyed by Fuseli in this accurate but heightened form: 'If you think
it inconceivable how any part of the body but the head can be
endowed with the power of thought, then learn here how the
creative hand of the artist could animate matter'.

V

This piece was followed rapidly in the next few months by several
other translations from Winckelmann's works, all of which appeared
in the *Annual Register*. That Fuseli was responsible for them is

[20] All references to Winckelmann's works, with the exclusion of his letters,
will be to the edition published as *Werke*, 2 vols., Stuttgart, 1847, and will
hereafter be cited as WW. The piece under discussion appeared in Vol. II, pp.
67-9.
[21] Vol. VIII, pp. 180-2.

virtually indubitable, for they revealed, in their style and ordonnance, the techniques by which he governed himself. They dealt with materials that Winckelmann had published on Herculaneum, and on the influence of climate upon the growth of the arts. They had appeared originally in the previous year in his long *Geschichte*. Included in the second article was Winckelmann's criticism of Milton's images—they may have been sublime, but they had 'no archetype in nature', an observation which may have been one of the seeds of the subsequent British hatred of Winckelmann, although not of his adulation of the Greeks.[22] The only other periodical translation from Winckelmann that Fuseli appeared to have completed was an unsigned piece in the *Universal Museum* in 1768: 'Description of the Apollo in Belvedere and the Borghese Gladiator. From the Idea of Abbé Winkelmann'.[23] Fuseli seemed to have tuned this last translation not only to Winckelmann's text itself, but also to his knowledge of what Winckelmann, in the late 1750s, was writing to his other friends (and probably to Johann Caspar Füssli as well) about his reactions to the statue:

> Die Beschreibung des Apollo erfordert den höchsten Stil, eine Erhebung über alles was menschlich ist. Es ist unbeschreiblich, was der Anblick desselben für eine Wirkung macht.
> (The description of the statue of Apollo demands the highest style, a transcending of everything mortal. It is indescribable in its effect upon those who even give it a mere glance.)[24]

That Fuseli was responsible for a work which appeared in England in 1771, the year after he had left for Italy, and which dealt with aspects of Herculaneum is uncertain.[25]

There is, however, not the slightest twinge of uncertainty about Fuseli's most important group of Winckelmann translations, which appeared in April 1765, under the imprint of Andrew Millar: *Reflections on the Painting and Sculpture of the Greeks: with Instructions for the Connoisseur, and An Essay on Grace in Works of Art. Translated from the German Original of the Abbé Winkelmann, Librarian of the Vatican, F. R. S. &c. &c. By Henry Fusseli, A. M.* It was eminently fitting that Millar should undertake the venture, for, more than twenty years before the Fuseli work, he had published two now exceedingly rare works by George Turnbull which made a palpable contribution to the stirring of interest in

[22] Ibid., pp. 182-9 and 250-3.
[23] Vol. IV, February 1768, p. 56.
[24] WB, I, p. 212.
[25] *Critical Account of the Situation and Destruction by the First Eruption of Mt. Vesuvius, of Herculaneum, Pompeii, and Stabie. From the Celebrated Abbe Winckelmann, Antiquarian to the Pope. Who Was Unfortunately Murdered at Trieste*, London, 1771.

neo-hellenism.[26] And throughout the preparation and sale of this edition (a second followed in 1767), Millar acquitted himself commendably. To Sulzer Fuseli wrote on 17 April 1765—the work was officially published on 25 April—describing Millar's liberal profit arrangements, and concluding: 'Er verdienet ein monument' (He deserves a monument in his honour). Fuseli sent a prepublication copy to Sulzer and explained, somewhat ruefully, 'Hr Murdoch hat mich dediciren gemachet' (Murdoch made me write the dedication).[27]

Murdoch's advice was excellent, however much Fuseli detested any notion of the courting of a patron. The dedicatee of the work, Lord Scarsdale, had been an influential sponsor of Robert Adam, whose classically correct drawings were the basis for the remodelling of Kedleston, Scarsdale's estate. Moreover, Scarsdale had met Winckelmann in Rome, although what he had thought of him is not recorded. There is no indication that Scarsdale did anything for Fuseli as a result of this dedication, however. But if he stimulated the sale of the work among his friends, that would have been enough for the young Fuseli at this time. Perhaps the second edition came about through this kind of indirect intercession.[28]

The first edition, which appeared in the same year as Samuel Johnson's *Preface to Shakespeare* and Bishop Percy's *Reliques*, offered, within its own sphere, as much to the cultivated reader as these two other works of indigenous writers. For Fuseli far outstripped his publisher's hopes by giving translations not only of the *Gedanken*, but also of several shorter, yet highly charged works by Winckelmann: *Sendschreiben über die Gedanken* (1756); *Erläuterung der Gedanken* (1756); *Nachricht von einer Mumie in dem Antiken-Kabinet in Dresden* (1756); *Errinerung über die Betrachtung der Werke der Kunst* (1759); and *Von der Gratie in Werken der Kunst* (1759). Fuseli's anthology constituted a superb series of choices, for it contained Winckelmann's most seminal shorter writings; there was only an expansion of their contents in the *Geschichte*, not an alteration. Moreover, whatever Fuseli translated, he translated fully; no sections were omitted. He prided himself, in his letter to Sulzer, for rescuing for the English reader works that had been 'begraben', buried in Nicolai's *Bibliothek*. Clearly he had a sense of mission about the whole enterprise.

[26] George Turnbull, *A Treatise on Ancient Painting*, London, 1740; and *A Curious Collection of Ancient Paintings*, London, 1741.

[27] Arnold Federmann, *Johann Heinrich Füssli: Dichte und Mahler*, Zürich und Leipzig, 1927, p. 112.

[28] The second edition, published by both Millar and Cadell, described itself as 'Corrected' on the title page, but a comparison with the first edition shows that the type was not reset for the new edition, and consequently the same errors in spelling remained.

Fuseli's *Reflections* were reviewed, on the whole favourably, by the two most influential magazines of the day: the *Critical* and the *Monthly*. The latter periodical gave it much space, and quoted several passages at length. It objected to the expletives in the text (which were mostly Fuseli's), but it commended the first part of the book, the actual translation of the *Gedanken*, for being 'written with all that closeness and conciseness of expression, which is usual to men perfectly versed in their subject, and writing for the use of adepts'.[29] The *Critical Review* objected to Winckelmann's unqualified adulation of the Greeks, and feared that he might blind his readers to what they needed to perceive, that 'calmness and serenity is in fact insensibility and dullness'. As for Fuseli himself, he was described as 'master of his original'. The review, despite its animadversions against Winckelmann's emphasis on repose instead of energy, maintained that 'upon the whole, this book contains the best system of practical criticism upon painting and sculpture of any that has appeared in our or any other language'.[30]

Winckelmann was not made aware immediately of the favourable reception this project had received. There is, however, internal evidence from Fuseli's letters that several letters to Winckelmann had gone astray. Fuseli's impatience at what he conceived to be Winckelmann's slight of his talents and efforts to disseminate his works caused him to pen what was doubtless a most extraordinary communication. The original is now lost, but of it Winckelmann wrote to Usteri:

> Herr Fuessli aus London hat mich neulich gefraget, ob ich sein Freund seyn wolle oder nicht; weil ich ihm auf einen seiner Briefe nicht geantwortet. Ist dergleichen Gewaltthätigkeit in Bekanntschaften bey euch Gebrauck, so es ist mir zu verzeihen, wenn ich diese Frage selten finde; verfahrt man aber in England so, ist es eine neue Mode daselbst; denn ich habe Engl. Bücher von der Freundschaft gelesen, wo man nicht mit diesem Ton spricht. Dieses aber sey und bleibe unter uns.
> (Fuseli in London has asked me anew whether I intend to be his friend or not; for I have not answered one of his letters. Is it customary where you are to exercise such force in the pursuit of friendship? I have rarely come across a problem of this kind: perhaps it is the new mode in England. I have read books about friendship in English, but no one in them spoke in such a tone. However the case may be, let us keep this between ourselves.)[31]

[29] XXXII, 1765, pp. 456-68, especially 456-7.
[30] XIX, 1765, pp. 443-50, especially 448-9.
[31] WB, III, p. 290.

Plate VII   Chardin, *Les attributs de la musique*. Reproduced with the permission of La Musée de Versailles.

Winckelmann was used to more effeminate and seductive wooing than Fuseli was apparently willing, or able, to give. Nonetheless, they appeared to have been in relatively amicable communication until Winckelmann's murder; although no letters exist that can be connected with their correspondence, the letters of each of them to others indicated that this was so. Winckelmann came to admire Fuseli's translation; the *Gedanken*, especially, was 'fort bien traduit', he wrote to Count Cobenzl, and thus he was revising his *Geschichte* so that Fuseli might undertake an English translation based on a definitive text.[32] In this Fuseli exulted; it accorded with his new sense of his own capacities, as well as with his growing affection for England and his determination to convey it by serving her as best he could. Thus he begged Bodmer for another copy of Winckelmann's *Geschichte*, in a note written in September 1766, asserting that whoever sent him more Winckelmann material 'wird mir und vielleicht der engländischen Welt einen Dienst tun' (would do me, and perhaps even the entire English-speaking world, a service).[33] His plan to translate Winckelmann's *magnum opus* was not, then, motivated by a desire for financial gain—he was supporting himself adequately, although not opulently, as a tutor, an artist, and a periodical writer. Rather, it appeared to have been stimulated by his positive feelings for what England was offering him and permitting him to become. Such feelings were crystallised by him at the end of the century in a statement he made to William Roscoe of Liverpool when he presented him with a magnificent allegorical (Fuseli would have called it 'historical') painting, *The Union of England and Ireland*, for the Union Society of Liverpool: Fuseli would take no money for the work, as he wished it to serve as 'a trifling pledge of my gratitude to the country which has reared the humble talent I may possess'.[34]

VI

However, the question which poses itself with regard to the *Reflections* volume has to do with what its purchasers, and especially William Blake, actually acquired when they bought it. Did they get Winckelmann pure, or Winckelmann as comprehended by Fuseli, or only Fuseli manipulating Winckelmann? The candid answer must be that they got the essence of Winckelmann as interpreted by Fuseli, and Fuseli himself, not manipulating, but relating to Winckelmann. The translations were still paraphrastic,

[32] Ibid., p. 283.
[33] Johann Heinrich Füssli, *Briefe*, Basel, 1942, p. 140.
[34] Roscoe Papers, Liverpool Public Libraries, 1686.

Plate VIII *Judith et Holopherne*, engraved by Cornelius Galle after a lost painting by Rubens.

but with the unique Fuseliesque orientation. Fuseli was extremely sensitive to Winckelmann's emotional and conceptual nuances. He was hence able to grasp both the manifest and latent contents of Winckelmann's insights, not only what the German paraded, but what he portrayed, and often to make them more lucid and imperative.

The only way to indicate how Fuseli ordered matters is to discuss each work which he included in the volume separately, and to attempt to give a sense of what Winckelmann was saying and how Fuseli enhanced his manner of saying it. Fuseli was wise in commencing this work with the translation of the *Gedanken,* for in this short tract (the German word *Streitschrift* conveys its nature better) all of Winckelmann's later writings are prefigured.[35] It was this pamphlet that exerted the greatest influence upon his contemporaries.

Fuseli's translation of the *Gedanken* communicated its essence intact and its arguments clearly. Further, he facilitated the English reader's comprehension of Winckelmann's outstanding points by dividing the work into sections (Nature, Contour, Drapery, Expression, Workmanship in Sculpture, Painting, Allegory) which the original German text lacked. Fuseli did not force materials under these rubrics; he simply acknowledged that Wincklemann's discussion revealed them logically, and he simply named them when he felt that Winckelmann had adequately developed one topic and was ready to move on to another. The English reader, then, was presented with Winckelmann's main tenets: that the only way to become great is by the imitation of the Greeks; that among the moderns only Raphael, Michelangelo, and Poussin recognised this; that the unique excellence of Greek art stemmed from the felicitous climate of the country and the beauty of the natives' bodies, cultivated through sports and gymnastics; that the Greek civilisation was a free one, rejoicing in the controlled development of the body and the freedom of the soul; and that artists pursued and achieved ideal beauty in their works. He cautioned against the excesses of a modern like Bernini, whose contorted forms were for Winckelmann a travesty of the calm and repose with which the Greeks conveyed the highest forms of passion. Winckelmann urged not the copying of Greek art in a slavish sense, but an imitation of its principles of unity, restraint, and proportion. Finally, he called for the composition of an allegorical lexicon, depicting the best images from Greek artefacts and literature which the modern

---

[35] WB I, p. 172. To his friend Uden, Winckelmann wrote on the eve of the work's appearance: 'Von der Schrift wird mein ganzes Schicksal abhängen' (My whole destiny will depend upon the reception of this work).

artist could take over and systematise, to invest his concepts with the reality of visual embodiments understood universally.

Where Fuseli modified and expanded some of Winckelmann's specific points, he revealed both his own developing convictions and those of his contemporaries. For example, in a passage where Winckelmann contrasted sensual beauty, which gave a heightened awareness of reality, with ideal beauty, which communicated an emotion of the sublime ('Die sinnliche Schönheit gab dem Künstler die schöne Natur; die ideale Schönheit die erhabenen Züge'),[36] Fuseli introduced a crucial word: 'Sensual beauty furnished the painter with all that nature could give; ideal beauty with the awful and sublime'.[37] The key word here was 'awful', which Winckelmann had not used. But had he implied it? The answer must be in the affirmative, if we recognise that for Winckelmann awe was an emotion not of transport but of calm; used adjectivally before 'sublime' it could be read as an enforcement of his basic meaning. For Fuseli, however, who had so eagerly devoured Edmund Burke's treatise on the sublime before he came to London, and who discussed it with Sulzer during his long stay with him (Fuseli specifically mentioned Sulzer's essay on the sublime, which was still in its embryonic stage, as one of the pieces on which they worked together),[38] awe was more akin to active terror than to sedate ennoblement. The cultivated English reader would certainly have known Burke's work. Would he also have known John Baillie's *An Essay on the Sublime*, published in 1747, in which sublimity was regarded as calming the mind and infusing it with 'a solemn sedateness'?[39] The answer here must be uncertain, for Baillie's essay was relatively obscure. My point may seem to be a small one, but when it is considered in the context of Fuseli's feelings about the sublime, which he was always to link with terror, and in the framework of contemporary English understanding of the sublime, as phrased by Burke, it assumes significant proportions. What Fuseli did here, then, was not merely to clarify or reinforce Winckelmann's meaning; he actually modified it by introducing, subtly, and doubtless unconsciously, its polarity. He thus prefigured one of the reasons for his vehement rejection of Winckelmann later in life, a rejection which I shall explore at the end of this essay.

In other specimen instances, Fuseli enhanced the meaning aptly: 'höchsten Manier' became 'Grand Style'; 'schönen Contour' became 'correct Contour'; 'gebrochene' Drapery was rendered as 'un-

---

36 WW, II, pp. 8-9.
37 *Reflections*, p. 14.
38 *Briefe*, p. 92.
39 John Baillie, *An Essay on the Sublime* (1747), Samuel Holt Monk (ed.), Los Angeles, 1953, p. 10.

dulating', truly a masterstroke on Fuseli's part. A kind of poetic licence was also indulged in: Venetian draperies, which Winckelmann had characterised as 'steif und hölzern', Fuseli described as 'stiff as brass', thus evoking a sense both of their rigidity, and of the tinsel quality of the whole school of painting which, even as a young man, he held in only middling esteem. Finally, he rendered what was to become Winckelmann's most famous phrase, 'eine edle Einfalt, und eine stille Grösse', as 'a noble simplicity and [a] sedate grandeur'.[40] By using 'sedate' instead of the more literal 'calm' or 'quiet' he externalised, as Winckelmann had done in the body of his work, the entire context of the neo-classic hierarchy of genres. Flemish or Dutch still life could be quiet in its inferiority or tedious over-elaboration, but sedate was reserved for heroic or poetic painting, the highest type. Of course, for Fuseli even terror could be sedate, and thus he made a subtle fusion between the best practice of the Greeks and Winckelmann's prescriptive feelings about certain kinds of modern art on the one hand, and the concrete aspirations of his English contemporaries and himself on the other. Only one alert to current and practical developments in painting and art theory could have so packed a seemingly objective phrase with a value-judgment.

Despite his own slight packing of the text, however, Fuseli kept within the paraphrastic bounds and produced a translation which, like the original, was, to adapt the words of Nicolai when he reviewed the *Gedanken,* 'nachdrucksvoll und körnigt',[41] emphatic and pithy. And Fuseli maintained this level in his renderings of the *Sendschreiben über die Gedanken (A Letter Containing Objections Against the Foregoing Reflections),* a series of extremely amusing but piddling objections which Winckelmann published anonymously against his own work, so that he could demolish them effectively and strengthen his position, and in a work which Fuseli also translated in the same style, *An Answer to the Foregoing Letter, and a further Explication of the Subject* (Winckelmann's *Erläuterung der Gedanken*). To the last, Fuseli added helpful notes about Winckelmann's trip to Rome, and a surprisingly vitriolic footnote about Oeser's present circumstances. Winckelmann had acknowledged the stimulating aid of Oeser during the composition of the *Gedanken*; Fuseli had just met Oeser in Leipzig and had been very impressed by him. In the footnote he called him 'one of the most extensive geniuses which the present age can boast of', and stated that he 'now lives at Dresden; where, to the honour of his country, and the emolument of the art, he gets his livelihood by

40 WW, II, p. 11; *Reflections*, p. 28.
41 Nicolai, *Bibliothek*, I, 1757, p. 346.

teaching young blockheads of the Saxon-race, the elements of drawing'. This Fuseli signed with a flourish: 'N. of Transl.'[42]

The three remaining pieces in Fuseli's collection were handled equally as well as the others. Winckelmann's meticulous description of a mummy, its wrappings, and its case was admirably conveyed by Fuseli. The other two essays, *Instructions for the Connoisseur (Erinnerung über die Betrachtung der Werke der Kunst)* and *On Grace (Von der Gratie in Werken der Kunst)*, were rendered with a paraphrastic perceptiveness that contained a considerable amount of self-revelation on Fuseli's part. In the essay on connoisseurship Fuseli made numerous additions to the Winckelmann text. Some clarified it; others illuminated the direction in which Fuseli himself was moving in his own evolvements of critical theory. A few examples will suffice: what for Winckelmann had been merely 'gewöhnlichen', ordinary or real forms, became for Fuseli 'vulgar' forms; what Winckelmann had described as the changing of facial expression in art (for this he used the verb *verändern*), became for Fuseli an achievement of 'characteristic distinction'; what for Wincklemann was simply 'völlig auszuführen' became for Fuseli 'strongly fancied and masterly [*sic*] executed'; what for Winkelmann was 'der Deutlichkeit und kräftige Fassung der Gedanken' became for Fuseli 'the clearness and fluency and nervousness of . . . diction'.[43] Implicit here was Fuseli's detestation of what he called 'vulgarity' and what the romantic writers were to worship as realism. But with the word 'characteristic' a new pull entered the translation, for characteristic to Fuseli meant individual, not typical. How to reconcile the individual with the real without debasing it became for Fuseli, as for many artists of this uneasy period, a primary problem, one seldom solved without much expense of spirit. The emphasis upon fancy was Fuseli's way of assuring the reader that conception was as important as execution. Moreover, in this essay Fuseli added much documentation of Winckelmann's points from the practice of Renaissance and Baroque painters, and even from Shakespeare, but he did it with finesse and acuity, as well as with an excellent sense of timing.

The final essay, *On Grace*, was handled similarly by Fuseli. A splendid example of his technique was in the definition of grace itself, which Winckelmann had described as 'das vernünftig Gefällige. Es ist ein Begriff von weitem Umfange, weil er sich auf alle Handlungen erstreckt'. This was simultaneously condensed and amplified by Fuseli into: 'Grace is the harmony of agent and action. It is a general idea: for whatever reasonably pleases in things and

42 *Reflections*, p. 237.
43 WW, II, pp. 61-4; *Reflections*, 251-70.

actions is gracious'.[44] By introducing the word 'harmony', implicit in Winckelmann's definition, Fuseli pointed up the vital relationship between harmony and reason in neo-classical aesthetics, certain to please a cultivated audience not concerned with numbering the streaks of the tulip but with apprehending the general principle as revealed in the particular action.

In the entire anthology Fuseli consistently employed a terminology in translating which was the closest to the original sources that originally inspired Winckelmann—the writings of Shaftesbury, Addison, Jonathan Richardson, Spence, Blackwell, and Turnbull—sources with which Fuseli had been made familiar in Zürich. To abide by what must have been an unconscious decision on Fuseli's part, but one of which the consequences become obvious to the modern reader of his book, Fuseli rendered 'Geist' as 'genius', not 'spirit'; 'Beurteilung' as 'connoisseurship', not 'judgment'; 'Urbild' as 'model', not 'archetype'; 'Nachahmung' as 'imitation', not 'counterfeiting'; 'natürlich' as 'easy', not 'natural'—and so forth. His English version fairly leaps with many of the *Modewörter* of the period: allegory, invention, conception, sublimity, motion, ideal, beauty, expression, passion, taste, grandeur, form, nature, and execution. Thus the informed English reader could relish the stimulating interplay and tension between familiar critical terms and their novel synthesis. Future British criticism of the period would be favourable towards Winckelmann on the whole. The only dissent would stem from artists opposed to his pessimistic view of the effect of British climate upon the development of the fine arts.[45]

[44] WW, II, p. 65; *Reflections*, p. 273.
[45] Wiliam Carey was one of the few Englishmen who protested against Winckelmann's doctrines of imitation in *Variae: Historical Observations on Anti-British and Anti-Contemporarian Prejudices*, London, 1822. After a long excerpt from Fuseli's translation of the *Reflections*, Carey concluded with a castigation of the 'mean and frigid system of Winckelmann and his drivelling disciples', claiming that, in Winckelmann's case, 'blind admiration of antiquity closed his eyes and hardened his heart to living beauty. . . . Notwithstanding all his profound knowledge of their manners and customs, he permitted their spirit, their glorious, rational spirit, to escape his notice. He overlooked the fact that the Greeks attained to their excellence, and became *inimitable*, by making it their pride to be *unimitative, original*, and purely Grecian, in all their institutions' (pp. 88-9 and 47-8).
The most devastating blow to Winckelmann's climate theories was given by the artist James Barry in his *Inquiry into the Real and Imaginary Obstructions to the Acquisition of the Arts in England*, London, 1775, in which he decided that England's lag was due to moral and social conditions, and not to those of climate. Nevertheless, the doctrines of Winckelmann persisted, and well into the next century they were inspiring British artists with either defeatism or truculence. Thus Prince Hoare, in his *Epochs of the Arts*, London, 1813, still found it necessary to write: 'The ridiculous dogmas of Du Bos and Winckelmann on the subject of atmospheric and other physical obstacles of genius, have been long overthrown, but disdainful criticism has by no means lost her powers of

VII

But Fuseli was to be opposed to much more than Winckelmann's ideas of climate, which the German critic had actually lifted substantially from Du Bos and Montesquieu. After Fuseli's return from Italy to London in 1779 after a sojourn of eight years, he developed a vehement hostility against Winckelmann. This he publicised in the reviews he wrote for the *Analytical Review* in the 1780s and the 1790s: he took every opportunity he could to charge Winckelmann with frigidity, tameness, and specious system-making. Yet not only had Fuseli, with his early translations, supplied the resources for the creation of a taste in England for everything that Winckelmann championed, but he also had begun to use the term 'eclectic' (in a pejorative sense) of artists like the Caracci, a usage which he derived directly from Winckelmann. Moreover, Fuseli was defending publicly most of Winckelmann's tenets: the need for simplicity, grandeur, unity, sublimity, grace, beauty, discrimination, form, and the like, as aesthetic controls and criteria. Why the falling out, then?

The preface which Fuseli composed for the 1820 edition of his Royal Academy *Lectures* contained a partial answer. Winckelmann, he wrote, 'was the parasite of the fragments that fell from the conversation or the tablets of Mengs, a deep scholar, and better fitted to comment a classic than to give lessons on art and style'. Therefore, concluded Fuseli, Winckelmann

> reasoned himself into frigid reveries and Platonic dreams on beauty. As far as the taste or the instructions of his tutor directed him, he is right, whenever they are, and between his own learning and the tuition of the other, his history of art delivers a specious system and a prodigious number of useful observations. He has not, however, in his regulation of epochs, discriminated styles, and masters, with the precision, attention, and acumen, which from the advantages of his situation and habits might have been expected; and disappoints us as often by meagreness, neglect, and confusion, as he offends by laboured and inflated rhapsodies on the most celebrated monuments of art. To him Germany owes the shackles of her artists, and the narrow limits of their aims; for him they have learnt to substitute the means for the end, and by hopeless chace after what they call beauty, to lose what alone can make beauty interesting, expression and mind.[46]

brilliancy' (p. 84). And much later, in 1825, Haydon observed in his *Diary* that 'the ridiculous assertions of Winckelmann . . . , though refuted over and over again, have still their effect' (III, 28).

[46] John Knowles, *The Life and Writings of Henry Fuseli, Esq., M.A., R.A. The Former Written and The Latter Edited by John Knowles, F.R.S.*, London, 1831, Vol. II, pp. 13-14.

And although Fuseli criticised Winckelmann as an art historian first, the heaviest burden of his opposition was contained in the charge that the exhortations of Winckelmann, if followed, would diminish or destroy 'expression and mind', which for Fuseli epitomised artistic excellence.

While Fuseli had already been alerted to the value of 'Ausdruck', expression, in Zürich, it was not until his long stay in Italy, from 1770-8, when he studied intensively the works of Michelangelo, that he elevated dynamic expressiveness above self-contained beauty. It is ironic that in his last essay in the Winckelmann anthology, he had taken Winckelmann's description of Michelangelo, already censorious, and had made it even more so; he claimed that Michelangelo had 'debauched' his imitators, using a word that Winckelmann had not even approximated in the German original. But the first-hand experience of Michelangelo had induced a radical alteration of Fuseli's views, and he came to despise Winckelmann's mincing criticism of the Italian for not remaining within the boundaries of grace. He could not forgive Winckelmann's demotion of Michelangelo beneath the Raphael-Titian-Correggio trinity. In the remaining works of Michelangelo Fuseli, who also adored the Greeks, thought he had found a dynamic objectification of Greek practice as he apprehended it: expression, passion, sublimity, presided over by a Leibnizian energy.

Fuseli was further appalled by Winckelmann's obsession for codifying emblems and allegories. He would not admit allegory into the higher forms of painting, 'because wherever it enters, it must rule the whole'.[47] Like Wordsworth, who regarded allegory as a mechanical device unless it was negotiated with the emotions, 'the purest sensations', Fuseli asserted that 'none ever peopled a barren fancy and a heart of ice with images or sympathies by excursions into the deserts of mythology or allegory'.[48] A choking-off of innovative originality would, it seemed to Fuseli, be the consequence of elevating allegorical painting to the same level as epic painting with its sublime symbols—although what Fuseli sometimes explicated as symbols we would, in many cases, regard as allegories. But within his own working system, where expression and mind mattered above all else, Fuseli's animadversions made sense. When he spoke on the question in 1801, and censured 'the laborious pedantry of emblems . . . by which arbitrary and conventional signs have been substituted for character and expression', when he excoriated 'this hieroglyphic mode of exchanging sub-

[47] Ibid., pp. 197-9.
[48] Ibid., Vol. III, p. 126.

stance for signs',[49] in a basic sense he defended his own practices
as an artist and struck at Winckelmann's precepts as well. That
he should retain his hatred of these precepts for such a long period
of time demonstrated how forcefully he felt himself threatened
by them.

VIII

In his own artistic practice, Fuseli's final stance on the subjects
of expression, allegory, symbol, and mind bears a strong analogy
to Blake's. While Blake's stated views of allegory seem, at first reading, to be significantly different from Fuseli's, actually they are not.
Fuseli and Blake lived for expression, not beauty; both lived, as
Blake put it, 'to renew the lost Art of the Greeks'.[50] Yet Blake
ordered his values to conform to 'living Gothic forms' as against
'mathematical Greek' ones; Fuseli perceived both his variants of
Gothicism and Hellenism within the *Gestalt* of Michelangelo's
works. In their maturity, then, both Blake and Fuseli forsook what
they construed as Winckelmann's premises. Composing original,
working definitions for themselves, both Blake and Fuseli, as artists
and critics, invested ideas with senses, instead of submerging senses
in schemata, and elevated the emblems of classical allegory to the
symbols of unique vision.

49 Ibid., Vol. II, p. 201.
50 William Blake, *Letters*, New York, 1956, 16 August 1799.

The Influence of Pierre Bayle's Defence of Toleration on the Idea of History expressed in the Dictionnaire Historique et Critique

J. J. Cashmere

On 17 September 1697, Bayle answered Pierre Jurieu's criticisms of the *Dictionnaire historique et critique*[1] by asserting 'En un mot, tout ce que j'ai fait se trouve enfermé dans le ressort ou dans la jurisdiction d'un Ecrivain, qui donne une Histoire accompagnée d'un Commentaire Critique'.[2] Since the eighteenth century, the significance of this assertion has been obscured by an excessive concern with the reputation Bayle has acquired as the irreligious and sceptical 'philosophe de Rotterdam'. Bayle's answer to Jurieu was not an idle assertion, however, for in fact the *Dictionnaire* may best be described as a monumental work of history, which is devoted, in its critical footnotes, to arguing the reasonableness of the principle of universal religious toleration. The work is unique because two elements are fused together in its footnotes: it is at one and the same time a work of historical criticism and a disjointed polemical treatise. It will be the purpose of this paper to demonstrate one feature of the reaction of these two elements upon each

1 Quotations are taken from my own copy of the *Dictionnaire historique et critique, quatrième édition, revue, corrigée et augmentée avec la vie de l'auteur par Mr. Des Maizeaux*, 4 vols., Amsterdam and Leyden, 1730. The spelling of this edition has been followed for all quotations. The citation of Bayle's own footnotes is made according to the title of the article, which is capitalised (e.g. BEAULIEU), and the alphabetical letter of the note (e.g. note B).

2 'Suite des réfléxions sur le prétendu jugement du public', *Dictionnaire*, IV, p. 660.

other, and their importance to any interpretation of the meaning and intention of the *Dictionnaire*.

Although it cannot be denied that the *Dictionnaire* exercised a profound influence upon the eighteenth century in general, it is a mistake to assume that the intention of the work necessarily corresponds to the inferences drawn from it by the *philosophes*. This fact was clearly summed up by Paul Dibon in 1959 when he wrote: 'Il y a un mythe de Bayle, tenace parce qu'il est commode. Il consiste à imaginer un Bayle sceptique, un Bayle déjà voltairien sous prétexte que son *Dictionnaire Historique et Critique* servit d'arsenal aux polémistes des générations suivantes'.[3] This myth largely explains why the positive aspects of Bayle's philosophy of history have been given such inadequate consideration. As recently as 1963, H. T. Mason wrote: 'When a philosophy of history was required Bayle had little advice to give, and Voltaire, like the eighteenth century in general, had painfully to elaborate and systematize his outlook as well as his times would permit.'[4] Although the *philosophes* did elaborate and systematise Bayle's ideas, their interpretation of the *Dictionnaire* often failed to consider whether a disparity existed between Bayle's motives and their own.

The fact that on this occasion Bayle chose to compose an encyclopaedic dictionary, and the natural prolixity he displayed in his writing, probably gave impetus to the eighteenth-century myth concerning the *Dictionnaire*. As Edward Gibbon noted in August 1762: 'He could not have chosen a better plan. It permitted him everything, and obliged him to nothing. By the double freedom of a dictionary and of notes, he could pitch on what articles he pleased, and say what he pleased on those articles.'[5] While this plan allowed Bayle considerable flexibility in developing his defence of toleration, it also encouraged the *philosophes* to pillage the book more freely, and more frequently, than they might otherwise have done. They came to regard the *Dictionnaire* as a veritable mine of information, as a storehouse of destructive and anti-religious arguments which anticipated their own program for reform. Consequently, they plagiarised not only arguments, but in some cases entire articles, from the work to support their own polemical needs.

The reputation of an irreligious sceptic which Bayle subsequently acquired received its original currency in France. The *Dictionnaire* appears to have been one of the most widely read works in that country during the eighteenth century, appearing in the

[3] *Pierre Bayle, le philosophe de Rotterdam, études et documents*, Paul Dibon (ed.), Amsterdam and Paris, 1959, p. viii.
[4] *Pierre Bayle and Voltaire*, London, 1963, p. 133. As well as Mason, both Ernst Cassirer and Alfred Cobban express this view.
[5] *Miscellaneous Works*, London, 1814, Vol. V, p. 238.

catalogues of 288 out of 500 private libraries between 1750 and 1780.[6] Voltaire's debt to the *Dictionnaire*, for example, must remain beyond doubt, especially since it provided the inspiration for his own *Dictionnaire philosophique*. He referred to Bayle's work as 'le premier ouvrage de ce genre où l'on puisse apprendre à penser'.[7] He also described Bayle as 'le premier des dialecticiens et des philosophes sceptiques'.[8] It was in the *Poème sur le désastre de Lisbonne*, however, that he expressed perhaps his best known interpretation of Bayle's intentions:

> C'est là ce que m'apprend la voix de la nature.
> J'abandonne Platon, je rejette Épicure.
> Bayle en sait plus qu'eux tous; je vais le consulter:
> La balance à la main, Bayle enseigne à douter,
> Assez sage, assez grand pour être sans système,
> Il les a tous détruits, et se combat lui-même:
> Semblable à cet aveugle en butte aux Philistins,
> Qui tomba sous les murs abattus par ses mains.[9]

Although Voltaire can never be regarded as merely 'Un Bayle bilieux',[10] he did have sufficient regard for the arguments which he discovered in Bayle's work to refer to him in a footnote to this passage from the *Poème* as 'l'avocat général des philosophes'.[11]

Voltaire's views were also shared by Baron d'Holbach who referred to the author of the *Dictionnaire* as 'L'illustre Bayle, qui apprend si bien à douter . . .'.[12] Diderot, who plundered the *Dictionnaire* most industriously, considered that 'le Scepticisme n'eut ni chez les anciens, ni chez les modernes, aucun athlete plus redoutable que Bayle'.[13] In the same article from the *Encyclopédie*, in a passage which was withheld from publication by Le Breton, Diderot added: 'Pour pallier son pyrrhonisme, lorsqu'il l'établissoit, c'étoit toujours sous prétexte de ramener la révélation qu'il savoit bien sapper, quand l'occasion s'en présentoit'.[14] One wonders what discomfort Bayle may have felt had he known how entirely the *philosophes* had taken him to their bosom.

---

6 Daniel Mornet, 'Les Enseignements des bibliothèques privées (1750-1780)', *Revue d'histoire littéraire de la France*, Vol. XVII, 1910, pp. 463-4.
7 *Oeuvres historiques*, Texte établi, annoté et présent par René Pomeau, Paris, 1957, p. 1008.
8 *Mélanges*. Préf. par Emmanuel Berl; texte établi et annoté par Jacques van den Heuvel, Paris, 1961, p. 1197.
9 Ibid., p. 308.
10 Emile Faguet, *Dix-huitième siècle: études littéraires*. Paris n.d., p. 20.
11 *Oeuvres complètes de Voltaire*, Paris, 1877-85, IX, p. 476n.
12 *Système de la nature* (Paris, 1821), repr. Hildesheim, 1966, Vol. II, p. 354 n.l.
13 *Encyclopédie*, Neufchastel, 1765, XIII, p. 612.
14 Douglas H. Gordon and Norman L. Torrey, *The Censoring of Diderot's Encyclopédie and the Re-established Text*, New York, 1947, p. 77.

While the *philosophes* proclaimed Bayle's scepticism, his religious critics added further testimony to the myth by denouncing his irreverent attitude towards religion. His famous debate with Leibniz, and the publicity received by such articles as DAVID, MANICHEENS, PYRRHON, and the *Eclaircissement sur les athées* gave rise to complaints that Bayle was largely to blame for the deplorable decline in morals and a decreasing respect for the authority of the Catholic Church in eighteenth-century France. The Jesuit Abbé Porée declared Bayle to be the enemy of religion whether he appeared to be defending or attacking it. He blamed Bayle for the increasing spread of libertinism and atheism, protesting that he taught his readers to believe nothing, to know nothing, to despise authority and to suspect truth.[15] In 1752 there appeared a work entitled *Remarques critiques sur le Dictionnaire de Bayle* in which its author, the cleric P. L. Joly, claimed that the *Dictionnaire* had given considerable strength to the cause of scepticism and irreligion 'qui ne s'est malheureusement que trop répandu depuis le funeste présent que cet Ecrivain a fait au Public'.[16]

In contrast to France, the reception of the *Dictionnaire* in England was generally more impartial. Dr Johnson, for example, who referred to the work constantly, concluded dispassionately that 'Bayle's Dictionary is a very useful work for those to consult who love the biographical part of literature, which is what I love most'.[17] Joseph Addison, who also made great use of the *Dictionnaire*, reported the opinion in the *Spectator* for 15 June 1711 '. . . that *Bayle's Dictionary* might be of very great Use to the Ladies, in order to make them general Scholars'.[18] On the other hand, David Hume, who was undoubtedly influenced by Bayle, scarcely mentions his name. Perhaps the most reliable assessment of Bayle's intentions comes from the historian Edward Gibbon who comments:

> A calm and lofty spectator of the Religious tempest, the Philosopher of Rotterdam condemned with equal firmness the persecution of Lewis xiv; and the Republican maxims of the Calvinists; their vain prophecies and the intolerant bigotry which sometimes vexed his solitary retreat. In reviewing the controversies of the times, he turned against each other, the arguments of the disputants: successively wielding the arms of the Catholics and protestants, he proves that neither the way of authority, nor the way of examination can afford the multitude any test of Religious truth; and dextrously concludes,

[15] See Howard Robinson, *Bayle The Sceptic*, New York, 1931, p. 279.
[16] *Remarques critiques*, Paris, Dijon, 1712, I, p. viii.
[17] Boswell, *Life of Johnson*, G. B. Hill (ed.) Rev. L. F. Powell, Oxford, 1934-50, p. 425.
[18] *The Spectator*, Donald F. Bond (ed.), Oxford, 1965, I, p. 390.

that custom and education must be the sole grounds of popular belief . . . His critical Dictionary is a vast repository of
facts and opinions; he balances the *false* Religions in his
sceptical scales, till the opposite quantities, (if I may use the
language of Algebra) annihilate each other.[19]

In this passage Gibbon highlights the issue which completely
dominated Bayle's interests. His was an age of violent religious
controversy in the years on either side of the Revocation of the
Edict of Nantes in 1685. While French Huguenots were suffering
persecution from the dragoons of Louis XIV, Catholic and Protestant theologians were thundering away at each other over such
questions as the nature of religious orthodoxy, the validity of the
authority claimed by each church and the moral justifications for
the persecution or toleration of religious heretics. Considering the
fact that Bayle had suffered as much at the hands of the apocalyptic
visionaries of his own Calvinist faith as he had at the hands of the
religious zealots of the Catholic Church, it is scarcely surprising
that his distaste for religious disputes, fanaticism, and intolerance
should have dominated his intellectual interests.

In announcing the *Dictionnaire* to be an arsenal of irreligious
and sceptical arguments, the *philosophes* failed to appreciate the
limited area in which Bayle intended his ideas to be applied. If his
footnotes were destructive, it was only because they were intended
to subvert the intolerant dogmatism of religious controversies,
which he considered to be a principal cause of religious persecution.
The arguments which he used solely to undermine the rational
basis of theological controversy were later applied by the *philosophes* to a more general criticism of society, both civil and religious,
a program which Bayle had never envisaged. The limited scope of
his vision in the *Dictionnaire* is reflected nowhere better than in
his idea of the purpose of history which clearly indicates his preoccupation with the issue of religious toleration.

To a considerable extent, Bayle's discussion of history in the
Dictionnaire presumed an acceptance, in its broad framework, of
the seventeenth-century humanist philosophy of history, in which
the purpose of history was seen to be the provision of historical
examples which would implicitly teach moral or political lessons.
The originally high ideals of the Italian humanists became perverted in France during the seventeenth century, and as Carl
Becker commented 'We then find humanists "exploiting the past"
in the interest of classical learning, patriots in the interest of
national or royal prestige, Protestants in the interest of the new

---

[19] *Memoirs of My Life* (edited from the manuscripts by Georges A. Bonnard),
London, 1966, pp. 64-5.

religion, Catholics in the interest of the old faith'.[20] Bayle reacted strongly against this tendency, which represented all the elements of intolerance against which he was fighting. His whole theory of tolerance, and the principle of liberty of conscience upon which it was based, relied upon the notion that morality was an idea directly instilled in man by God, and was in no way dependent upon institutional religion. Consequently Bayle saw the purpose of history as essentially non-sectarian, capable of teaching universal moral lessons.

Initially his view of the instructive moral value of his new venture was quite modest as is suggested in a letter which he wrote to Jacques du Rondel at Maestricht University on 5 May 1692:

> mais on m'avoüera, Monsieur, qu'une infinité de personnes peuvent profiter moralement parlant de la lecture d'un gros Recueil de Faussetez Historiques bien avérées; quand ce ne seroit que pour devenir plus circonspects à juger de leur prochain, & plus capables d'éviter les pieges que le Satire & la Flaterie tendent de toutes parts au pauvre Lecteur.[21]

He regarded history as nothing more than a catalogue of the errors, sins, follies, and passions of mankind, and considered that there was nothing so trivial, whether fact or falsehood, from which men could not glean some lesson. This is why he resolved to present an encyclopaedic correction of Louis Moreri's *Le Grand Dictionnaire Historique*.[22]

Between the announcement of Bayle's original design for the *Dictionnaire* and the publication of the first edition on 24 October 1696,[23] a situation arose which caused him to alter radically his original plan. In 1690 an anonymous pamphlet entitled *Avis important aux réfugiéz* was published in Amsterdam warning the

---

[20] *The Heavenly City of the Eighteenth-Century Philosophers*, New Haven, 1961 (original ed. 1932), p. 90.

[21] 'Dissertation qui fut imprimée au devant de quelques Essais ou Fragmens de cet Ouvrage l'an MDCXCII, sous le Titre de Projet d'un Dictionnaire Critique, à Mr. du Rondel, Professeur aux belles Lettres à Maestricht', *Dictionnaire*, IV, p. 614. This letter was originally published under a separate cover in 1692, but was appended to all editions of the *Dictionnaire* from 1720 onwards.

[22] *Le Grand Dictionnaire Historique, ou le Mélange Curieux de l'Histoire Sainte et Profane*, 1674.

[23] There is some confusion about the date of this first edition. Henri-F. Bergeron places it in November 1697, with the first volume having been printed in 1695. (See 'Le manichéisme de Bayle et Plutarque', *XVIIe Siècle*, Vol. 68, 1965, p. 45.) Elisabeth Labrousse places it on 24 October 1696. (See Bayle, *Oeuvres Diverses* (La Haye, 1727-31), repr. Hildesheim, 1964-9, Vol. III, p. xv.) Most other authors assert that it was published in 1697. I accept Mme Labrousse's opinion, for apart from the obvious scholarship upon which it rests, Bayle himself speaks of the work's being on sale in bookshops in December 1696. (See 'Suite des réfléxions sur le prétendu jugement du public', *Dictionnaire*, IV, p. 662.)

Huguenots of the Refuge that their exile would be permanent if they continued to disparage the cause of religious pacifism and to advocate theories of popular sovereignty. Jurieu condemned the pamphlet, accusing Bayle of its authorship.[24] The bitter feud which developed between these two men erupted into a fierce pamphlet war which split the Huguenots in exile into two opposing factions. By the time that Jurieu finally had Bayle dismissed from his professorship at the *École illustre* in 1693, circumstances were already compelling Bayle to transform the original plan for the *Dictionnaire* into yet another defence of the principle of universal religious toleration.

Although Bayle resisted the idea that historians should themselves interpolate the moral lessons of history, he personally applied his idea of the moral purpose of history to the practical end of providing a historical foundation for his defence of toleration. He directed his moral lessons to specific elements of society, and drew upon his wide knowledge of biblical, classical and what was for him modern history to establish these moral lessons.

The fundamental statement which incorporated Bayle's practical ideas on the use and purpose of history occurs in the well-known article MACON. Here he treated the subject of the French Wars of Religion, that sixteenth-century holocaust which saw open civil war in France, presses running hot with treatises on popular sovereignty and some of the most horrible examples of religious persecution known to man. It was an abominable century, the memory of which was scarred with bitterness, hatred, passion, and suffering. Should historians even consider touching upon such barbarities? Bayle asked. It was a reasonable question, he admitted, for it might rekindle dying hatreds, revive settling passions. He had been personally accused of doing this very thing. Nevertheless, as much as one might wish that the memory of those years could be obliterated, the fact remained that numerous history books, which still exist, had dealt with the subject, and 'comme toutes choses ont deux faces, on peut souhaiter pour de très-bonnes raisons que la mémoire de tous ces effroiables desordres soit conservée soigneusement'.[25] The 'très-bonnes raisons' to which he alluded are the moral lessons to be drawn from the events of the sixteenth century, which would benefit all readers, but to which three types of people ought to pay particular attention, 'Ceux qui gouvernent . . . Ceux qui conduisent les affaires Ecclésiastiques . . . [et] ces Théologiens remuans, qui prenent tant de plaisir à innover . . .'.[26]

[24] See Walter Rex, *Pierre Bayle and Religious Controversy*, The Hague, 1965, pp. 233-4.
[25] MACON, note C.
[26] Ibid.

Like Montaigne, Descartes, Milton, Spinoza, and Locke before him, Bayle realised that liberty of conscience and religious toleration could only exist in a country where social and political stability and religious peace prevailed. Although relative peace and stability had existed in France under Louis XIV until the Revocation of the Edict of Nantes, the situation after 1685 changed rapidly. War, social upheaval, and religious disputes threatened to destroy any hopes the Huguenots might have had of returning to their homeland peacefully. It is significant that the three groups to whom Bayle directed his moral lessons correspond broadly to the three elements of French society in whom Bayle saw the greatest threats to political stability and religious peace in France: Louis XIV, the Catholic Church, and the exiled Huguenot clergy. As we shall see, he used numerous historical examples, particularly from the sixteenth century, in his effort to undermine the political and social threats which these three elements represented.

The anarchy and persecution which existed in France in the sixteenth century lay heavily on Bayle's conscience. Firmly etched in his mind were the horrors of Vassey and St Bartholomew's Night, and the whole religious holocaust which accompanied them. By contrast, he was acutely aware of the relative peace and stability which France had enjoyed under Louis XIV. It is not surprising, then, that he should have dismissed with a wave of his hand the new democratic idealism which burst forth in the Refuge after 1685:

> Qu'on fasse ce qu'on voudra, qu'on bâtisse des Systêmes meilleurs que la République de Platon, que l'Utopie de Morus, que la République du Soleil de Campanella, &c.: toutes ces belles idées se trouveroient courtes & défectueuses, dès qu'on les voudroit réduire en pratique. Les passions des hommes, qui naissent les unes des autres dans une variété prodigieuse, ruïneroient bientôt les espérances qu'on auroit conçues de ces beaux Systêmes.[27]

He asserted that the disorders in France during the early part of the seventeenth century arose only because the royal authority was being undermined by the aristocracy. Once Richelieu had fettered the nobility and obliged them to submit to Louis XIII, peace was restored to the nation, and the stability which France had experienced since that time under Louis XIV testified to the value of absolute monarchy.[28] Despite the fact that Bayle persistently criticised Hobbes and his political system, both men shared at least one conviction: the need to justify and encourage obedience to the

[27] HOBBES, note E.
[28] GUISE, Louis de, note A.

absolute monarchies of their sovereigns. It is more than coincidence that Bayle's own political beliefs bear a striking resemblance to this precis which he gives of the *Leviathan*:

> Le précis de cet Ouvrage est, que sans la paix il n'y a point de sûrété dans un Etat, & que la paix ne peut subsister sans le commandement, ni le commandement sans les armes; & que les armes ne valent rien si elles ne sont mises entre les mains d'une personne; & que la crainte des armes ne peut point porter à la paix ceux qui sont poussez à se batre par un mal plus terrible que la mort, c'est-à-dire, par les dissensions sur des choses nécessaires au salut.[29]

History provided frequent examples to prove the value of absolute monarchy over democracy. Bayle used Caesar's Rome, for example, to show that democratic republics could only remain faithful to popular sovereignty if they desisted from foreign conquests and concentrated their popular energies within the confines of a small state. Once republics embarked upon a program of conquest, popular sovereignty was soon replaced by the power of a few individuals, as occurred in Rome with Caesar, Brutus, and Cassius.[30] It was rare, in fact, for any democracy to succeed. Even a small democracy like Athens could boast its tyrannies: 'Vous chercheriez en vain dans la Macedoine, qui étoit une Monarchie, autant d'exemples de Tyrannie, que l'Histoire Athenienne vous en présente'.[31] His conviction that religious toleration could only develop under stable political conditions left Bayle no alternative but to uphold the absolute government of Louis XIV:

> L'Auteur du Testament Politique de Mr. de Louvois a bien mieux conu le genié de la Nation. Il pose en fait que le seul & le vrai moien d'éviter en France les guerres civiles est la puissance absolue du Souverain, soutenue avec vigueur, & armée de toutes les forces nécessaires à la faire craindre . . . Il se pourroit tromper par raport à certains païs; mail il n'y a point d'aparence qu'il se trompe à l'égard de sa Nation. . . .[32]

This insistence upon the legitimacy, or rather the necessity, of absolute monarchy in France was not without its qualifications. The first of the moral lessons to be learned from history to which Bayle refers in the article MACON was directed specifically to Louis XIV. He seems almost to be anticipating the eighteenth-century concept of enlightened despotism when he points to the

[29] HOBBES, note F.
[30] BRUTUS, M. J., note F.
[31] PERICLES, note Q. See also the comment on democracy in CAPPADOCE, note A.
[32] LOUIS XIII, note A.

many imperfections and weaknesses from which monarchies suffer. He identified religion as the greatest weakness of monarchies and stressed, in the article ABDAS, that religion, far from being an artifice invented by sovereigns to encourage the obedience of their subjects, was more frequently an inhibition to the monarch's own power.[33] The examples of Henry of Navarre,[34] and more immediately of James II of England, indicated that if monarchs did not profess the religion of their subjects, they ran the danger of losing their crowns.

Bayle insisted that, as a general rule, monarchs who sacrificed their religious beliefs to the political welfare of their state increased their power and the prosperity of the nation. Ecclesiastics lead weak princes by the nose; the strong prince always considers politics before religion.[35] Henri II of France, who preferred to exterminate the Protestants of his kingdom rather than overwhelm his greatest enemy, Austria, did irreparable harm to the power and prestige of the monarchy in France.[36] 'Il est aisé de prouver aussi que l'exercice de cette autorité fut la principale source des miseres du Roiaume depuis l'an 1562 jusqu'à l'an 1594.'[37] Furthermore, Louis XIV was making precisely the same mistake:

> C'est ainsi que l'on a vu la même Cour laisser perdre les occasions les plus favorables de s'agrandir l'an 1684, afin de s'apliquer uniquement à la supression de l'Edit de Nantes. Ceux qui se laissent posséder de cet esprit n'ont qu'à renoncer au titre de Conquérant.[38]

Elsewhere Bayle applauded the fact that Queen Elizabeth of England had avoided this mistake, and had maintained herself upon the throne by carefully distinguishing between political expedience and religious conviction.[39]

The second moral lesson which Bayle drew from the French Wars of Religion concerns the threat by Louis XIV's Jesuit advisers to the peace and stability of France. He remained convinced that the Roman Catholic Church, particularly the Jesuit order, was ultimately responsible for the Revocation of the Edict of Nantes and the dreadful persecutions which had followed it. Louis XIV

[33] Note B.
[34] In SAMBLANÇAI, Guillaume de Beaune, Baron de, note C, Bayle remarked of Henry IV: 'Voilà un Roi bien souverain: il ne peut pas même obtenir que ses sujets aient la bonté de lui permettre de servir Dieu selon les lumieres de sa conscience; & c'est une honte au Christianisme d'avoir introduit dans l'Univers un si grand renversement de l'ordre. C'est aux sujets à demander la liberté de conscience à leur Souverain; & en voici qui la lui refusent'.
[35] EMMA, note A.
[36] HENRI II, note D.
[37] HOSPITAL, Michel de l', note K.
[38] HENRI II, note D.
[39] ELISABETH, note G.

had finally been persuaded to use his secular power in a religious matter, an action which Bayle sincerely deplored. The spectre of Vassey loomed again, and in the hope of reversing the trend, he once again set about clarifying the separation of the sovereign's temporal power from any connection with spiritual power.[40] As far as Bayle was concerned, the days of King David were past history; the monarchy should now be not only absolute, but secular as well.

He was intransigent towards those ecclesiastics who made use of the secular sword to persecute heretics. History was filled with their exploits and the degradation to which they had brought their countries. The influence of the Jesuits at the court of Versailles was notorious, and Bayle spelled out the moral lesson clearly:

> . . . on ne sauroit s'empêcher de plaindre la destinée des Souverains, & leur dépendance inévitable de leur Clergé. Dévots ou non, ils seront toûjours obligez de la ménager & de le craindre: c'est un véritable *Imperium in Imperio*. Il est vrai, le Regne de Jesus-Christ n'est point de ce monde; il l'a dit lui-même: mais ceux qui le réprésentent ne laissent pas d'être bien souvent les maîtres des Rois de la terre, & d'ôter ou de donner des couronnes; & ceux qui nous parlent tant de l'Eglise militante ont plus de raison qu'ils ne croient.[41]

Although the reference is not direct, there seems little doubt that Bayle was thinking about Louis XIV's Jesuit advisers when he wrote this. They were one of the principal obstacles to the implementation of religious toleration in France, and their church, far from being a pillar of society, was more frequently a source of instability:

> Lisez bien l'Histoire de l'Eglise Romaine, vous trouverez que les plus grans [sic] Princes du monde ont eu plus à craindre les passions que les zélateurs excitent, que les armes des Infideles: ainsi ce qui devroit être l'affermissement de la République, & de la Majesté de l'Etat, est bien souvent l'obstacle le plus invincible que les Souverains rencontrent à l'exécution de leurs ordres.[42]

Bayle acknowledged that it was not easy for the French king to resist Jesuit pressure. As a religious order, the Jesuits were ultramontanist in sympathy, and argued firmly for the Pope's right to depose sovereigns. As recently as 1681, he remarked, a new edition

---

[40] It is interesting to note that at the time of the Revocation, this principle of the separation of powers was also coming under attack from Jurieu's faction in Holland. See Rex, *Pierre Bayle*, p. 215. Bayle dealt extensively with this subject in the *Commentaire philosophique*.

[41] BROSSIER, note E.

[42] JUNIUS, François [père], note B.

of Thomas Barlow's book *An Historical Treatise on the Subject of Excommunicating and Deposing Kings* was published in France. The author maintained that it was still an article of the Roman faith that the Pope retained the right to depose sovereigns, and because of this, the book, which was originally published during the Titus Oates affair in England, had aroused a great deal of sentiment against the Catholics there.[43] Bayle denounced the doctrine as completely untenable. If the sovereign had no right to dabble in religious affairs, equally the Pope had no right to interfere in secular matters. The logic of this is exposed in the article GREGOIRE VII, where he explained:

> Qu'on supose tant qu'on voudra que Jesus-Christ a établi un Vicariat dans son Église, le bons sens, la droite raison, ne laisseront pas de nous aprendre qu'il l'a établi, non pas en qualité de souverain Maître, & de Créateur de toutes choses . . . Ce Vicaire ne pourroit tout au plus que décider de la doctrine qui sauve, ou qui damne . . . Ainsi ceux-mêmes qui ont été le plus fortement persuadez que le Pape est le Vicaire de Jesus-Christ, ont dû regarder comme un abus du Vicariat tout ce qui sentoit la jurisdiction temporelle, & l'autorité de punir le corps.[44]

Doubtless Bayle hoped that this second moral lesson would enlighten the king as much as it would serve as a warning to the Catholic clergy. If Louis continued to listen to the advice of his Jesuit counsellors, he would plunge his realm into civil war and risk the danger of losing his crown.

The third moral lesson to be learned from the history of the French Wars of Religion was specifically directed to the Huguenot clergy in exile. Pierre Jurieu and most of the other Huguenots in exile had already renounced their support for Louis XIV and turned towards the new theories of popular sovereignty and resistance. Isolated though he was by this turn of events, Bayle realised that Jurieu and his followers posed a new and dangerous threat to the stability of France, this time from the refuge of Holland and England. The revived doctrines of popular sovereignty for which Bayle had only contempt, became the subject of innumerable tracts and pamphlets which flooded these countries after 1685, and increased especially in number and intransigence after the Glorious Revolution of 1688 in England.[45] An open split, which occurred among the Huguenots in exile after the Revocation, culminated in two factions, the 'moderates', who included Bayle

43 BARLOW, note B.
44 Note S.
45 In ARNISAEUS, note A, Bayle remarked on the fact that in the year 1699 books on this subject were more numerous and popular than ever.

among their number, and the 'zealots', unofficially led by ·Pierre Jurieu.

Jurieu and his faction clamoured for a united Protestant crusade to drive Catholicism from France,[46] and the passion of their appeal increasingly alarmed Bayle. He was deeply concerned with the fate of those Huguenots still remaining in France and bearing the burden of the persecutions. With William of Orange on the English throne, and most of the European powers united in a war against Louis XIV,[47] it must have seemed to Bayle that Jurieu's cry for a religious crusade against France must have already been answered. He was acutely aware that while Louis XIV was so hard pressed, he was hardly likely to lend a sympathetic ear to any appeals to his reason and conscience to restore religious toleration in France. On the contrary, it was more probable that the Huguenots would be blamed for France's reversal of fortune, and their persecution intensified. To make matters worse, Jurieu had put forward the claim that his co-religionaries were no longer bound by their oath of loyalty to Louis XIV. With many young Huguenots already serving in the armies of William of Orange and the German princes, the French king could hardly be expected to have sympathy for his Protestant subjects. Under such circumstances, Bayle felt obliged to intensify his appeal for toleration, and to denounce not only the revived theories of resistance but the men who advanced them as well.

The exiled 'zealots', living as they were in the Low Countries, mingled with a wide variety of intellectuals—refugees from the Exclusion Crisis in England, republicans, and an assortment of Protestant clergymen. In such an intellectual environment, Jurieu could scarcely avoid being put in touch with the current theories of popular resistance, many of which were derived from the Monarchomach doctrines revived during the English Exclusion Crisis. The criticisms which he levelled at Louis XIV initially covered a variety of subjects, but following the English Revolution there appeared in his *Lettres pastorales* (1686-1689) an open call to his fellow subjects to rebel against their king. The justification for such a call to arms lay in his belief that there was an implicit contract in existence between subjects and ruler, and as in all such contracts, there were mutual obligations. For the monarch, there was the obligation to protect and safeguard the physical and spiritual liberty of his subjects. When he violated this obligation,

---

[46] See Rex, *Pierre Bayle*, p. 216. Rex also mentions the interesting fact that Jurieu claimed to have had the sanction of William of Orange for his doctrines, and was used by the English government to co-ordinate a spy ring (p. 225n.84).

[47] England, Spain, Holland, Austria, and most of the German states were at war with France by November 1688.

his subjects were under an obligation to resist him. Such an obligation should be invoked, Jurieu claimed, especially when the
monarch violated the supreme liberty of worshipping according to
conscience. Contact with the English Whigs had left its mark in his
uncompromising stand on sovereignty. When the king exceeded
the limits of his authority, Jurieu claimed, his subjects had the right
to depose him. They alone had no need to be right for their actions
to be valid.

Bayle had little patience with Jurieu's political *volte-face* from
supporting to criticising the French monarchy: 'Généralement par-
lant c'est une preuve que les passions font parler ou pour ou contre
le droit des Princes, que de voir que les mêmes gens disent là-
dessus le ouï & le non à mesure que les intérêts de leur cause se
trouvent changez'.[48] He was not content to let the matter rest there,
however. Once again he mustered his historical resources, this time
for a direct attack on Jurieu's doctrines. If we turn to the article
ELISABETH, the text affords us with an account of the persecutions inflicted upon the English papists as a result of their slanders
and libels against Queen Elizabeth and her government. It was
a clear allegorical warning to Jurieu that his own diatribes against
Louis XIV would only result in intensified persecution of the remaining Huguenots in France. If Huguenots preached the right of
subjects to depose their sovereigns, Louis would never grant them
toleration.

Bayle's principal attack upon the idea of popular resistance is
to be found in the article LOYOLA.[49] In this article he mentions
two doctrines which were ardently supported by the Jesuits: that
the authority of kings is inferior to that of the people, and that
kings may be punished by their subjects in certain instances. The
Jesuits, he remarked, were not the inventors of these doctrines,
but they were responsible for putting them into the most odious
practice. At the same time he condemned the notion that sovereigns
were given their power to persecute heretics. The reasoning of the
Jesuits on this subject was that if sovereigns refused to use their
power to persecute heretics, then the people, the true sovereign,
had a responsibility to assume the task, and the king should be
dethroned. If, however, because of some threat to the security of
the state, the king should be obliged to grant toleration, the concession should remain only while the danger existed, and then
the persecution should once again be resumed. At this point, Bayle
remarked that the Third Estate of France condemned all such
doctrines as pernicious. Then followed the significant thrust at

48 KNOX, note H. See also BARCLAI, Guillaume, note E.
49 Note S.

Jurieu. This French pastor, he continued, reasoned in a similar manner to the Jesuits, viz. *Les Princes peuvent faire mourir les heretiques, donc ils doivent les faire mourir,*[50] only this time the heretics were not Protestants, but Catholics.

Although the footnote under which all of this is discussed is ostensibly a criticism of the Jesuits, the general condemnation of the ideas of popular sovereignty and resistance indicate that it is equally an allegorical criticism of Jurieu's own political beliefs. That Bayle should have used allegory as a means of criticising Jurieu is not surprising, since Jurieu's political influence in Holland is an established fact.[51] In 1693 he had already used this influence with the Walloon Consistory to secure Bayle's dismissal from his professorship in Rotterdam, the excuse being that Bayle was an enemy of the Prince of Orange. This zealous pastor would undoubtedly have interpreted criticism of himself as an act of treachery against both William and Holland. Prudence forbad Bayle to write too explicitly against the political beliefs of his arch-antagonist. In fact in this very article he admitted as much himself:

> L'opinion que les Souverains ont reçu de Dieu le glaive pour punir les Hérétiques est encore plus universelle que la précédente, & a été réduite en pratique parmi les Chrétiens depuis Constantin jusques à present, dans toutes les Communions Chrétiennes qui on dominé sur les autres, & à peine ose-t-on écrire en Hollande contre une telle opinion.[52]

This is even more significant if we consider Jurieu's appeal for a religious crusade against France. William of Orange was now in a position to lead such a crusade, and Jurieu was bound to look with disfavour upon any attempts to prevent this.

A more open attack upon Jurieu's political beliefs is to be found in the article GELDENHAUR. In this article, Bayle exposed Jurieu's caprice in maintaining against the Catholics the very arguments which the Jesuits had used against the Protestants. The irony of the situation, he pointed out, was that the early Church fathers had not intended to deprive princes of the power of the sword which they held from God. They only meant to signify that this power should not be used against errors of conscience, since sovereigns had no commission from God to persecute people for their religious beliefs. He continued:

> Et ce qui est bien plus étonnant, d'où vient que depuis quelques années un Ministre de Hollande [Jurieu] a tâché de

---

[50] Ibid.
[51] See note 46 above. Also Rex, *Pierre Bayle,* pp. 233-4.
[52] LOYOLA, note 5.

rendre odieux les Tolérans, par la raison qu'ils ôtoient aux
Souverains un des plus beaux droits de leur Majesté? N'est-ce
pas être plus malin & plus injuste que les Paiens ne l'étoient
contre les Peres de la primitive Eglise, ausquels ils ne repro-
choient point ce prétendu attentat sur les droits des Souverains,
ou ce prétendu crime d'Etat? Mais pour montrer l'illusion de
ce Ministre, il suffit de lui demander pourquoi il ôte aux Rois
Catholiques le droit du glaive par raport aux Protestans?
Pourquoi se croit-il permis ce qu'il blâme dans les autres
comme un crime de leze-majesté? Je parle pour la vérité,
dira-t-il; mais sa prétention est celle de tout le monde.[53]

On the subject of allegory in the *Dictionnaire*, Walter Rex has
noted two further points. In his erudite and detailed analysis of
the article DAVID, he claims that in the first edition of the
Dictionnaire, when Bayle condemned King David for joining the
Philistines to fight his own people, the Israelites, he really had in
mind the contemporary problem of the Huguenots.[54] Jurieu had
claimed that France's Protestants were no longer bound by their
oath of loyalty to Louis XIV, and were free to enlist in the foreign
armies which were at that time at war with France. Since many
young Huguenots had readily accepted this advice, Bayle's condemnation of David is quite rightly seen by Rex as an allegorical
criticism of Jurieu and those who accepted his doctrines. The second
point which Rex makes is that note G of the article DAVID can
be seen as an allegorical treatment of the deposition of James II
and the revolutionary content of Jurieu's *Lettres pastorales*.[55]

On this latter point there is further evidence, in the article
ELISABETH, of Bayle's keen awareness of the importance of the
1688 Revolution to the Huguenots. P. J. S. Whitmore has noted in
his thesis the use to which Bayle has put English history and learning in the *Dictionnaire*,[56] and while I consider that he rather over-
inflates the importance of Bayle's specifically English knowledge,
there can be no doubting the value which Bayle placed upon
1688 as a piece of historical evidence. We learn, for example, in
note I of ELISABETH, that the excuse the English used in 1688
to depose James II was that Queen Elizabeth had once broken a
promise to maintain the Catholic religion in England when she
came to the throne. 'Ainsi les Anglois', he continued, 'ont pu se
persuader que Jacques II ne craindroit point les mauvaises suites

[53] GELDENHAUR, note F. See also MAHOMET, note O.
[54] Rex, *Pierre Bayle*, pp. 238-9.
[55] Ibid., pp. 239-41.
[56] P. J. S. Whitmore, 'The use made of English thought and learning in the
works of Pierre Bayle, with special reference to the *Dictionnaire*'; Dissertation,
University of London, 1952.

d'un manquement de parole en matìere de Religion . . . ' An oath once broken by a monarch had made the English cautious a second time, and in their eyes this seemed to justify the deposition of James II. But in a sense Louis XIV had also broken his oath to the French Huguenots by revoking the Edict of Nantes, and Bayle could foresee what capital Jurieu would, and did, make of this. This zealous pastor's proclamation of a holy war against France, allied to the fact that the deposed English king was not only a close friend of Louis XIV, but also enjoyed his protection, seemed to Bayle evidence enough that the French monarchy was in dire peril.

Bayle's involvement in the political and religious crisis of the French Huguenots in exile at the end of the seventeenth century gave him a perspective which had altered radically by the time Voltaire took up his pen. The cause of religious toleration and liberty of conscience was a living issue for Bayle, and it formed the framework within which his intellectual interests developed. To regard him as a sceptical philosopher is to misread the meaning and intention of the *Dictionnaire*. Bayle was primarily a polemicist and propagandist who drew upon every branch of knowledge and every weapon at his disposal in his fight against religious dogmatism and intolerance.

The effect of his defence of toleration upon his view of history, in particular, was profound. In this paper I have only been able to suggest its significance for his view of the purpose of history, but a careful reading of the *Dictionnaire* reveals much more than this. Bayle's defence of toleration determined his view of the relationship between man and Providence in historical causation, as well as the division he drew between religious and secular history and the principles he laid out for historical criticism. In addition, I believe that a significant part of the explanation for his discussion of such questions as the relationship between faith and reason, the origin of evil, manicheanism, pyrrhonism and the nature of truth, which have been regarded by many scholars as philosophical digressions, is to be found in their relationships to this same defence of toleration. If the eighteenth century *philosophes* failed to appreciate this, it was because the Bayle whom they discovered in the *Dictionnaire* was a far more convenient ally in their struggles with the ideologies and practices of the *Ancien Régime*.

Historical Scepticism in Scotland before David Hume

Thomas I. Rae

Although David Hume is the best known and most popular Scottish historical writer of the eighteenth century, it is necessary to remember that he was neither the only nor the first Scot to write important historical works. Contemporary with him, and sharing many of his ideas, was William Robertson, Principal of Edinburgh University, author not only of a *History of Scotland* but also of a *History of America* and a *Life of Charles V*; and behind him lay a strong cultural tradition of Scottish historical writing expressed in the works of John Fordun, Hector Boethius, George Buchanan, William Drummond of Hawthornden, Robert Wodrow, and many others. In making a tentative backward exploration into some of the ideas which influenced this Scottish historical tradition, it is possible that some light may be thrown on the more notable Enlightenment figures of the Athens of the North, and it is perhaps appropriate in view of Hume's reputation as a sceptic to examine the reaction of two earlier Scottish historians to the problem of historical scepticism.

The seventeenth century had seen the growth in western Europe of what was to many people a devastating philosophical viewpoint, that of total scepticism. Partly through the intellectual religious warfare between Roman Catholic and Protestant, who continually attacked and counter-attacked in an attempt to undermine the positions held by their religious opponents, and partly through the rediscovery in the sixteenth century of the thought of the classical sceptics who provided the guns and ammunition for this battle, many thinkers were forced into a position of complete doubt about the nature of reality and complete doubt about the possibility of knowing that nature.[1] In as much as on both sides some of

---

[1] For the development of scepticism, see Richard H. Popkin, *The History of Scepticism from Erasmus to Descartes*, New York, 1964.

the attacks had been concentrated on destroying the historical foundation of the entrenched positions, this situation posed fundamental problems for the study of history; the reliability of all historical data came to be questioned and doubt was expressed on the ability of man to learn anything of the past let alone anything from it. Sceptical arguments could be raised against any claim to certainty in historical matters.

Many historians and antiquaries ignored this problem and continued their work in much the same manner as they had done before. Others, however, were seriously disturbed by these arguments, especially those involved in religious history, and felt it necessary to abandon their studies; William Harrison, one of those active in compiling Holinshed's *Chronicles*, wrote as early as 1577 that he 'will give over not onelie to write more at this present, but for ever hereafter of anie historicall matters, sith I see that this honest kind of recreation is denied me, and all time spent about the same in these daies utterly condemned, as vaine and savouring of negligence and heathenish Impietie'.[2] Some felt forced to attempt to seek a solution to the problem in order to justify their activities, and in the attempt brought forward new and improved historical methods. The crisis affected historians throughout western Europe, including those in Scotland, physically if not culturally on the fringe of that continent. Sir George Mackenzie of Rosehaugh, and the Rev. Thomas Innes were two Scottish historians who each played a part in facing this problem of historical scepticism.

Mackenzie, born in 1636 and descended from a noble family, was by profession a lawyer, who reached the climax of his career in 1677 on being appointed King's Advocate in Scotland, a position of considerable political and administrative power. During his tenure of office, showing a hatred of religious fanaticism which itself bordered on fanaticism, he was responsible for the physical persecution of the Covenanters, a popular but extremist Presbyterian sect, thus earning the well-deserved appellation 'Bloody Mackenzie'. At the same time he was devoted to literature, and, before his death in 1691, saw the Advocates' Library, which he had himself virtually founded, fully established. His social gifts and his own extensive writings led Dryden to describe him as the 'noble wit of Scotland', an equally well-deserved epithet. His flamboyant and extrovert career contrasts with that of Innes, who, born in 1662, came from a relatively poor Catholic family in Aberdeenshire. At an early age Innes went to study at the Scots College in Paris,

2 William Harrison, 'The Description of Scotland', p. 21, in Raphael Holinshed, *The Historie of Scotland*, London, 1577.

of which his brother later became Principal; after becoming a priest he served for a period in the Scottish mission—a dangerous and uncomfortable experience during which he was hunted from glen to glen in continuous danger of his life—bringing his religion to the Catholic clansmen inhabiting the Highland regions. Eventually he returned to Paris to lead the life of a scholar until his death in 1744. The contrast between these two men, the Episcopalian lawyer, politician, and polymath, and the adventurous, studious, Roman Catholic priest, is no greater than the contrast between their historical thought, a contrast which is the more marked because both chose to deal with the same period and subject, the establishment of the Scottish race in Scotland and the government of their early kings.

In medieval and Renaissance times most of the countries of western Europe had their legends of origin. Just as ancient Rome was supposedly founded after the wanderings of Aeneas, the French and English traced their origins to other wandering Trojan heroes, Francion and Brutus. The Scottish legend was perhaps more original. Scota, the daughter of Pharaoh, and her husband Gathelos, a Greek prince, were exiled from Egypt for their lack of enthusiasm in persecuting Moses and the children of Israel, and travelled westwards to the Atlantic until they reached Portgathel (Portugal). The race they founded eventually settled, under the leadership of Scota's son, Hyber, in Ireland (Hibernia), and a branch of it migrated to present-day Scotland four centuries before Christ to found a dynasty of kings which reigned without interruption until the seventeenth century. First recorded by the ninth-century writer Nennius, this myth played an important part in the thirteenth century as part of the historical justification for the Scottish claim to political independence from Edward I. Medieval Scottish writers, such as John Fordun in the fourteenth century and especially Hector Boethius in the early sixteenth, added detail to it, and it received its final form at the hands of the Renaissance humanist George Buchanan in his *Rerum Scoticarum Historia*, published at Edinburgh in 1582, although by this time the Egyptian origins of the Scottish race had been dropped.

With Buchanan's authority behind it, the story of the ancient lineage of the Scottish kings caught the imagination of the Scottish people. Charles I referred to himself in 1641 as the 108th King of Scots in a letter addressed to Parliament seeking loyal support from the Scottish people. The Scottish painter George Jamesone is said to have painted a series of portraits of all the Scottish kings for Charles I's visit to Scotland in 1633, at the same time as he painted a portrait of Charles himself.[3] In 1684-5 the Dutch painter Jacob de Wett painted the series of 110 portraits which still hangs in Holyrood Palace in Edinburgh. John Johnston, a Scottish Latinist poet, wrote a series of odes to all the Scottish kings, *Inscriptiones Historicae Regum Scotorum*, published at Amsterdam in 1602. At Dalry House near Edinburgh, a Latin motto dated 1661, commemorating the kings, formed part of the plaster ceiling of the spacious dining room.[4] The legend permeated all Scottish society and, of course, the tradition of these kings lay behind all Scottish historical writing of the period. There were many reasons for the all-pervading popularity of this historical myth. It maintained the picture of Scottish independence from England at a time when the Scottish monarchs, now kings also of England, were being increasingly drawn to English ways. It maintained the glory and renown of the British monarchy as kings with the most ancient uninterrupted royal lineage in Europe. It maintained the tradition of the independence of the Scottish people against their kings, for Buchanan had imposed his democratic ideas of an elective monarchy and the right of rebellion on his picture of primitive monarchic government in Scotland. And, finally, it justified the Presbyterian form of Scottish church government; for Scotland, according to this view of history, had been Christianised under King Donald early in the second century, and had possessed a form of church organisation under presbyters for three centuries before the first bishop, St Palladius (probably also mythical), was sent from Rome. Royalist Episcopalians and revolutionary Presbyterians, at variance in almost every other thought in this period of religious warfare, could agree in accepting the ancient history of the Scottish race and its continuous line of kings. Politically it was a most important historical doctrine for Scotland.

As elsewhere in Europe sceptical attacks were being made on this historical mythology. Humphrey Lhuyd, the Welsh antiquary, writing shortly before Buchanan, had cast doubts on the Scottish royal lineage in an essay entitled *Commentarioli Descriptionis Britannicae Fragmentum* published in 1572, after Lhuyd's death, in conjunction with Ortelius's *Theatrum Orbis Terrarum*. He was followed by William Camden and James Ussher, who objected to many details of the story. But, with the exception of John Major, who as early as 1521 had expressed a sceptical attitude towards

---

[3] Jamesone's portraits of the 108 kings have not survived, although they were possibly at Newbattle in the early eighteenth century: see *Correspondence of Sir Robert Kerr, first Earl of Ancrum, and his son William, third Earl of Lothian*, David Laing (ed.), Edinburgh, 1875, Vol. II, p. 535.

[4] 'Nobis haec invicta miserunt 108 proavi'; John Smith, 'Dalry House: its lands and owners', in *Book of the Old Edinburgh Club*, Vol. XX, 1935, p. 27.

part of the legend, no Scot had lifted his pen against the popular traditional picture.[5] The really critical attack came from England in 1684 when William Lloyd, Bishop of St Asaph, published his *Historical Account of Church Government*; he was supported the following year by his friend Edward Stillingfleet, Bishop of Worcester, in the preface to his *Origines Britannicae*. These two men, concerned to establish historically the episcopal character of church government throughout the British Isles, asserted that the Scots as a race had not settled in Scotland until the sixth century A.D., and that any tradition of the Christianising of the early Scots related to the Scots in Ireland and was totally irrelevant to the history of Scotland. At one blow Scotland was deprived not only of some 900 years of its accepted history but also of 40 of its kings, including those on whom Buchanan had based his historical justification of elective monarchy. While Sir George Mackenzie as an Episcopalian would welcome an interpretation of history which robbed the Presbyterian extremists in Scotland of historical justification for their religious and political views, he could not, as a devoted Royalist and an important state servant of the house of Stuart, accept anything derogatory to his king, 'since the Honour of the Ancient and Royal Race of our Sovereigns is the chief thing, wherein we glory'. To him, the two bishops Lloyd and Stillingfleet were virtually guilty of treason—'a degree of *Lese-Majesty* to injure and shorten the *Royal Line* of their kings'.[6] Accordingly in 1685 he countered Lloyd by publishing his *Defence of the Antiquity of the Royal Line of Scotland*, following it, after Stillingfleet had counter-attacked, with *The Antiquity of the Royal Line of Scotland further cleared and defended*, printed in 1686.

These were not his first published historical works; Mackenzie already had a significant reputation in Scotland as an antiquary and searcher-out of historical documents, though perhaps mainly in the field of heraldry and genealogy. But this is the first occasion on which we can detect his overall attitude towards historical studies, the philosophy of history he expounds early in his *Defence*. He sums up his position in one short paragraph. 'History requires, nor admits, no Mathematical, nor Legal Proof, but is satisfi'd with such Moral certainty, as is infer'd from probable Tradition, old Manuscripts, credible Historians, the Testimony of foreign

---

[5] 'De hac prima profectione de Grecia et Aegypto figmentum reor'; John Major, *Historia majoris Britannaie tam Angliae quam Scotiae*, Paris, 1521, fo. xvii.

[6] Sir George Mackenzie, *A Defence of the Antiquity of the Royal Line of Scotland*, London, 1685, dedication to the king, A4; ibid., p. xi (hereafter cited as *Defence*); *The Antiquity of the Royal Line of Scotland further cleared and defended*, London, 1686 will be hereafter cited as *Antiquity*.

Authours, and probable Reasons.'[7] From this it is clear that Mackenzie accepted the sceptical viewpoint that it is impossible to know with total certainty exactly what happened in the past. Earlier historians are not omniscient: 'we consider that even the Historians of this present age, cannot themselves see everything they relate; nor can all be prov'd by the Testimony of Witnesses'. Documents and manuscripts are not infallible: 'for the Authour of the Manuscript might have been mistaken, or byass'd'.[8] Yet Mackenzie believes that knowledge of the past can be achieved with some degree of certainty, a degree he categorises as 'moral certainty'.

In using this term to combat total scepticism about the past, Mackenzie is not being original; he is taking it over from earlier writers both in England and in France who had sought to maintain that a degree of certainty in knowledge can be attained. These earlier writers, for example Pierre Gassendi and Marin de Mersenne on the continent and William Chillingworth and John Tillotson in England, were mainly concerned with justifying religious certainty. They sought a middle way between the total scepticism of Montaigne and the disciples of Descartes, and the blind dogmatism of the protagonists both of the Roman Catholic and the Protestant churches. Absolutely infallible certainty, especially on religious matters, they accepted as being beyond human reach, but they distinguished two different types of certainty which were adequate for human purposes. Firstly the certainty a man has based on evidence in which in human terms there is no possibility of error, but which in absolute terms does not exclude the possibility of error. (Certain mathematical propositions are of this nature, hence the use by these writers of phrases such as mathematical certainty. The lawyer Mackenzie, it will be recollected, includes law within this degree of certainty.) Yet because this degree of certainty is infrequent in human affairs, these writers distinguished a second degree of certainty, the certainty of everyday life which every normal man has in going about his day-to-day business, the certainty based on the evidence of his senses, his accumulated experience, and the testimony of others. The possibility of error and deception exists and undoubtedly they occur, but for practical purposes the certainty derived in this way—the 'moral certainty' of Chillingworth, the 'sufficient assurance' of Tillotson—is adequate; without it life would be impossible. This is the certainty, these writers argued, on which religious belief is based. Later writers, such as Joseph Glanvill and Robert Boyle in England,

[7] *Defence*, p. 3.
[8] Ibid., p. 5.

developed the idea to cover scientific knowledge, and Mackenzie was not alone in applying it to history.[9]

It was recognised that there were degrees of moral certainty. The kind of proof acceptable in one subject would be inadequate in another, and one must seek only the proof, and hence the certainty, appropriate to that subject—as Mackenzie puts it, 'right Reason requires onely in all cases, such Proofs, as the Nature of the Subject can allow'. The historian can rely neither on the evidence of his own senses nor on his personal experience of past events. He is forced to rely in one form or another on 'the Testimony of Witnesses', the evidence of the past which has survived from the past. This evidence Mackenzie asserts consists of tradition, documents, and the work of former historical writers both native and foreign, and is to be used to build up in the light of reason a consistent, probable picture of the past. All the available evidence must be considered: 'I must intreat my Readers to lay all these together, and not to judge by parcels'.[10]

Had Mackenzie gone no further in his analysis of the nature of history this would have been a perfectly acceptable view for the time in which he wrote. He did, however, make qualitative distinctions about his different categories of admissible evidence which suggests that as a historian he was backward- rather than forward-looking in his attitude. Some forms of evidence, in his opinion, were more reliable than others, and had to be given greater weight in the final assessment. Documentary evidence he does not rate highly, accepting, as we have seen, the sceptical argument that the writer might have had no real knowledge of the facts, and might have been mistaken or biased in his views. He deliberately refuses to see that the same argument could be used against the evidence provided by historical writers, evidence which he places in a much higher category. Mackenzie's argument here is somewhat confusing, no doubt owing to the illogical nature of the position he was attempting to maintain, for he realises that the historical writers he extols must have 'Warrands' (i.e. sources) for their work. But, he argues, the completed historical work of a reputable historian is more important than his sources. 'I conceive also that in Reason, Historians already receiv'd in the World with applause, need not shew their Warrands, whereupon they proceed.' Accordingly historians need not be 'curious to preserve old Manuscripts and Records, after they have form'd their Histories by them: for else no Historian could ever be secure, if the not

9 Popkin, *History of Scepticism, passim*; Henry G. Van Leeuwen, *The Problem of Certainty in English Thought, 1630-1690*. International archives of the History of Ideas, Vol. III, The Hague, 1963, *passim*.

10 *Defence*, p. 4.

being able to show their Warrands after many ages, might discredit their History'.[11] The sources cited by Herodotus, Livy, and Josephus no longer exist, Mackenzie argues, but no one therefore challenges their authority. It is the reputation of a historian, not the quality or quantity of his sources, which makes him a reliable guide to our knowledge of the past.

Mackenzie continues his argument by asserting that the best and most reputable historians of ancient times based themselves on the tradition of their own people: 'men satisfie themselves in most things, with the general belief, and Tradition of those among whom they live'. The Roman Livy, he quotes, maintained that 'the best Records were the faithfull Remembrance of things past'; and, he comments, 'the *Jewish History* also had no Historical warrand for the first 2000 years, but Tradition'. Mackenzie concludes: 'the surest Foundation then of all Histories, is the common belief and consent of the Natives'.[12] In his final position, he twists his conception of a history based on the rational analysis of historical evidence into one based on the semi-rational acceptance of the authority of tradition, in fact a restatement of dogmatism.

This position is remarkably similar to that taken four years previously by Jacques Bénigne Bossuet, Bishop of Meaux, in his *Discours sur l'histoire universelle*. Bossuet was also concerned to maintain dogmatically the tradition of past authority against sceptical attack, and in doing this was troubled by the glaring discrepancies he found in the chronologies of the peoples of the eastern Mediterranean; he resolved the problem by taking his stand firmly on the Holy Scriptures, and by asserting that the lost histories of the Greeks would probably have confirmed them had they survived.[13] Mackenzie probably knew the work of Bossuet, for his patron, James Drummond, Earl of Perth and Lord Chancellor of Scotland, had been converted to Catholicism by Bossuet's works, and corresponded regularly with him;[14] but it is not necessary to postulate the connection to explain Mackenzie's attitude. His very nature was Royalist; he could not stomach rebellion against the Crown in any form; he equated the writing of Lloyd and Stillingfleet with the rebellion of Monmouth and Argyll against James II. 'The agreement of Men of different Professions, almost at the same time, against the Royal Line, is very remarkable; some endeavouring by their Swords to cut it short at that end which lay next to them;

[11] Ibid., p. 8.
[12] Ibid., pp. 5-7.
[13] Jacques Bénigne Bossuet, *Discours sur l'histoire, universelle*, Paris, 1681, pp. 41ff.; see also Paul Hazard, *The European Mind*, London, 1953, p. 210.
[14] François Gaguère, *Vers l'unité Chrétienne: Drummond et Bossuet*, Paris, 1963.

Whilst others, by their Pens, have undertaken what derogates from its glory, by lopping off its remoter end'.[15] Perhaps Mackenzie was justified in this view for within three years Lloyd was one of the seven bishops imprisoned in the Tower of London by James II for their protest against his Declaration of Indulgence. In his own view Mackenzie could maintain the historical glory of British (i.e. Scottish) Royalty only by maintaining the true historical nature of the Scottish tradition.

In the execution of his work Mackenzie faithfully followed his historical philosophy; or rather, the work shows why his philosophy took the form it did. Classical authors and early historians such as Bede (the 'Warrands') were combed for references to the Scots, their coming to Scotland, and their kings; but these references were few, and their interpretation doubtful, though Mackenzie makes the most of them as evidence. Eventually, as foretold in his philosophical prelude, he is forced to rely on established authors, on George Buchanan, and thus on Hector Boethius who was Buchanan's main source. Boethius,[16] writing in 1526, had based his narrative of the first forty Scottish kings on the then recently discovered manuscript histories by Veremundus, Turgot, and John Campbell; but these manuscripts had since disappeared. Hence the philosophical necessity for Mackenzie to minimise documentary sources to the point of suggesting that they all might as well be lost, and to elevate the reputations of historians as a criterion of reliability. For both Boethius and Buchanan were undoubtedly men of vast reputation: 'in a letter concerning him, *anno* 1530, insert in the Life of *Erasmus*, he [i.e. Erasmus] remarks, that *Boethius was a person who could not lie*'; 'Mr *Dryden* also my friend, whom I esteem a great Critick, as well as Poet, prefers *Buchanan* to all the Historians that ever wrote in *Britain*'. 'And,' Mackenzie pertinently adds with regard to Buchanan, 'he was not so much a favourer of Monarchy, to have allow'd it the advantage of so singular an Antiquity if he had not found the same due to it . . .'.[17] The detractors of the antiquity of the Scottish kings were not men of such reputation. Glossing over Camden, Mackenzie describes the work of Humphrey Lhuyd as 'the vain and silly scruples of an obscure Authour', attributes to Ussher, 'picqu'd by *Dempster's* severity, to his Uncle *Stanihurst*, . . . an undigested, and formless lump of all writers, good and bad', and accuses William Lloyd of having 'drawn a new Model, without bringing new materials, and has Translated even the fabulous Non sense of

---

[15] *Antiquity*, Epistle dedicatory, A4.
[16] Hector Boethius, *Scotorum Historiae a prima gentis origine*, Paris, 1527.
[17] *Defence*, pp. 29, 38.

these ignorant Authours, into polite *English*, putting that confus'd Rabble in Rank and File'.[18] Such men are clearly unreliable witnesses, not worthy of our respect in basing our 'moral certainty' on their evidence. In effect, Mackenzie does not answer his adversaries by argument but by seeking to denigrate them.

Less than a year elapsed between the publication of Lloyd's attack on the antiquity of the Scottish race and Mackenzie's defence. Mackenzie's work was hastily put together, but shows evidence both of extensive reading in the sources and of the working of a keen legal mind. He was undoubtedly helped in the compilation of the sources by others—Sir James Dalrymple, Sir Robert Sibbald, Harry Maule, later *de jure* Earl of Panmure—all likeminded men, Episcopalian if not Roman Catholic in religion, and staunch supporters of the Stuart monarchy.[19] Thomas Innes, writing some forty years later,[20] was of a similar stamp, a Roman Catholic priest and an adherent of the Stuarts now in exile in Rome. Political and religious motives influenced his work, as he himself admits. His *Critical Essay* he considered a necessary preliminary to a larger work, a history of the Scottish Church which he did not live to complete, in which he would prove that Christianity in Scotland had always, until the Reformation, been episcopal and Roman in organisation. At the same time the *Essay* served for Innes the political purpose of upholding the Divine Right of the Stuart monarchy, by exposing as historical errors the seditious democratic principles based on the fabulous history of the early kings to which George Buchanan had given such prominence. Yet in the *Critical Essay* neither of these motives shows itself in any ostentatious way; with only slight digressions into religion and politics, the work reads as a straightforward account by an antiquarian scholar, who had spent many years in study, seeking historical accuracy.

Innes nowhere expresses his philosophy of history as clearly and as succinctly as did Mackenzie. His ideas must be brought together from hints scattered throughout his book, from comments in letters to his antiquary friends, and from the execution of the work

18 Ibid., pp. 10-11.

19 Sir James Dalrymple, *Collections concerning the Scottish History Preceeding the Death of King David the First*, Edinburgh, 1705, p. i; letter of Thomas Innes to James Edgar, 8 April 1730: 'As to My Lord Panmure, you know he was one of the principal Assistants to Sir Geo. Mackenzie in his two Books agt. St Asaph and Stillingfleet in defence of the 40 kings . . . '. Edinburgh University Library MS. La. III. 346.

20 Thomas Innes, *A Critical Essay on the Ancient Inhabitants of the Northern Parts of Britain, or Scotland*, 2 vols., London, 1729 (hereafter cited as *Essay*); reprinted, with an introduction by George Grub, as Volume 8 (1879) of *The Historians of Scotland*, Edinburgh, 1871-80. Page references in brackets are to the reprinted edition.

itself. He was aware that a problem relating to historical knowledge existed, but considered that it had been solved. 'We live
in an age in which all ancient accounts of history, however con-
fidently delivered in the finest dress by modern writers, are brought
back to a trial, and, whatever vogue they may have had for an
age or two, are allowed by the best judges of these kind of performances no more credit than what is due to their vouchers'.[21]
His activities as a historian he describes as 'my sincere endeavours
to search impartially after truth, and a fixed resolution to prefer,
upon occasions, what I conceived most conformable to it, before
all prejudices whatsoever';[22] and he requests to be 'allowed to speak
out what I conceive is most conformable to truth, leaving to evry-
one [sic] the freedom to contradict or refute, as he shall find
reason, what I may happen to advance'.[23] The 'trial' to which
history is brought is the operation of a sceptical attitude of mind;
'what I conceive is conformable to truth' is the 'moral certainty'
of Chillingworth, Tillotson, and Mackenzie, to be obtained and
judged by the 'vouchers'—Mackenzie's 'Warrands'—or historical
evidence. Innes combats total historical scepticism in the same way
as Mackenzie, just as the seekers after religious certainty countered
religious scepticism and as the scientists of the late seventeenth
century justified scientific knowledge, by relying on evidence considered impartially. Scepticism is being replaced by criticism, and
Innes regarded himself as living in an era of 'the renewall of
criticism'. At the same time he recognises that this process, and the
'truth' or knowledge derived from it, is purely personal, and that
others, examining the same evidence, are at liberty to accept or
reject his conclusions. Philosophically this is a point of some
significance.

Where Innes differs totally from Mackenzie is in his attitude
towards the nature of valid historical evidence. The native tradition
of the people, which Mackenzie revered so highly, is of negligible
importance to Innes, 'the uncertain and fabulous relations of bards,
a set of illiterate men'. 'Nothing', Innes asserts, 'is more capable
to decry the history of any country . . . than for an author to put
the bards' accounts of it, in remote ages, on a level with the
histories written in times of learning, and to seem to give equal
credit to both, and make use indifferently of them for vouchers'.[24]
Unconfirmed oral tradition is the least valuable form of historical

[21] *Essay*, Vol. I, p. xv [5-6].
[22] Ibid., p. xi [4].
[23] Letter of Thomas Innes to Harry Maule, 27 February 1731: Scottish
Record Office, GD45/14/387; printed in *Registrum de Panmure*, John Stuart
(ed.), Edinburgh, 1874, Vol. I, p. cxxii.
[24] *Essay*, Vol. I, pp. 123-4 [83-4].

evidence, and is an unreliable guide to any conformity with truth.

With one exception—George Buchanan—Innes regards earlier Scottish historical writers highly as far as their reputation is concerned. But, unlike Mackenzie, he does not feel that, because former writers were men of good repute and wrote in good faith, their works must be accepted as totally trustworthy authorities, or as valid historical evidence. Their writings must be examined critically, compared with those of other writers and with other sources, and their vouchers tested. This is what Innes means when he writes, in a letter to Harry Maule describing the *Critical Essay*, 'the schemes of our history by all our famed historians are discussed to the bottom'; and this is confirmed by an examination of the *Essay* itself. In the same letter Innes draws attention to a very revealing part of his method: 'I have taken all the care I could . . . by describing the times, circumstances, and prejudices that reigned when they [i.e. earlier historians] wrote . . . [to show] that in those circumstances they could not write otherwise than they did, and that if we had lived under alike circumstances we had probably believed and given the same account of our history and antiquities as they have done'.[25] Innes realised that a former historian was a creature of his own time, subject to the beliefs and pressures existing at that time, and that this must be considered as part of the critical operation of judging the validity of the evidence he has to offer. The work of a former historical writer, although he is to be considered seriously as living nearer the time about which he was writing, must, in Innes's view, be examined critically before being accepted as evidence to provide a conformity with truth.

The most valid pieces of historical evidence for Innes are actual relics of the times being examined. He is aware of the value of archaeological specimens, and he tentatively uses the linguistic evidence of place names; but most important to the historian are contemporary documents. He praises Fordun, who in the fourteenth century 'spared neither labour nor diligence to restore the history of his country: and for that end travelled over all *Scotland,* searching everywhere the libraries, churches, monasteries, colleges, universities, and towns, gathering together whatever remains he could meet with to his purpose'.[26] He himself, at great personal danger (for Roman Catholic priests were still subject to severe penal laws), searched likewise, visiting the Advocates' Library in Edinburgh in 1724, examining the Cottonian and Harleian manu-

25 Letter of Innes to Maule, 5 April 1729, printed in *Panmure*, Vol. I, p. cxviii.
26 *Essay*, Vol. I, p. 204 [124-5].

scripts in London, persuading private individuals to open their charter-chests to him, and studying the archives of his own Scots College in Paris. To him documents are essential as sources for history: 'as all ancient histories depend upon the credit of their vouchers, so, besides other qualities, the more the transactions related in a history are ancient and extraordinary, the more ancient must also be the vouchers that attest them'.[27] Hence documents must be preserved: 'I cannot hinder myself from adding, that it were to be wished . . . that greater care had been . . . taken by the publick . . . for the preservation of the few remains we have still left of ancient records'.[28] And not only preserved, but published: 'Nothing could contribute more to the honour of the *Irish* nation, in this critical age, than that some of their learned men would . . . render publick such vouchers of [their history] as may bear the test of these times; . . . [and] publish in a body of history, as other polite nations have done, and daily continue to do, their chronicles and annals . . .'.[29] These documents must 'bear the test of these times'. In other words they must be critically examined to eliminate the possibility of historical error arising from prejudice, ignorance, or even downright forgery. Here Innes is adopting the standards of documentary criticism evolved some forty years before by Jean Mabillon, whom he had known personally. Only when documents had passed such tests could their evidence begin to be used to assess the past.

Allied to this modern attitude towards documentary evidence Innes had a decidedly academic attitude towards the layout of his book, which he provided with detailed footnote references and appendices of transcripts of manuscripts. 'In all the more important occasions, I have set down and quoted my authorities, and those either from authors already published, or from MSS. to which the access is easy, and I have printed in the appendix such short MS. pieces as seemed more curious, or more proper to give light to the subject, and serve for proofs.'[30] These transcriptions of difficult manuscript originals can scarcely be bettered by present-day scholars.

It was not easy for Innes to use his historical method rigorously in his study of the early Scottish monarchy, for documentary evidence from this period was virtually non-existent. Much of his *Critical Essay*, therefore, is devoted to a critical examination of what we today would call the secondary sources, the same sources in fact that Mackenzie had examined from a more prejudiced

27 Ibid., Vol. II, p. 419 [235].
28 Ibid., Vol. I, pp. xxix-xxx [11].
29 Ibid., Vol. II, p. 505 [278].
30 Ibid., Vol. I, p. xlix [19].

viewpoint. His critical techniques were almost certainly based on those evolved by Pierre Bayle, whose *Dictionnaire* Innes undoubtedly knew, for his friend Harry Maule possessed a copy.[31] Included in his analysis was a study of some of the 'modern' Scottish writers, particularly Fordun, Boethius, and Buchanan, in which he showed that the attitude they adopted reflected the times in which they wrote, and, in Buchanan's case, the workings of a psychologically complex character. Buchanan, Innes asserted, deliberately distorted the past against all reason to support the tenets of his political philosophy, an opinion which Innes supports by rational argument, in contrast to Mackenzie's crude denigratory methods of dealing with his opponents.

The crux of Innes's argument, however, is a comparative analysis of the lists of the early Scottish kings, and it was here that he was able to use, in a relatively modern way, his techniques of documentary criticism. In his searches throughout British and Continental libraries Innes had succeeded in discovering several versions of the names of the early Scottish kings, lists written at different times between the eleventh and the fifteenth centuries, the earliest one in Gaelic. An analysis of these lists showed a growing distortion of the names of the kings, through misunderstanding by Latin-writing scribes of the Gaelic original and through self-perpetuating scribal errors. Innes then compared these lists with the succession of kings as given by Hector Boethius, the succession on which the whole picture of early Scottish history was based in the seventeenth century; it was this succession which Boethius had derived from his mysterious lost authorities Veremundus and Campbell, who, according to him, were writers of the eleventh and twelfth centuries. Innes was able to show that many fictitious names had been added and that the forms of the names of the kings which Boethius gave (and therefore those which he found in his alleged twelfth-century sources) were in fact corruptions of the corrupt fifteenth-century lists of kings, not of the twelfth-century lists and still less of the earlier Gaelic list. Boethius's sources, especially Veremundus, Innes concludes, could not have come from the twelfth century, but were fifteenth-century forgeries which Boethius had accepted in good faith; and Innes typically goes on to advance a hypothesis why, in the political conditions of late fifteenth-century Scotland, such forgeries should have been made. If Veremundus was a forgery (and no manuscript had survived for Innes to analyse) then not only Boethius's history of the period but also Buchanan's fell utterly to the ground, and the whole history of the

---

[31] *Panmure*, Vol. I, p. lxxiii.

early kings of Scotland, including the democratic principles on which their rule was conducted, was exposed as a myth.

In Mackenzie's view Boethius, as a man of honour and good repute, must provide an acceptable view of the past, even though his 'Warrand' Veremundus was no longer in existence, just as Livy had given a picture of the early days of Rome which in spite of his lost sources was generally accepted. Innes, sceptical of the missing manuscript of Veremundus, in effect reconstructs the evidence it must have contained and finds it, in comparison with genuine documents, wanting.

Both men solved the problem of total historical scepticism by positing a view of history based on the impartial examination of the evidence of the past. Both men were concerned to uphold the influence and power of the Stuart monarchy and of an episcopal church. Where they differed was in their attitudes towards historical evidence; Mackenzie revered tradition and authority and accepted this as valid evidence, while Innes, trained in critical historical analysis, could accept only what had been tested to the furthest point. The writing of Mackenzie reads like the speech of an advocate defending a cause rather than the work of a historian searching for the truth about the past. Innes, although he admits to prejudice, gives the impression of a more impartial approach; his ideal historian was William Camden, whom he describes as a writer who 'had candor and equity, that preserved him from being biassed, and judgment to discern what might be relied upon . . .'.[32] By this impartial and critical interpretation of the historical evidence, Innes constructed a picture of early Scotland which, in its broad outlines, is still acceptable to present-day historians of the period. But, equally important, he discovered more than half the vital documentary sources which these historians must still study, and also, however crudely, laid the foundations of the critical method they must still use.

Innes, then, is a forward-looking historian. Does he look forward to the historians of the Scottish Enlightenment, David Hume and William Robertson? Both these writers, of course, had a much wider conception of the nature of history and a clearer idea of the processes of historical change, and it is this that made them great historians. They looked at the society of the past as a whole, not as a series of historical events; they knew that change was inevitable in society, and that the function of history was to describe and analyse these changes, not to justify the present by reference to the past. Both Hume and Robertson, basing their opinion on Innes's arguments, rejected the idea of the ancient

[32] *Essay*, Vol. I, p. xxxiv [13].

democratic constitution of the Scottish kings, realising not only that the growth of democratic ideas in the seventeenth century was part of a natural social development, but also that these ideas did not need to be justified historically as a restoration of ancient liberties, and could not be overthrown by attacking their 'historical' basis. Neither Mackenzie nor Innes could have understood this conception of the nature of history; for them, especially Mackenzie, society was unchanging and unchanged, and the purpose of history was to guide and warn, by example from the past, the governors of the present day, and to justify their policies.

There is one philosophical point in which Innes, although he did not express his ideas in philosophical form or language, can be regarded as a precursor of Hume. Through admitting and allowing for his prejudices, he believed he could attain a more impartial interpretation of the past and thus a closer approximation to historical truth; yet he was the first in Scotland to realise, many years before Hume made the same point, that complete impartiality was impossible and that ultimately any historical interpretation was an individual, a personal, glimpse of the past.

Both Hume and Robertson followed Innes in the critical examination of sources, taking great pains to establish their facts with exactitude. Robertson, for example, in writing his *History of America* in the early 1770s, compiled a detailed questionnaire which he circulated widely in America, Spain, and France, in order to gain reliable information about the American Indians, information which he subjected to critical analysis.[33] Hume, as Keeper of the Advocates' Library in Edinburgh, had full access to the books and manuscripts there which provided the facts he critically analysed. This critical method was part of the climate of the time, yet it is significant for Scottish historical writing that these Enlightenment figures were not the first to use it.

In one important respect, in his use of rigorous methods of documentary criticism, Innes was looking beyond these Enlightenment historians. Neither Hume nor Robertson, although they cite references to manuscript material, followed Innes in this method. Hume refers on a few occasions to manuscripts in the Advocates' collection, but, even if he had wanted to (and it probably would not have been congenial for him), he could not have subjected these particular manuscripts to documentary analysis, for the items he cites are not original documents but copies made by earlier Scottish antiquaries.[34] In his development of documentary criticism

[33] National Library of Scotland, MS. 3954, ff.11-94.
[34] For example, in his *History of England under the House of Tudor*, Vol. II, London, 1759, Hume refers on several occasions (pp. 502, 514, 516, 574, etc.) to Advocates' Manuscripts A.3.28 and 29 (now in the National Library of Scotland,

in Scotland, Innes is a precursor not of these notable eighteenth-century writers but rather of those Scottish historians of the nineteenth century who, through their critical analysis and publication of manuscript sources as advocated by Innes, laid a secure foundation for the modern study of Scotland's past.

Adv.MS. 35.1.1). These volumes were compiled about 1700 by David Crawfurd of Drumsoy, who had copied the text from manuscripts of earlier Scottish antiquaries, who in turn had copied from various Cotton manuscripts in the Caligula series. Hume was aware of and acknowledged the fact that he was citing copies of Cotton manuscripts, but there is no evidence that he checked his copies with the originals or examined the originals critically. With the exception of one other item, cited as Lord Royston's manuscript, which was probably also a series of transcripts made in the eighteenth century, Hume refers to no other manuscript source in his major historical works.

Modernisation, Mass Education and Social Mobility in French Thought, 1750-1789[1]

James A. Leith

During this century of philosophers the general cry is that it is necessary to educate men. Everybody sets himself up as tutor of the human race.

Letter to the editor of the
Journal de Troyes, 1784[2]

The development of the modern state has been marked by the centralisation of political authority, the creation of specialised ministries, the standardisation of administrative regions, the secularisation of functions hitherto performed by the church, and by the substitution—at least in principle—of talent and training in place of privilege as criteria for bureaucratic appointments. Viewed from the twentieth century, France in 1750 appears to have been a half-modernised state. French kings had centralised political authority, but their power was still restricted by local customs and refractory officials secure in ownership of their offices. Many modern ministries did not yet exist—among them departments of the interior, justice, commerce, public works, and the post office. Underneath the superstructure of the central state lay a bewildering patchwork of military, civil, judicial, financial, and ecclesiastical divisions. Even economic unity was incomplete with about a third of the country remaining outside the customs union established by Colbert. The church still performed many functions later considered

[1] This paper is a by-product of preparation of a two-volume study of educational ideas in the last half of the eighteenth century in France, to be entitled *Education for Citizenship*, one volume dealing with the Old Régime, the other with the Revolution. In discussing mass education here I do not intend to treat education for girls since this would make the paper much too lengthy.

[2] 'A. M. le Rédacteur . . .', *Journal de la Ville de Troyes et de la Champagne Méridionale*, 1784, IIIe année, No. 14, 7 avril, p. 54.

the responsibility of the state. And government reflected a social structure divided into various orders and permeated with special privileges. The efforts of various reformers under the Old Régime and the more extreme measures of the revolutionaries can be seen partly as attempts to modernise this obsolescent state.

Nowhere was the half-modernised condition of France in the middle of the eighteenth century more obvious than in the sphere of education. Over the centuries a network of educational institutions had grown up, but central government direction and administrative uniformity were incomplete. There was no ministry of education and the state interested itself in educational matters only spasmodically and to a limited extent. It was most active at the top of the educational pyramid, subsidising various academies, supporting special schools for the army or navy or certain professions, paying the professors of the prestigious Collège de France, and financing the Observatory and the Jardin des Plantes in Paris. Even at this level the universities were usually left on their own. There was no budgetary provision for education generally. In so far as the central government did intervene in educational matters it often had to share its role with the powerful sovereign courts or parlements. And most educational institutions remained more or less directly under the control of the church.

Secondary education was largely in the hands of the colleges of the teaching congregations or the arts faculties of the universities. These offered a six-year course in the humanities, plus another two years of 'philosophy', for boys who at about the age of ten had already learned to read and write and do some arithmetic at a primary school or elsewhere. The curriculum remained centred on the classics, especially Latin authors and composition, although some teaching orders were already introducing more science and history. Philosophy was still dominated by a scholastic approach. Since most colleges were under the control of teaching orders religious instruction and services still bulked large in the life of these institutions. There were approximately 562 colleges on the eve of the Revolution providing for more than 70,000 students of whom about 40,000 held bursaries of some sort. There were, of course, some more students in seminaries and other secondary institutions, but judging by recent demographic tables all these schools probably provided facilities for about three-and-a-half per cent of college age males.[3]

<hr/>

[3] One of the best sources of statistical information about colleges under the Old Régime is still the appendix to the report by Abel-François Villemain, *Chambre des Pairs. Session de 1843-1844. Projet de loi sur l'instruction secondaire, précédé de l'exposé des motifs par M. Villemain, ministre de l'instruction publique. Séance du 2 février 1844*, Paris, n.d. For a breakdown of the French

Elementary education was provided in a number of ways, but was very unevenly distributed throughout the country. In the late seventeenth and early eighteenth centuries a series of royal decrees had called for establishment of schools in every parish, but these decrees were aimed not so much at creating a national system of primary schools as at providing Catholic indoctrination for all children in the wake of revocation of the Edict of Nantes. In any case since there were no state grants to back up these decrees many communities had difficulties raising the necessary funds. At this level too education remained largely in the hands of the church. To teach in a *petite école* masters had to have a licence, renewable annually, issued by a representative of the bishop. The state in the person of the intendant had to confirm the appointment, but only to ensure that the contract between the teacher and his employers was being observed. Licensed teachers were entitled to charge fees which varied greatly from region to region. In fact in some places no fees were exacted because the schools had been endowed by benefactors. In the capital and some large towns there were writing schools run by the Scriveners' Corporation. In many parishes the local priest started an elementary school financed by church funds and staffed by himself or his curate. Other charity schools were founded by private individuals or religious orders. The results of this mixed bag of primary schools were extremely uneven, but in all of France on the eve of the Revolution less than half the bridegrooms could sign their names—and that is not a very exacting test of literacy.[4]

From the mid-century onwards scores of writers proposed reforms of this antiquated and incoherent educational system. They poured out their pleas in books, essays, journal articles, letters to editors, and even occasional poems. The majority called for some means of government control so that the schools would turn out citizens dedicated to the state. Also they demanded thorough revision of

population by age groups see the chapter by J. Bourgeois-Pichat, 'The General Development of the Population of France since the Eighteenth Century', in *Population in History*, D. V. Glass and D. E. C. Eversley (eds.), London, 1965, pp. 474-506, especially the table on p. 479.

[4] On the eve of the educational reforms introduced by Jules Ferry, the historian of education Louis Maggiolo was commissioned to mobilise teachers throughout France to accumulate statistics about those capable of signing marriage registers at different periods. His report, *Ministère de l'instruction publique. Statistique Rétrospective. Etat récapitulatif et comparatif indiquant, par département, le nombre des conjoints qui ont signé l'acte de leur marriage, au XVIIe, XVIIIe et XIXe siècles. Documents fournis par 15,928 instituteurs*, Paris, n.d. is still very useful, although the probe was less thorough in some regions than in others and was weak in the large cities where primary schools were more plentiful. Maggiolo's tables are the basis for the maps in M. Fleury and P. Valmary, 'Les Progrès de l'instruction élémentaire de Louis XIV à Napoléon III', *Population*, XII année, 1957, pp. 71-92.

the curriculum so that the graduates would be trained to adapt to and contribute to modern society instead of being foreigners in their own country as some authors put it. For these reformers the new criterion of social utility tended to push other values aside. They demanded less Latin and more living languages, modern history, social geography, political studies, mathematics, physics, and technology. They contended that in an enlightened century the old curriculum was completely out of date. 'Is Gothic architecture still in use?' asked one writer sarcastically in 1762.[5]

The agitation of these educational reformers coincided with other attempts to modernise the obsolescent French state—to strengthen central authority, to streamline the administration, to reduce fiscal anomalies, to complete economic unification, to abolish guild restrictions, to secularise citizenship by granting toleration, and even to create an aristocracy based on merit rather than birth. Most educational reformers were intent on laying the cultural and psychological basis for a modern society and more effective state. 'The whole object of education is to produce men, citizens useful to the fatherland', the Abbé Pellicier argued in 1763.[6] His viewpoint was constantly restated in the following decades. The proponents of educational reform were convinced that in order to improve society and renovate the state they would have to remake men's minds.

But education for citizenship seemed to demand public schools, since only they could be given a uniform purpose under government direction. In the seventeenth century and the early eighteenth the stress had been on private education. D'Alembert's provocative article 'College' in the *Encyclopédie* in 1753 might be seen as a turning point. Admittedly he damned the existing public schools and recommended private education for those who could afford it, but significantly he proffered this advice provisionally. He contended that only the government was powerful enough to challenge the existing antiquated system. 'But while waiting for this reform which our descendants perhaps will have the good fortune to enjoy', he wrote, 'I do not hesitate to believe that college education, such as it is, is subject to many more disadvantages than private education . . .'.[7] In the following decades most educational reformers

[5] [Jean-Baptiste Daragon] *Lettre de M.xxx à M. L'Abbé.xxx, professeur de philosophie en l'Université de Paris, sur la nécessité et la manière de faire entrer un cours de morale dans l'éducation publique*, Paris, 1762, p. 55.

[6] Abbé Pellicier, *Mémoires sur la nécessité de fonder une école pour former des maîtres, selon le plan d'éducation donné par le parlement en son arrêt du 3 septembre 1762*, Paris, 1763, p. 2.

[7] Jean le Rond d'Alembert, 'Collège', *Encyclopédie* . . . , 17 vols., Paris, Neufchastel, etc., 1751-65, Vol. III, pp. 634-7. Quotation p. 637. Roland Mortier, '*Les Philosophes* and Public Education', *Yale French Studies*, No. 40, 1968,

believed that public education could be transformed. But if a reno-
vated public school system was created, whom should it serve? How
much instruction should be provided for the masses?

Several objectives of these educational innovators might seem to
have involved mass education. Many of the reformers campaigned
for a national system of education which in time would create
an identical outlook throughout France. The very title of La
Chalotais's *Essai d'éducation nationale,* which appeared in 1763,
had revolutionary implications, but the magistrate from Rennes did
not spell out the administrative changes which would have been
necessary to create a national school system.[8] Subsequently Rolland
d'Erceville, who draughted the proposals of the Paris parlement,
advocated a vast educational structure which he claimed would
eventually knit the country closer together by imbuing all Frenchmen with the same outlook. The University of Paris would oversee,
not only the colleges of its region, but also the provincial universities, which in turn would supervise the colleges in their districts.
The colleges would then regulate the lower educational institutions.
Rolland and most later reformers demanded uniform state textbooks as one means of stamping a national character on all
Frenchmen.[9]

The faith that education could bring about moral progress might
likewise be expected to have produced a demand for popular education. Guyton de Morveau, the attorney-general of the parlement
at Dijon, was typical of many educational reformers in his confidence that education could regenerate society. While he conceded
that the idea of the natural goodness of men might be questionable
from a moral point of view, it was valuable from a political
standpoint. The idea of innate perversity gave rise to a dangerous
fatalism. It was far better to assume that wickedness was a product
of wrong education. Guyton hoped that the schools would in time
be able to break the vicious cycle of generations which perpetuated
immorality in the home. By inculcating social morality the schools
could produce parents better able to provide moral training for
preschoolers. The schools would then find it easier to engender
civic virtues in these children. Over several generations the schools

---

pp. 62-76, does not point out that d'Alembert clearly implied that public education could possibly be reformed to his liking.

[8] L.-R. Caradeuc de la Chalotais, *Essai d'éducation nationale, ou plan
d'études pour la jeunesse,* n.p., 1763, *passim.*

[9] B.-G. Rolland d'Erceville, *Recueil de plusieurs des ouvrages de M. le Prési-
dent Rolland, imprimé en exécution des délibérations du Bureau d'administration du Collège de Louis-le-Grand des 17 janvier et 18 avril 1782,* Paris, 1783,
pp. 8-24. On textbooks, pp. 128-9, 184-5, 216-23, and 770-1.

could approach the goal of perfecting social behaviour.[10] Soon some reformers spoke of creating *une génération toute nouvelle*.[11]

Moreover the hope of improving productivity through application of modern knowledge might also be expected to have led to a demand to educate every Tom, Dick, and Harry. For example the Comte de Vauréal, a former army engineer, argued that national education was the sole means of improving production. 'It is the only way that the nation can perfect its agriculture, its commerce, and become illustrious and flourishing', he wrote half a dozen years before the Revolution.[12] The Promethean vision of an utter transformation of nature which has inspired some modern revolutionaries was not yet fully developed. That would have to await observation of the advances in production during the nineteenth century. But already in eighteenth-century France many reformers believed that the latest information about agriculture and manufacturing could substantially improve both the quantity and quality of production.

The highest hope of the proponents of mass education was for a generally enlightened citizenry. Such an ideal can best be seen in the utopian novels of writers such as Louis-Sébastien Mercier who entitled his vision of the future *L'An 2440*. Such utopian visions often reveal the highest aspirations of an age, just as dreams may reveal the deepest yearnings of an individual. Significantly Mercier's ideal society was set, not in some imaginary land or undiscovered island, but in France itself. In this new France a free, universal, compulsory state system of schools aims at the happiness of all Frenchmen. In these schools, whose program embodies most of the content commonly advocated by eighteenth-century reformers —living languages, modern science, practical arts, moral instruction, and civic indoctrination—children are moulded into united, virtuous, productive, rational citizens.[13] Evidently Mercier rejected Voltaire's pessimistic view that the rabble, mired in poverty and

---

[10] L.-B. Guyton de Morveau, *Mémoire sur l'éducation publique avec le prospectus d'un collège suivant les principes de cet ouvrage*, s.l., 1764, pp. 12-21.

[11] C.-A. Comte de Thélis, *Plan d'éducation nationale, en faveur des pauvres enfans de la campagne . . .* , s.l., 1779, pp. 16-17.

[12] Comte de Vauréal, *Plan ou essai d'éducation général, ou la meilleure éducation à donner aux hommes de toutes les nations*, Bouillon, 1783, p. 6. See also p. 57 where he speaks of the need for *la patrie* to use all available means of strengthening social bonds 'if she wishes to perfect her economic structure'.

[13] Louis-Sébastien Mercier, *L'An Deux Mille Quatre Cent Quarante. Rêve s'il en fût jamais*, London, 1772, 3e édition, 3 vols. [Amsterdam], 1786, Vol. I, pp. 76ff and Vol. II, pp. 161ff. Similar views were expressed by Guillaume Grivel, *L'Isle inconnue, ou mémoires du Chevalier Des Gastines*, Paris, 6 vols., 1783-7, although Grivel was less certain of the perfectibility of man.

ignorance, would always outnumber thinking men one hundred to one.[14]

Some reformers were willing, not only to promote mass education, but to accept and even encourage the social mobility which this might produce. For example in an *Essai sur les moyens de réformer l'éducation* published in 1764 Fleury, a retired professor of mathematics and engineering, called on the state to direct education so as to turn out useful citizens on a massive scale. Moreover his whole system was devised to create opportunities for the lower classes whose talented offspring were often lost to the state because of financial difficulties. 'It is easy to see that it is my intention that even citizens of the lowest rank not be neglected', he wrote. 'Yes, let us speak plainly, the poor themselves, the children of the poor will be raised up forever from poverty and be placed without distinction alongside the leaders of the state'. Children of all classes would attend primary schools which would be free for indigent students. Able students would then advance to various professional academies.[15] Fleury thus showed no fears of mass education and upward mobility, but many of his fellow reformers had serious misgivings about too much education for the people.

One common fear was that the over-educated peasant or artisan would become a troublemaker because he would no longer know his place in society. In a letter to the *Journal de la ville de Troyes*, which featured a controversy over country schools in 1784, one correspondent expressed this view humorously, supposedly passing on the observations of his cousin who was a country priest. He agreed that a peasant who, in addition to some religious training, knew only how to read, write, and calculate a little was certainly no scholar. But teach him a smattering of 'Jography', some 'Jometry', and a bit about 'Lectricity', tell him that the sun, which he believes is no bigger than the opening to his oven, is a million times larger than the earth, and you will produce a social disturber:

> My cousin says that with all these things you will turn the head of your peasant, you will make him into a dangerous man, you will push him beyond the limits of his understanding. He will confuse everything and will become an all the more insufferable ignoramus because he will think that he is a first class scholar. He will despise his equals and even his priest.[16]

[14] Voltaire, *Oeuvres complètes*, L. Moland (ed.), 52 vols., Paris, 1877-85, Vol. XXX, p. 549. This pessimistic view was expressed in 1777 shortly before his death.
[15] N.-M. de Fleury, *Essai sur les moyens de réformer l'éducation particulière et générale, destiné à l'instruction des pères et mères, à celle des directeurs de collèges et de tous les éducateurs* . . . , Paris, 1764, pp. 23-53. Quotation pp. 48-9.
[16] 'Lettre au Rédacteur . . .', *Journal de la Ville de Troyes et de la Champagne Méridionale*, 1784, IIIe année, No. 38, 22 septembre, pp. 151-2.

Above all many educational reformers dreaded that exposure to literature and science would create in peasants and artisans a distaste for those tasks which were painful but essential to society. La Chalotais warned that it was always dangerous to increase the number of those who consumed what others produced instead of producing themselves. France in his opinion had too many priests, too many lawyers, too many writers. Even labourers and artisans were sending their children to colleges in the smaller cities where the cost of living was not too high. These children learned to disdain their fathers' occupations and frequently became harmful citizens. La Chalotais criticised the Christian Brothers for teaching children to read and write who only needed to be shown how to manipulate a plane or file but no longer wanted to do so. 'Every man who sees beyond his dreary craft will never carry it out patiently and courageously', the magistrate contended.[17]

As they developed a repugnance for their humble chores peasants would depopulate the countryside by flocking into the cities. 'People complain that the fields lack workers, that the number of artisans decreases, and that the class of vagabonds increases', wrote Philipon de la Madeleine, a royal attorney in Franche-Comté. 'Let us look for the cause no further than the multitude of schools with which our towns and villages abound. There is not a hamlet which does not have its grammarian'.[18] This fear of rural depopulation strikes the modern historian as somewhat odd since we know that the population had expanded steadily, producing numerous beggars in many provinces. France was probably overpopulated given the existing productivity of her agriculture, but only a few contemporaries such as the Abbé Eyrard pointed out that there were plenty of potential labourers provided that they trained to do something useful.[19] Many Frenchmen feared that too much schooling might leave agriculture, the very basis of national prosperity, with insufficient muscle power.

And as they migrated from the countryside peasants would be exposed to the alleged moral contagion of city life. The Comte de Thélis, author of a whole series of memorials on national educa-

---

17 La Chalotais, *Essai d'éducation*, pp. 23-7. Quotation p. 26.

18 Louis Philipon de la Madeleine, *Vues patriotiques sur l'éducation du peuple tant des villes que de la campagne; avec beaucoup de notes intéressantes*, Lyon, 1783, p. 17.

19 Abbé François Eyrard, *Observations sur l'éducation publique pour servir de réponse aux questions proposées par MM. les agens généraux du clergé de France à N.N.S.S. les archevêques et érègues de l'Eglise gallicane*, Paris, 1786, pp. 46-47. Later during the revolution the Comité de mendicité concluded that in fact France had an excess population relative to agricultural production and employment opportunities.

tion as the means of achieving a moral revolution, was extremely anxious to protect peasants from the baneful luxury and licentiousness of big-city life.[20] At the same time the Comte de Vauréal, another proponent of national education as the means for establishing the ethical foundation of the state, depicted the city as an artificial and unhealthy milieu. The urban child developed much less naturally than the youngster raised in the country. He babbled words he did not understand and exhausted himself physically even before he reached maturity. 'Should people be surprised', asked the Count, 'that his life is one prolonged lie, an error, a delirium, and that his imagination contains all the reveries destined to amuse our posterity . . .?'[21] However, since the eleventh century the city had been the source of most of the economic advances, technological improvements, and administrative innovations in western civilisation. Paradoxically many educational modernisers feared the well-spring of modernity.

But in *le siècle éclairé*, when men rejoiced over the dissemination of knowledge, it was difficult to oppose mass education. A few spoke out openly against too much education for the lower classes. Many more revealed their misgivings by their silences and omissions. Others designed plans for schools which reflected the existing hierarchical social structure. And some who appeared to be champions of popular education proposed an extremely limited curriculum for ordinary primary schools and provided for very little progression into higher institutions. Or they reassured those who feared mass education that change would be so slow that the social repercussions would be minimal. Misgivings affected all social groups, but viewpoints varied, not only according to the class origins of the authors, but also to their personal convictions and attitudes. Often men who were very progressive in advocating state control and curriculum reform proved very conservative in their reluctance to shake the existing social order.

Many of the clergy showed little enthusiasm for extending mass education, although in the 1750s and 1760s four successive church assemblies had called for more parish schools. In the 1770s churchmen who wrote about education usually ignored the lower classes.[22]

---

[20] C.-A. Comte de Thélis *et al.*, *Mémoires concernant les écoles nationales*, Paris, 1781 (-1789), 18 fasc. rel. en 1 vol., No. 1, pp. 12-14. See also No. 5, pp. 6-7 where the Duc de Charost argues that emigration of country folk to the cities exposes them to libertine influences.

[21] Vauréal, *Plan ou essai*, p. 81.

[22] Abbé Le More, *Principes d'institution, ou la manière d'élever les enfans des deux sexes par rapport au corps, à l'esprit et au coeur*, Paris, 1774, was typical in that the author sketches a program for ecclesiastics, officers, and magistrates, but not for lower-class occupations. The Abbé Athanase Auger, *Discours sur l'éducation, prononcés au collège royal de Rouen*, Rouen, 1775, proposed a

A decade before the Revolution the Assembly of the French clergy did order its agents to distribute a questionnaire to all priests asking for suggestions as to how public education could be improved, but the questions reveal that the clergy were primarily concerned about secondary education. Those ecclesiastics who wrote lengthy replies focused entirely on reform of the colleges. In a work entitled *De l'éducation publique* the Abbé Proyard advocated various reforms including creation of a special institution for training teachers, but the fact that it would graduate only six principals and fifty professors each year revealed that the Abbé had no intention of opening colleges to the masses. In fact he speaks of supplying teachers for one hundred colleges, many fewer than already existed. And he relegated discussion of education of peasants—the bulk of the population—to a footnote.[23] The Abbé Eyrard, who also wrote in response to the church questionnaire, defended educating poor countryfolk, but he was mainly concerned with allowing a few of them to become priests, thus siphoning off some potential vagabonds. He too gave almost all his attention to secondary schools.[24]

The sword aristocrats who wrote on public education also revealed their distrust of too much schooling for the masses. The Comte de Thélis, who as we have seen was a persistent advocate of a national educational system, dreaded disruption of the social hierarchy and emigration to the cities. He advocated boarding schools in the country staffed with former army officers to train poor lower-class children to be both good soldiers and able workers. Above all he wanted these schools to inculcate a work ethic which would prepare lower-class youths for their arduous tasks in society. Indigent young nobles were also to be admitted to these schools; however, they would be preparing for positions of command. The offspring of the two classes would take religious training together and drill together, but they would study and live separately because in later life their roles would be different.[25] The Comte de Vauréal, another champion of national education, argued that it would be madness to extend education indiscriminately. Order in nature as confirmed by modern science would be used to teach the child to accept the place in society which fate had allotted him, 'that perfection in each category alone brings the pleasures which

---

scheme for national education, but he too discussed only the needs of the privileged classes.

[23] Abbé Proyart, *De l'éducation publique, et des moyens de réaliser la réforme projetée dans la dernière assemblée générale du clergé de France*, Paris, 1785, pp. 63-7 and 151-2.

[24] Eyrard, *Observations*, pp. 46-51.

[25] In addition to the two works by Thélis already mentioned see his *Règlement concernant les écoles nationales, du 12 février 1780*, Paris, n.d.

expand existence and create real distinctions between one man and another'.[26] And although his book claimed to put forward a general plan for education he made no proposals for improving popular education.

The magistrates of the various parlements who wrote about education at the time of the suppression of the Jesuits and closure of their colleges revealed their fears of too much education for the common people. At Rennes La Chalotais who, as we have seen, feared lest education make the peasant or artisan discontented with his lot, urged that training in reading and writing be confined to those who actually needed such skills for their work and called for abolition of many colleges.[27] 'National education will then be aimed at only a million men while twenty million will not be taken into account', protested Crevier, a historian and professor of rhetoric,[28] but La Chalotais's fellow magistrates sided with him. At Dijon Guyton de Morveau, fearing that the arts and sciences might lure too many men from useful tasks, advocated abolishing the first class—the 'sixth' as it was called—in order to make preparatory education prohibitively expensive. In addition he suggested limiting large colleges, where advanced work was done, to provincial capitals. Only the best students from the smaller colleges would be admitted.[29] At Paris Rolland d'Erceville proposed a very restricted curriculum for primary schools, limitation of full-scale colleges to large centres, and reduction of the total number of college students. And in a compilation of his various reports totalling almost a thousand pages he devoted only three to discussing popular education.[30]

Spokesmen for the universities and colleges shared the fears of the magistrates. Combalusier, who wrote on behalf of the University of Paris at the time of closure of the Jesuit schools, argued that the government could not give too much attention to education. 'The Nation where children received the best education possible would doubtlessly be the most formidable, the most prosperous, the happiest', he wrote, 'because there all duties would be performed with understanding and precision, there everything would be centred on the Citizen, there everything would be directed to the service of the State'.[31] However, it soon became clear that he is

[26] Vauréal, *Plan ou essai*, pp. 9 and 98-100. Quotation pp. 111-12.
[27] La Chalotais, *Essai d'éducation*, pp. 23-7.
[28] Jean-Baptiste-Louis Crevier, *Difficultés proposées à M. le Caradeuc de la Chalotais . . . sur le mémoire institué 'Essai d'éducation nationale . . .',* Paris, 1763, pp. 10-18. Quotation p. 13.
[29] de Morveau, *Memoire*, pp. 42-51.
[30] d'Erceville, *Recueil*, pp. 24-7.
[31] François de Paule Combalusier, *Mémoire de l'Université sur les moyens de pouvoir à l'instruction de la jeunesse et de la perfectionner*, n.p., n.d. p. 4.

primarily interested in educating an élite. If too widely spread education might deprive the state of useful workers and create a mediocre group of malcontents. Although he stated that real talent should be allowed to advance for the benefit of the state, he too argued that there were too many colleges and wanted the masses confined to learning the true principles of religion, reading, and writing.[32] Other professors, such as Mathias, principal of the college at Langres, in their discussions of public education, simply ignored the masses altogether.[33]

One might expect the upper clergy, titled aristocrats, high-court magistrates, or even university professors to display social conservatism, but one is more surprised to find their misgivings echoed by some progressive intellectuals. D'Alembert opposed free places in the colleges, apparently because he felt that the influx of students lowered the level of teaching.[34] 'I thank you for proscribing study among farm labourers', Voltaire wrote when La Chalotais's book appeared. 'I who cultivate the soil ask you to provide me with manual workers, and not tonsured clerics'.[35] In one of his diverse moods Rousseau remarked in *Emile* that the poor had no need for education.[36] The philosopher Abbé Coyer wanted colleges confined to one in each provincial capital, high fees to keep out the multitude, and reduction of the student body in Paris by about a half through exclusion of external students.[37] Condillac designed a lengthy course of study for the Prince of Parma, but did not discuss popular education.[38] Diderot advocated free compulsory primary education, plus bursaries to allow bright students to go on to higher institutions, but only a few were to move upward.[39]

---

[32] Ibid., pp. 45-8.

[33] [Mathias], *De l'enseignement public, par M.xxx, principal du Collège de Langres*, Paris, 1776. Another later example would be the book by Jean-André Perreau, a law professor at the Collège de France, *Instruction du peuple divisée en trois parties. 1re partie: De la morale; 2e partie: Des affaires; 3e partie: De la santé*, Paris, 1786. Perreau advocated a very limited education for common folk and opposed peasants and artisans sending their children to colleges where they were not trained for any practical occupation and contracted tastes beyond their families' means.

[34] D'Alembert, 'College', p. 637.

[35] Voltaire, *Correspondence*, Th. Besterman (ed.), 107 vols., Genève, 1953-65, Vol. LI, Jan.-Mar. 1763, 10238 (28 février). See Roland Mortier, 'Voltaire et le peuple', *The Age of the Enlightenment: Studies Presented to Theodore Besterman*, W. H. Barber *et al.* (eds.), University of St Andrews, Edinburgh and London, 1967, pp. 137-51.

[36] Rousseau, *Emile*, Paris, 1964, p. 27.

[37] [Abbé Gabriel-François Coyer] *Plan d'éducation publique*, Paris 1770, pp. 254-8 and 334-5.

[38] Etienne Bonnot, Abbé de Condillac, *Cours d'études pour l'instruction du prince de Parme*, 12 vols., Genève, 1780 [First edition, 16 vols., Parma, 1775].

[39] Diderot, *Plan d'une université pour le gouvernement de Russie ou d'une éducation publique dans toutes les sciences* in *Oeuvres complètes*, J. Assézat and M. Tourneaux (eds.), Paris, 1875-7, Vol. III, pp. 410-534. Although he argues

Helvétius, one of the most enthusiastic champions of education—
l'éducation fait tout—attacked those who wished to keep the people
in subjection through ignorance, but he ended up by assuring one
correspondent that the spread of enlightenment would be so slow
that it would not prove dangerous.[40] Among the major *philosophes*
only d'Holbach seems to have had no forebodings about mass
education.[41]

The economists, especially the Physiocrats, men such as Le
Mercier de la Rivière, Quesnay, Turgot, Mirabeau, and Dupont de
Nemours, were among the strongest proponents of mass education
because they saw it as a means of spreading their ideas and increasing productivity,[42] but some of their associates revealed their misgivings. For example the Abbé Baudeau, the editor of the sect's
periodical, was an eloquent proponent of a national system of
education. 'The nation is waiting for a universal system, uniform
and invariable legislation covering every sort of public school, a
complete code of study', he wrote. 'Such is the wish of all good
patriots.' The Abbé wanted this code to be administered by a special
government bureau. But he went on to advocate five varieties of
public schools corresponding to the five classes into which he divided
French society—the king and princes of the blood, the nobility,
the upper bourgeoisie, the petty bourgeoisie, and the common
people. Thus although he advocated a certain amount of enlightenment for the lower classes, his system was designed to mirror
rather than disturb the hierarchical social structure.[43]

Philipon de la Madeleine deserves special attention because later
in the Convention at the peak of the Revolution Grégoire, a member of the Committee of Public Instruction, praised his book *Vues
patriotiques sur l'éducation du peuple* as a pre-revolutionary

---

in favour of mass education up to a certain level—see pp. 416-18—he asserts—p.
519—that too many colleges would be a calamity. On Diderot's attitude toward
the lower classes see Roland Mortier, 'Diderot et la notion de "peuple" ', *Europe*
(numéro spécial sur Diderot), 41e année, Nos. 405-6, janvier-fevrier, 1963, pp.
78-88. See too Denise Jacqueline Chevalier, 'Diderot et l'éducation', *La Pensee*,
août 1969, No. 146, pp. 128-41.

[40] Helvétius, *Sur l'instruction du peuple*, Oeuvres complètes, Paris, 1795, Vol.
XIV, pp. 97-109.

[41] Paul Henri Thiry, baron d'Holbach, *Ethocratie ou gouvernement fondé
sur la morale*, Paris, 1776, pp. 194ff.

[42] The ideas of the Physiocrats on education deserve further research, but
there is a pioneering study, V. H. Gourdon, 'Les Physiocrats et l'éducation
nationale au 18e siècle', *Revue pédagogique*, Vol. XXXVIII, 15 juin 1901, No. 6,
pp. 577-89.

[43] Abbé Nicolas Baudeau, 'De l'éducation nationale', *Ephémérides du citoyen*,
Vol. I, No. 7, 25 nov. 1765, pp. 97-112; Vol. II, No. 5, 17 jan. 1766, pp. 65-80;
Vol. III, No. 2, 7 mars 1766, pp. 17-32; Vol. IV, No. 4, 12 mai 1766, pp. 49-64;
Vol. V, Nos. 10-13, 4 août-15 août 1766, pp. 145-208. Quotation, Vol. I, No. 7,
pp. 100-1.

appeal for popular education. Philipon did indeed emphasise the importance of educating the labouring masses. It was they who provided husbandmen to nourish the state, artisans to enrich it, and soldiers to defend it; however, they could also be the source of disturbers of the peace, bloodthirsty assassins, armed brigands, and parasitic vagabonds. Their education ought therefore to be financed by the state, but it should be confined to preparing them to perform and accept their arduous lot in life. A solid grounding in reading would be essential, but writing would almost be forbidden. Children of the common people would also learn elementary arithmetic, useful geometry, simple drawing, basic physics, practical medicine, and some veterinary science. Rough physical exercises would prepare them for the hardships of later life. Music would also be taught because in future they would need a gay distraction from their chores. Above all moral and religious indoctrination would inculcate a work ethic. But if the state went any further in educating the masses, it would not only lose useful workers, but it would risk creating half-educated social disturbers like Peter Waldo or John Hus. 'But if to this word instruction one attaches the idea of studying languages, sciences, literature, and the fine arts, one ought to keep it out of the reach of the people', argued Philipon. 'I know of no more dangerous weapon than knowledge in the hands of the people.'[44] One wonders if Grégoire had read more than the title of Philipon's book.

Philipon also proposed a number of social controls designed to reconcile the lower classes with their lot once they emerged from these limited primary schools. School authorities would sponsor athletic and paramilitary associations for young graduates to maintain them in shape for work, keep them out of taverns, train them for public works, and prepare them to rally in case of some emergency in the community. The government would promote rural festivals for all age groups designed, not to distract the common people from their work, but rather to teach them the dignity of their calling and encourage competition. Village dances were to be employed to deflect the lower classes from harmful activities. There would also be various educational institutions for the toiling masses—reading rooms, special lectures, agricultural societies— all aimed at improving production and reinforcing the work ethic. A special collection of proverbs, entitled *La Philosophie du Peuple*, would bolster this effort. For example,' All that glitters is not gold' would be used to inform the common people that the rich whom they envy also suffer from various afflictions. And throughout life

[44] Philipon de la Madeleine, *Vues patriotiques*, pp. 1-26. Quotation pp. 13-14.

the church would assist in teaching the commonalty to love their work.[45]

Later Philipon de la Madeleine wrote a book calling for reform of the colleges without proposing any scheme by which gifted children from the lower classes would be assisted in passing from the elementary stream to these more advanced institutions.[46] This dramatises the partial solution which many pre-revolutionary French educational reformers arrived at in the effort to reconcile their desire to reshape the masses with their fears of disturbing the social order. They would extend education horizontally but not very far vertically. By providing education for all young males they would be able to increase state control, engender national patriotism, instil a new social morality, increase productivity, and even achieve a degree of general enlightenment—in short produce a citizenry useful to society and dedicated to *la patrie*. Also by providing a few free places for poor but talented children some of them could claim to be substituting the modern criterion of utility for the old one of privilege. But by restricting the content of universal education, by limiting upward progression, by creating national schools in layers suited for different classes, and sometimes by advocating certain social controls or distractions, they hoped to preserve the existing social order. Reformers could thus be progressive and conservative simultaneously.

Their misgivings about the repercussions of mass education persisted into the opening phase of the Revolution. The absence of any ringing appeal for mass education in the cahiers of the Third Estate suggests that many members of the middle class were still inhibited by the same doubts that had haunted La Chalotais.[47] In the spate of books, pamphlets, and articles on education which appeared in 1789 a few continued to favour domestic instruction, some still advocated different levels of schooling for each class,[48] others focused on the colleges, and still others clearly preferred to train an élite. The author of a series of articles in the *Journal Encyclopédique* argued that all citizens ought to be able to read and write, but he obviously feared going too far. 'Admittedly this

---

[45] Ibid., pp. 225-92.

[46] Louis Philipon de la Madeleine, *De l'éducation des collèges par l'auteur de l'Education du peuple'*, Londres et Paris, 1784.

[47] A.-E.-S. Duméril, *Des vœux des cahiers de 1787 rélatifs à l'instruction publique*, Toulouse, 1880; Ernest Allain, *La Question d'enseignement en 1789, d'après les cahiers*, Paris, 1886; and Louis Bourilly, *Les Cahiers de l'instruction publique en 1789. Étude documentaire*, Paris, 1901.

[48] [—] Fauleau, *Plan d'un éducatoire national*, Orléans, 1789, like the Physiocrat Abbé Baudeau more than twenty years earlier, proposed five levels of schooling to match the social hierarchy—labourers, artisans, petty bourgeois, men of ease, and the very wealthy—lest too much education unfit the lower classes for their humble tasks. Pp. 23-7.

restricted knowledge inspires the desire to acquire more', he wrote, 'but there are obstacles which can be opposed to this desire, and tests to which talent can be submitted . . .'.[49] Not surprisingly he ended up advocating a drastic reduction in the number of colleges.

Nevertheless the advent of revolution brought mounting pressures in favour of the idea of mass education directed by the government. Authors repeatedly emphasised the need for such a system if the representatives gathered at Versailles were to succeed in creating a new order. For example the doctor Le Clerc argued as early as the spring of 1789—a footnote indicates that his two volumes went to press on 15 May—that national reconstruction would depend on imbuing future citizens with a new civic morality. 'But TO CHANGE THE MASS OF MORALS ONE MUST ATTACK THE MASS', he wrote, capitalising his declaration to hammer home his point.[50] In the following months others reiterated his plea for a national educational system embracing all classes.[51] Despite lingering fears of disturbing the social order, the dawn of the age of the democratic revolution thus intensified the demand for mass education, bringing western man in this sphere to the threshold of modern times. Yet even when the dawn of the age of the democratic revolution seemed to make extension of popular education imperative, authors seldom advocated much social mobility. Their motto might still have been: education for the masses, *mais pas trop.*

[49] 'Première lettre sur l'éducation . . .', *Journal encyclopédique ou universel,* Vol. VII, pt 1, 1er octobre 1789, pp. 103-15; 'Deuxième lettre . . . ', Vol. VII, pt 2, 15 octobre 1789, pp. 281-9 and pt 3, 1er novembre 1789, pp. 465-77; and 'Troisième lettre . . . ', Vol. VIII, pt 1, 15 novembre 1789, pp. 68-80. Quotation, Vol. VII, pt 1, p. 108.

[50] Nicolas-Gabriel Clerc *dit* Le Clerc, *Abrégé des études de l'homme fait, en faveur de l'homme à former, dédié aux représentans de la nation,* 2 vols., Paris, 1789, p. lxix.

[51] For example Bertrand Verlac, *Nouveau plan d'éducation pour toutes les classes de citoyens . . . avec un traité de la nature de la liberté en général, de la liberté civile,* Vannes, 1789, advocated making attendance obligatory for children of peasants and artisans. Pp. 100-11.

Hawkesworth's Voyages

W. H. Pearson

It was in June 1773 that Hawkesworth's *Voyages* was issued in 2,000 sets of three volumes, containing the authorised account of the circumnavigations of John Byron, of Wallis, Carteret, and Cook, and within three or four months a second issue of 2,500 sets was made, of which 610 were still unsold twelve years later[1] Nevertheless by the end of 1744 there had been cheaper and apparently unauthorised editions in Dublin and New York, a French translation that appeared in four distinct editions, and translations into Dutch and German. At the one English public library whose borrowing records have survived, Hawkesworth's *Voyages* was the most frequently borrowed book between 1773 and 1784—201 times in 12 years, 115 of them in the first three years.[2] There were four further English-language editions within sixteen years—a total of eight; there were two further German editions by 1786, there was an Italian translation in 1794, and two further French editions by 1796; and Hawkesworth's version of Cook's first voyage was incorporated in part or in full, verbatim or in paraphrase, often without his name, in uncounted collections of voyages or lives of Cook or editions of Cook's voyages in several European languages.[3] There was no other published account of the first contact between Europe and Tahiti till 1948 and until Admiral Wharton's edition of the *Endeavour* journal in 1893, as

[1] John Hawkesworth, *An Account of the Voyages . . . by Commodore Byron, Captain Wallis, Captain Carteret, and Captain Cook, in the Dolphin, the Swallow, and the Endeavour:* . . . . , 3 vols., London, 1773; Robert D. Harlan, 'Some Additional Figures of Distribution of Eighteenth Century English Books', pp. 160-70, *Papers of the Bibliographical Society of America*, New York, Vol. 59, 1965, p. 167.

[2] Paul Kaufman, *Borrowings from the Bristol Library 1773-1784,* Charlottesville, Va., 1960. Comparative frequencies were Anson, 10; Bougainville in J. R. Forster's translation, 48; Dalrymple's Collection, 14, and for the years 1777-1784, Cook's second voyage, 113; George Forster, 65, Parkinson, 17. I am indebted to Mr Alan Frost of La Trobe University for this reference.

[3] Details of French and German editions are from Rolf du Rietz, *Bibliotheca Polynesiana*, Oslo, 1969, pp. 176-7, 181, and *Bibliography of Captain James Cook*, M. K. Beddie (ed.), 2nd ed., 1970, pp. 125, 126-8, 229-30.

J. C. Beaglehole puts it, 'so far as the first voyage was concerned, Hawkesworth was Cook'.[4]

Hawkesworth considered himself fortunate and many envied him. The Admiralty paid for the engravings and gave him sole ownership of the projected book.[5] William Strahan the publisher paid £6,000 for it and in a remark that has been given little notice by scholars, Horace Walpole says that Joseph Banks paid him a further £1,000 for including his own journal.[6] Yet the book in its time was as angrily attacked as it was widely bought and read, and Fanny Burney attributed Hawkesworth's death in November of that year to the harassment of the reviewers.[7] Some of the grounds of contemporary attack are of slight interest now: for example, Hawkesworth's firm refusal to allow that it was divine intervention that rescued the *Endeavour* from the Great Barrier Reef, or the charges of pruriency in his delineation of Tahitian sexual practice. Of more substance are the complaints of Cook that views were attributed to him that he had not entertained and that a 'general conclusion' was drawn 'from a particular fact'[8]—objections apparently unimportant to one who prided himself on his large views and esteemed philosophers above sea-captains, or George Forster's objection to the subjectivity and shallowness of Hawkesworth's interpretation of his material.[9]

Another criticism of Hawkesworth belongs to the twentieth century; I suppose it began with Henry Adams and it has been most forcefully put by Hoxie Neale Fairchild.[10] It concerns Hawkesworth's responsibility in the reaction of intellectual Europe to the apparent discovery of a contemporary Golden Age on a remote island where people lived in abundance and happiness and with a sexual morality that combined the greatest of enjoyment with the least of anxiety. In England the immediate reaction was fiercely puritanical (though there was one lone voice regretting that a

---

[4] *The Journals of Captain James Cook on his Voyages of Discovery*, J. C. Beaglehole (ed.), 3 vols., Hakluyt Society, extra ser. Nos. 34-6, Cambridge, 1955-68 (hereafter *Journals*), Vol. I, p. ccliii.

[5] John Hawkesworth to Charles Burney, 6 October 1771, National Library of Australia MS 332/2.

[6] Horace Walpole to Rev. William Mason, 15 May 1778, in Horace Walpole, *The Letters of Horace Walpole, Earl of Orford*, Peter Cunningham (ed.), 9 vols., London, 1858, Vol. V, p. 463.

[7] Fanny Burney, *The Early Diary of Frances Burney 1768-1778*, A. R. Ellis (ed.), 2 vols., London, 1880, Vol. I, pp. 271-3.

[8] James Boswell, *Boswell: The Ominous Years 1774-1776*, Charles Ryskamp and F. A. Pothe (eds.), London, 1963, p. 308.

[9] George Forster, *A Voyage Round the World*, 2 vols., London, 1777, Vol. I, pp. x-xi.

[10] Henry Adams, *Tahiti, Memoirs of Arii Tamai* (Paris, 1901), repr. New York, 1947 (R. E. Spiller, ed.), pp. 55-6; H. N. Fairchild, *The Noble Savage*, New York, 1928, pp. 104-12.

simple people had been unsettled by Europe's dissatisfactions) in a series of scurrilous verses at the expense of Joseph Banks and his aristocratic hostess Purea, known from Hawkesworth as 'Oberea Queen of Otaheite'. So far as the Tahitian entered English literature at all in any stance of dignity it was in the familiar role of critical visitor from the East. In France the Tahitian appeared not only in this role, he appeared too as a noble representative of sensibility and sentiment and as the enlightened savage, whose polity, founded on the principles of Nature and Reason, was consciously designed to avoid the mistakes of Europe. One can in part trace such a view to the journals of Bougainville and of George Forster who accompanied Cook on his second voyage. It has frequently been held—in fact it is a cliché in popular books on the Pacific—that Hawkesworth was in large measure responsible for the idealisation of the Polynesian as what, in a phrase that has not been subjected by the historians of ideas to the sceptical scrutiny it needs, is called the Noble Savage.

It is my claim that this imputation is wrong, that a comparison with the logs and journals that Hawkesworth worked from shows that in the many alterations he made he was guided not by the attitude A. O. Lovejoy was later to describe as 'primitivism'[11]— the desire to idealise pre-literate societies—but by quite other principles. In an excellent but unpublished thesis written thirty years ago Clara Lesher, taking Hawkesworth's book as a self-contained whole, cleared it of imputations of primitivism,[12] and J. C. Beaglehole in his very full and sensible discussion of Hawkesworth has illuminated the strategies by which he satisfied, or thought he satisfied, the conflicting claims of authenticity and authorship. But no one has undertaken a detailed comparison of Hawkesworth's text with the logs and journals to which he had access. There are fifty-seven or so of them and Hawkesworth clearly did not try to use them all. So in attempting this task I have concentrated on a close comparison with the half-dozen journals from which Hawkesworth can be shown to have worked, consulting only for specific incidents the three dozen or so supplementary logs and journals of the *Swallow* (Captain Carteret) and the two voyages of the *Dolphin* (in turn, Captains Byron and Wallis). For the supplementary journals of the *Endeavour* it would be difficult to do better than rely on the annotations in Beaglehole's editions of the journals of Banks and Cook. With the question of primitivism in mind I have confined myself to those areas which might provide

[11] A. O. Lovejoy and G. Boas, *Primitivism and Related Ideas in Antiquity*, Baltimore, 1935, pp. 7-11.
[12] Clara Lesher, The South Sea Islanders in English Literature 1519-1798, Ph.D. thesis, University of Chicago, 1937.

the greatest opportunity to moralise or distort—tropical Polynesia because of its apparent affinities with Arcadia, and more briefly, Eastern Australia and Tierra del Fuego since they might attract comment from an exponent of the spartan or stoic virtues of food-gathering by primitive techniques.

Hard primitivism, to use Lovejoy's term, was a recurrent sentiment that found such virtue in the life of hunters or pastoralists in inclement climates or infertile terrains; it was an attitude that earlier in the century had ennobled North American Indians and Corsicans. Cook shows an unusual moral enthusiasm when he contemplates the life of the Australians of the eastern coast:

> From what I have said of the Natives of New Holland they may appear to be some of the most wretched people upon Earth, but in realty they are far more happier than we Europeans being wholy unacquainted not only with the Superflous but the necessary Convenience so much sought after in Europe, they are happy in not knowing the use of them.[13]

Cook argues that their happiness lies also in the sufficiency of their natural environment in satisfying the needs they are aware of. At a similar place in his journal Banks argues the same case, but with less conviction, and the two passages probably reflect a mutual discussion. If Hawkesworth had been sympathetic to these opinions it would have been in keeping with his practice to elaborate them into one of those dissertations with which he makes his narrative morally instructive. But in fact at this point he omits them. That he did not do so without due thought is suggested by the marginal annotation of the relevant paragraph in Cook's manuscript with two entries 'happy' and 'good Climate'. But he did not entirely omit the discussion; he shifted it, as Bernard Smith detects, from Australia to Tierra del Fuego.[14] What Hawkesworth makes of Cook's argument in relation to the Indians at the Bay of Success is in these words:

> What bodily pain they might suffer from the severities of their winter we could not know; but it is certain, that they suffered nothing from the want of innumerable articles which we consider, not as the luxuries and conveniences only, but the

¹³ James Cook, Journal of the *Endeavour*, P.R.O. Adm. 55/40 f. 165a (AJCP Reel 1580). I have thought it necessary to quote from the manuscript used by Hawkesworth, but for convenience and since the only textual differences in the passages quoted in this essay from the MS. used by Beaglehole are in spelling and punctuation, I also give the parallel references in Beaglehole's edition of Cook's *Journals*; in this case, Vol. I, p. 399. Cf. Joseph Banks, *The Endeavour Journal of Joseph Banks*, J. C. Beaglehole (ed.), 2 vols., Sydney, 1962, Vol. II, p. 130.

¹⁴ Bernard Smith, *European Vision in the South Pacific 1768-1850*, Oxford, 1960, p. 22.

necessaries of life: as their desires are few, they probably enjoy them all; and how much they may be gainers by an exemption from the care, labour and solicitude, which arise from a perpetual and unsuccessful effort to gratify that infinite variety of desires which the refinements of artificial life have produced among us, is not very easy to determine: possibly this may counterbalance all the real disadvantages of their situation in comparison with ours, and make the scales by which good and evil are distributed to man, hang even between us.[15]

Cook had said that his primitive people were 'far happier than we Europeans'. Hawkesworth said only, 'they were content' and possibly the scale may hang even between us. There has been a distinct drop in enthusiasm.

But if Hawkesworth himself does not provide a clear answer to the question, the context into which he has shifted it does. On the Fuegians the journalists were unanimous. Neither Byron, Carteret, Wallis, nor Robertson, nor for that matter Bougainville, whom Hawkesworth had apparently read, envied the canoe Indians (Alakaluf or Yahgan) of the Straits of Magellan with their early Neolithic technology, living by gathering shellfish and hunting seals, eating raw food, shivering naked or clad at most in waist-length capes of the untreated skin of seals or guanacoes, sleeping in wigwams unfitted to protect them from one of the worst climates of the world. And Cook himself described the foot Indians (the Haush) at the Bay of Success as 'perhaps as miserable a set of People as are this day upon Earth'.[16] So that by transferring the discussion to concern a people whose life all were agreed was unenviable Hawkesworth is tactfully avoiding the incivility of disagreeing with Banks for the use of whose journal he was so grateful and the commander in whose person he purported to be writing.

He takes up the discussion again in Wallis's voyage, a task he undertook after he had finished Cook's voyage. This time there is no question of editorial tact and in a passage based on the journal of George Robertson, master of the *Dolphin*, the editor shows that his opinion on this question is opposed to Cook's:

> Their perfect indifference to every thing they saw marked the disparity between our state and their own, though it may preserve them from the regret and anguish of unsatisfied desires, seems, notwithstanding, to imply a defect in their nature; for those who are satisfied with the gratifications of a brute, can have little pretension to the prerogatives of men.[17]

[15] Hawkesworth, II, 59. See Smith, *European Vision*, p. 22.
[16] Cook, Adm. 55/40, 16 January 1769; *Journals*, I, 45.
[17] Hawkesworth, I, 172.

It is in the light of the discussion on the happiness of primitive life begun by Banks and Cook in the Arafura Sea that one should read that remark on Tahitians which has frequently been cited to illustrate Hawkesworth's admiration for the noble savage. He echoes Cook's 'far more happier than we Europeans':

> Yet if we admit that they are upon the whole happier than we, we must admit that the child is happier than the man, and that we are the losers by the perfection of our nature, the increase of our knowledge, and the enlargement of our views.[18]

Greater happiness Hawkesworth conceded, but only 'upon the whole' and it was at the expense of the ability to reflect on the past or anticipate the future which he denied equally to Fuegians, and Tahitians, and children. Who before Blake and Wordsworth would have exchanged the completion of education and physical and mental growth that is implied by 'perfection' or the increased knowledge and enlarged views of maturity for the precarious happiness of a child?

II

It was contrary to the universal moral system Hawkesworth chose in his *Adventurer* essays to expound and no doubt inculcated at the young ladies' school he directed, that indolence should be rewarded or unashamed sexual gratification be condoned. In examining the imputation frequently made—that Hawkesworth is a 'soft primitivist'—I have sought to establish whether those remarks praising Tahitian behaviour were copied from his sources or invented, whether he omitted any remarks unfavourable to Tahitians or any remarks favourable. It is clear from this exercise that Hawkesworth's alterations did not tend towards soft primitivism. Some of the remarks that have been used to support the imputation can be matched in Banks and Cook and show that he had more claim than has been supposed to see himself as 'little more than an amanuensis for others'.[19] In several cases it is Banks who is more enthusiastic than his editor. For example, Hawkesworth omits Bank's observation that Tahitians appeared to be exempt from the curse of Adam, having to earn their bread with the sweat of their brow.[20] If his compliment to the six-year-old girl at Ra'iatea seems extravagant, Hawkesworth leaves out the very inference a primitivist would have welcomed. The girl, heiress to

---

[18] Hawkesworth, II, 104-5.

[19] Hawkesworth 'Preface to Second Edition', 1773, sig. [A] 3.

[20] Hawkesworth, II, 197; Banks, I, 341-2. An identical passage in Cook, Adm. 55/40, f. 57a, *Journals*, I, 121, appears to be copied from Banks. See Beaglehole in Cook, *Journals*, Vol. I, pp. cciii-ccv.

a high ancestral line, presided at a reception for Banks and
Solander and as she held out her hand to receive the beads they
offered her, Hawkesworth says, 'no Princess in Europe could have
done it with a better grace'. But Banks had written a warmer
tribute:

> had she been a princess royal of England giving her hand to be
> kiss'd no instruction could have taught her to have done it
> with a better grace. So much is untaught nature superior to
> art that I have seen no sight of the kind that has struck me
> half so much.[21]

When Hawkesworth commends Tahitians as 'a people who show
an intelligence and influence which would do honour to any system of government, however regular and improved', he does not go
so far as Banks's description of 'a policy at least equal to any
we had seen in civilized countries, exercisd by people who never
had any advantage but meer natural instinct uninstructed by the
example of any civilizd countrey'.[22] So too when Hawkesworth
describes the same people as 'brave, open and candid, without either
suspicion of treachery, cruelty or revenge' he has compounded the
statement from Banks and Cook. When he is lyrical about the
rural beauties of Tahiti or likens it to Arcadia or thinks of Greek
bards and minstrels when he hears a performance of the travelling
musicians, it is Banks who preceded him or provided the hint.[23]
    It is misleading to complain, as H. N. Fairchild does, of his
'knack for explaining away savage faults'.[24] Hawkesworth's Tahiti
has many undesirable features: there is a plague of flies, the
children and common people pick lice from their heads and eat
them; he accepts Bank's feudal model of Tahitian social structure,
and he follows Banks on a subject Cook does not mention, the
stubbornness of Tahitian fighting and the ruthlessness of the victor towards the defeated.[25] The common people are thieves and
their chiefs are no better, one chief who steals is exposed and in
the unexplained theft of Banks's pistols and coats the guilt of his
hostess, though never proved, is assumed. He goes further than
Banks when he writes: 'the people of this country, of all ranks,
men and women, are the errantest thieves upon the face of the

---

[21] Hawkesworth, II, 263; Banks, I, 324.

[22] Hawkesworth, II, 88; Banks, I, 256.

[23] (a)Hawkesworth, II, 188; Banks, I, 334; Cook, Adm. 55/40, f. 58a. *Journals*,
I, 124. (b) Hawkesworth, II, 194; Banks, I, 340. (c) Hawkesworth, II, 83; Banks,
I, 252. (d) Hawkesworth, II, 148; Banks, I, 290.

[24] Fairchild, *The Noble Savage*, p. 118.

[25] (a)Banks, I, 260; Hawkesworth, II, 97. (b) Banks, I, 337; Hawkesworth, II,
189. (c) Banks, I, 384; Hawkesworth, II, 242. (d) Banks, I, 386; Hawkesworth, II,
244.

earth'.[26] If in a passage for which neither Banks nor Cook provides a precedent, Hawkesworth seeks to explain the lapse of the chief whose personal name was apparently Tupura'a, it carries the condescension of a member of a technologically more advanced society:

> he was at length exposed to temptations which neither his integrity nor his honour was able to resist. They had withstood many allurements, but were at length ensnared by the fascinating charms of a basket of nails.[27]

The role of participant in a superior technology does not sit easily with belief in a return to nature, nor does that of paternalist, a posture that shows in Hawkesworth's frequent insistence on an analogy between Tahitian conduct and the behaviour of children. For example, he retells from Banks an incident in which some Tahitians begged mercy for the ship's butcher, who was being flogged for stealing an adze from them; when Cook refused, they wept. It was an incident that was not overlooked in France, but of the several inferences that might have been drawn from it the one that Hawkesworth makes has no model in his source:

> Their tears indeed, like those of children, were always ready to express any passion that was strongly excited, and like those of children they also appeared to be forgotten as soon as shed.[28]

If he was accused of prurience in his account of Tahitian sexual mores, especially of the aspect that so shocked England, the promiscuity and infanticide practised by the society of travelling performers called *ario'i*, Hawkesworth clearly condemned it:

> there is a scale in dissolute sensuality, which these people have ascended, wholly unknown to every other nation whose manners have been recorded from the beginning of the world to the present hour, and which no imagination could possibly conceive.[29]

There is in fact very little praise of Tahiti that cannot be found in Hawkesworth's originals. There are two observations on the disinterested devotion of the people towards their gods, 'a reverence and humility that disgraces the christian'—which is no more than a new version of a fashionable enough truism.[30] There is one comment that Hawkesworth volunteers which if it were not contradicted by so many other statements in the *Voyages*, might be

26 Banks, I, 263; Hawkesworth, II, 100.
27 Hawkesworth, II, 129.
28 Hawkesworth, II, 103-4. Cf. Banks, I, 264-5, 266-7.
29 Hawkesworth, II, 207, Cf. Cook, Adm. 55/40, f. 59b, *Journals*, I, 128.
30 Hawkesworth, II, 241; Banks, I, 383.

adduced to support the imputation of primitivism. Banks had falsely accused Tupura'a of stealing a knife; when the knife was found Tupura'a broke into tears in reproach of Banks for his suspicion. Hawkesworth comments:

> these people have a knowledge of right and wrong from the mere dictates of natural conscience; and involuntarily condemn themselves when they do that to others, which they would condemn others for doing to them.

He proceeds to a statement of moral relativism uncharacteristic of the rest of the *Voyages*: 'We must indeed estimate the virtue of these people, by the only standard of morality, the conformity of their conduct to what in their opinion is right'. But as his argument proceeds the tone revealed is that of technological superiority. We should not judge theft by Tahitians as harshly as theft by Europeans because

> an Indian among penny knives, and beads, or even nails and broken glass, is in the same state of trial with the meanest servant in Europe among unlocked coffers of jewels and gold.

What began as a tribute to the 'natural conscience' has passed through moral relativism to patronising contempt. Here the analogy is not with a child but with a servant; the attitude not paternalistic but colonial.[31]

It is clear then that it was not Hawkesworth's desire to present primitive society as more attractive than civilised. If his work includes laudatory passages he trims the generosity of Banks and more than once he exceeds Banks in condemning Tahitian practice; he never surrenders his claim to pass judgment. For many years Hawkesworth was the English reader's introduction to the South Pacific. If sentimentalists found the children of nature, there were those who found the children of Satan, like the missionaries of the *Duff* who came to Tahiti in 1797 forewarned of the wickedness of the savage heart.

Hawkesworth was guided in his alterations by preoccupations quite other than the question whether men were happier in nature than in civil society.

III

As his contemporaries describe him Hawkesworth was a self-taught man with his eye on success and enough confidence in his intellectual ability to pass judgment on many topics, but defensively conscious of his humble origins. Fanny Burney observed a

31 Hawkesworth, II, 101-2. Cf. Banks, I, 264.

'stiffness and something resembling pedantry' which wore off on further acquaintance; he talked at the dinner table as if he were reading one of his own essays: 'I never heard a man speak in a style which so much resembles writing. He has an amazing flow of choice words and expressions.'[32] When Dr Burney spoke for Hawkesworth to the Earl of Sandwich on 14 September 1771, Hawkesworth was so pleased at his nomination as editor of the journals that he could not wait for Sandwich's formal application and enlisted Garrick to ensure his appointment.[33] He hoped to make the book 'another Anson's Voyage'—then in its 14th edition. From 6 October 1771 when he had the Admiralty journals in hand, to May 1772, a date mentioned by Miss Burney, he was engaged on the work, and probably for many months more since it was not until May 1773 that he tested what Joseph Cradock called his 'Preface' (probably the Dedication rather than the General Introduction) on a meeting at the Admiralty convened for the purpose.[34] He claims that he worked first on the voyage of the *Endeavour* so that it could be approved by Cook before he sailed on his second voyage and that he completed this section (two of the three volumes) in four months.[35] Cook declared that he 'never had the perusal of the Manuscript nor did I ever hear the whole of it read in the mode it was written'. But there is a report by Boswell which on its least forced interpretation gives the impression that in conjunction with Banks Cook read, or at least had read to him, part of the manuscript and revised it or discussed revision, but that Hawkesworth refused to alter it.[36] Before the publication of this part of Boswell's journal the fullest treatment of this question was by Beaglehole, to whose discussion I would add only the suggestion that if Boswell is right Hawkesworth made only such revisions from his own manuscript as Banks insisted on, that it was Banks who gave him the confidence to override the objections of one of the original journalists.

Hawkesworth might well have taken pride in his authorship

[32] F. Burney, *Diary*, I, 47, 207.

[33] Hawkesworth to Dr Charles Burney, 18 September 1771, N.L.A. MS 332/1; F. Burney, I, 139-40.

[34] Hawkesworth to Charles Burney, 6 October, 1771, N.L.A. MS 332/2; F. Burney, I, 175; Joseph Cradock, *Literary and Miscellaneous Memoirs*, London, 1838, Vol. I, 135. Hawkesworth had the first volume of Banks's journal by 19 November. Beaglehole in Cook, *Journals*, I, ccxlvi n.2.

[35] Hawkesworth, I, v.

[36] Cook, *Journals*, II, 661; Boswell, *Ominous Years*, 308-9. Boswell's words are: 'He said it was not true that Mr. Banks and he had revised all the book; in what was revised Hawkesworth would make no alteration (I think he said this too)', I take 'Mr' and 'he' to mean Banks and Cook and not (as is possible) Banks and Hawkesworth, and 'revised' to mean corrected by the original journalists from Hawkesworth's version, and not rewritten by Hawkesworth from the journals. Boswell is not even certain about Hawkesworth's obduracy.

of the work to which Sandwich had given him the legal right. When he has used more than one account of the same voyage, Cook and Banks or Wallis and Robertson, the blending, as Beaglehole says, is 'not unskilful',[37] and the occasional cross-reference or transfer of a passage from a daily entry to a chapter of general description reflects a concern for the form of the work as a whole. In fact the greatest changes to the journals are stylistic. It is obvious that the editor considered himself a better writer than the seamen and thought their journals in need of serious revision, so that the plain scrupulous prose of Cook, the hard-won humane writing of Robertson and even the spirited pace of Banks are converted into the predictably measured fluency of Hawkesworth's balanced sentences. The stylistic change is a pervasive one. The 'miscellaneous writer' brings forward his learning—small though Reynolds thought it—and his worn metaphors. Tut⌐ha sits under a tree 'like an ancient Patriarch', Banks's 'grave-looking' old men become 'venerable': Purea's courage becomes 'greatness of mind'.[38]

A number of incidents are expanded and dramatised, for example Banks's discovery of Purea in bed with her lover or Cook's account of the reunion of two chiefs one of whom had been arrested as a hostage against the return of a stolen quadrant. Cook says simply that the scene 'was realy moving, they wept over each other sometime', but Hawkesworth 'expresses' the emotion in stylised postures: Tupura'a 'pressing forward, ran up to Tootahah, and catching him in his arms, they both burst into tears, and wept over each other, without being able to speak'.[39]

There are several comic incidents that remind us that Hawkesworth had written a stage farce. None of them has any manuscript authority and four of them occur in the second voyage of the *Dolphin* which the editor tackled after Cook and for whose journals he seems to have shown less respect than for those of Cook and Banks. Wallis says that the people who first boarded the *Dolphin* off the east coast of Tahiti jumped overboard when they saw goats and sheep; Hawkesworth invents the incident, frequently cited in popular histories of the Pacific, of a Tahitian being butted from behind by a goat.[40] Wallis notes the people's surprise at the gunner cooking his food in a pot: 'they are Quite Ignorant of what Boiling Water, is'. Hawkesworth marginally

---

[37] Beaglehole in Cook, *Journals*, I, ccxlvii.
[38] (a) Cook, Adm. 55/40, 5 May 1769, *Journals*, I, 90; Banks, I, 271; Hawkesworth, II, 117. (b) Cook, Adm. 55/40, 20 June 1769, *Journals*, I, 102; Hawkesworth, II, 152.
[39] (a) Banks, I, 267; Hawkesworth, II, 107. (b) Cook, Adm. 55/40, 2 May 1769, *Journals*, I, 88; Hawkesworth, II, 114.
[40] Samuel Wallis, Log of the *Dolphin*, P.R.O. Adm. 55/35 (AJCP Reel No. 1579), 18 June 1767; Hawkesworth, I, 214.

notes 'Astonished at a pot' and invents an incident where one of Purea's attendants scalds himself and howls like a child.[41] There is not even such slight authority for the incident at Purea's house where the surgeon feeling hot, takes off his wig: 'the whole assembly stood some time motionless, in silent astonishment, which could not have been more strongly expressed if they had discovered that our friend's limb had been screwed on to the trunk'.[42] Any or all of these Hawkesworth might have picked up at the Admiralty or from Sandwich, but there is no evidence that he met Wallis or Robertson or that to him the *Dolphin*'s voyage was of anything like the interest of the *Endeavour*'s. It is notable that most of these comic additions play upon the technological backwardness of the Tahitians.

Some changes reflect Hawkesworth's special obligation to Banks. In the Introduction to the voyage of the *Endeavour* his gratitude in having the journal of a fellow-philosopher and wealthy gentleman is generously, perhaps fulsomely, acknowledged and this alone would explain a series of tactful omissions, which must have saved Banks from embarrassment or more ridicule than he suffered from the lampoonists as a result of what Hawkesworth had included of his dealings with Purea. He at least omitted what they assumed, that she had offered herself to him when she discarded her lover; and he prudently drops Banks's explanation that another woman was his 'flame'.[43] There are occasions when Hawkesworth adds a commendation as if from Cook. Cook had written that Banks 'is always alert upon all Occasions wherein the Natives are Concern'd'. Hawkesworth went further: 'Mr Banks . . . who upon such occasions declined neither labour nor risk, and who had more influence over the Indians than any of us'.[44]

There are several omissions that can be explained on the ground of lack of space in a book that was to grow in plan from two to three volumes, or on the ground of economy, where of two or three similar episodes yielding the like 'instruction' only one is used. The neo-classic principle of consistency operates in his handling of Purea's grief at Wallis's departure. Her tears are mentioned as often as by Wallis and indeed are dwelt on when her final gesture in Wallis ('She Shook us all by the hand and then put of the Canoe') becomes in Hawkesworth:

> our Indian friends, and particularly the queen, once more bade us farewel, with such tenderness of affection and grief, as filled both my heart and my eyes.

41 Wallis, Adm. 55/35, ff. 43b-44a; Hawkesworth, I, 246.
42 Hawkesworth, I, 243.
43 (a) Banks, I, 279. (b) Banks, I, 276; Hawkesworth, II, 125.
44 Cook, Adm. 55/40, 2 May 1769; Hawkesworth, II, 112.

It is a charming rather than a heroic grief, and as creditable to the commander as to his hostess. Robertson, who was no sentimentalist, was deeply moved by Purea's tears, and it is his words that are the warrant for Hawkesworth's addition to Wallis:

> this Great freindly Woman took no manner of notice of what She got from us, but Shaked hands with all that she could come near, she wept and cryd, in my oppinion with as mutch tenderness and Affection as any Wife or Mother, could do, at the parting with their Husbands or children.[45]

But the moral to be drawn from Hawkesworth's version is neither Robertson's perception of common human feeling nor the sentimentalist's axiom of the natural tenderness of the uninstructed heart, but a triumphant vindication of the initial firmness of policy with which Wallis had subdued Tahitian resistance to his landing (bombarding them and destroying their fleet) and which had apparently produced obedience and gratitude. Banks had hinted at insincerity in the farewell to which the *Endeavour* was exposed and 'Oberea', due to appear in a later act as an adulteress and suspected thief, could not be cast in the role of tragic heroine.[46]

There is, however, some duplicity in Hawkesworth's handling of the sexual encounters between the English seamen and the Tahitian women. It was easy to castigate Purea's adultery or the promiscuity and infanticide of the *ario'i* society, but Banks himself had made no secret of his own light-hearted amours. One recalls that it was maliciously alleged that the *Adventurer* essays (the soundness of whose morality had moved the Archbishop of Canterbury to confer on their author a doctorate) were written to advertise the trustworthiness of the direction of the school for young ladies managed by Hawkesworth and his wife.[47] It was also alleged, no less maliciously, that his principles and opinions changed to accord with those of his new acquaintance as he became habituated to lunching with Sandwich at the Admiralty or dining at his London house.[48] Hawkesworth of course did not overlook his role as public moralist; he censored a number of passages that might have offended nice sensibilities or a patriotic self-image. Readers are spared the scene of Purea feeling and exclaiming at the thickness

45 George Robertson, *The Discovery of Tahiti*, Hugh Carrington (ed.), London, Hakluyt Society, 2nd sec., No. 98, 1948, p. 227.
46 (a) Hawkesworth, I, 248, 251, 257, 258-9. Cf. Wallis, Adm. 55/35, 22, 27 July 1767; Robertson, *The Discovery of Tahiti*, pp. 224-5, 226, 227. (b) Robertson, Adm. 51/4539 (ASCP Reel 1559), 27 July 1767, f. 68 (this is in Robertson's first, briefer and unpublished Journal); Banks, I, 313.
47 John Hawkins, *The Life of Samuel Johnson, Ll.D.* (abridged), B. H. Davis (ed.), London, 1961, pp. 128-9.
48 Cradock, I, 185.

of Robertson's thighs and legs.[49] Even so, he was not prudish and there is a change in tone, not only from the Adventurer essays but from the journals to the *Voyages*. It was not Wallis who introduced the waggish tone into the account of the stealing of nails by the *Dolphin*'s crew. The chiefs, greatly desiring the new material iron, had instructed the young women to increase the size of the nail asked as fee for sexual accommodation and Wallis was seriously concerned that most of the hammock nails had been drawn and also the spikes from the belaying cleats. Hawkesworth phrases Wallis's discovery of the trade in nails:

> When I was acquainted with it, I no longer wondered that the ship was in danger of being pulled to pieces. . . .[50]

It is a phrase that attracted him; he had used it before in the entry of 21 July. But it is an exaggeration, an arch witticism that might have passed in the new company he dined with. Wallis brings up the matter three times but nowhere does he complain of the removal of nails from the body of the ship.[51] Nor was it Cook who described the public act of coition on a Sunday in terms so irreverent as:

> Such were our Matins; our Indians thought fit to perform Vespers of a very different kind. A young man, . . . performed the rites of Venus with a little girl. . . .[52]

The explanation seems to lie in the chameleon-like quality of Hawkesworth's attitudes, consequent on his obsequiousness to wealth and learning and power. Robertson's language was plain: 'fine Young Girls', 'Smart Sensable People', 'fine brisk-spirited women', but the graceless prose of a ship's master, however forceful, could not command the respect due to the diary of a country gentleman whose references to his own sexual affairs were more adept and glancing. The instinct of the lampoonists was right: it was not Hawkesworth but Banks who was ultimately responsible for many of the features unacceptable to contemporary readers.

IV

Hawkesworth accepted the neo-classic literary canons including the gradation of 'kinds'. In his view prose fiction, though a lesser form, had its justification in morality, in that 'the precept becomes more forcible and striking as it is connected with example'. History

[49] Robertson, *The Discovery of Tahiti*, pp. 211-12.
[50] Wallis, Adm. 55/35, f. 42a; Hawkesworth, I, 261.
[51] Wallis, Adm. 55/35, 7, 11, 21 July 1767, all reported in Hawkesworth, I, 239, 241, 248.
[52] Hawkesworth, II, 128.

did not even have this merit since, though it gratifies curiosity, it seldom excites terror and pity.[53] The same defect was common to voyages:

> Voyages and travels have nearly the same excellences and the same defects: no passion is strongly excited except wonder; or if we feel any emotion at the danger of the traveller, it is transient and languid, because his character is not rendered sufficiently important; he is rarely discovered to have any excellences but daring curiosity, he is never the object of admiration, and seldom of esteem.[54]

It was a defect Hawkesworth set out to remedy, perhaps his only attempt at literary innovation. He created, throughout the four voyages, one heroic character designated only as 'I', who is consistent in his behaviour and admirability, but not distinctly recognisable as Byron or Wallis or Carteret or Cook. Far from celebrating the noble savage, Hawkesworth is creating the prototype of that hero of Victorian boys' sea fiction, the magnanimous British commander, and for all that Cook was embarrassed by his editor's inaccuracies and intrusions, the edition of his first voyage was the first contribution to his ennoblement as a national hero. In his General Introduction Hawkesworth outlines the debate, no doubt a private one, that was resolved in his decisions to use the first person rather than the third and to cross-relate the experiences of the journalists and insert any observations of his own. He has annexed for himself two editorial liberties—to speak in the person of each commander and to add his own comments in the commander's person; the journals are not at one remove, but two. His intrusions, his occasional disquisitions on what Beaglehole calls 'large questions' occur when the journals illustrate, or appear to illustrate, a general truth, or open up a fashionable topic of debate; they are random and unsystematic and if at these moments he is consciously displaying his merits as a philosopher he is at least in keeping with his heroic role.

It is this heroic figure who is Hawkesworth's creation. The noble British commander is serene in his confidence of military and technological superiority over the 'Indians' he meets with; he is understanding, imperturbable but unyielding, magnanimous in victory, and seeks only trade and friendship, even if he has to establish it by force. There are sufficient hints of this figure in the journals and Hawkesworth could have claimed he was only giving a firmer outline to a lightly sketched figure. There are Cook's rules

---

53 *Adventurer*, No. 16, 30 December 1752, and No. 4, 18 November 1752.
54 Ibid.

for trading with Tahitians: 'to cultivate a friendship with the natives and to treat them with all imaginable humanity'; and Wallis's instructions off Nukutavake, one of the Tuamotu group: 'to make a landing, but act so as not to offend the Inhabitants if possible to be avoided' and 'to endeavor to traffic with them . . . at the same time not to give them any Offence but endeavor by civil means to get refreshments from them'.

But Hawkesworth omits to say that when Wallis's first blandishments failed at Nukutavake, he gave orders for a forced landing if his men were opposed, an eventuality only prevented by the Tuamotuans vacating the island, or that the English fired twice to frighten them away. The hostility of the people here is presented rather as shyness perhaps born of unfamiliarity with the magnanimity of Europeans.[55] At the end of the second skirmish at Tahiti on 21 June 1767 Hawkesworth adds a passage justifying Wallis's policy: 'and others returned again to the ship to traffic, which is a proof that our conduct had convinced them that while they behaved peaceably they had nothing to fear, and that they were conscious they had brought the mischief, which had just happened upon themselves'. It is not in Wallis, though it can be inferred from Wallis's account of his second lieutenant's speech at the surrender ceremony of 27 June, when Furneaux showed an old man the stones found in the war canoes 'and endeavored to make him sensible that we had acted as we did thro' necessity'.[56]

During the *Endeavour's* stay in Tahiti an inhabitant was shot for making off with a musket. Hawkesworth's account of this eases the conscience of the English reader in a number of ways. He dwells on the motives of the marines who fired in a way that exonerates the commander; he is more convinced than Cook that the Tahitians accepted Banks's explanation of the incident; he is firmer than Cook in his suspicion that the firing might have prevented an attack, and he ends with the real circumstances of the affair unexplained so that no blame can certainly be attached to anyone.[57]

But the noble commander is more concerned at the effects of his actions than those who suffer from them. In one case Hawkesworth not only improves on Cook but he converts Banks's doubts into Cook's afterthoughts. On 14 June 1769 Cook, in retaliation for

[55] (a) Wallis, Adm. 55/35, F. Wilkinson, Log of the *Dolphin*, Adm. 51/4541 (AJCP Reel 1560), 8 June 1767; Robertson, *The Discovery of Tahiti*, p. 118. (b) ibid., p. 121; also 8 June 1767 in the logs of T. Furneaux, F. Pender, and H. West, Adm. 51/4542-4 (AJCP Reels 1560-1). (c) Hawkesworth, I, 204-6; Robertson, *The Discovery of Tahiti*, AJCP 118-21; Wallis, Adm. 55/35, 8 June 1767.

[56] Hawkesworth, I, 218.

[57] Hawkesworth, II, 91-2; Banks, I, 257; Cook, Adm. 55/40, 15 April 1769, *Journals*, I, 79-80.

the theft of a coal-rake, impounded twenty-two canoes full of catches of fish and threatened to burn them. The rake was returned but he now demanded the return of other stolen goods before he would release the canoes. Banks doubted the wisdom of the policy since the canoes belonged to people unconcerned in the thefts, but he thought that, having chosen this course of action, Cook should see it through. At this point, however, Hawkesworth omits Banks's doubts; he repeats Cook's justification and adds to it. Cook says he did it because he was displeased with the daily thefts, Hawkesworth that he planned to end the thefts by making it the common interest of the Tahitians to prevent them. Cook nevertheless defended his policy that thieves should not be fired at, on the two grounds that it would allow the sentinels to shoot on the least occasion, and that if he allowed muskets to be fired with powder only it would reduce the inhabitants' fear of the weapons. Hawkesworth adds moral arguments to Cook's pragmatic reasons. Not only are the common sentinels not fit to be entrusted with the power of life and death, but he argues that since theft (as he thought) was not a crime in Tahiti the English had no right to impose their own code of law and punish it with death. It is an argument more enlightened than Cook himself proposes; and it involves some distortion of the record that Cook has to be made to live up to this view. Cook's policy in fact succeeded only in stopping trade and on 20 June (six days after the theft) he decided to release the canoes. According to Banks they were not released till 22 June, and some of them held for a further ten days. Hawkesworth, however, perhaps approaching one of the neo-classic unities, or perhaps to save the fish, compresses the whole affair into two days and incorporates as Cook's second thoughts Banks's insistent doubts of 15 June, that Cook's action would result in famine for people who were not guilty of the theft. The noble commander, who confesses himself (in Hawkesworth but not in Cook) 'not a little mortified at the bad success of my project' is not above learning from his own mistake, and the editor by engaging the reader's passions has taught a moral lesson. Cook's dismay at the handling of his journal is not surprising.[58]

Generally, however, the tendency of Hawkesworth's treatment of disputes with the inhabitants is towards self-congratulation. He arrives at a smug conclusion in his account of the arrest of the high chiefs on 10 July as hostages against the return of two deserters. If any incident lent itself to moralising or second

---

[58] Banks gives different dates, 22 June and 2 July, for the actual release of the canoes, apparently in two stages. Hawkesworth, II, 148-50; Cook, Adm. 55/40, 14, 15, 20 June 1769, *Journals*, I, 100-1, 103; Banks, I, 290-1, 294, 306.

thoughts it was this, because neither Banks nor Cook was happy with its conclusion—the prisoners' unforgiving resentment and the shame of the English at being offered and having to refuse a reproachful gift from the prisoners who would take nothing in payment. Cook argued that he could have recovered the deserters by no other means, but he was unhappy. But instead of the English embarrassment at their hostages' passive resistance, Hawkesworth manages to suggest a moral triumph in their refusal to take anything without fair payment from a simple people so overjoyed with their release that they wanted to express their gratitude:

> Upon this occasion, as they had done upon another of the same kind, they expressed their joy by an undeserved liberality, strongly urging us to accept of four hogs. These we absolutely refused as a present, and they as absolutely refusing to be paid for them, the hogs did not change masters.[59]

The tone of self-commendation is at its most obvious in the valedictory assessment of the visitors' relations with their hosts. Cook, within the assumptions of his time, is both unpretentious and scrupulous in his self-examination. He recognised that there had been differences due partly to misunderstanding and partly to thefts, but these differences had not been fatal except once and that he was sorry for. Hawkesworth uses the rhetoric of a public oration. He speaks of having lived together 'in the most cordial friendship, and a perpetual reciprocation of good offices'. The differences had been 'accidental', they were 'sincerely regretted' on both sides, and they had arisen not only from the causes Cook mentions but 'from our situation and circumstances, in conjunction with the infirmities of human nature'. The fatal 'accident' had led him to undertake 'measures . . . to prevent others of the same kind'. All his measures during his stay had been governed by the hope of avoiding bloodshed and he wished sincerely that his successor might be 'still more fortunate'.[60]

Hawkesworth's alterations proceed from a mixture of motives, literary, social, and patriotic: his desire to write a work that was interesting and instructive and would sell, to display his merits as a writer, to raise the status of voyages as a literary kind, to please Banks and protect his good name, to protect the reputation of the British navy and promote a national self-image and a model of trading relations with peoples of inferior technology. As his General Introduction makes clear he favoured the expansion of trade, and he was only slightly disturbed that a number of casual-

---

[59] Cook, Adm. 55/40, 11 July 1769, *Journals*, I, 115-16; Banks, 1, 312; Hawkesworth, II, 179.

[60] Cook, Adm. 55/40, 13 July 1769, *Journals*, I, 117; Hawkesworth, II, 182.

ties should be the price of the immense benefits he had no doubt would result from contact with European knowledge and commerce.[61]

On can understand his reluctance to let Cook revise his work. He had imported into his editing an inventive energy of which he might justly have been proud had it been his fortune to have employed it on material more original than other men's journals. But in Beaglehole's words he created 'a sort of classic . . . unacknowledged by the historians of literature . . . a classic . . . of English adventure'.[62] With its neo-classic elements it was an odd work of the eighteenth century to be accepted so uncritically, even if anonymously, by the nineteenth century. Its attraction lay, apparently, in those sentiments of Hawkesworth's that were in key with that century's sense of mission. In this respect, Hawkesworth's *Voyages* has more in common with the pejorative view of pre-literate societies that was taken in the first forty years of the nineteenth century by the agents of the London Missionary Society than with the Enlightenment's envy of their closeness to the simple promptings of Nature.

61 Hawkesworth, I, xvii-xix.
62 Beaglehole in Cook, *Journals*, I, ccliii.

Of Silkworms and Farthingales and the Will of God

Louis A. Landa

I propose to examine a phase of eighteenth-century rationalism hitherto little known or neglected. This rationalistic strain of thought manifests itself in a variety of literary works whose authors used prevalent economic ideas, ideas themselves rooted in the diffused rationalistic philosophy of the times. Since the subject is greatly ramified I will restrict myself to one significant aspect, a theme involving a creature both fascinating and disconcerting to contemporaries—the lady of quality or fashion, the Clarindas and Belindas and Celias of the reigns of Queen Anne and the first two Georges; and I submit that this lady of fashion becomes a figure of special interest and complexity if we view her in the context of the economic ideas which swirled around her head. She will be seen to play a vital part in a universe rationally designed and providentially ordered to accommodate her. Because the eighteenth century held firmly to the Aristotelian conviction that nature does nothing in vain, it found a rationale for the lady of fashion in the cosmic scheme of things. And perhaps it is not untenable to maintain that the lady of fashion, like the seas, the mountains, and the other artifacts of nature, was herself part of that design and harmony in the universe which truly demonstrated the existence of a deity.

The image of the lady of fashion relevant to present purposes emerges from two minor poems of 1729, the first of which is James Ralph's *Clarinda, or the Fair Libertine*, where the poet writes: for ladies of fashion

> the Silk-worm spins his silken Store,
> For them *Peru* exports its silver ore;
> For them the Gold is dug on *Guinea*'s Coast
> And sparkling Gems the farthest *Indies boast*,

> For them *Arabia* breathes its spicy Gale,
> And fearless Seamen kill the *Greenland* Whale.[1]

Here we observe the lady of fashion, not as a fully delineated character or personality but as a kind of economic abstraction, the figurative embodiment of luxurious taste and indulgence, an idealised consumer of economic goods for whose delectation the entire universe is exploited and operated as a vast mercantile enterprise. It is of this creature that John Gay had written (in *Rural Sports*, 1713):

> So the gay Lady, with Expensive Care,
> Borrows the Pride of Land, of Sea, and Air.[2]

And in a similar vein, again in 1729, Soame Jenyns, in his poem, *The Art of Dancing*, addressed the lady of fashion thus:

> For you the Silkworms, fine-wrought Webs display,
> And lab'ring spin their little Lives away;
> . . . .
> For you the Sea resigns its pearly Store
> And Earth unlocks her Mines of treasur'd Ore.[3]

But let me take a more familiar point of departure, a passage from Pt IV of *Gulliver's Travels*, in which this attractive consumer is repudiated. She is, indeed, converted into a female Yahoo. Gulliver is conversing with his master in Houyhnhnmland: 'I assured him', Gulliver says, 'that this whole Globe of Earth must be at least three Times gone round, before one of our better female *Yahoos* could get her Breakfast, or a Cup to put it in'. This remark, which comes as Gulliver is nearing the apogee of his disenchantment, is part of a long passage primarily economic in substance. The wise and rational Houyhnhnm listens to Gulliver describe

---

1 James Ralph, *Clarinda, or the Fair Libertine. A Poem. In Four Cantos*, London, 1729, pp. 37-8.

2 John Gay, *Rural Sports: A Poem to Mr. Pope*, 1713, in *Poetical Works of John Gay*, G. C. Faber (ed.), London, 1926, p. 658.

3 Soame Jenyns, *The Art of Dancing. In Three Cantos*, London, 1729, pp. 8-9. See also J. D. Breval, *The Art of Dress*, 1717, dedicated to the 'Toasts of Great Britain':

> For you, th' Italian Worm her Silk prepares,
> And distant *India* sends her choicest Wares,
> Some Toy from ev'ry Part the Sailor brings,
> The Semptress labours and the Poet sings. (p. 17).

Elsewhere I hope to write (but not extensively) about the silkworm in eighteenth-century literature, that 'wondrous worm' (to use a phrase from Du Baztas) which caught the attention and stirred the imagination of poets and clergymen, of scientists and merchants and statesmen. To contemporaries the silkworm was, as Henry Barhan, F.R.S., wrote in 1719, an 'incomparable creature, which is even a miracle in nature' (*An Essay upon the Silk-Worm*, London, 1719, p. 151).

certain aspects of life in England: the unequal distribution of wealth, the fine clothes and noble houses available to the rich, the indulgence in costly meats and drinks. And here Gulliver finds that he must explain to the Houyhnhnm what these costly meats are: 'I enumerated', he says, 'as many Sorts as came into my Head, with the various Methods of dressing them, which could not be done without sending Vessels by Sea to every Part of the World, as well for Liquors to drink, as for Sauces, and innumerable other Conveniences'. It is at this point that Gulliver remarks on the extensive economic activity—encircling of the globe three times —necessary to provide one of the better female Yahoos of England with her breakfast. The comment of his master among the Houyhnhnms—that a country unable to furnish its inhabitants with food and drink must be miserable—is mild in contrast to Gulliver's own indictment of his countrymen, who, he tells us, send away the necessities in exchange for 'the Materials of Diseases, Folly, and Vice'.[4]

---

[4] *The Prose Works of Jonathan Swift*, Herbert Davis (ed.), Oxford, 1941, XI [235]-236. Hereafter cited as *Prose Works*. An interesting parallel in medical literature to Swift's attack on sauces and liquors as emblems of luxury and intemperance may be found in John Woodward, *The State of Physick, and of Diseases*, London, 1718: 'Our Error in Diet consists partly of the Nature and Sort of it: in high Seasoning, strong Sauces . . . new Modes of Cookery, brought amongst us by the Foreigners that have come over . . . for about 30 Years past. The so frequent Use of Chocolate, of Coffee, Limonade, Punch: but more especially of Tea, drank now in so great Excess, all over the Kingdom; to the Neglect of the much better and more wholsome Products of our own Country, the Misspending our Treasure, and carrying it even to the most distant and remote Parts of the World: or to the Exchange of our own usefull Manufactures, not only for Trifles, and Things of no real Use, but for such as are detrimental, and injurious. To these Sauces, and these Liquors, our vertuous, wise, stout, healthy Ancestors were Strangers. By the former, Intemperance and Excess is promoted. . . . By the Liquors, Way is made for a fresh Appetite, and new Charge; these Swilling the Indigestion, and vitious Contents of the Stomach, into the Blood . . . Hence the great Increase of the Stone, Gout, Rheumatism, Nervine and other Affections. . . . The Consequence of this great Increase of the Arts of Luxury and Intemperance, are Vice and Immorality: Irreligion, Impiety, Passion, Animosity, Contention, Faction: Neglect of Thought, Studyes, and Business, Misspending of Time, Ignorance, Stupidity, Poverty, Discontent, Sickness, Disease.' (pp. 194-5). A similar indictment in a different context is found in R. Campbell, *The London Tradesman*, London, 1747, p. 277: 'We abhor that any thing should appear at our Tables in its native Properties; all the Earth, from both the Poles, the most distant and different Climates, must be ransacked for Spices, Pickles, and Sauces, not to relish but to disguise our Food . . . This depraved Taste of spoiling wholesome Dyet, by costly and pernicious Sauces, and absurd Mixtures, does not confine itself to the Tables of the Great; but the Contagion is become epidemical; Poor and rich live as if they were of a different Species of Beings from their Ancestors, and observe a Regimen of Diet calculated not to supply the Wants of Nature, but to oppress her Faculties, disturbe her Operations, and load her with, till now, unheard of Maladies.' But cf. Thomas Fuller, *The Holy State and the Profane State* (1642), J. Nichols (ed.), 1841, p. 109: 'God is not so hard a master, but that he alloweth his Servants sauce . . . to eat with their meat'.

Characteristically Swift brings the passage to a close with a burst of Juvenalian indignation in a catalogue of the vices and follies which inevitably result from a foreign trade thus misdirected. The fundamental point of this passage in *Gulliver's Travels* needs little attention. It is a general statement of a prevalent theoretical position in mercantilist economic thought of the period, that the importation of luxuries is *not* economically desirable, the logic being that imported luxuries have an adverse effect on the balance of trade. In a compendium of mercantilist dogma published in 1713, Sir Theodore Janssen, a director of the South Sea Company, codified the prevailing view in these words: 'That the importing Commodities of mere Luxury is so much real Loss to the Nation as they amount to'.[5]

It is well known that Swift often expounded this view—in his various Irish tracts, in his correspondence, even in one of his sermons, *Causes of the Wretched Condition of Ireland,* where he maintained that the importation of luxuries is a primary cause of Ireland's impoverishment. A year or so after the publication of *Gulliver* he wrote that a people should 'import as few Incitements to Luxury, either in Cloaths, Furniture, Food, or Drink, as they possibly can live conveniently without'—a remark which restates the economic principle of the passage in *Gulliver* here under discussion.[6]

We might expect in his Irish tracts that Swift's statement of this view would be less fervid than in *Gulliver's Travels,* where he is using it for the satirical exposé of a wasteful and corrupt society and for the denunciation of man's nature; but even in the cooler context of purely economic discussion Swift does not restrain himself. The intensity with which Gulliver inveighs against foreign importations derives from Swift's appraisal of the harsh realities of Ireland's economy, to which he bore witness so frequently in pleading for economic reforms which might achieve a measure of national self-sufficiency.[7]

But this passage in *Gulliver's Travels,* which I call the Female Yahoo's Breakfast, contains more than appears on the surface. It has ramifications and implications reaching into several fields of thought; and in using the woman of quality, this better female Yahoo, to define his economic predilections Swift had ample pre-

5 [Charles King], *The British Merchant: A Collection of Papers relating to the Trade and Commerce of Great Britain and Ireland,* 2nd ed., London, 1743, p. 5 [1st ed. 1721]. The quoted 'maxim' is from Sir Theodore Janssen's *General Maxims of Trade,* 1713.
6 *Prose Works,* XII, p. 7.
7 For a general discussion of Swift's economic views, see my article, 'Swift's Economic Views and Mercantilism', *ELH: A Journal of English Literary History,* Vol. X, Dec. 1943, pp. 310-35.

cedent. She was already known in one guise or another well before *Gulliver's Travels* was published; and I wish to suggest that when Swift's contemporaries found her in the *Travels* she would have been recognised as a stock figure, or even as a convention in literary works using economic themes. She would have generated a variety of emotions, by no means all of them emotions attendant on rejection, as in Swift. Furthermore, the more knowledgeable contemporaries would have realised that the female Yahoo's breakfast was indeed a complex matter, one that went beyond merely economic considerations into considerations of medicine and national health, geography and international relations, and theology. It is not merely her imported breakfast which disturbed Swift. As this better female Yahoo emerges from his writings of the 1720s her power to consume is enlarged beyond, in Swift's words, exotic liquors, such 'Indian poisons' as tea, coffee, and chocolate. There is also an array of 'unnecessary finery—muslin, laces, silks, holland, cambric, calico', characterised by Swift as 'the instruments of our ruin', imported 'to gratify the vanity and pride, and luxury of the women, and of the fops who admire them'.[8] The opening lines of Swift's poem, *The Lady's Dressing Room* (1732), are appropriate here:

> Five Hours, (and who can do it less in?)
> By haughty *Celia* spent in Dressing;
> The Goddess from her Chamber issues,
> Array'd in Lace, Brocades and Tissues.[9]

Celia in 'Lace, Brocades and Tissues' is merely a poetic version of the Irish women who so preoccupy Swift's thoughts in these years. It is to them that he often appealed, to 'vie with each other in the fineness of their native linen', assuring them that their beauty and gentility would shine no less than if they were covered with diamonds and brocade.[10] Three years after the appearance of *Gulliver's Travels* we find Swift again erupting with blazing intensity against these fine ladies. With Bishop Berkeley he believed an Irish woman arrayed in French silks and Flanders lace to be 'an enemy to the Nation'.[11] He wrote with passion of 'those detestable Extravagancies of Flanders lace . . . Italian or Indian Silks, Tea, Coffee, Chocolate, Chinaware, and . . . profusion of wines':

---

[8] *Prose Works*, XII, pp. 63ff., 126.

[9] *The Poems of Jonathan Swift*, Harold Williams (ed.), 2nd ed., Oxford, 1958, II, p. 525.

[10] *Prose Works*, XII, p. 127.

[11] Ibid., XI, p. 16. See George Berkeley, *The Querist*, No. 141, 1735: 'Whether a woman of fashion ought not to be declared a public enemy', in *Works*, A. A. Luce and T. C. Jessop (eds.), London and New York, 1953, VI, p. 117.

> Is it not [he asked] the highest Indignity to human nature,
> that men should be such poltrons as to suffer the Kingdom
> and themselves to be undone, by the Vanity, the Folly, the
> Pride, and Wantonness of their Wives, who under the present
> Corruptions seem to be a kind of animal suffered for our sins
> to be sent into the world for the Destruction of Familyes,
> Societyes, and Kingdoms . . . who by long practice can recon-
> cile the most pernicious forein Drugs to their health and
> pleasure, provided they are but expensive . . . who . . . can
> sleep beyond noon, revel upon Indian poisons, and spend the
> revenue of a moderate family to adorn a nauseous unwhole-
> some living Carcase.[12]

Here, then, in the Irish tracts, passionately denounced, is Gulliver's
better female Yahoo, a creature of indulgence, given to 'unwhole-
some drugs' and 'Unnecessary finery', an emblem of ruinous economic consumption. And we get a brief flashing vision of the vast
machinery of foreign trade, functioning wastefully and absurdly
to satisfy this demanding consumer.

I may mention in passing that Swift's pleas for national frugality
would have evoked sympathetic responses in many of his contemporaries, but my concern here is to observe other writers of the
period—Addison, Pope, and Defoe, among them—who have employed this economic theme and who contrast sharply with Swift.
I turn first to a work not belletristic, but one in which the conception of man's nature and of society has affinities with that of
Swift, Bernard Mandeville's brilliant *Fable of the Bees* (1714).
Mandeville was concerned with a paradox that made his own and
a later generation uneasy: how to achieve a society whose members
are frugal and honest and at the same time opulent. Mandeville
thought it *not* possible. A frugal and honest society, he maintained,
could arise only when men practised 'Native Simplicity': 'let them
never be acquainted with Strangers or Superfluities, but remove
and keep them from every thing that might raise their Desires . . .'.
An opulent nation, on the other hand, was based upon the refined
appetites and enlarged desires of its people. Thus Mandeville tells
those who want 'an opulent, knowing, and polite Nation' to value
'commerce with Foreign Countries . . . if possible get into the Sea'.
'Promote Navigation', he urges, 'cherish the Merchant, and
encourage Trade in every Branch of it; this will bring Riches,
and where they are, Arts and Sciences will soon follow . . .'.[13] From
the vantage of national wealth (ethical considerations are something else again) Mandeville finds nothing to condemn in sending

[12] *Prose Works*, XII, p. 80.
[13] *The Fable of the Bees: Or, Private Vices, Publick Benefits*, F. B. Kaye (ed.),
Oxford, 1924, I, p. 184.

a ship thrice around the world for a female Yahoo's breakfast. 'What Estates', he writes, 'have been got by Tea and Coffee!'[14] It would be a difficult Task', he asserts, 'to enumerate all the Advantages and different Benefits, that accrue to a Nation on account of Shipping and Navigation'. And Mandeville details the multitudinous web of activities and the abundance of stores necessary for building and manning even one ship: timber, tar, resin, grease, masts, nails, cables, the employment of smiths and mariners, and the maintenance of the families of those employed—all of this spreading in a widening circle of economic activity involving large numbers.[15]

Dispassionately Mandeville looks at this universal mercantile economy—the vast nexus of enterprises—to observe 'What a vast Traffick [i.e. trade] is drove, what a variety of Labour is performed in the World to the Maintenance of Thousands of Families that altogether depend on two silly if not odious Customs; the taking of Snuff and smoking of Tobacco . . .'.[16] By this logic the woman of quality becomes not 'an Enemy to the Nation' (Swift's epithet) but a public benefactor. Her *private* vices are *public* benefits. Mandeville considers the farthingale: that 'silly and capricious Invention of Hoop'd and Quilted Petticoats', he declares, has done as much as, if not more than, the Reformation for the enrichment of nations.[17] As for a fine scarlet cloth designed for a garment: 'what a Bustle is there to be made in several Parts of the World' before it can be produced, 'what Multiplicity of Trades and Artificers must be employ'd!'[18]

In a brilliant passage Mandeville evokes the mercantile complexities involved, the vast seas to be traversed, the varied climates to be endured, the fatigues and hazards to be undergone, even the ramifications involved in so obvious a matter as providing the ingredients of the dye, ingredients 'dispers'd thro' the Universe that are to meet in one Kettle': argol from the Rhine, vitriol from Hungary, saltpetre from the East Indies, cochineal from the West Indies. 'While so many Sailors are broiling in the Sun and sweltered with Heat in the *East* and *West* of us, another set of them are freezing in the *North* to fetch Potashes from Russia'.[19] All of this to satisfy the desire for a garment of scarlet cloth.

We observe then in Mandeville a fuller expression of the theme treated all too sparsely by Swift; and Mandeville gives us the details

---

14 Ibid., I, p. 359.
15 Ibid., I, pp. 359-60.
16 Ibid., I, p. 359.
17 Ibid., I, p. 356.
18 Ibid.
19 Ibid., I, pp. 356-8.

not supplied by Gulliver when that disillusioned traveller is dis-
approving of ships that encircle the world to bring back vanities
for indulgent female Yahoos. Indeed, Swift might have enriched
this part of the *Travels* had he been as vivid as Mandeville in
employing concrete details.

This evocation of particulars in support of the economic theme
I am discussing is vividly present in the *Spectator*. As we know,
Addison and Steele celebrate the dignity of commerce on many
occasions, most obviously in the person of Sir Andrew Freeport, a
man concerned with foreign trade, a man, we are told, of noble
and generous ideas, better company than a scholar, one whose ships
sail to every point of the compass.[20] He is the type, Addison and
Steele are convinced, responsible for England's wealth and greatness. It is therefore not surprising that Mr Spectator, visiting the
Royal Exchange, should look about him with satisfaction and
remark that there 'are not more useful members in a commonwealth than merchants'. Mr Spectator glows with satisfaction as he
considers *foreign* trade, and his rhetoric likewise glows as he comments on seaborne traffic:

> Our Ships [he says] are laden with the Harvest of every
> Climate: our Tables are stored with Spices, and Oils, and
> Wines: Our Rooms are filled with Pyramids of *China*, and
> adorned with the Workmanship of *Japan*: Our Morning's-
> Draught comes to us from the remotest Corners of the Earth:
> We repair our Bodies by the Drugs of *America*, and repose our
> selves under *Indian* Canopies. My Friend Sir Andrew calls the
> Vineyards of *France* our Gardens; the Spice-Islands our Hot-
> bed; the *Persians* our Silk-Weavers, and the *Chinese* our
> Potters.[21]

The heightened tone, the particularity, the accumulation of consumer items in the essay I am quoting, No. 69, suggest a kind of
mercantile appetite or zestfulness.

Little wonder that the Tory foxhunter depicted by Addison in
the *Freeholder,* No. 22 (5 Mar. 1716), of the landed gentry and
disdainful of foreign commerce, is out of countenance when he

---

[20] *Spectator*, No. 2, 2 Mar. 1711, Donald F. Bond (ed.), Oxford, 1965, Vol. I, pp.
10-11.

[21] Ibid., No. 69, 19 May 1711, Vol. I, pp. 295-6. See Edmund Waller's poetic
version of this theme in 1665:

So what our earth, and what our heav'n denies,
Our ever-constant friend, the sea supplies.
The taste of hot Arabia's spice we know,
Free from the scorching sun, that makes it grow:
Without the worm, in Persian silks we shine;
And, without planting, drink of ev'ry wine.

('A Panegyric to My Lord Protector, of the Present Greatness, and Joint
Interest, of his Highness, and the Nation', stanzas 14-15).

discovers that the punch he loves so well contains such imported items as brandy, sugar, lemon and nutmeg. The only English ingredient is water. And what of the woman of quality, Swift's 'enemy to the Nation', Gulliver's better female Yahoo, Mandeville's lady encased in a hooped petticoat, whose desires and consumer's appetite keep the vast machinery of international trade in motion? For Mr Spectator she is a vision of delight; and he envelops her along with the merchant, in his swinging eloquence and orotundity.

> The single Dress of a Woman of Quality [he declares] is often the Product of an Hundred Climates. The Muff and the Fan come together from the different Ends of the Earth. The Scarf is sent from the Torrid Zone, and the Tippet from beneath the Pole. The Brocade Petticoat rises out of the Mines of *Peru*, and the Diamond Necklace out of the Bowels of *Indostan*.[22]

Far from being an object to condemn, this woman adorned with 'the Products of an Hundred Climates', is for Mr Spectator an emblem of cosmopolitanism, a citizen of the world transcending national boundaries; and as he visualises her his imagination goes winging out over oceans to far away lands, into the frozen wastes and the steaming tropics, on a mercantile progress more extended than any royal progress ever was.

If we look back for a moment to Addison in his guise as Mr Bickerstaff in the *Tatler,* we find him, like Mandeville, glancing with the eye of both economist and moralist at the quilted and hooped petticoat. With this 'monstrous invention' Addison was ready to sacrifice economic advantage for good taste and good sense in fashions. In an amusing essay (the *Tatler,* No. 116) he depicts Mr Bickerstaff as presiding over a Court of Judicature in which the hooped petticoat is the criminal defendant. Although counsel for the defendant argues that the hooped variety in contrast to the ordinary petticoat has greatly improved the woollen trade, the ropemaker's trade, and the Greenland trade, by utilising more cloth, more cordage, and more whalebone, the decision nevertheless goes against the defendant. At the same time Mr Bickerstaff hastens to declare himself a defender of luxuries and fashions which do *not* pervert nature:

> I consider woman as a beautiful romantic animal, that may be adorned with furs and feathers, pearls and diamonds, ores and silks. The lynx shall cast its skin at her feet to make her a tippet; the peacock, parrot, and swan shall *pay contributions* to her muff; the sea shall be searched for shells, and the rocks

for gems; and every part of nature furnish out its share towards the embellishment of a creature that is the most consummate work of it. All this I shall indulge them in; but as for the petticoat I have been speaking of, I neither can nor will allow it.[23]

The light tone of the essay does not obscure Addison's concern, shared by his contemporaries, over the conflicting claims of commerce and morality; but he was not inclined, either by temperament or general outlook, to view the conflict with the austerity and intensity of a Swift. Mr Bickerstaff's apostrophe to woman, just quoted, in which he maintains that the animal and physical worlds are properly exploited for the embellishment of women, reveals that Mr Bickerstaff and Mr Spectator are in no respect at odds.

Pope presents us with a more subtle insinuation into literature of the theme we are observing. In *The Rape of the Lock* (1714) we enter a world where serious economic considerations ostensibly do not intrude. It is, of course, a world catered to by the luxury trades (to use modern parlance), a world of glitter and fine feathers, a filigree world of jewels and brocades, of Indian screens and amber snuff boxes, all an appropriate context for Pope's heroine, Belinda, whose charm and gaiety are such that to place her among the economically wasteful female Yahoos seems unforgivably churlish. When 'Belinda smiled . . . all the world was gay'. And Pope envelops Belinda in such vivid and memorable lines of poetic beauty that we may miss the economic implications. Yet Belinda at the toilette table at the close of Canto I would I believe, have arrested the attention of any contemporary reader sensitive to economic ideas. The relevant lines depict Belinda being made up by her maid, Betty, for the daily round of pleasure and social conquest. Pope describes the objects of the toilette:

> Unnumber'd Treasures ope at once, and here
> The various Off'rings of the World appear;
> From each she [Betty] nicely culls with curious Toil,
> And decks the Goddess with the glitt'ring Spoil.
> This Casket *India's* glowing Gems unlocks,
> And all *Arabia* breathes from yonder Box.
> The Tortoise here and Elephant unite,
> Transform'd to *Combs* the speckled and the white.
>
> (Canto I, ll. 129-36)

[23] *Tatler*, No. 116, 5 Jan. 1709-10, in *The British Essayists, with Prefaces, Biographical, Historical, and Critical*, Lionel Thomas Berguer (ed.), London, 1823, Vol. III, pp. 175-6.

Here, in a somewhat different guise and transmuted into poetry, we have Addison's woman of quality whose desires caused timber to be felled, hemp and resin to be imported, ships to be built, and sailors sent to remote lands, that she may be adorned. Her adornment is 'the Product of an Hundred Climates', in Addison's phrase; or as Pope himself says, Belinda was 'decked with all that Land and Sea afford' (Canto V, l. 11), with 'the various Off'rings of the World'—and a Swift or a Mandeville, visualising the ships traversing the seas, to India for gems, Arabia for perfumes, and Africa for ivory, would be aware of the mercantile complexities implied by these poetic lines. Pope calls this ritual of the toilette the 'sacred Rites of Pride' (Canto I, l. 128), a piece of overt social or ethical indictment, without any explicit economic coloration. Perhaps there is a sly, dark hint in the phrase 'glitt'ring Spoil', but I should not want to insist on the pejorative impact of even that phrase. And the submerged theme, the suggestion of a universal mercantile economy operating for the enhancement of Belinda's beauty, is in a context of such tolerance and amiability that Pope's mild rebuke tends to dissolve in the sunshine of Belinda's charm.

But consider for a moment the reaction to Belinda of a convinced mercantilist with his austere conviction that imported luxuries are an economic evil. How would he view this beguiling young lady? What would he say of her silks, spun not by *domestic* silkworms but by the *foreign* worms of Persia, France, and Italy? Of her ivory and tortoise shell from Africa? Of her sparkling gems from India? Of her Arabian perfumes transported laboriously by camel caravan across the Arabian desert and thence down the incense road to a Mediterranean port, eventually to reach London?

The answers are obvious—and painful. But we may find some relief in what was doubtless of English manufacture, the stays of her corset covered with tabby (taffeta), the one article of her underclothing likely to be domestic, and as well her stockings and her shoes. The only conclusion possible is that Belinda, economically speaking, was a menace to the welfare of her country.

I return to Addison for a moment, for suggestions of a richer, more philosophic view of this theme, a larger vision prevalent in the period and earlier which assimilated the idea of trade and the merchant into both the natural order and the divine order. The eulogists of commerce in the eighteenth century would have been untrue to their rationalistic heritage if they had failed to see the spectacle of a universal mercantile economy as an aspect of the ordered and harmonious universe in which all parts cohere and have specific functions. A clue comes, significantly, from Addison's choice of an epigraph for the *Spectator,* No. 69, a quotation from Virgil's *Georgics* of several lines (I, ll. 54-61) concerned with regional differences. Virgil points out that nature has imposed diversity in the products of the soil:

> This Ground with *Bacchus,* that with *Ceres* suits:
> That other loads the Trees with happy Fruits:
> A fourth, with Grass, unbidden, decks the Ground.
> Thus *Tmolus* is with yellow Saffron crowned.

The genius of the soil which produces this diversity is paralleled by the genius of each nation, whose products reveal the specialised and distinctive quality of its culture:

> *India,* black Ebon and white Ivory bears;
> And soft *Idume* weeps her od'rous Tears.
> Thus *Pontus* sends her Beaver Stones from far;
> And naked *Spanyards* temper Steel for War:
> *Epirus,* for the *Elean* Chariot breeds,
> (In hopes of Palms) a Race of running Steeds.
> This is the Orig'nal Contract; these the Laws
> Impos'd by Nature, and by Nature's Cause,
> On sundry Places. . . .[24]

From Virgil down through the middle ages and into the seventeeth century the idea of regional differences received more than passing comment. Its significance was observed by geographers, theologians, and poets, by writers on travel and by those interested in commerce. The readers of Du Bartas in the late sixteenth and in the seventeenth centuries found the idea elaborately set forth in *The Divine Weekes;* and it may be that the English translations of the 'Second Week' in the early seventeenth century help to disseminate the view that the entire world is an exchange, a mart, analogous to a city, such a city as London, so Joshua Sylvester, the translator of Du Bartas (1606) would have it, *'wherein dwell People of all conditions, ... continually trafficking together and exchanging their particular commodities for benefit of the Publicke'.*[25] Consider the following lines from Du Bartas:

> *And All's but an Exchange, Where (brieflie) no Man Keeps ought as private: Trade makes all Things Common*
> So come our Sugars from *Canary* Isles:
> From *Candy,* Currance, Muskadels, and Oyles:

---

24 *Spectator,* No. 69, 19 May 1711, Vol. I, pp. 292-3. Dryden's translation.
25 Du Bartas [Guillaume de Saluste Sieur], *Dubartas His Divine Weekes and Workes translated . . . by Joshua Sylvester,* London, 1613, p. 352.

From the *Moluques* Spices: Balsamum
From *Egypt*: Odours from *Arabia* come:
From *India*, Drugs, rich Gemmes, and Ivorie:
From *Syria*, Mummie: black-red Ebonie,
From burning *Chus*: from *Peru*, Pearl and Gold:
From *Russia* Furres (to keep the rich from cold):
From *Florence*, Silks: From *Spayn*, Fruit, Saffron, Sacks:
From *Denmark*, Amber, Cordage, Firres, and Flax:
From *France* and *Flanders*, Linnen, Wood, and Wine:
From *Holland* Hops: Horse[s] from the banks of *Rhine*.
In briefe, each Country (as pleas'd God distribute)
To the Worlds Treasure payes a Sundry Tribute.[26]

Writers of a religious cast of mind saw in this universal disper-
sion of products a divine intention, that widely separated peoples
would be bound together in amity, brought to cohesion and inter-
dependence by their need for one another. Bishop Joseph Hall,
whose *Quo Vadis?* (1617) is a 'Censure of Travel', nevertheless
grants that travel for purposes of trade is valid, because trade
derives from the providential ordering by which products have
been dispersed. God, he writes, 'hath made one country the granary,
another the cellar, another the orchard, another the arsenal, of
their neighbours, yea of the remotest parts'.

> It is an over rigorous construction of the works of God, that
> in moating our island with the ocean he meant to shut us
> up from other regions: for God himself, that made the Sea,
> was the Author of navigation; and hath therein taught us to
> set up a wooden bridge that may reach to the very antipodes
> themselves.

Thus Bishop Hall can remark that 'no parcel of earth' has been
stored by the deity as a 'private reservation', that 'Either Indies
may be searched for those treasures which God hath laid up in
them for their far distant owners', that 'a ship of merchants, that
fetches her wares from far, is the good housewife of the commonwealth'.[27] Little more than a decade later Baptist Goodall, an
obscure London merchant, stimulated by the wonders of travel

---

[26] Ibid., p. 353.
[27] *Works of the Right Reverend Joseph Hall, D.D.*, Philip Wynter (ed.), Oxford, 1863, IX, [529]. Hall writes:
> The sea and earth are the great coffers of God: the discoveries of naviga-
> tion are the keys, which whoever hath received may know that he is freely
> allowed to unlock these chests of nature without any need to pick the
> wards. In *Quo Vadis*, though Hall accepts the principle of the 'divinity of
> trade,' he is concerned to write a 'just censure of travel'; and as a result
> he strongly indicts the introduction into England of foreign fashions and
> manners. These have corrupted, he asserts, the judgment and manners of
> the English. The lady of fashion draws some of his strongest criticism:
> 'it were well if we knew our own fashions; better if we could keep them.
> What mischief have we amongst us that we have not borrowed? To begin

and trade to break into verse, catalogues the products of two score and more of nations ranging from the furs of Russia, the fruits of Spain, the wool and coal of England, to the pearls of China and the silks of India—with the conclusion that there is a divinity in this diversity:

> One succours other, traffic breeds affection,
> The whole is governed by the high protection,
> For winds, seas, sky and travel all agree
> To frame on earth a just conformity.[28]

Inevitably economic writers and the apologists for the great trading companies found this viewpoint congenial. Witness Charles Davenant, one of the able defenders of the East India Company, declaring in 1697 that 'the various Products of different Soiles and Countries is [sic] an Indication that Providence intended they should be helpful to each other, and mutually supply the Necessities of one another'.[29] There is, then, a long-established traditional view in the background of Mr Spectator's remark (No. 69) in 1711 that

> Nature seems to have taken a particular Care to disseminate her Blessings among the different Regions of the World, with an Eye to this mutual Intercourse and Traffick among Mankind, that the Natives of the several Parts of the Globe might

---

at our skin: who knows not whence we had the variety of our vain disguises . . .? The dresses being constant in their mutability, show us our masters. . . . Whom would it not vex, to see how that other sex hath learned to make antics and monsters of themselves? Whence came their hips to the shoulders and their breasts to the navel; but the one from some ill shaped dames of France, the other from the worse minded courtesans of Italy? Whence else learned they . . . those high washes which are cunningly licked on . . . Whence the frizzled and powdered bushes of their borrowed excrement: as if they were ashamed of the head of God's making . . . ?' (p. 556). This kind of tirade was, of course, a commonplace in homiletic literature. For our purposes it illustrates the juxtaposition in the same work of the principle that trade is inherent in the divine plan and the view of the moralist that it can be, as a practical matter, an evil force.

[28] *The Tryall of Travell*, London, 1630, sig. c³. I have modernised the spelling. The providential conjunction of winds and sea to further trade, as observed by Goodall, is a frequent theme in the seventeenth century. A typical example from an economic tract: 'And to the end there should be a *Commerce* amongst men, it hath pleased *God* to invite as it were, one Countrey to traffique with another, by the variety of things which the one hath, and the other hath not: that so that which is wanting to the *one*, might be supplyed by the *other*, that all might have sufficient.
Which thing the very windes and seas proclaime, in giving passage to all nations: the windes blowing sometimes towards one Countrey, sometimes towards another; that so by this divine justice, every one might be supplyed in things necessary for life and maintenance' (Edward Misselden, *Free Trade, Or the Meanes to Make Trade Flourish*, 2nd ed., 1622, p. 25). Misselden finds these providential winds mentioned in Seneca and Aristotle (p. 26).

[29] [Charles Davenant], *An Essay on the East India Company. By the Author of The Essay upon Wayes and Means*, London, 1696, p. 34.

have a kind of Dependance upon one another, and be united together by their common Interest.[30]

What Gulliver gloomily repudiated, Addison sees as the working out of a natural and rational and providential nexus: 'The Food [he writes] often grows in one Country, and the Sauce in another. The Fruits of *Portugal* are corrected by the Products of the *Barbadoes*: The Infusion of a *China* Plant is sweetened with the Pith of an Indian Cane'. It is, of course, by this same logic that Addison can cheerfully observe that 'the single Dress of a Woman of Quality is often the Product of an hundred Climates'. It is by this logic as well that merchants are recognised as instruments of a universal economy, fulfilling a principle of universal mercantile amity: Merchants, Mr Spectator writes, 'knit Mankind together in a mutual Intercourse of good Offices, distribute the Gifts of Nature, find work for the Poor, add Wealth to the Rich, and Magnificence to the Great'.[31]

This principle of universal mercantile amity is aptly termed by James Thomson, in his *Castle of Indolence* (1748) 'social commerce': social commerce joins 'land to land' and unites the poles. It raises 'renowned marts' and 'without bloody Spoil', brings home from either Indies 'the gorgeous stores'.[32] Into this concept of 'social commerce' contemporaries infused a richness of feeling well illustrated by George Lillo's popular play of 1731, *The London Merchant*. Here we are told that merchandise promotes humanity, 'as it has open'd and yet keeps up an Intercourse between Nations, far remote from one another in Situation, Customs and Religion; promoting Arts, Industry, Peace and Plenty; by Mutual Benefits diffusing Mutual Love from Pole to Pole'.[33]

Defoe, as we would expect from one who with justice may be called the laureate of commerce, utilises these various strains of thought with enthusiasm. Like Addison, Defoe envisions trade in

[30] *Spectator,* No. 69, 19 May 1711, Vol. I, pp. 294-5.
[31] Ibid., p. 296.
[32] *The Castle of Indolence and Other Poems,* Alan Dugald McKillop (ed.), Lawrence, Kansas, 1961, Canto II, stanza 20, p. 101. See Pope's variant of 'social commerce' in *Windsor Forest* (1713), ll.385ff. written as the Treaty of Utrecht was being completed. Pope presents a shining vision of a world peaceably united by commerce, with England, of course, as the central unifying force.
[33] Act III, sc. 1. In this scene the merchant, Thorowgood, says that trade is 'founded in reason and the nature of things' and Trueman, his virtuous apprentice, responds: 'I have observ'd those countries, where trade is promoted and encouraged, do not make discoveries to destroy, but to improve mankind by love and friendship; to tame the fierce and polish the most savage; to teach them the advantages of honest traffick, by taking from them, with their own consent, their useless superfluities, and giving them, in return, what, from their ignorance in manual arts, their situation, or some other accident, they stand in need of'.

274 STUDIES IN THE EIGHTEENTH CENTURY

larger, philosophic terms, in the context of the principle of universal correspondence, a principle which meant for contemporaries as I have indicated, a providential and rationalistic ordering of the universe by virtue of which the very differences in nations and peoples bind all men together. The restricted and specialised products of each nation and the national character which manifests itself by demanding certain products not indigenous—these are part of the providential design. England had been *naturally* and providentially endowed with the soil and climate for grain, Norway for lumber, Poland for flax, the Moluccas for spice. '. . . every Country', Defoe writes, 'Communicates to its other corresponding Country what they want, and these [that] can spare them *vice-versa* receive from that Country again what of their Growth these want; and not a Country so barren, so useless, but something is to be found there that can be had nowhere else'.[34] This variety in nature is paralleled by the varied and differing genius of each people which makes them seek in foreign climates what they cannot find at home. Gulliver saw only folly in 'sending Vessels by Sea to every Part of the World . . . for Liquors to drink . . .'. Defoe differs sharply. He views with satisfaction the inclination of English prelates for 'those liquors which we must fetch from abroad'.

> We cloth[e] [Defoe writes], all the Islands and Continent of *America*; and they in return, furnish us with Sugars and Tobaccoes, things by Custom becoming as useful to us as our cloths is to them. . . . What a Quantity of the *Terra Firma* has been carried from *Newcastle* in coles . . . what Cavities and Chasms in the Bowels of the Earth have we made for our Tin, Lead, and Iron. . . . These we carry abroad, and with them we purchase and bring back the Woods of *Norway*, the Silks of *Italy* and *Turkey*, the Wines and Brandies of *France*, the Wines, Oil, and Fruit of *Spain*, the Druggs of *Persia*, the Spices of *India*, the Sugars of *America*, the Toys and Gaiety of *China* and *Japan*.[35]

It is this variety, Defoe says, 'both of the Produce and Manufactures of the several Countries [which] are the Foundations of Trade, and [he says significantly] I entitle Providence to it . . .'. He adds: 'The Merchant by his Correspondence reconciles that infinite Variety which . . . has by the Infinite Wisdom of Providence been scattered over the Face of the World'.[36]

Like Addison, Defoe too can envelop the merchant in super-

---

34 *Review*, Vol. III, No. 2, 3 Jan. 1706.
35 Ibid.
36 Ibid.

latives and rhythmic prose; and he goes well beyond Addison in full statement of the religious and rationalistic implications of the mercantile theme. In fact, in two issues of the *Review* (3 Jan. 1706 and 3 Feb. 1713) Defoe goes so far in investing the merchant, that is, the person engaged in foreign trade, with the aura of divinity that Addison seems pale and secular by contrast. 'And what [Defoe asks] if . . . I should tell you there is a kind of divinity in the origin of trade . . .?' He then proposes to demonstrate that Providence has concurred in and prepared the world for commerce, that Providence has 'adapted nature to trade'. His demonstration begins, properly, with winds, oceans, and ships. Why is it, how does it happen, that 'Floaty Bodies, by natural levity' invariably swim upon the surface of the water; that a ship, 'toss'd by the Fury of the contending Elements, and mounted on the Surface of a Rolling Body of disordered Water', is saved from 'falling into a vast Gulph of Destruction' by these same waves, 'moved by the mighty Winds', hurrying 'into the hollow Place, and catching it [the ship] in their soft Arms . . . gently raise it up again . . . and . . . launch it forward?' To Defoe this is God acting 'in the order of Nature', to make navigation possible, 'to lay the Foundation of Commerce', to preserve 'the Communication of one part of the World with another'. Then Defoe turns to the world of man and animals. He sees here a similar 'superintendency of invisible Providence', for example, in the subjection of the lower animals to men, particularly in that wise provision whereby the useful creatures are tame and submissive and the less needful ones are left wild. Thus it is, Defoe informs his reader, that your sheep, 'the tamest, quietest, submissivest Creatures in the world . . . lay their backs to the shears. . . .'[37] The logic is inescapable: England's great staple, wool, is by divine arrangement.

It is of more than passing interest that Defoe, writing of navigation and commerce in these issues of the *Review*, uses the logic of the physico-theologies, those elaborate rationalistic demonstrations (popular in the period) that in every aspect of physical creation, in each 'visible work of God', can be traced 'his Wisdom in the Composition, Order, Harmony, and Uses of every one of them'. In the cosmic order God, the 'Wise Contriver', the divine Architect, managed so that all things are 'commodiously adopted

---

[37] Ibid. I, No. 54, 3 Feb. 1713. On the idea of regional differences and the providential arrangement by which 'God [furnished] all Countreys from the first beginning with some *Staple-commodities*, for the benefit of themselves and others, for the maintaining of that entercourse between Nation and Nation, which makes them link the closer in the bonds of Amity', see Peter Heylin, *Cosmography*, 9th ed., 1703, pp. 4-5.

to their proper uses'.[38] Defoe looks at the physical properties of ships ('Floaty Bodies'), at the nature of gravitation, wind, water, and waves, and he sees that they constitute a mingled measure, providentially designed, to make navigation and commerce possible. Shortly before Defoe wrote the second of the two *Reviews* under discussion Sir Richard Blackmore had published his poem, *Creation* (1712), possibly the most elaborate contemporary physico-theology in verse. The parallels between Defoe and Blackmore are striking: Blackmore writes:

> What, but a Conscious Agent, could provide
> The spacious Hollow, where the Waves reside?
> . . .
> What other Cause the Frame could so contrive,
> That when tempestuous Winds the Ocean drive,
> They cannot break the Tye, nor disunite
> The Waves, which roll Connected in their flight?
> . . .
> This apt, this wise Contexture of the Sea,
> Makes it the Ships driv'n by the Winds obey;
> Whence hardy merchants Sail from Shoar to Shoar,
> Bring *India's* spices home, and *Guinea's* Ore.

As for Defoe, so for Blackmore the 'wise Contexture of the Sea' acts in conjunction with the providential utility of the wind:

> Of what important Use to human Kind,
> To what great Ends subservient is the Wind;
> . . .
> Without this Aid the Ship would ne'er advance
> Along the Deep, and o'er the Billow dance,
> But lye a lazy and a useless Load,
> The Forest's wasted Spoils, the Lumber of the Flood.
> Let but the Wind with an auspicious Gale
> To shove the Vessel fill the spreading Sail,
> And see, with swelling Canvas wing'd she flies,
> And with her waving Streamers sweeps the Skies!
> Th' advent'rous Merchant thus pursues his Way,
> Or to the Rise, or to the Fall of Day:
> Thus mutual Traffick sever'd Realms maintain,
> And Manufactures change to mutual Gain;
> Each others Growth and Arts they sell and buy,
> Ease their Redundance, and their Wants supply.[39]

---

[38] The phraseology is from John Ray's *The Wisdom of God in the Works of Creation* (1691), 10th ed., 1705, Preface, sig. B¹.

[39] Richard Blackmore, *Creation, A Philosophical Poem. In Seven Books*, London, 1712, Bk I, ll. 632-50, pp. 41-2; Bk II, ll. 698-759, pp. 95-8.

In these lines and others we have Blackmore's more elaborate versification of the theme quoted earlier from the obscure merchant of the seventeenth century, Baptist Goodall:

> One succours other, traffic breeds affection,
> The whole is governed by the high protection,
> For winds, seas, sky and travel agree
> To frame on earth a just conformity.[40]

Blackmore continues his rationalistic physico-theological analysis of the wind with a typical catalogue of luxurious mercantile items:

> Ye *Britons*, who the Fruit of Commerce find,
> How is your Isle a Debtor to the Wind,
> Which thither wafts *Arabia's* fragrant Spoils,
> Gems, Pearls and Spices from the *Indian* Isles.
> From *Persia* Silks, Wines from *Iberia's* Shore,
> *Peruvian* Drugs, and *Guinea's golden* ore?
> Delights and Wealth to fair *Augusta* flow
> From ev'ry Region whence the Winds can blow.[41]

Here it is once again, that conventional inventory of luxuries which an eighteenth-century reader must inevitably have associated with the woman of quality—the aromatic gums of Arabia, the mineral wealth of the Indies, the woven silks of Persia, delights flowing into Queen Anne's England 'From ev'ry region whence the winds can blow'. Blackmore could assume that his inventory of shining luxuries would evoke the image of the fashionable lady. For a Swift or a Pope or an Addison, and for many others, his lines would bring her imaginatively forth.

As we observe, Defoe and Blackmore are among those who provide a rationale for this lady of fashion in terms of a providential and rationalistic scheme of things with a mercantile coloration. In the realms of economic theory and physico-theological speculation, the indulged and indulgent woman of quality had her place, so to speak, by divine right. From this vantage in theory she, like the merchant who laid at her feet 'the various Off'rings of the World', is a facet of a universal economy in which she plays a significant role; and if we accept the logic we ought not, in charity and tolerance, accuse her of vanity and ostentation. Rather with Defoe and his contemporaries we should realise that when she appeared, decked in India's sparkling gems and adorned with all that land and sea afford, she was merely fulfilling the will of God.

---

40 See above, n. 28.
41 Blackmore, *Creation*, Bk II, 11, 760-7, p. 99. See my article, complementary to this, 'Pope's Belinda, the General Emporie of the World, and the Wondrous Worm', in *The South Atlantic Quarterly: Essays in Honor of Benjamin Boyce*, Vol. LXX, Spring 1971, pp. [215]-235.

Swift and Satirical Typology *in* A Tale of a Tub

Paul J. Korshin

I

I shall be concerned in this essay with Swift's use of Biblical typology for satiric purposes in *A Tale of a Tub*, principally in Section VII, 'A Digression in Praise of Digressions', a brilliant and enigmatic portion of his satire on religion and learning which has not received the attention from scholars that it properly deserves. Satires on learning are often far more complex than the writings they attempt to expose, correct, or destroy. Certainly this is true of the digressions in *A Tale of a Tub*, the obscure and arcane allusions, shifting parodic style, and elaborate *personae* which have inspired intensive, difficult analysis, sometimes more profound than the materials of Puritanism, false inspiration, and intellectual error which Swift attacks.[1] Yet, despite the exhaustiveness of recent Swift studies, little has been said about the contribution of Section VII to the satirical effect of the rest of the *Tale*. It is usually regarded as a peculiar digression, more an attack on contemporary learning and scholarship than on religion, rhetorically capable but, as the title seems to imply, concerned primarily with ridiculing the device of digressions.[2] But, rhetorical brilliance aside, 'A Digression in Praise of Digressions' is integral to the central satiric purposes

---

[1] The most detailed recent studies of Swift's satire on religion are Ronald Paulson, *Theme and Structure in Swift's* Tale of a Tub, New Haven, 1960, and Phillip Harth, *Swift and Anglican Rationalism: The Religious Background of* A Tale of a Tub, Chicago, 1961, both of which pass over Section VII almost completely. Miriam K. Starkman, *Swift's Satire on Learning in* A Tale of a Tub, Princeton, 1950, pp. 136-8, sees Section VII mainly as ironic praise of the modern device of digressions and a condemnation of modern learning, but gives it little elaborate treatment.

[2] The 'Digression's' rhetoric has been analysed by Lamarr Stephens, ' "A Digression in Praise of Digressions" As a Classical Oration: Rhetorical Satire in Section VII of Swift's *A Tale of a Tub*', *Tulane Studies in English*, Vol. 13, 1963, pp. 41-9.

of the *Tale*, while its chief method of satirical attack is intimately involved with seventeenth-century religious and exegetical concerns. It contains, furthermore, an interesting, largely original method of exposure which both complements and augments the traditional techniques of ridiculing religious fanaticism commonly employed by the Anglican rationalists of the seventeenth century, and adds a new dimension to our assessment of Swift's satirical genius.[3]

I do not wish to force a typological interpretation on the reader, as if it were the principal, unique interpretative device capable of uncovering the meaning of 'A Digression in Praise of Digressions', without adequate examination of the relevant passages of Swift's text. Central to the discussion of this section is Swift's presentation, through the parodic pose of his fanatically inclined narrator, of what he describes as 'the noblest Branch of *Modern* Wit or Invention, planted and cultivated by the present Age, and, which of all others, hath born the most, and the fairest Fruit'.[4] To Swift's speaker, who represents not only the worst qualities of modern literary tendencies but also the depravities of contemporary theological error, all things *Modern* are superior to the 'Remains . . . left us by the *Antients*'. His contention is simply that this 'noblest Branch' owes nothing to earlier periods of intellectual achievement, but is completely self-generated, in the best modern manner. He continues:

> What I mean, is that highly celebrated Talent among the *Modern* Wits, of deducing Similitudes, Allusions, and Applications, very Surprizing, Agreeable, and Apposite, from the *Pudenda* of either Sex, together with *their proper Uses*. And truly, having observed how little Invention bears any Vogue, besides what is derived into these *Channels*, I have sometimes had a Thought, That the happy Genius of our Age and Country, was prophetically held forth by that antient typical Description of the *Indian* Pygmies; *whose Stature did not exceed above two Foot; Sed quorum pudenda crassa, & ad talos usque pertingentia.* Now, I have been very curious to inspect the late Productions, wherein the Beauties of this kind have most prominently appeared.[5]

[3] See Harth, *Swift and Anglican Rationalism*, p. 71.

[4] *A Tale of a Tub, to which is added The Battle of the Books and The Mechanical Operation of the Spirit*, A. C. Guthkelch and D. Nichol Smith (eds.), 2nd ed., Oxford, 1958, p. 146. This edition is cited throughout as *Tale*.

[5] *Tale*, p. 147. Eds. 1-4 read 'the *Genitals*' for 'the *Pudenda* of either Sex' (5th and all later eds.). To the words 'typical Description' Swift has a marginal gloss reading '*Ctesiæ fragm. apud Photium*'. Ctesias is a fourth-century Greek author whose historical writings, *Persica* and *Indica*, survive fragmentarily, principally in the *Myriobiblon* or *Bibliotheca* of Photius. See J. A. Fabricius, *Bibliotheca Graeca*, 4th ed., 12 vols., Hamburgi et Lipsiae, 1790-1809, Vol. II, pp. 740-3. The marginal reference to Photius on the fragments of Ctesias re-

Like much of the style of the digression, Swift's narrative is both vaguely prophetical and ostentatiously conscious of the fulfilment of an ancient prophecy in the greatness of modern genius. Prophetic narrative alone is neither new nor unfamiliar in seventeenth-century methods of interpreting secular history, so the prophecy of this fortunate fruition of modern learning, which is clearly a branch of secular history, might well be regarded as being fulfilled by present intellectual endeavour. But Swift has his narrator make clear that he is referring to a special kind of prophetical description, that which is here called 'typical'.

Throughout the seventeenth century, the sole meaning of this term most readily comprehensible to readers of the *Tale* was an explicitly typological one.[6] There can be no doubt that this is the connotation which Swift intended for it in this context. This typological reference is no accident: Swift and his narrator are attempting to show us something. The modern author displays the arcana of his learning, while Swift manipulates him toward a strongly prophetical, typological presentation. There are several interesting grammatical and artistic problems raised by the text in its own terms. First, the allusion to the *'Indian* Pygmies' from Photius has been doctored somewhat to fit the present situation more appropriately. Second, the typological reference is not isolated, but is actually the most visible peak of a chain of similar allusions and references throughout Section VII. And third, the mention of the physical image of the genitalia as typical of or shadowing forth modern learning bears significant resemblance to contemporary use of bodily imagery for satirical and polemic purposes.[7] Hence it may now be appropriate to pursue a few of the possible origins of Swift's attempt at typological satire here, not

calls Bentley's *Dissertation upon the Epistles of Phalaris*, also fragmentary and of dubious authenticity; see the 2nd ed., London, 1699, pp. 506-23, 535-40.

[6] See *O.E.D.*, s.v. 'Typical', 'Type', and their derivatives, esp. quotes. The customary modern meaning of 'typical', 'representative of a class or specimen', is a nineteenth-century development.

[7] See especially C. M. Webster, 'Swift's *Tale of a Tub* compared with Earlier Satires of the Puritans', *Publications of the Modern Language Association*, Vol. 47, 1932, pp. 171-8, esp. p. 175 and n. 18; see also Webster's 'Swift and Some Earlier Satirists of Puritan Enthusiasm', *Publications of the Modern Language Asociation*, Vol. 48, 1933, pp. 1141-53, and 'The Satiric Background of the Attack on the Puritans in Swift's *A Tale of a Tub*', *Publications of the Modern Language Association*, Vol. 50, 1935, pp. 210-23. Swift's allusions to Puritan sexual practices are in *Tale*, Section XI (pp. 201-2) and in *The Mechanical Operation of the Spirit* (1710), in *Tale*, pp. 283-7, where the sexual satire is also partly typological. Webster does not attempt to prove that Swift was acquainted with this vast literature, but it is likely that he had read much of it, certainly the best known works, like Thomas Edwards' *Gangræna* (1646), of which he owned a copy at his death. See Harold Williams, *Dean Swift's Library*, Cambridge, 1932, where this is lot 515 in the facsimile of the sale catalogue.

so much to determine his precise sources as to understand the intellectual context of Biblical typology at the time when Swift wrote *A Tale of a Tub*.

II

The popularity of typology as an exegetical technique in the seventeenth century was so great that few educated men could have been ignorant of its existence and the theoretical background concerning it. If it is possible to believe that Swift could have concluded his studies at Trinity College, Dublin without an intimate acquaintance with this popular branch of Scriptural exegesis, then we must assume that he became intimately acquainted with the subject during his years of reading, probably from 1692 to 1694, in preparation for ordination into the Church.[8]

To give more than a brief sketch of the role of typological exegesis in the seventeenth century is impossible in a short essay, so it will be necessary to limit ourselves. The basis of Biblical typology is the doctrine that the promise of redemption made in Paradise, which is fulfilled by the life and mission of Christ, was reinforced throughout the Old Testament for the chosen people of Israel by additional testimonies, signs, ceremonies, and events. The signs (Gr τυποι) in the Old Testament were interpreted by the Apostles, especially by Paul, as 'types and shadowes' of the life and mission of Christ.[9] Typology flourished in patristic times and during the middle ages. It was equally popular in Reformation exegesis, and received elaborate theoretical treatment during the sixteenth and seventeenth centuries. This resulted in two different conceptions of the role and application of the device.[10] The traditional

---

[8] See Louis A. Landa, *Swift and the Church of Ireland*, Oxford, 1934, pp. 1-6; Irvin Ehrenpreis, *Swift: The Man, his Works, and the Age*, Cambridge, Mass., 1962, Vol. I, p. 145; and Harth, *Swift and Anglican Rationalism*, pp. 158-64 on Swift's reading relative to the *Tale*.

[9] The phrase 'types and shadowes' is Milton's (*Paradise Lost*, XII.232-3), but precisely the same words and sentiments are used frequently throughout the century.

[10] There are numerous works which deal in part with typology. The most complete studies devoted solely to the subject are Patrick Fairbairn, *The Typology of Scripture, or, the Doctrine of Types . . . applied to the explanation of the earlier revelations of God*, 2 vols., Edinburgh, 1845-7; Jean Daniélou, *Sacramentum Futuri*, Paris, 1950, trans. Wulstan Hibberd as *From Shadows to Reality: Studies in the Biblical Typology of the Fathers*, London, 1960 and G. W. H. Lampe and K. J. Woollcombe, *Essays on Typology*, London, 1957. Important seventeenth-century theoretical works are the moderate Salomon Glassius, *Philologiae Sacrae, quae totius sacrosanctae, Veteris et Novi Testamenti Scripturae . . . Libri Quinque*, 3rd. ed., Francofurti et Hamburgi, 1653, pp. 314-36 ('De Typis') and the extreme exegeses of Johannes Cocceius (1603-69); see his *Opera Anecdota, Theologica, et Philologica*, 2 vols., Amsterdam, 1706, Vol. I, pp. 55-61, 62-75. Victor Harris, 'Allegory to Analogy in the Interpretation of Scripture', *Philological Quarterly*, Vol. XLV, 1966, pp. 1-23, discusses of the typological variations within this period.

typology of the Church, introduced by St Paul and refined and enlarged by the early Fathers, had been anything but conservative. Early typological theory and practice were influenced by the allegorising of Philo, the mystical readings of Origen, and the anagogism of the Gnostics. Despite these eclectic beginnings, traditional typology tends to confine its doctrine of Old Testament prefiguration of the New Testament principally to the life, mission, teachings, and sacraments of Christ. In addition, certain early writers, most notably St Augustine, argued that there were Old Testament types of the Christian Church and its history.[11] The method of typological exegesis which is most familiar in seventeenth-century Anglican apologetics, Biblical interpretation, Church history, and sermons generally limits itself along such lines as these. The popular exegetical writings of Andrew Willet, for example, continually emphasise typological relationships; John Wilkins's *Ecclesiastes* (1646), a popular handbook for preachers, lists most of the principal theoreticians on typology in its bibliography for students; Edward Stillingfleet shows acute awareness of Biblical types in his discussions of the Scriptural origins of pagan mythology.[12] Numerous other orthodox Anglicans made extensive use of typology in their normal theological concerns, as we may see from the frequency of

---

[11] On the early Fathers, see Daniélou, *From Shadows to Reality, passim;* for the Reformation and post-Reformation period, Frederic W. Farrar, *History of Interpretation*, London, 1886, pp. 307-94, and *The Cambridge History of the Bible: The West from the Reformation to the Present Day*, S. L. Greenslade (ed.), Cambridge, 1963, pp. 25-6, 335-7. On the seventeenth century, see C. A. Patrides, *Milton and the Christian Tradition*, Oxford, 1966, pp. 128-30 and, more generally, pp. 121-52; Barbara K. Lewalski, *Milton's Brief Epic: The Genre, Meaning and Art of Paradise Regained*, Providence, 1966, pp. 164-82; William G. Madsen, *From Shadowy Types to Truth: Studies in Milton's Symbolism*, New Haven, 1968, pp. 18-47; and Dennis P. Quinn, 'John Donne's Principles of Biblical Exegesis', *Journal of English and Germanic Philosophy*, Vol. 61, 1962, pp. 313-29. A recent general study of typology and literature is Robert E. Reiter, 'On Biblical Typology and the Interpretation of Literature', *College English*, Vol. 30, 1969, pp. 562-71.

[12] Willet's *Hexapla in Genesin* (1605; 6 eds. by 1633) and *Hexapla in Exodum* (1608; 3 eds. by 1633) are his best known exegeses, but his *Hexapla in Danielem* (1610) and *Hexapla in Leviticum* (1631) are equally important; all these works employ typology on hundreds of occasions, but with continual awareness of the dangers of excessive 'mystical' reading, which the author regularly condemns in other Renaissance exegetes. See Wilkins, *Ecclesiastes, or, A Discourse concerning the Gift of Preaching*, 3rd ed., London, 1651, pp. 38-9, 71-2. On the subject of the typological significance of figures from classical mythology, see Stillingfleet, *Origines Sacrae, or A Rational Account of the Grounds of Christian Faith*, 4th ed., London, 1675, pp. 577-98, but the most laborious work on the subject is that of the polymathic Samuel Bochart, *Geographia Sacra seu Phaleg et Canaan* (1646), in his *Opera Omnia*, 4th ed., 3 vols., Lugduni Batavorum, 1712, Vol. I, pp. 1-13. See also Lewalski, *Milton's Brief Epic*, pp. 172-5 and Edgar Wind, *Pagan Mysteries in the Renaissance*, London, 1958, pp. 24-30.

types in a popular genre of sermons like the hundreds of surviving 30 January sermons on the martyrdom of Charles I.[13]

Throughout Anglican writings on typology the notion of general rather than excessively particular application is coupled with an insistence on rational restraint. Willet, in the midst of a typological interpretation of the tabernacle in Exodus XXVII, cautions his reader: 'It is sufficient if we have the bodie and substance shadowed forth; though we cannot find out every particular; every thing must not be forced to a typical signification'.[14] This tone of judicious moderation is common in Anglican discussions of theories of interpretation, especially in the post-Restoration period, when the movement for plainer styles of preaching intensified and excessively metaphorical or allegorical readings of Scripture are often identified with early mystical heresies like gnosticism or with contemporary enthusiasm and mysticism.[15] Samuel Parker's objections to the excesses of neo-Platonism provide evidence of the Anglican position on the fanciful, inventive notions of the seventeenth-century mystics:

> *Plato* and his Followers have . . . communicated their Notions by Emblems, Symbols, Parables, heaps of metaphors, Allegories, and all sorts of Mysticall Representations (as is vulgarly known). All which upon the account of their Obscurity and Ambiguity are apparently the unfittest signes in the world to expresse the Train of any man's thoughts to another: For besides that they carry in them no intelligible Affinity to the Notices, which they were design'd to imitate, the Powers of Imagination are so great, and the instances in which one thing may resemble another are so many, that there is scarce any thing in nature, in which the Fancie cannot find or make a Varietie of such symbolising resemblances; so that Emblems, Symbols, Fables, Allegories, though they are pretty *Poetick*

[13] On the 30 January sermons, see Helen W. Randall, 'The Rise and Fall of a Martyrology: Sermons on Charles I', *Huntington Library Quarterly*, Vol. 10, 1947, pp. 135-67. For two examples, among many others, of sermons employing typology in this genre, see Joseph Glanvill, *A Loyal Tear Dropt on the Vault of Our Late Martyred Sovereign*, London, 1667, pp. 16-17, and Nathaniel Hardy, *A Loud Call to Great Mourning*, London, 1668, pp. 17, 19, 20, 26-7, 34.

[14] Willet, *Hexapla in Exodum*, 2nd ed., London, 1633, p. 520.

[15] Part of the Restoration attitude involves the question of style: see George Williamson, 'The Restoration Revolt against Enthusiasm', *Studies in Philology*, Vol. 30, 1933, pp. 571-603; Richard Foster Jones, 'The Attack on Pulpit Eloquence in the Restoration: An Episode in the Development of the Neoclassical Standard for Prose', *Journal of English and Germanic Philology*, Vol. 30, 1931, pp. 188-217; Jackson I. Cope, *Joseph Glanvill, Anglican Apologist*, St Louis, 1956, pp. 144-66, and works there cited. On the association of excessively figural exegesis with enthusiasm and mysticism, see Henry More, *Enthusiasmus Triumphatus* (1655) in *A Collection of Several Philosophical Writings of Dr Henry More*, 4th ed., London, 1712, pp. 4, 17-18, 39; and Meric Casaubon, *A Treatise concerning Enthusiasme*, 2nd ed., London, 1656, pp. 179-260.

> *Fancies,* are infinitely unfit to expresse Philosophical Notions and the discoveries of the Natures of things.[16]

Although Parker assails figurative language here, as he often does in the *Free and Impartial Censure*, it is clear that the basis of the reasoning he attacks is identical with the fertile and farfetched interpretations used by typological writers.

The other side of the coin reveals how deeply the doctrine of correspondence between the Old and New Testaments was engraved upon certain theologians. A writer from the first third of the seventeenth century can demand,

> How many Things represented him in everie thing? How many Tongues forespake all that he did, or said? When, and in what was not Christ typed, or prophecied? Each Type was a silent Prophecie of him; each Prophecie a speaking Type. All things in Holy Writ were said by, of, or for him; The Word of God implying, or unfolding nothing more, than God the Word.[17]

Such enthusiastic, mystical interpretation of Scripture, which tends to find types of Christ in everything, gradually lost popularity in late seventeenth-century Anglicanism. By the 1650s the practice of reckoning every important text in the Old Testament, to say nothing of numerous occurrences in the contemporary world, as a 'Type and Shadow' of Christ was increasingly identified with the theological methods of Puritanism and its various sects. It is difficult to specify a date at which this change becomes evident, for typology is so universal in the writings of orthodox Christians in the first half of the seventeenth century that, inevitably, it continues as an exegetical device in the works of Anglican churchmen until well into the following century. There is a vital difference, however, between the moderate typological reading of the Old Testament which Tillotson, Barrow, Glanvill, South, and others employ and the codifications of Scriptural types which Nonconformists like

---

[16] *A Free and Impartial Censure of the Platonick Philosophie*, 2nd ed., London, 1667, pp. 70-1.

[17] John Gaule, *Practique Theories: or Votive Speculations upon Jesus Christs Prediction, Incarnation, Passion, and Resurrection*, London, 1629, p. 21; cf. also pp. 23, 25. Gaule's 'Monodie' (p. 44) is even more explicit:

> The Priest (of Old)
>   Altar, and Sacrifices,
> Were Types that did
>   him promis't represent:
> Robes, Vessels, Offrings,
>   Beasts, Birds, Flowre, & Spices
> Sign'd what he should
>   both Be, and Doe, when sent.

Benjamin Keach and Samuel Mather formulated with elaborate detail.[18]

Mather isolates seven classes of types, from the personal and occasional, which deal with individuals and things, to the 'Legal Sacrifices and Purifications' and the Jewish Festivals.[19] Early in the seventeenth century both Catholics and Protestant reformers accepted liberal theories of typological exegesis, as we may see from the writings of orthodox Anglicans, Protestant exegetes on the Continent, the medieval *Glossa Ordinaria*, which employs a four-fold allegorical method of glossing each Biblical text, and the Douay Bible and some of its commentaries.[20] Yet even early in the century, in the writings of popular Anglican commentators like Willet, the cautionary note against too much figural interpretation appears. As religious controversy widens later in the century, particularly during the Civil War and in the years leading up to the Restoration, a polarisation in exegetical techniques begins to develop. As a result of this evolution, we find that the Anglican apologists of the post-Restoration period start to censure *excessively* metaphorical, allegorical, symbolic, and typological exegesis. It is essential to emphasise that Anglican apologetics and homiletics do not abandon such methods of interpretation; they simply argue for rational restraint in their use. For, as Henry More pointed out in *Enthusiasmus Triumphatus*, 'The Enormous Strength of *Imagination* [is] the Cause of Enthusiasm', which was widely regarded as a form of excessive zeal and false inspiration.[21] An overactive imagination is also necessary to the inventiveness of the typological interpreter of Scripture—this had been evident to Christians since the mystical interpretations of Origen.[22] The Anglicans of the later seventeenth century were quick to respond to what they regarded as abuses of typology by comparing them to mysticism, cabalism, gnosticism, and other heresies.

Now typology, properly used, is an acceptable, even a standard device for relating Scriptural, especially Old Testament, history to its spiritual meaning in the context of Christ's mission. It is an orthodox exegetical tool to prove that the New Testament Christ is the Messiah who was shadowed forth in the Old Testament.

---

[18] See Keach, *Tropologia*, 2nd ed., London, 1779, pp. 225-36; Samuel Mather, *The Figures or Types of the Old Testament*, Dublin, 1683, pp. 67-75. Mather's work was one of the most popular on the subject written in England; it reached a fourth edition in 1705.

[19] Mather, *Figures or Types*, p. 675-6.

[20] See Lewalski, *Milton's Brief Epic*, p. 170; cf. Victor Harris, *Philological Quarterly*, Vol. XLV, 1966, p. 9 and n.13.

[21] *Philosophical Writings* (1712), p. 4 (each work separately paged).

[22] See Jean Daniélou, *Origen*, trans. Walter Mitchell, London, 1955, pp. 139-73, on Origen and the Bible.

But when misused, or applied loosely, typology becomes a tremendously versatile method for relating Scriptural history to contemporary affairs and, through subtle analogising, for paralleling the situation of the oppressed and embattled chosen race of the Old Testament with that of the elect but persecuted Nonconformists and Puritans of the seventeenth century. If, for Samuel Mather, 'the Flood, *Sodom and Gomorrah*, *Egypt*, *Jericho*, Babylon, *Edom*, were *Types of Rome and Hell*',[23] it is not difficult for us to see how typology might be distorted from its Biblical framework to serve as a figural justification for the sufferings of seventeenth-century Nonconformists at the hands of their persecutors. Nor should we find it strange that Anglican apologists should seize upon what they considered the mystical and figural excesses of many Puritan writers as a mark of an enthusiastic zeal worthy of parody. The parodic style appears in John Eachard's defence of *The Grounds & Occasions of the Contempt of the Clergy and Religion* and brief shafts of satiric light illuminate other Anglican works, but the greatest parody of the excesses of Puritanism is indisputably *A Tale of a Tub*.[24]

III

It would be interesting to know precisely where Swift acquired his knowledge of typology, but it is difficult to determine his sources exactly. That he was intimately acquainted with the basic works of patristic theology, Renaissance and post-Reformation exegesis and controversy, and contemporary Anglican and Puritan apologetics is certain, as the complex allusions of the *Tale* demonstrate.[25] We may see from the sophisticated application of the abuses of typology which he scatters about the early portions of the *Tale* that he was extremely well versed in the Puritans' method of relating the typology of Scripture to the situations of everyday life. For example, in the voice of his fanatic Puritan narrator, he explains the device of the oratorial machines in 'The Introduction' in the mystical terms of figural exegesis:

> NOW this Physico-logical Scheme of Oratorial Receptacles or Machines, contains a great Mystery, being a Type, a Sign, an Emblem, a Shadow, a Symbol, bearing Analogy to the

23 Mather, *Figures or Types*, p. 675. On the popularity of historical paralleling see John M. Wallace, 'Dryden and History: A Problem in Allegorical Reading', *Journal of English Literary History*, Vol. 36, 1969, pp. 280-1.

24 Eachard's *Grounds & Occasions* . . . London, 1670, was attacked by an anonymous pamphlet, *An Answer to an Enquiry into the Grounds &c*, London, 1671; see his reply, *Some Observations upon the Answer* . . . , 4th ed., London, 1672, pp. 69-71, 72-4, 144, for parody upon Puritan style, sermons, and learning.

25 For an example of one year of Swift's reading (1697), see *Tale*, pp. lvi-lvii and the whole section on Swift's preparation for the *Tale*, pp. liii-lx.

spacious Commonwealth of Writers, and to those Methods by which they must exalt themselves to a certain Eminency above the inferiour World. By the *Pulpit* are adumbrated the Writings of our *Modern Saints* in *Great Britain*, as they have spiritualized and refined them from the Dross and Grossness of *Sense* and *Human Reason*. The Matter, as we have said, is of rotten Wood, and that upon two Considerations; Because it is the Quality of rotten Wood to give *Light* in the Dark: And secondly, Because its Cavities are full of Worms: which is a Type with a Pair of Handles, having a Respect to the two principal Qualifications of the Orator, and the two different Fates attending upon his works.[26]

Students of Swift will immediately notice the parody of Puritanical style and inspiration and the attack upon mechanist reductionism and the doctrine of the inner light. Furthermore, his manner and satirical style are obviously typological. True, he describes the 'great Mystery' of the machines not only as a type, but as five other terms as well, all taken from the terminology of contemporary Biblical exegesis. But it is clear that the notion of adumbration applies particularly well to the mainly typological conception of early history as in some way prefiguring later or, in this case, modern history as a kind of consummation of an earlier promise. The typological narrative as Swift introduces it here is ridiculous but it has certain basic satirical ingredients. These include the almost prophetic obscurity, the inventive foreshadowing of the future, the mystical and incomprehensible relationship between the type, sign, emblem, shadow, etc. and the antitype, that which is shadowed forth (in this case, modern learning, particularly the writings of the Puritans), and, finally, the manifest absurdity of the interpretation of the type. For Swift's typology in *A Tale of a Tub* is always parodic, and hence satirical of the extremes of figural abuse by Puritan exegetes and apologists.

Typology, moreover, is so familiar an exegetical device to Swift's narrator that he enters into its intricacies with an ease and naturalness born of long acquaintance, as in the first of the digressions in the *Tale*, 'A Digression Concerning Criticks' (Section III). Here, as he traces the genealogy of the '*True Critick*', he makes the agreeable discovery that the history of modern criticism has been foreshadowed by the most ancient writers through a convenient application of typology to history.

Yet whatever they touch'd of that kind, was with abundance of Caution, adventuring no farther than *Mythology* and *Hieroglyphick*. This, I suppose, gave ground to superficial

[26] *Tale*, pp. 61-2.

Readers, for urging the Silence of Authors, against the
Antiquity of the *True Critick*; tho' the *Types* are so apposite,
and the Applications so necessary and natural, that it is not
easy to conceive, how any Reader of a *Modern Eye* and *Taste*
could overlook them.[27]

Swift's typological inventiveness here is considerably obscure: his
narrator uncovers prefigurations of modern criticism in texts of
Pausanias, Herodotus, Ctesias, Diodorus, and Lucretius. The classical allusions themselves—asses with horns, an army put to flight by
the braying of an ass, a plant with poisonous flowers—are less important than their method of introduction. To the enthusiastic
narrator, these allusions are cunningly concealed allegories ('nothing can be plainer'), 'cautious and mystical' signs introduced by the
ancients for the particular comprehension and guidance of the
chosen *illuminati*, wise in the ways of obscurity. To the Modern
they are clear evidence of the prefiguration of the present by early
history.

The abuse of Scriptural typology consists in the narrator's
imaginative interpretation of an extant, early text, charging it with
symbolic, figural signification far beyond what seventeenth-century
hermeneutics, especially as practised by the Anglican Church, considered permissible. Contemporary theory expressly rules out the
attribution of typical meaning to just *any* text, as Swift's narrator
does with such impunity in 'A Digression Concerning *Criticks*'.
According to the opinion of one exegete, 'True types have God
for the Author of them. God bade the prophet here take one stick
and another stick, and write upon them; and thereby to type out
the houses of Judah and Israel. Had he [i.e., Ezekiel] taken these
of his own head, they had been nothing, bastardly types, not true
types'.[28] The Modern narrator is not simply guilty of devising false
types, but also of transgressing the boundaries of legitimate allegorising of a 'dark' text. A plain Scriptural text, according to an
author like Benjamin Keach, might legitimately be treated as a
type, and interpreted accordingly to educe the historical and prophetical meaning of an Old Testament sign.[29] The Modern violates
propriety in his choice of texts, for not only is their meaning
plain, but they have nothing to do with Scripture. His abuse of
typology appears in the perversion of a standard hermeneutical
device to prefigure not Christ and his glory but rather modern

[27] *Tale*, p. 97.

[28] William Greenhill, *An Exposition of the Prophet Ezekiel, with useful
Observations thereon*, 2nd ed., James Sherman (ed.), London, 1839, p. 746, on
Ezekiel XXXVII, 20-2.

[29] See *Tropologia*, London, 1682, pp. 26-9, 41-5.

learning and *its* glories.[30] He justifies the need for typological interpretation of the plainest passages in the Ancients: 'The Reason
why those Antient Writers treated this Subject only by Types and
Figures, was, because they durst not make open Attacks against
a Party so Potent and so Terrible, as the *Criticks* of those Ages
were'.[31] In this way Swift again creates, sustains, and justifies typological narrative for satiric purposes. It is unique because, although
typology is generally confined in the seventeenth century to Scriptural and other theological concerns, Swift applies this branch of
hermeneutics to modern learning, partly because his narrator per-
sonifies all the excesses of modern scholarship, both religious and
secular, partly no doubt because Swift is eager to correlate the
abuses of modern learning with the enthusiastic zeal and self-
righteousness of the Puritans.

The inspirational application of typology to all subjects, including the supposed perfections of contemporary learning, associates
the obscurantism of the typologists, like Swift's Modern, with the
similarly fantastic religious delusions of the occultists against whom
portions of *A Tale of a Tub* are directed.[32] We find in the brief
analogy between a tailor and a '*True Critick*' that typology may be
used with good effect in any obscure allusion: 'The *Taylor's Hell*
is the Type of a Critick's *Common-Place-Book* and his Wit and
Learning held forth by the *Goose*'.[33] In the satire on the sartorialists
in Section II of the *Tale*, Swift presents their icons, a tailor-figure
and his goose, as the objects of idolatrous devotion. So here the
'*Taylor's Hell*', the eschatological result of idolatry, prefigures
the intellectual errors of modern critical documents, of which
the commonplace book is the ideal representation. Typology becomes the essence of his analogical relationship between false
religious inspiration and false learning. As a prominent device in
Biblical hermeneutics, its application to secular matters tends to dis-
figure them to the same degree that the excesses of typology blemish
true religion. Hence when Swift refers to the Aeolists (Section VIII)
as '*All Pretenders to Inspiration whatsoever*' he also alludes to those

---

[30] The narrator's allusions are to plain, literal texts in that they are comprehensible on the literal plane without four-fold interpretation: 'But *Herodotus* holding the very same *Hieroglyph*, speaks much plainer, and almost *in
terminis*. He hath been so bold as to tax the *True Criticks*, of Ignorance and
Malice; telling us openly, for I think nothing can be plainer, that *in the Western Part of* Libya, *there were ASSES with HORNS*' (*Tale*, p. 98). This is his
idea of a 'clear' type of modern criticism.

[31] *Tale*, pp. 98-9.

[32] On Swift's satire on occultism, see Harth, *Swift and Anglican Rationalism*,
pp. 59-67; see also Guthkelch and Smith's appendix, 'Notes on Dark Authors',
in *Tale*, pp. 353-60, which collects the most important allusions to occult
writers, none of them, unfortunately, from Section VII.

[33] *Tale*, pp. 101-2.

equal idolaters, the worshippers of modern learning. We see this best in Section VII of the *Tale*, 'A Digression in Praise of Digressions', his longest and most effective attempt at typological satire which, though it contains only one clear type, is constructed in such a way that we may plausibly infer deliberate typological meaning throughout.

IV

The principal typological *locus* in Section VII is the narrator's assertion that the genius of modern learning 'was prophetically held forth by that antient typical Description of the *Indian* Pygmies; *whose stature did not exceed above two Foot; Sed quorum pudenda crassa, & ad talos usque pertingentia.*' The abuse of typology in this allusion to the fragments of Ctesias, the historian of India and Persia whose writings are preserved only in the *Bibliotheca* of Photius, is similar to that of earlier mistaken applications of types in the *Tale*. To interpret an obscure, non-Biblical text in a typological sense is tenuous and uncertain, to say nothing of being a flagrant violation of the rules of exegesis. To assert, as Swift's narrator does so categorically, that the grotesque Pygmies, with their tiny bodies and exaggeratedly large genitalia, prophetically foreshadow the greatness of modern learning, or anything else, is absurd, if not obscene. The only Latin text of Photius available to Swift, that of André Schott, does not present Ctesias' account of the Pygmies in precisely the same words as Swift uses, though its meaning is substantially the same; evidently he wished to clarify the implication of Ctesias by deliberate economy of style.[34] More important, however, than the small alterations to Photius is his introduction of the gross physical image of the deformity of the Pygmies as representative of the achievements of modern learning. The narrator is guilty of the modern failing 'of deducing Similitudes, Allusions, and Applications, very Surprizing, Agreeable, and Apposite, from the *Pudenda* of either Sex, together with *their proper Uses'*, while simultaneously he establishes the

---

[34] See Photius, *Bibliotheca. Sive Lectorum a Photio librorum recensio . . . e Graeco Latine reddita . . . Andreae Schotti Antuerpiani*, Augsbourg, 1606, p. 57: 'Narrat praeter ista, in mediae India homines reperiri nigros, qui Pygmaei appellentur. Eadem hos, qua Indi reliqui, lingua uti, sed valde esse parvos, ut maximi duntaxat cubiti sum dimidio altitudinem non excedant . . . Veretrum illis esse crassum ac longum, quod ad ipsos quoque pedum malleolos pertingat. Pygmaeos hosce simis esse naribus, & deformes'. Swift's edition of Photius, edited by David Hoeschelius and Schott, Rothomagi, 1653, pp. 145-6, has the same text; see Williams, *Dean Swift's Library*, where this work is lot 104 in the sale catalogue. On the early editions of Photius, see the *Bibliothèque*, René Henry (ed.), 4 vols., Paris, 1959-65, Vol. I, p. xxxvii.

small body-large genitalia image of the pygmies as a suitable type
of his own intellectual pursuits.

Once we identify this image as Swift's debasement or parody of
a true type, it becomes possible for us to discern a complex yet
unmistakable strain of typological satire in Section VII constructed
around analogies to this figural centre. Analogous to the pygmy
image are other images which utilise, in the same prefiguring or
typological manner, a small body with exaggeratedly dispropor-
tionate genitals, posteriors, privities, or hinder parts. The swollen
or erect genitals (crassa) of the Indian pygmies are latent with more
than one typological meaning. These distended members hold
forth not just the happy genius of the modern age of cant and
hypocrisy, but a particularly inflated, enthusiastic kind of modern
learning. The potential ejaculation of sperm which the pygmy-
genitalia image implies closely parallels, in the imagistic scheme
of Section VII, the discharge of the seeds of spiritual inspiration
portended by the swollen bodies of Swift's Aeolists and by the inflated rhetoric of enthusiastic Puritanism and mysticism.[35] Sexual
erection becomes clearly analogous to spiritual inspiration here,
as it does in *The Mechanical Operation of the Spirit,* where he
describes an enthusiastic fit in such terms: 'The *Saint* felt his
Vessel full *extended* in every Part (a very natural Effect of strong
Inspiration)'.[36] The association of carnality (physical excess) with
fanaticism (false inspiration or enthusiasm) is common in seventeenth-century anti-Puritan writings, but it also is likely that Swift
seeks to exploit an additional pejorative relationship, which draws
as well on a rich figural tradition, between sexuality and idolatry.
Prominent Anglican apologists like Parker and Stillingfleet allude
to the idolatrous cults of phallic or priapic worship and their symbolism; the well-known studies of idolatry by Gerardus Vossius
and Athanasius Kircher discuss the phallic myths of the ancient
Egyptians and Greeks in detail; and Swift himself alludes to the
'Types and Symbols' of the Osiridic and Bacchanalian rites.[37]

Analogous to the Pygmy-type of modern genius is the equally

[35] See Sherman H. Hawkins, 'Swift's Physical Imagery', unpublished dissertation (Princeton, 1960), pp. 412-13, 423.

[36] *Tale,* p. 283; cf. pp. 280-2.

[37] See Parker, *A Free and Impartial Censure of the Platonick Philosophie,*
pp. 99-103; Stillingfleet, *Origines Sacrae,* p. 591; Vossius, *De Theologia Gentili,
et Physiologia Christiana; sive de origine ac progressu Idolotriae Libri IX*
(1641), in *Opera,* Isaac Vossius (ed.), 6 vols., Amsterdam, 1695-1701, Vol. V, pp.
12-14; Athanasius Kircher, *Oedipus Aegyptiacus. Hoc est Universalis Hiero-
glyphicae Veterum Doctrinae Temporum iniuria abolitae Instauratio,* 3 vols.
in 4, Romae, 1652-4, Vol. I, pp. 223-30. Cf. Swift, *The Mechanical Operation of
the Spirit,* in *Tale,* p. 284. On the Osiris and Dionysius cults and their phallic
worship, see Sir James G. Frazer, *The Golden Bough,* 3rd ed., London, 1935-6,
Vol. VI, pp. 3-23, 112-13; Vol. VII, pp. 1-34.

obscure image of the Scythian mares which, with their artificially inflated privities, are also typical of the contemporary scholarship of which the narrator boasts so proudly. Yet everything unnaturally enlarged will eventually collapse: thus the small body of modern learning with its swollen appendages is essentially temporary, constantly in danger of running dry of newly invented matter. We have more than a figural joke here on the sexual and intellectual potency of Swift's contemporaries. The narrator's solution continues the typological relationship started by the Pygmy image between the small body-large appendages concept and contemporary genius. He proposes, therefore, 'that our last Recourse must be had to large *Indexes*, and little *Compendiums*; . . . To this End, tho' Authors need be little consulted, yet *Criticks*, and *Commentators*, and *Lexicons* carefully must'.[38] Once again, we continue with the prophetical foreshadowing of the present age by the 'antient typical Description of the *Indian* Pygmies', since the greatest achievement of modern learning is a small compendium with a large, one is tempted to say a swollen, index.

The triumph of all this scholasticism is an author trained by the best methods of the modern school: 'BY these Methods, in a few Weeks, there starts up many a Writer, capable of managing the profoundest, and most universal Subjects. For, what tho' his *Head* be empty, provided his *Common-place-Book* be full'. The typological methodology prolongs the relationship adumbrated earlier: the accomplishment of the mysterious prophecy of the Pygmy-type is achieved by a writer whose intellectual body (or head) is unnaturally small, but whose literary appendage, the universal compilation or commonplace book, is swollen with seminal thoughts derived from other writers. This is what Swift calls 'the *Sieves* and *Boulters* of Learning', the intellectual detritus of scholarship. The traditional movement from type to antitype is one from prefiguration to fruition, from shadows to reality, from darkness and obscurity to light and truth. The narrator treats his text, the *dicta* of Ctesias, in the same way that the Puritans and the enthusiastic exegetes of the seventeenth century treat the Old Testament, as an obscure prophecy charged with mysteries. All true types are such. The ultimate perfection of this type, the true modern work of genius, is a neat treatise which, 'when the Fulness of time is come, shall haply undergo the Tryal of Purgatory, in order *to ascend the sky*'. This mock glorification or resurrection of a desperate piece of hack writing, complete with somewhat sour Scriptural echoes, recalls the enthusiastic prognostications of salvation which appear so commonly in the writings of the early Gnos-

38 *Tale*, pp. 147-8.

tics and more recent mystics like Boehme and Thomas Vaughan. It is also the final accomplishment of the type, from darkness to light, or from death to resurrection.

Typological satire, as Swift develops it in Section VII, is based on the creation of an absurd, mock-mysterious correspondence between the works of the ancients and the productions of his contemporaries. The pygmy image, however, is the only one in the entire digression which the narrator clearly describes as 'typical'. This is not unusual, for a seventeenth-century author employing typological exegesis could assume enough knowledge of the device among an educated audience to make corroboratory references to types later in his text unnecessary. An exegeticist can thus mention the chief typical figures and events of the Old Testament without specifically informing us that these are types and that they prefigure certain later persons and situations. Such correspondences would have been obvious to his audience. Through the guise of his narrator, Swift introduces allusions to the body of modern learning which, although we are never told of their 'typical' nature (within the context of typological abuse which the narrator habitually favours), clearly relate to the prophecy-fulfilment conception of the digression and to the parodic, distorted typology of the pygmy image. Much of the satire on learning in the *Tale* consists of an ironical demonstration of the superiority of Modern over Ancient learning. Just as Ancient learning was partial and imperfect, so that of the Moderns is the *pleroma*, the fulfilment of the promises held forth by earlier authors.

Swift's description of contemporary intellectual methodology is such an accomplishment:

> The most accomplisht Way of using Books at present, is twofold: Either first, to serve them as some Men do *Lords*, learn their *Titles* exactly, and then brag of their Acquaintance. Or Secondly, which is indeed the choicer, the profounder, and politer Method, to get a thorough Insight into the *Index*, by which the whole Book is governed and turned, like *Fishes* by the *Tail*. For, to enter into the Palace of Learning at the *great Gate*, requires an Expence of Time and Forms; therefore Men of much Haste and little Ceremony, are content to get in by the *Back-Door*. For, the Arts are all in a *flying* March, and therefore more easily subdued by attacking them in the *Rear*. Thus Physicians discover the State of the whole Body, by consulting only what comes from *Behind*. Thus Men catch Knowledge by throwing their *Wit* on the *Posteriors* of a Book, as Boys do Sparrows with flinging *Salt* upon their *Tails*. Thus Human Life is best understood by the wise man's Rule of *Regarding the End*. Thus are the Sciences found like *Hercules's*

Oxen, by *tracing them Backwards*. Thus are *old Sciences* un-
ravelled like *old Stockings*, by beginning at the *Foot*.[39]

We may disregard the first way of using books, for the narrator
obviously finds the second method infinitely preferable. What is
most striking about the second method and its ramifications is that
all of them deal with the rear of learning, the hinder or lower parts
of the body of contemporary intellect. Just as a knowledge of the
index is the key to the book, so the posteriors of learning, wit,
the arts and sciences, the human body itself, are the true entrance
into the inverted world of modern genius. There is a parallel in
this passage to the later typology of the pygmy image, since the
narrator sees learning and its acquisition, in figural terms, as virtually identical with what the pygmies shadow forth. The promise
which the pygmies foreshadow is the stunted body of present-day
originality with its large addition of commentary, appendix, and
index. Analogously, through a group of deliberately imperfect types,
the speaker describes the refinements of modern genius as a series
of actions which stress the relative importance of the back door
to learning and the relative insignificance of the proper acquisition
of knowledge. These actions parallel and typify that modern vein
of obscene allusion which is in danger of running dry unless
modern wits emphasise still more the superficies of learning or have
further recourse to indexes, systems, and abstracts.

Like the rest of Swift's typological satire, this section is filled
principally with nonsensical figural interpolations whose meaning
and application to the Modern narrator's subject are purposely
obscure. Doubtless Swift intends to parody the obscure imagistic
revelations of mystics like Vaughan or writers of the alchemical
school like Paracelsus, Agrippa, and Robert Fludd. But more to his
purpose in this account of modern intellectual methodology is the
knowledge that these profane parodies of real learning prefigure
the accomplishment of the nonsensical promise of contemporary
greatness. He even creates a patrology of modern knowledge which
is responsible for much of the felicity of the present age: 'For this
great Blessing we are wholly indebted to *Systems* and *Abstracts*, in
which the *Modern* Fathers of Learning, like prudent Usurers,
spent their Sweat for the Ease of Us their Children. For Labor
is the Seed of *Idleness*, and it is the peculiar Happiness of our
Noble Age to gather the *Fruit*'. The early patristic writers, for
whom typology was a central exegetical device, were important for
seventeenth-century Anglicans as the first heresiologists, notable for

[39] *Tale*, p. 145.

their success in confuting the pre-Nicene heretics.[40] But in the twisted patrology of the *Tale*, the labour of the '*Modern* Fathers of Learning' is the seed or type which yields the fruition of 'our Noble Age'. The motion of typology, as we have seen, is a rising one, from promise to consummation. There is a clear parallel in the typological narrative of 'A Digression in Praise of Digressions', for Swift moves from the partial and imperfect signs of modern genius, all of which point to the hinder part of knowledge, to the ultimate accomplishment of modernity, '*Systems* and *Abstracts*'. These are, after all, simply books in which the compilation of an index or other posterior pedantry has become the whole instead of the part.

V

The cleverest example of Section VII's attack upon the abuses of modern learning is its opening image which, taken separately, seems simply an allusion to a scholastic triviality. But it is closely connected with the intricate typological narrative of the entire 'Digression'. The narrator begins enigmatically, 'I HAVE sometimes *heard* of an *Iliad* in a *Nut-shell*; but it hath been my Fortune to have much oftner *seen* a *Nut-shell* in an *Iliad*. There is no doubt, that Human Life has received most wonderful Advantages from both'.[41] This image is a classic instance of how readily the narrator inverts every proposition he touches, no matter how absurd. The '*Iliad* in a *Nut-shell*' is one of the more preposterous scholastic riddles that Swift introduces into the *Tale*. Although the origin of the conception is obscure, even in Roman times it seems to have been the subject of an arid scholastic dispute (one can imagine it as the *quaestio*: *An possit includere in nuce Iliadem Homeri carmen membrana?*). More recent writers refer to the riddle, including Cowley in his ode 'To the Royal Society' prefixed to Thomas Sprat's *History of the Royal Society* (1667), which Swift quite likely had read.[42] The cream of the jest occurs in the miscellaneous writings of Bishop Huet, who asks the question just presented and then reveals how the paradox can be accomplished by very small

[40] See Danièlou, *From Shadows to Reality*, pp. 1-7; cf. the interesting summary account in Berthold Altaner, *Patrology*, trans. Hilda C. Graef, Edinburgh and London, 1958, pp. 138-60.

[41] *Tale*, p. 143, and n. 1, where the editors record allusions to this fanciful idea in Pliny, Scaliger, and Rabelais. There are other texts which Swift might have known, but once again his distortion of an allusion is more important than the allusion itself. Cf. Wilma L. Tague, 'Stephen Gosson and "Homer's Iliades in a Nutte Shell" ', *Notes & Queries*, Vol. 205, 1960, pp. 372-3.

[42] The lines in Cowley's Ode which include this reference were removed from the poem in all collected editions of Cowley's works, including the 1668 Folio, so Swift could only have encountered the phrase in Sprat's *History of the Royal Society*.

writing on a large piece of vellum which then might be folded up into an exceptionally large nutshell ('il pourroit être enfermé dans une coque de noix d'une bonne grosseur').[43] Thus the '*Iliad* in a *Nut-shell*' becomes broadly symbolic of scholastic nonsense. But the narrator has only *heard* of this paradox; what he has actually *seen* quite often is 'a *Nut-shell* in an *Iliad*' which, so far as he is concerned, has been equally beneficial to the world. This nutshell, whether contained in or containing an *Iliad*, becomes both the symbol for the very digression he is writing and a foreshadowing or type of the 'great *Modern* Improvement of *Digressions*' from which human life has derived so many advantages. Section VII leads up to an affirmation of this nutshell-digression equation, for the narrator emphasises it at the very end when he informs his audience, 'THE Necessity of this Digression, will easily excuse the Length; and I have chosen for it as proper a Place as I could readily find. If the judicious Reader can assign a fitter, I do here empower him to remove it into any Corner he pleases'.[44] The nutshell in the *Iliad*, then, is both a type of modern scholasticism, which is so refined by digressions, paradoxes, and obscure allusions that it lacks coherence, and a symbol of the disease of contemporary knowledge, that canting mysticism and enthusiastic fanaticism which are frequently the objects of Swift's satire in the *Tale*.

This is the most interesting aspect of the introductory image of Section VII. Swift's narrator insists that the '*Nut-shell* in an *Iliad*', or the modern device of digressions, is not only common but beneficial. Significantly, it is not the contents of the nutshell, the kernel or (in the paradox) the enclosed *Iliad*, which the Modern has encountered often; it is rather the shell itself, the rind or superficies of things, which may be found in any modern work, most notably in *A Tale of a Tub*. The nutshell-*Iliad* is not without its mystical signification. The shell-kernel image is not uncommon in religious writings—the shell is commonly visualised as the surface obscurity of a Biblical or other text which the interpreter must pierce or crack to uncover the kernel or meaning. Donne, for example, states at one point in a sermon, 'We must doe in this last, as we have done in our former two parts, crack a shell, to tast the kernell, cleare the words, to gaine the Doctrine'.[45] Donne describes a per-

---

[43] See *Huetiana, ou Pensées Diverses de M. Huet, Evesque d'Avranches,* Paris, 1722, pp. 135-8, Pensée LX: '*S'il est vrai que l'on ait pû mettre l'Iliade d'Homere dans une coquille de noix?*' The French court, according to Huet, were delighted by the small writing and the solution of the problem. Although *Huetiana* appeared too late for Swift to have used this account, it seems clear that the paradox was widely known.

[44] *Tale*, p. 149.

[45] *The Sermons of John Donne*, Evelyn M. Simpson and George R. Potter (eds.), 10 vols., Berkeley and Los Angeles, 1953-62, Vol. IX, p. 226. For various

fectly rational exegetical act, analogous to Origen's penetrating the 'vast forest of the Scriptures'. But Eugenius Philalethes, the pseudonymous narrator of Thomas Vaughan's *Anthroposophia Theomagica*, uses the image somewhat differently. Vaughan attempts a lengthy justification, complete with digressions and liberal citation from dark authors, of the necessity of mystical interpretation of the Scriptures, for not only the Bible but many theologians, he argues, divide their writings into that which is secret and mystical and that which is evident and better known. Many texts have always been misunderstood, their full meaning lost, for 'It hath been the common error of all times to mistake signum for *signatum*, the shell for the kernel'.[46] Intensive analysis of all the 'mystical speeches contained in Scripture' is requisite to a thorough understanding of what has commonly been taken literally or historically. This approach is an old one, which begins at least as early as Philo and Origen, but it is relevant to Swift's satire on mysticism in the *Tale* because of its contemporaneity and because of his known acquaintance with seventeenth-century mysticism. The nutshell is therefore symbolic, for the Modern narrator, of the surface of things which takes precedence over the naked truth within because of its supposed mystical significance. It burlesques the tendency of the English Puritans, in their sublimer moments, to uncover vast spiritual meanings in the most common ingredients of everyday life.

In this manner Jack's over-vivid imagination tends 'to reduce all Things into *Types*' and, like other Puritans, to refine 'what is Literal into Figure and Mystery'. In a similar inquiry into the nature of things in 'A Digression concerning Madness', the narrator finds 'that in most Corporeal Beings, which have fallen under my Cognizance, the *Outside* hath been infinitely preferable to the *In*'; that is, true wisdom proceeds from a minute observation of what Swift calls 'the *Superficies* of Things'.[47] To prefer deliberate obscurity to plain, simple truth and reason, consciously to create a style compounded of allusions to dark authors and arcane symbols, then, is the narrator's great achievement. For Swift, this is the height of intellectual error in modern learning, both theological and secular. The '*Nut-shell* in an *Iliad*', although not a perfect Swiftian type of 'the happy Genius of our Age and Country', symbolises learned and nonsensical obscurantism in modern writing. Moreover, be-

---

proverbial phrases employing 'Nut' or 'Nutshell' see Morris Palmer Tilley, *A Dictionary of the Proverbs in England in the Sixteenth and Seventeenth Centuries*, Ann Arbor, 1950, N358-N366. Cf. O.E.D., s.v. 'Kernel' *sb*.1,8.

46 *The Works of Thomas Vaughan: Eugenius Philalethes*, Arthur Edward Waite (ed.), London, 1919, pp. 36-8, esp. p. 38.

47 *Tale*, pp. 189-90 and Section XI *passim;* pp. 173, 174.

cause the nutshell represents the device of digression and prefigures the mock-mystical darkness of the central portion of 'A Digression in Praise of Digressions', it is also consistent with the typological structure and narrative of Section VII. Part of the success of the typological exegete depended upon his audience's familiarity with his method, so that it was unnecessary to introduce a special explanation with every new shadow or type. This is certainly part of Swift's genius in his parody of the excesses of typology in the *Tale*. We recognise that he has introduced typological analysis in several places and, through examination of other portions of his carefully constructed satire, we may perceive figural analogies and similarities to the typological sections which join to help create his full-fledged satire of modern critical and theological methodology.

VI

I have argued that in portions of the *Tale* and especially in the digression of Section VII Swift introduces what I have called typological satire. This is, so far as I know, a phrase with no precedent in the study of seventeenth- and eighteenth-century English literature. It is a tentative term, limited here to his attempts to parody the theological and literary techniques of some of his contemporaries. In the religious sphere, this would include many of the English Puritans of the seventeenth century, as well as other advocates of false spiritualism and mysticism. The *Tale* touches on many of the points at issue in the *rabies theologorum* of the Reformation, but it is important to note again that the typological method is not confined to any one group, even during Swift's lifetime. Although the Anglican Rationalists in the years after the Restoration were widely opposed to a florid, heavily imagistic style in pulpit oratory, they were still capable of the closely reasoned arguments and strict logical coherence which carefully used typological exegesis must always employ if it is to avoid the extremes of inspired mysticism.[48]

A distinct expression of the moderate school of thought on analogical applications is contained in the following remarks of the dissenting Whig clergyman Robert Ferguson:

> There must be a proportion and Similitude between the things themselves, whereof the one is applyed to ground, illustrate,

[48] See Irène Simon, *Three Restoration Divines: Barrow, South, Tillotson. Selected Sermons*, Bibliothèque de la Faculté de Philosophie et Lettres de l'Université de Liège, Fasc. 181, Paris, 1967, p. 23, on the logical methods of Calvinism; see also pp. 75-148 for Miss Simon's excellent discussion of Anglican Rationalism. On the style of sermons, see pp. 1-73, and cf. George Williamson, *The Senecan Amble*, Chicago, 1951, and W. Fraser Mitchell, *English Pulpit Oratory from Andrewes to Tillotson*, London, 1932, both *passim*.

manifest, and support the other. Nor must the Analogy be strained and far fetched, but obvious and pertinent. Much less must we superstruct any Doctrine upon Allusions how accommodated soever, unless where the Holy Ghost hath preceded us, as in some cases he hath. Where God himself hath informed us that though such a passage was originally and principally spoken of one thing, that yet he intended to signifie some other thing by it, there we may with safety build, but no where else . . . For as there are many passages in the Old Testament, which though in their Immediate significations and meaning they relate to Persons, Things and Actions that were, yet so that those Persons, Things and Actions were solemnly designed, ordained and *instituted* to prefigure Christ and the things belonging to his Kingdom.[49]

Hence we cannot lay the fault of excessive allegorism and imagism in hermeneutics only at the door of the Puritans, for intellectual error, as a moderate like Ferguson describes it, can occur anywhere. The object of Swift's satire in Section VII is ostensibly the Puritans; but we know that he was opposed to '*All Pretenders to Inspiration whatsoever*'. He would have agreed with a prominent Anglican rationalist like South, who wrote in a sermon, probably of the 1690s, 'He who thinks and says he can understand all *Mysteries*, and resolve all *Controversies*, undeniably shews, that he really understands none'.[50] And this is precisely the point of the profundity of Swift's typological narrative in 'A Digression in Praise of Digressions'. The Modern narrator has great acquaintance with the mysteries of arcane learning, and finds all sorts of unlikely parallels and analogies in this otherwise worthless knowledge to prove the genius of his own age. The narrator's Modern bias is nourished by many things. The nature of typology, with its rising motion from darkness to light, its interpreting apparently obscure historical events as prophesying the present and a still better future, and its tendency to reinterpret the past to suit the needs of the present, is especially appropriate to the Modern's needs in Section VII, his great *apologia* for digressions and all that they contain.

Early in this essay I stated my wish to avoid forcing upon the

[49] *The Interest of Reason in Religion; with the Import & Use of Scripture Metaphors*, London, 1675, pp. 312-13. For general discussion of Biblical imagery, see pp. 297-314.

[50] Robert South, *Sermons Preached Upon Several Occasions*, 6 vols., London, 1737, Vol. III, p. 250. The entire sermon, 'Christianity Mysterious, and the Wisdom of God in Making it so', preached 29 April 1694 (Vol. III, pp. 211-52), is a strong defence of Anglican Rationalism and a thorough attack upon those Christians who find mysteries even in literal texts of Scripture. Swift's 'great Philosopher of *O. Brazile*' (*Tale*, p. 125), may be derived from or related to South's derisive term for a mystical interpretation of scripture, 'some *O Brazil* in divinity' (III, p. 250). Like Swift, South animadverts against an arbitrary mysticism which leads to nothing but delusion.

reader a typological interpretation of Section VII, for one can visualise all too easily being indicted for excesses in critical reading not dissimilar to those for which Swift attacks the Moderns in *A Tale of a Tub*. It would be possible to interpret Section VII simply as a satire on the abuses of modern learning without any reference to typology. However, Swift deliberately introduces a theological pattern into his satire which is closely related to the *Tale*'s ridicule of abuses in religion. Thus the effect of using parodic types and typological exegesis in this digression is to associate pretended inspiration in scholarship and secular learning with similar pretence in religion. The typological mode is not pervasive in Section VII, but the narrator introduces typical references with strategic frequency so that the general impression of the 'Digression' is one of a parodic exposition of the rise of modern genius from its shadowy beginnings. Yet the limits of the typological reading of *A Tale of a Tub* are clearly worthy of emphasis. For example, Swift writes in 'A Digression in the Modern Kind' of how far the Moderns surpass the Ancients: 'WHEN I consider how exceedingly our Illustrious *Moderns* have eclipsed the weak glimmering Lights of the *Antients*, and turned them out of the Road of all fashionable Commerce, to a degree, that our choice Town-Wits of the most refined Accomplishments, are in grave Dispute, whether there have been ever any *Antients* or no'.[51] This passage suggests that the present has accomplished more than the past, but it would be erroneous to see typology here because there is no predictive, prophetical, or prefiguring relationship, either real or implied. But, on the other hand, in his brief history of fanaticism and idolatry in *The Mechanical Operation of the Spirit*, Swift not only tells us that the early pagan ceremonies, myths, and rituals 'were so many Types and Symbols' of later fanatics and their rites, but also introduces imagery dealing with the posterior parts of the body and of books that is strongly reminiscent of virtually all of the typological passages in Section VII.[52]

Hence we may expect to find Swift's typological satire heralded by specific mention of typology and accompanied by deliberately obscure literary and physical (often sexual) imagery. The style is profoundly figural and the imagery itself is often interpreted

---

[51] *Tale*, pp. 124-5.

[52] *Tale*, pp. 283-5. Compare, for example, 'They [the Bacchantes] bore for their Ensigns, certain curious Figures, perch'd upon long Poles, made into the Shape and Size of the *Virga genitalis*, with its *Appurtenances*, which were so many Shadows and Emblems of the whole Mystery, as well as Trophies set up by the Female Conquerers. Lastly, in a certain Town of *Attica*, the whole Solemnity stript of all its Types, was performed in *puris naturalibus*, the Votaries, not flying in Coveys, but sorted into Couples' (p. 285). As this passage indicates, Swift almost never mentions types without some satiric purpose.

in a mystical, if not a typical, sense.[53] His narrator is intellectually associated with the spiritual excesses of the English fanatics, so we may expect that in his typological style his interpretations of what *he* identifies as types will employ the freedom of imagination which is so characteristic of English mysticism and Puritanism.[54] Like Origen, the narrator of the *Tale* finds mysteries and figurative meanings everywhere. He is like Jack, who finds 'that the Matter was *deeper* and *darker*, and therefore must needs have a great deal more of Mystery at the Bottom'.[55] The narrator, then, is guilty of a number of Modern sins. His rhetorical exuberance, imagistic excesses, mystical interpretations, and devious misapplications of typological method, especially in Section VII of the *Tale*, associate him closely with the undercurrents of Puritan dissent in the years after the post-Restoration reaction against the civil strife and religious controversy of the Civil Wars and Commonwealth. His language and methods are emphatically those of an earlier age: they look backward across the great chasm separating the ideologies of the Renaissance from those of the eighteenth century. Thus, by connecting his Modern narrator with the errors of an earlier, more turbulent era, Swift intensifies his satiric scorn against fanaticism and its intellectual mistakes.

---

[53] Sherman H. Hawkins shows, in 'Swift's Physical Imagery', that Swift employs physical allusions as a method of setting forth the error of the enthusiasts in all its naked deformity; see pp. 449, 473. The deformity of the Pygmies is just such an instance of this technique.

[54] One will find satisfactory examples of pervasive mystical interpretation in many seventeenth-century authors, but I will only suggest one of the most popular, Jacob Boehme; see, e.g., *The Epistles of Jacob Behmen, aliter, Teutonicus Philosophus*, London, 1649, pp. 11, 49-50, 109; and cf. *The Remainder of the Books Written by Jacob Behme*, London, 1662, pp. 26-8.

[55] Origen, *Homiliae in Genesim*, x.1 (*Patrologia Graeca*, Vol. XII, p. 215). 'Quae leguntur mystica sunt, in allegoricis exponenda sunt sacramentis'. Cf. Danièlou, *Origen*, pp. 182-5.

The Politics of Gulliver's Travels

Michael Wilding

Generally when we talk or write about political fiction we think of works written from the mid-nineteenth to the twentieth century. Earlier works are not usually admitted to the category, and neither M. E. Speare's *The Political Novel* (1924) nor Irving Howe's *Politics and the Novel* (1957) are concerned with the eighteenth century. Irving Howe, indeed, writes that 'from the picaresque to the social novel of the nineteenth century there is a major shift in emphasis'[1] and he makes a further shift in emphasis between the social and the political novel:

> The ideal social novel had been written by Jane Austen, a great artist who enjoyed the luxury of being able to take society for granted; it was *there*, and it seemed steady beneath her glass, Napoleon or no Napoleon. But soon it would not be steady beneath anyone's glass, and the novelist's attention had necessarily to shift from the gradations within society to the fate of society itself. It is at this point, roughly speaking, that the kind of book I have called the political novel comes to be written—the kind in which the *idea* of society as distinct from the mere unquestioned workings of society, has penetrated the consciousness of the characters in all of its profoundly problematic aspects, so that there is to be observed in their behavior, and they are themselves often aware of, some coherent political loyalty or ideological identification.[2]

And in arguing against 'the notion that abstract ideas invariably contaminate a work of art and should be kept at a safe distance from it' Howe writes:

> No doubt, when the armored columns of ideology troop in *en masse*, they do imperil a novel's life and liveliness, but ideas, be they in free isolation or hooped into formal systems, are indispensable to the serious novel. For in modern society ideas raise enormous charges of emotion, they involve us in our

1 Irving Howe, *Politics and the Novel*, 1961 ed., London, p. 18.
2 Ibid., p. 19.

most feverish commitments and lead us to our most fearful betrayals. The political novelist may therefore have to take greater risks than most others, as must any artist who uses large quantities of 'impure' matter. . . .[3]

Some of these ideas and phrases that Howe uses in defining the political novel have a relevance to *Gulliver's Travels*. The 'feverish commitments' and the 'most fearful betrayals' resulting from political ideas find their counterpart in Gulliver's commitment to the ideology of the Houyhnhnms and his rejection, his betrayal of humanity. While the 'coherent political loyalty or ideological identification' which Howe argues the characters of a political novel possess, is evidenced in Gulliver's conversations with the King of Brobdingnag. Gulliver's commitment to the political system of England and his eulogies of its procedures provoke first mirth, when the King having heard Gulliver's account 'could not forbear taking me up in his right Hand, and stroaking me gently with the other; after an hearty Fit of laughing, asked me whether I were a *Whig* or a *Tory*'. (p. 91);[4] and later they produce contempt in the King's famous denunciation that 'I cannot but conclude the Bulk of your Natives, to be the most pernicious Race of little odious Vermin that Nature ever suffered to crawl upon the Surface of the Earth'. (p. 116)

I have been citing Howe not from contention, but because his study is the most valuable one to date of political fiction. I want to argue, however, that the political novel has an earlier origin than the mid-nineteenth century, and I want to emphasise the non-naturalistic tradition of English political fiction. Seeing the political novel as a development of the social novel, Howe is inclined to emphasise the social, the naturalistic connections of political fiction. But an equally important tradition of the fable and the non-naturalistic utopian narrative leads through Swift to William Morris, Huxley, and Orwell.

In his first three travels Gulliver never encounters primitive peoples. The only people with which he communicates or spends time are all members of highly developed societies. They are all political societies.

From the beginning Gulliver's presence in Lilliput presents political problems and he becomes the focus of political intrigue: 'It seems that upon the first Moment I was discovered sleeping on the Ground after my Landing, the Emperor had early Notice of it by an Express: and determined in Council that I should be tyed in

---

[3] Ibid., pp. 20-1.
[4] *The Prose Works of Jonathan Swift*, Herbert Davis (ed.), Vol. XI, *Gulliver's Travels*, Oxford, 1941. All quotations are from this edition.

the Manner I have related . . .'. (p. 10) The immediate notification of Gulliver's arrival to the King, the summoning of a council, stress the fact the Lilliput is envisaged as a political world.

The political events and political practices of Lilliput have been related by a number of commentators to the political history of England during the years 1708 to 1715.[5] But the power of the book is not restricted to these particular political allusions: the methods of promotion to ministerial office in Lilliput are parodic of the procedures in England but the absurdity and meaninglessness of these methods, their total irrelevance to the requirements of public life and their inherent ridiculousness, are not restricted to any specific historical time or place:

> When a great Office is vacant, either by Death or Disgrace, (which often happens) five or six of those Candidates petition the Emperor to entertain his Majesty and the Court with a Dance on the Rope; and whoever jumps the highest without falling, succeeds in the Office. (p. 22)

Yet allied with such absurd comedy in the manner of appointment is the evil that the appointed can go on to practise—something again not limited to the specific practices of early eighteenth-century England. When Gulliver falls from favour for refusing to gratify the King's desire for absolute domination of Blefuscu by the capture of their fleet, the Council hold long discussions about whether to poison, starve, or blind him. The cruelty of the Lilliputians in power is as strongly established as the absurdity of the methods of gaining power.

These same qualities of absurd methods of appointment to office, allied with a great appetite for extending power and exercising it with cruelty, are shown in the account of English public life that Gulliver gives to the King of Brobdingnag. The King

> was perfectly astonished with the historical Account I gave him of our Affairs during the last Century; protesting it was only an Heap of Conspiracies, Rebellions, Murders, Massacres, Revolutions, Banishments; the very worst Effects that Avarice, Faction, Hypocrisy, Perfidiousness, Cruelty, Rage, Madness, Hatred, Envy, Lust, Malice, and Ambition could produce. (p. 116)

and he tells Gulliver that

> You have clearly proved that Ignorance, Idleness and Vice are

5 Sir Charles Firth, 'The Political Significance of Gulliver's Travels', Proceedings of the British Academy, Vol. IX, 1920, pp. 237-59; Irvin Ehrenpreis, 'The Origins of Gulliver's Travels', Publications of the Modern Language Association of America, Vol. LXXII, 1957, pp. 800-99; Arthur E. Case, Four Essays on Gulliver's Travels, Princeton, 1945.

the proper Ingredients for qualifying a Legislator. That Laws are best explained, interpreted, and applied by those whose Interest and Abilities lie in perverting, confounding, and eluding them . . . It doth not appear from all you have said, how any one Perfection is required towards the Procurement of any one Station among you; much less that Men are ennobled on Account of their Virtue, that Priests are advanced for their Piety or Learning, Soldiers for their Conduct or Valour, Judges for their Integrity, Senators for the Love of their Country, or Counsellors for their Wisdom. (p. 116)

Swift's concern here has mainly been with the corruption of the officers and offices of public life. He has established this in Gulliver's statements, and in the presented behaviour of the public figures of Lilliput. But although this is a comment on political activity, it is not really a political statement. Given the absurdities and corruptions, we can move on to a number of political conclusions. We can conclude, for instance, that political action is hopeless because power corrupts, because men in power are absurd and evil; or we can conclude that we need moral, upright men in political positions; or we can conclude that a correct belief will prosper whatever the corruptions of the political operatives; or we can conclude that there are no sincere beliefs, merely ideologies that serve as a cloak for personal ambitions.

The situation in Lilliput shows the role of political beliefs and political parties in both the domestic and foreign affairs of the state. Internally Lilliput is divided between 'two struggling Parties . . . under the Names of *Tramecksan*, and *Slamecksan*, from the high and low Heels on their Shoes, by which they distinguish themselves'. (p. 32) The implication is that this is all that distinguishes them. At the same time Lilliput and Blefuscu are at war over the issue of which end to break eggs, the traditional way of breaking them at the larger end having been proscribed in Lilliput after the present King's grandfather cut his finger when, as a child, breaking the big end. As a result of the Lilliputians' resentment of the order to break the smaller end of their eggs

> their have been six Rebellions raised on that Account; wherein one Emperor lost his Life, and another his Crown. These civil Commotions were constantly fomented by the Monarchs of *Blefuscu*; and when they were quelled, the Exiles always fled for Refuge to that Empire. It is computed, that eleven Thousand Persons have, at several Times, suffered Death, rather than submit to break their Eggs at the smaller End. (p. 33)

Essentially Swift is saying here that the political beliefs motivating political action are as absurd as he has shown the officers and offices of political life to be. Certainly this is satire, and caricature and absurdity are methods of satire; certainly the low and high heels, the big and little endians, represent specific political issues in England. But Swift is not merely using the manner of satire, adopting the appropriate decorum and so denoting serious matters by absurd terminology. Rather he is questioning that any of the issues are serious by comparing them to issues of the height of heels, or the end on which to break an egg. The huge disproportion between the triviality of those beliefs and their consequences in terms of political actions, rebellion, death, exile, express a high contempt for the political. It seems that for Swift political confrontations are reducible to such absurdities: indeed, he would not think there was any reduction involved. This is the stature of political causes. Issues of economic power, of parliamentary representation, of governmental responsibility have no place in this confrontation 'during which Time we have lost Forty Capital Ships, and a much greater Number of smaller Vessels, together with thirty thousand of our best Seamen and Soldiers; and the Damage received by the Enemy is reckoned to be somewhat greater than ours' (p. 34). Swift sees it merely as two absurd intransigent sides each trying to foist absurd doctrines on to everyone. The particular causes, the particular beliefs, are not presented as having any serious foundations.

When absurd issues are allied with corrupt political practitioners and ridiculous methods of appointing statesmen, the total account is one of unmitigated hostility towards the political world, towards political commitment, towards the assumption that there is any value in any political position. It is that attitude Conrad expresses in *Nostromo*. The reported views of the King of Brobdingnag offer a contemptuous dismissal of the political realm. But, as I shall argue later, his dismissal is an ethical dismissal—he rejects the immorality of the practitioners and the triviality of issues, but does not question the political structure of society. His advocacy of an alternative is powerful; the King

> gave it for his Opinion; that whoever could make two Ears of Corn, or two Blades of Grass to grow upon a Spot of Ground where only one grew before; would deserve better of Mankind, and do more essential Service to his Country, than the whole Race of Politicians put together. (pp. 119-20)

But his statement does not go on to recommend the abolition of all political structures, and a vision of decentralised, corn-growing communities. Kings, cabinets, legislation are accepted as facts. The judgments are all against the delusions and corruptions of the politicians and leaders; and against, too, the rabble, who are

presented as mindless, violent, hostile, disruptive. When Gulliver
is in the temple in Lilliput he is

> left with a strong Guard, to prevent the Impertinence, and
> probably the Malice of the Rabble, who were very impatient
> to croud about me as near as they durst; and some of them
> had the Impudence to shoot their Arrows at me as I sate on
> the Ground by the Door of my House. (p. 15)

Corrupt ambitious politicians, fanatics, a malicious rabble; absurdity and triviality of beliefs and behaviour; an absence of serious
political theory: this is the picture Swift presents of the political
life. From here he can develop various possible positions. One
would be an attitude of utter rejection—and Swift has often
enough been seen as utterly negative, as rejecting the world, life,
humanity. This rejection is Gulliver's position with regard to mankind at the end of Book IV. But although withdrawal and rejection are certainly possibilities considered in *Gulliver's Travels*,
Swift also considers certain positive political attitudes.

One obvious position is to advocate firm authority. Having made
a diagnosis of society so fearful, the imposition of law and order
merely for the sake of law and order can seem appealing in the
face of the impending chaos. It is not, however, something Swift
advocates. It is not true to say, as George Orwell wrote, that Swift's
'political aims were on the whole reactionary ones'.[6] Reactionary
power, absolute authority, come off badly in *Gulliver's Travels*.
The King of Lilliput, when Gulliver has prevented an invasion from
Blefuscu by capturing their fleet, develops absolutist ambitions. He

> desired I would make some other Opportunity of bringing all
> the rest of his Enemy's Ships into his Ports. And so unmeasur-
> able is the Ambition of Princes, that he seemed to think of
> nothing less than reducing the whole Empire of *Blefuscu* into
> a Province, and governing it by a Viceroy; of destroying the
> *Big-Endian* Exiles, and compelling that People to break the
> smaller End of their Eggs; by which he would remain sole
> Monarch of the whole World. But I endeavoured to divert him
> from his Design, by many Arguments drawn from the Topicks
> of Policy as well as Justice: And I plainly protested, that I
> would never be an Instrument of bringing a free and brave
> People into Slavery: And when the Matter was debated in
> Council the wisest Part of the Ministry were of my Opinion.
> This open bold Declaration of mine was so opposite to the
> Schemes and Politicks of his Imperial Majesty, that he could
> never forgive me. . . . (p. 37)

[6] George Orwell, 'Politics vs Literature: an examination of *Gulliver's Travels*'
in *The Collected Essays, Journalism and Letters of George Orwell*, Sonia Orwell
and Ian Angus (eds.), IV, London, 1968, p. 220.

In Brobdingnag, of course, the situation is reversed. Here Gulliver advocates to the horror of the King the marvels of gunpowder 'that would have made him absolute Master of the Lives, the Liberties, and the Fortunes of his People'. (p. 119)

For all his presenting political issues and political ambitions as petty, trivial, and comic, in his opposition to absolutism Swift is utterly serious. His turning away from the political arena in mocking despair is not a final attitude.

Swift's opposition to absolutism depends on his acceptance of the theory of the mixed monarchy—the theory that the three estates of the realm, king, nobles, and commons, were of equal importance in the state. Z. S. Fink has shown how this is expressed in the course of the political discussions between the King of Brobdingnag and Gulliver.[7] At the end of the discussions, Gulliver explains the existence of a militia of citizens in Brobdingnag:

> I was curious to know how this Prince, to whose Dominions there is no Access from any other Country, came to think of Armies, or to teach his People the Practice of military Discipline. But I was soon informed, both by Conversation, and Reading their Histories. For, in the Course of many Ages they have been troubled with the same Disease, to which the whole Race of Mankind is Subject; the Nobility often contending for Power, the People for Liberty, and the King for absolute Dominion. All which, however happily tempered by the Laws of that Kingdom, have been sometimes violated by each of the three Parties; and have more than once occasioned Civil Wars, the last whereof was happily put an End to by this Prince's Grandfather in a general Composition; and the Militia then settled with common Consent hath been ever since kept in the strictest Duty. (p. 122)

Here Swift has abandoned his presentation of all political involvement as being absurd, corrupt or criminal. Here he presents the three estates as having their three, independent, class interests. Certainly he refers to this as a 'disease'—with perhaps the implication that it is something that has been caught and that might be cured. But nonetheless, this is an analysis of political interest, of competing interests, that gives politics a far more significant role than the cavortings of the Lilliputians, or Gulliver's account of the English to the King of Brobdingnag, would allow.

However, it is not clear that Swift recognised his analysis of the three orders as political. He presents it not as a political theory but rather as a fact about human nature. That Brobdingnag has

7 Z. S. Fink, 'Political Theory in *Gulliver's Travels*', *ELH: A Journal of English Literary History*, Vol. XIV, 1947, pp. 151-61.

experienced civil wars might have allowed for some political speculation. A radical thinker might, for instance, have argued that as
long as a state has a monarchy and nobility there will always be
civil wars; but Swift considers democratic republicanism no more
than he considers any other political theories. Political theories
are the absurdities of high and low heel and big and little end
factionists. Civil wars are innate to man because the three social
orders are innate. Swift never acknowledges that this is but another
hypothesis, another ideology. Although he offers a serious political
analysis, he presents it not as a political theory but as a fact of
human nature. We might wonder why it is that Lilliput, Brobdingnag, and Laputa all have social structures of the three orders.
The expectation of satire might provide a partial explanation: we
have to be offered societies whose structures are like those of the
England that is being satirised. But the real explanation, I think,
is that Swift believed that the three orders were innate to man.
He finds it necessary to have Gulliver explain why there should be
armies and war in Brobdingnag, when 'there is no Access from any
other Country'. Today with our current ideologies we would not
find it necessary to explain that: we would argue that aggression
is innate to man. Today we would find it necessary to explain why
in this isolated community a society of the three orders of king,
nobles, and people should have developed.

The most radical critique of domestic political life offered in
Gulliver's Travels is that voiced by the King of Brobdingnag. But
the questions the King asks of Gulliver and the statements Gulliver
gives make a moral critique of English political practice:

> He asked, what Methods were used to cultivate the Minds and
> Bodies of our young Nobility; and in what kind of Business
> they commonly spent the first and teachable Part of their
> Lives. What Course was taken to supply that Assembly, when
> any noble Family became extinct. What Qualifications were
> necessary in those who are to be created new Lords: Whether
> the Humour of the Prince, a Sum of Money to a Court-Lady,
> or a Prime Minister; or a Design of strengthening a Party
> opposite to the publick Interest, ever happened to be Motives
> in those Advancements. What Share of Knowledge these Lords
> had in the Laws of their Country, and how they came by it,
> so as to enable them to decide the Properties of their Fellow-
> Subjects in the last Resort. Whether they were always so free
> from Avarice, Partialities, or Want, that a Bribe, or some
> other sinister View, could have no place among them. (p. 113)

This is not a political critique of English political theory. The
sorts of questions asked about educating the nobility and creating
a new nobility, and the ensuing questions about the Commons and

bribing voters, accept as an implicit ideal the model of English political structures. There is no questioning at all about the principles of a hereditary nobility with its political representation in the House of Lords: the only questions are about moral education and about the principles of creating new lords—unquestioningly accepting an aristocracy as a permanent social and political force. The King of Brobdingnag's political theory and the social organisation of his state are an expression of the theory of the mixed monarchy; but it is not recognised as a theory that can be questioned or challenged. The questions and challenge relate to ethical behaviour within that system.

The most memorable treatment of the conflict of interests of the various estates or classes is that given in the account of the relationship of the flying island to the lands below it in Book III. In recognising the competing interests, Swift offers here an advocacy of a politics of compromise:

> The King would be the most absolute Prince in the Universe, if he could but prevail on a Ministry to join with him; but these having their Estates below on the Continent, and considering that the Office of a Favourite hath a very uncertain Tenure, would never consent to the enslaving their Country.
>
> If any Town should engage in Rebellion or Mutiny, fall into violent Factions, or refuse to pay the usual Tribute; the King hath two Methods of reducing them to Obedience. The first and the mildest Course is by keeping the Island hovering over such a Town ... But if they still continue obstinate, or offer to raise Insurrections; he proceeds to the last Remedy, by letting the Island drop directly upon their Heads, which makes a universal Destruction both of Houses and Men. However, this is an Extremity to which the Prince is seldom driven, neither indeed is he willing to put it in Execution; nor dare his Ministers advise him to an Action, which as it would render them odious to the People, so it would be a great Damage to their own Estates that lie all below; for the Island is the King's Demesn.
>
> But there is still indeed a more weighty Reason . . . the King, when he is highest provoked, and most determined to press a City to Rubbish, orders the Island to descend with great Gentleness, out of a Pretence of Tenderness to his People, but indeed for fear of breaking the Adamantine Bottom; in which Case it is the Opinion of all their Philosophers, that the Loadstone could no longer hold it up, and the whole Mass would fall to the Ground. (pp. 155-6)

There is, then, a limit on the exercise of power here. For if the King attempts to exercise absolute power by bringing down the full weight of the island to crush the people below, he will damage the very instrument of his power. Similarly, the people are inhibited from too great an exercise of independence or rebelliousness for fear of the possibility of such an action. Neither side can win. It is a very neat fable for compromise.

It might be objected that the fable is of limited applicability, that the damage to the bottom of the island is something limiting the exercise of absolute power only in this rather exceptional community. But the fable is not dependent on the mysterious qualities of the flying island. The ministers would never agree on such a policy since 'it would be a great Damage to their own Estates that lie all below'. Their wealth and power depend on the continued existence of the people to farm their estates. There can be no common cause between King and nobility, for the King's lands are all on the island; and if the nobility did agree to the destruction of their own estates beneath, they would be dependent on the King's goodwill for their continuing economic support and 'the Office of a Favourite hath a very uncertain Tenure'. Any such alliance could only be temporary.

The three interests of king, nobility, and people that are stated in Book II are here realised in fictional form, the concepts are expressed in the imagery and events of the novel. And by the introduction of these concepts, we can see book III as offering an advance in political sophistication and analysis on Book I. With the recognition of inevitable conflicting interests, Swift both takes political behaviour more seriously than in Lilliput, and can offer some positive suggestions of compromise. We have been led, through a series of examples and discussions, to a deeper understanding. Yet looked at in another way Swift's attitudes in Book III offer little advance from Book I and indeed are dependent on the judgments expressed in Books I and II on political activity. When political behaviour and activity have been presented as absurd, comic, cruel, irrational, and based on no theories or ideas, it is easy to advocate a compromise of the warring factions. A scepticism about the value of every political position, a suspicion about every scheme that claims to offer a solution, makes the advocacy of compromise easy: there is no problem about surrendering a position for a compromise when no position is serious or worthwhile.

And after all, the political positions of the three orders of the state are not presented as deriving from theory or argument: they are given as inevitable, instinctual roles, not subject to thought or debate. If three groups are born as warring, as having different interests, then there is an inevitability about competition and a need for compromise, and an impossibility that any one can be correct. Since this conflict is innate in society, no other political position, no party, can ever hope to gain total support. The competing interests of the three estates are presented as inevitable, as pre-existing and transcending any issues of authority, economics, religion and property. The only political opinion possible is to discourage factions, new beliefs, alternatives, and to try to reconcile the three positions into compromise: and it is compromise, not a tripartite pluralism, that is advocated.

Given the nature of *Gulliver's Travels* a reader might well expect to meet in at least one of the episodes some primitive peoples, noble savages or unfallen creatures. After the political societies of the first three books, the Houyhnhnms at first appear to be unfallen, uncorrupt, rational, possibly ideal beings. They present themselves to Gulliver as having a society that does not need the corruptions of political life. 'Power, Government, War, Law, Punishment, and a Thousand other Things had no Terms, wherein that Language could express them; which made the Difficulty almost insuperable to give my Master any Conception of what I meant. . .'. (p. 228). And after Gulliver has given his account of European society, his 'Master' comments

> That, our Institutions of *Government* and *Law* were plainly owing to our gross Defects in *Reason,* and by consequence, in *Virtue*; because *Reason* alone is sufficient to govern a *Rational* Creature. (p. 243)

After the succession of political activities that the preceding books have presented, we are in as ready a state as Gulliver to welcome a society that can operate without politics, with neither parties nor institutions nor competing orders. But the realities of the Houyhnhnm society do not accord with the official account. They have no words for 'Power, Government' and so on which makes it difficult for Gulliver to talk to his 'Master'; but they clearly have the concepts of authority and rule, for one of them is in the role of master to Gulliver. The contradiction is firmly established by Swift but left implicit. It is not a contradiction that Gulliver is willing to recognise.

But although the Houyhnhnm society may seem superior to European society in its absence from political corruptions, the absurdities of party and ideology, the competition of varied interests, it achieves this apparent superiority only at the expense of certain freedoms that we accept as basic to the political world. In the course of the preceding books Swift's belief in the mixed monarchy has become clearer. It is a doctrine of compromise, of course, and because of that the clarity and singleness of the Houyhnhnms' rationality might seem appealing; but the virtues of political compromise, of the adjustable balances have emerged in contrast with the ambitions of the various parties and the three orders to have their own belief and interest adopted with a singleness of purpose that represses all alternatives. Just such an absolutism has been achieved in the Houyhnhnm society. George Orwell has indicated the totalitarian nature of the Houyhnhnm society, though without recognising that Swift has established in the preceding books the means for a critique and rejection of it. But although Orwell misunderstands Swift's attitude towards the Houyhnhnms, he gives an account of them that cannot be bettered:

> In a Society in which there is no law, and in theory no compulsion, the only arbiter of behaviour is public opinion. But public opinion, because of the tremendous urge to conformity in gregarious animals, is less tolerant than any system of law. When human beings are governed by 'thou shalt not', the individual can practise a certain amount of eccentricity: when they are supposedly governed by 'love' or 'reason', he is under continuous pressure to make him behave and think in exactly the same way as everyone else. The Houyhnhnms, we are told, were unanimous on almost all subjects. The only question they ever *discussed* was how to deal with the Yahoos. Otherwise there was no room for disagreement among them, because the truth is always either self-evident, or else it is undiscoverable and unimportant. They had apparently no word for 'opinion' in their language, and in their conversations there was no 'difference of sentiments'. They had reached, in fact, the highest stage of totalitarian organization, the stage when a conformity has become so general that there is no need for a police force.[8]

The closed nature of the society, the unawareness of other possibilities, is given a fine underlining just before Gulliver leaves. Standing on a height he sees a small island: 'but it appeared to the Sorrel Nag to be only a blue Cloud: For, as he had no Conception of any Country beside his own, so he could not be as expert in distinguishing remote Objects at Sea, as we who so much converse in that Element' (p. 265). This is not only a reminder of the Houyhnhnms' lack of vocabulary and lack of concepts: it relates too to their overall political philosophy, the sorrel nag's having 'no conception of any Country beside his own'. The political insights of *Gulliver's Travels* come largely from Swift's having such various conceptions of other countries, of being able to illuminate the political nature of his own society by comparison with other countries and the conceptions of hypothetical countries, of utopias and anti-utopias. But the Houyhnhnms see not another country,

---

8 'Politics vs Literature', pp. 215-16.

not another island, but a blue cloud. Had it been a white or a
grey or a black cloud, we might have more confidence in their
judgment and sympathy for their eyesight: a mistake due to incomplete observation. But the nag does not explain the unknown
in terms of something known; rather he invents the unknown—a
blue cloud—to explain something, the proper explanation of which
would upset his world picture.

Orwell's classic essay indicates the non-institutional aspects of the
political form of Houyhnhnm society. But for all the lack of
political vocabulary, the society also has its political institutions.
The quaternial 'Representative Council of the whole Nation' (p.
254) is, indeed, no other than a parliament, and Gulliver's 'Master'
who attends it 'as the Representative of our District' is no other
than a member of parliament. The political nature of the assembly
is made clear in the topics discussed; for, in addition to redistribu-
ting foodstuffs, they had 'their old Debate, and indeed, the only
Debate that ever happened in their Country . . . Whether the
Yahoos should be exterminated from the Face of the Earth'. (p.
255). And with the abruptness of the introduction of the issue, and
the extremeness of its formulation, we are brought to realise that
like all the other societies encountered, that of the Houyhnhnms
is political too.

The nature of the proposed extermination cannot be defined
until the nature of the Yahoos is defined. Our judgment of the
event will be different depending upon whether we see the Yahoos
as domestic animals, or as subservient human beings. The ambiguity
about the Yahoos is of course basic to the satiric effects Swift
achieves. That they seem indeterminately men and beasts is in itself
a comment on human motivations and activities: their sexuality
and their hoarding of 'certain *shining Stones*' (p. 244) are particularly presented in this way to illuminate the bestial aspects of
European society.

But to understand the political issues we have to separate out
the strands of the ambiguities. Is Swift offering us here a comparable reversal to that of the first two books with its big and
little men? Horses and men in reversed roles, so that the Yahoos
are in this context animals. Or are the Yahoos essentially human
beings who are treated as animals? One of the suggestions in the
debate about extermination is that 'the *Houyhnhnms* should be
exhorted to cultivate the Breed of Asses, which, as they are in
all respects more valuable Brutes; so they have this Advantage, to be
fit for Service at five Years old, which the others are not till Twelve'
(p. 257). That there are asses to carry out the functions of beasts
of burden indicates that the Yahoos are not to be seen simply as

the equivalent of horses in Europe for this Houyhnhnm society. By removing them from their servile role, the social ecology would not necessarily be disrupted; there are asses to fill their niche. The possibility is that the Yahoos are not in their necessary or appropriate role in the Houyhnhnm society. That they are treated as humans treat animals may tell us more about the people who treat them so than about their true nature. We remember the writer of *A Modest Proposal* who is able to suggest using the Irish children as animals for food and skins; he talks about the human population in terms of farming—'a Child, *just dropt from its Dam*', 'Two hundred Thousand Couple whose Wives are Breeders'. By thinking of humans as animals, they can be treated as animals. The Houyhnhnms think of the Yahoos as animals, propose exterminating them as animals, skin them for Gulliver's canoe.

But what if the Yahoos are not animals? Their stressed similarity to Gulliver is important in this context. Commentators indicate how this emphasises the bestiality of man, taking their cue from Gulliver's reactions; but the comparison also works in the opposite way. The Houyhnhnms are concerned to keep the Yahoos as servile, as animals; but if indeed they are like Gulliver, then the possibility of educating them, of civilising them, perhaps exists. Now such an education is an ambivalent issue: on the one hand it might be argued that there is no point in educating the Yahoos, for they would simply be brought to the state of man, and man, we have seen, is so debased. To educate the Yahoos would be simply to enable them to add to their basic unpleasantness a European sophistication in evil. On the other hand, debased as European man is presented to be, he is certainly less debased, less bestial than the Yahoos. The importance of the kindness of the Portuguese captain is that it contrasts both with the cold rationality of the Houyhnhnms and with the degraded bestiality of the Yahoos, one of whom in Gulliver's eyes he appears to be: 'I wondered to find such Civilities from a *Yahoo*' (p. 270).

Perhaps the Yahoos could achieve such civilities. This would certainly seem likely if they originated in the way tradition recorded:

> the two *Yahoos* said to be first seen among them, had been driven thither over the Sea; that coming to Land, and being forsaken by their Companions, they retired to the Mountains, and degenerating by Degrees, became in Process of Time, much more savage than those of their own Species in the Country from whence these two Originals came. (p. 256)

The fact that Gulliver who also arrives by sea does not degenerate but abhors the behaviour of the Yahoos is an argument for the possibility for the rehabilitation of the Yahoos. Man has a potential for degeneration as the Yahoos show; but this degeneration is insisted on and desired as an irremediable, permanent state by the Houyhnhnms. It would not suit the Houyhnhnms if the Yahoos were civilised and educated. Because Gulliver does not degenerate and become like the Yahoos, he has to be driven out of the country. He presents a threat to the security of the Houyhnhnms' society that is essentially a political threat.

Gulliver is told by his 'Master'

> That in the last general assembly, when the Affair of the *Yahoos* was entered upon, the Representatives had taken Offence as his keeping a *Yahoo* (meaning my self) in his Family more like a *Houyhnhnm* than a Brute Animal. That, he was known frequently to converse with me, as if he could receive some Advantage or Pleasure in my Company: That, such a Practice was not agreeable to Reason or Nature, or a thing ever heard of before among them. The Assembly did therefore *exhort* him, either to employ me like the rest of my Species, or command me to swim back to the Place from whence I came. That, the first of these Expedients was utterly rejected by all the Houyhnhnms, who had ever seen me at his House or their own; For, they alledged, That because I had some Rudiments of Reason, added to the natural Pravity of those Animals, it was to be feared, I might be able to seduce them into the woody and mountainous Parts of the Country, and bring them in Troops by Night to destroy the *Houyhnhnms* Cattle, as being naturally of the ravenous Kind, and averse from Labour. (p. 263)

The Houyhnhnms, then, resent the breakdown in segregation resulting from the way Gulliver is treated by his 'Master', and they fear a slave revolt; they fear that Gulliver will lead an insurrection that will threaten their property and withdraw their slave labour. Gulliver has to be expelled for fear he will subvert the whole order of Houyhnhnm society. The rationality, order and social uniformity of the Houyhnhnms is founded on the existence of a subjugated people that they treat as animals, using them for their work (drawing sledges) and for their skins and tallow.

The treatment of the Yahoos as animals encourages us to accept them as animals in this society. But in his description of them Swift emphasises their humanity. When Gulliver's 'Master' unties one of them from the stable to show him, Gulliver has a reaction of horror:

> My Horror and Astonishment are not to be described, when I observed, in this abominable Animal, a perfect human

Figure; the Face of it indeed was flat and broad, the Nose depressed, the Lips large, and the Mouth wide: But these Differences are common to all savage Nations, where the Lineaments of the Countenance are distorted by the Natives suffering their Infants to lie grovelling on the Earth, or by carrying them on their Backs, nuzzling with their Face against the Mother's Shoulders. The Fore-feet of the *Yahoo* differed from my Hands in nothing else, but the Length of the Nails, the Coarseness and Brownness of the Palms, and the Hairiness on the Backs. (pp. 213-14)

The Yahoos, then, are given negroid features. The effect of this is not to suggest Negroes are more debased, nearer to the bestiality of the Yahoos: but to present the Houyhnhnm society as a type of a colonial or slave owning society. The Augustan rationality of the Houyhnhnm is founded on a system of slavery, just as Britain's attempts at those Augustan values had an economic foundation in the slavery of the West Indian plantations.

The attack on colonialism in the final chapter of *Gulliver's Travels* takes on more point if we accept this interpretation of the Houyhnhnm society and the status of the Yahoos. Gulliver's exemption of English colonial practice from his attacks (hence drawing our attention to it), and the encounter with the Portuguese Don Pedro, set a general context for an indictment of colonialism; one particular race is not denoted. The features of the Yahoos are negroid, but their long hair and the 'brown Buff Colour' (p. 207) of their skins might associate them also with the South American subjects of Spanish colonialism.[9] The Yahoos, of course, invade the land of the Houyhnhnms; and Gulliver's complaint about colonialism is due to a fear the European Yahoos will destroy the society of the Houyhnhnms. But the irony is, that the European Yahoos will destroy the Houyhnhnms' society by introducing into it a system of behaviour that the Houyhnhnms already employ on the Yahoos. The Houyhnhnms' treatment of the Yahoos is the only example of a slave owning or colonial society in action that we are given. But if Europeans arrived, then they would naturally treat the Houyhnhnms as beasts of burden, since they look like horses: what this means is indicated by the way the Houyhnhnms already treat the Yahoos. Although the Yahoos were not the indigenous aboriginals invaded and colonised by the Houyhnhnms, the way they are treated gives substance to the attack on colonialism that Gulliver concludes with. That attack is not an unintegrated diatribe, but an explicit handling of a theme that the previous

[9] The girl Yahoo who Gulliver claims attacked him sexually has red hair as a conventional indication of her lubriciousness. This symbolic coloration need not upset the overall presentation of the Yahoos as blacks.

chapters of the book have been presenting in action, in character:

> A Crew of Pyrates are driven by a Storm they know not whither; at length a Boy discovers Land from the Top-Mast; they go on Shore to rob and plunder; they see an harmless People, are entertained with Kindness, they give the Country a new Name, they take formal Possession of it for the King, they set up a rotten Plank or a Stone for a Memorial, they murder two or three Dozen of the Natives, bring away a Couple more by Force for a Sample, return home, and get their Pardon. Here commences a new Dominion acquired with a Title by *Divine Right*. Ships are sent with the first Opportunity; the Natives driven out or destroyed, their Princes tortured to discover their Gold; a free Licence given to all Acts of Inhumanity and Lust; the Earth reeking with the Blood of its Inhabitants: And this execrable Crew of Butchers employed in so pious an Expedition, is a *modern Colony* sent to convert and civilize an idolatrous and barbarous People. (p. 278)

The subjugation of the Yahoos is the subjugation of a people, of a race. It bears a relationship to specific English practice, just as Book I relates to the relationships between England and France in the early eighteenth century, and as Lagado relates to specific practices of the Royal Society.

This account of the Houyhnhnms' treatment of the Yahoos suggests then an increase in political sophistication in the analyses presented through *Gulliver's Travels*. From the triviality and absurdity of Lilliputian politics where no ideas can be taken seriously, we move to the presentation of the theory of the mixed monarchy where the conflicting interests are presented as serious but innate, not really 'political', and conclude with the modern analysis of the Houyhnhnms' society as one founded on economic oppression.

The revelation of the political nature of the Houyhnhnm society relates to the political themes of the earlier books in an important way: the revelation comes in terms of foreign policy. Swift's denunciation is of English colonialism: the Houyhnhnms and Yahoos are not members of the same race or nation, but quite distinct from each other; their relationship is one of racial or national domination, not of class oppression. Similarly the indictment of Lilliput emerges as a result of the King's wanting to subjugate another nation, Blefuscu, not from the internal conduct of the kingdom. Writing about the domestic politics of Lilliput, Blefuscu, Brobdingnag, Laputa, Swift does not deal with internal class oppression. In so far as he analyses internal policies it is in terms of their absurdities or idiocies. He does not allow that there can be legitimate

internal clashes. He accepts the theory of three orders of the mixed
monarchy, but deduces from it harmonious compromise, not continual conflict. Although in Book IV Swift is led to a criticism of
economic practices in England, this is not developed. It is important that this is introduced in the book in which he is showing
the economic basis of exploitation of the Yahoos, suggesting again
a deepening of seriousness of analysis. But the sort of indictment is
of the moral nature of the King of Brobdingnag's attacks on English
practice. Gulliver relates that

> the rich Man enjoyed the Fruit of the poor Man's Labour, and
> the latter were a Thousand to One in Proportion to the former.
> That the Bulk of our People was forced to live miserably, by
> labouring every Day for small Wages to make a few live
> plentifully. I enlarged myself much on these and many other
> Particulars to the same Purpose: But his Honour was still to
> seek: For he went upon a Supposition that all Animals had a
> Title to their Share in the Productions of the Earth; and
> especially those who presided over the rest. (p. 235)

That last phrase makes it clear that though there are immoral inequalities in English practice, the essential theory is sound; the
communistic 'all Animals had a Title to their Share in the Productions of the Earth' is explicitly defined as not communistic
with the 'and especially those who presided over the rest'. Some in
England are rewarded with too little. But the structures of
authority, feudal ownership, capitalist investment—whatever their
form—are not challengeable; the bosses 'especially' must profit.
Some are more equal than others.

In his attitudes to internal, to domestic political issues, Swift, as
Orwell pointed out, though in many matters 'a rebel and icono-
clast', 'cannot be labelled "Left"'.[10] But when he deals with the
relationships between nations, then he recognises and denounces
oppressions. The explanation no doubt lies in part in his direct
experiences of England's treatment of Ireland. There Swift encountered the receiving end of oppression, but in terms of the
domestic life of Ireland or England, his social position committed
him to the perpetuation of a hierarchical system, and protected him
from experiencing oppressions. The plan of the King of Lilliput
to subjugate Blefuscu is seen as a serious issue: different nations
should exist in equality.[11] With the different orders, the three
classes, Swift's commitment to co-existence, to balance, ensures his
hostility to the attempts of either monarch, nobility, or people

10 'Politics vs Literature', p. 216.
11 In his article 'Hobbes' *Leviathan* and the Giantism Complex in the First
Book of *Gulliver's Travels*', *Journal of English and Germanic Philology*, Vol.
LX, 1961, pp. 228-39, John D. Seelye has related the image of Gulliver covered

to achieve absolute domination; but it is a co-existence, within a hierarchical system. That seems not to disturb him.[12] The hierarchical system by which the Houyhnhnms oppress the Yahoos is exposed to criticism because Swift can see the relation of the Houyhnhnms to the Yahoos as one of a different species, a different race, a different nation to each other: he can see it in terms of subjugation, colonialism, exploitation. But he has nothing to say, it is important to note, about the defined classes within the Houyhnhnm society—the white, sorrel, and iron-grey horses born in an inferior station.

Many of the standard approaches and themes of English political fiction can be seen in *Gulliver's Travels*. The emphasis on party political life in Lilliput rather than any examination of the economic and social bases of the society is an emphasis repeated by Conrad in *Nostromo*; and the consequent rejection of political life there, the reduction of it to barbarity and self-interest, is very similar to Swift's. Through *Kangaroo, 1984* and Alan Sillitoe's *Travels in Nihilon* (1971) the continuing theme of English political fiction has been a rejection of political life as destructive, self-seeking and corrupt. Unlike William Morris's fable *News from Nowhere*, however, the fable of *Gulliver's Travels* offers no alternative to a structured, hierarchical political society. As the reader is led along through stages of developing political sophistication and complexity in the first three books, there is the expectation that Book IV will offer a society freed from politics; but the pessimistic irony is that the Houyhnhnms are politically organised after all. The final statement is that all societies are political and that all political societies are corrupt or exploitive or both. Moral improvements can be attempted. But man cannot escape from the political world. And the political world is a fallen world. Swift's Christian

---

with a swarm of pygmies when he is tied down to the image of Hobbes' Leviathan composed of a vast crowd of tiny people, and he argues that Swift is presenting 'a satire upon Hobbes' *Leviathan* and the paradox of absolutism'. Since Gulliver is not one of the individual figures that comprise the Leviathan of the state of Lilliput, since he 'is not corporeally identifiable with the Emperor or Lilliput', then it is absurd for him to recognise the rule and authority of the Emperor of Lilliput. Swift attacks Hobbes

> first, by Gulliver's ridiculous, unquestioning obeisance to the tiny Emperor, and then by his indignant escape from Lilliput when the ambition and tyranny of the ruler makes his situation perilous, The social contract, Swift would seem to imply, is only as good as Leviathan wills it to be, and the law of self-preservation is more powerful than the invisible chains of government. (p. 237).

It is important that Swift can only make this attack by using someone from another nation. His radical traits of thought emerge in the international context.

[12] Irvin Ehrenpreis gives a valuable summary of some of Swift's political thinking and indicates the contradictions in his conservatism in 'Swift on Liberty', *Journal of the History of Ideas*, Vol. XIII, 1952, pp. 131-46.

pessimism is akin here to Milton's argument in *The Tenure of Kings and Magistrates*. Men were originally created free, Milton argues, and

> they livd so, till from the root of *Adams* transgression, falling among themselves to doe wrong and violence, and forseeing that such courses must needs tend to the destruction of them all, they agreed by common league to bind each other from mutual injury, and joyntly to defend themselves against any that gave disturbance or opposition to such agreement. Hence came Citties, Townes and Common-wealths. And because no faith in all was found sufficiently binding, they saw it needfull to ordaine some authorities . . . These for a while governd well, and with much equitie decided all things at thir owne arbitrement: till the temptation of such a power left absolute in thir hands, perverted them at length to injustice and partialitie. . . .[13]

Political and social organisations were established because man was fallen; and because man was fallen, they themselves were inevitably corrupt as institutions. They are both unavoidable and imperfectible.

---

[13] *The Prose of John Milton*, J. Max Patrick (ed.), New York, 1967, pp. 351-2.

Satire and Self-Expression in *Swift's* Tale of a Tub

Gardner D. Stout, Jr

It . . . [is] as hard to get quit of *Number* as of *Hell.*

Which way I fly is Hell; myself am Hell;
And in the lowest deep a lower deep
Still threat'ning to devour me opens wide . . .

I

That *A Tale of a Tub* would prove enigmatic Swift well knew. He anticipates us with unnerving prescience:

> The Reader truly *Learned* . . . will here find sufficient Matter to employ his Speculations for the rest of his Life . . . I do here humbly propose for an Experiment, that every Prince in *Christendom* will take seven of the *deepest Scholars* in his Dominions, and shut them up close for *seven* Years, in *seven* Chambers, with a Command to write *seven* ample Commentaries on this comprehensive Discourse. I shall venture to affirm, that whatever Difference may be found in their several Conjectures, they will be all, without the least Distortion, manifestly deduceable from the Text.[1]

Like Swift's frequent references to the *Tale's* 'sublime Mysteries' and '*Arcana*', this passage is not simply a travesty of dark authors and their learned commentators. For Swift's satire on dark authors expresses his sense that his own *Tale* is a mysterious work and that widely differing, even conflicting speculations are deducible from its text.

In this essay I wish to suggest that the *Tale* can be experienced and understood most fully as a complex, enigmatic expression of

---

[1] Swift, *A Tale of a Tub, to which is added The Battle of the Books, and the Mechanical Operation of the Spirit*, A. C. Guthkelch and D. Nichol Smith (eds.), 2nd ed., Oxford, 1958. All quotations from these works are from this edition.

Swift's personality and state of being as its author and speaker.[2] As embodied in the *Tale* he tells, Swift's personality is essentially coherent and yet self-contradictory, powerfully self-assertive and yet fragmented by intense conflicts. He indulges and exhibits repressed impulses, mainly towards regressive sexual and excremental self-gratification.[3] At the same time, he seeks to negate these guiltily enjoyed impulses by projectively embodying them in his satiric targets, thus dissociating himself from their latent sources in his own personality. His state of being in the *Tale* is partly epitomised by his observation that: 'It . . . [is] as hard to get quit of *Number* as of *Hell*'. Swift unrelentingly struggles to get quit of the depravities of the crowd, of the libidinous and undifferentiated '*Number*' of human egoism and sensuality, by satirising the crowd. But he thereby condemns himself to the '*Hell*' of '*Number*' by obsessively demonstrating, in covert and largely unconscious ways, his hateful, and pleasurable, complicity in the depravities of his satiric butts.[4]

II

Responding to the *Tale*'s detractors, Swift asserts in the Apology that he '*wrote only to the Men of Wit and Tast*'. They alone '*will observe*' that '*there generally runs an Irony through the Thread of the whole Book*', and that

> *some of those Passages in this Discourse, which appear most liable to Objection are what they call Parodies, where the Author personates the Style and Manner of other Writers, whom he has a mind to expose . . . But this is enough to direct those who may have over-look'd the Authors Intention.*

2 On the currently prevalent view that the speaker in the *Tale* is usually a persona, see p. 325 and n.5, below.

3 For a general study of these aspects of Swift's personality, see especially Phyllis Greenacre, *Swift and Carroll: A Psychoanalytic Study of Two Lives*, New York, 1955. In *Life Against Death: The Psychoanalytic Meaning of History*, Middletown, Conn., 1959, Norman O. Brown examines Swift's 'startling anticipations' of psychoanalytic theories about anal erotism and sublimation. Like Brown, I admire Swift's extraordinary ability to apply 'his own doctrines to himself'. But I feel that Brown's insistence on the sane objectivity of Swift's 'excremental vision' of 'the universal neurosis of mankind' neglects Swift's individuality and the obsessive elements of his art in the *Tale*, its anxious compromises between conflicting impulses, and its brilliantly self-expressive strategies and significance, which are explored in the present essay.

4 The theoretical assumptions of my essay are generally indebted to Frederick Crews's discussion of psychoanalytic criticism in *Psychoanalysis and Literary Process*, F. Crews (ed.), Cambridge, Mass., 1970, pp. 1-24. In an excellent essay entitled 'Order and Cruelty: A Reading of Swift (with some Comments on Pope and Johnson)', *Essays in Criticism*, Vol. XX, 1970, pp. 24-56, which came to my attention after the present essay was completed, Claude Rawson explores the 'interplay between deliberate attacking purposes (and tactics), and certain tense spontaneities of self-expression' in Swift's satire, especially in the *Tale* and the *Travels*. Professor Rawson examines with subtlety and precision strategies and stylistic qualities of Swift's satire which are complementary to some of the psychological patterns I consider here. I thoroughly agree with his con-

Swift thus opposes himself and the élite few for whom he writes—the true wits—to the witless 'mob' who have mistaken his aims and performance. In telling his *Tale*, Swift often parodies his satiric butts by personating them: a hack, an egotistical modern, a frenzied adeptus or Aeolist is conjured up before us by the mocking histrionics of a brilliant mimic who wittily travesties their foolish depravities—while simultaneously maintaining an ironic, often sarcastic commentary on them. Swift's satiric parodies are mainly reductive: his mimicry of his targets, particularly in the *Tale's* literary satire, arrogantly asserts his superiority and control over them. By insisting on a radical dichotomy between himself and the objects of his scorn, Swift's satire affords him (and his audience) the aggressive, and self-defensive, pleasures of sudden glory. On the other hand, the sustained vitality of Swift's mimicry is such that his voice as satiric speaker often tends to merge with the voices of his satiric victims, and bespeaks his antagonistic kinship with them. In attacking his satiric butts, Swift covertly expresses his complicity both in their depravities and in their perverse satisfaction in subverting the norms of decency, common sense, and rational moderation and orthodoxy which he consciously seeks to vindicate in the *Tale*. Swift's vivid parodies and personations are often projective embodiments of repressed aspects of his own personality as the *Tale's* author. His parodies allow his buried self to speak through him, while enabling him to maintain that the voice he is parodying is antithetic to himself as satiric speaker. Swift's mimicry is thus a kind of psychic ventriloquism. It simultaneously projects his denied wishes onto despised 'others'—and takes them into himself so he can utter them with his own tongue. It thereby achieves a precarious compromise between the demands of his buried life for expression and gratification, and the repressive dictates of his conscience-stricken sense of ethical and aesthetic integrity, and identity.

Swift's success in dissociating himself from his buried life may be gauged by the recent vogue of persona-oriented criticism, according to which the speaker in the *Tale* is generally a foolish character, antithetic to Swift, who unwittingly epitomises the targets of the satire. Failing to grasp the *Tale's* thread of irony and to perceive Swift's latent kinship with his satiric butts, such readings mistake his consciously preferred self-image for the whole man. They thus respond narrowly to the *Tale's* self-defensive, repressive aspects, thereby presenting a spectacle Swift anticipated in his mocking image of satire: 'Tis but a *Ball* bandied to and fro, and every Man carries a *Racket* about him to strike it from himself among

---

cluding suggestion that in the depths of his being Swift 'was and sensed that he was, in all rebellious recalcitrance, himself Yahoo'.

the rest of the Company'.[5] On the other hand, readings of the work as wholly anarchic and nihilistic ignore its tense compromise between conflicting psychic impulses—a compromise which satisfies the demands of Swift's punitive conscience as well as those of his repressed feelings and fantasies.

One way of grasping the principles which generate and govern the *Tale*'s pervasive ambivalence is suggested by Freud's discussion of psychological 'negation':

> the content of a repressed image or idea can make its way into consciousness, on condition that it is *negated*. Negation is a way of taking cognizance of what is repressed . . . though [it is] not, of course, an acceptance of what is repressed . . . With the help of negation only one consequence of the process of repression is undone—the fact, namely, of the ideational content of what is repressed not reaching consciousness . . . [Through] negation, thinking frees itself from the restrictions of repression and enriches itself with material that is indispensable for its proper functioning.[6]

Satiric negation released in Swift repressed aspects of his own personality and made them accessible to his creative consciousness in writing the *Tale*. It thus enabled him to create satiric fictions representing and gratifying his repressed impulses and fantasies, while simultaneously denying them. Satiric negation thereby satisfied the demands of conscience and defended his unstable sense of identity against the potentially disintegrative forces of repressed aspects of his own being. The entire *Tale*, especially the 'Digression Concerning Madness', exhibits a principle of satiric energy suggested by Freud's theory: the more powerful the satiric negation, the more vital will be the satiric fiction. The intense vitality of Swift's satiric fictions and the creative energy with which he conjured them into life are paradoxically dependent on his relentless, frustrated effort to annihilate them. Satiric negation enabled Swift to enrich the imaginative range and power of his satire, by allowing him to

---

[5] In 'Speaker and Satiric Vision in Swift's *Tale of a Tub*', *Eighteenth-Century Studies*, Vol. II, No. 2, 1969, pp. 175-99, I have presented a detailed critique of persona-oriented criticism of the *Tale*, arguing that Swift, as the *Tale*'s satiric author, is the speaker throughout; that the work's complex ironies express shifts in Swift's tone and pose as speaker, not in the stance of a protean, foolish persona (or character) who is the butt of Swift's satire; and that a major aspect of the work's purpose and significance is Swift's self-mocking and yet sympathetic probing of the satirist's character, aims, and achievements, especially of his own character and performance as author, and speaker, of the *Tale*.

[6] Freud, 'Negation', *Standard Edition of the Complete Psychological Works of Sigmund Freud*, James Strachey *et al.* (eds.), London, 1953- , Vol. XIX, pp. 235-6. Freud's discussion of negation is also cited by Norman O. Brown, in *Life Against Death*, and by Denis Donoghue, in *Jonathan Swift: A Critical Introduction*, Cambridge, 1969.

slip down his conscience in the service of his own 'Lewdness as well as Nastiness'—projectively embodied in his satiric vision of the lewdness and nastiness of that hateful and detestable 'animal called man'.[7]

Let us consider some characteristic examples of the ways Swift represents his inner conflicts in disguised forms through satiric negation.

In the religious allegory, Swift assumes 'the character of an Historian' who chronicles the careers of Peter, Jack, and Martin in a curiously equivocal manner. His portraits of Peter and Jack are contemptuously degrading, and his description of Martin's sane moderation expresses his conscious commitment to the common forms of Anglican orthodoxy. As has often been noted, however, Martin is as much a foppish bully-boy as his brothers until his last-minute transformation into an Anglican rationalist, after which he disappears from the narrative. Martin embodies Swift's genuine, self-defensive commitment to rational moderation and restraint. But Martin's pallor reflects the emotional weakness of that commitment: though he has all the orthodoxy, Peter and Jack have all the imaginative vitality.[8] Swift recounts their depraved careers in a tone which, hovering between contempt and fascination, expresses his ambivalent relationship to them. Their successful efforts to subvert their father's will by allegorising its plain meaning into self-serving mysteries is a curious parody of one of Swift's own favourite procedures in the *Tale*. Peter's tyrannical paternalism toward his subservient brothers is disturbingly akin to Swift's aggressive egoism and determination to subdue others to his 'own *Power*, his *Reasons*, or his *Visions*'. Jack's masochistic pleasure in '*a handsom Kick on the Arse*' and a box from milady on his erected ears; his delight in playing with excrement, pissing in the spectators' eyes and bespattering them with mud; and above all, his manic determination—for the '*Love of God*'—to '*Strip, Tear, Pull, Rent, Flay off all*' so as to '*appear as unlike the Rogue* Peter *as it is possible*'—all these characteristics exhibit, in transmuted forms, impulses and fantasies that pervade the *Tale*. Mysterious forces of attraction and identification continually bring Jack together with Peter and cause him to be taken for his brother. Their latent kinship symbolises Swift's unconscious identification with them as surrogates of his own detested, yet pleasurable, impulses

---

[7] Swift, *Correspondence*, Harold Williams (ed.), Oxford, Vol. III, 1965, p. 103.
[8] Cf. F. R. Leavis's observation: 'The clean skin of the Houyhnhnms . . . is stretched over a void; instincts, emotions and life, which complicate the problem of cleanliness and decency, are left for the Yahoos with the dirt and the indecorum' ('The Irony of Swift', in *Discussions of Swift*, John Traugott (ed.), Boston, 1962, p. 42).

toward aggression, regressive sexuality, and anal erotism. The besetting tensions of Swift's psychic conflicts are disguisedly portrayed
in Jack's predicament: the more strenuously Jack seeks to dissociate himself from Peter, the more inevitably he becomes identified with him, in a symbolic drama of the return of the repressed:

> it was among the great Misfortunes of *Jack*, to bear a huge
> Personal Resemblance with his Brother *Peter*. Their Humours
> and Dispositions were not only the same, but there was a close
> Analogy in their Shape, their Size, and their Mien . . . This we
> may suppose, was a mortifying Return of those Pains and Pro-
> ceedings, *Jack* had laboured in so long; And finding, how
> directly opposite all his Endeavours had answered to the sole
> End and Intention, which he had proposed to himself; How
> could it avoid having terrible Effects upon a Head and Heart
> so furnished as his?

Jack's frustrated efforts to dissociate himself from Peter are emblematic not only of the absurd antagonisms among religious extremists, but also of Swift's efforts to dissociate himself in the *Tale*
from consciously disapproved traits of his own character. In the
Apology, Swift defends the *Tale* with an aggressiveness which
covertly acknowledges the justness of his detractors' charges that
the work is in part obscene, heterodox, even blasphemous. In
pledging that *'he will forfeit his Life, if any one Opinion can be
fairly deduced from that Book, which is contrary to Religion or
Morality'*, he protests too much. Indeed the entire Apology betrays,
I think, Swift's uneasy sense of the discrepancy between his actual
performance in the *Tale* and his determination to satirise the
'gross Corruptions in Religion and Learning' and the *'Follies of
Fanaticism and Superstition'*. Like Jack, Swift is caught in a
charmed circle, demonstrating his hateful, and latently pleasurable,
kinship with his opposing self by seeking to deny him.

As I suggested at the outset of this essay, Swift's use of mimicry
and parodic personation is another of the principal means by
which he expresses his buried life in disguised forms. In personating
a Grub Street hack, a hermeticist, a member of the Royal Society,
Swift satirically praises and mimics the pretences of 'our Illustrious
Moderns' to universal knowledge, their fatuous pride in their
spurious accomplishments, and their bogus zeal 'for the universal
improvement of mankind'. And yet, in parodying such writers, he
indirectly expresses, as in his satire on Peter, the egoism of his
own unstable personality.

Swift's attack on the ephemeral productions of Grub Street and
of all the mountebank purveyors of literary and spiritual fads is

especially intense in dedicating his *Tale* to Prince Posterity. His contempt for 'the Productions of human Wit, in this polite and most accomplish'd Age' manifests itself in the veiled sarcasm with which he ironically complains against Time's 'inveterate Malice' to the Moderns. But his complaint is not simply a travesty of a modern hack's pretenses to literary immortality. In protesting Time's peculiar malice toward 'our vast flourishing Body, as well as . . . my self', Swift is acknowledging that like every production of human wit, his *Tale* (and he himself as its author) is subject to 'the transitory State of all sublunary Things'. The description of Time, with his 'large and terrible *Scythe*', rending nails and teeth, and 'baneful abominable *Breath*, enemy to Life and Matter', has a grotesque surrealism which screens and expresses Swift's latent fear that his unstable identity, as embodied in his *Tale of a Tub*, will be annihilated by the 'furious Engins' of an aggressor he imagines as an absurd, horrible figure from a nightmare. For, like those in religion, conquest, and philosophy, literary innovations, including the *Tale* itself, are engendered by 'Vapours, ascending from the lower Faculties, to water the Invention, and render it fruitful'. Like the other acquirements of his mind, man's literary achievements are a superficial, ephemeral dress covering their true sources in the lewdness and nastiness of the corrupt body beneath. Their origins and destiny, like their authors', can be discovered by peeping in their breech and by tracing them to a *'Jakes'* or a *'Bawdy-House'*.

Swift's dedication of his *Tale* to Prince Posterity epitomises the indirections, ironies, and brilliant (occasionally surrealistic) wit and humour of the entire work. Describing the three oratorical machines requisite for exalting oneself above the crowd, Swift classifies the *Tale* as a product of the Stage-Itinerant, that great seminary of 'Westminster *Drolleries, Delightful Tales, Compleat Jesters*, and the like; by which the Writers of and for GRUB-STREET, have . . . so nobly triumph'd over *Time*; have . . . filed his teeth, . . . [and] blunted his Scythe'. In the *Tale*, Swift plays the role of a bewilderingly elusive, protean jester, and presents a series of ostensibly zany fantasies, allegories, projects, and speculations whose witty extravagance expresses his repressed feelings through humorous denial. Posing as a mountebank peddling crack-brained theories and bogus nostrums in *A Tale of a Tub Written for the Universal Improvement of Mankind*, Swift is able to exploit that ancient strategy of the jester's trade—mystification. In the twilight zone between jest and earnest, he can simultaneously reveal and conceal himself. His jesting should not be dismissed as the senseless ravings of a foolish, even mad character antithetic to him.

Nor should it be mistaken simply for a rhetorical strategy intended to manipulate his reader or to protect himself from public censure. His protean poses allow him to play the licensed fool in the court of conscience. He can thus represent, in riddling, fantastic symbols, thoughts and feelings which might invite retaliation if uttered soberly by his official self. Through playful jesting, he can partially liberate, without consciously acknowledging, the refractory, regressive child within him who enjoys punning, mystification, number games, magical thinking, and nonsense comedy of all kinds, as well as the pleasures of aggression, excremental play, and regressive sexual fantasising. But we should also be sensitive to the tensions of Swift's incessantly shifting role-playing: his performance self-assertively combats, and betrays, the anxieties of a fragmented personality uncertain of its own identity and fearful of the threat posed to its sense of moral and psychological integrity by the partial release of its repressed impulses.

As I suggested earlier, Swift's role as a protean jester liberated a rich vein of fantasy in him and thereby allowed him to express his buried life, while dissociating himself from it. Swift frequently represents his repressed feelings by ascribing them projectively to some zany sect of philosophers or mystery-mongers. The *Tale*'s 'Scheme of Oratorial Receptacles or Machines', its explication of Aeolist doctrines and the theory of vapours deduced therefrom, the history of the tailor sect who worship the god of fashion—all these furnish Swift with what he sarcastically refers to as 'a Type, a Sign, an Emblem, a Shadow, a Symbol' enabling him to represent, in veiled terms, his own repressed feelings and fantasies. He repeatedly attacks those 'whose peculiar Talent lies in . . . refining what is Literal into Figure and Mystery' and boasts with sardonic irony that, as a member of the republic of dark authors, he has written a treatise filled with 'sublime Mysteries'. In satirising those who mistake darkness for profundity, however, he tacitly acknowledges his own propensity for conveying his forbidden impulses 'shut up within the Vehicles of Types and Fables'. He indirectly describes his own strategies by observing that ancient writers self-defensively attacked critics in a *'Hieroglyph'*. The ancients spoke in hieroglyphic 'Types and Figures' because 'they durst not make open Attacks against a Party so Potent and Terrible'. Swift's jesting description of the ancients' veiled manner of treating their critics typifies his own way of representing his repressed impulses in covert defiance of his conscience, by embodying them in types and fables. He notes, however, that the self-defensive advantages of speaking mysteriously may be offset by the risks of being wholly misunderstood, thus anticipating those who have mistaken his emblematic, riddling fables for the nonsensical ravings of a demented modern. Swift observes that in contemplating the mysterious 'Vehicles of Types and Fables':

> the transitory Gazers have so . . . fill'd their Imaginations with the outward Lustre, as neither to regard, or consider, the Person or the Parts of the Owner within. A Misfortune we undergo with somewhat less Reluctancy, because it has been common to us with *Pythagoras, Aesop, Socrates,* and other of our Predecessors.

Swift's account of the tailor-worshipping sect epitomises his use of enigmatic types and figures to express himself in disguised, negative terms. He begins with an extravagant account of the fashionable world's worship of the tailor god, 'a sort of *Idol*, who, as their Doctrine delivered, did daily create Men, by a kind of Manufactory Operation . . . At his left hand, . . . *Hell* seemed to open, and catch at the Animals the Idol was creating'. This equivocal fable simultaneously ridicules man's subservience to fashions and serves as a dark allegory of Swift's obsessive fear that his identity is the mechanical product of ephemeral fashions generated by the tailor god (as the 'God of Seamen' [semen]) and devoured by his yawning *'Hell'*. Unfolding with an energy which seems to flow impersonally from the metaphors themselves, Swift's explication of the sartorists' extravagant doctrines gradually metamorphoses into a disturbingly plausible allegory of the human condition:

> To conclude from all, what is Man himself but a *Micro-Coat,* or rather a compleat Suit of Cloaths with all its Trimmings? As to his Body, there can be no dispute; but examine even the Acquirements of his Mind, you will find them all contribute in their Order, towards furnishing out an exact Dress: To instance no more; Is not Religion a *Cloak,* Honesty a *Pair of Shoes,* worn out in the Dirt, Self-love a *Surtout,* Vanity a *Shirt,* and Conscience a *Pair of Breeches,* which, tho' a Cover for Lewdness as well as Nastiness, is easily slipt down for the Service of both.

The passage's impersonal explication of the ostensibly fantastic beliefs of a crazy sect allows Swift to represent (in a self-defensively 'hieroglyphic' form) a fearful obsession that is central to the entire *Tale*: the 'higher' faculties, the 'Acquirements' of man's 'Mind', are merely a superficial, modish cover tenuously hiding the 'lower Faculties' of genitals and anus. Like Gulliver, Swift discovers that clothes are a deceptive, ineffectual denial of his kinship with the excrementally filthy and sexually degenerate Yahoos. The discovery is at once deeply threatening to his sense of his moral identity, and gratifying in its sado-masochistic self-disgust and its perverse pleasure in the excremental and sexual functions. As Empson has noted of the entire *Tale*,[9] the language itself plays into Swift's hands here: the *breeches* of conscience are essentially indistinguishable from the *breech* they cover. The self-defensively impersonal observation that conscience is 'easily slipt down' for the 'Service' of lewdness and nastiness implies that the act is deliberate and morally reprehensible, while at the same time making it seem impersonal and involuntary. The metaphor can thus be interpreted as symbolising the psychological and literary processes I have been analysing here: through a satiric negation dictated by conscience, Swift evades his conscience for the service of his repressed impulses. Small wonder he insists on satire's impotence to reform human nature.[10] For by attacking what he considered lewdness and nastiness, Swift paradoxically slipped down his conscience and liberated his own lewdness and nastiness.

As Empson remarks (*Pastoral*, p. 60), for Swift everything spiritual and valuable has a gross and revolting parody, very similar to it—only unremitting judgment can distinguish between them. In the *Tale* Swift relentlessly attempts to distinguish goodness from its contemptible, demoralising parody. But in seeking to distinguish goodness from its parody, and the higher faculties from the lower, he demonstrates their kinship, even their identity. The more resolutely he struggles to deny and transcend his affinities with the crowd, the more inextricably he mires himself in man's common body and fate. The more energetically he attempts to get quit of the undifferentiated '*Number*' of common humanity, to escape the guiltily pleasurable hell of sensuality, the more obsessively he circles back to it. Satiric negation brings the return of the repressed. By a fearful irony, conscience panders will.

The following passage brilliantly expresses Swift's experience of this paradox:

> And, whereas the mind of Man, when he gives the Spur and Bridle to his Thoughts, doth never stop, but naturally sallies forth into both extreams of High and Low, of Good and Evil; His first Flight of Fancy, commonly transports Him to Idea's of what is most Perfect, finished, and exalted; till having soared out of his own Reach and Sight, not well perceiving how near the Frontiers of Height and Depth border upon each other; With the same Course and Wing, he falls down plum into the lowest Bottom of Things, like one who travels the *East* into the *West*; or like a strait Line drawn by its own Length into a Circle. Whether a Tincture of

9William Empson, *Some Versions of Pastoral*, London, 1935, p. 60. Cited hereafter as *Pastoral*.
10 See my essay cited n.5, above, esp. pp. 184-91.

Malice in our Natures, makes us fond of furnishing every bright Idea with its Reverse; Or, whether Reason reflecting upon the Sum of Things, can, like the Sun, serve only to enlighten one half of the Globe, leaving the other half, by Necessity, under Shade and Darkness: Or, whether Fancy, flying up to the imagination of what is Highest and Best, becomes over-shot, and spent, and weary, and suddenly falls like a dead Bird of Paradise, to the Ground. Or, whether after all these *Metaphysical* Conjectures, I have not entirely missed the true Reason; The Proposition, however, which hath stood me in so much Circumstance, is altogether true; That as the most unciviliz'd Parts of Mankind, have some way or other, climbed up into the Conception of a *God*, or Supream Power, so they have seldom forgot to provide their Fears with certain ghastly Notions, which instead of better, have served them pretty tolerably for a *Devil*. And this Proceeding seems to be natural enough; For it is with Men, whose Imaginations are lifted up very high, after the same Rate, as with those, whose Bodies are so; that, as they are delighted with the Advantage of a nearer Contemplation upwards, so they are equally terrified with the dismal Prospect of the Precipice below.

This passage is a paradigm of the artistic and psychological patterns we have been examining: the effort to escape what Swift regards as the debased, disturbingly attractive depths of human nature inevitably compels one to circle back to those depths. Quixotically sallying forth, the mind seems to transport itself, with incipient madness, to delusively fanciful ideas of disembodied, exalted perfection. But its soaring flight spent, the mind impotently falls from High to Low, plummeting with the 'same Course and Wing' into the debased 'Bottom of Things' along the trajectory of the original flight. Swift's '*Metaphysical* Conjectures' intuitively describe the return of the repressed. As he insists in the digression on 'Madness', inspired attempts to rise above the genital and anal fundamentals of human nature are an insanely fanciful, self-defeating denial of the inextricable involvement of spirit in flesh. Indeed, as Empson suggests (*Pastoral*, p. 60), at its farthest reach Swift's self-lacerating irony implies that what man takes to be spiritual is merely physical: *spirit* (the word plays into Swift's hands) is a *vapour* generated from semen and excrement. The physical, especially the sexual, sources of the energy which transports the mind of man into fanciful visions of an exalted perfection are implied by Swift's analogy between Fancy and the Bird of Paradise, which 'flying up to the imagination of what is Highest and Best, becomes over-shot, and spent', and suddenly falls dead to the ground. As Swift puts the matter in *The Mechanical Operation of the Spirit*: 'the *Thorn in the Flesh* serves for a *Spur* to the *Spirit*'—and 'Too intense a Contemplation [upwards toward Heaven] is not the Business of Flesh and Blood; it must by the necessary Course of Things, in a little Time, let go its Hold, and fall into *Matter*'.

The circular flight of the Bird of Paradise in its energetically doomed ascent and inevitable fall to the ground, represents an important aspect of the movement of Swift's satire and of his state of being in the *Tale*. To represent his intuitive sense of his own state, Swift denies that he is describing himself, by embodying his own feelings in a projective image of 'the mind of Man'. Attempting to escape the libidinous impulses of his own being, Swift strives to transcend them through various forms of denial, in order to become a Bird of Paradise devoid of the feet which blazon those impulses. But the very effort to transcend the repressed ensures its obsessive return with redoubled energy. Straining upward, Swift's satire circles back on itself 'like a strait Line drawn by its own Length into a Circle', and 'falls down plum into the lowest Bottom of Things'. As the word 'plum' suggests, the 'Mind' falls through a leadenly gravitational attraction to its debased counterpart. Swift thus explores the shadow-line where the 'Frontiers of Height and Depth border upon each other', through the defensively hieroglyphic metaphors and wit of his satiric fiction. He thereby indulges through denial, his repressed impulses. This indulgence is as threatening as it is gratifying, for it invites retaliation from his punitive conscience.

The patterns of pain and pleasure embodied in the *Tale* are complex. Its indulgences and brilliant insights are earned partly through a conscience-stricken, satiric self-laceration which combines sadistic and masochistic pleasures: as Swift sardonically observes of all satire (generalising his own experience): 'the World [is] soonest provoked to Praise by *Lashes*, as Men are to *Love*'. Swift's predicament is epitomised partly by his scornful description, in *The Mechanical Operation of the Spirit*, of the philosopher who, 'while his Thoughts and Eyes were fixed upon the *Constellations*, found himself seduced by his *lower Parts* into a *Ditch*'—and partly by his concluding assertion in the Bird of Paradise passage, that it is 'with Men, whose Imaginations are lifted up very high, . . . as with those, whose Bodies are so; that, as they are delighted with the Advantage of a nearer Contemplation upwards, so they are equally terrified with the dismal Prospect of the Precipice below'.

III

By partially liberating his buried life, Swift's covert exploration in the *Tale* of the frontiers of height and depth within himself called his very sanity into question. The 'vehemence and rapidity of mind' and 'vivacity of diction' Dr Johnson noted as characteristic of the *Tale*'s 'distinct and peculiar . . . mode',[11] defend Swift against his latent fear that, without continuous self-assertion, his tenuous sense of identity may disintegrate, and he will, like the Bird of Paradise, plummet into the 'lowest Bottom of Things'. His effort to negate and transcend his own repressed impulses energetically conjures them into dismaying life. His violent self-disgust paradoxically enables him to gratify the desires and tendencies he consciously abhors. To someone who equates his probity and conscious identity with a repressive mastery of his buried life, the dismal prospect of the precipice beneath his feet is terrifying *and* inviting—a seductive hell which, threatening to devour him, opens wide.

The 'Digression Concerning Madness' urgently expresses Swift's obsessive fear about his sanity, a fear which recurred in his foreboding that he would die at the top. He masters that fear and explores the shadowy frontiers between High and Low, sanity and madness, by questioning, and asserting, his own sanity through an indictment of mankind's insanity. As elsewhere in the *Tale*, Swift expresses himself in veiled terms which conceal and reveal his own involvement in a bedlamite nightmare which attacks the reader's sense of his own sanity. Swift disguisedly represents the sexual and excremental impulses of his own personality, in explicating the theory that revolutions in conquest, philosophy, and religion are insane products of 'Vapours, ascending from the lower Faculties, to water the Invention, and render it fruitful'. Anatomising madmen whose higher faculties are possessed by their frustrated sexual and excremental impulses, Swift explores the ways their mad, aggressive egoism is communicated to others by a kind of mechanical operation of the spirit. There is, he observes:

> a peculiar *String* in the Harmony of Human Understanding, which in several individuals is exactly of the same Tuning. This, if you can dexterously screw up to its right Key, and then strike gently upon it; Whenever you have the Good Fortune to light among those of the same Pitch, they will by a secret necessary Sympathy, strike exactly at the same time. And in this one Circumstance, lies all the Skill or Luck of the Matter; for if you chance to jar the String among those who are either above, or below your own Height, instead of subscribing to your Doctrine, they will tie you fast, call you Mad . . . It is therefore a Point of the nicest Conduct to distinguish and adapt this noble Talent, with respect to the Differences of Persons and of Times . . . For, to speak a bold

[11] 'Life of Swift', in *Lives of the English Poets*, G. B. Hill (ed.), Oxford, 1905, Vol. II, p. 51.

> Truth, it is a fatal Miscarriage, so ill to order Affairs, as to pass for a *Fool* in one Company, when in another you might be treated as a *Philosopher*.

Thus 'the sole Point of Individuation' between madness and sanity is merely a fortuitous, mechanical concurrence of external circumstances and 'the Force of certain *Vapours* issuing up from the lower Faculties'.

Swift's anatomy of the world's madness is defensive. His insistence on mankind's insanity reassuringly asserts his own sanity and yet insists, with self-protective, humorous irony, thàt he too has had 'the Happiness to be an unworthy Member' of the company of Bedlam. Swift's survey of 'all those mighty Revolutions, that have happened in *Empire*, in *Philosophy*, and in *Religion*', universalises his obsessive doubts about his own sanity so as to displace the fearful burden of those doubts onto the 'shoulders of the World'. As a satirist bent on 'subduing Multitudes to his own *Power*, his *Reasons*, or his *Visions*', he may be merely another visionary who, crazed by vapours from his lower faculties, should be tied fast and called mad:

> For, what Man in the natural State, or Course of Thinking, did ever conceive it in his Power, to reduce the Notions of all Mankind, exactly to the same Length, and Breadth, and Height of his own? . . . The more [a man] shapes his Understanding by the Pattern of Human Learning, the less he is inclined to form Parties after his particular Notions; because that instructs him in his private Infirmities, as well as in the stubborn Ignorance of the People. But when a Man's Fancy gets *astride* on his Reason, when Imagination is at Cuffs with the Senses, and common Understanding, as well as common Sense, is Kickt out of Doors; the first Proselyte he makes is Himself, and when that is once compass'd, the Difficulty is not so great in bringing over others; A strong Delusion always operating from *without*, as vigorously as from *within*.

Swift's commitment to common sense is heartfelt. But his *Tale* explores the paradox that what he terms the 'natural State' of man, governed by common sense in accord with the common forms, is largely a fanciful ideal alien to human nature.

To ignore the possibility of one's own madness is to purchase serenity by yielding to another madness: 'For what is generally understood by *Happiness*, as it has Respect, either to the Understanding or the Senses . . . will herd under this short Definition: That *it is a perpetual Possession of being well Deceived*'. To exempt oneself from the madness of mankind is to condemn oneself to the hellish number of the deluded herd of mankind—to surrender one's claim to an individual integrity defined partly by one's capacity to discover the unpleasant facts covered by plausible appearances. But the stress of achieving such integrity is expressed in the detached pathos of Swift's rhetorical question: 'How fade and insipid do all Objects accost us that are not convey'd in the Vehicle of *Delusion*?'—and in his warning that:

> If this were seriously considered by the World, as I have a certain Reason to suspect it hardly will; Men would no longer reckon among their high Points of Wisdom, the Art of exposing weak Sides, and publishing Infirmities; an Employment in my Opinion, neither better nor worse than that of *Unmasking*, which I think, has never been allowed fair Usage, either in the *World* or the *Play-House*.

Swift thus expresses the anxious conflicts he endured in unmasking and dis-covering his buried self in the *Tale*'s satiric glass. Recoiling from his own satiric vision, he observes:

> In the Proportion that Credulity is a more peaceful Possession of the Mind, than Curiosity, so far preferable is that Wisdom, which converses about the Surface, to that pretended Philosophy which enters into the Depth of Things, and then comes gravely back with Informations and Discoveries, that in the inside they are good for nothing.

The generalising detachment of this bleak observation and its implication that delusion is a form of mad 'Possession' defensively screen Swift from his intuitive sense that in the *Tale* he has entered into the depths of himself and returned with the conscience-stricken discovery that in the inside he is, apparently, good for nothing. And yet, he shapes into a compelling artistic vision the discoveries with which he returned from that inward descent. Torn between credulity and curiosity, Swift embraces and rejects both, and leaves us with an enigmatic recommendation of 'the sublime and refined Point of Felicity, called, *the Possession of being well deceived*; The Serene Peaceful State of being a Fool among Knaves'.

The 'Digression Concerning Madness' concludes with Swift's audacious acknowledgment of his doubts about his own sanity. Enumerating the 'mighty Advantage' the commonwealth would gain by recovering from Bedlam those madmen whose talents are 'now buried, or at least misapplied', Swift observes:

> all these would very much excel, and arrive at great Perfection in their several Kinds; which, I think, is manifest from what I have already shewn; and shall inforce by this one plain Instance; that even, I my self, the Author of these momentous Truths, am a Person, whose Imaginations are hard-mouthed, and exceedingly disposed to run away with his *Reason*, which

> I have observed from long Experience, to be a very light
> Rider, and easily shook off; upon which Account, my Friends
> will never trust me alone, without a solemn Promise, to vent
> my Speculations in this, or the like manner, for the universal
> Benefit of Human kind. . . .

The extravagance of this acknowledgment and its position at the
very end of the 'Digression Concerning Madness' are significant.
Having obliquely explored the shadowy frontiers of sanity and madness in himself by exploring those frontiers in mankind, Swift
suddenly concludes by challenging his own sanity, thereby venting
with humorous self-defensiveness his deep fears about his own possible madness. And by immediately digressing to another subject, he
protects himself from the threat that voicing those fears posed
to his precarious equilibrium. Swift's success in dissociating himself
from his repressed impulses and in warding off their menace to
his sense of sanity may be gauged by the tendency of some readers
to misconstrue this passage, and indeed much of the *Tale*, as the
utterance of a madman (or fool) antithetic to him. Such readings
respond to Swift's negation of those tendencies in himself which he
finds threatening and demoralising. He instinctively recognised
that some of his readers would seek to tie him fast and call him
mad. Indeed, so sharply do the *Tale*'s paradoxes divide his readers
that Swift's admonition may well give pause to any explicator of
the '*Arcana*' of his book: 'it is a fatal Miscarriage, so ill to order
Affairs, as to pass for a *Fool* in one Company, when in another you
might be treated as a *Philosopher*'.

IV

In order to experience and understand the *Tale* fully we cannot,
I believe, ignore its obsessive, neurotic qualities; rather, we should
respond to them as major sources of its extraordinary power and
vitality, and of its brilliant artistry. Its role-playing, fantasies,
zany extravagance, and fragmentary digressiveness express the
anxious conflicts of an unstable, strongly self-assertive personality.
In the Preface to *The Battle of the Books*, Swift sardonically
observes that '*Satyr is a sort of* Glass, *wherein Beholders do generally discover every body's Face but their Own*'. In the *Tale*, Swift
fashioned a glass which enabled him simultaneously to cover and
dis-cover, to mask and unmask before the world the protean, conflicting roles he played in the inner drama of his being. He thus
found a style answerable to the deepest imperatives of his personality—a style which could embrace its powerful conflicts. By
negating the repressed desires and fantasies he found so threatening

and yet so compelling, he succeeded in giving them creative life while satisfying his conscience. Those aspects of the book which have been mistaken for the ravings of a madman are, rightly interpreted, often a mysterious type, sign, and symbol of Swift's buried life. As he himself sensed: 'Reason reflecting upon the Sum of Things, can, like the Sun, serve only to enlighten one half of the Globe, leaving the other half, by Necessity, under Shade and Darkness'—no commonplace observation in the Enlightenment. The *Tale* is a dark work which illuminates the shaded half of Swift's being, and of human nature, through metaphor, typology, symbolic allegory. By means of wit, Swift brilliantly represents his experience of what his admirer Yeats termed the 'uncontrollable mystery on the bestial floor'.

By reading the *Tale* as an expression of Swift's whole state of being as its author and speaker, we can, I believe, more fully experience and account for its paradoxes and conflicts. Such a reading enables us to respond to Swift as a man, rather than substituting for the man a shadowy, delusive paragon of moral integrity and artistic detachment. We can thus share Swift's experience of the besetting predicaments of what he felt to be the 'ridiculous tragedy' of the human condition and, like him, dis-cover and unmask our faces in the *Tale*'s satiric glass.

Swift: Some Caveats

Donald Greene

What I have to say here about Swift may seem to mature and thoughtful Swift scholars the most obvious commonplace. Yet perhaps it is worth saying at the present time. More and more as I read new monographs and articles on Swift by younger scholars, I get the uneasy feeling that Swift, from being the complex, disturbing, gigantic figure he used to appear, has diminished into a small, neat stereotype, whose dimensions have all been taken. We know Swift's views on all the important questions; those views are clear, simple, easily grasped, and unvarying; the future of Swift studies, then, is merely a matter of analysing the techniques with which he expressed them. Fortunately, he was a subtle technician of rhetoric, and the bulk of his writings is so great that many more monographs can still be written. Otherwise, the industry would come to a halt, for in effect we now know all there is to know about Swift's thought.

Let me reassure you, to begin with, that I am not going to deal here with the matter of how the Fourth Book of *Gulliver* is to be interpreted, except to observe that recent opinion about what Swift is trying to say to us in it has also been hardening into dogma. Now only a few veterans like Professor Landa and Professor James Clifford still have some doubts about what has come to be the orthodox interpretation. This interpretation maintains that Swift is satirising the Houyhnhnms at least equally with the Yahoos, and is advising us to take a pleasant *via media*, an easy 'compromise' between too much reason on the one hand and too much emotion on the other—as though the human race had ever suffered from an excess of either! The young tend not to be so afflicted, and many recent products of graduate schools are surprised to learn that any other interpretation has ever been thought possible. Rather, I want to deal with a more general topic, the prevalent image of Swift as the archetypal right-winger—the reactionary Tory, the extreme High Churchman, the hater of modern science and modern empiricism in general. To give a detailed documentation of the occurrence of this stereotype might seem unnecessarily and personally invidious, and for this reason I will not attempt it here. So let me, without being specific, give an example of what I mean— a recent study, on the whole excellent, sober, full of sound learning, of Swift's short but highly important late piece of verse, 'The Day of Judgment', in which the whole of the human race appears before Jove to be judged, and Jove disconcerts them by laughing at 'You who in different Sects have shamm'd/And come to see each other damn'd' and then disappoints them by refusing to damn anyone at all.[1] In an early version of the study—the writer later modified his view—the poem was automatically read as an attack by the High Anglican Swift on the various Dissenting bodies, and the occasion for it was argued to be some contemporary public action involving the Irish Presbyterians that had particularly irritated Swift.

But nothing in the text of the poem warrants the interpretation that it is only Dissenters who are capable of such perversion of religion, or that when Jove addresses his audience as the 'Offending Race of Human Kind,/By Nature, Reason, Learning, Blind', Anglicans are *ipso facto* excluded. What, on the face of it, seems to be a wonderfully audacious, devastating, and comprehensive *attack* on religious partisanship as a ubiquitous manifestation of the original sin of pride has been reduced to a petty and bad-tempered *expression* of religious partisanship: because we know, *a priori*, that one of the controlling elements in Swift's thinking was rigid religious partisanship, the interpretation of the text of the poem must be adjusted to fit that preconception. We have lost a magnificently searching and compelling comment on the universal human condition, and Swift, as a writer and thinker, has dwindled from a giant into a pygmy.

I was also bothered—but less so, since such statements are encountered so frequently—by an incidental comment, stemming from a suggestion that the poem had been praised as an expression of religious tolerance by a contemporary of well-known Whig views, that Swift, after having been for so many years a Tory of the Tories, would have been most offended by being associated with the term 'Whig' in any way. Of the three elements of Swift's thought I should like to discuss—his political views, his religious views, and his views on 'modern' science and epistemology—let us begin with this, the question of Swift's political labelling and what it means. It is not hard to rebut the theory of Swift's abhorrence in later life of the

---

[1] Swift, *Poems*, Harold Williams (ed.), Oxford, 1958, pp. 578-9. Another early text reads 'You by differing churches shammed'.

word 'Whig': one merely turns to a letter which he wrote to the
Countess of Suffolk at almost exactly the same time the poem seems
to have been written (27 July 1731), in which he states quite
flatly, 'I am a good Whig'.[2] It will be useful to note other places
in his post-1710 correspondence where he makes the same declaration: on 8 January 1733, to Lady Betty Germain, 'I know you
have been always a zealous Whig, and so am I to this day', and
again, 'As to myself, I am of the old Whig principles, without the
modern articles and refinements'; to Francis Grant, 23 March 1734,
he writes of 'septennial Parliaments, directly against the old Whig
principles, which have always been mine'. Those who are accustomed to attribute to Swift a set of responses in political and
ecclesiastical matters similar to that of such Non-Jurors as his
contemporary Thomas Hearne should read his comment on the
Non-Jurors, in a letter of 13 November 1716, to Archbishop King:
'The Tory Clergy here'—and it is evident that Swift is sharply dissociating himself from 'the Tory Clergy'—'seem ready for Conversion, provoked by a Parcel of obscure Zealots in *London*, who, as
we hear, are setting up a new Church of *England* by themselves.
By our Intelligence it seemeth to be a Complication of as much
Folly, Madness, Hypocrisy, and Mistake, as ever was offered to the
World', and later (22 December), ironically, 'The System of the
new Zealots . . . must be very suitable to my Principles who was
always a Whig in Politicks'.

How odd that modern students refuse to take Swift's own word
for how his politics are to be described! Older commentators did
him this honour, notably Samuel Johnson, whose life overlapped
Swift's by thirty-six years and who presumably had some qualifications to speak on the subject: 'By his political education he was
associated with the Whigs, but he deserted them when they
deserted their principles, yet without running into the contrary
extreme'[3]—that is, presumably, High Toryism. Swift's Whig 'political
education' was, let us remember, long and exceedingly thorough.
A refugee from Ireland for fear of Jacobite violence just as he
completed his education, he could almost be described as a child
of the Revolution. For many years he lived under the aegis of the
Whig Establishment, in the household of its renowned elder
statesman, Temple, where William of Orange himself taught him
to cut asparagus in the Dutch manner. He edited Temple's *Works*,
with a dedication to King William and with prefaces highly com-
plimentary to Temple and to such Whig ministers as Sunderland

---

[2] Swift, *Correspondence*, Harold Williams (ed.), Oxford, 1963-5, under the
dates shown.
[3] 'Life of Swift' in *Lives of the English Poets*, G. B. Hill (ed.), Oxford, 1905,
Vol. III, pp. 52-3.

and Godolphin. His most important early work—perhaps his greatest—*A Tale of a Tub*, is dedicated in the most engagingly laudatory manner to the great theorist and chief of propaganda of Revolutionary Whiggism, Somers. His *Discourse of the Contentions in Athens and Rome*, recently superbly edited by Frank Ellis, was a masterly piece of propaganda in defence of the Whig *junta*, Somers, Sunderland, and the rest, against Tory attacks. Of his four early Pindaric odes, two, those to King William and Temple, praise their politics; the remaining two, those to the Athenian Society and to Archbishop Sancroft, deal with the other two subjects I wish to discuss in this paper, Swift's attitudes toward science and religion; and I am not sure that, taken together, the four odes do not represent as full and accurate a statement as anything we have of Swift's fundamental views on these subjects throughout his life.

After Temple's death, Swift went to Ireland as chaplain to the Whig Earl of Berkeley, Lord Justice of Ireland, a position which, together with a prebend in St Patrick's Cathedral, placed him close to the centre of the Whig Establishment in Dublin, and it was not surprising that he should have been chosen by the Whig Archbishop King of Dublin for the important position of chief negotiator with the Godolphin administration in London for the abolition of the imposts of the First Fruits and Twentieth Parts on the clergy of the Church of Ireland. The story of what then happened has often been told: Swift's consistent refusal to accept the condition which the ministry attached to such abolition, the repeal of the Irish Test Act denying public employment to Dissenters unwilling to receive communion in the established Church, a refusal based on the ground (in effect) that this was the first step toward the disestablishment of that Church; his gradual conviction that there was more hope of obtaining the terms he wanted from the leaders of the opposition, Harley and St John, who were on the point of overthrowing the Godolphin régime; eventually, his whole-hearted alliance with Harley and St John and his becoming their chief of propaganda in the great campaign to bring the war with France to a close.

How is this shift in Swift's political allegiance in 1710 to be described and interpreted? The usual phraseology is—to quote a recent book on Swift's politics—'his transformation into a Tory stalwart', or the like. That radical transformations in political ideology take place so facilely in intelligent and highly politically experienced men of forty-three, one may venture to doubt, especially considering Swift's later insistence on his continuing Whiggism. The question of the precise signification of political partisan labels, especially during the reign of Anne, is still much debated by historians. Robert Walcott, in what still seems to me the most useful treatment of the subject,[4] follows Sir Lewis Namier's handling of it in the later part of the century in suggesting that then, as later, it would be foolish to take 'Tory' and 'Whig' as representing two opposing clear-cut and well-defined opposing ideologies. These labels were merely attached by historical accident or, sometimes, for propaganda effect, to various shifting alliances of individual politicians not normally greatly motivated by political ideology in the abstract but, as politicians usually are, by the desire of power and the enhancement of their own and their associates' personal interests. And, interestingly, this view has the support of Swift himself: in *The Sentiments of a Church of England Man*, after reprobating the fact that 'there should be so much Violence and Hatred in religious Matters, among Men who agree in all Fundamentals, and only differ in some Ceremonies; or, at most, meer speculative Points'—a proposition to which I shall presently refer again—he continues:

> Yet is not this frequently the Case between contending Parties in a State? For Instance; do not the Generality of *Whigs* and *Tories* among us, profess to agree in the same *Fundamentals*; their Loyalty to the Queen, their Abjuration of the *Pretender*, the Settlement of the Crown in the *Protestant* Line; and a *Revolution Principle*? Their Affection to the Church Established, with Toleration of *Dissenters?* ... so that the Differences fairly stated, would be much of a Sort with those in Religion among us; and amount to little more than, *who should take Place*, or *go in and out first*, or *kiss the Queen's Hand*; and what are these but a few *Court Ceremonies?* or *who should be in the Ministry?* And what is that to the Body of the Nation, but a meer *speculative Point?*[5]

Swift says the same thing in other and later places—as did Johnson when Boswell asked him for a, so to speak, official formulation of his views on the difference between Whig and Tory, 'A wise Tory and a wise Whig, I believe, will agree. Their principles are the same'.[6] How odd that modern students cannot bring themselves to accept Swift's and Johnson's carefully thought out words on the subject, but insist on clinging desperately to the belief that the labels 'Tory' and 'Whig' furnish some magic, metaphysical clue to two opposing total philosophies of life! It is particularly surprising in American students, who would be hard pressed if they had to define the essence of the political labels 'Republican'

[4] *English Politics in the Early Eighteenth Century*, Cambridge, Mass., 1956.
[5] Swift, *Prose Works*, Herbert Davis (ed.), Oxford, 1939-68, Vol. II, pp. 13-14.
[6] Boswell, *Life of Johnson*, G. B. Hill (ed.), rev. L. F. Powell, Oxford, 1934-50, Vol. IV, p. 117.

and 'Democrat' in their own country and who learn every day from votes in Congress that Republicans and Democrats, whether 'wise' or not, do in fact very frequently agree.

This is not to deny, of course, that on concrete matters of disputed political action Swift could involve himself very deeply on one side or the other of a current issue. It mattered to him very much that the position of the national Church of Ireland should not be undermined by encroachment from the Irish Presbyterians; that an end should be put to the great war with France, which, as he thought, had degenerated into an unnecessary shedding of blood prolonged for the benefit of the Marlborough-Godolphin faction; that the Irish economy should be defended against subversion by English ministries; and he could become very hostile indeed to those who upheld the opposing positions. But this is quite different, I think, from saying that Swift's political ideology was transformed, in the fifth decade of his life, from Whiggism to Toryism. The danger in the glib use of these partisan labels by the modern student is that, consciously, or unconsciously, we attach to them our own, later meanings, and then distort the biography and the writings of the individual to whom we have attached them so as to fit those meanings. I once protested about the workings of this process with Samuel Johnson: 'Given that Johnson was a Tory, we can immediately deduce the essential facts not only about his political opinions, but about his critical principles, which must have been authoritarian, his religion, which must have been "High", his morality, which must have been prescriptive . . . It is very useful to know all this *a priori*, for it saves us the trouble of having to read what Johnson actually wrote on such matters'[7]—or, at least, to read it carefully. Swift, I think, has been subjected to the same kind of distortion. If he is to be saved from it, let us at least take seriously his own consistent affirmation throughout his life of his fundamental Whiggism, which we have not the least reason to doubt. It has been said that 'the nearest test one can apply for whiggery' is 'exclusionism'[8]—support of the movement in the late 1670s to exclude the future James II from the throne. When Swift was in his late sixties, he read and annotated William Howells' *Medulla Historiae Anglicanae,* later presenting it to his friend Mrs Whiteway's daughter, the future Mrs Deane Swift. 'It was a popular Whig history', Herbert Davis comments, 'and Swift took care [in his annotations] that she should have plenty of warning against the bias and the nonsense to be found in it'. Nevertheless, when Swift encounters in Howells the report, 'A Bill was

---

[7] Donald Greene, *The Politics of Samuel Johnson,* New Haven, 1960, p. 1.
[8] John Carswell, *The Descent on England,* London, 1969, pp. 206-7.

voted to be brought in to EXCLUDE THE DUKE OF YORK from succeeding to the Crown', he adds the marginal note, 'Wd to God it had
passed'[9]—a sentiment which, by the way, Johnson would have
heartily seconded.

Swift's staunch loyalty to the Church of Ireland has been exaggerated in many recent discussions into little less than bigotry—
witness the comment on 'The Day of Judgment' mentioned earlier
—and the term 'High Church', though at least as unhelpful a one
as 'Tory', is applied to him as a matter of course. It is true enough
that he greatly feared what seemed to him a deliberate campaign
of encroachment by the Irish Presbyterians on the position of the
established Church; that, like the vast majority of his contemporaries, he regarded with the deepest horror the events of the
1640s, culminating with the execution of the King and the Archbishop of Canterbury and the dissolution of the episcopal structure
of the Church of England; that, as a result, he maintained a life-
long suspicion of at least certain groups of Dissenters, notably the
Presbyterians, and sometimes talked about them in much the same
way as Johnson talked about 'Whigs'—'Sir, the first Whig was the
devil' and the like. But, as with Johnson, it is possible to take such
surface manifestations too seriously. Are we really to define the
core of Swift's religious beliefs as *extra ecclesiam Anglicanam
nulla salus*—a doctrine which Anglicanism itself has always repudiated? When he writes in *The Sentiments of a Church of England
Man*, 'We look upon it as a very just Reproach . . . that there
should be so much Violence and Hatred in religious Matters,
among Men who agree in all Fundamentals, and only differ in
some Ceremonies; or, at most, meer speculative Points',[10] are we to
believe that he is insincere? What are we to make of 'The Day of
Judgment', where, as I read it, *all* self-regarding religious partisanship by those 'who come to see each other damn'd' is stingingly
rebuked? Or of the account of religion in Lilliput, where the strife
between the Big-Endians and Little-Endians has caused the loss of
a total of eleven thousand lives? Little-Endianism is the state, the
established religion, but Swift's account makes it seem in no way
more attractive than dissenting Big-Endianism. Swift, though
strongly opposed to the repeal of the Test Act—as indeed were
William III and the great majority of Englishmen until 1829—
was quite ready to accept the Toleration Act, which guaranteed
freedom of worship to Protestant Dissenters and was, it may be
remembered, the legislative expression of Locke's powerful argument in his *Letters on Toleration* that it is itself contrary to the

9 *Prose Works*, Vol. V, pp. xxxv, 264.
10 See n.5, above.

Christian religion to attempt to make another change his religion by the use of force. 'A MAN truly Moderate', says Swift in one of his most serious statements, his sermon on brotherly love, 'is steady in the Doctrine and Discipline of the Church, but with a due Christian Charity to all who dissent from it out of a Principle of Conscience; the Freedom of which, he thinketh, ought to be fully allowed, as long as it is not abused, but never trusted with Power'[11] —that is, political power. My argument is that if we fail to recognise the central importance to Swift's thought of 'moderation' and 'Christian charity' in this sense we do him a great injustice and make a pitiful travesty of the transcendent greatness of his moral teaching.

Swift, I think, has not always been well served here by his editors and commentators. I recently turned to the long-awaited index volume to the Blackwell edition of his prose works, in general so excellently compiled by Professor Ehrenpreis and his associates, in search of passages that might help me to understand what Swift meant by the term 'fanatic'. I was taken aback to discover no entry except the cross-reference, 'Fanatics and Fanaticism: *see* DISSENTERS', and, when I turned to the entry 'Dissenters', to find the gloss '(commonly called "fanatics" by JS)'.[12] This is index-making with a vengeance. Is it really true that to Swift 'dissenter' and 'fanatic' were synonymous? To Johnson, as to most other users of the English language, they were not. According to his *Dictionary*, a 'dissenter' is 'one who, for whatever reasons, refuses the communion of the English church', whereas a 'fanatick' is 'An enthusiast; a man mad with wild notions of religion'.[13] To affirm that Swift did not distinguish between these two classes is to affirm a great deal. If all dissenters are men mad with wild notions of religion, it is hard to see how Swift could have approved of the privileges afforded them by the Toleration Act. Even in one of his most extreme anti-Puritan statements, the sermon on the anniversary of Charles I's execution, he distinguishes: speaking of 'the meanest person', who, if he 'hath common understanding', finds it easy 'to know whether he be well or ill governed', he asserts:

> If his religion be different from that of his country, and the government think fit to tolerate it, (which he may be very secure of, let it be what it will) he ought to be fully satisfied, and give no offence, by writing or discourse, to the worship established, as the dissenting preachers are too apt to do.

11 *Prose Works*, Vol. IX, p. 178.
12 *Prose Works*, Vol. XIV, pp. 136, 157.
13 The special sense of 'enthusiast'—'one who vainly imagines a private revelation'—should be noted.

Which seems to imply that there are some, at least, who do not give offence in this way. 'But', Swift continues,

> if he hath any new visions of his own, it is his duty to be quiet, and possess them in silence, without disturbing the community by a furious zeal for making proselytes.

Which seems to imply that there are some dissenters, at least, who do *not* have such visions. 'This', Swift goes on,

> was the folly and madness of those antient Puritan fanatics: They must needs overturn heaven and earth, violate all the laws of God and man, make their country a field of blood, to propagate whatever wild or wicked opinions came into their heads, declaring all their absurdities and blasphemies to proceed from the Holy Ghost.[14]

The distinction is surely clear between the 'antient Puritan fanatic', proclaiming his revolutionary doctrines to be the direct inspiration of the Holy Spirit, and the sober dissenter of 1726, the possibility of whose existence Swift at least admits, quietly and legally worshipping in his own fashion and refraining from attacking the established Church.

As a kind of test of the extent of Swift's intransigence in this matter, it might be interesting to speculate, on the basis of one's presuppositions about Swift's views, what his attitude toward John Bunyan would be. Bunyan, it will be recalled, was a devout member of a small Baptist sect, who became convinced that it was his duty to preach, by doing so ran afoul of the law, and was imprisoned for several years. This, however, did not silence him, and he spent his time in prison writing copiously for publication. His books, composed with intense religious passion and great artistic skill, were widely sold and read, and no doubt influenced many people. Did Swift consider him a fanatic to be suppressed? The one reference to Bunyan I have found in Swift's works—no thanks to the Blackwell index, which lists neither Bunyan's name nor the title of his great work—is in the *Letter to a Young Gentleman Lately Entered into Holy Orders*, where Swift is giving advice on composing sermons:

> SOME Gentlemen abounding in their University Erudition, are apt to fill their Sermons with philosophical Terms, and Notions of the metaphysical or abstracted Kind . . . I have been better entertained, and more informed by a Chapter in the *Pilgrim's Progress*, than by a long Discourse upon the *Will* and the *Intellect*, and *simple* or *complex Ideas* . . .[15]

[14] *Prose Works*, Vol. IX, p. 227.
[15] *Prose Works*, Vol. IX, pp. 76-7.

Does this recommendation come as a surprise? It should not. The laws which Bunyan offended against by his preaching had been superseded by the Toleration Act, which would have permitted it. Bunyan did not profess private verbal inspiration by the Holy Spirit. His book in no way attacks the Church of England, but preaches, in the most vivid and memorable fashion, the Augustinian theology of the Prayer Book and many other works of Christian devotion—those 'fundamentals' on which Swift pointed out most Christians agree, whatever their differences in ceremonies and speculative points. It should be remembered that for a dissenting preacher to be licensed under the Toleration Act, he had to subscribe to virtually all the doctrinal articles of the Thirty-Nine, omitting only those dealing with church discipline; though Baptists were also allowed to omit that dealing with infant baptism. Swift, in short, is not attacking dissent simply as dissent; his fulminations are against the activities beyond the intentions of the Toleration Act in which he thinks some of them engage or plan to engage.

The Blackwell indexers, however, believe Swift incapable of distinguishing between a Bunyan, a Baxter, an Isaac Watts on the one hand, and a Lodowick Muggleton and the Fifth-Monarchy Men on the other, and under their rubric 'Dissenters' we are referred to such topics in *A Tale of a Tub* as 'fanaticism', 'zeal and ignorance', 'ridicule of their views on doctrine, ritual, church decoration, etc.' Now, interestingly, the word 'dissenters' occurs in the *Tale*, so far as I can tell, only in a few footnotes taken over from Wotton's *Observations* and added to the fifth edition, 1710—added with just what motive is hard to say. Guthkelch and Nichol Smith, while calling their inclusion 'a humorous revenge on the *Tale's* chief critic', go on merely to say, 'In the course of his hostile remarks Wotton explained a large number of difficulties in the allegory. These explanations were inserted, word for word, in the new notes, and thus the critic was turned into the "learned commentator".'[16] It is hard to see in what way this is either humorous or a revenge—if the notes are as illuminating and helpful as suggested, the result could only redound to Wotton's credit. I suggest —and this is only a hypothesis thrown out for examination—that Swift was sardonically amused by Wotton's obtuseness in extending his scathing remarks on 'fanatics', 'enthusiasts', and 'Aeolists' to all dissenters, and hoped the exposure of it might embarrass him.

Quite apart from the question of motive, however, the first of

---

[16] Swift, *A Tale of a Tub* [etc.], A. C. Guthkelch and D. Nichol Smith (eds.), 2nd ed., Oxford, 1958, p. xxv.

those notes in the *Tale* proper—in Section II—has long puzzled me simply in itself. This is the one that reads 'By these three sons, Peter, Martin, and Jack, Popery, the Church of England, and our Protestant Dissenters are designed'. Let us keep in mind that not Swift, but Wotton, the 'chief critic' of the *Tale*, is the author of this assertion. What has puzzled me about it is a simple matter: if you are going to invent an allegorical person to represent the Church of England, why, of all possible names to bestow on him, choose that of 'Martin'? Martin Luther, after all, was not an Anglican. If you wanted the character specifically to represent the Church of England and nothing else, it would seem more logical to name him after some worthy *of* that Church, 'Thomas' perhaps, after Cranmer, or 'William' after Laud. It may well be that Swift saw in Luther's theology and attitudes toward church discipline and church-state relations the essence of what he approved in Anglicanism. But if so, the Church of England has far from an exclusive claim to him; Martin, in the *Tale*, must also represent at least the very extensive Lutheran bodies in Germany and Scandinavia. Likewise, Wotton's equation of 'Jack' with 'our Protestant dissenters' is not completely satisfying. If Jack's name comes from Calvin, not all English dissenters were Calvinists or the descendants of Calvinist movements. There were, for instance, the General Baptists, whose doctrine was Arminian and whose Mennonite heritage antedates Calvin; there were even a few Lutherans who in England would be classified as Dissenters—Prince George of Denmark, Queen Anne's husband, himself a Lutheran, maintained a chapel for them at St James's.

Long as Wotton's identification of the three brothers has been accepted without question, the only authority for it, after all, is Wotton's *ipse dixit*. If we try to forget it—and to forget our presupposition of Swift's religious exclusiveness, not to say bigotry, to which that identification has contributed much—and try to work out the allegorical significance of the brothers from the *text* of the *Tale*, as it seems to me sound critical method requires, we may arrive at a different solution. I suggest that it will relieve us of many difficulties in reading the *Tale* and more accurately express Swift's real intention if we redefine Martin as representing, not the Church of England, but moderate Protestantism in general, and Jack as extreme or fanatical Protestantism. Let us remember, when we encounter the Aeolists and read about 'enthusiasm' in the 'Digression Concerning Madness' and the ecstatic and hallucinatory manifestations there and in *The Mechanical Operation of the Spirit*, that the doctrine of the direct verbal inspiration of individual preachers by the Holy Spirit was, then as now, confined to a very small number of eccentric sects—it was in particular attributed to the early Quakers, the one dissenting sect mentioned by name in the next of the *Tale*—and was quite as repugnant to most ordinary Baptists, Presbyterians, and Congregationalists as it is now and as it was to Swift; so too were, and are, manifestations like 'speaking with tongues' and what is vulgarly called 'holy rolling', which is what Swift seems to be satirising. It is true, certainly, that Swift distrusted dissenters in general, and perhaps rubbed his hands in glee when Wotton made the extension he did. But it is also true that Swift was too well informed and fundamentally sensible a person to believe, or to think that intelligent readers could be made to believe, that the doctrines and practices he so vividly and repulsively attributes to the followers of Jack were those of the majority of the ordinary sober Baptists, Congregationalists, and Presbyterians of his time.

If so, what then *was* Swift trying to communicate about religion to his readers in the work? Professor Ehrenpreis has complained that Martin is the weakest character in the story; that 'in a book dominated by the [religious] principles which Swift shared with Temple'—this, of course, is only Ehrenpreis's theory—'the figure representing Swift's positive religious values could not be strong'; that 'in seventeenth-century England it would scarcely have been feasible for a writer to communicate his love for the Established Church by the medium of mock-insults. Swift would have accomplished his aim best by leaving Martin out'.[17] This line of reasoning is possible only if, like Professor Ehrenpreis, one takes Swift's central purpose in the religious part of the *Tale* to be the communication or inculcation of 'love for the Established Church'. Audacious as the hypothesis may seem to modern Swiftian scholarship, I venture to suggest that Swift's purpose was a wider one, namely, the inculcation of Christianity;[18] and that the central and indispensable figure for that purpose *is* Martin, who represents much more than the Church of England by law established, with Queen Anne at the top, Archbishops Tenison and Sharp beneath her, and so on. The key passage in the *Tale* proper—the allegory of the three brothers—has always seemed to me the one near the end of Section VI where we are told that Jack 'entered upon the matter' of removing the embroidery from his coat 'with other thoughts and a quite different spirit' from those of Martin. 'For, the Memory of *Lord Peter*'s Injuries produced a Degree of Hatred and

17 Irvin Ehrenpreis, *Swift: The Man, His Works; and the Age*, Cambridge, Mass., 1962, I, p. 188.
18 C. S. Lewis's opinion on this subject carries some weight: 'If Swift were (as I do not think he is) primarily a Church of England man, only secondly a Christian . . .' (*Selected Literary Essays*, Cambridge, 1969, p. 158).

Spight, which had a much greater Share of inciting Him, than any Regards after his Father's Commands, since these appeared at best, only Secondary and Subservient to the other'. Jack exclaims,

> '*Ah, Good Brother* Martin . . . *do as I do, for the Love of God; Strip, Tear, Pull, Rent, Flay off all, that we may appear as unlike the Rogue* Peter, *as it is possible*' . . . But *Martin,* who at this Time happened to be extremely flegmatick and sedate, *begged his Brother of all Love, not to damage his Coat by any Means; for he never would get such another*: Desired him *to consider, that it was not their Business to form their Actions by any Reflection upon* Peter, *but by observing the Rules prescribed in their Father's* Will. That *he should remember,* Peter *was still their Brother, whatever Faults or injuries he had committed; and therefore they should by all means avoid such a Thought, as that of taking Measures for Good and Evil, from no other Rule, than of Opposition to him.*[19]

All this is close to the central teaching of the Christian ethic. An eye for an eye, a tooth for a tooth will not do as the basis of a code of conduct. Nor is it the mere outward performance of stipulated acts thought to be 'good' in themselves that is important —the Pharisee's fasting and prayer and payment of tithes; here the removal of illegal embroidery. What matters is the motive, the inward state, which causes them to be done. They are to spring from love of God and one's fellow man, as with Martin, not from hatred, as with Jack. 'Works done before the grace of Christ, and the inspiration of his Spirit', says Article Thirteen of Swift's church, 'are not pleasant to God . . . yea rather, for that they are not done as God hath willed and commanded them to be done, we doubt not but they have the nature of sin'. No, Swift's purpose here is much more than to persuade his readers of the exclusive validity of the Anglican Church and the invalidity of all others. The mild irony of '*Martin* . . . at this Time happened to be extremely flegmatick and sedate', and, later, '*MARTIN* had still proceeded as gravely as he began; and doubtless, would have delivered an admirable Lecture of Morality, which might have exceedingly contributed to my Reader's *Repose, both of Body and Mind*: (the true ultimate End of *Ethicks*)', is intended to remind us that the Church of England too is an institution composed of fallible human beings, is *semper reformanda*.[20] It was, no doubt, such

19 *A Tale of a Tub,* pp. 137, 139.
20 In considering this passage, it is well to keep in mind Swift's sarcasm against the 'dull divines' (including a 'crazy prelate') of the Church of England, who are alarmed because 'S— had the sin of wit, no venial crime . . . Humor and mirth had place in all he writ;/He reconciled divinity and wit' ('The Author upon Himself').

touches of proper humility that convinced Queen Anne and her Archbishops that Swift was unfit for the episcopate of that Church.

Finally, we come to the question of Swift's attitude toward scientific empiricism. I have been suggesting that Swift in the *Tale* of Peter, Martin, and Jack is writing primarily as an Augustinian Christian, endeavouring to defend 'those very foundations, wherein all Christians have agreed', as he puts it in his 'Apology'. Elsewhere, I have argued that orthodox Christianity in the late seventeenth century by no means entailed suspicion of the principles of Bacon and the Royal Society;[21] that, on the contrary, they were regarded as mutually reinforcing; that so great a scientist as Robert Boyle[22] could entitle a book *The Christian Virtuoso: Shewing that by Being Addicted to Experimental Philosophy a Man is Rather Assisted than Indisposed to Be a Good Christian*; that Thomas Sprat, bishop of the Church of England, Doctor of Divinity and Fellow of the Royal Society, could draw a specific parallel between the intellectual humility and mistrust of one's own innate mental ability which Bacon and his followers see as the essential quality of the experimental scientist, and the spiritual humility and self-distrust inculcated by Augustinian Christianity. Is Swift, then, an opponent of this way of thinking? The adversary whom Bacon sets up as representing what he is attacking—the glorification of the power of human *nous* to arrive at knowledge through the exercise of syllogistic logic without any need to observe external phenomena—is, of course, Aristotle and the scholastics. What does Swift think of Aristotelian and scholastic 'reason'? R. S. Crane has drawn attention to the place of scholastic logic in Swift's undergraduate education and his distrust of it.[23] In *A Tale of a Tub* we have devastating satire of scholastic 'reasoning' in the exegesis of the will and Peter's 'thundering proof' of transsubstantiation. In *The Battle of the Books*, Scotus and Aquinas are classified among the moderns; and Aristotle, though an 'ancient', 'observing *Bacon* advance with a furious Mien, drew his Bow to the Head, and let fly his Arrow, which *mist* the valiant *Modern*',[24] and hit Descartes instead.

If *The Battle of the Books* is a piece of straightforward partisanship of the Ancients against the Moderns by Swift, as it has often been taken to be, anomalies like these need to be explained—not

[21] Cf. Donald Greene, *The Age of Exuberance*, New York, 1970, pp. 103-4, and 'Augustinianism and Empiricism', *Eighteenth-Century Studies*, Vol. I, 1967, pp. 55-7.

[22] Though, to be sure, Swift could mock his pomposity in *A Meditation upon a Broomstick*.

[23] R. S. Crane, 'The Houyhnhnms, the Yahoos, and the History of Ideas', in *The Idea of the Humanities*, Chicago, 1967, Vol. II, pp. 275-82.

[24] *A Tale of a Tub*, p. 244.

to mention the fact that the whole work is a hilarious burlesque of that great 'Ancient' form, the Homeric epic. The heart of the work is, of course, the episode of the Spider and the Bee. Bacon had earlier used the image to inculcate his empiricist point of view: describing the unhealthy intellectual and emotional life of scholasticism, he wrote:

> This kind of degenerate learning did chiefly reign amongst the schoolmen, who having sharp and strong wits and abundance of leisure and small variety of reading, but their wits being shut up in the cells of a few authors (chiefly Aristotle their dictator) as their persons were shut up in the cells of monasteries and colleges, and knowing little history, either of nature or time, did out of no great quantity of matter and infinite agitation of wit spin out unto us those laborious webs of learning which are extant in their books. For the wit and mind of man, if it work upon matter, which is the contemplation of the creatures of God, worketh according to the stuff, and is limited thereby, but if it work upon itself, as the spider worketh his web, then it is endless, and brings forth indeed cobwebs of learning, admirable for the fineness of thread and work but of no substance or profit,

and again,

> The men of experiment [i.e. 'empirics' in the pejorative sense, aimless collectors of desultory facts] are like the ant: they only collect and use; the reasoners resemble spiders, who make cobwebs out of their own substance. But the bee [the empirical scientist as Bacon conceives him, who makes inductions from his observations] takes a middle course: it gathers its material from the flowers of the garden and of the field, but transforms and digests it by a power of its own.[25]

Can it be denied that Swift, in his episode, is saying exactly the same thing, that it is merely a restatement of Bacon's manifesto of empiricism as against Aristotelian and scholastic rationalism?

> *Erect your Schemes* [says Aesop to the spider] *with as much Method and Skill as you please; yet, if the materials be nothing but Dirt, spun out of your own Entrails (the Guts of* Modern *Brains) the Edifice will conclude at last in a Cobweb ... As for* Us, *the* Antients, *We are content with the* Bee *to pretend to Nothing of our own, beyond our* Wings *and our* Voice: *that is to say, our* Flights *and our* Language. *For the rest, whatever we have got, has been by infinite Labor, and search, and ranging thro' every Corner of Nature: The Difference is, that instead of* Dirt *and* Poison, *we have rather chose to fill*

[25] *The Advancement of Learning*, p. 225; *The New Organon*, p. 360; in *Francis Bacon: A Selection of His Works*, Sidney Warhaft (ed.), Toronto, 1965.

> *our Hives with* Honey *and* Wax, *thus furnishing Mankind*
> *with the two Noblest of Things, which are* Sweetness *and*
> Light.[26]

The *locus classicus* of Swift's 'hatred of modern science' is, of
course, Gulliver's Third Voyage. Marjorie Nicolson and Nora
Mohler, in their important study,[27] show the similarities of many
of the experimental projects of the members of the Academy of
Lagado to some reported in the *Philosophical Transactions* of the
young Royal Society and by other scientists of the late seventeenth
century. No doubt; but are we justified, as some modern studies
of Swift have done, in proceeding from Swift's satire here to the
conclusion that he was a hater of modern science in general, of
all attempts to improve the material condition of the human race
by the experimental method and by advances in technology—that
he was, in short, a reactionary obscurantist preaching a return to
the Middle Ages? A few years ago in the United States there was a
widely publicised attack on a number of modern scientific research
foundations, which often reads very much like Swift's description
of the Academy of Lagado—accounts of how millions of dollars
were squandered in fantastic projects of no conceivable use, devised
by scientific workers whose motive was not the advancement of
scientific knowledge or the welfare of mankind, but simple empire-
building, for their own personal aggrandisement and glorification.
The leaders of this attack were not a group of churchmen, or neo-
conservative philosophers, or even of irate taxpayers. On the contrary, they were a number of the most distinguished scientists
in the country, men of great international reputations, some of them
Nobel laureates, whose objection to this kind of racketeering was
that it was *not* scientific—that it represented the prostitution of
science to bare-faced self-seeking.

I submit that Swift's implied attack, in Book III of *Gulliver*, on
the activities of certain members of the Royal Society no more
entails a rejection of the philosophy which the Royal Society was
organised to foster than the attack of the distinguished scientists I
have mentioned on certain scientific 'research' foundations entails
their rejection of 'science'. To suggest that Swift was incapable of
grasping the old maxim, *abusus non tollit usum*, is to make him
out to be a very simple-minded person indeed—but then, I am
afraid, the tendency of too much recent comment on Swift *has* been
to make him out to be very simple-minded, not to say stupid.
The attacks in Book III on scientific experimentation—on certain

26 *A Tale of a Tub*, pp. 234-5.
27 'The Scientific Background of Gulliver's Third Voyage', in Marjorie Nicolson, *Science and Imagination*, Ithaca, N.Y., 1956.

kinds of scientific experimentation—are acidulous, certainly. But they must be read together with two deservedly famous passages in Book II, put into the mouth of the King of Brobdingnag, who is clearly Swift's spokesman here: while protesting his abhorrence of the invention of gunpowder, he affirms 'Few Things delighted him so much as new Discoveries in Art or in Nature', and a little later,

> he gave it for his Opinion; that whoever could make two Ears of Corn, or two Blades of Grass to grow upon a Spot of Ground where only one grew before; would deserve better of Mankind, and do more essential Service to his Country, than the whole Race of Politicians put together.[28]

How are we to reconcile these statements with the view that Swift was a stubborn opponent of modern attempts to improve technology by means of scientific discovery?

One student has, indeed, proposed that they can be reconciled in the following manner: since it is given—since we *know*—that Swift was a hater of modern science, it follows that he must have had an ironic purpose in putting these speeches in the mouth of the King; he goes on from this to argue that the whole of Book II is a devastating satire on the mistaken values of the Brobding-nagians—much as other students have concluded, using a similar methodology, that Book IV is a devastating satire on the mistaken values of the Houyhnhnms (they actually observe the Ten Commandments, and neither lie, steal, nor commit adultery; how could Swift possibly be recommending so absurd and boring a way of life?), and, most recently, that *A Project for the Advancement of Religion* is satiric—since we *know* that Swift disliked 'projects', therefore it follows, etc., etc.

Too many modern literary students seem unable to grasp that *petitio principii*—begging the question—is an invalid mode of reasoning. It used to be taken for granted that if a hypothesis encountered a fact that contradicted it, the hypothesis had to be modified. Too often with Swift, the reverse has been true—if our presuppositions about the way Swift's mind works encounter a passage in a text by Swift that seems to contradict those presuppositions, it is the inconvenient passage that bites the dust, by being dismissed as another piece of Swiftian 'irony'.[29] In this case, I propose, as an alternative way of dealing with the inconvenient passages in *The Battle of the Books* and Book II of *Gulliver*, that the hypothesis of Swift as a simple-minded partisan of 'Ancients' versus 'Moderns', as an opponent of modern scientific empiricism,

28 *Prose Works*, Vol. XI, pp. 119-20.
29 This, I think, is the gist of R. S. Crane's attack on the methodology of some Swift scholars in the essay mentioned in note 23 above.

will not do. On the contrary, what is wrong with the 'scientists' of Lagado and the 'Moderns' in the *Battle* and the *Tale* is that they are not sufficiently scientific, not sufficiently empirical, not sufficiently 'modern' in the Baconian sense. They are not examples of the scientific and intellectual humility that Bacon recommends; they are eaten up with the same foolish pride in their own innate mental capacity, the same impenetrable self-centredness, that Bacon reprobates in the scholastics—for whom Swift makes it very clear he has no love. They do not keep their eyes and ears open and alert to gather wisdom from observing God's creation, as Bacon advises; on the contrary, they continually have to be recalled to an awareness of external reality by being beaten over the head with bladders. Their motive for their experiments and their writings is not the welfare of mankind, but the glorification of their 'images' and the gratification of their egos. It is not 'modernity' or 'science' that Swift objects to; it is the persistence or recrudescence in those who proudly label themselves 'moderns' or 'scientists' of the same eternal faults of human nature—pride, egocentricity, competitiveness, and the irascibility and malevolence which flow from them—that Bacon and Sprat and Glanvill detected in the 'intellectuals' of an earlier era. *Naturam expellas furca, tamen, recurrit*: it is Swift's great service as a moralist to remind us of this, whatever complacency-generating labels we attach to ourselves, 'moderns', 'scientists', 'Whigs', 'Puritans'—even 'Anglicans', even 'intellectuals': of all the great English moralists, Swift is supremely 'the apostle to the intellectuals'. He needs more than ever to be read today—that is, what he is saying needs to be read, not what, to spare our own complacency, we would like to think he is saying.

David Garrick, Poet of the Theatre: A Critical Survey

John Hainsworth

David Garrick will be known as an actor for as long as the English theatre continues to exist. As a theatre manager he is remembered for the innovations, notably in stage lighting and scenic design, that were introduced at Drury Lane during his management. As a playwright he survives still—if only because of *The Clandestine Marriage* written in collaboration with George Colman the elder. His brilliance as a letter-writer is evident in the magnificent three-volume edition of his letters brought out by D. M. Little and G. M. Kahrl in 1963.[1] And, of course, he is known as an associate of Dr Johnson and a member of the famous Club. But David Garrick as a poet? This aspect of his achievement has been almost lost sight of. Yet verse-writing was an activity that he persisted in throughout his busy and successful adult life. 'It seems', says his friend and biographer Arthur Murphy, 'that his close connection with Dr. Johnson at Litchfield [*sic*], gave him an early turn for versification . . . If we except the pleasures he enjoyed in conversation with his friends, poetical composition was his chief recreation from the fatigue of his profession.'[2] There has been no new edition of these poems since Kearsley published *The Poetical Works of David Garrick, Esq.* in 1785. Professor Mary E. Knapp, it is true, brought out a check-list of his poems in 1955,[3] and lists, in all, 479 items,[4] some of them unknown to Kearsley. But the only other significant recognition of him as a poet that I know of, has come from David Nichol Smith, who includes two items by Garrick in *The Oxford Book of*

---

[1] *The Letters of David Garrick*, David M. Little and George M. Kahrl (eds.), 3 vols., Cambridge, Mass., 1963.

[2] Arthur Murphy, *The Life of David Garrick*, London, 1801, Vol. II, pp. 187-8.

[3] Mary E. Knapp: *A Check List of Verse by David Garrick*, Charlottesville, 1955.

[4] A few items are listed more than once, under different titles. On the other hand, this number does not include songs Garrick wrote for musical plays.

Eighteenth Century Verse.[5] One of his choices is the song Garrick wrote for his patriotic pantomime *Harlequin's Invasion*, usually known by the first line of its chorus, 'Heart of Oak', and so traditional that its authorship has been widely forgotten. Nichol Smith's other choice is two stanzas of the poem Garrick wrote *To Mr. Gray, on the Publication of his Odes*:

> Repine not, Gray, that our weak dazzled eyes
>   Thy daring heights and brightness shun;
> How few can track the eagle to the skies,
>   Or like him gaze upon the sun!
>
> The gentle reader loves the gentle Muse,
>   That little dares, and little means,
> Who humbly sips her learning from *Reviews,*
>   Or flutters in the *Magazines.*

These lines owe their effectiveness to the imagery, and especially to the eagle imagery of the first stanza and the way the final verb 'flutters' is played off against it. But what Garrick actually says about Gray through this imagery is extremely vague and general. This vagueness and generality are failings typical of Garrick whenever he ventures outside the field of light verse. From his *Ode on the death of Mr. Pelham*,[6] for instance, no impression emerges of an individual person or even of a recognisable type. The qualities which Garrick perceives in the deceased prime minister are merely ideals:

> No selfish views t' oppress mankind,
> No mad ambition fir'd thy mind,
>   To purchase fame with blood;
> Thy bosom glow'd with purer heat;
> Convinc'd that to be truly great,
>   Is only to be *good.*

There is nothing beyond uninspired commonplace to be found, either, in the Ode on Shakespeare[7] that Garrick wrote to be delivered by himself at the great Stratford Jubilee, where he would clearly have wished to be at his best; or in the various epitaphs that he wrote for his friends. One is even tempted to take seriously the remark of Samuel Foote that he was afraid of dying before Garrick, in case Garrick should write his epitaph.[8]

Garrick was more in his element with the comic epitaph. His

5 Nos. 263 and 264.
6 *The Poetical Works of David Garrick, Esq.*, G. Kearsley (ed.), London, 1785, I, pp. 3-7.
7 Ibid., I, pp. 57-71.
8 Cited J. Genest, *Some Account of the English Stage*, Bath, 1832, V, p. 606.

famous quip on Goldsmith was delivered extempore at a meeting of the Club:

> Here lies Nolly Goldsmith, for shortness call'd Noll,
> Who wrote like an angel, but talk'd like poor Poll.[9]

Garrick also claimed extemporaneousness for his couplet on Dr John Hill, the well-known purveyor of patent medicines, who had reviled the Drury Lane management after his farce *The Rout* had been badly received:

> For physic and farces,
> His equal there scarce is;
> His farces are physic,
> His physic a farce is.[10]

Such verse as this is merely an extension of conversational wit, and so strongly suggestive of its social origin that one is tempted to speculate on who was present in the company that first heard it. Garrick also has a slightly longer piece relating to this affair of John Hill and his farce. This is a step further in the direction of literature and shows Garrick's muse *fluttering* 'in the Magazines'. It makes use of the fact that, at the first performance of *The Rout*, the playwright's name had been withheld, and he had been designated merely as 'A Person of Honour':

> Says a friend to the Doctor, 'Pray give it about
> That this farce is not yours, or you'll miss of the pelf;
> What had come of your *Nerves*, or your *P[o]x* or your *Gout*,
> Had these embrios crawl'd forth as begot by yourself?
> Let your Muse, as your pamphlets, come forth (I advise ye)
> Like a goddess of old, with a cloud cast upon her.'
> 'You're right,' quoth the Doctor, 'and more to disguise me,
> I'll give myself out for a *Person of Honour*.'[11]

This is still more witticism than wit, however, and writing it in verse serves only to make it sound a little more clever. It is instructive to set these lines beside Charles Churchill's account of Hill in *The Rosciad*. Churchill's superiority is that his lines are more than just witticism: they make a statement more complex than Garrick's and they use the peculiar resources of poetry to achieve their complexity. Churchill's account of Hill is accurate enough: he had been an actor, if not a very successful one; he contributed a regular

[9] Peter Cunningham printed both the epigram and Garrick's account of how it came to be composed, from 'the original in Garrick's own handwriting' in his edition of *The Works of Oliver Goldsmith*, London, 1854, I, p. 78.

[10] Kearsley, II, p. 489. For the circumstances of composition, see Little and Kahrl, Letter 222.

[11] Knapp, *Check List*, No. 218. The text is taken from R. W. Lowe, *A Bibliographical Account of English Theatrical Literature*, London, 1888, pp. 175-6.

letter entitled 'The Inspector' to *The London Advertiser;* and he was a botanist of distinction, as well as a medical man. A cursory glance might even give the impression that Churchill was praising Hill, as he reminds us of these remarkably varied achievements.

> For who, like him, his various pow'rs could call
> Into so many shapes, and shine in all?
> Who could so nobly grace the motley list,
> Actor, Inspector, Doctor, Botanist?[12]

The use of the word 'shapes', however, makes one think of an actor or a mimic changing his shape, and suggests that there is an element of pretence in Hill's achievements.[13] 'Motley', as well as meaning 'diverse', carries a suggestion of folly. And the falling rhythm (trochees and dactyls) of the fourth line clashes sharply with the rising iambic rhythm that has conveyed a sense of achievement in the three preceding lines. The impression one is finally left with is that Hill deserves a certain amount of credit for all that he has done, but not as much as he himself would claim. One is made to feel, too, that the poet is carefully weighing what he says, and so deserves to be taken seriously. This is poetry because of the peculiarly poetic means by which Churchill gains his effect. It can also be placed in a specific poetical tradition. One can see its connection with Dryden, and especially with the portrait of Zimri in *Absalom and Achitophel.*

It is not, of course, fair to show up the deficiencies of Garrick's verse by comparing lines he wrote for a magazine with an extract from a consciously literary work like *The Rosciad.* A fairer comparison would be between *The Rosciad* extract and lines from Garrick's poem *The Fribbleriad.* This is a more ambitious literary project, a contribution to that mock-heroic genre to which *The Rosciad* also belongs—a genre so popular at this time that Christopher Smart had even written a *Hilliad* about Dr Hill. A 'fribler' [sic] had been defined by Richard Steele in *Spectator* No. 288 as 'one who professes rapture and admiration for the woman to whom he addresses, and dreads nothing so much as her consent'. There is a character called Fribble in Garrick's play *Miss in her teens.* According to Garrick's friend Arthur Murphy, he represents a phenomenon of the times, 'the pretty gentlemen, who chose to unsex themselves, and make a display of delicacy that exceeded

---

[12] *The Poetical Works of Charles Churchill,* Douglas Grant (ed.), Oxford, 1956, pp. 6, 11, 109-12.

[13] For this sense of 'shapes' cf. *The Rosciad,* 11, 395-6, on the actor and mimic Samuel F[oo]te:
> By turns transform'd into all kinds of shapes,
> Constant to none, F(OO)TE laughs, cries, struts, and scrapes.

See also O.E.D., s.v. *Shape,* s.b., 8a.

female softness'.[14] In the course of acting the role of Fribble, Garrick was said to mimic eleven fashionable gentlemen of the time.[15] The poem *The Fribbleriad*,[16] however, was not published till 1761, fourteen years after the first performance of the play. It was a rejoinder to attacks on Garrick's abilities as an actor made in print by a certain Thaddeus Fitzpatrick. In his poem, Garrick comically takes it for granted that these attacks were a belated act of vengeance, prompted by 'fribbles' who had recognised themselves in the play. The poem describes a 'Panfribblerium'—a meeting of fribbles at Hampstead to discuss the form of their revenge on Garrick. At one stage the Chairman, Fizgig, who represents Fitzpatrick, calls on Sir Diddle, a character who has already appeared in *Miss in her teens*, to address the meeting:

> Sir DIDDLE then he thus address'd—
> "'Tis yours to speak, be mute the rest.'
> When thus the knight—'Can I dissemble?
> 'Conceal my rage, while thus I tremble?
> 'O FIZGIG! 'tis that Garrick's name,
> 'Now stops my voice, and shakes my frame—
> 'His pangs would please—his death—oh lud!
> 'Blood, Mr. FIZGIG, blood, blood, blood!'
> The thought, too mighty for his mind,
> O'ercame his powers; he star'd; grew blind:
> Cold sweat his faded cheek o'erspread,
> Like dew upon the lily's head;
> He squeak'd and sigh'd—no more could say
> But blood—bloo—blo—and died away.
> Thus when in war a hero swoons,
> With loss of blood, or fear of wounds,
> They bear him off—and thus they bore
> Sir DIDDLE to the garden-door.

The obvious criticism of such verse is that the tetrameters limit metrical flexibility and make for an effect of doggerel. This is not entirely a fair criticism, as it is largely this effect of doggerel that deflates the heroics into mock-heroics and makes the epic similes sound comic. The device is a simple one, but then the end in view is also simple. Garrick's aim is merely to ridicule his fribbles. The more complex and serious kind of statement that Churchill has achieved is not attempted.

One has to go to Garrick's prologues and epilogues to find a complexity in any way approaching Churchill's. It is on these

---

[14] Murphy, *Life*, I, p. 118.
[15] See *The Autobiography and Correspondence of Mary Granville, Mrs. Delany*, Lady Llanover (ed.), London, 1861, II, p. 453.
[16] Kearsley, I, pp. 21-34.

theatrical pieces that Garrick's claim to be remembered as a poet must mainly rest. And yet, of course, the complexity there achieved is not of the same kind as that to be found in a literary work like *The Rosciad*. For the prologues and epilogues are not literature but drama. They were part of that varied theatrical entertainment that, in Garrick's day, stretched from six p.m. until about eleven o'clock, and included—as well as the comedy or tragedy that was the mainpiece for the evening—music, singing or dancing, and an afterpiece, usually a short farce. Being theatrical entertainment, prologues and epilogues are not meant just to be read with the eye, nor even just to be recited to a company; they are meant to be performed to an audience. The medium is not just words, but words acted: it is not just the voice of an actor that is required, but his whole person and personality. In Mrs Frances Sheridan's comedy *The Discovery*, Sir Anthony Branville is an elderly beau who, in spite of his age, manages to fall in love with two women. The method Garrick had hit on of playing this character involved a deliberate checking of the movement of his face and body, to achieve a startling contrast between Sir Anthony's passionate sentiments and the calm voice and stiffly formal mien in which he uttered them; and an equally sharp contrast with the extreme mobility of face and body that usually characterised Garrick's acting. 'Sir Anthony Branville's Address to the Ladies'[17]—the epilogue which Garrick wrote for Mrs Sheridan's play—gives him a further opportunity to exploit this way of acting. Such a piece is designed to create an audience, which is not just a company of people assembled in an auditorium, but a company of people controlled and transformed by the arts of dramatist and actor. Stepping right out of the play, Sir Anthony now subjects the ladies of the audience to his decorous blandishments:

> LADIES, before I go, will you allow
> A most devoted slave to make his bow?
> Brought to your bar, ye most angelic Jury!
> 'Tis you shall try me for my am'rous fury.
> Have I been guilty pray of indecorum?
> My Ardors were so fierce I could not lower 'em;
> Such raging passions, I confess an evil,
> In flesh and blood like mine, they play the devil!
> Bound on the rack of love poor I was laid,
> Between two fires, a *Widow* and a *Maid*!
> My heart, poor scorched Dove, now pants for rest,
> Where, Ladies, shall the flutt'rer find a nest?
> Take pity, fair ones, on the tortur'd thing,
> Heal it, and let it once more chirp, and sing:

[17] Kearsley, II, pp. 318-19.

Yet to approach you were infatuation;
If souls like mine so prone to inflammation,
Shou'd meet your tinder hearts—there wou'd be
    conflagration!
Indeed so prudent are most men of fashion,
They run no danger, for they feel no passion:
Tho' fairest faces smile, they can defy 'em,
Tho' softest tongues shou'd plead, they can deny 'm,
Mankind wou'd cease, but for such loving Fools as I am.

Twice in the last eight lines quoted, a triplet occurs in which feminine rhyme-words lead on to an alexandrine and a pause which effectively takes in, and, indeed, stimulates laughter. So wholly dramatic is this piece that an audience is implied even in the movement of the verse.

The imagery and wit of Garrick, in his prologues and epilogues, were singled out for special praise in his own day. Thus, in a prologue delivered at the Haymarket theatre in 1775, the speaker excuses his own lack of these things on the grounds that they are in short supply: Garrick is making so much use of them elsewhere:

> In Prologue Writing, modern Bards agree,
> The only Art, is Wit and Simile;
> But *for* that Art, we ever must complain,
> While ROSCIUS uses it at Drury-Lane.[18]

Both wit and imagery are very effectively used in Garrick's Epilogue to the Rev. John Brown's tragedy of *Athelstan*,[19] and used in a way that is peculiarly appropriate to the theatre. Mrs Cibber, who has just been playing the tragic heroine, tells of the different ways in which different sections of the audience react to tragedy:

> As men with different eyes a beauty see,
> So judge they of that stately dame—Queen Tragedy.
> The Greek-read critic, as his mistress holds her,
> And having little love, for trifles scolds her:
> Excuses want of spirit, beauty, grace,
> But ne'er forgives her failing, time and place.
> How do our sex of taste and judgment vary?
> Miss 'Bell adores, what's loath'd by lady Mary:
> The first in tenderness a very dove,
> Melts, like the feather'd snow, at Juliet's love:
> Then, sighing, turns to Romeo by her side,
> 'Can you believe that men for love have dy'd?'

---

[18] Prologue to *The Snuff Box; or, A Trip to Bath* (1775), by William Heard. Quoted Mary E. Knapp, *Prologues and Epilogues of the Eighteenth Century*, New Haven, 1961, p. 15.
[19] Kearsley, I, pp. 150-2.

This is a passage which well repays an analysis of its dramatic merits. The 'Queen Tragedy', referred to at the beginning, is no mere allegorical figure whom the audience have to imagine. Mrs Cibber is clearly intended, by a significant change in her deportment, to take the role upon herself, her past achievements in this theatre, and not just her performance this evening, making her a a strong candidate for the throne in question. 'The Greek-read critic' is at first titillated with the idea of having Mrs Cibber as his mistress, and then wittily abused as one so lacking in true feeling that he would care more about whether she arrived at the right time, in the right place, than about her personal qualities. The imagery associated with Miss Bell is satisfyingly rich on a purely literary level:

> The first in tenderness a very dove,
> Melts, like the feather'd snow, at Juliet's love.

Dove, it is true, is a conventional enough image for tenderness, but the conventionality is redeemed by what follows. The richness can be demonstrated if one asks what the connection is between the two images *dove* and *snow*. They are associated because both are white, because snow-flakes are like feathers (compare Hopkins: 'Flake-doves sent floating forth at a farm-yard scare!'[20]), and because the dove represents tenderness, which, like snow, turns to water *(melts)*. The imagery is not just literary, however; it involves a dramatic relationship. Juliet, in whom the tears originate, is not just a random representative of tragedy, but one of the roles in which Mrs Cibber herself most excelled. And Miss Bell, to whom the imagery relates, is supposed to be someone in the audience Mrs Cibber is addressing—some members of the audience, that is, are recognising themselves in the portrait—recognising themselves, though, with a certain amount of comic detachment, because the imagery contains also an element of poetic exaggeration, of which both speaker and audience are aware. Comedy gains the upper hand at the end of the passage quoted, in the stock joke about the shallowness of men's love. There is more here than just a joke, however, for the suggestion that Romeo and Juliet may be located in the audience as well as on stage, carries the serious implication that the stage world and the real world are essentially one—or, at least, that the one mirrors the other.

This is to labour over a passage that would make its impact in the theatre without any need of analysis. The point of analysing it is to show that it can only achieve its full impact in the theatre.

[20] 'The Starlight Night', in *The Poems of Gerard Manley Hopkins*, W. H. Gardner and N. H. Mackenzie (eds.), 4th ed., London, 1967, pp. 66-7.

Other prologue writers use imagery at least as effectively as Garrick, from a *literary* point of view, but they are seldom as effective dramatically. This is true even of so good a prologue writer—and so good a playwright—as George Colman the elder. There is, for instance, the tightrope imagery in his Prologue to Francklin's tragedy, *The Earl of Warwick*:

> While Shakspere vaults on the poetic wire,
> And pleas'd spectators fearfully admire,
> Our bard, a critic pole between his hands,
> On the tight-rope, scarce balanc'd, trembling stands;
> Slowly and cautiously his way he makes,
> And fears to fall at every step he takes.[21]

The imagery here serves to make more vivid the point that a multiplication of critics has restricted the modern playwright's scope and also made his lot more precarious, but that is all. These lines, unlike the ones by Garrick, might just as well be read in the study as heard in the theatre.

Yet, dramatic as Garrick's prologues and epilogues are, they are not dramatic in quite the same way that a play is dramatic. For a play involves a sustained fiction; the actor is consistently pretending to be someone else; the audience are all the time being asked to assume the reality of the fictitious world they see before them on the stage. There always is an element of fiction in a prologue or epilogue, even when the speaker addresses the audience in his own person. For he is pretending to speak his thoughts extempore, whereas, in fact, they have been carefully prepared and versified; and they are not his own thoughts, either, unless author and speaker happen to be the same person. Yet the fiction is never as complete as in a play, for even when the speaker of an epilogue acts the role he has just been playing, as in 'Sir Anthony Branville's Address to the Ladies', he is now in a different and more personal relationship with the audience, addressing them directly from the apron, and sometimes with the curtain dropped behind him.

'Sir Anthony Branville's Address' illustrates particularly well this incompleteness of the fiction. It was not attached to Mrs Sheridan's comedy until this was revived in 1776, thirteen years after the first production. The original epilogue had been spoken by Mrs Pritchard, who was now dead. Indeed, Garrick, as Sir Anthony, was the only one of the original performers left. For some of the audience, at any rate, Garrick would stand before them, not just as Sir Anthony, but also as the sole survivor and representative of the original cast. The Epilogue to the tragedy of *Barbarossa*[22]

---

[21] Quoted from John Bell's edition of the play, London, 1792, pp. iv-v.
[22] Kearsley, I, pp. 127-9.

shows Garrick exploiting the ambiguous role of the speaker for humorous effect. Here, Henry Woodward, in the character of a fine gentleman, expresses his doubts whether the kind of fare they have been having that evening—tragedy—is really suited to an English audience. The effectiveness of his conclusion comes from the audience's awareness that the actor, who is an author as well, has a vested interest in the recommendations made by the character he is playing:

> Banish your gloomy scenes to foreign climes,
> Reserve alone to bless these golden times,
> A Farce or two—and Woodward's pantomimes.

Another variation on this effect is in the prologue Garrick wrote for Arthur Murphy's *The Desert Island*.[23] Here Garrick appears as 'a drunken poet'—the author of a play, which he says, the manager has not the wit to put on, though it compares very favourably with what is being performed that evening. After a little flattery of the audience in an attempt to sell copies of his play, the drunken author staggers off stage exclaiming to himself 'A little flattery sometimes does well', a line from Colley Cibber's version of Shakespeare's *Richard III*,[24] the play in which Garrick had first established his reputation as an actor, in a role vastly different from the one he is playing now. The audience's applause would be the louder for this reminder of Garrick's past achievements and his extraordinary versatility.

In the writing of prologues and epilogues, certain problems were involved that were common to all those who attempted them at that time. Not the least of these arose simply from the fact that the custom of having prologues and epilogues had lasted for so long. Already, by 1704 even, Nicholas Rowe, in the Epilogue to his play *The Biter*, was complaining about this:

> OF all the Taxes which the Poet pays,
> Those Funds of Verse, none are so hard to raise
> As Prologues and as Epilogues to Plays.
> So many mighty Wits are gone before,
> Th' have rifled all the Muses sacred Store.[25]

By the time of Garrick the variations in approach that were within the scope of a prologue or epilogue writer had been virtually exhausted. In these circumstances the writer deserves credit for the extent to which he is able to give new life to a stock device. The incongruity of the convention that the tragic heroine should rise

---

23 Kearsley, I, pp. 159-60.
24 Noted by Knapp, *Prologues and Epilogues*, p. 103.
25 Quoted Knapp, *Prologues and Epilogues*, p. 24.

from death to deliver a comic epilogue had been turned into a source of laughter by John Dryden in 1669, in his notorious epilogue to *Tyrannic Love*.[26] There, after Nell Gwynn, as tragic heroine, had been slain, she resisted attempts to carry her off the stage, exclaiming:

> Hold, are you mad? you damn'd confounded Dog,
> I am to rise, and speak the Epilogue.

As late as 1756, in the epilogue to *Athelstan*[27] spoken by Mrs Cibber, Garrick is still able successfully to make fun out of the incongruity—paradoxically by introducing into the situation another old joke—one about women's talkativeness. Each joke provides the other with a new context. The listener is agreeably surprised, and amused, that they can still be freshened up in this way.

> To speak ten words, again I've fetch'd my breath;

says Mrs Cibber, the deceased tragic heroine:

> The tongue of woman struggles hard with death.

Another hackneyed device is where it is pretended that the prologue meant for this evening has been lost, and therefore the actual prologue really is an extempore effusion, and is not just pretending to be one. Garrick puts this device to brilliant use in his prologue to the tragedy of *Barbarossa*.[28] Before the play, a serving-lad enters in search of his master, the author of the play, who is wanted urgently because he has the script of the prologue in his pocket. The lad, who is from the country, expresses his astonishment at what he sees from the stage:

> Law! what a crowd is here! what noise and pother!
> Fine lads and lasses! one o' top o' other.
> (*Pointing to the rows of Pit and Gallery.*)
> I could for ever here with wonder geaze!
> I ne'er saw church so full in all my days!

This leads him on to tell of other astonishing experiences that have befallen him since he came to London: how he has fled from the service of his first employer on seeing him eat turtle:

> Law! how I star'd! I thought—who knows but I,
> For want of monsters, may be made a pye.

[26] *The Poems and Fables of John Dryden*, James Kinsley (ed.), London, 1961, p. 119.
[27] Kearsley, I, pp. 150-2.
[28] Kearsley, I, pp. 124-6.

His second master, a lord, has offended him by his total absorption in card-playing. His third was a lady:

> A lady next, who lik'd a smart young lad,
> Hir'd me forthwith—but troth, I thought her mad,
> She turn'd the world top down, as I may say,
> She chang'd the day to neet, the neet to day!
> I was so sheam'd with all her freakish ways,
> She wore her gear so short, so low her stays,
> Fine folks shew all for nothing now-a-days!

Now he is 'the poet's man'. His wages depend on this night's venture. If it is not successful, he will 'pack up all, and whistle whoame again'. The young lad from the country was played by Garrick, who showed off his versatility as an actor in the tragedy that followed—where, as Selim, a king's son of Algiers, he over-threw the tyrant who had murdered his father and planned to ravish his mother. In the Epilogue of this play, the fine gentleman played by Woodward who forces his way on to the stage to protest against the country boy's criticisms of upper-class life, provides yet another variation on the pretence that this is not the speech intended.

Another device popular with prologue-writers was to make the speaker, who could see the audience, since the candles in the auditorium were lit throughout the evening, address the various sections of it individually. Garrick does this in the Epilogue that he wrote for Mrs Cibber to the tragedy of *Virginia*,[29] and, in doing so, he brings out vividly the audience's diversity. In the shilling seats in the upper gallery are the poorer folk:

> No high-bred prudery in your region lurks,
> You boldly laugh and cry, as nature works.

From among the middle-class spectators of the middle gallery, 'some maiden dames' are picked out:

> So very chaste, they live in constant fears,
> And apprehension strengthens with their years.

In the boxes are the 'Fine ladies', and in the pit the men of fashion:

> Ye bucks, who from the pit your terrors send.

Also in the pit, as other epilogues inform us, were the more critical and intellectual part of the audience.

In the writing of prologues and epilogues, the various and some-times conflicting predilections and prejudices of this audience

[29] Kearsley, I, pp. 122-3.

had to be taken note of, and, as far as possible, reconciled. The moral scruples of the middle-class 'citizens', for a long time now an important element in the audience, had to be propitiated. So, in speaking Garrick's Epilogue to Hoadly's *The Suspicious Husband*,[30] Mrs Pritchard abandons the role of the gay young Clarinda she has just been playing:

> Tho' the young Smarts, I see, begin to sneer,
> And the old sinners cast a wicked leer:
> Be not alarm'd, ye Fair—you've nought to fear.
> No wanton hint, no loose ambiguous sense,
> Shall flatter vicious taste at your expense.

Political and religious sensitivities, too, had to be carefully considered, for on these issues Garrick's audience was easily roused to violence. James Boswell and two of his friends brought cudgels, not to mention catcalls, with them, when they went to the opening of *Elvira*, a tragedy by David Mallet, a free thinker and supporter of the unpopular minister, the Earl of Bute.[31] Garrick had put on a *Chinese Festival* at Drury Lane in November, 1755, when feeling against the French was running high. Chinese the Festival may have been, but the company of dancers involved in it had come from Paris. Fighting broke out between pro-French aristocrats and enraged patriots, severe damage was done to the theatre, and even the windows of Garrick's house were smashed. No doubt it was partly as a discouragement to such excesses that patriotic sentiments had become so conventional an ingredient in prologues and epilogues. Garrick's Prologue to Mallet's masque *Britannia*,[32] in the writing of which Mallet also seems to have had a hand, is jingoistic in a more than usually clever way. Garrick staggers on stage as a drunken British sailor who says he has promised to take his girlfriend to a show before going back to beat the French. He chooses the tragedy of *Zara*, the mainpiece at Drury Lane that evening, because of the similarity of its name to that of his girlfriend Sarah. The masque that is to accompany the tragedy also arouses his enthusiasm:

> But what is here, so very large and plain?
> BRI-TA-NIA—oh Britania!—good again.
> Huzza, boys! by the Royal George I swear,
> Tom coxen, and the crew, shall strait be there.
> All free-born souls must take Bri-ta-nia's part,
> And give her three round cheers, with hand and heart!

[30] Kearsley, I, pp. 93-5.
[31] See *Boswell's London Journal, 1762-1763*, Frederick A. Pottle (ed.), London, 1950, pp. 152, 154-5.
[32] Kearsley, I, pp. 133-5.

No doubt, as Professor Knapp has suggested,[33] this display of patriotism was occasioned by a regrettable fact: that the tragedy of
Zara was translated from the French!

Prologues and epilogues had to be appropriate to their speakers
as well as to the audience. The choice of speakers was limited to
some extent by convention. They were drawn from the leading
members of the company. A prologue was almost invariably
assigned to an actor, and an epilogue to an actress, though it could
be given to a comic actor instead. The prologue or epilogue was
generally considered to belong to the actor or actress it was first
assigned to. If it was called for again after the first three nights
of a play's run, the normal occasions when prologue and epilogue
were attached to a play, then that particular actor or actress had
to deliver it. A story is told of Tom King's being summoned from
home late at night to repeat, at the insistence of the audience,
who sat waiting for him, a prologue he had given earlier in the
evening. Says King, in the prologue Garrick wrote for Colman's
farce *The Spleen*:[34]

> While living call me, for your pleasure use me,
> Should I tip off—I hope you'll then excuse me.

This is Garrick dramatising Tom King's own humorous and
likeable character. He often does this for a speaker when he has
no fictitious role for him. Another example is the epilogue he
wrote for Mrs Woffington to speak at the opening of Garrick's
first season in management, in 1747.[35] Here Mrs Woffington, whose
fondness for the opposite sex was notorious, is made to complain
against the new policy of prohibiting public access behind the
scenes:

> Each actress now a lock'd-up nun must be,
> And priestly managers must keep the key.

It was Mrs Woffington who, flushed with her success in the part
of Sir Harry Wildair, boasted to James Quin that half the town
believed her to be a man. 'Madam', replied Quin, 'the other half
know you to be a woman'.[36] In the epilogue in question, Garrick
was actually trying to gain acceptance for the policy he makes
Mrs Woffington complain of. He hoped, unrealistically as it turned
out, that opposition would be dissolved by laughter.

In the skill with which he tailors prologues and epilogues to
their speakers, Garrick is without rival. This is hardly surprising,
since his success as a manager depended on his being able to

33 *Prologues and Epilogues*, p. 38.
34 Kearsley, II, pp. 322-4.
35 Kearsley, I, pp. 96-8.
36 Murphy, *Life*, I, p. 37.

gauge with accuracy the abilities of actors and actresses. An interesting illustration of the pains Garrick would take in this matter is the epilogue he wrote for the occasion of Mrs Pritchard's retirement from the stage.[37] To try to ensure *her* satisfaction, in the copy of the epilogue he sent her, he marked lines she could omit if she wished, and offered variant readings.[38] Knowing that Mrs Pritchard would be deeply moved by the occasion, he makes her say:

> I now appear myself, distress'd, dismay'd,
> More than in all the characters I've play'd.

And the epilogue is so worded that any tears she sheds will help rather than hinder the effect aimed at. 'She spoke her farewell epilogue,' says Thomas Davies, 'with many sobs and tears, which were increased by the generous feelings of a numerous and splendid audience.'[39]

It was obviously important that a piece should make no demands on the speaker that were beyond his competence—that an epilogue for Mrs Cibber, for instance, whose gifts lay in tragedy, should not demand too much in the way of comic acting. It was no less desirable that a speaker should be given a chance to display his own special abilities. Of particular interest, from this point of view, are the prologues and epilogues which Garrick wrote to deliver himself. It was in his ability to transform himself physically, rather than in the vocal aspects of acting, that Garrick's greatest excellence lay. 'Damn him,' exclaimed Mrs Clive, 'he could act a gridiron.'[40] The point of this remark is that a gridiron does not talk—Garrick did not need speech to create a role. The Rev. William Mason, a contemporary, remarks particularly on Garrick's powers of facial expression, and says 'he disliked to perform any part whatever, where *expression of countenance* was not more necessary than recitation of sentiment'.[41] The epilogue Garrick wrote for his own farce *The Lying Valet*[42] provides supporting evidence in this matter. It is an apology for his behaviour in the play by its leading character, the Lying Valet, played by the author. In illustrating how widespread is the vice of lying, Garrick passes rapidly through impersonations of a gouty lawyer, a dishonest doctor, a boastful poet, and Lady Dainty, a pretended prude,

---

[37] Kearsley, II, pp. 248-9.
[38] See Little and Kahrl, Letter 498.
[39] *Memoirs of the Life of David Garrick, Esq.*, London, 1780, II, p. 185.
[40] Cited Lily B. Campbell, 'The Rise of a Theory of Stage Presentation in England during the Eighteenth Century', *Publications of the Modern Language Association of America*, Vol. XXXII, 1917, p. 187.
[41] Quoted James Boaden, *Memoirs of Mrs. Siddons*, London, 1827, II, pp. 162-3.
[42] Kearsley, I, pp. 82-4.

switching to and fro between these and his basic role of valet. Finally he gives himself the opportunity to hit off a Dutchman, a Frenchman, a German and a Spaniard, all within the space of two lines. One is reminded of Johnson's reply to a remark by Dr Burney that Garrick's face was beginning to look old: 'Why, Sir, you are not to wonder at that; no man's face has had more wear and tear'.[43] Garrick's prologue to *Much Ado About Nothing*,[44] written twenty-four years later, for a Royal Command performance that marked his return to the stage after eighteen months abroad, is only slightly less exacting. It allows him to impersonate a truant schoolboy returning fearfully to school, a 'youth of parts' cocking his glass at the aging Garrick in the street and commenting on his fatness, and, finally, a Chelsea pensioner, still ready, like Garrick himself, to serve his King:

> Should the drum beat to arms, at first he'll grieve
> For wooden leg, lost eye—and armless sleeve;
> Then cocks his hat, looks fierce, and swells his chest;
> 'Tis for my King, and, zounds, I'll do my best!

The prologue to the Royal Command performance of *Much Ado About Nothing* was written to be performed by a particular actor and tailored to his particular abilities; it was also written for one particular, and in this case, non-recurrent occasion, and for one quite specific audience. These limitations, though present here in an extreme form, in some measure affected all prologue writers. The preoccupation with what was particular was a restriction the writer must necessarily accept, but for Garrick it was also a source of strength. For one thing, it helped to prevent the vagueness that is so often a fault in his non-dramatic verse; for another, no one understood better than he did the tendencies of the audience, the potentialities of the speakers, the subtle and ambiguous relationship that existed between the one and the other, and all the particular circumstances of the theatre where he was manager, principal actor and occasional dramatist, as well as purveyor-in-chief of prologues and epilogues.

His intimate and many-sided knowledge of his theatre provided Garrick with a much firmer foundation for his poetry than any literary tradition could do—which is, no doubt, the main reason why these theatrical pieces are, generally, superior to anything else he wrote. This is the basis, too, for his eminence, if not preeminence, amongst writers in this genre. Dr Johnson even compared him favourably with Dryden. 'Dryden has written prologues

---

43 Boswell, *Life of Johnson*, G. B. Hill (ed.), rev. L. F. Powell, Oxford, 1934-50, Vol. II, p. 410.
44 Kearsley, I, pp. 201-3.

superiour to any that David Garrick has written; but David Garrick has written more good prologues than Dryden has done'.[45] With the first part of this statement there can be no quarrelling. For sheer dramatic effectiveness, nothing in Garrick can quite equal, for instance, Dryden's Epilogue to *An Evening's Love*.[46] Here the way the actress mimics the audience's behaviour and makes fun of their critical attitudes allows her to show off her abilities, and, at the same time, involves the audience, in a delightfully provocative way, in her performance. She also makes them laugh at French manners, but wittily justifies the author's borrowing of a French plot. If she is a good deal more bawdy than Garrick could permit, the bawdiness is made to seem not adventitious, but a genuine and amusing revelation of the speaker's character. Dryden shows in this epilogue that he can excel Garrick even in those dramatic qualities where Garrick is strongest. The first part of Dr Johnson's verdict is unassailable, therefore. It is doubtful, however, if the second part of it—that 'David Garrick has written more good prologues than Dryden has done'—is soundly based in arithmetical calculations. But whatever Garrick's status relative to Dryden, or indeed, to anyone else, there are reasons enough why a modern reader might find a study of his prologues and epilogues worthwhile. Many of them still make lively and enjoyable reading —that is one reason. But for anyone interested in the history of the theatre they have a special importance. In them, in quite a unique way, the dead facts of history are brought to life again. As Garrick himself has pointed out in his Prologue to *The Clandestine Marriage*,[47] the art of the actor lacks the durability of other arts:

> The painter dead, yet still he charms the eye;
> While England lives, his fame can never die:
> But he, who *struts his hour upon the stage*,
> Can scarce extend his fame for half an age;
> Nor pen nor pencil can the Actor save,
> The art, and artist, share one common grave.

Prologues and epilogues—and especially those of Garrick—to some extent ameliorate this situation. In them, so carefully tailored, as they often are, to the aptitudes of a particular speaker, there is captured something, at least, of the art and stage personality of the dead performer. Also accessible through them is the audience to which they were originally addressed—and to which they were also tailored. And this not just because of the vivid portraits of

45 Boswell, *Life*, Vol. II, p. 325.
46 *The Poems and Fables of John Dryden*, pp. 123-4.
47 Kearsley, I, pp. 203-4.

that audience which they occasionally provide, but in a more exis-
tential way, too. For the imaginative reading and re-reading of these
verses provides the nearest possible approximation to actually
becoming oneself a part of that eighteenth-century audience. They
bring to life for the reader a theatrical community, and this not
in any merely external way, but by enabling him to feel for himself
the tensions within it, by giving him a personal and unique experience of its intimate life.

Cato in Tears:
Stoical Guises of the Man of Feeling

Ian Donaldson

I

Nearly forty years ago, the late R. S. Crane showed how the early growth of the eighteenth-century cult of Sensibility was stimulated by a feeling of hostility—particularly on the part of the Latitudinarian divines—towards a contemporary revival of interest in the teachings of the Stoics.[1] The Man of Feeling, that familiar figure of eighteenth-century sentimental literature, might also be seen (Crane suggested) as a deliberate answer to a forbidding model of the neo-Stoics: the Man Without Passions.[2] I intend in this paper to look at one or two of the ways in which this hostility towards Stoical teaching is reflected in the imaginative literature of the period.

Hostility; and something more complex than hostility. It is tempting to think of the Stoic and the Man of Feeling as radically opposed: the one (we might say) is interested in the suppression of feeling, the other in its expression. To a man such as Harley, the ludicrously demonstrative hero of Henry Mackenzie's *The Man of Feeling* (1771), tears, sighs, blushes, exclamations, and acts of charity seem to come swiftly and spontaneously; his face and his hand are forever betraying the feelings of his heart. There is no good reason why a Man of Feeling should behave like this; feeling is still feeling, after all, even if it is not expressed. Yet it is worth noticing one important aspect of such a character as Harley:

---

[1] R. S. Crane, 'Suggestions towards a Genealogy of the "Man of Feeling"', *ELH: A Journal of English Literary History*, Vol. I, 1934, pp. 205-30. See also Henry W. Sams 'Anti-Stoicism in Seventeenth- and Early Eighteenth-Century England', *Studies in Philology*, Vol. XLI, 1944, pp. 65-78.

[2] Antoine Le Grand's *Le Sage des Stoiques ou l'homme sans passions. Selon les sentimens de Seneque* (1662) was translated into English in 1675 by 'G.R.' as *Man Without Passion: Or, the Wise Stoick, According to the Sentiments of Seneca*.

that he is spontaneous despite himself; that he often tries—as, in another way, a Stoic tries—to suppress his natural feelings, to exercise self-denial and restraint; only (as a rule) to fail, signally but not dishonourably. Harley tries to keep to himself the major passion of his life, refusing—through 'extreme sensibility'—to tell Miss Walton that he loves her; but the book ends with Harley's final breathless confession of the secret, followed by his immediate fatal collapse in Miss Walton's arms. The formula is not uncommon in sentimental literature of the period. Comedies such as Steele's *The Conscious Lovers* (1722) and Hugh Kelly's *False Delicacy* (1768) turn upon similar acts of heroic self-denial, in which lovers suffer in silence—even going so far as to betroth themselves to partners for whom they have no affection—rather than declare the true objects of their love. This pseudo-Stoicism of the sentimental hero (as it might be called) deserves to be explored a little further.

Jacques Barzun's suggestive definition of Sentimentalism as 'the cultivation of feeling without ensuing action' is particularly relevant here. 'Habitually to enjoy feelings without acting upon them', Barzun wrote, 'is to be a sentimentalist'.[3] We might say that the sentimentalist often attempts simultaneously to indulge and to restrain his feelings; and that in this respect he is significantly different from the Stoic, who attempts to extinguish the feelings altogether.[4] Here is a simple example of the kind of thing I have in mind; the passage occurs in the opening chapter of *The Mysteries of Udolpho* (1794). The heroine's father, St Aubert, has two sons, both of whom die in infancy. This is how Mrs Radcliffe tells us of St Aubert's reaction:

> He lost them at that age when infantine simplicity is so fascinating; and though, in consideration of Madame St. Aubert's distress, he restrained the expression of his own, and endeavoured to bear it, as he meant, with philosophy, he had, in truth, no philosophy that could render him calm to such losses.[5]

[3] Jacques Barzun, *Classic, Romantic and Modern*, New York, 1961, p. 75.
[4] This view of Stoicism was widely held in the period. 'I had rather follow *Aristotle's* opinion than *Seneca's*', wrote Jean François Senault in *The Use of the Passions* (the English translation, by Henry Cary, Earl of Monmouth, in 1671 of *De l'Usage des Passions*, 1641), 'and rather govern passions than destroy them' (p.130). This insistence on the need to govern rather than destroy the passions is found in many works of the period, such as William Ayloffe's *The Government of the Passions* (1700). Cf. *Spectator*, No. 408 (possibly by Pope): 'We must therefore be very cautious, least while we think to regulate the Passions, we should quite extinguish them, which is putting out the Light of the Soul . . .'.
[5] Ann Radcliffe, *The Mysteries of Udolpho*, Bonamy Dobrée (ed.), London, New York, Toronto, 1966, p. 5.

St Aubert tries to restrain the 'expression' of his grief; the grief itself, it is implied, is always there. St Aubert does not impose this restraint because of callousness, but rather out of tenderness towards his wife. That the attempt fails is the final guarantee of his goodness. It was decent of him to try to behave like a Stoic; it was heroic of him to fail in the attempt. A few chapters further on we find St Aubert himself at the point of death, offering his daughter these last words of consolation. Mrs Radcliffe here sets out in an even more explicit way the idea of sensitive restraint:

> 'Above all, my dear Emily,' said he, 'do not indulge in the pride of fine feeling, the romantic error of amiable minds. Those, who really possess sensibility, ought early to be taught, that it is a dangerous quality, which is continually extracting the excess of misery, or delight, from every surrounding circumstance. And, since, in our passage through this world, painful circumstances occur more frequently than pleasing ones, and since our sense of evil is, I fear, more acute than our sense of good, we become the victims of our feelings, unless we can in some degree command them . . . Always remember how much more valuable is the strength of fortitude than the grace of sensibility.[6]

Here is a similar feinting movement; in the midst of a novel which is itself lavishly given over to the cause of sensibility, we are warned of the perils to which sensibility exposes us, and are reminded that it is the tougher virtues that really matter. St Aubert is not, however, suggesting that Emily should suppress her 'fine feeling' altogether ('I would not teach you to become insensible, if I could'), but rather that she learn to control that feeling 'to some degree'. 'You see, my dear,' he goes on, 'that, though I would guard you against the dangers of sensibility, I am not an advocate for apathy.' 'Apathy' is a word much used in the period in connection with the philosophy of the Stoics;[7] Emily is advised to acquire some, but not all, of the Stoical virtues, to behave, one might almost say, like a sensitive Stoic. Once again there is a slight air of paradox, of having it both ways, about the whole proposition; whether Emily now collapses or bears up bravely does not greatly matter, for either action would represent a victory of a sort. Moreover, whatever the outcome, we might find it hard to escape the suspicion that St Aubert's long, sententious speech about fortitude has been introduced simply to heighten the pathos of the moment. Despite the surface meaning of St Aubert's words, the scene remains stubbornly sentimental.

---

[6] Radcliffe, *The Mysteries of Udolpho*, ch. VII, pp. 79-80.

[7] See for instance David Hume, 'The Stoic', *Essays, Moral, Political and Literary*, Oxford, 1963, pp. 147-56; especially p. 152.

The formula is capable of being more subtly deployed, and I shall come in due course to a number of similar passages that show a more delicate and complex balance than Mrs Radcliffe achieves here. I have begun with a couple of death-bed scenes, and there will be more to follow. I shall be dealing in particular with two situations which seem to have laid a strong hold on both philosophical and imaginative writers in the period: in the first, a man becomes aware of the imminence of his own death; in the second, he is told of the sudden death of his child. All writers on the subject of the passions in this period readily conceded that these two situations provided the supreme tests of human self-control.[8] The Stoics argued that one man in particular had shown exemplary coolness in a circumstance of this kind, and held that his conduct proved the possibility of other men and women doing likewise. That man was Marcus Porcius Cato, the hero of Utica. It is to the fortunes and transformations of Cato in the late seventeenth and early eighteenth centuries that I shall now turn.[9]

II

Seneca had taken Cato's suicide at Utica as his crowning example of the way in which man, in the face of the worst adversity, might remain the free and rational master of both his passions and his fate. 'If it might be imagin'd, that the *Almighty* should take off his Thought from the Care of his Whole Work', he wrote in a pasage in *De Providentia* which was well known in the eighteenth century, 'What more Glorious Spectacle could he reflect upon, than a Valiant Man Struggling with Adverse Fortune: Or *Cato's* standing Upright, and Unmov'd, under the Shock of Public Ruin?'[10] Not all writers in this period were convinced that the Almighty would have been so entranced, or even that Cato in fact died in the manner Seneca evidently believed. In *The Christian Hero* (1701) Sir Richard Steele picks up Plutarch's hints that Cato was far from relaxed on the night of his death, and proceeds to give his

8 See Gwin J. Kolb, 'The Use of Stoical Doctrines in *Rasselas*, ch. XVIII', *Modern Language Notes*, Vol. LXVIII, Nov. 1953, pp. 439-47.

9 J. W. Johnson has surveyed Cato's reputation in eighteenth-century England in his book *The Formation of English Neo-Classical Thought*, Princeton, 1967, pp. 95-105. Mr Johnson is principally concerned to show how Cato was admired in this period. The present paper attempts to show how that admiration was often tempered by a spirit of criticism.

10 *De Providentia*, II.10. The free translation given here is that of Sir Roger L'Estrange in *Seneca's Morals by Way of Abstract*, first published in 1678 and frequently reprinted throughout the eighteenth century. Addison quoted this passage in *Spectator*, No. 237, and later attached it as a motto to his tragedy of *Cato*.

own version of the probable manner of Cato's death.[11] Cato kills
himself (in Steele's new version of history) simply because he is
afraid of Caesar. He works himself up into a bad temper and goes
off to bed to read '*Plato*'s Immortality, and Guesses at a future
Life'. He behaves disgracefully towards those who are trying to
restrain him from killing himself:

> Among the rest, a fond Slave was putting in his Resistance, and
> his Affliction, for which he dash'd the poor Fellow's Teeth out
> with his Fist, and forc'd out of the Room his lamenting Friends,
> with Noise, and Taunt, and Tumult; a little while after had
> his Hand with which he struck his Servant dress'd, lay down,
> and was heard to Snore; but sure we may charitably enough
> believe, from all this unquiet Carriage, that the Sleep was dis-
> sembled, from which as soon as he awak'd, he Stabb'd himself,
> and fell on the Floor; His Fall alarm'd his wretched Depen-
> dants, whose help he resisted by tearing open his own Bowels,
> and rushing out of Life with Fury, Rage, and Indignation . . .
> Thus did *Cato* leave the World, for which indeed he was very
> unfit. . . .[12]

By discrediting Seneca's account of the manner of Cato's death,
Steele is questioning the fundamental Stoical assumption that in
extreme crises man may continue to act as though in an emotional
vacuum (Christ himself, Steele reminds us, was not without emotion at the time of his death).[13] He is asking, too—as Milton asks
at the opening of Book IX of *Paradise Lost*—what there is to
admire in the kind of fortitude traditionally celebrated as heroic.
Is there no pattern of 'better fortitude' for a Christian to follow
than that set by a defeated pagan who takes his own life?[14]

Although Steele's account of the death of Cato has virtually no
warrant in classical authority, the questions he asks in *The
Christian Hero* are by no means new. Fundamentally they are the
same questions which St Augustine asked in *Civitate Dei* (XIX, iv),
when he challenged the heroic status traditionally accorded to Cato
and other pagan figures, and ascribed Cato's suicide not to fortitude
but to impatience. The habit of speculating on the manner of

---

[11] Richard Steele, *The Christian Hero: or, No Principles but those of Reli-
gion Sufficient to make a Great Man*, Rae Blanchard (ed.), London, 1932. Blan-
chard's introduction is particularly helpful on the background to Steele's work.
For Steele's change of mind about Cato, see *The Guardian* Vol. XXXIII, 18
April 1713, and *The Englishman* Vol. XXV, 1 December 1713; Vol. XXXIV, 22
December 1713.

[12] *The Christian Hero*, pp. 20-1.

[13] Ibid., pp. 48-9.

[14] For a review of the various attitudes to suicide in this period see Lester
G. Crocker, 'The Discussion of Suicide in the Eighteenth Century', *ELH: A
Journal of English Literary History*, Vol. XIII, 1952, pp. 47-72.

Cato's death and the motives which lay behind it—censured by Montaigne in his essay 'Du Jeune Caton'—continued briskly throughout the seventeenth century. It became common to allege that Cato had died passionately and ignobly. Jean-François Senault in 1650 accused Cato of vanity, cowardice, illogicality, despair, and a perverted desire for self-gratification: his suicide 'seemed so pleasing to him, as he endeavoured to spin it out, that he might longer taste the pleasure thereof'.[15] Jacques Abbadie argued that although Cato masqueraded as a patriot he was in fact an ambitious egotist who had his eye solely upon 'Consideration, Glory, and Dignities'.[16] William Ayloffe in 1700 dismissed Cato's suicide as a 'furious Act' of despair.[17] So discredited did Cato become that the neo-Stoics themselves were sometimes forced to abandon him as a model. Antoine Le Grand, for instance, author of the work translated into English under the title *Man Without Passion: Or, the Wise Stoick*, freely asserts Cato's despair as a fact, and as 'an evident sign of his imbecility: he did not kill himself, but because he envyed *Cesars* fortunes, and set not the Dagger to his breast, but because he could not bear the prosperity of a victorious Antagonist'.[18]

By the early eighteenth century, then, two radically opposed traditions concerning Cato continued to exist side by side: the tradition of the cool Cato, master of his passions, and the tradition of the desperate Cato, mastered by his passions. The century's most famous and influential account of Cato—Addison's tragedy of *Cato*, first presented at Drury Lane in April 1713—is to be seen in the light of this double tradition.[19] It is clear that Addison was uneasily aware of Cato's ambiguous reputation. The view of Cato which Addison expresses in a number of *Spectator* papers is far from being one of unqualified admiration. At times, it is true, Addison is content to repeat Seneca's high praise of the man: that his death was a sight worthy of the attention of the gods; that when we are alone we should imagine that Cato is before us, watching everything we do.[20] Elsewhere, however, Addison is not

15 Jean-François Senault, *Man Become Guilty* (the English translation by Henry Cary, Earl of Monmouth, 1650, of *L'Homme Criminel*, 1644), p. 153.

16 Jacques Abbadie, *The Art of Knowing One-Self: Or, An Enquiry Into the Sources of Morality* (the English translation by 'T.W.', Oxford, 1695, of *L'Art de se connoitre soy-meme, ou la recherche des sources de la morale*, 1692), pp. 263-4.

17 William Ayloffe, *The Government of the Passions*, London, 1700, pp. 93-4.

18 Le Grand, *Man Without Passion*, pp. 250-1. In addition to the above examples, see Sir Thomas Browne, *Religio Medici*, I, 25, 44.

19 On Addison's *Cato* see Peter Smithers, *The Life of Joseph Addison*, Oxford, 1954, pp. 250ff.; John Loftis, *The Politics of Drama in Augustan England*, Oxford, 1963, pp. 56-61 and *passim*; M. M. Kelsall, 'The Meaning of Addison's *Cato*', *The Review of English Studies*, N.S., Vol. XVII, 1966, pp. 149-62.

20 *Spectator*, Nos. 237, 231.

only sharply critical of the extreme doctrines and practices of the Stoics—their refusal to show concern for the misfortunes of others, their supreme trust in 'indifference' rather than pity, etc.[21]—but he is also far less enthusiastic about the kind of virtues which Cato represents. Speaking in *Spectator* No. 169 of Sallust's account of Cato, for instance, Addison remarks that 'A Being who has nothing to pardon in himself, may reward every Man according to his Works', and adds that compassion, humanity, benevolence, and good nature are not much in evidence in Cato's character. Cato, says Addison in a phrase later to be echoed by Hume, is a man 'rather awful than amiable'.[22] In *Spectator* No. 349 Addison comments with equal severity that 'the indifference which [Cato] showed at the Close of [his life] is to be looked upon as a piece of natural Carelessness and Levity, rather than Fortitude'. As an example of better fortitude, Addison instances a Christian hero, Sir Thomas More, whose simple good humour at the time of his death was of a piece with the natural cheerfulness and sanctity he showed throughout his life.

It is possible to imagine a tragedy on the subject of Cato which might express the kind of mixed feelings which Addison shows in these essays. Its hero might be a man admirable in his sense of duty, his self-discipline, his consistency to principle, but fatally lacking in warmth, humour, generosity, and, finally, in real knowledge of himself and of the motives which drive him to suicide. The hero of Addison's *Cato* is not, however, a man of this kind. Where he has found the historical Cato deficient, Addison has chosen not to expose this deficiency, but rather to change and soften the character. This is the kind of character that emerges; Cato's daughter, Marcia, is speaking:

> Though stern and awful to the foes of *Rome*,
> He is all goodness, *Lucia*, always mild,
> Compassionate, and gentle to his friends.
> Fill'd with domestic tenderness, the best,
> The kindest father! I have ever found him
> Easie, and good, and bounteous to my wishes. (V. iv)

Addison is attempting to transform the Cato of Seneca—and of all the early commentators—into an eighteenth-century Man of Feeling. Equally anxious to avoid the desperate Cato and the cold

[21] *Spectator*, No. 397.
[22] David Hume, 'An Enquiry concerning the Principles of Morals' Appendix IV; *Essential Works of David Hume*, Ralph Cohen (ed.), New York, Toronto, London, 1965, p. 287. Hume, like Addison, is discussing Sallust's comparative account of the characters of Caesar and Cato. Professor Claude Rawson points out to me that the contrast between 'awful' (or 'admirable') virtues and 'amiable' virtues is to be found in several places in Fielding's work.

Cato, Addison gives us instead what might be called the tender
Cato: Cato domesticated, the kindly father of his family. The real
Cato's domestic life was not, in fact, entirely above reproach, and
Addison is forced to maintain a discreet silence about at least one
aspect of this 'domestic tenderness':

> Heroic, stoic Cato, the sententious
> Who lent his lady to his friend Hortensius

makes no appearance in Addison's play, as he was later to do in
the less reverent pages of Byron's *Don Juan* (VI. vii).

Addison concentrates not on Cato's role as a husband but as a
father; and here, too, he is forced to tamper a little with history.
Plutarch tells us that Cato was accompanied to Utica by one son,
Marcus Porcius, who was with him to the end. Adopting a trick
that he had already censured in other writers of tragedy, Addison
attempts to increase pathos by increasing the number of children
who are with Cato on his last day, giving Cato two sons (whom
he calls Marcus and Portius), and a daughter, Marcia; these
children are accompanied by various lovers.[23] The sub-plot which
Addison creates by the addition of these characters is a curiously
sentimental one, especially for a play which seems to celebrate
the conduct of a hero of the Stoics. Within seconds of the opening
of the play Portius is in tears as he realises that he and his brother
Marcus are rivals for the hand of Lucia, and the sub-plot continues
on the same high note of hectic passion. As John Dennis pointed
out in his lengthy and hostile 'Remarks upon *Cato*, A Tragedy',
this whole area of the play is puzzlingly contradictory, and a reader
may well be unsure whether he is being introduced to a 'Nest of
Stoicks', or to a collection of 'whining Amorous Milk-Sops'.[24] A
curious disjunction may be felt to exist at the heart of the play, as
though Addison were trying to celebrate two quite contrary modes
of behaviour, the passionate and the austere. Cato's alleged tenderness towards his family is never allowed to complicate his final
decision to take his life; he does not hesitate to debate the issue,
but moves boldly and (we are told) smilingly to his death. The

---

[23] See *Spectator*, No. 44. It is not known precisely how many children the
real Cato had; by his first wife, Atilia, he had one daughter, Porcia, and one
son, Marcus Porcius Cato; by his second wife, Marcia, he had one son (?Lucius
Porcius Cato) and two daughters. Plutarch (*Cato Minor*, 52.3) tells us that
when Cato decided to follow Pompey into exile, he took with him his elder
son, sending his younger son (apparently not yet adult) to Munatius in Brut-
tium for safe-keeping, and leaving his daughters with his wife Marcia, whom—
after Hortensius's death—he had just re-married. (I am grateful to Dr Beryl
Rawson for guiding me, here and elsewhere, through the intricacies of Cato's
family relationships.)

[24] *The Critical Works of John Dennis*, E. N. Hooker (ed.), Baltimore, 1943,
ii, pp. 41-80; the quotation is from p. 54.

play's ideas about stoicism and sensibility are never brought into meaningful relationship with each other, but are simply allowed loosely and incongruously to co-exist. For all his efforts, Addison has not been able to bring alive his somewhat abstract idea of the tender Cato; we are left instead with the cold Cato and his sentimental children.

It could of course be argued that, short of violating history even more grossly, Addison could not have done otherwise; that the trouble arises fundamentally from his decision that Cato might be considered a suitable subject for tragedy. 'All stoicism is undramatic', Lessing was to declare in *Laocoön*, and without debating the general truth of this dictum, one might agree that the death of Cato is not a theme which is likely to arouse the Aristotelian emotions of pity and terror.[25] John Dennis, again, is the first to describe the difficulty:

> For his Philosophy has taught [Cato] to check his Passions, to conceal them, and to shorten them; so that a *Stoick*, if his Manners are made convenient, can never be shewn, as *Oedipus* and some other principal Characters of Tragedy are shewn, *viz.* agitated and tormented by various violent Passions, from the opening of the Scene to the very Catastrophe.[26]

Behind the general chorus of praise for Addison's tragedy in the eighteenth century, this objection from time to time makes itself heard. William Guthrie thought that Cato could be 'no object of compassion, one great end of tragedy', and regretted that Addison should have tried 'to raise compassion in circumstances, wherein he ought of all things to have avoided such an attempt, in drawing the character of a professed stoic'.[27] Edward Young in his *Conjectures on Original Composition* found the theme so lacking in pity and terror that the play itself became 'a sort of suicide, and that which is most dramatic in the drama dies'.[28] Schlegel made the point less prescriptively and with greater subtlety:

> Cato, who ought to be the soul of the whole, is hardly ever shown to us in action; nothing remains for him but to admire himself and to die. It might be thought that the stoical determination of a suicide, without struggle and without pas-

---

25 'Alles Stoiche ist untheatralisch; und unser Mitleiden ist allezeit dem Leiden gleichmässig, welches der interessierende Gegenstand äussert': G. E. Lessing, *Laokoon*, Dorothy Reich (ed.), Oxford, 1965, p. 60.

26 Dennis, 'Remarks', p. 50.

27 William Guthrie, *An Essay Upon English Tragedy*, London, n.d., p. 24. E. N. Hooker cites some similar contemporary criticisms, *The Critical Works of John Dennis*, II, p. 452.

28 *The Complete Works, Poetry and Prose, of the Reverend Edward Young, L.L.D.*, London, 1854, II, p. 576.

sion, is not a fortunate subject; but correctly speaking, no subjects are unfortunate, every thing depends on correctly apprehending them.[29]

All these criticisms of Addison's play—with the possible exception of Schlegel's—reveal the writers' commitment to an Aristotelian view of tragedy. The real interest of many such comments, however, lies in the ease with which they move from the aesthetic to the moral argument. John Dennis, for example, with no very keen regard for consistency, criticises Addison's Cato both for his freedom from passion and for his readiness to yield to the passion which, he conjectures, must have prompted his suicide:

> Is this, after all, his boasted Firmness? Is this the Courage of a valiant Soldier, or the Magnanimity of a *Roman* General, or the Impassiveness of an habitual *Stoick,* or the undaunted invincible Resolution of an admired Assertor of Liberty? Did ever weak Woman despair sooner, or yield more tamely to a threatening Accident, before she knew the Event of it?[30]

Dennis's questions are the very questions which Steele had asked a few years earlier in *The Christian Hero.* Like Steele (and like those later critics who felt uneasy about the fact that Addison's tragedy apparently condoned an act of suicide),[31] Dennis is asking what is fundamentally a moral question: what is there in the fortitude of a Cato that can properly be regarded as heroic?

Such questions as these provide both context and rationale for much early eighteenth-century experimentation in the mode of mock-heroic. Swift's poem 'On Clever Tom Clinch, Going to be Hanged', for instance, ironically poses a similar question about the nature of certain kinds of 'heroic' fortitude:

> My Conscience is clear, and my Spirits are calm,
> And thus I go off without Pray'r-Book or Psalm.
> Thus follow the Practice of clever *Tom Clinch,*
> Who hung like a Hero, and never would flinch.[32]

Tom Clinch's brand of fortitude is much the same as that of Fielding's Jonathan Wild, who flings himself with heroic resolution into the sea—only to return a few minutes later to his boat, having had some misgivings about the desirability of an early death (II, xi-xii). But mock-heroic is not the only weapon at Fielding's

---

[29] A. W. Schlegel, *A Course of Lectures on Dramatic Art and Literature,* trans. John Black, 1846, Lecture XXVIII, pp. 484-5.

[30] Dennis, 'Remarks', p. 52.

[31] See, for example: [F. Gentleman], *The Dramatic Censor,* London, 1770, p. 454.

[32] *The Poems of Jonathan Swift,* Harold Williams (ed.), Oxford, 1937, II, p. 400.

disposal in *Jonathan Wild*; and this demonstration of Wild's preparation for death is balanced by the scene in which Heartfree
prepares to meet his execution. Heartfree's attitude is not one of
stoical fortitude, but rather of sensitive restraint: he shows Christian
resignation and composure, but also an active concern for the
plight of his family after his death; he is both cool and compas-
sionate. And it is significant that Fielding compares Heartfree not
to Cato, who voluntarily ended his life (as Wild attempted to do),
but to Socrates, who had the penalty of death imposed upon him
(III. i-ii).[33]

Fielding's awareness of the precise shades of meaning implied in
such comparisons may be seen again in his description of the
behaviour of Allworthy, when he is told in *Tom Jones*, V. 7, that
he is unlikely to survive his present illness:

> Mr. Allworthy, who had settled all his affairs in this world,
> and was as well prepared, as it is possible for human nature
> to be, for the other, received this information with the utmost
> calmness and unconcern. He could, indeed, whenever he lay
> himself down to rest, say with Cato in the tragical poem
> > —Let guilt or fear
> > Disturb man's rest, Cato knows neither of them;
> > Indifferent in his choice, to sleep or die.
>
> In reality, he could say this with ten times more reason and
> confidence than Cato, or any other proud fellow among the
> antient or modern heroes: for he was not only devoid of fear;
> but might be considered as a faithful labourer, when at the
> end of harvest, he is summoned to receive his reward at the
> hands of a bountiful master.

'Ten times more reason and confidence', because Allworthy is not
taking his own life, but is meekly preparing to have it taken from
him; and because he prepares to meet his death with the consolation not of Plato's *Phaedo* but of the Christian religion. Such
fortitude as this, Fielding implies, is more genuinely to be admired
than is the behaviour conventionally celebrated in heroic literature,
ancient and modern; beside Allworthy, Cato is no more than a
'proud fellow'.

Fielding is not the only writer of the period who attempts to
criticise and recast the character of Addison's Cato in this way.
Exactly two years after the first performance of Addison's play,
Nicholas Rowe's tragedy of *Lady Jane Grey* was presented at Drury
Lane (April 1715). In the fourth act of Rowe's play the heroine is

---

[33] The law in Athens specified that the condemned man should administer
the death penalty to himself by drinking hemlock. See J. M. Rist, *Stoic Philosophy*, Cambridge, 1969, ch. 13.

discovered on the eve of her execution reading the same book
which Cato studied on the night of his death:

> 'Tis Plato's *Phaedon,*
> Where Dying *Socrates* takes leave of Life,
> With such an easy, careless, calm Indifference,
> As if the Trifle were of no Account,
> Mean in it self, and only to be worn
> In honour of the Giver.

The incident links Lady Jane in our minds not only with Socrates,
but also—by its recall of Addison's play—with Cato. Socrates in
his last hours had been forced to send away his shrewish wife
Xanthippe, who 'cried out and said the kind of thing that women
always do say' on such occasions; Socrates sees fit to die in the
company of men. The clear implication of Rowe's tragedy is that a
woman is perfectly capable of showing the kind of heroic courage
we normally associate with the names of Socrates and Cato; Lady
Jane is a female Socrates, a female Cato. But Rowe is not simply
making a feminist point here; in a passionate final scene between
Lady Jane Grey and her lover, Lord Guilford Dudley, he shows
that the 'indifference' of which his heroine speaks is quite unlike
the indifference of Socrates or of Cato; her stoicism, Rowe suggests,
is maintained only with difficulty, and is continually threatened
by the force of her passion.

A more spectacularly transformed Cato is to be found in George
Lillo's *The London Merchant* (1731). In the play's last act George
Barnwell is discovered on the eve of his execution reading not
Plato, but the Bible, a work which—so far from encouraging 'in-
difference'—drives him to more vehement passion:

> How shall I describe my present state of mind? I hope in
> doubt, and trembling I rejoice. I feel my grief increase, even
> as my fears give way. Joy and gratitude now supply more tears
> than the horror and anguish of despair before. (V. ii)

The allusion to Addison's tragedy seems plain,[34] but the distance
between the two plays is even more remarkable: Lillo's Barnwell
is a Cato in tears, a man who, at the point of death, is capable of
subduing his fears but not his other, more generous emotions of
'joy and gratitude'. The villainous Millwood, who has seduced
Barnwell and encouraged him to murder his uncle, goes to meet
her death like a Stoic, 'Dauntless and unconcerned', only to lapse,
the moment before her execution, into 'anguish and despair'. In

---

[34] William H. McBurney sees another echo of Addison's famous scene in
Lillo's *Fatal Curiosity,* II, iii; see McBurney's edition of the play for the
Regents Restoration Drama Series, London, 1967, p. 35.

the dedication to *The London Merchant* Lillo speaks admiringly
of Addison's *Cato*, but goes on to remark that he himself has
attempted in his play to 'enlarge the province of tragedy'. What
Lillo has attempted to enlarge is not merely the traditional idea
of the station in life to which a tragic hero may belong, but also
the traditional idea of the kind and quality of fortitude which a
tragic hero may display at the point of death. Like Fielding and
Rowe, Lillo reminds us of Addison's play only to mark his distance
from it. The hero of the Stoics, the Man Without Passion, has been
extravagantly transformed in Lillo's play into a tearful and peni-
tent Christian Man of Feeling.

III

So far I have looked at a number of scenes in which a man or
a woman prepares, with more or less composure, to meet his or
her own death. I turn now to a related group of scenes, in which
a parent is suddenly told of the death of his child. We have just
left a weeping Cato, and it should perhaps be recalled that there
is in fact one famous scene in Addison's tragedy where his hero,
too, is reduced to tears. In the fourth act of the play Cato's son,
Portius, enters hurriedly to announce to his father that his brother
Marcus has just met his death in battle, bravely and against great
odds. Cato's response is dry and short: 'I'm satisfy'd'. Marcus's body
is brought in, accompanied by weeping senators; Cato is still unmoved, and remarks that he is sorry that it is possible to die only
once for one's country. Then he turns to his weeping companions
to deliver this rebuke, which serves in turn to bring on his own
tears—not for his son, but for Rome:

> Alas, my friends!
> Why mourn you thus? let not a private loss
> Afflict your hearts. 'Tis *Rome* requires our tears.
> The mistress of the world, the seat of empire,
> The nurse of heroes, the delight of gods,
> That humbled the proud tyrants of the earth,
> And set the nations free, *Rome* is no more.
> O liberty! O virtue! O my country!
> *Juba. (aside)* Behold that upright man! *Rome* fills his eyes
> With tears, that flow'd not o'er his own dead son. (IV. iv)

Cato's tears over Rome are attested by Plutarch.[35] The whole
affair of the death of Marcus, however, is Addison's invention;
as we have seen, no second son of Cato is known to have been

[35] *Cato Minor*, 54.7; 63.6. Lucan in his account of the African journey speaks
of 'Sorrows that might tears, ev'n from Cato, gain,/And teach the rigid Stoic
to complain': *De Bello Civili*, IX, ll. 47-50; Rowe's translation.

present at Utica.[36] Nothing in Plutarch's account suggests that Cato was a man insensible to personal grief; Plutarch remarks, indeed, that at the death of his half-brother Caepio, Cato showed quite immoderate and extravagant lamentation.[37] Addison's Cato, however, is a man who is at once preternaturally stoical about his private sufferings, and preternaturally sensitive to the sufferings of his country; a balance of virtues which in some ways resembles that with which Swift was later to endow his Houyhnhnms.[38] Pope praised Addison's attempt in this scene to arouse in his audience a unique kind of tragic response:

> He bids your breasts with ancient ardor rise,
> And calls forth Roman drops from British eyes.[39]

'Roman drops': these are special tears, noble, disinterested, patriotic.

They are also very odd tears, as the energetic John Dennis was not slow to point out. When we weep for our country, Dennis argued, we do not weep for an abstraction but for the people who belong to our country; and it is only natural that we should care most for those people who are nearest to us. Thus 'for a Man to receive the News of his Son's Death with dry Eyes, and to weep at the same time for the Calamities of his Country, is a wretched Affectation and a miserable Inconsistency'.[40] Dennis's commonsensical remarks were commended by Dr Johnson in his *Life of Addison*,[41] and it is tempting to think that the episode from *Cato* may have been at the back of Johnson's mind when he wrote in the eighteenth chapter of *Rasselas* of the philosopher who preached the virtues of 'rational fortitude' and enumerated 'many examples of heroes immovable by pain or pleasure' before being told of the death of his daughter. 'What comfort, said the mourner, can truth and reason afford me? of what effect are they now, but to tell me, that my daughter may not be restored?' Gwin J. Kolb has shown that it was common in neo-Stoical writings of the time to remark that a particular fortitude was necessary to endure the

---

36 See p. 384 n. 23. Addison is possibly thinking of the fortitude shown by Cato the Censor—Cato of Utica's great-grandfather—at the death of his son, Marcus Porcius Cato Licinianus, *c.* 152 B.C. See Plutarch, *Cato Maior*, 24.6, 27.9; Cicero, *Tusculanae Disputationes*, 3.28, 70: *Cato Maior*, 68.

37 *Cato Minor*, 11.1.

38 For Swift's admiration of the historical Cato, see Johnson, *The Formation of English Neo-Classical Thought*, pp. 101-2; M. M. Kelsall, 'Iterum Houyhnhnm: Swift's Sextumvirate and the Horses', *Essays in Criticism*, XIX, 1969, pp. 35-45.

39 'Prologue to Mr Addison's Tragedy of Cato', 11.15-16.

40 Dennis, 'Remarks', p. 67.

41 Samuel Johnson, *Lives of the English Poets*, G. B. Hill (ed.), Oxford, 1905, Vol. II, pp. 135-6.

death of a close friend or relative; Johnson's allusion may well be general.[42] Yet not even Seneca—who had declared that 'to Lament the Death of a Friend, is both Natural and Just', and who had added that 'there's no applying of Consolation to fresh, and Bleeding Sorrow'—had taken such an extreme view on this matter as is implied by Addison in the scene in question.[43] Addison is prepared to improve not only on history but on Stoic philosophy as well. Johnson could scarcely have found a treatment of this topic which more richly invited his irony.

It is possible that *Cato* may form the link between this scene in *Rasselas* and another scene to which it is sometimes compared, in chapter eight of the fourth book of *Joseph Andrews*—a novel which Johnson evidently had not read.[44] Parson Adams is here rebuking Joseph for being 'too much inclined to passion'—he cites Abraham's readiness to sacrifice Isaac as an example of the way in which the natural affections may properly be suppressed—when news is suddenly brought that Adams's youngest son is drowned.

> He stood silent a moment, and soon began to stamp around the room and deplore his loss with the bitterest agony. Joseph, who was overwhelmed with concern likewise, recovered himself sufficiently to endeavour to comfort the parson; in which attempts he used many arguments that he had at several times remembered out of his own discourses, both in private and public (for he was a great enemy to the passions, and preached nothing more than the conquest of them by reason and grace), but he was not at leisure now to hearken to his advice. 'Child, child', said he, 'do not go about impossibilities. Had it been any other of my children, I could have borne it with patience; but my little prattler, the darling and comfort of my old age—the little wretch to be snatched out of life just at his entrance into it; the sweetest, best-tempered boy, who never did a thing to offend me.'

[42] See p. 380 n.8. The observation is not confined to neo-Stoical writers; see, for instance, Jeremy Taylor, *The Rule and Exercises of Holy Living*, Ch. II, §VI 'Of Contentedness': 'Death of Children, or nearest Relatives and Friends', in *The Whole Works of Rt. Rev. Jeremy Taylor D.D.*, London, 1839, IV, pp. 133ff.

[43] Roger L'Estrange, *Seneca's Morals by Way of Abstract*, 9th ed., 1705, pp. 266, 272.

[44] *Life of Johnson*, Boswell, G. B. Hill (ed.), rev. L. F. Powell, 1934-50, Vol. II, p. 174. O. F. Emerson noted the possibility that Fielding has in mind Cicero's allusion in *Tusculanae Disputationes*, 3.28.70, to the hero Oïleus (in a lost tragedy by Sophocles) who, having consoled Telamon for the death of Ajax, breaks down when he hears of the death of his own son. (O. F. Emerson (ed.), *The History of Rasselas, Prince of Abyssinia*, 1895, p. 160). It is in the same section of this work that Cicero describes Cato the Censor's fortitude on hearing of the death of his son.

It is one of the several ironies of this passage that Adams, that 'great enemy to the passions', has been represented to us as a warm admirer of Addison's *Cato*—'the only English tragedy I ever read' (III. v)—a tragedy which he declares to be one of the only two plays 'fit for a Christian to read' (III. xi). Once again, Fielding is showing us a man who is like, and yet unlike, Addison's Cato, a man whose Stoicism reaches only to a certain point. So far is Fielding from merely ridiculing Adams for his *volte-face* that— like Mrs Radcliffe in her description of St Aubert coping unsuccess- fully with his grief at the death of his sons—he is giving us a double guarantee of the man's goodness. It would have been easy to allow the incident to demean Adams, as Johnson in some ways demeans the bereaved philosopher in *Rasselas*, or as Fielding in *Tom Jones* V. 2 more decisively demeans the stoical Square, who, while lecturing Tom learnedly on the need to cultivate the forti- tude which will allow him to disregard such trifles as a broken arm, is unfortunate enough to bite painfully on his own tongue. It is important that the incident in *Joseph Andrews* occurs near the end of the novel, when Adams's goodness and humanity are already fully established; we know full well that Adams's animosity towards the passions is neither hypocritical nor inhumane, and that it is directed—despite the apparently broad sweep of Adams's language —not against all passions but against some. By way of contrast, we know nothing of Johnson's philosopher, save that his actions fail to live up to his fine words. Johnson cuts the philosopher down to size, showing us that he is only human. Fielding's incident, on the other hand, humanises Parson Adams in a way that increases rather than diminishes our affection for him. Fielding humanises without sentimentalising; it is a wonderful touch that Adams should *stamp* for grief, rather than burst into tears, as a bereaved hero in Mrs Radcliffe's world might do.

To feel pain at a bereavement, Fielding writes in his essay 'Of Remedy of Affliction for the Loss of Our Friends' in 1743, 'is a malady to which the best and worthiest of men are chiefly liable'.

> For this reason the calm demeanour of Stilpo the philosopher, who, when he had lost his children at the taking of *Meghra* by *Demetrius*, concluded, *he had lost nothing, for that he carried all which was his own about him*, hath no charms for me. I am more apt to impute such sudden tranquillity at so great a loss, to ostentation or obduracy, than to consummate virtue. It is rather wanting the affection than conquering it. To overcome the affliction arising from the loss of our friends, is great and praiseworthy; but it requires some reason and time. This sudden unruffled composure is owing to mere in-

sensibility; to a depravity of the heart, not goodness of the understanding.[45]

Those who command their passions perfectly may be thought to have few passions to command; it is for this reason that Stilpo the philosopher, like Addison's Cato, is regarded by Fielding as a doubtful model of virtue. Parson Adams is, as it were, the antitype to both Stilpo and Cato, a man whose passionate grief assures us he is no victim of 'mere insensibility'. Through Adams's admiring references to *Cato* in *Joseph Andrews*, Fielding ironically throws out a false trail for the reader. Like Joseph—whom Adams has rebuked for an emotional outburst in an earlier chapter—Adams might more aptly align himself with a bereaved father from a very different tragedy: Shakespeare's Macduff, whose words Joseph has passionately misquoted:

> I will bear my sorrows as a man,
> But I must also feel them as a man.
> I cannot but remember such things were,
> And were most dear to me.—[46]

Sorrows that are borne, as Adams discovers, are still sorrows that are felt.

One more bereaved father from eighteenth-century fiction remains to be considered. Walter Shandy is 'a man of deep reading —prompt memory—with *Cato*, and *Seneca*, and *Epictetus*, at his finger ends' *(Tristram Shandy,* V. vi), and when the news arrives that his son Bobby is dead he is in one sense armed for the occasion. It would have been no surprise or disgrace, says Tristram, if his father had wept at the news, for the best of scholars allow this to be a natural response:

> 'Tis either *Plato,* or *Plutarch,* or *Seneca,* or *Xenophon,* or *Epictetus,* or *Theophrastus,* or *Lucian*—or some one perhaps of later date—either *Cardan,* or *Budæus,* or *Petrarch,* or *Stella*— or possibly it may be some divine or father of the church, St. *Austin,* or St. *Cyprian,* or *Barnard,* who affirms that it is an irresistable and natural passion to weep for the loss of our friends or children—and *Seneca* (I'm positive) tells us some-where, that such griefs evacuate themselves best by that par-ticular channel.—And accordingly we find, that *David* wept for his son *Absolom*—*Adrian* for his *Antinous*—*Niobe* for her

[45] 'Of the Remedy of Affliction for the Loss of Our Friends', in *The Com-plete Works of Henry Fielding,* W. E. Henley (ed.), London, 1903, Vol. XVI, *Miscellaneous Writings,* Vol. III, pp. 97-109; the passage quoted occurs on p. 99. For an excellent account of Fielding's attitude to Stoical thought see Henry Knight Miller, *Essays on Fielding's Miscellanies. A Commentary on Volume One,* Princeton, 1961, pp. 254-71, and *passim.*
[46] Joseph Andrews, III.xi; cf. *Macbeth,* IV.iii.220-3.

children, and that *Apollodorus* and *Crito* both shed tears for *Socrates* before his death. (V. iii)

But instead of yielding to such weighty authority and weeping in the 'irresistable and natural' way for the death of his son, Walter begins to remember, at first with bitterness and then with rapidly increasing pleasure, 'how many excellent things might be said upon the occasion' of such a death. Walter's oration upon death is learned and wide-ranging in its allusions, and occasions deepening bewilderment and distress to his brother Toby, who—innocently missing the allusions and assuming a passage out of Servius Sulpicius to be an autobiographical confession—concludes that his brother is out of his mind.

> 'May the Lord God of heaven and earth protect him and restore him', said my uncle *Toby*, praying silently for my father, and with tears in his eyes.
> —My father placed the tears to a proper account, and went on with his harangue with great spirit.

Like the only other tears which are shed on this occasion—those of Susannah the chambermaid—Toby's tears spring not from the primary fact of Bobby's death but from a secondary source of emotional disturbance.

Sterne is here playing an unexpected variation upon a situation that had by now become thoroughly hackneyed not only in philosophical writing but—as we have seen—in fictional writing of the period as well. Sterne's wit, like Fielding's, vitalises an old cliché. Like Fielding, Sterne reminds us that the emotions may not always show themselves in conventional and predictable ways; that a man who does not weep at the death of his son may still be deeply moved. Conversely, tears do not always signal grief, as Tristram points out as he tells of the pleasure which Walter gained from his retort to Obadiah after the disastrous matter of the Arabian horse that gave birth to a mule:

> —See here! you rascal, cried my father, pointing to the mule, what have you done!—It was not me, said *Obadiah*—How do I know that? replied my father.
> Triumph swam in my father's eyes, at the repartee—the *Attic* salt brought water into them—and so *Obadiah* heard no more about it.
> Now let us go back to my brother's death.

By contrast to such a touch as this, the emotional signals of an Addison or a Mrs Radcliffe are crude and obvious: grief is conveyed through tears, tears are the sign of grief; neither writer shows any understanding of the phenomenon of displaced emotion, which

Sterne so skilfully exploits throughout *Tristram Shandy*. When Addison's Cato weeps over Rome after remaining unmoved at the sight of his dead son, there is no possibility that these tears are the tears of delayed private grief. Addison's signal is a simple one: we are to understand that Cato cares more about public calamities than about private ones. It is because Addison's play rarely leaves this level of emotional simplicity that we may be justified in describing it as being, despite its theme, a sentimental work. It is, on the other hand, the wit and psychological complexity of *Tristram Shandy* that requires us to describe that work as being, despite its reputation, something more than that.

IV

I have spoken of several figures who, at various times, have been adduced as models of fortitude; and I conclude with this slightly unusual example from Montaigne's *Apologie de Raimond Sebond*:

> The Philosopher Pyrrho being at sea, and by reason of a violent storme in great danger to be cast away, presented nothing unto those that were with him in the ship to imitate but the securitie of an Hog which was aboard, who, nothing at all dismaied, seemd to behold and outstare the tempest.[47]

One enjoys the 'securitie' of a hog only by making a certain sacrifice: the sacrifice of one's human sensibility. It is precisely this kind of fortitude which most of the writers I have mentioned are determined to reject. Cato, Stilpo, Tom Clinch, Millwood, Jonathan Wild, the philosopher of Cairo are all made to appear (for a time at least) a little too successful in their fortitude, a little too like Pyrrho's pig. The successful Stoic, aspiring to the highest virtue, becomes no better than a beast. The eighteenth-century hostility to Stoicism which I have discussed is not a simple thing, but it is fundamentally based on a belief like this. Better to bear and feel one's sorrows 'like a man' than to achieve no more than the brutal valour of Pyrrho's pig.

---

[47] *The Essayes of Michael Lord of Montaigne*, trans. John Florio, London and New York, 1965 (Everyman edition), II, 189.

Nichol Smith Collections in Edinburgh and Oxford

A. S. Bell

I. PRINTED BOOKS

'After my long residence in Oxford—over 50 years now—every breath that I breathe in Edinburgh seems to be a gentle tonic.' Thus David Nichol Smith wrote to his friend and pupil John Butt, when the latter was appointed to the Regius Chair of Rhetoric and English Literature in the University of Edinburgh.[1] Nichol Smith always regarded Edinburgh with the greatest affection, and is himself remembered affectionately by the senior staff of the National Library of Scotland, who knew him as a generous and considerate benefactor. Although the last academic affiliations of his life determined the eventual sale of many of his books to the National Library of Australia, he recalled his early career when arranging for the disposal of several cherished groups of books from his distinguished library.

At the end of World War II he presented to the National Library of Scotland a number of Restoration plays, formerly in the library of his friend Sir Charles Firth, which filled several gaps in its collections and which he supplemented in 1957 by the gift of over a hundred eighteenth-century editions of English plays. But he had a larger benefaction in mind, and after further discussions he wrote in 1950 to the Earl of Crawford and Balcarres, Chairman of the Library's Board of Trustees, that he was preparing a formal bequest:

> As an Edinburgh boy, born and bred, I do not forget what I owed to the Advocates' Library when I worked in it some fifty years ago, and the desire to do something in acknow-

[1] Letter to John Butt, 9 August 1959, presented to the National Library of Scotland by the addressee. Nichol Smith remarked that Butt was the sixth holder of the Chair he had known, from his own teacher, Masson, onwards; and Aytoun had taught his father.

ledgement of my debt to it has increased since it became the National Library of Scotland under management which I have more and more admired.[2]

The codicil he made just before his departure for Australia in 1950 bequeathed to the Library 'all books in French, Latin, Greek and Italian printed before 1800'.

In 1959, however, he anticipated his own bequest by presenting these books to the Library. Prior to this major donation, he had given to the Library several sets of eighteenth-century literary and scientific periodicals, but the foreign books formed the major benefaction. Not the least of his many kindnesses to the Library was his preparation of a detailed account of the formation of his foreign collection:

> They are the books which I left to the N.L.S. in the will drawn up in 1950 before my wife and I set out for Australia. They form a little collection by themselves consisting mainly of French books and translations from and into French before 1800, and of a smaller number of Latin, Greek, and Italian books also printed before that date. I began collecting them in the 'nineties when I was working on the relations of French and English criticism and acquired many on the quais in Paris, and others were found in John Grant's open-air boxes. Later sources were Dobell, and, after 1908 when I came to Oxford, Blackwell. The collection began as a kind of foundling hospital, and it never quite lost that character. I was never put off by broken binding or the absence of a half-title, and sometimes of a more important page, as in the first edition of La Bruyère's *Caractères*, or in the fragment of the French translation of the Vulgate that is earlier than Tyndale. I yielded to the temptation of a very ugly chunk of a book by the 'Seigneur des Accords' because it aroused my curiosity— which is still unsatisfied. Occasionally I gave room to an odd volume in the hope of learning more about the edition. The result is that there is a section of the collection which may not unfairly be described as ramshackle. So I ask you very earnestly to reject what you do not think good enough for the N.L.S. In doing so you will do me a kindness, for I do not wish this collection to be disfigured by anything unworthy of it. I shall be disappointed if you do not find that as a rule the books are—to borrow words from a famous preface— perfect in their limbs and absolute in their numbers of the pages.
>
> There is the other question of sound books of which copies are already in the N.L.S. There I must fall in with your wishes, but there are some possible duplicates which I should like to

2 Letter to Lord Crawford, 21 May 1950, in the Library archives.

remain with their companions, e.g. the copies of *Scaligeriana*
and *Scaligerana*, and *Menagiana*, and Le Bossu's *Epic*. Do not
hesitate to tell me when you think that a duplicate might
be returned to me. . . .³

After the books had been received and sorted, it was found that
only 58 of the 771 volumes were duplicates, and several of these
were retained for sentimental reasons. For example, his Aristotle,
Poetica, vulgarizzata per L. Castelvetro (Basilea, 1576) was 'the
nucleus of the critical collection', acquired as a result of attending
S. H. Butcher's lectures while Butcher was preparing his edition
of the *Poetics* (1895). Heliodorus, *Aethiopicorum libri X* (Lutetiæ
Parisiorum, 1619), was pleaded for (and of course retained), because 'it was one of the first books I ever bought. I could not read
it, but I ventured a whole half-penny for it'.⁴

There are some early books, including a French Bible, *Cy com-
mence la bible en francoys . . .* (A. Lotrian, Paris, *c.* 1525), in
Gothic type with four woodcuts, but nothing in the main collection is later than 1800. Some works are of Italian interest. The
first edition of Lodovico Dolce's *Osservatione* (Venice, 1550), a
study of the Italian language, is one of the earlier Italian critical
works. G. B. Marini, *L'Adone* (Paris, 1623) is the first edition of
the poem composed while Marini was living in France under the
protection of Marie de Medici. But the main interest of the collection is, as Nichol Smith remarked, 'largely concerned with the
literary criticism of the late seventeenth and early eighteenth
century, and the relations then of French and English literature'.⁵

The spirit in which Nichol Smith collected his French books is
illustrated by his edition of Boileau's *L'Art poétique* (1898).
It was, he said, 'the first critical edition published in this country',
and was intended to be as useful to students of English literature
as of French. Nichol Smith owned many critical and controversial
works of importance, which enabled him to situate Boileau in the
literature of his time: Scudéry's *Observations sur le Cid* (1637), the
first shot in a famous battle; Furetière's satirical *Nouvelle allé-
gorique* (1658), Boileau's own *Oeuvres diverses* (1675), and later
editions of his works; Le Bossu's *Traité du poème épique* (1675),
with later editions, French and English. Perhaps most interesting,
however, is the extent to which the prose and poetry Boileau knew,
and frequently cited in evidence, is represented in the collection.
Here are the epics: Chapelain's *La Pucelle* (1657); Pierre Le
Moyne's *Saint-Louys* (1658), and Brébeuf's translation of the

³ Letter to W. Beattie, 29 May 1959, in the Library archives.
⁴ Ibid., 11 October 1959.
⁵ Ibid., 28 September 1959.

Pharsalia (1658). The writers of burlesque have a large place: Saint-Amant's works of 1642-3, and several collections of the works of Scarron, to which may be added Cyrano de Bergerac's *La mort d'Agrippine* (1656). There is one outstanding novel, the rare first edition of Furetière's *Roman bourgeois* (1666). Boileau's critical theories were distilled from his reactions to such works, which provide the essential context for the study of those theories and of the basic tenets of French classicism. There could be no better corrective to later misrepresentations, French and English.

The National Library of Scotland had not been strong in early editions of seventeenth-century French literature. The eighteenth century was better represented, but the Nichol Smith collection added much, particularly in categories such as early eighteenth-century criticism, theatrical collections, and periodicals. Among major writers, Montesquieu and Rousseau are represented, but the outstanding items are works by Voltaire, which include a first edition of the *Henriade* and John Lockman's version of *Letters concerning the English nation* (1733), published a year before the French original, of which there is also a first edition in the collection.

Voltaire writing on the English illustrates a major theme of the Nichol Smith collection, that of Anglo-French literary and intellectual relations. From the seventeenth century, the collection contains Sir Thomas Browne, *La religion du médecin* (1668), the first translation into French. Pascal's *Lettres provinciales* was translated into English almost at once (1657), as was Rousseau's *Nouvelle Héloïse* (1761) a century later. For the eighteenth century, the collection is strongest in translations from the English. *Les voyages de Gulliver* (Paris, 1727), is the first edition of the French translation by the Abbé Desfontaines, and the collection also contains *Le nouveau Gulliver*, Desfontaines's so-called 'translation'. Another of his real translations is Henry Fielding, *Les avantures de Joseph Andrews . . .* (Londres, 1743), 'Traduites par une Dame Angloise'. The translation of *Le ministre de Wakefield* (Londres et Paris, 1767) has been variously attributed to the Marquise de Montesson and to M. Rose.

Not all great works were translated as soon after publication as those of Pascal or Rousseau. The *Theatre Anglois* (1745-9), translated by P. A. de la Place, contains the first translations of the complete plays of Shakespeare; *Paradise Lost*, included in the collection in Louis Racine's prose translation of 1755, also remained untranslated until the eighteenth century. The Milton, like so much else in the collection, reminds one once again of Nichol Smith's interest in the theories of criticism: he once wondered how Boileau, who condemned the Christian epic, would have reacted had he known Milton.

Nichol Smith made a series of smaller benefactions after his foreign collection was transferred. Some were related to the main collection, with which they are placed; others have been shelved as separate groups. These donations illustrate strikingly the breadth of their collector's interests, ranging from three dozen volumes of poetry of Sir Walter Scott's period (a reminder that Nichol Smith chose Scott's poetry as the subject of his Edinburgh University Scott Lectures in 1950), to a valuable little group of fourteen early books in which Anglo-Saxon types are used. Most of them were printed in the seventeenth and eighteenth centuries, but the collection includes a copy of Aelfric's *A Testimonie of Antiquitie* [STC 159 (i)], printed by John Day in London in 1566 or 1567, the first book in which Anglo-Saxon types appear. Nichol Smith also gave the Library some miscellaneous books to fill gaps in the Copyright Act accessions of the nineteenth century, and continued his donations of eighteenth-century volumes until the end of his life. These later gifts include a small but useful Defoe collection which Lady Firth had given him: it contains, for example, a copy of the uncommon London [1705] edition of *A Journey to the World in the Moon*.

They are all volumes of some interest, not least in their association with Nichol Smith himself. 'They have formed a little collection', he wrote to Lord Crawford, 'and I should have been sorry if after they had lived together in good companionship they should have had to be scattered again by the bookseller. They have, I think, an interest as a group over and above what they have individually.'[6]

II. CORRESPONDENCE

Most academic correspondence, concerned as it is with the conduct of university affairs, makes remarkably uninteresting reading. Only when the correspondents are men of distinction, charm, malice, or wit, do their letters rise above the common round of academic business and stale controversy. Nichol Smith selected the letters of fourteen distinguished colleagues for preservation in the National Library of Scotland, and this bequest contains several sets of correspondence which are of permanent interest. It has been given the reference MS. Accession 3349, pending final cataloguing.

There are about sixty letters from, or concerning, George Saintsbury, beginning with cryptic postcards on Nichol Smith's first paid

6 Letter to Lord Crawford, 21 May 1950, in the Library archives.

work, reading the proofs of Saintsbury's *Nineteenth-Century Litera-ture*. This was the task which led Nichol Smith to the conclusion 'that the only dates in which [Saintsbury] could be trusted to be minutely accurate were the dates of vintages'[7] Saintsbury's later letters, arranging testimonials, acknowledging books, and discussing examinations, continue to the end of his life. They are brief and conversational: 'Short as his letters might be, in their wit or un-expected turns of phrasing, in their allusiveness or their precision, I can hear him speaking'.[8] Many are almost illegible, and Nichol Smith's interlinear glosses (themselves often incomplete) are very useful for the more difficult words.

Two sets of letters from French scholars have been preserved. Thirteen letters from the literary historian and diplomat J. J. Jusserand cover the years 1896-1908, and open with offers of hospi-tality to the young scholar during the year he spent at the Sorbonne —the important time in the formation of his collection of French criticism. There are later comments on Nichol Smith's edition of Boileau's *L'Art Poétique* (Cambridge, 1898), and on his transla-tion of *Brunetière's Essays in French Literature* (London, 1898). A larger collection of letters from Emile Legouis (30 in number, 1912-33) is full of comments on the progress of his work on Words-worth, Spenser and others, and on the *Short History of English Literature* (Oxford, 1934), which Nichol Smith read in proof for Legouis.

J. H. Lobban was an early friend, and his letters span a long period (58 letters, 1899-1908, 1926-34). Lobban was on Blackwood's staff when Nichol Smith was editing Macaulay's *Life of Johnson* (1900) and Hazlitt's *Essays on Poetry* (1901) for their English Classics series. Lobban later moved to London to work for Hodder and Stoughton, and wrote vivid and good-humoured letters about his work in a publishers' office. The correspondence unfortunately breaks off shortly after Lobban had started teaching at Birkbeck College, London, in 1908. By the time the correspondence resumes, Lobban had established his academic position, and the later letters are largely concerned with university business.

Nichol Smith's first academic appointment was as Assistant to Walter Raleigh at Glasgow. Some 150 letters from Raleigh open with a cordial welcome to his new colleague in 1902, marking the start of a long and intimate friendship. By the time they were separated—Raleigh going to Oxford as first Professor of English Literature, and Nichol Smith to the Newcastle chair—Raleigh was

---

[7] *The Saintsbury Centenary Oration . . .* , privately printed for the Saints-bury Club, London, 1946, p. 3; and *A Last Vintage: Essays and Papers by George Saintsbury*, 1950, p. 12.

[8] *Oration*, p. 5; *A Last Vintage*, p. 13.

writing long, characteristic letters which continued nearly to the end of his life. The letters for several years from 1905 are largely concerned with the planning of the Oxford Shakespeare, a project which Raleigh and the Clarendon Press regarded as a relatively simple undertaking, to be completed in a few years.[9] On 5 January 1905, Raleigh wrote of English Literature at Oxford: 'What is wanted is a school, a real one of about half a dozen [that] could make things buzz'. By the end of Raleigh's life the School was buzzing satisfactorily, and its growth is well chronicled in his letters. Nichol Smith joined him in Oxford in 1908, and the subsequent letters deal with appointments, syllabuses, lecture arrangements, the establishment of a Faculty Library, and the literary business of the University Press, with which Raleigh was closely concerned. There are many pungent comments on contemporaries, and local administrative disputes are discussed with remarkable gusto. Extracts from some of his letters to Nichol Smith were published in 1926, in *The Letters of Sir Walter Raleigh (1879-1922)*, edited by Lady Raleigh (a dozen of whose letters are preserved with her husband's), with a sensitive biographical preface by Nichol Smith himself.[10]

The few years which Nichol Smith spent at Armstrong College[11] were the foundation of his long correspondence with Henry Ellershaw, Professor of English in the associated Durham Colleges, 1910-32, and Master of University College, Durham, from 1919. The 160 letters begin just before Nichol Smith left for Oxford, and contain much interesting Durham and Newcastle university news, scattered in routine correspondence about examinations and

[9] See the Appendix below, and also J. R. Sutherland's obituary of D.N.S. in *Proceedings of the British Academy*, Vol. XLVIII, 1962, p. 455. The letter quoted there was recently bequeathed to the National Library of Scotland by J. Dover Wilson, with his own voluminous correspondence and working papers.

[10] Another interesting general comment on Raleigh has survived in some fragments of a memorial lecture delivered by D.N.S. in May 1922 (Bodl. MS. Eng. misc. c. 384, ff. 197-200): 'But R. though he was a professor all his life could never be subdued to the purely academic. He had a profound respect for scholarship, but he really disliked the academic, & he was a better professor of English literature for that very reason. Many of his colleagues here did not quite understand his methods. They did not suspect that what often seemed to them to be a lack of method was part of a deliberate policy. He was afraid that his school, like some other schools in this university, might become a mere clanking machine, & he set himself to prevent this. More than any other teacher in recent times in this university he has been the life and spirit of his school. He has controlled it even when he seemed—perhaps even to himself—to be exerting no control. To hundreds of his students Raleigh has been the English school. And he had only one fear for it,—the fear that the requirements of organisation and routine might make it stereotyped . . .'.

[11] See his reminiscences of 'Armstrong College Fifty Years Ago' in *Durham University Journal*, Vol. L, 1958, pp. 49-57.

appointments. The picture they give of an overworked and under-paid teaching staff, and of the grave financial difficulties of Durham University between the wars, is particularly interesting. Ellershaw contributed *Keats: Poetry and Prose* (1922) to Nichol Smith's Clarendon Series of English Literature, and a number of letters relate to this edition.

The letters of George Gordon are in many ways similar to Raleigh's. The Nichol Smith collection contains 139 of Gordon's letters, 1909-39, including a few from his family, and is supplemented by fourteen of Nichol Smith's (1913-35), returned to him by Mrs Gordon in 1942. As will be known from the many extracts printed in *The Letters of George S. Gordon, 1902-1942*, edited by M. C. G[ordon] (Oxford, 1943), these letters are vigorous, affectionate, and exceedingly well-tempered. The most numerous belong to the period of Gordon's tenure of the English chair at Leeds, when the friends corresponded frequently. There is much about academic business, but, as Gordon remarked in a letter of 15 April 1919, 'how trivial [are] these politics compared with our friendship . . .' Gordon's wartime letters are fairly sampled in his widow's selection, and the letters of 1919-21 give a vivid impression of the stresses of a busy period of reorganisation: 'Now—in this reconstructional mood—Professors are no longer either scholars or Professors, but "Heads of Depts."; and we have conferences, and committees, and interviewing, and reports all day long'.[12] Nevertheless, Gordon found time to edit several volumes of selections for the Clarendon English Literature series, which are discussed in the correspondence. In 1922 he returned to Oxford as Raleigh's successor; the later letters are naturally less frequent, but will provide much of interest to the historian of the Oxford School of English Literature.

Sir Charles Firth played an influential part in the formation and early management of the School, and became a close friend of Nichol Smith's. They met constantly in Oxford, and Firth's letters (80, 1911-36) therefore contain little of major importance, but a fine letter on his retirement from the English Board (25 March 1932) testifies to his long-standing interest in its development. Many of the letters refer to their common interest in Swift (it will be recalled that Nichol Smith took over Firth's notes on *Gulliver's Travels*). The manuscripts of a few articles by Firth, including that of an essay on the Union of 1707, have been preserved with the letters. Nichol Smith advised Lady Firth on the disposal of Sir Charles's fine library, and many of the forty letters from her which he kept refer to this work. She gave him many of her hus-

---

[12] Letter of 21 January 1920, quoted by M.C.G., *The Letters of George S. Gordon*, p. 133.

band's Restoration plays and Defoe books, which he later presented to the National Library of Scotland.

Nearly a hundred letters from Sir Walter Greg to Nichol Smith cover thirty-five years (1923-58) of regular correspondence on matters of mutual scholarly interest, and on the administration of learned bodies, such as the British Academy and the Malone Society, with which they were both intimately concerned. Greg's letters are full of interesting comments, such as his reply to a letter on *The Calculus of Variants* (1927): 'really there is nothing mathematical in it —at least in the symbolism. This is really very simple, though I agree that the argument is stiff at times . . .'. A discussion of the draft of Greg's obituary of McKerrow[13] led them both into reminiscences of their early work. Greg's literary executors later presented to the Library two very long letters from Nichol Smith on the McKerrow obituary, one of which is important enough to be printed in the Appendix to this paper.

Three other scholars are well represented in the bequest. A packet of forty-two letters, 1898-1918, from C. H. Herford, Professor of English at Manchester, opens with an invitation to edit *Henry VIII* for the Warwick Shakespeare, a task which occupied only three months of Nichol Smith's time in 1899. He subsequently edited *King Lear* for the same series—a year's work in 1901-2. Most of Herford's later letters are concerned with university examining, but one (21 May 1918) contains comments on Nichol Smith's draft proposals for the Oxford English School. Many of the sixty-two letters from H. J. C. Grierson, 1918-53, relate to the preparation of *Metaphysical Poetry: Donne to Butler* (Oxford, 1921) which, as Grierson acknowledged, 'owed a mighty lot to your prompting and suggestions'. About forty letters from Oliver Elton, 1927-45, are preserved, together with three early letters on examinations. They deal with British Academy business, including the obituary of Saintsbury which Elton prepared for the *Proceedings,* and with the translations from Slavonic languages which he made in his later years. Three of Nichol Smith's own letters to Elton have also been kept.

Amongst the smaller groups are twenty-four letters from Logan Pearsall Smith, which divide into those relating to the selections of Donne's Sermons (1919) and of Jeremy Taylor (1930) which he prepared for the Clarendon Press (under Nichol Smith's general editorship), and several wartime letters, some of which refer to *Milton and his Modern Critics,* which Nichol Smith read for the Oxford University Press before its publication in 1940.

Nichol Smith wrote an introduction to Volume VIII of the

[13] *Proceedings of the British Academy,* Vol. XXVI, 1940, pp. 489-515.

Ashley Library Catalogue (1926), and many of the thirty-two letters, 1925-36, from Thomas James Wise concern its preparation. Wise's letters are interesting in showing his achievement as a collector, which his more notorious activities tend to obscure. But Nichol Smith amusedly placed a letter from R. W. Chapman to himself with the Wise letters. On 23 March 1923, Chapman wrote: 'Wise lunched with us at Amen Corner on Monday. His knowledge and fluency are amazing, and I never met a bibliographer with his range—Dekker to Conrad, or thereabouts. He told us many scandalous tales of fakes and their detection'. Outraged respectability was ever part of Wise's stock-in-trade.

Altogether, the general impression left by this important correspondence is one of the establishment and expansion of a whole academic profession, both in Oxford and at other universities. There are as yet only a few of Nichol Smith's own letters in the National Library of Scotland, but these and his incoming correspondence show his steadying influence quietly at work, and amply confirm Mr D. J. Palmer's view of the Oxford English School after the first war: 'there were those who continued to integrate and direct its work, none with greater distinction than the late David Nichol Smith, during his long tenure of the Merton Chair of English Literature from 1929 to 1946'.[14]

III. LECTURE NOTES

Those of Nichol Smith's lecture notes and working papers which he chose to retain were given to the Bodleian Library by Mrs Nichol Smith in accordance with his wishes. The collection has been bound up and is now shelf-marked MSS. Eng. misc. c. 383-5, d. 539-55, e. 483 and 551; a typed inventory is available in the Library. All Nichol Smith's main interests are represented, and the manuscripts range in date from material for his Edinburgh University Heriot Fellowship essay on 'Dryden and the Rise of Literary Criticism in English' (1895), to the text of his reminiscent Arthur Skemp Memorial Lecture, delivered at Bristol in 1962.

The lecture notes vary in detail according to the standard of the audience and the formality of the occasion, but most of the outlines may be followed with ease. Many were delivered several times (especially on foreign journeys), and the dates and places are carefully recorded. There is a good deal of preparatory material for courses such as 'The History of English Studies' and 'Sources and Authorities for the Study of Elizabethan Literature', which were

---

[14] D. J. Palmer, *The Rise of English Studies*, London, New York, Toronto, 1965, p. 150.

delivered to advanced students in Oxford over several years, but few notes for undergraduate lectures have been preserved. Amongst the working papers, the notes on the history of French criticism are particularly interesting in relation to the Edinburgh bene-faction; the early reading-lists are virtually desiderata-lists for his foreign collection. A whole volume contains preparatory material (and a good deal of correspondence on manuscripts) for the Oxford English Texts edition of *The Poems of Samuel Johnson* (1941). Like many of the other files, such as those on eighteenth-century newspapers and periodicals, it contains numerous cuttings from booksellers' catalogues, usually marked in R. W. Chapman's characteristic scrawl.

There is an occasional striking phrase or a piece of out of the way information in this *Nachlass*, but I suspect that little of it will not be found elsewhere in Nichol Smith's extensive published work. Nor should any of it be taken as evidence of his final opinion: his frequent and scrupulous revision of his lecture scripts indicates their tentative nature. But the lecture notes do give a valuable impression of the range, progress, and above all the methods, of Nichol Smith's work.

APPENDIX

Extract from a letter of David Nichol Smith to Sir Walter Greg, 23 November 1940:

. . . And now for a little bit of personal history, in which I am tempted to indulge by the pleasure which your two letters have given me. The incompetent editor [mentioned anonymously in a previous letter] is now writing to you. Raleigh came to Oxford in 1904 convinced that Samuel Johnson was the greatest of Shake-speare's editors. Johnson had said that 'whoever has any of the folios has all', and that after beginning by collating them all he 'afterwards used only the first'. Raleigh's perusal of the Clarendon Press facsimile of the First Folio (ed. S. Lee), a book in which he took great delight, convinced him that English scholarship de-manded a reprint of the First Folio with a scantling of variants from the Quartos, all passages peculiar to the Quartos to be given at the bottom of the page, and he had no difficulty in persuading Cannan, who had become interested in old spelling editions since the publication of Beeching's Milton in 1900. Boas's Kyd followed in 1901, and Bond's Lyly in 1902. I had two very happy years with Raleigh in Glasgow, from 1902 to 1904, and about 1906, when I was in Newcastle, Raleigh personally and by word of mouth invited me to be the editor of the new Shakespeare for the Clarendon

Press. I was at that time unknown to Cannan. My foolhardy acceptance of this invitation had not a little to do with my appointment
to the Goldsmiths' Readership in 1908.

I came to Oxford expecting that Shakespeare was to be my main
work for the next dozen years or more, not altogether happy in
the prospect but buoyed up by youthful ambition and the recognition of a great opportunity. I had my new lectures to prepare,
but for four or five years I gave all my spare time to Shakespeare,
and during these years I learned practically all that I now know
about textual criticism. But problems arose in legions. Raleigh
used to say that once I had got the plan of the page the rest would
follow easily. Whenever I presented him with a problem he never
seemed to me quite to see it, and if I presented him with more
than one he soon grew weary. Henry Bradley was very kind, but
he was more critical than constructive. I found nobody in Oxford
who was prepared to worry out the problems from the beginning.
I began to think of other things. The Clarendon Press asked me
to revise Courtney's Bibliography of Johnson, and I edited a
volume for the Roxburghe Club. By this time the war had come,
and when it ended I did not return to Shakespeare. I was still
thought enough of a Shakespearian to be asked to write the chapter on 'Authors and Patrons' in *Shakespeare's England*, and I was
called in for the final revision of the proofs of the two volumes.
But the edition of Shakespeare was no longer for me. It had become a mill-stone, and it gradually dropped from my neck. Had I
had more courage I should have thrown it off.

I was beaten, and nobody here seemed quite to know why. I had
been knocking my head against a stone wall, and got a headache
which, I am sorry to admit, has to some extent affected my liking
for textual criticism. My liking for it only, not my recognition of
its importance, nor my admiration of the advances which have
recently been made and which distinguish this age. Those four
years were not wholly lost, though I was inclined to think at the
time that they were. I learned what was being done in London.
I remember the excitement with which I read your articles in
The Library on 'False dates in Shakespearian Quartos' and in the
the following year Pollard's *Folios and Quartos*. (I have always
thought that the lead was yours and that Pollard played a skilful
backing hand.) I worked out the question of formes with the
Quartos of *King Lear*,—the play to which I gave most attention.
But I never dreamed even of the possibility of such a treatise as
The Variants in the First Quarto of 'King Lear'. The most I can
say is that I then learned enough to know how good it is, and how
important.

An incidental gain was that I came to know Aldis Wright on a visit to the Capell collection. I dined with him in Trinity and found him most benevolent—perhaps because I was introduced to him by a lady who had known him since her childhood and whom he remembered in his will. He was precise enough in his talk, but after dinner he took me to his rooms and showed me book after book. He said to me—'If you edit Shakespeare, do not have a colleague',—from which, and from his interest in the old spelling, I gathered that the plan of the Cambridge Shakespeare was not wholly to his liking. I am very glad to have had this talk with the last great representative of the old school. I do not think that McKerrow quite does him justice in his *Prolegomena*. And he was not wholly of the old school, though he could not see the school that was coming. I wonder if you remember his note on the text of Bacon's Essays in the Golden Treasury edition, —pp. 350 to 353. It is a remarkable note for 1862.

But why have I written at such length? It is your letters that have extracted the secret and made me talkative. The only other man to whom I have said so much is F. P. Wilson.

Note: I am grateful to the Librarian and Trustees of the National Library of Scotland for permission to quote from documents in their collections and in the Library's own archives. Professor William Beattie, then Librarian, encouraged me to write this paper, and my colleagues Robert Donaldson and L. J. G. Heywood have contributed substantially to the parts dealing with English and foreign printed books respectively.

Bodley's Librarian and the Keeper of Western Manuscripts kindly allowed me to examine and describe the Lecture Notes discussed in section III.

Quotations from Nichol Smith's own letters are made by kind permission of his daughters, Mrs Cannon, Mrs Gray and Mrs Phipps.

Index

Abbadie, Jacques, 382
Aberdeen Philosophical Society, 115, 116, 122, 123, 128, 129
Abrams, M. H., 33, 122n.
Adam, James, 169
Adam, Robert, 175
Adams, Henry, 240
Addison, Joseph, 2, 114, 182, 190, 264, 266-7 *passim*, 380n., 382-6, 388, 389, 93, 394-5
Adventurer, 252-3
Albani, Cardinal Alessandro, 169
Alemán, Mateo, 28-30, 33, 35
d'Alembert, Jean le Rond, 226, 234
Allain, Ernest, 237n.
Alter, Robert, 32-3, 51, 52n.
Altaner, Bernhold, 296n.
Amory, Hugh, 19n.
Analytical Review, 183
Anderson, P. J., 116n., 117n.
Annual Register, 173
Anson, George Anson, Baron, 239n., 248
Antal, F., 110
Aquinas, St Thomas, 354
Aristotle, 95, 259, 272n., 354, 399
Audra, Emile, 1-2, 8, 9
Auger, Abbé Athanase, 231n.
Augustine, St, 11, 283, 381
Austen, Jane, 77, 303
Avis important aux réfugiez, 192-3
Ayloffe, William, 378n., 382

Bacon, Francis, 90, 118, 123, 124, 128, 131-5 *passim*, 354, 355, 358
Baillie, John, 179
Baird, Theodore, 76, 79, 80
Baker, E. A., 76n.
Banks, Joseph, 240-52 *passim*, 254-6 *passim*
Barbauld, Mrs Anna Letitia, 71
Barhan, Henry, 260n.
Barlow, Thomas, 198
Barrow, Isaac, 285

Barruel, Abbé Augustin, 11
Barry, James, 182n.
Barzum, Jacques, 378
Basire, James, 163
Bataille, Georges, 161-2
Battestin, Martin C., 19n., 32n.
Batteux, Charles, 148n.
Baudeau, Abbé Nicolas, 235, 237n.
Baudelaire, Charles, 157
Bauerhorst, Kurt, 113n.
Bayle, Pierre, 2, 11, 187-203, 218
Beaglehole, J. C., 240, 241, 242n., 244n., 248, 249, 253, 257
Beattie, James, 115, 116, 117, 134, 135
Becker, Carl, 191
Bénac, H., 158n.
Benot, Yves, 144n.
Bentley, Richard, 281n.
Berger, Peter, 49
Bergeron, Henri-François, 192n.
Bergson, Henri, 21, 35
Berguer, Lionel Thomas, 268n.
Berkeley, George, Bishop of Cloyne, 78, 146, 263, 263n.
Bernini, Giovanni Lorenzo, 178
Bertrand, Elie, 14
Bevilacqua, Vincent M., 135n.
Bible, The, 84-5, 90, 212, 284, 289, 398, 399
Blackmore, Sir Richard, 276-7
Blackwell, Thomas, 182
Blake, William, 163-4, 171n., 177, 185, 244
Boaden, James, 373n.
Boas, G., 241n.
Boccaccio, Giovanni, 32
Bochart, Samuel, 283n.
Bodmer, J. J., 168, 171-2, 177
Boehme, Jacob, 294, 302n.
Boethius, Hector, 205, 207, 213, 218-19
Boileau, Nicolas, 149
Bolingbroke, Henry St John, Viscount, 344

Designed by Roderick Shaw. Text set in 10 pt lino Baskerville,
one point leaded, and printed on 85 gsm Burnie English Finish
at The Griffin Press, Adelaide, South Australia.